THIS IS ORSON WELLES

THIS IS ORSON WELLES

ORSON WELLES
and
PETER BOGDANOVICH

JONATHAN ROSENBAUM: EDITOR

HarperPerennial
A Division of HarperCollins*Publishers*

A portion of the original interviews that comprise this volume is available on audiocassettes from HarperAudio. The set received a Grammy nomination in 1992.

Photograph credits follow the index.

A hardcover edition of this book was published in 1992 by HarperCollins Publishers.

HarperCollins books may be purchased for educational, business, or sales promotional use. For information please write: Special Markets Department, HarperCollins Publishers, Inc., 10 East 53rd Street, New York, NY 10022.

First HarperPerennial edition published 1993.

Designed by Ruth Kolbert

The Library of Congress has catalogued the hardcover edition as follows:

Welles, Orson, 1915–
This is Orson Welles / Orson Welles & Peter Bogdanovich ; edited by Jonathan Rosenbaum. — 1st ed.
p. cm.
Includes index.
ISBN 0-06-016616-9
1. Welles, Orson, 1915– —Interviews. 2. Motion picture producers and directors—United States—Interviews. 3. Actors—United States—Interviews. I. Bogdanovich, Peter, 1939– . II. Rosenbaum, Jonathan. III. Title.
PN1998.3.W45A3 1992
791.43'0233'092—dc20
[B] 92-52601

ISBN 0-06-092439-X (pbk.)
93 94 95 96 97 DT/CW 10 9 8 7 6 5 4 3 2 1

CONTENTS

ACKNOWLEDGMENTS

For invaluable assistance on this book through its many stages, Peter Bogdanovich would like to thank the late Eugene Archer, Sherry Arden, Eileen Bowser, Iris Chester, Gary Graver, the late Richard Griffith, the late Margaret Hodgson, Oja Kodar, Joseph McBride, Craig Nelson, Polly Platt, Peggy Robertson, Ann Rogers, Jonathan Rosenbaum, Andrew Sarris, Daniel Selznick, Cybill Shepherd, L. B. Straten, Daniel Talbot, Beatrice Welles-Smith, Elizabeth Wilson, the late Richard Wilson, and Mae Woods.

For assistance on this book in its latter stages, Jonathan Rosenbaum would like to thank Piet Adriaanse, Jr., Adriano Aprà, Sherry Arden, Frank Beacham, Catherine Benamou, John Berry, Peter Bogdanovich, Fred Camper, Rebecca Cape, Iris Chester, Michael Dawson, David Ehrenstein, Bernard Eisenschitz, Pamela Falkenberg, George Fanto, Carolyn Fireside, Tag Gallagher, Ciro Giorgini, Miriam Hansen, J. Hoberman, Dave Kehr, Oja Kodar, Allan Zola Kronzek, Todd McCarthy, J. Fred McDonald, Alain Maes, the late Fletcher Markle, James Naremore, Craig Nelson, James Pepper, Bill Reed, Michael Rosenbaum, Alexander Sesonske, Alessandro Tasca di Cuto, Sandra Taylor, Beatrice Welles-Smith, Bart Whaley, and Bret Wood. And in particular, for their devoted, scrupulous, and untiring generosity, I would like to thank Bill Krohn, Gary Graver, and the late Richard Wilson.

PREFACE

These interviews were recorded on reel-to-reel tape. Why they have taken so long to reach print is a complicated story.

When Peter Bogdanovich first met Orson Welles in Los Angeles toward the end of 1968, he had already published monographs on Welles, Howard Hawks, and Alfred Hitchcock for the Museum of Modern Art, as well as interview books with John Ford and Fritz Lang, and directed one feature *(Targets)*. During those same years, Welles had made *The Trial* (1962) and *Chimes at Midnight* (1966) and acted in a good many other films while trying to raise money for his other film projects.

Bogdanovich's sixteen-page *The Cinema of Orson Welles* (1961) —written for the first Welles retrospective in the United States, one organized by Bogdanovich for the Museum of Modern Art—differs strikingly from other American critical treatments of Welles, especially during this period, by arguing that Welles "developed much further both technically and intellectually" after *Citizen Kane*: e.g., "The photography and what remains of Welles' original editing mark [*Mr. Arkadin*] as perhaps Welles' most ambitious film to date"; "Technically, *Touch of Evil* is Welles' most advanced film."

Bogdanovich recalls their 1968 meeting and their mutual decision to do a book together in the Introduction which follows, written especially for this volume. The interviews began in Welles' bungalow at the Beverly Hills Hotel and resumed as Bogdanovich joined Welles on location for *Catch-22* in Guaymas, Mexico, and then continued sporadically at various places in Europe and the United States. During this same period—1969 to 1972—Bogdanovich published two lengthy broadsides defending Welles against his detractors—"Is It True What They Say About Orson?" in the *New York Times*, and "The *Kane* Mutiny" in *Esquire*. According to Bogdanovich, as the book developed, its collage structure and its emphasis on the fact that the interviews occurred in different locations stemmed from Welles himself, and one can see in both these conceptual ideas rather precise parallels to the films Welles was making over the same period—the giddy globetrotting in *F for Fake* and *Filming "Othello"* and the array of diverse overlapping "documentary" materials in the still unreleased *The Other Side of the Wind*.

As Bogdanovich describes it, what usually happened was that he would edit and arrange the material after it had been transcribed and submit versions of each section to Welles. Months later, Welles would send these back, either retyped or with handwritten changes; some chapters went through two or three such revisions, with Welles often rewriting Bogdanovich's comments as well as his own.

With the pressures of Bogdanovich's mushrooming career as a Hollywood director—given special impetus by the enormous successes of *The Last Picture Show* (1971), *What's Up, Doc?* (1972), and *Paper Moon* (1973)—and Welles' continual (if unsuccessful) efforts to launch new features of his own, months stretched into years. The book passed through two contracts—one with Atheneum, another with *Harper's* Magazine Press—without coming to fruition. Then the project was effectively abandoned after Welles signed another contract to write his memoirs. When they had to return the publishers' advances, which they had shared equally, Bogdanovich was more solvent and covered the costs himself. (Similarly, when Welles' plans to write his memoirs yielded only a few pages—published in the Christmas 1982 issue of the French *Vogue*—Oja Kodar, a Yugoslav sculptor, actress, and writer and Welles' companion and collaborator since the early 1960s, paid back the corresponding advance.) Welles and Kodar were living at Bogdanovich's house, where parts of *The Other Side of the Wind* were being shot. Scripted by Welles and Kodar, the film centers on a birthday party being held for an aging macho film director, Jake Hannaford (played by John Huston), and Bogdanovich was cast first as an interviewer and then—in a far more important role, replacing Rich Little—as a successful director and friend of Hannaford at the party; Kodar played the lead actress in Hannaford's latest film.

Around this time, Bogdanovich's own commercial status was becoming precarious with *Daisy Miller* (1974), *At Long Last Love* (1975), and *Nickelodeon* (1976), and many of his possessions—including all of the materials relating to the Welles book—wound up in storage. In part because of the varying fortunes of Welles and Bogdanovich and some unsuccessful efforts to come together on a number of film projects, their friendship cooled by the late 1970s, although they remained in touch. During this time Bogdanovich continued to help Welles with his projects and career; unofficially, he helped the American Film Institute in its efforts to honor Welles with its third Life Achievement Award in 1975.

Bogdanovich's life took a much darker turn in 1980 with the brutal murder of Dorothy Stratten, his companion, who had just played a featured role in his film *They All Laughed*—a tragedy dealt with at length in his book *The Killing of the Unicorn* (1984), the TV movie *Death of a Centerfold* (1981), and Bob Fosse's film *Star 80* (1983). In 1985, he went into bankruptcy after purchasing and releasing *They All Laughed*. In the course of these vicissitudes, the book was effectively lost for five years; Bogdanovich knew it was somewhere in storage, but was unable to lay his hands on it.

Welles died on October 10, 1985, and at a warm and moving tribute to him held at the Directors Guild in Hollywood (which I attended), Bogdanovich served as emcee and Oja Kodar spoke. A few weeks later, I invited both of them to another Welles tribute that I was presenting at the Rotterdam Film Festival; Peter was too busy at the time to attend, but Oja agreed, and we met for the first time there in early 1986. (I was to meet Peter for the first time at the same festival three years later.) Over the next year, I persuaded Oja to publish one of Welles' last unrealized screenplays, *The Big Brass Ring* (Santa Barbara: Santa Teresa Press, 1987), and contributed an afterword to it.

Then, in the late summer of 1987, after Bogdanovich had told her he had no time at the present to put the book into final publishable shape and to bring it up to date, Oja asked me to edit this book—a legendary manuscript I had been hearing about since the early 1970s. A couple of years later, in Chicago, I started to receive a copy of the last draft of the manuscript—1301 pages long, but still unfinished—in separate installments in the mail. What impressed me the most, as I started reading it, was how differently Welles regarded his own work and career from the ways the rest of us did. Here he was, at the height of the power of the auteur theory—the time when American directors were being discovered and praised as never before, with Welles himself enthroned in most people's minds as the veritable symbol of the director's authority—declaring that the importance of the director was vastly overrated, particularly in relation to the role of the actor. The glorious iconoclasm that he had repeatedly shown as an artist—never producing the film (or radio show or stage production) that was expected of him, always staying several nimble steps ahead of his commentators—was equally apparent in the fascinating perspectives that he had about his work and so much else.

About a year later, I received the tapes (which Peter had found in 1987, and had turned over to Oja)—approximately twenty-five hours of interview representing more than five sixths of the original material, which expanded the range of my choices still further (a couple of tapes had unfortunately been lost). The earlier drafts—or as many of them as could be found inside diverse boxes in storage, comprising thousands of more pages—arrived in early 1991, and then, during my brief visit to Los Angeles the following summer, Oja managed to uncover still other drafts with Welles' revisions. Like Welles' work as a whole, which I was concurrently trying to catalogue, this book was obstinately growing every time I thought I had it under some form of control.

So it's been a kind of unfolding serial for me since the beginning, complete with unraveling mysteries, protracted cliff-hangers, and last-minute revelations—spurred along by advice and assistance from Peter (who was working on four separate pictures during this period), Oja (who was making *her* first feature), and many others. Above all, I should single out Bill Krohn—a friend who introduced me to Oja and has been a constant source of help on this book—but two of Welles' most faithful collaborators, Gary Graver and the late Richard Wilson, gave tirelessly and generously to this project as well.

It's a sad fact that when Orson Welles died in the fall of 1985, responses in the United States tended to differ sharply from those in the rest of the world. While the obituaries outside America devoted themselves almost exclusively to Welles' many accomplishments over more than half a century, the repeated refrains in his home country seemed to concentrate on his weight and on the specter of failure—almost as if these two fixed concepts seemed to "explain" and justify each other. In a culture increasingly bent on defining success, history, and reality itself in terms of currently marketable items, Welles' artistic career seemed to consist of a spectacular debut followed by forty-odd years of inactivity.

It's an oddly comforting scenario for those who feel that both the marketplace and industry choices made on our behalf are always right. But for those who have followed Welles' career more closely, his increasingly low visibility as a filmmaker during his lifetime suggests a highly troubling paradox—that the most universally revered of all American filmmakers found himself unable to make another studio picture over the last three decades of his life. The reasons for this impasse are too complex to be dealt with adequately here, although it is important to stress two factors: that the nature and proclivities of the film industry are every bit as pertinent to *this* "failure" as Welles' own eccentricities, and that, far from being inactive, Welles continued to do creative work for the remainder of his life, even when he had to finance it himself. For these reasons, among others, Welles' work and career remain exemplary and highly subversive rebuttals to many received ideas about art and commerce that continue to circulate in this culture; they are ideological "disturbances" in the best sense.*

* The only major area where there was any editorial disagreement is one that could be described as social and political etiquette. While Welles remained pas-

With significant portions of Welles' work still out of reach (for a variety of reasons), and many other portions unknown or forgotten, the need to clarify his legacy in some detail has never seemed more pressing. Welles' youngest daughter, Beatrice Welles-Smith, recently authorized a restoration and rerelease of *Othello*, and Oja arranged for a premiere of *Don Quixote* in Spain. If certain legal and financial obstacles can be overcome, *The Other Side of the Wind* will finally see the light of day as well. Although the two most neglected areas of Welles' work—his prodigious output in radio and his extensive involvement in politics—are only touched on in the first eight chapters of this book, I've given them extensive coverage in the concluding career summary, which also contains some additional interview material, as well as information about some of his lesser-known activities in theatre and film. For Welles fans who tend to judge his work mainly in relation to a handful of features, it's worth recalling that the most productive stretch in his career occurred before he even went to Hollywood; he was just short of twenty-three when he made it onto the cover of *Time*.

Insofar as it's been possible, I've tried to respect Welles' and Bogdanovich's intentions while drawing the best material from all the sources available to me. In the cases where Welles' facts differ from the ones at my disposal, or where I believe that other sources or information might be helpful, I've mentioned this in my notes.

JONATHAN ROSENBAUM
April 1992

---

sionately progressive throughout his career, his irreverence was equally constant, and I personally differed with some of the cosmetic changes made in his language and the deletion of certain remarks—alterations that Peter maintains Welles would have made himself.

INTRODUCTION:
A Nice Little Book

> "Now I am going to tell you about a scorpion. This scorpion wanted to cross a river, so he asked the frog to carry him. 'No,' said the frog. 'No, thank you. If I let you on my back you may sting me, and the sting of the scorpion is death.' 'Now, where,' asked the scorpion, 'is the logic of that?' (for scorpions always try to be logical). 'If I sting you, you will die, and I will drown.' So the frog was convinced, and allowed the scorpion on his back. But just in the middle of the river he felt a terrible pain and realized that, after all, the scorpion *had* stung him. 'Logic!' cried the dying frog as he started under, bearing the scorpion down with him. 'There is no logic in this!' 'I know,' said the scorpion, 'but I can't help it—it's my character.' Let's *drink* to character. . . ."
>
> —ORSON WELLES, *Mr. Arkadin* (1955)

This book began for me with a program note I did on Welles' *Othello* for a New York revival house over thirty-two years ago. The note—I had called the picture the best Shakespeare film ever made—came to the attention of the Curator of the Museum of Modern Art Film Library who, as a result, asked me to organize the first U.S. Welles retrospective and to write an accompanying monograph on his pictures. Welles was unable to attend any of the programs, which ran at the museum from June 11 through August 12, 1961—he was in Europe preparing *The Trial*—so I had no communication with him at all for the show or for my little critical study, though a copy was sent off to some address overseas. I didn't know if he received it or not—until seven years later.

The phone rang one afternoon—I had by then married for the first time and moved to Los Angeles—and when I answered, a familiar male voice asked for me and after I had identified myself, said, "Hello, this is Orson Welles—I can't tell you how much I've wanted to meet you." I laughed—he had taken "my line," I said and asked, incredulously, *why?* "Because you have written the *truest* thing ever published about me," he said, then added: ". . . in English." Could I meet him at the Polo Lounge of the Beverly Hills Hotel tomorrow at 3:00 for a coffee and a talk?

It was near the end of 1968 and I had been working in the business about thirteen years—having acted and directed without great acclaim in the theatre, done all right as a show-biz magazine writer, published a few small movie books and monographs (the Welles had been my first), directed (and acted in) one very low-budget movie. I had already interviewed and got to know a good number of the great legendary names of the movies, from John Ford and Alfred Hitchcock to Cary Grant and John Wayne. But Orson Welles was the first whose presence did not awe me so much as it inspired an openness and ease I would not have thought possible since a quarter century separated us. There was a strangely conspiratorial quality Orson and I fell into almost at once; I felt as though we had known each other for a long time.

He was so extraordinarily disarming that I felt quite comfortable telling him only the truth: I even said the one film of his I didn't really like was *The Trial*. He said, explosively, "I don't *either!*" This joint confession seemed to me to solidify our sense of agreement on everything. By the end of two hours, as we were leaving the restaurant, Welles flipped through the pages of my just-published interview book with John Ford (he was Orson's favorite American director; I had quoted Welles in the work and brought him a copy). "Isn't it too bad," Orson said, "that you can't do a nice little book like this about me."

Why couldn't I? Now that I was directing, he said (my first film had been released that year), probably there would be no time. I said that I would love to do an interview book with him, that it wouldn't take so long, after all. "Fine," Orson said, "then let's do one." I was twenty-nine years old at that time, and Welles was fifty-three—exactly my age now, as that "nice little book" is finally published.

Why it took such a long time to appear has at least something to do with that "scorpion/frog" fable Orson told so memorably in his *Mr. Arkadin:* a metaphor on the basic inability of people to alter their true nature or to escape the fate to which their personalities lead them. Even in our first—from my viewpoint, euphoric—meeting of the minds, things turned out to be quite different than I had understood them. Less than a year later, we were talking about *The Trial* again and when I began to discuss in detail what bothered me about it, Orson suddenly said sharply: "I wish you wouldn't keep on *saying* that." "Oh," I said, "I thought you didn't like the picture either." "No, I only said that to please you, I like it very much," Orson said. "But I have a much poorer opinion of my life's work than you possibly could guess, and every negative thing that I hear from a friend, or read from a person that I vaguely respect, reduces the little treasure that I have." Naturally, I felt terrible and Orson used to rub it in from then on by always referring to *The Trial* as "that picture you hate." But, of course, by then we were on our ride across the river.

Orson and I played scorpion and frog to each other more than once, switching roles back and forth a number of times. That "old Arab fable," which Orson said he heard once and incorporated into his picture, is expressive of perhaps his most basic theme—realizing that most people in life, like Orson himself, are both scorpion and frog, victims of others' natures and destinies as well as their own. In pictures Welles brilliantly embodied scorpions as different as Charlie Kane and Harry Lime, frogs as dissimilar as Othello and Falstaff, scorpion/frogs like the Cop in *Touch of Evil*, about whom the Gypsy says after his death: "He was *some kind of a man*. What does it matter what you *say* about people?"

Orson wrote that line, wishing it didn't matter what people said about him but knowing it did; the main reason he cared so much was that the often grossly inaccurate stories and exaggerated legends told of his exploits made it that much tougher for him to work as a filmmaker. The whole point of the book he had invited me to do with him, he said, was to "set the record straight," something he seemingly wished to do on nearly everything that had happened in his life. And, by that last year of the sixties when we started to become friends, Orson Welles had been in professional show business for nearly forty years as director/actor; had conquered all the known media—theatre, radio, and film—before he was twenty-five; had, as it turned out, directed all the plays and all but three of the pictures—two documentaries and one still unreleased feature—that he would complete in his lifetime, which had yet to go almost another two decades.

At that first meeting, I didn't realize what desperate and discouraged straits Orson was in—his personal life was in disarray, his continued work as a film director in peril. Yet within the previous six years he had finished two of his most ambitious pictures: adaptations of Kafka's *The Trial* and of Shakespeare's Falstaff into *Chimes at Midnight*, arguably his best film. But neither of these relatively small-budget European-based coproductions received adequate distribution and, though reviews were moderately favorable, neither even did art-house business. After these, and a memorable French-produced television adaptation of Isak Dinesen's *The Immortal Story* (his first released work in color), Welles' European financing dried up. Whereas he had long hoped to make Joseph Heller's novel *Catch-22* as a picture, he had ended up having to accept a small supporting role in the movie that Mike Nichols was making.

We arranged to begin taping the interviews at his bungalow in the next day or so and then for me to come down to Guaymas, Mexico, and tape some more while he was acting in the Nichols film. I would eventually write about some of this in the early 1970s (in *Esquire*):

> One afternoon . . . Orson and I got a bit soused in an elegant bar. . . . They'd given him most of the day off, so we retired to do some taping. . . . Now, Orson doesn't relish talking about himself, and especially not about his pictures—like pulling teeth is not an exaggeration—so to ease the pain, we had a few drinks. Actually, Orson didn't *get* drunk—he only became more eloquent, projected his voice a little more, and reacted more emotionally than usual. (He has since given up drinking altogether.)
>
> I told him the evening before how difficult it was for many of the older directors we both admired to get a job. This was nothing new, really. The movie business has always been rough on its old men. Griffith, who invented so much of it, didn't make a film the last seventeen years of his life.

An annotated list followed of virtually identical director's life stories: Josef von Sternberg, Fritz Lang, King Vidor, Jean Renoir, all of whom I had also interviewed and in some cases had got to know a bit, so my reports were firsthand:

> I had given Orson a similar rundown and had seen that he was deeply affected. . . . The next day (we were in the bar now), he brought up the subject again. "You told me last night about all these old directors whom people in Hollywood say are 'over the hill,' and it made me so sick, I couldn't sleep. I started thinking about all those conductors—Klemperer, Beecham, Toscanini—I can name almost a hundred in the last century—who were at the height of their powers after seventy-five. And were conducting at eighty. Who *says* they're over the hill!"
>
> The waiter came by, but Orson waved him away. "It's so *awful*," he said. "I think it's just terrible what happens to old people. But the public isn't interested in that—never has been. That's why *Lear* has always been a play people hate."
>
> "You don't think Lear became senile?"
>
> "He became senile by giving *power* away. The only thing that keeps people alive in their old age is power. . . . But take power away from de Gaulle or Churchill or Tito or Mao or Ho or any of these old men who run the world—in this world that belongs only to young people—and you'll see a 'babbling, slippered pantaloon.' "
>
> There was a long pause. I thought of how easy it was now for young men to get a job directing. In fact, I recently had said not too facetiously that after *Easy Rider*, the simplest way to get to make a picture was never to have made one.
>
> "It's only in your twenties and in your seventies and eighties that you do the greatest work," Orson went on. "The enemy of society is the middle class, and the enemy of life is middle age. Youth and old age are great times—and we must treasure old age and give genius the capacity to function in old age—and not send them away. . . ."
>
> The day after, Orson told me he planned to make his next picture on precisely this subject: the last days of an aging director, which eventually became *The Other Side of the Wind*, a by now legendary film Welles began shooting with his own money late in 1970, and which he continued to shoot off and on for several years. John Huston plays the director and the cast included Lilli Palmer, Mercedes McCambridge, Edmond O'Brien, Pat O'Brien, George Jessel, Jack Nicholson, Henry Jaglom, Paul Mazursky, Oja

> Kodar, Dennis Hopper, many, many others, and me. The little I have seen . . . is among the finest Welles has done.

This last paragraph appeared in 1985, the year Orson died; the film is still tied up, the editing incomplete.

There are so many memories and stories of Orson—too many that fall outside the scope of this piece: Like Orson moving hurriedly through my study in the afternoons, on his way to his bedroom, anxious not to miss a second of his favorite rerun, *The Dick Van Dyke Show*. Or the time he accidentally put his lit cigar into the pocket of his white terry-cloth robe which, after a while, caught on fire—he tossed it into the bathtub but missed, burning up part of the white rug too. Orson in Paris pacing up and down the street at night, arguing with himself as to who should play the old director, he or Huston—wanting to keep the plum role for himself: "Why should I give that great part away!?"—but feeling Huston was better for it. I remember Orson in the passenger seat, told to put on his seat belt, flipping it over his shoulder like a scarf; or Orson, jumping into a New York cab, giving the address and adding, in his most swashbuckling voice: ". . . and a gold doubloon if you get us there before nightfall!"

But the central motivating factor for everything we did (though I don't believe it was ever discussed between us) had to do with one basic cause: good pictures. Each in our own way, Orson and I had both fallen in love not only with the movies, but with the vast potential of the movies as well. That potential was encouraged when good pictures were made and discouraged when bad ones dominated. By the end of the 1960s the golden age of pictures certainly had passed, but if Orson Welles could keep working, all hope was not gone.

This was to me a guiding factor for my activities, though certainly they were interpreted in other ways, and would have their diminishing returns for Orson and for me. I remember one time we were getting ready to go to a big Hollywood party together, in the mid-1970s, around the height of my first success and the peak of interest in Orson's (final) return to Hollywood. He said by all means we should not arrive together at the party. Why not? I asked. "Oh, God," he said, "they hate us enough already. Can't you imagine? We enter arm-in-arm—it's almost calculated to

annoy every single person in the room." I laughed, but didn't really want to believe him.

Of course it was Welles who suggested the shape of "the book," as we always called it—we never did arrive at a title we both liked. He said we should set the interviews wherever we had been together, even if we hadn't necessarily done any taping sessions there. He also felt the conversations should not be strictly chronological, according to his life, but more loosely organized, as our conversations actually were. And to break them up with relevant letters, memos, reviews, etc., gathered from the Welles/Mercury files that the late Richard Wilson—among Orson's most loyal former lieutenants—had kept in safekeeping for years. (These are almost all now at the Lilly Library at Indiana University.) I then edited and organized the material into chapters and sent them to Welles one at a time—typed as he had requested, the left side of the page blank for him to rewrite.

Eventually, a few months later, a chapter would come back, thoroughly revised, heavily rewritten at times (including some of my remarks). I understood Orson occasionally altered things for dramatic purposes, and if it was good for the "cause" to have me a little more gauche or pushy, why would it matter? Only one anecdote never happened at all: my leaving the De Filippo play in Rome (see chapter 1). But since it was a quick way of illustrating a good point, why not? Looking back, I certainly *was* gung ho for American subjects and for the director-as-author, my experiences of life and work still tremendously limited, especially compared to Orson's.

Besides the conversations, Welles said, and I came to agree, there was a need to substantiate Orson's side of the story of his career. This seemed all the more necessary after three very damaging books (by Charles Higham, Pauline Kael, and John Houseman) came out in the late sixties and early seventies that did nothing to increase Orson's chances of getting a job as a director. One book grudgingly gave him only *Kane*, the other two tried to take even this away.

On a personal level, I could see what these writings did to him, how deeply he was discouraged and demoralized by them. (I had noticed how sensitive he was to criticism: I tactlessly said an early draft of a script he had done "needs work" and he exploded: "Every script '*needs work*'! There is no script that *doesn't* 'need work'! I hate that expression!" He never discussed that project with me again.) To be used eventually for our book, I did pieces for the *New York Times*, and for *Esquire*, trying to refute the charges and opinions in those three books, giving Orson's views a chance, with plenty of corroboration from other key witnesses (see Editor's Notes to chapters 2 and 4).

From 1969 through 1977, besides working on and off on the book and numerous picture projects of his and mine and ours, I also functioned for a while somewhat as Orson's agent: encouraging him to return to America and try to make pictures here again, helping to arrange his first triumphant TV appearances on David Frost's syndicated program and Dick Cavett's network show. After one of these, Orson went out to dinner with Norman

Mailer; I joined them. The first thing Norman did after we sat down was to ask Orson about a particular shot from *Kane*, and Orson said with a groan, "Oh, no, please, Norman, not *Citizen Kane!*" Mailer looked surprised for a moment, then nodded and said, "Oh, yeah, OK—it's like me and *The Naked and the Dead.*" "Yeah," Orson said, and roared with laughter. The one picture everyone always asked him about was the one he *least* wanted to discuss, mainly perhaps because it was the *only* one anybody ever brought up. In fact, he didn't like talking about any of his past works at all.

At the beginning of this period, while I was trying to get a second picture started, I accompanied him a number of times to meals with prospective backers or producers (Orson often picked up the tab, even though he was constantly broke; at that point, so was I). Welles was extraordinarily dazzling in these social situations—with hilarious stories, graciousness, and charm, mesmerizing when he described a picture—but all the while I could sense from his would-be financiers that they weren't going to come across with anything. After one of these dinners in New York, walking back to the hotel, I said the spectacle of his entertaining these people wonderfully and probably getting nothing in return had made me sad and angry. He looked at me, slightly surprised, then bemused by my reaction. "It's funny," he said, "I've been doing that for so long I guess I'm used to it." The truth is that Orson was nearly always right in his artistic advice about pictures; his business acumen was not of the same caliber. Nor was his ability to be politic always well developed—sometimes Orson would not suffer fools easily. People could be frightened of him. I once told him that somebody was scared of him and he got irritated: "Oh, I hate that!" he said. "What am I supposed to do? Say 'Boo!'?"

One of Orson's most affecting qualities, I think, was his seemingly perpetual youth: he never became an old veteran, a gray sage, but rather kept to the end a sense of that first flash of irreverent and innovative genius with which he fired all the art forms he touched, all the other artists he inspired. *Citizen Kane* was certainly the first *modern* American picture, the first that seemed to say, "Let's cut the bullshit: things are not really how you've been taught or led to believe—life often works out exactly like this." I remember Orson around 1974 leaning over the breakfast table yelling at an amazed Cybill Shepherd (amazed at the intense vehemence perhaps even more than at the content), "Everything you've ever learned in school is balls! Do you understand? Balls!"

Certainly nobody else in American pictures in 1941 was illustrating the thesis that capitalism and success could perhaps lead to spiritual impoverishment and the failure of emotion. In its style the picture also had something else that was unique: an absolutely certain sense of the sound, look, and feel of America *combined* with a worldly, aristocratic sophistication and intellect. One of the most disturbing aspects of Welles' work lies in the tension between the essential pessimism of his outlook and the essential optimism inspired by the brilliance of his style. He summed this up in a poetic way at the end of his documentary *F for Fake*, when he said in effect that all man's achievements finally turn to dust but: "Keep on singing!"

After my next two films became popular, I was in a much better position to help Orson, and a number of pictures almost did get made. But something always seemed to go wrong: a thriller with BBS/Columbia; an adaptation of a Conrad novel for The Directors Company/Paramount (Orson was paid for his screenplay on this, but then the rights to the novel fell apart). I think this turned out to be the last time—it was in the mid-1970s—that Welles was paid as writer or director by a major studio. About that same time period, the AFI gave Orson its third Life Achievement Award, which irritated a lot of the old-line Hollywood people, especially those who were more successful and felt they deserved recognition before Welles: the older generation still considered him something of a troublesome and overrated upstart. I found myself in the middle on this affair—trying to assist producer George Stevens, Jr., to bring off a terrific show and at the same time to please Orson, who was terribly anxious about the entire event—worried it was somehow going to make him seem finished as an active director. He gave a memorable speech of encouragement to the "mavericks" who, like himself, needed to scramble to make what they believed in. Everyone had tears of inspiration in their eyes and applauded wildly—but no one offered him a job or financing.

When my stock went down because of a couple of flops, I suddenly had trouble convincing the studio even to pay Orson his normal salary as an actor on a movie I was directing. When this project was suddenly canceled because of a dispute with the studio in which Orson had encouraged me to fight in the name of quality, he made what I thought at the time was a strange remark: "Well, that's the end of my career in Hollywood." It felt as though *I* should be saying that, but Orson was right once more—nothing again worked out into a deal for him in America.

We had, up to this point, first become very close, and then drifted apart a bit. He had stayed at my Bel Air home while I was in town and out (in aggregate, for nearly two years). He shot many scenes there for his *Other Side of the Wind.* One other picture almost got made for Orson but after many delays two of the partners in the project wanted *me* to direct and, because of my commitment in a legal and personal way to one of them, I eventually felt obliged to do the film. Orson said he understood but in effect this ended our work together. What had been a kind of specter behind our friendship—that I was in some way playing Prince Hal to his King Henry IV (or Falstaff)—had finally become a reality neither of us had wanted. It was the role I actually did play to Huston's aging "king" in *The Other Side of the Wind*—the old director supplanted or, in mythic terms, killed by the younger one. I had never looked at it that way in my relationship with Orson, but clearly he had, or else he would not have written the character in his film so much like me (at least in the role's external aspects). The dramatic situation was one that Orson dealt with in numerous films (including a bullfight picture he had conceived long ago—young matador versus aging matador), but our having to play it out in life broke us apart.

By that time, he had already told me that our book—for which we had taken advances from two publishers—could not come out in the foreseeable future. *McCall's* had offered him a quarter of a million dollars to write his memoirs and he had no choice but to agree. This was OK with me: it was *his* life and one of the few ways he had of getting money to pay not only for his family's expenses, but also for the real work he was doing—his many directing projects.

Orson, of course, always knew his difficult position only too well. One time he made a remark about my being "a popular artist," and I asked if he had meant that as a put-down. "No," he answered, with mildly amused irritation, and turning sardonic, "it was not meant as a 'put-down,' but rather as a statement of fact—you *are* a popular artist. Shakespeare was a popular artist. Dickens was a popular artist. The artists I personally have always enjoyed the most are popular artists. I *wish* I were one—but I'm not. I'm more like Céline—writing away at books no one ever reads." Then he erupted into a wave of wildly explosive laughter. If the public didn't always see his work, however, other serious picture people always did, so his influence became pervasive. Yet not in any way that *he* felt he was really valuable.

Welles' father had been an inventor, his mother an artist, and Orson combined the characteristics of both. He had some of the impatience of a visionary innovator who sees the work so deeply and profoundly finished in his mind and heart that the actual making is anticlimactic and can never have the chance to equal the image he had of it—the process is too complicated by politics, money, history, and the imponderables of human behavior for the original, pure form to be realized. A gentleman inventor—like Orson's father and like Joseph Cotten's character in *The Magnificent Ambersons*—is one who invents not for the money but for the common good or for the fun of it. If he can get no support for his invention, part of him remains satisfied because *he* himself has seen it, after all, even if no one else will.

On the other hand, Welles was an artist too—a dark poet true to his vision, no matter how unpopular, and, as Robert Graves (one of his favorite authors) might have expressed it, Welles had paid the final tribute in honor of the Muse he served.

> A certain great and powerful king once asked a poet, "What can I give you of all that I have?" He wisely replied, "Anything, sir . . . except your secret."
>
> —Opening title, *Mr. Arkadin*

Robert Graves also said that it was impossible for any artist not to be a part of the times in which he lived—no matter how much he might be *against* his own time or ahead of it. Orson was both. He also was an extremely sensitive man who went through all the tragically confused and stupefyingly fast chain of historical and artistic events that happened from May 6, 1915—World War I already under way, women not yet allowed to vote, the movies' first great attraction, *The Birth of a Nation*, released that year—a chain in which he eventually played a very noticeable part until October 10, 1985. There were the influences on Orson from his nineteenth-century Midwestern parents to consider; in a world already out of control, his personal life went awry at an early age: his mother dying when Orson was nine, his father when he was fifteen. Whatever Eden Orson may have known—and he claims only one in this book—he certainly was removed from it at a very young age.

In Welles' little-known, brilliant but damaged *Mr. Arkadin*, a young adventurer is hired by a fabulously wealthy international figure to research and prepare a "confidential report" on all of the rich man's activities prior to his emergence as a power. Arkadin, the scorpion in this tale, wants Van Stratten, the frog, to find out the possible dirt about his early life so that he can then destroy all evidence and kill all witnesses. This was Orson's original story and script, and there were times when I seemed to play a variation of Van Stratten to Welles' personal version of Arkadin, because during our talks (on or off the record), he would get particularly agitated and annoyed about connections made between his work and his own life.

One time, while he was staying with me in L.A., I heard someone lightly playing the piano in the living room and when I looked in found Orson standing over the keyboard, speculatively trying a chord or two with one hand. Oh, I had said, I didn't know he could play. "I don't," he said and stopped. "I haven't for years. I used to play." I asked why he stopped. "I stopped after my mother died. I never played another note." Yet when I tried to connect the loss of Orson's mother to Kane's loss of *his* mother—and therefore of the "Rosebud" of his youth—Orson would have none of it. He angrily denied any such connection, at the same time attacking the whole modern school of criticism that relates authors' lives to their works. But, I said, the French believe there *are* no works, only authors. "Well, I disagree," Orson said heatedly, "I believe there are only *works*."

But the strange, nightmarish description Orson wrote of his mother's death (published in French *Vogue* in 1982) hints at a far greater loss than Welles ever seemed to acknowledge. The closeup of the mother in *Citizen Kane* when she calls for her son to send him away; the closeup of Kane when he responds to the remark "You know what mothers are like" with a quiet and misty "Yes"; the son's apology to his dead mother at the end of *Ambersons*—these are perhaps the warmest, most moving moments in Orson's film career. In a conversation about John Ford's tendency to sentimentalize his women characters, we somehow moved on to a story about Welles' own mother: At the age of six or seven, Orson evidently threw something of a fit one afternoon about practicing his piano. To make the point very clear to his piano teacher, Orson climbed onto the window ledge of their apartment building and threatened to jump if the teacher insisted any further. The poor man had gone running frantically in to see Orson's mother: "Mrs. Welles, he says he's going to *jump!*" Outside on the ledge, Orson could hear his mother's quiet response: "Well," she said, "if he's going to jump, he's going to jump. . . ." Soon after that, Orson said, he sheepishly returned to his lessons.

Welles would not, however, connect incidents like these to his work, any more than he would normally agree to be photographed without makeup—the only role he ever played with no makeup at all was Harry Lime in *The Third Man*—or allow a character to laugh the way he himself did. So much a part of any memory of Welles is his volcanic, infectious laugh, loud and sustained, often resonating through its very length and intensity into further levels of the labyrinthine comedy of life. One time, when I tried to write his laugh into a role we were preparing for him in a picture, he impatiently refused to hear of it. It was all part of Orson's acute sense of privacy. A cryptic remark he made once—"The moon is very important to me"—could refer to the moon-possessed poet Graves writes of in *The White Goddess*, a book Orson recommended I read in the mid-1970s (along with Graves' *Greek Myths*). Another time I asked about his religion and he said gruffly that it was none of my business—then relented slightly, said he had been *raised* Catholic. "And," he had a faintly ironic smile, "once a Catholic, always a Catholic, they say."

Our work on the book brought us closer and it was inevitable our private lives would be exposed to each other. Being in many ways an Old World gentleman, Welles was extremely discreet about his personal relationships. On official public occasions, he was sometimes accompanied by his third wife, Paola Mori, and their lovely daughter Beatrice. Tragically, Paola was killed in a car accident about a year after Orson died. His closest friend and associate through all the years I knew him was Oja Kodar, the Croatian actress, sculptor, and writer who collaborated with Welles on most of his projects the last two decades of his life. That Oja's first language and mine were the same (Serbo-Croatian) was for me a happy coincidence.

Orson never did write his memoirs. Eventually, when he asked what had become of our book, it was lost somewhere in the depths of a storage facility while I was going through a personal and financial crisis (leading to bankruptcy and a kind of general breakdown in the summer of 1985, just a few months before Orson died). During one phone conversation he had said he hoped I wouldn't "just publish" the book after he was dead—implying that I knew where it was and was just hanging on to it. That upset me and so when we finally could get back into storage and the boxes turned up, I sent all of them over to Orson—not keeping copies of anything—with a note saying, in effect, it was his life, and here it was for him to do with as he saw fit. Orson called me as soon as he got it—he was very touched, he said, and thanked me profusely. He went on to explain that there wasn't much he could leave to Oja, and if anything happened to him, he was planning to will the book to her.

When Oja asked me to help prepare the book for publication, my professional and private life was still in no shape to take any time away for anything else. However, I thought her idea of asking Jonathan Rosenbaum to edit was excellent and later I put her in touch with my literary agent who at Jonathan's suggestion brought the manuscript to Craig Nelson at HarperCollins. Craig and Jonathan had worked together before, and have been a great help in bringing this to a form close to what Orson and I had envisioned. Neither Orson nor I ever found the time to do a really final draft on any of this material, and I can't say with certainty what things he might finally have cut, even less what he would undoubtedly have added. I know there are still remaining a few negative opinions of other artists that he might have deleted, and I would have agreed: Orson used to say there were enough critics around, artists didn't need to add to their number.

There are quite a few things I didn't agree with Orson about in those days, but most assuredly I do now. Age and experience. I still don't go along with his views on John Wayne or Josef von Sternberg, or a number of Ford's movies (especially *The Grapes of Wrath* and *How Green Was My Valley*, which seem to me among the most enduring of the director's work). I thoroughly agree that the actor's role in pictures was for a time overly downgraded and the director's overly inflated.

Another thing I have now come around to is *The Trial*. In 1973 or '74 we were in Paris and Orson said, "You know why you don't like *The Trial?* You haven't seen how funny it is—how funny I meant it to be. Tony Perkins and I were laughing all the way through the shooting." To prove his point, he invited me to go with him to a special Parisian showing of the picture, a black-tie affair at which Orson was being honored. During this showing, sitting beside Welles, I finally saw his intentions quite clearly—a kind of tragic satire on the power of the law to play on people's innate sense of guilt, even though often unnamable. The two of us were laughing at any number of scenes no one else in the stuffy, academic audience found even remotely funny: after all, Kafka and Welles were Serious Art. People kept shushing Orson and me throughout. But then it is certainly the blackest kind of black comedy. Orson told me the next day that on the bohemian Left Bank there had been a screening the same night at which everybody laughed.

In 1991, on its fiftieth anniversary, *Citizen Kane* was revived in theaters around the country and it did well. People talked of how modern it seemed. So Welles had been fifty years ahead of his time. Also, what he was saying in the lost original version of *The Magnificent Ambersons* about technology's destruction of the environment and the quality of life had become all too real. The complete *Ambersons* certainly is the most tragic loss to pictures besides the complete *Greed*, and both showed a terrible darkening vision of America's problems, which now, unfortunately, seems not so much pessimistic as prophetic.

The one thing most people are still certain to ask about Welles is: What happened after *Citizen Kane?* This book actually started out to answer the question conclusively, so that Orson could continue to "fulfill his promise." Now, I hope that it may supply a few answers for those who, in the future, would be inspired by Welles' work. He was a remarkably courageous man, yet he was perilously sensitive and vulnerable in a far more painful way than his confident demeanor or his boisterous exterior personality would suggest. There was tremendous assurance combined with tremendous insecurity. When I asked if he had ever met his two favorite authors, Isak Dinesen and Robert Graves, he shook his head no. Why not? I asked. He said, "I was afraid I would bore them." I laughed, but he was deadly serious. There were some who accused him of having lost his nerve: years of being told you were no good, and of not being allowed to function in your field, could normally lead to bouts of discouragement, depression, even fear. Yet at his deepest level, Orson had an ever-valiant nature that seemed all the more indestructible in the face of the odds he fought nearly all his life.

The better question to ask about Welles would be: How did he accomplish so much in a commercial medium without ever having a commercial success? We were talking about Greta Garbo once and I was saying what a pity she had been in only two really good pictures and Orson said, "So what? You only need *one*." By his own standards, then, Welles' "small treasure" is immense. As his posthumous fame and stature grow, I recall that he predicted this accurately, too (though not at all happily), muttering under his breath, "Oh, how they'll love me after I'm dead."

For some of us, Orson was a kind of artistic conscience. In my life and work, his influence left an indelible mark. He tried to maintain an integrity and purity as a director, and in order to finance these activities he allowed the actor/personality side of his career to be degraded and devalued. That the American artist who electrified the stage, transformed and defined radio, pointed the way (no one followed) for television, and made films that inspired more picturemakers than any other director since D. W. Griffith should end up selling wine on TV commercials is somehow more a cautionary comment on the cultural fall of our society than it is on Orson's personal predicament.

One time, while I was bemoaning the end of the golden age of pictures, Orson laughed and said, "Well, come on, what do you expect? Even the Renaissance lasted only sixty years!" Along the same lines, we should not be consumed with thoughts of how much we didn't get of Orson Welles, but rather how much he did manage to achieve that has lasting value. G. B. Shaw said it was very difficult to have any continuing influence as an author, because if successful he will be made either into a classic, whom no one reads, or an entertainer, whom no one takes seriously. How much more difficult when the serious artist must allow himself to be subsidized by the entertainer in him. It is a tightrope over an abyss that a number of American artists have had to walk, and with this additional obstacle considered, Orson's legacy becomes all the more extraordinary.

Max Beerbohm, another of Welles' favorite writers, divided people into two categories: hosts and guests. Orson said he was obviously a host but he admitted he was often a reluctant guest who then found himself the last one to leave. For the book, when I asked him if he divided his world into scorpions and frogs, he said, with a smile, "No, there are a lot of other animals." The sharks, for example, in Welles' *Lady from Shanghai*, who eat each other and end up eating themselves. Orson had a fascination with the contradictory elements in people and their behavior, perhaps because he himself was such a contradictory person. Once I saw him on a TV talk show late in the 1970s and the attitude he expressed about me over the air did not seem the attitude of a friend. I dropped him a note, saying I had tuned in to see how he was feeling and guessed I had found out. The next day an envelope arrived from Orson which, it turned out, contained two separate letters he had written to me plus a note. The top letter was a terse, cool two paragraphs, saying in effect that I deserved a touch of bad-mouthing and shouldn't be so hypersensitive. The second letter was much longer, abjectly apologetic, deploring his actions as a form of betrayal. The note he attached said that since each letter had validity, he had sent both.

Actor/author Micheál Mac Liammóir, who played Iago to Orson's Othello, knew him far better than I ever could, right from Welles' first professional acting roles at age sixteen; Mac Liammóir wrote:

> Orson's courage, like everything else about him, imagination, egotism, generosity, ruthlessness, forbearance, impatience, sensitivity, grossness and vision, is magnificently out of proportion.

And the great French poet/picturemaker Jean Cocteau wrote:

> Orson Welles is a giant with the face of a child, a tree filled with birds and shadows, a dog who has broken loose from his chains and gone to sleep on the flower bed. He is an active loafer, a wise madman, a solitude surrounded by humanity.

I used these quotes in my monograph before I had met Orson and discovered how accurate they actually were. I also had quoted what thirty years ago seemed to me Orson's credo, and still does today:

> I want to use the motion picture camera as an instrument of poetry.

I could see the other Orson scowl, saying that was the kind of statement one made at European film festivals and his majestic laugh would sweep me along again. Did it matter what he said? His best films had the real answers, and these are placed ever more securely among the true masterworks of the age.

The last time we spoke was only a couple of weeks before his death. We had been laughing, and then I said something about having made some terrible mistakes. He said, suddenly serious, that *he* had made so *many* mistakes, and that it seemed to be almost impossible to go through life without making an incredible number of them. Orson was interrupted just then by a long-distance call from Oja in Yugoslavia; we said we would talk again soon. We never did. Later, I came to realize our last conversation had been a kind of apology from both of us for having made mistakes about each other. It was a sober acknowledgment from two scarred and somewhat numbed but still alert survivors of the wars on earth. These same wars that all of Orson's pictures, finally, were about: the battles between men and men and between women and men, which lead to their mutual destruction and ultimately to a world poised on the brink.

That our relationship had begun and ended on the phone seems weirdly appropriate for two workers in our technological age of art, the first in history, and both of us therefore guinea pigs in the experiment. That our friendship managed to survive well enough that we could with empathy admit our failures to each other seems to me, in the circumstances, something of a miracle—like scorpion and frog getting across the river alive. I'll always be especially grateful for that, as I profoundly am for having known Orson at all.

My favorite memory of him? There are many, as I said, but one that keeps coming back is Orson under the trees at night on a Beverly Hills sidewalk lithely doing a little tap dance and song routine from a musical he had written in school at the age of thirteen. There was a full moon, and Orson's face was beaming at us, looking remarkably like an out-to-please teenager, unburdened by legends, lies, mistakes, triumphs, or failures, the whole world still out there for him to conquer.

PETER BOGDANOVICH

THIS IS ORSON WELLES

Orson Welles in his Mercury Theatre office, February 1938.

ROME

THEATRE ▪ *MOBY DICK–REHEARSED* ▪ RADIO ACTING ▪ D. W. GRIFFITH ▪ HOLLYWOOD ▪ JOHN BARRYMORE ▪ *THE GREEN GODDESS* ▪ JOHN FORD ▪ *HEART OF DARKNESS* ▪ *THE SMILER WITH A KNIFE* ▪ COMICS ▪ *TOO MUCH JOHNSON* *HEARTS OF AGE* ▪ BULLFIGHTING ▪ IRELAND

ORSON WELLES: A couple of years before I went to Hollywood, Metro-Goldwyn-Mayer had loaned a then unknown actress named Hedy Lamarr to Walter Wanger and he'd produced a picture with her and Charles Boyer called *Algiers*, a frame-for-frame remake of *Pepe le Moko*. The movie and Hedy were both very successful. And Metro realized they had a new star on their hands and couldn't figure out what to do with her. They called an enormous conference—all the producers, associate producers, casting people, in-laws and relatives, even a few writers—a great council presided over by Louis B. Mayer. (I got this story from Ben Hecht, who was there.) "We've got to find another foreign thing," somebody said. "This dame is exotic—let's put her in China or some place like that." And L. B. said, "We gotta have some kind of leading man who'll go with it. Who is there? Robert Young looks sort of like a Chinaman but you couldn't call him exotic. We don't have anybody like that." (And indeed they didn't—Rod La Rocque was long finished.) So who was it going to be? Hecht ventured a suggestion: "There's that young actor in New York—Orson Welles. He looks kind of weird. . . ."

"Welles—that's who we want! Get him. Who's his agent?"

"He doesn't have an agent."

"What?!"

"No, he's on the radio and he's running a theatre in New York called the Mercury."

"Get him."

Because of the time difference, it is now about two o'clock in the morning on the East Coast; ten secretaries are put on the job. "Get him out of bed," cries Mayer, "wherever that may be. Get me Welles." The secretaries start wildly searching by long-distance telephone: "We hear he's at the Stork Club." "No, El Morocco." From Harlem to Chinatown, the telephone dragnet spreads out over Manhattan; and for four or five hours the conference proceeds. . . .

Finally a secretary, breathless with victory, throws open the door: "I've got him for you!" she exclaims, "I've got Orson Welles!"

Then somebody says, "What does *he* want?"

For the moment, that was the end of my career in movies.

A restaurant in Rome.

PETER BOGDANOVICH: Your first love was the theatre.

OW: Peter, if that's a statement, it's wrong; if it's a question, the answer is no.

PB: But you started in the theatre.

OW: Because I was broke and didn't want to go back to America and go to school. I earned my first money in the theatre, but I *started* in music—as a sort of imitation musical *Wunderkind.* That had to do with my mother, who was a most gifted pianist. I've never played a note since she died. I was nine when that happened, and already I'd started to paint. That's what I've loved the

Orson at fourteen.

most. Always. If only I'd been better at it, I'd still be painting. Anyway, that's how I happened to be in Ireland. I'd been traveling around with a donkey and cart and a big box of paints all summer. The days were getting short and so were my financial resources. I started acting just to eat. There was this dreaded scholarship for Harvard. To stay out of school, I went on the stage. I only fell in love with it afterwards.

PB: That seems to be a pattern. You told me once you didn't fall in love with movies, either, until you started to make them.

OW: I wish I hadn't fallen quite so hard.

PB: Why?

OW: Because movies take too long to make and cost too much money. Because the money takes too long to raise. I've spent most of my life, as it turns out, just *trying* to make movies. Think of all the years I could have salvaged if I'd been a little more polygamous.

PB: And you don't love the theatre anymore?

OW: I love empty theatres.

PB: That sounds rather perverse.

OW: During rehearsals, I mean. The physical fact of one of those dusky old candy-boxes with just the actors in it—*making* what's going to happen. The moment the people are let in, it loses some of its magic. Anyway, that's the only kind of stagestruck I've *ever* been.

PB: You wrote a play which was supposed to be a rehearsal: *Moby Dick—Rehearsed.*

OW: The idea was to conjure up some of that empty-theatre magic. We had to do it with an audience out front, of course; it was a sort of magic trick. In London, anyway, I think it worked. That show was the last pure *joy* I've had in the theatre. Great cast—most of them are stars now. Kenneth Williams, Joan Plowright—it was her first important role; she was extraordinary in it as little Pip. And Patrick McGoohan, who'd now be, I think, one of the big actors of his generation if TV hadn't grabbed him. He can still make it. Well, he was tremendous as Starbuck. Then, too, all of the small-part dancer-actors were pretty super, too. And all of them ready and willing to work around the clock, fourteen to sixteen hours a day.

But that was London. Nowadays, on Broadway, they rather tend to watch the clock and check you out with the fine print in the union rule book. A show as intricate as *Moby Dick* needs impossible, uncounted overtime. After all, once that first night's behind him, an actor's hours are pretty easy. The truth is, Peter, when you try for anything approaching total theatre, for those two or three terribly short weeks when you put the whole thing together, you've got to throw away the rulebooks and time clocks. Just to do our storm at sea, you know—to make an audience believe that the whole theatre was tossing on the waves—that was very athletic, acrobatic, and very precisely choreographed. In New York, I guess, it didn't get that, so they bombed.

Kenneth Tynan concluded his review in the London Observer (*reprinted in his collection* Curtains [*New York: Atheneum, 1961*]):

"... As the actor-manager, [Welles] makes what seems to be a final statement on the relationship of actor to audience: 'Did you ever,' he says, 'hear of an unemployed audience?' It is a good line; but the truth is that British audiences have been unemployed for far too long. If they wish to exert themselves, to have their minds set whirling and their eyes dazzling at sheer theatrical virtuosity, *Moby Dick* is their opportunity. With it, the theatre becomes once more a house of magic."

Welles in Moby Dick—Rehearsed.

PB: Would you still like to work in theatre?
OW: Not in New York. Just one critic and too much money—a boom-or-bust economy where you've got to be the greatest thing that ever happened or a disgrace. That makes for a certain . . . tension.

That's why the theatre in London—at least until recently—was still attractive and amusing. You could afford to go in and have a flop and still have your friends speaking to you. Anyway, in New York, in what's called "legitimate" theatre, you're basically a second-class citizen, because Broadway is so musical-oriented now that a "straight" show is just something dignified and nice that happened to get into one of the smaller houses. I can imagine producing a play in a university or a provincial theatre—that's a funny European expression, but we really can't call it "the road" anymore, because there aren't any more road shows, no touring companies. No, the real theatre glamour for me isn't Broadway, but small-time show business. A touring tent show, or anything like that—someday I want to make a movie about that kind of thing. I love that atmosphere—"the fit-ups." It's still going on in Ireland, you know, where they build up a stage in a town hall—that kind of thing.

I'm one of the last actors left who actually likes to tour! Then, I don't mind being in the same play. You're facing a different audience all the time, and I love moving around from town to town. I never got on a train in my life without my spirits rising. I was out on the road for a whole year with Katharine Cornell in the thirties. . . .

PB: The last thing you did in New York was *Lear*, wasn't it?

OW: Yes, and in rehearsals, and every evening right on the dot of six, the actors (most of them, anyway) downed tools and marched out. We had similar problems with the technicians in the Mercury. Sometimes we'd pretend to go home—and when all the union guys had left, we'd sneak back in and work through till dawn lighting the show. I remember one night we broke one of the switchboard handles and had to gimmick it so it would seem to break when the stagehands touched it. Our lighting plots were tremendously complicated. One show, *Danton's Death* (an enormous, thundering flop—it nearly closed us), had over 350 cues. Under normal commercial-theatre conditions, that requires an amount of rehearsal time that there's no way of getting. Maybe things are better now *Off* Broadway. But I've never been there. I've never even *been* to an Off Broadway play.

PB: Why?

OW: Peter, I've hardly been to New York since that part of the theatre country was opened up. In my whole life, I've seen fewer plays than you might imagine or than I'd like to admit. Oh, I used to go as a kid. I was taken—and thrilled to *be* taken. Saw all the great ones, from Werner Krauss to Kachalov. This hand that touches you now once touched the hand of Sarah Bernhardt—can you imagine that? She had a wooden leg and she was playing vaudeville, and I was brought backstage, aged four or five, I guess, and led into a bower of dark-red roses where that marvelous old lady sat in her wheelchair refreshing herself from a tank of oxygen. That hand I took was a claw covered with liver spots and liquid white and with the pointy ends of her sleeves glued over the back of it. When she was young, Mademoiselle Bernhardt had taken the hand of Madame George, who had been the mistress of *Napoleon!* . . . Peter—*just three handshakes from Napoleon!* It's not that the world is so small, but that history is so short. Four or five very old men could join hands and take you right back to Shakespeare. You could put all the popes since Saint Peter right here in this restaurant—with nobody waiting for a table.

What were we talking about—going to the theatre? Well, we're going tonight. I'm taking you.

PB: Great. The trouble is, I don't understand Italian.

OW: You understand acting, don't you? Tonight we're going to see the greatest actor in Europe.

PB: You just said you weren't much of a playgoer. And you told me you practically stopped going to movies after you went to Hollywood.

OW: Well, making movies does rather tend to take the fun out of going to them. In front of every scene you see the ghost of the slate boy. That well-known suspension of disbelief—I suffered some kind of injury to that when I got behind the camera. I also suffered an injury to my back. I used to climb mountains—rather small ones—in my teens, and I took a big fall one afternoon and damn near killed myself. Since then the nicest theatre seat can be a fairly major source of misery. That's really what's kept me so much out of touch all these years with the main currents in the arts of the Drama and the Cinema—my aching back. And yet, you know . . . even a slipped disc can't make me like an intermission.

PB: Yeah, I understand in the Mercury you did away with intermissions entirely.

OW: In lots of shows, yes. We also pioneered the two-part, one-intermission formula, which nowadays is pretty standard. A lot of our shows ran without a break, and all of them were *short*. For me, you know, almost everything is too long. One of our productions, *Shoemaker's Holiday*, ran less than an hour, and nobody ever asked for their money back.

PB: I wonder if maybe there's a connection with films—

OW: How?

PB: Well, they also play through uninterrupted.

OW: Not here, boy—not in Italy. We sit and watch the lady trying to sell us Eskimo Pies for twenty-five minutes right in the middle of the picture.

PB: Every picture?

OW: It's written right into the scripts: "Part One," "Part Two." It's all programmed for the candy and ice-cream bars. The worst thing is that first moment, when they throw on the lights and everybody's sort of caught there sitting together in an empty building.

That, of course, is what a movie theatre always is. And there's nothing up onstage except a loudspeaker crouching behind the screen. No matter how many customers there are, it's still an empty building.

PB: You once said, "The theatre is a collective experience and the film is the work of one man—the director."

OW: I hope you've got that slightly wrong. A movie, of course, is a collaborative effort. When it's a work of art, then it goes without saying that the collaborators were at the service of a single and unique conception—the film author's. You must have winkled that quote out of one of those foreign interviews conducted in a language I don't speak very fluently. Maybe it lost something in the translation.

PB: What about the theatre being a collective experience? You want to take that back?

OW: Well, I don't want to take any bows for it, it's so goddamn obvious. The *living theatre* is *alive*—it's just that simple. A movie's not only dead, it's not even very *fresh*. It comes in a can. To make a picture—not just to shoot it, but to plan it and then finish it—takes time. Because time passes, the very latest film is always bound to be slightly shop-soiled, subtly old-fashioned. That movie opening next week is last year's movie.

PB: You've been quoted as saying that the theatre is on its last legs—

OW: Sure . . .

PB: —but that it's always been dying.

OW: Everybody's said that, ever since the Greeks. *The Fabulous Invalid*, that was what Kaufman and Hart called the theatre. I don't know who *they* were quoting, but they wrote a play with that title, and one of the characters was based on me, I'm proud to say.

PB: They wrote *The Man Who Came to Dinner*, too, and wasn't *that* character—?

OW: The gent in the wheelchair was much more Alex Woollcott than me. But George and Moss did admit that there were elements —the radio broadcasts, particularly—

PB: Radio. Shall we talk about that?

OW: OK, but first, for the record, I hope I didn't seem to be saying that the theatre is finished. Great artists continue to perform in it, but it's no longer hooked up to the main powerhouse. Theatre persists as one of those divine anachronisms—like grand

opera (which I much prefer) and classical ballet (which I don't really dig at all). A performing art, more than a creative one, a source of joy and wonder, but not a thing of *now*.

PB: The "thing of now," of course, being film?

OW: Number One. And then there's television, still largely undiscovered territory. . . .

PB: How about radio?

OW: An abandoned mine.

PB: That means radio has become another anachronism?

OW: Sure, like silent movies—a victim of technological restlessness. Radio still functions in a way, of course; but the silents are wiped out. That's like giving up all watercolors because somebody invented oil paint. And black-and-white is going the same silly route. For me, radio's a personal loss, I miss it very much. . . . What's that, for God's sake—more notes?

PB: It says here that you got into radio in 1934.

OW: Yes, I'd been turning up for auditions and never landing a job, until I met Paul Stewart. He's a lovely man; for years he was one of the main pillars of our Mercury broadcasts. He can't be given too much credit. Well, he started me off—got me on to something called *Cavalcade of America*—"brought to you every Sunday evening by Du Pont." I played old John D. Rockefeller—rather too unsympathetically for the taste of the Du Ponts—and for a while that set back my career in radio. The first chink of light was what used to be called a "sustaining show," which meant no sponsors and very little money. It went on the air, as I remember, at seven o'clock in the morning. Educational, they called it—*School of the Air*—and it paid $18.50 a shot. Jo Cotten and I used to count it a lucky week when one of the two of us got one of those. Then suddenly—I've forgotten just how, but quite abruptly—I was a big wage-earner.

PB: With your own show, you mean?

OW: No, for a whole lot of shows, none of them mine. With a whole series of voices, all of them anonymous. There were a few of us back in radio's golden age who used to make quite important bread by skipping nimbly from one soap opera to another. Soon I was doing so many that I didn't even rehearse. I'd come to a bad end in some tearjerker on the seventh floor of CBS and rush up to the ninth (they'd hold an elevator for me), where, just as the red light was going on, somebody'd hand me a script and whisper, "Chinese mandarin, seventy-five years old," and off I'd go again.

Orson Welles on The Shadow.

Some days I had to commute between the networks by ambulance. If there's a law that says you've got to be sick to hire one, at least I was never arrested for breaking it.

PB: It was in those years that you did *The Shadow*.

OW: Lamont Cranston, that was me.

PB: You didn't write those things?

OW: My God, I didn't even know what was going to happen to me while I was *in* 'em. Not rehearsing—which was part of my deal with Blue Coal, the sponsor—made it so much more interesting. When I was thrown down the well or into some fiendish snake pit, I never knew how I'd get out.

PB: You had nothing to do with that marvelous opening speech—

OW: "Who knows what evil lurks in the hearts of men . . . ?" Well, I *said* it every week for years.

PB: And the laugh that followed.

OW: Me again—*and* all the kids in America—back in those days.

PB: Marvelous—it's become part of American mythology.

OW: $185 every week—you bet it was marvelous.

PB: That was good money in those days.

OW: For a few hours' work, it's good now. Some shows paid less, a few of them more. But without a single radio listener having ever heard my name, I was taking home about $1,500 weekly. But

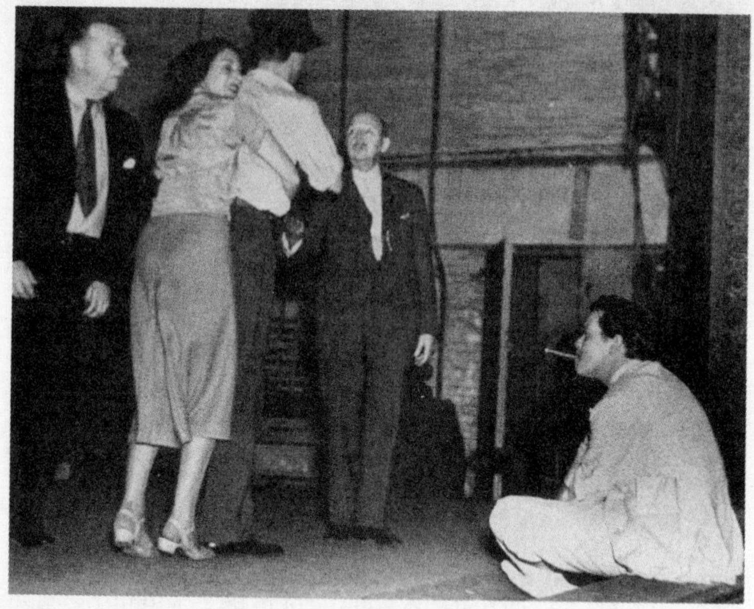

Welles directing Arlene Francis, Joseph Cotten, and others in Horse Eats Hat, *Maxine Elliott Theatre, 1936.*

"taking home" isn't accurate; a big hunk of that went to the government.

PB: Taxes bad even then?

OW: I trapped you into that.

PB: What do you mean?

OW: Anything about the WPA in those horrid little notes of yours?

PB: Yes, yes—Works Progress Administration. The government ran theatres during the Depression to give work to unemployed actors.

OW: Right.

PB: You were part of that, but it doesn't sound like you were unemployed.

OW: I was so employed I forgot how to sleep.

PB: You ran one of those federal theatres?

OW: Ran two of them, with Jack Houseman. One up in Harlem —an all-black project except for us—and the lovely Maxine Elliott on Broadway. There were lots of those projects all over the country. It was the only moment in history when America had a sort of national theatre. Joe Losey was part of that, too. There were endless committees, as you might imagine, and impenetrable jungles of red tape. It used to take guys like Joe as much as eight months just to get one of their shows together. Requisitions in triplicate clearing through twenty offices—you know the sort of thing.

Our plays got on much quicker and were much more handsomely mounted, thanks to *The Shadow* and *Big Sister* and stuff like that. The radio loot gave us the edge; that's what I meant by saying that so much of what I made went to the government. Roosevelt once said that I was the only operator in history who ever illegally siphoned money *into* a Washington project.

PB: You got to know Roosevelt in the WPA?

OW: Political campaigning. It was during the third one, as I remember, that he said that.

PB: Not part of a political speech.

OW: God, no—part of a private conversation late at night over some drinks on the presidential train.

PB: The Mercury Theatre grew out of the WPA. How about your Mercury radio show—did that grow out of your radio acting?

OW: Well, really it was through radio production that we made it into the theatre. I'd been with most of our leading actors in radio —people like Agnes Moorehead, Joseph Cotten, Everett Sloane, Ray Collins, George Coulouris, Erskine Sanford, Frank Readick. The ones who played in *Kane* were all from radio.

PB: Which would you say were some of the best Mercury shows?

OW: *Dracula* was a good one.

PB: It would make a good movie.

OW: *Dracula* would make a marvelous movie. In fact, nobody has ever made it; they've never paid any attention to the book, which is the most hair-raising, marvelous book in the world. It's told by four people, and must be done with four narrations, as we did on the radio. There's one scene in London where he throws a heavy bag into the corner of a cellar and it's full of screaming babies! They can go that far out now. Bram Stoker was the stage manager of Henry Irving, and *Dracula* was based on him; it was Stoker's vengeance on Henry Irving. He was a very considerable writer, Stoker—an old drunk Irishman—wrote some very good books. And he offered *Dracula* to Irving to make a play of it, but he didn't do it, and two fellows named Deane and Balderston did

—wrote this corny, terrible play with two sets. It's awful, and it became one of the biggest money-makers of all time. It works terribly well in the theatre—I did it once, played Dracula, and enjoyed doing it. And all the movies are based on the *play*, not the book. Nobody has ever gone back to the book.

PB: How about radio acting, Orson—would you say that it's similar to the acting required for movies? I mean, in the sense that—

OW: That you don't have to make yourself heard in the gallery? The famous difference between stage acting and acting for the camera? It's all nonsense, you know. There's just good acting and bad.

PB: You don't believe in playing down for the camera?

OW: You can play *up* for the camera. With enough energy behind it, you can't ever go too high. When it looks like you're pushing—well, then it's because you *are* pushing. It's because you can't get up there *without* pushing.

PB: But surely there's a limit, Orson. The camera isn't a theatre.

OW: The camera is an eye. And an ear. It takes you where it's *put*. The theatre is where you *get* put.

PB: OK, but are you saying it's impossible for acting to be too broad in front of the camera? That there's no such thing as hamming?

OW: Hamming is faking. It's opening a bag of tricks instead of turning on the juice. The right actor—the true *movie actor*—can never be too *strong*. What he must not be is too *broad*. What you're after isn't *spread*. You don't want to smear it all over the screen like pancake batter. Big acting isn't wide. It's sharp, pointed, vertical. Power, real explosive power, but never the explosion. The real stuff doesn't diffuse, it stays right on target. Hamming has no target, its only aim is to please. You can tell an actor from a whore only if he's totally in the service of his material. The public's pleasure and approval are incidental rewards.

"Playing down to the camera"? Never play down. *Up* is your direction. You shouldn't play *to* the camera at all. A camera isn't a girl. It isn't a mirror to pose in front of. Ham actors are not all of them strutters and fretters, theatrical vocalizers—a lot of them are understaters, flashing winsome little smiles over the teacups, or scratching their T-shirts. Cagney was one of the biggest actors in the whole history of the screen. Force, style, truth, and control—he had everything. He pulled no punches; God, how he projected! And yet nobody could call Cagney a ham. He didn't bother about reducing himself to fit the scale of the camera; he was much too busy doing his job. Toshiro Mifune: his movie performances would register in the back row of the Kabuki.

PB: But, Orson, don't you think there's still something called movie acting?

OW: There are movie *actors*. Cooper was a movie actor—the classic case. You'd see him working on the set and you'd think, "My God, they're going to have to retake that one!" He almost didn't seem to *be there*. And then you'd see the rushes, and he'd fill the screen.

PB: How do you explain that?

OW: Personality. I wouldn't presume to explain that mystery. It always matters more than technique. Who, for instance, knows more about technique than Olivier? Certainly, if screen acting depends significantly on *camera technique*, Larry would have made himself the master of it. And yet, fine as he's been in films, he's never been more than a shadow of that electric presence which commands the stage. Why does the camera seem to diminish him? And enlarge Gary Cooper—who knew nothing of technique at all?

Chaliapin—an actor whose genius was equal to his enormous stature as a personality. And believe me, Peter, that's really saying something. He was by far the *biggest* actor of our century. [Singer and actor Fyodor Chaliapin (1873–1938), much admired by Meyerhold, appeared in G. W. Pabst's 1934 film version of *Don Quixote*.] No contest; nobody could make his weight. And what was he onscreen? Just marginally impressive . . . Frank Fay, the vaudevillian's vaudevillian. What would Jack Benny have been without him? Fay made it from the Palace to legit, and made it very big—but not to Hollywood. On the screen he was a ghost. And now—right now, in fact, because it's time to go—you're going to see a marvelous example of this mystery we've been talking of: Eduardo de Filippo. [Actor, dramatist, theatrical producer, and film director, de Filippo was born in Naples in 1900, appeared in Vittorio De Sica's *Gold of Naples* (1954) and was co-screenwriter of *Yesterday, Today and Tomorrow* (1964).] On the stage nobody in Europe can come close to him. But nobody. In movies he just ceases to *happen*.

A street café at midnight on a small, deserted piazza near the theatre where Orson had taken me to see Eduardo de Filippo. Understanding about two words of Italian, I've only lasted for an act, and Orson is indignant; his theory is that you can actually judge acting better *if you* don't *understand the language.*

OW: It's easier to focus on it, Peter, if you simply can't get interested in the plot.

PB: Well, of course I could see he was *good*—

OW: Good? Eduardo? For God's sake, he's *great!* But some time you'll catch him in a movie, and then you'll see what I was talking about. The camera *doesn't like him.* This, by the way, is Akim Tamiroff's theory, not mine. "De box looks at vun fella," he says, "and de box says, 'Yes, dot vun is for me!' It looks at annoder, and it says, 'Nawww!' Who knows why?" He's right, of course—nobody knows why. And why does the camera *like* people? A second-rate stage actor like Emil Jannings—what made him first-rate on the screen? All right—a first-rate *overactor,* if you will. But whence came all that huge authority in front of the camera?

PB: *You're* sometimes criticized for overacting.

OW: I know, I know. . . .

PB: But looking at your films, as I've been doing—running them three and four times—it strikes me that your real style is understatement.

OW: Well, that's the *intention.*

PB: But, then, you've been attacking understatement—

OW: Peter, the *camera does not make understatement obligatory.* We're back now in this spooky business of personality. There are personalities who seem to be overstatements *in themselves.* Unhappily, I'm one of those. The camera doesn't just enlarge—it blows me up.

PB: You just said that nothing an actor does can ever be too big—

OW: Nothing can be too *strong.* If you just naturally displace too much air, that puts a limit on the size of your attack. You yourself provide the limitation, not the camera.

PB: But in acting—acting in general—some things do work better in closeup. Will you give me that?

OW: Dear Peter—I'll give you all the closeups you want. Personally, I don't much like them, as you know. I tell actors, "Look out—if you aren't good enough, we'll have to move in for a close shot."

PB: You've just now made a movie almost entirely in closeups.

Laurence Harvey and Oja Kodar in The Deep.

OW: *The Deep.* Well, it all happens on two small boats: what else could I do? I'll give you something else, Peter—there is indeed such a thing as a *closeup actor.* He's the one who doesn't score unless you frame him just under the chin. Rin Tin Tin and Lassie are good examples of the type.
PB: The camera's supposed to be a great lie-detector. Do you think it shows when the emotion is false?
OW: Sure, a kind of litmus-paper effect. What registers is the presence or absence of *feeling.* Quality counts, but the precise nature of the emotion isn't always automatically clear—and can be all too easily altered, as you know, or totally revised in the cutting room. I've said there can't be too much force, too much energy. *Emotional force* can charge up a living theatre, but on the screen there's often trouble keeping it in focus. Strong feelings can get very messy. What the camera does, and does uniquely, is to *photograph thought.* Don't you agree?
PB: Maybe. I'd like to have a little time on that one.
OW: That's my profoundest conviction in this whole business of moviemaking: the camera is not so much a lie-detector as a Geiger counter of mental energy. It registers something that's only vaguely, suppositionally detectable to the naked eye, registers it

clear and strong: thought. Every time an actor *thinks*, it goes right on the film.

PB: How about the microphone?

OW: Emotions—that's more the business of the sound track. You can *hear* a phony feeling before you can see it.

PB: I think that's very true. So where does that put radio?

OW: I was happy in it, Peter, the happiest I've ever been as an actor. It's so . . . what do I want to say, impersonal? No, *private*. It's as close as you can get, and still get paid for it, to the great, private joy of singing in the bathtub. The microphone's a friend, you know. The camera's a critic. I guess I'd say that radio's a lot closer to film than the theatre—and not just because it's another attentive machine substituting for the audience. No, with the microphone, as with the camera, you've got a choice of placement. You don't just sit out there snuffling in the darkness. You move around—you change angles.

> *A wire from Alexander Woollcott after the Mercury's Mars broadcast (October 30, 1938), when a good part of the country was frightened into believing that New Jersey had been invaded by Martians; on the rival network at the same time were Edgar Bergen and Charlie McCarthy; Orson had it posted in his office for years:*
>
> This only goes to prove, my beamish boy, that the intelligent people were all listening to a dummy, and all the dummies were listening to you.

PB: I've often wondered if you had any idea, before you did it, that *The War of the Worlds* was going to get that kind of response.

OW: The *kind* of response, yes—that was merrily anticipated by us all. The *size* of it, of course, was flabbergasting. Six minutes after we'd gone on the air, the switchboards in radio stations right across the country were lighting up like Christmas trees. Houses were emptying, churches were filling up; from Nashville to Minneapolis there was wailing in the street and the rending of garments. Twenty minutes in, and we had a control room full of very bewildered cops. They didn't know who to arrest or for what, but they did lend a certain tone to the remainder of the broadcast. We began to realize, as we plowed on with the destruction of New

Press conference after War of the Worlds *broadcast, 1938.*

Jersey, that the extent of our American lunatic fringe had been underestimated.

PB: You claimed innocence afterwards.

OW: There were headlines about lawsuits totaling some $12 million. Should I have pleaded guilty?

PB: What happened to the lawsuits?

OW: Most of them, as it turned out, existed in the fevered imagination of the newspapers. They'd been losing all that advertising to radio, so here, they reckoned, was a lovely chance to strike back. For a few days, I was a combination Benedict Arnold and John Wilkes Booth. But people were laughing much too hard, thank God—and pretty soon the papers had to quit.

PB: What about CBS?

OW: The day after the show, all you could find were sound mixers and elevator men. There wasn't an executive in the building. During rehearsals they'd been rather edgy, but what was there to censor? We were told not to say "Langley Field," because that was a real place, so we wrote in "Langham Field"—little things like that, so they couldn't complain when the lid blew off. But as I say, we were surprised ourselves by the size and extent of it.

PB: Is it a true story that when Pearl Harbor was announced, nobody believed it because—?

OW: Dead right. Particularly since I had a patriotic broadcast that morning and was interrupted in the middle of it. I was on the full network, reading from Walt Whitman about how beautiful America was, when they said Pearl Harbor's attacked—now, doesn't that sound like me trying to do that again? They interrupted the show to say that there had been an attack. Roosevelt sent me a wire about it. I've forgotten what—I don't have it. Something like "crying wolf" and that kind of thing. Not the same day—he was too busy!—but about ten days later. [*This thought was used as dialogue in Howard Hawks'* Air Force *(1943), in a scene in which flyers are hearing the Pearl Harbor reports on radio. —PB*]

PB: Then the Martian broadcast didn't really hurt you at all. Would you say it was lucky?

OW: Well, it put me in the movies. Was that lucky? I don't know. Anyway, thanks to the Martians, we got us a radio sponsor, and suddenly we were a great big commercial program, right up there with Benny, Burns and Allen, and the *Lux Radio Theatre* with C. B. De Mille. The next step was Hollywood. . . .

Now there's a station-break, if I ever heard one.

In the early 1960s, Orson wrote the following for the first issue of a new Spanish film magazine, the name for which he had suggested to its editor, Juan Cobbs, who was his assistant on Chimes at Midnight. *The name was used, and the magazine is still called* Griffith*:*

I met D. W. Griffith only once and it was not a happy meeting. A cocktail party on a rainy afternoon in the last days of the last year of the 1930s. Hollywood's golden age, but for the greatest of all directors it had been a sad and empty decade. The motion picture which he had virtually invented had become the product—the exclusive product—of America's fourth-largest industry, and on the assembly lines of the mammoth movie factories there was no place for Griffith. He was an exile in his own town, a prophet without honor, a craftsman without tools, an artist without work. No wonder he hated me. I, who knew nothing about films, had just been given the greatest freedom ever written into a Hollywood contract. It was the contract he deserved. I could see that he was not at all too old for it, and I couldn't blame him for feeling I was very much too young. We stood under one of those pink Christmas trees they have out there, and drank our drinks and stared at each other across a hopeless abyss. I loved and worshipped him, but he didn't need a disciple. He needed a job. I have never really hated Hollywood except for its treatment of D. W. Griffith. No town, no industry, no profession, no art form owes so much to a single man. Every filmmaker who has followed him has done just that: followed him. He made the first closeup and moved the first camera. But he was more than a founding father and a pioneer, his works will endure with his inventions. The Griffith films are far less dated today than they were a quarter of a century ago when we drank together under the pink Christmas tree and I failed so dismally to express what he means to me—to all of us. I have failed again. He is beyond tribute.

Another restaurant in Rome, Cesarina's—a favorite haunt of Orson's (and his friend Fellini's).

OW: When I first came to Hollywood, I wanted to make a movie about the great days of the silents. It would have been easier then. You could be freer now, but less true, maybe. Now we're so much farther away from it—

PB: Do your really think Griffith is the best director in history?

OW: Well, "best" is a bad word. There are only a few artists in *all* the arts who can be called the best without any argument. I can only think of two—Mozart and Shakespeare. . . . Velázquez, for my money, but there you can get arguments. The "best" is a very dicey kind of thing to try to decide. But if you're backed up against the wall on the matter of movie directors, isn't it going to have to be the founding father?

PB: Griffith's often accused of being overly sentimental.

OW: There's no defense against that charge, of course. He was very much of his epoch. He was an actor from Belasco's kind of theatre—and in that tradition, sentimentality was a big ingredient.

PB: Did his films exert an influence on you, do you think?
OW: He's influenced everyone who's ever made a movie.
PB: What did you think of Hollywood when you first got there?
OW: The movie town had its delightfully ridiculous moments and nobody in their right mind took it seriously. But American films and our film industry in its good days should be taken seriously now.
PB: I'm sure you didn't have the attitude toward Hollywood that so many people had—you know, that it's simply a place where sellouts go and there's nothing good ever made there.
OW: Well, the town is pretty terrible, you know—the community and the life it leads. But it used to be great fun also—I enjoyed it a lot. Still, I spent as little time there as I could. The minute a day's work was over, I was on a plane—weekends going down to Mexico or up to San Francisco.

But that's not a criticism of what you mean by Hollywood—the whole institution, as opposed to the movie colony. It deserved respect, and got it from me—guarded but genuine. I was friends with all the old-time sultans and taipans. Even in the days when I was supposed to be blowing it all up, I was having dinner with the likes of Sam Goldwyn and Jack Warner. Dinner, you understand. I was careful not to work for them. And they were pretty careful, too.
PB: You knew a lot of the older directors?
OW: Most of them—Vidor, Ford, Capra, Fleming, Milly [Lewis] Milestone, Woody Van Dyke. They weren't all of them so old then, of course—but at that epoch they looked a bit old-timey to me.
PB: W. S. Van Dyke—he wasn't a bad director.
OW: Woody made some very good comedies. And what a system he had! Did you know that his retakes sometimes took longer than his original shooting schedule?
PB: What do you mean?
OW: He'd shoot a *Thin Man* or something like that in about twenty days. Then he'd preview it and come back to the studio for thirty days of retakes. For comedy, when you're worried about the laughs, that makes a lot of sense. He gave me some advice I remember: "Just keep it close," he said, "and keep it moving."
PB: Did you follow it?
OW: Not really. I stay *away* from closeups when I can, you know—and when my actors are good enough.
PB: But you do keep it moving.

OW: The story, maybe. The camera? Only when there's a reason to—not just for the fun of it, or to show off. I was reading a review of somebody's movie the other day—the critic hated it: "Not since *Othello*," he said, "has there been such an excess of camera movement." I guess he was talking about that one short scene where we tied the camera to a roller skate; while it was photographing me, I was pushing it around on a stick. That was supposed to be epilepsy, and it only ran about a hundred feet. The rest of the time, we didn't do much hustling about. No crane shots at all; we didn't even have a dolly—just a jeep with some air let out of the tires.

PB: Did other directors give you advice?

OW: No, but they were all very nice to me. The big ones, I mean. I took a lot of trouble getting to know them, and it was worth it—sort of rubbing movies into my pores. . . .

PB: Was it true that one director told you not to call them "movies," but "motion pictures"?

OW: Ah, that was a friend of yours, Peter—that was George Cukor, and remember, he was from the New York stage. That probably had something to do with it. Nowadays, I'm afraid the word is rather chic. It's a good English word, though—"movie." How pompous it is to call them "motion pictures." I don't mind "films," though, do you?

PB: No, but I don't like "cinema."

OW: I know what you mean. In the library of Elèonora Duse's villa in a little town in Veneto where we've been shooting just now [*The Merchant of Venice*], I found an old book—written in 1915—about how movies are made, and it refers to movie actors as "photoplayers." How about that? Photoplayers! I'm never going to call them anything else.

PB: I have a book from 1929, and they list 250 words to describe a talking picture, asking readers to write in their favorites. And "talkie" was only one of them. Others were things like "actorgraph," "reeltaux," and "narrative toned pictures."

OW: I went with my father to the world premiere in New York of Warner's first Vitaphone sound picture, which was *Don Juan* starring Jack Barrymore. I think it was the opening night. It was really a silent, with a synchronized sound track full of corny mood music, horse hooves, and clashing swords. But it was preceded by a few short items of authentic talkies—Burns and Allen, George Jessel telephoning his mother, and Giovanni Martinelli ripping hell out of *Pagliacci*. My father lasted about half an hour and then went up the aisle dragging me with him. "This," he said, "ruins the movies forever." He never went back to a movie theatre as long as he lived. Anyway, he was a chum of Barrymore's, and that must have been the very worst Jack ever was. They'd put this little curly blond wig on him—and he just looked diseased.

PB: I heard a story about Barrymore. This was when he was making some B picture at RKO. . . .

OW: You mean the time he went into May Robson's dressing room and peed all over the old lady's wardrobe? Toward the end Jack was making rather a specialty of relieving himself in scandalous places. Weak bladder, I guess. But something else, too. That was a highly complicated man, Peter—a golden boy, a tragic clown grimacing in the darkness, gritting his teeth against the horror—a gallant old acrobat limping over the abyss on a tightrope that was badly frayed. But the spectacle, you know, wasn't invariably sad. He could be wildly funny. I guess you know what he did at the opening of *Kane?*

PB: No, what happened?

OW: That's the only one of my openings I ever went to. King Vidor gave a little dinner party. He asked me who I wanted to bring and I said Jack. There was some worry that he wouldn't or couldn't make it, but he turned up right at the appointed hour, resplendently dinner-jacketed and cold sober. And he was still apparently very much on his best behavior when we progressed, in our various rented limousines, to Grauman's Chinese or wherever it was. You know the scene—the screaming fans, arcs sweeping the sky. "Here comes Miss Shearer's car!" "Here's Cary *Grant!*" The greeter with the dry teeth and the microphone. Because of my radio show, they were on full network right across the country. "Well, well, Mr. Barrymore!" says the master of ceremonies in that bright commercial voice. "I see you've come with Mr. Welles. Have you got something you can tell us—speaking as a personal friend of his?" Jack took the microphone and held a slight pause. "I'm not a friend of his," he said; "you might say that I'm a *relative.*" "A relative? You don't mean to say Mr. Welles is a Barrymore?" Our genial radio host was very excited. Here was a red-hot scoop for all those listeners across the country. "Tell us about it."

Jack flashed him one of those tender, evil smiles of his. "Yes," he said, "I think it's time the public heard the truth—Orson is, in fact, the bastard son of Ethel and the Pope." . . . Now tell your story.

PB: Later. Mine isn't funny, and it's going to lead us—I hope—

Welles and Susan Fox in The Green Goddess, *1939.*

into another area. You were friendly with Barrymore, weren't you, even before you went to Hollywood?

OW: I used to stand in the wings when he was playing *Hamlet*—matinees, that is; I was a baby then—holding his private bucket of champagne. Years later, I got into the habit of flying down to Chicago to visit Jack when he was stuck down there in a dreadful little charade called *My Dear Children*. Then later I was there myself, not just to visit, but in a dreadful little charade of my own—a tab version of *The Green Goddess*.

PB: What's a "tab version"?

OW: That's from the language of vaudeville—an institution that died before you were born. I helped to kill it.

PB: With *The Green Goddess?*

OW: A condensed or "tab" version of that ripe old piece of high comedy-melodrama. It had been my notion that this would appeal to what is known as "the popular taste"—a grave miscalculation. Too bad, because I'd dropped a lot of dough just then on a fairly highbrow piece called *Danton's Death*.

PB: So the melodrama was a sort of reaction?

OW: It was a doomed attempt to recuperate our losses. In Chicago we did four-a-day. And six-a-day, my God, in Steubenville, Ohio. While we were at the Palace, Jack used to come along and play afternoon shows with us.

PB: Barrymore played a part in that thing?

OW: Well, he walked on—if that's the word I'm after. You *might* say that he *improvised*. Stanislavsky would have been proud of him. Imagine the two of us, clowning around up there in front of those poor, bewildered little gatherings of people. And when I say "little," that's the word. I was closing vaudeville houses all over the country. Forever.

> *The following was written at the time [1939] by an anonymous publicity person in the Mercury operation and has never been printed before:*

> . . . Welles was told by all his friends that he should not go into vaudeville. When they heard he definitely was, they all told him they hoped for the sake of his career he would do something dignified. So instead of doing his magic act he decided to cut *The Green Goddess* down to twenty minutes. That was easy. In fact, after seeing the twenty-minute version it is hard to believe how George Arliss got two hours out of it. He opened in Chicago and all went fairly well until the time came for a quick change before the last scene. As the Maharajah of Rook, Welles wore a turban, a long robe and black patent-leather boots. Under this were the rolled-up trousers of the dress suit he wore in the next scene—simply by dropping them. When he made the quick change, his dresser carefully removed the robe and then just as carefully put it back on him. This happened twice in the dark. So did several other things. Finally, after the music cue had been played for the third time by the anxious orchestra and extras were getting lost out on the stage, Welles made his entrance as the presumably nonchalant and immaculate Rajah, with his snap-on tie and collar reversed, pants still rolled up and an unlit and broken cigar in his hand. Welles couldn't understand the wonderful laughter he got with his opening speech . . .

PB: When all those things went wrong, I understand you made a speech to the audience and told them to demand their money back.
OW: True.
PB: That must have endeared you to the management.
OW: There weren't enough people in the audience to matter one way or another. . . . Funny thing, Peter—it seemed like, every house we played, the chief of the stage crew always introduced himself as the brother of John Ford.

PB: He must have had a lot of brothers!
OW: Why not? Those Irish families do.

> *In a 1967 interview for* Playboy, *Orson said that the film directors who appealed the most to him were the "old masters—by which I mean John Ford, John Ford and John Ford . . . With Ford at his best, you feel that the movie has lived and breathed in a real world—even though it may have been written by Mother Machree."*

PB: I think maybe you were influenced by some of Ford's pictures.
OW: I don't quite see that, but then, I'm such a fan of his that it wouldn't be surprising. Once, after I'd made a couple of pictures of my own, I got a sort of diploma from him—you might call it a citation. This had been put together in a bar in some sleazy fishing village in Baja California, and it was written, none too soberly, on the back of an old piece of cardboard. Many ornate and official-looking stamps were pasted all over this document, including several Mexican beer labels. Well, of course I had it framed. For many years, until somebody pinched it, it was the only award I ever used for decoration in my office.
PB: What did it say?
OW: The text was brief. There was just this simple statement: "Orson Welles has been elected."
PB: To what?
OW: The name of the institution doing me this honor wasn't given, but Duke Wayne had scrawled his signature as vice-president of something illegible across the Great Seal of Cresta Blanca. And there were those other names you know so well, Peter—all those hairy good companions of Ford's famous clan.
PB: I didn't know you were a member.
OW: I wasn't; that's why I was so pleased and complimented to receive that document from John Ford and his merry crew. It wasn't a command to turn up at any meetings, you understand—it was more like a citation. I was just . . . *elected.*
PB: I could never see you as a clansman, as a matter of fact.
OW: Well, I'm not much of a joiner, really. But I do have a sort of dim, out-of-town membership in Sinatra's thing. . . . I was maybe his first friend in Hollywood, knew him when he was still a singer with the band. You're right, of course, I don't run with the

Rat Pack, but Frank and I are still quite close. . . . And then there's Hemingway, another chieftain. I've had visitor's cards to some of Ernest's clubs. He changed outfits through the years, but I guess you always knew who was president.

PB: You never really had a club of your own?

OW: God, no.

PB: Wasn't the Mercury?

OW: A family. An Anglo-Saxon-type family where the members leave each other pretty much alone. We had our fun together during working hours—and it *was* fun, you know. The atmosphere was like a sort of house party. To give you an idea, we always kept a good jazz-piano man on the set. Between jobs, though, we tended to go our separate ways.

PB: You've never worked for John Ford, but—

OW: I almost did. He offered me the lead in *The Last Hurrah*.

PB: What happened?

OW: When the contracts were to be settled, I was away on location, and some lawyer—if you can conceive of such a thing—turned it down. He told Ford that the money wasn't right or the billing wasn't good enough, something idiotic like that, and when I came back to town the part had gone to [Spencer] Tracy.

PB: When did you first get to know Ford?

OW: He came on the set while we were shooting *Kane*—to wish me luck, you know—and there was a first assistant (let's call him Eddie) who we later learned was an informer for the anti-*me* faction in the front office. Ford's greeting to him was the first hint we had of his real status. "Well, well," he said, "how's old snake-in-the-grass Eddie?" That was the tipoff.

PB: Did Ford know you'd been studying *Stagecoach*?

OW: Why should he? It wasn't what you'd call a big public event—I'd just been running it a lot.

PB: Why *Stagecoach* specifically?

OW: Why not? I wanted to learn how to make movies, and that's such a classically perfect one—don't you think so? Not by any means my favorite Ford, but what a textbook!

PB: I think the influence shows in *Kane*.

OW: Yeah?

PB: Well, for example, there are a couple of low ceilings in *Stagecoach* . . .

OW: Sure there are. I hope you don't think I ever pretended to be the inventor of the ceiling.

PB: A lot of people say you were.
OW: A lot of people ought to study *Stagecoach.*
PB: You said it's not your favorite—
OW: Oh, I love most of his pictures—*The Informer* and *The Quiet Man* least of all. Oh, and that thing with Duke Wayne in the South Pacific—
PB: *Donovan's Reef.*
OW: And *Grapes of Wrath*—he made that into a story about mother love. Sentiment is Jack's vice. When he escapes it, you get a perfect kind of innocence. *Young Mr. Lincoln*, for instance. How truly great that is! And what a sense he always has for *texture*—for the physical existence of things. *The Iron Horse*—I'll never forget what an effect that had on me as a child.
PB: Orson, you claim you weren't interested in movies as a child.
OW: I *loved* movies. It just didn't occur to me to want to make 'em. Peter, there are maybe dozens of people scattered over the world who care passionately about films and don't want to direct. I was one of them. Hey! What about his comedies? What about *Judge Priest?* He's such a fine comedy director—people tend to forget that.
PB: According to Peter Noble's book about you [*The Fabulous Orson Welles*, 1956], while you were preparing *Kane*, you also ran films by many other directors—Hitchcock, Lang, Vidor, Capra.
OW: I never really got to talk to Noble when he was doing that thing; he pasted it together out of newspapers and magazines, so it's no fault of his that the book is a perfect treasury of misinformation. No, *Stagecoach* was the only picture I looked at—in those terms, I mean. You see, I couldn't push my way onto other people's sets. Everybody'd stop and be polite and I'd just be in the way. But if I couldn't watch, how could I learn? As it turned out, the first day I ever walked onto a set was my first day as a director. I'd learned whatever I knew in the projection room—from Ford. After dinner every night for about a month, I'd run *Stagecoach*, often with some different technician or department head from the studio, and ask questions. "How was this done?" "Why was this done?" It was like going to school.

Orson's cutting room in a film studio on the Palatine Hill. I've come early for our appointment in order to watch him work. He has a large staff of assistants and uses three moviolas, jumping from one to the other. When it's time for the lunch break, we take sandwiches and a bottle of Chianti and sit out under the trees. Famous ruins are all around us, the Church of SS Giovanni Paolo looming over the studio itself. I have just seen the bell tower on one of the moviola screens, Orson as The Merchant of Venice*'s Shylock standing in front of it. The reverse angle of this scene was on the second moviola. This was shot in Venice. Another angle for the same scene, on the third moviola, was shot in Yugoslavia. Why Yugoslavia? Because the Venetian weather had closed in early this year and Orson had gone south to the Dalmatian coast, which, he says, having once been part of the Venetian Empire, is full of the right sort of architecture. Orson's closeup in front of the Roman church had been a retake due to scratches on the negative.*

OW: We've had to change labs three times. . . .
PB: You've never played Shylock before?
OW: No, but I've always wanted to. When Olivier started the National Theatre in London, I thought my chance had finally come. Ken Tynan, then the Number Two in that management, had asked me what I'd like to do with them. I said *The Merchant*. Ken made encouraging noises, and seven years went by. Another case of waiting for the phone to ring. Then, last spring, Larry asked me to direct him in it. I wasn't free for that, but he'd heard about my notion for Bassanio.

You remember the story of the three caskets—to win Portia's hand in marriage, a suitor has to pick the right one. Well, Bassanio is basically a fortune hunter. When he first talks about Portia he says, "In Belmont is a lady richly left—*and* she is fair. . . ." Taking that for a cue, my notion was for him to get three full tries at the casket—choosing in three different disguises. In other words, he comes on as [the Prince of] Aragon and the Prince of Morocco as well as himself; that way he *can't* lose. Larry wanted me to give him that for his own production, but I asked him to let me keep the gimmick for myself. You can only do it once.
PB: You want to do a lot of TV?
OW: Well, I want to make movies, Peter, and I'll do 'em for any size screen that's suitable.
PB: Getting back to our chronology, wasn't your original Hollywood deal to make *Heart of Darkness*?
OW: Pretty much. It was really to make anything, but then, in

the course of signing the deal, it was agreed that it would be *Heart of Darkness.* It was a direct result of radio—and we'd done *Heart of Darkness* on the radio. I came to Hollywood and wrote the script, which was going to be a film in the first person: the camera was going to be Marlow, which is ideal for that particular kind of story, because he's in the pilot house and he can see himself reflected in the glass through which you see the jungle. So it isn't that business of a hand-held camera mooching around pretending to walk like a man. It's kind of the perfect setup, because you needed a lot of narration, and you would see the man who was talking reflected in the glass as you went up the river, and so on. It would have worked, I think. . . . I did a very elaborate preparation for that, such as I've never done again—never could. I shot my bolt on preproduction on that picture. We designed every camera setup and everything else—did enormous research in aboriginal, Stone Age cultures in order to reproduce what the story called for. I'm sorry not to have got the chance to do it. The reason we didn't was because we couldn't knock $50,000 off the budget.

PB: Simple as that?

OW: Simple as that. We just came right up against it, and it was clear that that $50,000 couldn't go.

PB: Did you actually start rehearsing?

OW: No, I made a test scene with Robert Coote, who later played Roderigo in *Othello.* We did a big scene, Coote and two or three other people. We shot for one day.

PB: How did it look?

OW: I don't know. I guess it looked all right.

PB: What were you testing, actually?

OW: Really just seeing what would happen with me in a movie studio with a camera. It seemed to work all right, and Coote was terribly good in the scene.

PB: The first-person camera was later used by Robert Montgomery in *Lady in the Lake.*

OW: Yes. I never saw it. We did the test with a hand-held camera, which was unheard-of then. I finally tried the subjective camera in *The Magnificent Ambersons,* in a sequence which was cut out except for a little bit. I didn't think it worked very well. *Heart of Darkness* is one of the few stories that it's very well adapted to, because it relies so heavily on narration and because it's a movie that needs a lot of words. I haven't got anything at all against a lot of words in movies, by the way.

Welles examining model of the Heart of Darkness *temple with assistant director Edward Donohue.*

PB: No, if the words are good—

OW: And this was, of course, superb. Conrad—I don't see how you can do Conrad without all the words.

PB: It certainly is a gloomy piece.

OW: I don't know about that. It's tragic, yes, it's dark as anything can be. It *is* the heart of darkness, all right. I guess "gloomy" is as good a word as you could find. But the story is also so terrifying—

PB: What about it specifically appealed to you?

OW: I don't know. I think I'm made for Conrad. I think every Conrad story is a movie. There's never been a Conrad movie, for the simple reason that nobody's ever done it as written. My script was terribly loyal to Conrad. And I think that, the minute anybody does that, they're going to have a smash on their hands. Any of them. Think what *Lord Jim* could have been, if some attention had been paid to the original book.

PB: Is there any similarity in your mind between *Heart of Darkness* and *Kane*?

OW: Not at all. *Heart of Darkness* was a kind of parable of fascism. Remember the time I was working on that, 1939–1940. War hadn't

started, and fascism was the big issue of the time. It was a very clear parable.
PB: Is that what especially interested you?
OW: Part of it. The story is marvelously interesting, and it does have one thing which is in *Kane*, and which is a thing I like very much in pictures: the search for the key to something. It's a little bit like the plots of some of the best fairy stories.
PB: It's in *Mr. Arkadin*, too.
OW: Yes, that's right.
PB: You were going to play Marlow, and narrate it?
OW: Yes. So you'd see my reflection occasionally. There was some thought that I would play Kurtz as well, but I decided against that.
PB: Who would you have cast in the role?
OW: I hadn't cast it really—the decision not to play Kurtz was made right at the end, just before the picture fell through. I decided I was a little too obvious for Kurtz and it should be a more romantic kind of personality, less of a heavy man—even a young heavy man. I think it should have been a more surprising person as Kurtz than I would have been.

Anyway, after we gave it up, I suggested that, while I prepare something more serious, I do a picture for them called *The Smiler with a Knife* so the year wouldn't be lost. There was an actress under contract at RKO then making a picture, called Lucille Ball, who I thought was the greatest female clown around—she could have been just superb in this picture. And they said, "What do you want Lucille Ball for? She's practically washed up in pictures." This was thirty years ago—imagine how idiotic they were. They didn't know what they had. So we didn't make *Smiler with a Knife*.
PB: In your mind, what was *Smiler with a Knife* to be like visually? Something like *The Lady from Shanghai*?
OW: No. *Lady from Shanghai* was frankly an exercise in eroticism and exoticism—almost erotic for its time. And *Smiler with a Knife* would have been a farce about a very likable, handsome, extremely attractive young man who's planning to be the dictator of America —one of those plots where you don't know which cop is in his pay. The basic thing that I loved about it is that the girl doesn't dare go to any policeman, because she doesn't know which one has gone over.
PB: How does it turn out?
OW: Oh, it turns out all right. He comes to a bad end, but not

until she's been a department-store Santa Claus and a lot of other things—just the sort of thing that Lucille has done with enormous success on TV, fifteen years later. It was *exactly* what I wanted her to do then. And it was the only farce I ever got near to making.
PB: Is it true that Rosalind Russell and Carole Lombard turned it down because they didn't approve you as director?
OW: Totally untrue. Carole Lombard was a dear friend of mine, extremely close. Real, real pal. An ugly word, because by saying that I give the impression there was some kind of romance. There wasn't. She was busy falling in love with Gable and marrying him and being his bride all during that time. But we became tremendous friends, saw a great deal of each other, and performed many practical jokes. And she was all *for* me. She simply couldn't get released from the studio to which she was under commitment. I think Rosalind Russell may well have turned me down. I seem to remember somebody did—it may have been Russell. But my first choice was Lucille.
PB: Were you going to be in it?
OW: No, I wouldn't have been. Actually, I'd already started the *Citizen Kane* idea, which was going to take longer to write, and we were going to make *Smiler with a Knife* while that was being done. That's basically why Herman Mankiewicz was hired—so he could prepare a script of *Kane* while I was doing *Smiler with a Knife*.

> *Orson's room at the Hotel Eden in Rome. He has skipped dinner to finish the Shylock sequence and is making a late dinner of prosciutto and champagne. He rises every morning at six and writes until it is time to go to the studio, and now he's giving the tape recorder some very dirty looks. I feel rather guilty. Orson says that's just as it should be.*

OW: Tonight *you* do the talking.
PB: This isn't a book about me, Orson.
OW: Let's make it a book about Barrymore. Hey! What about your story?
PB: Barrymore was making a sort of guest appearance in a B picture with Sammy Kaye, the bandleader. For some unlikely reason, in the script he had to recite one of Hamlet's soliloquies, and it seems he pulled himself together and gave a really wonderful performance. The kind of thing that makes the stagehands burst into

applause. Only this time they couldn't applaud—everyone was in tears. The director came up to Barrymore and said, "There isn't any doubt about it, Jack, you're still the greatest actor in the world." Barrymore gave out one of those famous snorts. "Don't give me that," he said. "There are only two great actors—Charles Chaplin and Orson Welles."

OW [*after a slight pause*]: Now can we talk about Chaplin?

PB: What do you honestly think of that judgment?

OW: Biggest compliment of my life. Worth a truckload of Oscars.

PB: But do you agree?

OW: About Chaplin?

PB: Seriously. What do you think of yourself as an actor?

OW: I'm not sure, Peter. Usually I don't think of myself as an actor at all. Oh, I'm not ashamed of it, like Brando—

PB: Is he really?

OW: He says so, and I think he means it. As for me . . . well, I've seldom felt any sort of secure pride in that department. But, then, that's probably a lack everyone feels and suffers from except the real idiots. It might be thought that you have to be pretty well puffed up in self-esteem to be able to face the public at all. But the most interesting actors I've known are, every one of them, riddled with self-doubt. . . . As you can see, I'm trying to worm my way out of this one. How am I doing?

PB: Let's get at it another way—

OW: Let's talk about Chaplin.

PB: All right, are you as great an actor as he is?

OW: We aren't in the same league, Peter. Or even the same game.

PB: Are you a greater actor than Barrymore?

OW: Of course not. In his time (and mine), nobody in our language was ever as good as Barrymore . . . or as bad.

What I really do have in common with Jack is a lack of *vocation*. He himself played the part of an actor because that was the role that he'd been given by life. He didn't love acting. Neither do I. We both loved the theatre, though. I know I hold it, as he did, in awe and respect. A vocation has to do with the simple pleasure you have in doing your job. Charlie was a happier actor because he was born for it. . . . Let's talk about Charlie.

PB: You still haven't answered my question.

OW: I rather hoped we'd lost it in the shuffle.

PB: You've played most of the great parts—Macbeth, Brutus, Othello. . . .

OW: Yeah, I've been lucky—Lear, Richard III, Falstaff. It doesn't prove anything. Those parts are too big for any actor—the very biggest never manage to completely fill them. The nearest I've ever seen was Chaliapin—nobody came near to him for size, for sheer density. But almost any bum can get a crack at Boris [Godunov] or Lear. Sometimes the bums even make it with the public. Look at Maurice Evans. He took on practically everything in Shakespeare, the critics raved, and the people packed in to see him.
PB: And he was bad?
OW: Worse—he was poor. Mrs. Patrick Campbell said he had "the face of a bellhop." Garrick, of course, didn't have much of a face, but Evans didn't have much of a talent. More than anything, that's what drove me to Hollywood. With the notices he was getting and the business he was doing, I decided there wasn't much hope left for me on Broadway. Somebody had to get out of town. A personal prejudice, sure—but try to find an actor who has a good word for him. The great roles, you see, endow an actor with something that isn't necessarily related at all to his real merit—a place in the pecking order, prestige. . . . Are we changing the subject?
PB: You're still trying to.
OW: Yes, we aren't trying to find out what I think about Maurice Evans. In your dogged way, you're trying to get me to say what I think of myself.
PB: As an actor.
OW: All right—to presume to play the great parts you have to believe that you're a great actor—is that what you're getting at? Well, you have to think that just maybe you *could* be great. I'll give you that much.
PB: Sounds like false modesty to me.
OW: No, I never pretended to be modest, though I'm not the braggart I seem to be in my publicity. When I am guilty of boasting, it's defensive—when I've found myself in some sort of corner. Or when I lose my cool over some sort of Evans or Antonioni. Nobody who takes on anything big and tough can afford to be modest. But he cannot afford not to be humble. Is that grammar? It's logic, anyway.
PB: And you're humble?
OW: I try to approach the big, tough jobs with humility. I may not love to act, Peter, but I love the craft, the art of acting. If you work in any art form, you've simply got to love the form—the

institution—a whole lot more than you love yourself. Sounds pompous, but it's common sense.

What kind of actor am I? OK, let's try to level with that one. First, I'm less than I was. Less versatile. A thin man can play a fat man, and a young man can play an old man, but it doesn't work the other way around. As the years limit my range, I like to think that maybe I've gained a little bit in focus, in concentration. But I don't get enough *practice*. Another thing: You've got a hell of a lot going for you when you don't give a damn. And that's something else I've lost. Nowadays I do give a damn, and that puts me out of the Zen-archery range. I care a whole lot more than anybody guesses.

PB: Well, if you don't like acting, Orson, how *can* you "care"?

OW: I don't *enjoy* it. In front of the camera, it's less than pleasure for me and often very close to pain. But when I do it I'm anxious—very anxious indeed—to do it well. Even the lousiest jobs (and I have to accept a lot of those) never get less than the best I can give. The lousy ones take more out of you. If you're bad in a bad part—or small in a small part—you vanish. It takes a lot of effort just to remain *visible*.

PB: OK, I'll change the subject.

OW: Thank God.

PB: What movies did you like as a boy?

OW: The first one I can remember was *The Birth of a Nation*—a revival probably, but with a big symphony orchestra in the pit. It frightened and depressed me. I was batty about *Robin Hood* and *The Three Musketeers*. Fairbanks was my idol—Senior, of course. Larry Olivier's, too. He told me. We were both hooked on him. Nobody since has ever swashbuckled like that, or moved so beautifully, or seemed so charmingly, innocently *conceited* . . . *The Hunchback of Notre Dame*—that was a big event. Lon Chaney. I saw it last year again on TV and I still think it was great.

PB: In terms of acting?

OW: With Chaney it wasn't just the makeup. No, that was a fabulous silent-screen performance. Remember Laughton's performance? Charles could be superb, but as Quasimodo he was just one of those shambling village idiots. . . . As a child, of course, the movies I saw were the ones I got taken to. I went with my mother, I remember, to see *Nanook of the North*. She adored it. My father went to the movies for a nice afternoon snooze, and in the more comfortable of the movie palaces they didn't show foreign or "art" films, so I missed much of the cream of that period. And when we were in China, or even in Europe, we didn't seem to go to the movies at all. I did see some theatre—Russian and Middle European—and was very impressed by it.

PB: You never saw Lang's German films?

OW: Only those he did later in America—you did a book about them, didn't you? [PB's *Fritz Lang in America*, 1969.] But from the great UFA days, nothing. Anyway, I was always much more interested in the actors. I still am. Actors are the great underrated subject in this vast heap of literature that's piling up about films.

Before I went to Hollywood, I went to the movies for simple pleasure. I wasn't interested much in the directors. And I didn't much like the ones who were considered very fine back in the thirties.

PB: Like?

OW: Oh, like Mamoulian. Those kinds of movies bored me to death. And still do. . . . Then, even more than the straight actors, I loved the comics. Naturally, Laurel and Hardy—nobody has *ever* given them their due. Bill [W. C.] Fields. But Bill, if you can believe such a thing, was even funnier on the stage. They took me to see him in Ziegfeld's *Follies* and I laughed so hard they got worried and took me out of the theatre. All next day I had to be kept in bed. Quite literally, I'd laughed myself sick. Bill Fields only had to cross a room, you know, and I'd be retching with laughter. Harold Lloyd—he's surely the most underrated of them all. The intellectuals don't like the Harold Lloyd *character*—that middle-class, middle-American, all-American college boy. There's no obvious poetry to it, and—they miss that incredible technical brilliance. The construction of *Safety Last*, for instance—I saw it again only a few years ago. As a piece of comic architecture it's impeccable. Feydeau never topped it for sheer construction. He was, almost entirely, his own gag man. Really a writer who acted, if you know what I mean. To the silents, what Fred Allen was to radio. Someday he'll get his proper place—which is very high. Keaton was beyond all praise . . . a very great artist, and one of the most beautiful men I ever saw on the screen. He was also a superb director. In the last analysis, nobody came near him.

PB: Did you get to know any of these people?

OW: All of them. I got to know Lloyd through magic—we were both members of the same magical fraternity. What a lovely man!

Bill Fields was a friend of my father's. I used to see him quite a bit after I came to Hollywood. Keaton, too. I was lucky enough to get to know him fairly well just at the end of his days.
PB: When he was down and out.
OW: I guess so—he didn't give you any reason to suspect it. The Stage Door Canteen—a sort of cabaret-restaurant for servicemen run by show people—we both used to work there. I did magic and he washed dishes, for God's sake. Keaton, one of the giants! What about *The General*—that's a truly great movie, isn't it? Now, finally, Keaton's been "discovered." Too late to do him any good, of course—he lived all those long years in eclipse, and then, just as the sun was coming out again, he died. I wish I'd known him better than I did. A tremendously nice person, you know, but also a man of secrets. I can't even imagine what they were.
PB: What do you think of Jerry Lewis?
OW: When he goes too far, he's heaven; it's just when he doesn't go too far that he's unendurable [*laughs*]. Now he wants to be a respected member of the community, and it shows in every move of his body. But, *God*, he can be funny! He did a scene in a movie I saw in Paris about eight years ago where he keeps trying to fix the hat on a gangster's head—
PB: *The Ladies' Man.*
OW: And I got so sick laughing, it was like in my childhood with Fields—I really had a kind of heart attack from laughing. It was one of the funniest things I'd ever seen in my life. . . .

I know a lot more about Chaplin—a whole lot more. Shall we talk about Charlie?
PB: Yes, but later. Now let's talk about you. Your first movie . . .
OW: Ah, that was a documentary.
PB: A documentary? I never heard of that.
OW: Made it right here in Rome—a highly artistic study in 8mm of the big church that bears your name, featuring Significant Architectural Detail. This was hand-held throughout, mind you, so it was really way ahead of its time. I got fascinated with that fountain—Antonioni at the very summit of his powers never held a single shot so long. Then, to my horror, the very instant I'd run out of film, the great doors of the cathedral were flung open and, with a mighty fanfare of trumpets, out came the Pope on a palanquin surrounded by Swiss Guards and a hundred cardinals. Well, with an empty camera, you could say I missed the parade. After that experience, I retired as a filmmaker. If you're aiming to make

this study what they call "in depth," you might jot that down as traumatic. I was nine years old at the time.

PB: The first movie of which there is any formal record is some footage you made for one of your early stage productions.

OW: *Too Much Johnson.* One of our best things, I reckon, but aborted—only ran for a week's tryout. A summer theatre with no projection facilities. We didn't even get to town with the play. Hey, do you know, that film still exists!

PB: Where?

OW: Somewhere. I think in Madrid. Someday I'm going to give it as a birthday present to Jo Cotten. He's very funny in it . . . It's an imitation silent comedy—with a big chase over the roofs of the old chicken market in New York. Then there's a sequence in Cuba with a volcano erupting and Jo in a lovely white suit, carrying a big white umbrella and riding a big white horse. The horse had been Valentino's in *The Sheik,* and this was Jo's first experience as an equestrian. It was all quite dreamlike.

PB: What was its purpose to be within the play?

OW: *Too Much Johnson* had an elaborate farce plot that required a lot of old-fashioned, boring exposition to set it up. The idea was to take all that out and do the explaining in a movie. That way you could start right with the slamming doors.

PB: How did you shoot it?

OW: Got some kind of a silent camera and just went out and started cranking. . . . Lots of fun.

PB: And you still insist you weren't interested then in making movies?

OW: Well, I was interested in that.

Later I discovered what must officially be recorded as Orson's first film: it was made during the Summer Festival of Drama in Woodstock (1934), at the school he had attended as a boy, and was shot silent by William Vance, a young actor at the festival. It runs a little over five minutes and is called Hearts of Age.

The little film tells in a strange, surreal way of Death (played by Welles in grotesque old-age makeup as a kind of grinning joker) and how he comes to beckon the old lady (Virginia Nicolson, soon to become Welles' first wife, also much made-up) to her grave.

What's fascinating—apart from the obsession with old age

Joseph Cotten escaping from the Washington Market in Too Much Johnson, 1938.

> *which has continued almost as a leitmotif through Orson's pictures—is that the signature is so unmistakably his. The shots rush at you with amazing speed and variety—complex images of considerable strength; though clearly not a careful or even considered job, it has remarkable spirit and inventiveness.*
>
> *I asked him about it some time later, in New York, after letting him read my comments.*

OW: *Hearts of Age?* What does that mean, I wonder?
PB: Well, it was surrealistic.
OW: It was a send-up, Peter—just a charade. Sunday-afternoon fun out on the lawn. I don't much care for surrealism on the

screen. Never did. And how the hell did you find out about *that* little caper?

PB: The American Film Institute turned up a print and it's now in the Library of Congress.

OW: My God! I just love that "obsession-with-age" business you wrote—when I was trying to imitate Werner Krauss in *Caligari*, just as simple as that. In those days, *Caligari* was the cinéaste's dream picture, you know. It hasn't stood up, thank goodness, but it used to be considered a great classic. You saw it every time you went to New York. That and *Blood of a Poet* by Cocteau and Buñuel's *Un Chien Andalou*. It was a combination of all those. I've always been pretty much antisurrealist. But it was a put-on. Roger Hill had a movie camera. Simple as that. It was bought for the school.

> "Who's this Welles?" Pat asked of Louie, the studio bookie. "Every time I pick up a paper they got about this Welles."
>
> "You know, he's that beard," explained Louie.
>
> —F. Scott Fitzgerald,
> "Pat Hobby and Orson Welles"

Garden in the Roman Film Studios (another lunch).

PB: Why the beard?

OW: Why not? That's come to be kind of a famous question hurled regularly across the generation gap nowadays.

PB: Was there some sort of gap like that in Hollywood as far as you were concerned?

OW: The gap was mainly between the people I knew and the ones I didn't. The first group was friendly. Even the old dinosaur producers, the Goldwyns and the Warners—I was on cheerful dining-out terms with all of them right from the start. As for the beard—well, I'd worn it for *The Green Goddess*, I don't like shaving on trains, and when I got off at the station in Los Angeles and saw how much it was disturbing the community it seemed a good idea to keep it on for a while. It would have been useful for *Heart of Darkness* (if I'd made that picture, which of course I didn't). Then, too, maybe I hoped the whiskers would make me look a little less like a depraved baby.

PB: Didn't Guinn "Big Boy" Williams cut off your tie in a restaurant because of that beard?
OW: That was in Chasen's; we went outside and started a fight, but good friends pulled us apart. The whole thing was a formal affair, really, without much conviction on anybody's part. Errol Flynn sicked him onto me.
PB: I thought you were good friends with Flynn.
OW: Later. When I first came out, Errol was one of the leaders of the anti-Welles faction. Ward Bond was another.
PB: Then you mainly kept the beard for its irritation value?
OW: Let's say that I didn't fancy the idea of collaborating with prejudice.
PB: I think there was more to the prejudice than just the beard.
OW: Sure. There was the contract. Everybody wants a contract like that. Director-producer-writer-actor with absolute artistic control. Imagine! A certain amount of outrage always goes with hitting a gusher. Here was the unique gusher of all time—what everybody's always wanted—and here was a fellow who'd never even *been* in a movie who had it!
PB: Did you contractually have the right to the final cut?
OW: For the first time in the industry's history. And the important thing was that nobody, but *nobody*, could even see the rushes or come on the set.
PB: How did you know to ask for that?
OW: Well, for quite a while Hollywood had kept making me offers, which, in the natural order of things, kept getting better as I kept turning them down. I wasn't playing smart, you understand. Movies sounded like fun, but I was busy and happy with my own theatre and radio show. The more I didn't care, they more they did; and when they met the last and wildest of my demands, well, then, of course I gave in happily. Not, believe me, with any burning sense of vocation, but, rather, in the spirit that I'd become an actor in Ireland and a bullfighter in Spain.
PB: A bullfighter?
OW: When I left Dublin, you see, I'd also left the stage—
PB: To be a *bullfighter?*
OW: I was willing to be *anything* if it would keep me out of school.
PB: Fighting bulls seems a little drastic. . . .
OW: Well, I had this scholarship for Harvard. Even after that crazy Irish year, I still figured the damn thing might catch up with

me. So I took off for the Ivory Coast of Africa, made my way up through Morocco, and finally settled down in Seville, in the gypsy quarter of Triana. I had a nice apartment in what Billy House used to call a "fuzz castle" [brothel]—separate but equal. Had my own private carriage, too, and used to buy drinks for every bum in Andalusia. It cost me about fifty bucks a week to live like Diamond Jim Brady, and I made that by holing up every once in a while and grinding out stories for the pulps. What a year that was! I was popular and rich (in the reverse order) and untroubled by the slightest itch of ambition. . . .

You asked about the bulls. Well, in that corner of Spain—and in that corner of that town—the bulls are the whole meaning and purpose of life. If you were seventeen and a rich young prince of a pulp writer like me, you could get to be a bullfighter by the simple expedient of buying the bulls. So that was how I worked it. All on a very small, provincial scale, you understand, but towards the end, for a couple of times, I got paid myself. Almost nothing, but, still, for a few minutes there I was a pro—scared to death, of course, but having the time of my life.

Still, even with all that untold Yankee wealth of mine, I'd never have got myself out there on the sand in front of the twisted horns of a perfect cathedral of a *becerro* [calf]—and before audiences of short-tempered and supercritical small-town Andalusian bull experts—if I'd really *cared*. No, what made that little taurine caper possible was what had made it possible for me, a year earlier, to launch myself in show business not as a spear-carrier, but as a star.

PB: Let's hear about that.

OW: Well, that was the summer I'd been traveling through Ireland with a donkey and cart and a big box of paints. I was going to be a painter then—I cared about that, all right. And I still wish that I'd been good enough.

PB: You're sure you weren't?

OW: Yes, damn it.

PB: So you went into the theatre.

OW: I fell into it, Peter. It was the same kind of joke as the bulls.

PB: You paid to act?

OW: I had no money—that was how it happened. I'd been sleeping under the cart, but now winter was approaching and there was the threat of Harvard. The only way I could avoid being educated was to get myself some kind of job.

PB: You were sort of a dropout.

OW: Perfect.
PB: So you just said, "I want to be a star."
OW: I said I *was* a star *already*.
PB: You were sixteen.
OW: Ah, but I was smoking cigars, Peter—sort of making myself older to escape the truant officers. I'd worked up this deep voice that I'm still stuck with (a specialist once told me I was actually born with the vocal cords of a tenor). And I lied like a maniac.
PB: But why did they believe you?
OW: I was from America, and in Ireland, back in those distant days, anything American was possible, however unlikely. I informed the directors of the Gate Theatre that I was that same Welles they must have read about. Just for the lark of it, I told them I'd enjoy the experience of playing with their company for a play or two—that is, if any leading roles were available. Nowadays Hilton Edwards—that fine director and my dear old friend—will tell you that he didn't swallow a word of it. But he did manage to get some of it down, because he started me off with as juicy a principal part as any grizzled veteran could ask for, in *Jew Süss*. So that's how I began—right at the top. I've been working my way down ever since.
PB: You were a hit, too, weren't you?
OW: What is it, thirty-eight years ago? I've never really equaled that success. Certainly not in the bullring!
PB: Weren't you just a little frightened?
OW: By the bulls? There's nobody who isn't. But stage fright is a malady that comes with experience. Oh, I'm not pretending I was *apathetic*. What got me up there on the stage and out there in the bullring wasn't a lack of nerves, it was just an absolutely perfect lack of ambition. I saw no glorious future for myself in either episode.

2.

GUAYMAS

CITIZEN KANE ▪ HEARST ▪ PRESTON STURGES ▪ HERMAN J. MANKIEWICZ ▪ MUSIC ▪ DEEP FOCUS ▪ GREGG TOLAND ▪ CEILINGS AND CAMERA PLACEMENTS ▪ PARENTS ▪ DR. BERNSTEIN ▪ ROGER HILL ▪ MAKEUP ▪ *THE MARCH OF TIME* ▪ COLOR VS. BLACK-AND-WHITE ▪ *KANE*'S RELEASE ▪ OSCARS ▪ GRAND DETOUR

PETER BOGDANOVICH: What was your initial reaction to the Hearst blacklist on *Citizen Kane*?
ORSON WELLES: We expected it before it happened. What we *didn't* expect was that the film might be destroyed. And that was nip and tuck; it was very close.
PB: To the negative being burned?
OW: Yes. It was only *not* burned because I dropped a rosary.
PB: What?
OW: There was a screening for Joe Breen, who was the head of

censorship then, to decide whether it would be burned or not. Because there was tremendous payola on from all the other studios to get it burned.

PB: All because of Hearst's people?

OW: Yes. Everybody said, "Don't make trouble, burn it up, who cares? Let them take their losses." And I got a rosary, put it in my pocket, and when the running was over, in front of Joe Breen, a good Irish Catholic, I stood up and dropped my rosary on the floor and said, "Oh, excuse me," and picked it up and put it back in my pocket. If I hadn't done that, there would be no *Citizen Kane.*

> *Guaymas, Mexico. Orson is there acting in Mike Nichols' movie of* Catch-22, *and they've given him the day off, so we've settled ourselves outside a spacious hotel overlooking the bay. It's hot, and Orson has brought only winter clothes, so he is still wearing the lightweight army uniform that is his costume for the film. Yesterday we tried to talk about* Citizen Kane *and*

A postproduction gag.

Bogdanovich and Welles (with Buck Henry, at right) during the shooting of Catch-22.

> *got sidetracked—I suppose purposely—so I'm trying again, and Orson isn't too happy about it.*

PB: You act as though it's painful for you to remember any of these things.
OW: Oh, everything. Just awful.
PB: Are you up to trying *Kane*?
OW: Oh Christ! All right—let's get it over with. I can't be awfully good on the subject, because I haven't seen the picture since I ran the last finished print in an empty theatre in downtown Los Angeles, about six months before it was released.
PB: Wait a minute—you went to the premiere.
OW: I went to the premiere and went right out the side door when it started, the way I always do. Because it makes me nervous not to be able to *change* anything. It comes from being in the theatre —you used to go to the opening, then go backstage and change things. When I've got a play running, I go on changing it until the last day of the show. And it's awful to have it all locked up in a can forever. That's why I don't go to see them.
PB: I guess it's like some painters. My father's like that. And Cézanne, who kept going into people's houses after he sold the painting—

OW: Yes! They'd smell wet paint and know Cézanne had been in! That's just the way I feel. I'd like to go to the projection booth and start snipping away.
PB: Griffith did—all during the run of *The Birth of a Nation*, he'd be up in the booth making changes.
OW: Well, it was easier then. Silent picture—no damn sound to worry about.
PB: So when Hearst intervened . . .
OW: Hearst didn't really intervene—they intervened on his behalf. It began badly, because Louella Parsons had been on the set and had written a wonderful article about this lovely picture I was making. And it was Hedda Hopper, her old enemy, who blew the whistle. Think of the weapon that gave to the competition! After that it was the Hearst hatchet men who were after me, more than the old man himself.
PB: But wasn't Hedda Hopper supposedly your friend?
OW: Sure—but what a break for her as a newspaperwoman. Couldn't blame her. Imagine what that did to Louella!
PB: After *Kane*, you once said, "Someday, if Mr. Hearst isn't frightfully careful, I'm going to make a film that's really based on his life."
OW: Well, you know, the real story of Hearst is quite different from Kane's. And Hearst himself—as a *man*, I mean—was *very* different. There's all that stuff about [Robert] McCormick and the opera. I drew a lot from that, from my Chicago days. And Samuel Insull. As for Marion [Davies], she was an extraordinary woman—nothing like the character Dorothy Comingore played in the movie. I always felt he had the right to be upset about that.
PB: Davies was actually quite a good actress—
OW: And a fine woman. She pawned all her jewels for the old man when he was broke. Or broke enough to need a lot of cash. She gave him everything, stayed by him—just the opposite of Susan. *That* was the libel. In other words, Kane was better than Hearst, and Marion was much better than Susan—whom people wrongly equated with her.
PB: You once said that Kane would have enjoyed seeing a film based on his life, but not Hearst.
OW: Well, that's what I said to Hearst.
PB: When!?
OW: I found myself alone with him in an elevator in the Fairmont Hotel on the night *Kane* was opening in San Francisco. He and

my father had been chums, so I introduced myself and asked him if he'd like to come to the opening of the picture. He didn't answer. And as he was getting off at his floor, I said, "Charles Foster Kane would have *accepted*." No reply . . . And Kane *would* have, you know. That was his style—just as he finished Jed Leland's bad review of Susan as an opera singer.

PB: Where did Kane's trait of acquiring possessions come from?

OW: *That* comes directly from Hearst. And it's very curious—a man who spends his entire life paying cash for objects he never looked at. I know of no other man in history exactly like that. This jackdaw kind of mind. Because he never made any money, you know; his great chain of newspapers basically lost money. He was in every sense a failure. He just acquired things, most of which were never opened, remained in boxes. It's really a quite accurate picture of Hearst to that extent.

PB: There's only one moment in *Kane* where I thought your acting was self-conscious—

OW: Tell me. I'll tell you the bad moment for me—in the first scene with Susan, the closeup when I had the mud on my face. That's a real phony movie moment. Look at it again—it really is. I haven't seen it since I made it, but—

PB: It's not so bad as—

OW: Not so bad, but it's a real movie actor with mud on his face. What's yours?

PB: The closeup smile in the newspaper office when Cotten asks to keep the Declaration of Principles you wrote—

OW: Oh, but that's *supposed* to be a forced smile. It's because I don't think the document should be kept—I don't believe in it.

PB: Really?

OW: Of course.

PB: You mean Kane didn't mean what he'd written even as he wrote it?

OW: No.

PB: I didn't realize that.

OW: No. You weren't supposed to believe that smile. He's horrified that somebody wants to keep that as a document. It's going too far.

PB [*laughs*]: All right, then I take it back—it's a great moment!

OW [*laughing*]: Anyway, it's not supposed to be a real smile, but the smile of somebody deeply embarrassed, being caught out. There's a point to that moment. Nobody signals it, but that's what

I meant. Because I always believed that Kane doesn't mean all that. He only wants to convince the two fellows. He wants them to believe it because he wants them to be his slaves. But he doesn't believe in anything. He's a damned man, you know. He's one of those damned people that I like to play and make movies about.
PB: There's a film written by Preston Sturges called *The Power and the Glory* [1933] which has been said to have influenced you in the flashback style of *Kane*. Is that true?
OW: No. I never saw it. I've heard that it has strong similarities; it's one of those coincidences. I'm a great fan of Sturges and I'm grateful I didn't see it. He never accused me of it—we were great chums—but I just never saw it. I saw only his comedies. But I would be honored to lift anything from Sturges, because I have very high admiration for him.
PB: You were friends.
OW: Right up till the end of his life [in 1959]. And I knew him before I went to Hollywood; in fact, I first met him when I was about thirteen and going to school at Todd. Wonderful fellow, and I think a great filmmaker, as it turned out.
PB: Yes, and he wrote marvelous dialogue.
OW: Started in a hospital. He was a businessman until he was about forty. He got very sick and lay in the hospital and decided to write a play, *Strictly Dishonorable*, which ran eight years or something on Broadway. And that made him a writer. Then later he became a director. He had never thought of it before.
PB: What happened to him in Europe in the 1950s? He only made one film.
OW: He was just trying to raise money for a picture. Nobody would give him a job. Simple as that.
PB: The idea for the famous breakfast scene between Kane and his first wife [the nine-year deterioration of their marriage is told through one continuing conversation over five flash-pans]—
OW: —was stolen from *The Long Christmas Dinner* of Thornton Wilder! It's a one-act play, which is a long Christmas dinner that takes you through something like sixty years of a family's life—
PB: All at dinner—
OW: Yes, they're all sitting at dinner, and they get old—people wheel baby carriages by, and coffins and everything. That they never leave the table and that life goes on was the idea of this play. I did the breakfast scene thinking I'd invented it. It wasn't in the script originally. And when I was almost finished with it, I sud-

denly realized that I'd unconsciously stolen it from Thornton and I called him up and admitted to it.

PB: What was his reaction?

OW: He was pleased.

PB: Is he still a good friend?

OW: Yes. Wonderful writer. I haven't seen him in a long time, but his newest novel, *The Eighth Day*, is marvelous.

PB: Did the idea literally come to you on the set?

OW: Well, there were going to be several breakfast scenes—you can see how it would have been written in the script—many scenes with transitions. And my idea was simply to photograph it as a continuous breakfast scene without dissolves, just whipping back and forth. Some of the conversation was written before; a lot of it was invented on the set and two or three days before, during rehearsal.

PB: Just how important was [Herman J.] Mankiewicz in relation to the script?

OW: Mankiewicz's contribution? It was enormous.

PB: You want to talk about him?

OW: I'd love to. I loved *him*. People did. He was much admired, you know.

PB: Except for his part in the writing of *Kane* . . . Well, I've read the list of his other credits. . . .

OW: Oh, the hell with lists—a lot of bad writers have wonderful credits.

PB: Can you explain that?

OW: Luck. The lucky bad writers got good directors who could write. Some of these, like Hawks and McCarey, wrote very well indeed. Screenwriters didn't like that at all. Think of those old pros in the film factories. They had to punch in every morning, and sit all day in front of their typewriters in those terrible "writers' buildings." The way they saw it, the director was even worse than the producer, because in the end what really mattered in moving pictures, of course, was the man actually making the pictures. The big-studio system often made writers feel like second-class citizens, no matter how good the money was. They laughed it off, of course, and provided a good deal of the best fun—when Hollywood, you understand, was still a funny place. But basically, you know, a lot of them were pretty bitter and miserable. And nobody was *more* miserable, *more* bitter, and *funnier* than Mank . . . a perfect monument of self-destruction. But, you know, when the bitterness wasn't focused straight onto you, he was the best company in the world.

PB: How did the story of *Kane* begin?

OW: I'd been nursing an old notion—the idea of telling the same thing several times—and showing exactly the same scene from wholly different points of view. Basically, the idea *Rashomon* used later on. Mank liked it, so we started searching for the man it was going to be about. Some big American figure—couldn't be a politician, because you'd have to pinpoint him. Howard Hughes was the first idea. But we got pretty quickly to the press lords.

PB: The first drafts were in separate versions, so when was the whole construction of the script—the intricate flashback pattern—worked out between you?

OW: The actual writing came only after lots of talk, naturally . . . just the two of us, yelling at each other—not too angrily.

PB: What about the *Rashomon* idea? It's still there to a degree.

OW: It withered away from what was originally intended. I wanted the man to seem a very different person depending on who was talking about him. "Rosebud" was Mank's, and the many-sided gimmick was mine. Rosebud remained, because it was the only way we could find to get off, as they used to say in vaudeville. It manages to work, but I'm still not too keen about it, and I don't think that he was, either. The whole shtick is the sort of thing that can finally date, in some funny way.

PB: Toward the close, you have the reporter say that it doesn't matter what it means—

OW: We did everything we could to take the mickey out of it.

PB: The reporter says at the end, "Charles Foster Kane was a man who got everything he wanted, and then lost it. Maybe Rosebud was something he couldn't get or something he lost, but it wouldn't have explained anything. . . ."

OW: I guess you might call that a disclaimer—a bit corny, too. More than a bit. And it's mine, I'm afraid.

PB: I read the script that went into production. . . . There were so many things you changed on the set, or, anyway, after you'd started shooting. From the point of view of Kane's character, one of the most interesting is the scene where you're remaking the front page for about the twentieth time. In the script, Kane is arrogant and rather nasty to the typesetter. In the movie, he's very nice, even rather sweet. How did that evolve?

OW: Well, all he *had* was charm—besides the money. He was one of those amiable, rather likable monsters who are able to command people's allegiance for a time without giving too much in return. Certainly not love; he was raised by a bank, remember. He uses charm the way such people often do. So when he changes the first page, of course it's done on the basis of a sort of charm rather than real conviction. . . . Charlie Kane was a man-eater.

PB: Well, why was it in the script the other way?

OW: I found out more about the character as I went along.

PB: And what were the reactions of Mankiewicz to these changes?

OW: Well, he only came once to the set for a visit. Or, just maybe, it was twice. . . .

> *Here is a memo, dated August 26, 1940, which I came across after this conversation, from Herbert Drake, Mercury Productions' press agent:*
>
> RE: . . . TELEPHONE CONVERSATION WITH HERMAN J. MANKIEWICZ RE CUT STUFF HE SAW . . .
>
> 1. In Bernstein's office with Bill Alland: Everett Sloane is an unsympathetic looking man, and anyway you shouldn't have two Jews in one scene.
>
> 2. Dorothy Comingore [as Susan Alexander Kane] looks much better now so Mr. M. suggests you re-shoot the Atlantic City cabaret scene. [Miss Comingore had been carefully made up to look as bad as possible.]
>
> 3. There are not enough standard movie conventions being observed including too few closeups and very little evidence of action. It is too much like a play, says Mr. M.

PB: Before shooting began, how were differences about the script worked out between you?

OW: That's why I left him on his own finally, because we'd started to waste too much time haggling. So, after mutual agreements on story line and character, Mank went off with Houseman and did his version, while I stayed in Hollywood and wrote mine. At the end, naturally, I was the one who was making the picture, after all —who had to make the decisions. I used what I wanted of Mank's and, rightly or wrongly, kept what I liked of my own.

PB: As you know, Houseman has repeatedly claimed that the script, including the conception and structure, was essentially Mankiewicz's.

OW: It's very funny that he does that, because he deserves some credit himself. It's very perverse, because actually he was a junior writer on it, and made some very important contributions. But for some curious reason he's never wanted to take that bow. It gives him more pleasure just to say I didn't write it.
PB: I have the impression, somehow— Well, let's put it this way: do you believe John Houseman is an enemy?
OW: To rewrite an old Hungarian joke: if you've got him for a friend, you don't *need* an enemy. . . . The truth is, you know, that I cling to the pathetic delusion that I don't have such things as enemies. But Jack is the one who makes this sort of Christian Science a bit difficult.
PB: How did your partnership work in the Mercury?
OW: For the radio shows, he acted as super editor over all the writers; he produced all the first drafts. And that, in a way, was his function with Mank for that six or eight weeks of their separate preparation for *Kane*. In the theatre, he was the business, and also, you might say, the political, boss. That last was important, particularly in the WPA. Without his gifts as a bureaucratic finagler, the shows just wouldn't have got on. I owe him much. Leave it at that. . . . It's a story I don't think I want to tell.
PB [*after a pause*]: There's a scene in which Susan is singing for you the first time in her apartment, and that dissolves to her singing for you in an entirely different, much-better-decorated apartment—
OW: —which Kane set up for her, yes.
PB: And you applaud in that scene, which goes to a group of people applauding Cotten, who is making a speech saying that Kane "entered this campaign"—cut to you finishing the sentence, "with one purpose only," in another campaign speech. Was a thing like that done in the preparatory stages?
OW: Yes, but the last preparatory stages—we were already rehearsing.
PB: It has the beautiful economy of segue-ing on a radio show.
OW: Yes, in a way, except faster than you could on radio.
PB: What about something like the woman screaming offscreen during your fight with Susan in the picnic tent?
OW: That was invented after we shot it. I thought, looking at the rushes, that's what we needed.
PB: As a counterpoint?
OW: Yes, and the song that went with it ["This Can't Be Love"]

Kane "entered this campaign": Joseph Cotten as Jed Leland.

I'd heard Nat "King" Cole and his trio do in a little bar. I kind of based the whole scene around that song.

PB: There's a shot of a black singer at one point—

OW: It isn't him, but the music is by Nat Cole—it's his trio. He doesn't sing it—he's too legitimate, we got some kind of low-down New Orleans voice—but it was his number and his trio.

PB: How did you work with Bernard Herrmann on the score?

OW: Very intimately, as I always did for many years on radio. Almost note for note. Benny Herrmann was an intimate member of the family. I think his score was marvelous for the opera in the film, *Salammbô.* It was a delightful pastiche.

> *From a telegram sent by Welles to Herrmann on July 18, 1940, just a few days before shooting began on* Kane*:*

> Opera sequence is early in shooting, so must have fully orchestrated recorded track before shooting. Susie sings as curtain goes up in the first act, and I believe there is no opera

> of importance where soprano leads with chin like this. Therefore suggest it be original . . . by you—parody on typical Mary Garden vehicle. . . . Suggest *Salammbo* which gives us phony production scene of ancient Rome and Carthage, and Susie can dress like grand opera neoclassic courtesan. . . . Here is a chance for you to do something witty and amusing—and now is the time for you to do it. I love you dearly.

OW: There's some music in the film Herrmann didn't write, like that tune for "Oh, Mr. Kane." That's a Mexican march I heard once down here in the north someplace.
PB: When we go to Mrs. Kane's boarding house, the snow is falling, and the music is lovely, very lyrical; then the snowball hits the house and the music just stops, right in the middle of a phrase.
OW: Typical radio device. We used to do that all the time. That music is very good right there.
PB: What about the idea of the light bulb spluttering out when Susan's voice fails and fades? Was a thing like that in the script?
OW: No. It was worked out later, of course.
PB: How did that shot evolve where the camera went all the way from Susan singing to two stagehands in the flies—and then one holds his nose?
OW: The idea for the way it ended was contributed by our propman. His name was Red. We were just going to go up to them looking disgusted or something. Anyway, it was a big contribution.
PB: You've told me that everyone felt free to contribute—that was part of the atmosphere on the set.
OW: That's true—it was wonderful. We had a couple of spies on the set, as I told you, but everyone else hated them, so they were completely in quarantine. Of course, the first two weeks of the film were done without the studio knowing we were shooting a picture. We said we were making tests, because I had never directed a picture. That began part of the big legend: "Imagine, he's been fourteen days on camera tests with extras and actors in costume!" But we were shooting the *picture*. Because we wanted to get started and be already into it before anybody knew about it.
PB: So there wouldn't be pressure on you.
OW: Yes, that's right. It was Perry Ferguson's idea, the art director.
PB: Do you agree with André Bazin that deep-focus camera set-

ups increase the ambiguity of a movie, because the director doesn't make choices for the audience—they can decide who or what they want to look at in the frame?

OW: That's right. In fact, I did a lot of talking about that in the early days of my life as a filmmaker—when I was more shameless and used to sound off on theory. I talked a lot about that "giving the audience the choice" business. It strikes me as pretty obvious now; I don't know why I came on so strong about it.

PB: I don't think it's so obvious; and it certainly wasn't twenty-five years ago. What about a shot like the one after Susan has tried to commit suicide? There's a bottle in the foreground, and we see you break through the door in the background. Did you have to use an outsized bottle in order to hold focus?

OW: No, it was just an ordinary, standard size.

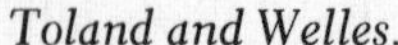

Toland and Welles.

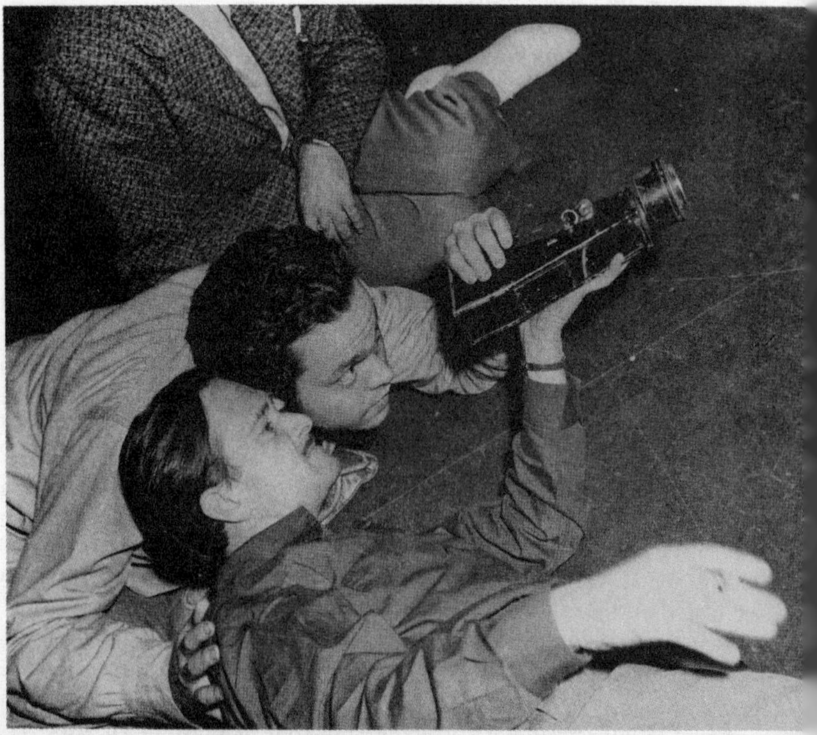

PB: It must have been very difficult to get a dark scene that still had enough light to hold focus.
OW: You bet. It was a very dark scene until the door opens and I come in—and *then* you see this ID bracelet I had on by accident because I had a girlfriend who made me wear it. Every time I think of that scene, I think of my reaching down and you see this awful love charm—nothing at all to do with Kane. That's all I really remember about that scene.
PB: I never noticed it. You must have cursed yourself watching the rushes.
OW: Yes, when I saw it I said, "Shall we go back, do it again?" "No." "Maybe he could have such—" "He never would have it." "They won't see it." And whenever I think of seeing this picture, the reason I don't want to is because I don't want to see that goddamn bracelet come down.
PB: I guess one always remembers the little things that nobody in the world would notice.
OW: Well, you'll notice it the next time you see it.
PB: That's true.
OW: It glitters on the screen!
PB: Some people have said that the look of *Kane* is a result of Gregg Toland's photography, but all your pictures have the same visual signature, and you only worked with Toland once.
OW: It's impossible to say how much I owe to Gregg. He was superb.

You know how I happened to get to work with Gregg? He was, just then, the number-one cameraman in the world, and I found him sitting out in the waiting room of my office. "My name's Toland," he said, "and I want you to use me on your picture." I asked him why, and he said he'd seen some of our plays in New York. He asked me who did the lighting. I told him in the theatre most directors have a lot to do with it (and they used to, back then), and he said, "Well, fine. I want to work with somebody who never made a movie." Now, partly because of that, I somehow assumed that movie lighting was supervised by movie *directors*. And, like a damned fool, for the first few days of *Kane* I "supervised" like crazy. Behind me, of course, Gregg was balancing the lights and telling everybody to shut their faces. He was angry when somebody finally came to me and said, "You know, that's really supposed to be Mr. Toland's job."
PB: You mean he was protecting you?

OW: Yes! He was quietly fixing it so as many of my notions as possible would work. Later he told me, "That's the only way to learn anything—from somebody who doesn't know anything." And, by the way, Gregg was also the *fastest* cameraman who ever lived, and used fewer lights. And he had this extraordinary crew—his own men. You never heard a sound on a Toland set, except what came from the actors or the director. There was never a voice raised, only signs given. Almost Germanic, it was so hushed. Everybody wore neckties. Sounds depressing, but we had a jazz combo to keep our spirits up.

PB: Toland didn't mind that?

OW: Not so you'd notice. With all his discipline, he was easygoing, and quite a swinger off the set.

PB: How did you get along with him after you found out that lighting was his job?

OW: Wonderfully. I started asking for lots of strange, new things—depth-of-focus and so on. . . .

PB: An elementary question: why did you *want* so much depth-of-focus?

OW: Well, in life you see everything in focus at the same time, so why not in the movies? We used split-screen sometimes, but mostly a wide-angle lens, lots of juice, and stopped way the hell down. We called it "pan focus" in some idiot interview—just for the fun of it—

PB: Didn't mean anything?

OW: Of course not; but for quite a while that word kept turning up in books and highbrow articles—as though there really *was* something you could do called "pan focusing"! . . . Christ, he was the greatest gift any director—young or old—could ever, ever have. And he never tried to impress us that he was doing any miracles. He just went ahead and performed them. *Fast.* I was calling for things only a beginner would have been ignorant enough to think anybody could ever do, and there he was, *doing* them. His whole point was, "There's no mystery to it." He said, "*You* can be a cameraman, too—in a couple of days I can teach you everything that matters." So we spent the next weekend together and he showed me the inside of that bag of tricks, and, like all good magic, the secrets are ridiculously simple. Well, that was Gregg for you—that was how big he was. Can you imagine somebody they now call a "director of photography" coming right out and admitting you can bone up on the basic technical side of it all in a weekend? Like magic again: the secret of the trick is nothing; what counts is not the mechanics, but how you can make 'em work.

PB: You gave Toland credit on the same card as yourself, which Ford had done, too, on *The Long Voyage Home.*

OW: Up till then, cameramen were listed with about eight other names. Nobody those days—only the stars, the director, and the producer—got separate cards. Gregg deserved it, didn't he?

PB: What made you put on so many ceilings?

OW: The simple thing is that movies still go on telling lies. First of all, they pretend there isn't a fourth wall—as in the theatre—that *has* to be because the camera is there. But then they pretend there's no ceiling—a big lie in order to get all those terrible lights up there. You can hardly go into a room without seeing a ceiling, and I believe the camera ought to show what the eyes see normally looking at something. That's all it was. Not because I thought the ceiling in itself had anything beautiful to say. It just seemed to me it was clearly a bad theatrical convention to pretend it wasn't there.

PB: Well, you also used a lot of low-angle shots that couldn't avoid seeing the ceiling. In fact, you're still fond of shots like that.

OW: I don't know why. I suppose it's because I think the picture looks better down there. Just that. I suppose I had more low angles in *Kane* just because I became fascinated with the way it looked—and I do it less now because it's become less surprising. But there are an awful lot of dull interiors—*Kane* is full of them—which are by their nature not very interesting and which look better when the camera is low. I think I overdid it.

PB: In the big scene between Kane and Leland after Kane loses the election, the whole thing is from an extreme low angle.

OW: Well, there's a purpose in that one—that was deliberate and wasn't just because the set looked better.

PB: What was the purpose?

OW: Oh, I don't know—I think if it doesn't explain itself, I can't explain it. There's this fallen giant. . . . I think that really called for the camera being there. And, of course, it was very low. We had to dig a hole, and they had to drill into the concrete floor for us to get down that low. And I'd sprained my ankle, so if you look carefully in that scene, you can see the steel brace I was wearing on my heel. I had fallen down the stairs in the scene where I threw Gettys out, and I was limping around in a steel brace. It took nerve to shoot from down there, with that steel brace right in front of the camera, but I thought rightly that at that point they'd be looking at Leland and not at me. Anyway, I wanted it like a big, kind of mythical encounter between the two. And also I wanted it to look outsized, because what they're saying is so prosaic, yet has reverberations—I had some such highfalutin idea. It still seems justified to me as I look back on it. But I don't have a general theory about low angles.

PB: How do you decide where you're going to put the camera?

OW: I don't make a conscious decision—I know instantly where it goes. There's never a moment of doubt. And I never use a viewfinder anymore.

PB: You look through the camera when it's set up?

OW: No. I place my hand where the camera goes and that's it. It never moves—I know exactly where it's going to be.

PB: But don't you then look at the setup?

OW: Then. And that's where it should be, and I'm right. For my money. I don't fish for it—or very seldom, only when I'm in real trouble. And then the fishing leads me nowhere and it's better if I go home or go to another scene. Because if I'm fishing it means I don't know, something's wrong.

PB: It's really instinctive rather than—

OW: Oh, it always is. I think I share with Hitchcock the ability to say what lens goes in the camera and where it stands without consulting a finder or looking through the camera. He does that, too, I believe.

PB: He sometimes draws a little sketch for the cameraman.

OW: Oh, I don't do that. I just walk over and say, "There it is." I may be dead wrong, but I'm so certain that nothing can shake it. It's the only thing I'm certain of. I'm never certain of a performance—my own or the other actors'—or the script or anything. I'm ready to change, move anything. But to me it seems there's only one place in the world the camera can be, and the decision usually comes immediately. If it doesn't come immediately, it's because I have no idea about the scene, or I'm wrong about the scene to begin with. It's a good sign, a kind of litmus paper for me. If I start to fish, something is wrong.

PB: Then it must be inconceivable to you, the idea of covering a scene from many different angles, as many directors do.

OW: That's right. Inconceivable. I don't know what they're fishing around for—they don't know what they're doing in the scene. Though I think the absolutely solid camera sense is *not* a sign of a great director. It's just something you have or you don't have. I think you can be a very great director and have only a very vague notion of what the camera does at all. I happen to think I have total mastery of the camera. That may be just megalomania, but I'm absolutely certain of that area. And everything *else* is doubtful to me. I never consult the operator or anything. There it is.

PB: Was it that way on *Kane*, too?

OW: Yes.

PB: Right away?

OW: Right away.

PB: It's instinctive.

OW: Yes, kind of instinctive, if you will—an arrogance that I have about where it's going to be seen from.

PB: I know it's difficult to dissect the creative process—

OW: Well, it's not even creative, because it *is* an instinctive thing, like a question of pitch for a singer. Where the camera goes. If you're absolutely sure, you may be wrong but at least it's one thing you can hang on to. Because I'm filled with doubts all the time about a movie: that the whole tone is wrong, that the level of it is wrong, that all the text, the performances, the emphasis, what they say, what it should be about—I'm constantly reaching and fishing and hoping and trying and improvising and changing. But the one thing I'm rocklike about is where it's seen from, by what lens and so on. That to me doesn't seem to be open to discussion. And it's something I must be grateful for: even if I'm wrong, I don't have that worry. But I always find scenes in a movie—I did in *Kane* and I have ever since—that I don't know how to photograph, and it's always because I haven't really conceived of it fully enough.

PB: Do you let those go until you're ready?

OW: Well, on *Kane*, I walked away once early in the morning—just quit for the day—and went home. Made a big scandal. I just had no idea what to do. Came back the next day.

PB: What was the scene?

OW: In Susan's apartment, the big confrontation, when Gettys [Ray Collins] comes in. He was named, by the way, after the father of the wife of Roger Hill, my teacher at Todd. That's another in-joke. But that was just a scene in a room, and it seemed to me so boring, I didn't know what to do. And I just went away.

PB: When you came back, it worked?

OW: Yeah. And I didn't figure it out on paper. But I think that scene is a little overstated, visually. It's a little overemphasized. It shows some kind of insecurity, I think, visually. I can see it now. It came from that moment of doubt. And I think it's like lion taming or being the conductor of an orchestra—you have to come in and know where the camera is, or there are all sorts of evil demons who will attack you, and the doubts will show on the screen and in everything. You have to be absolutely on top of it. Or pay no attention to it. One of the two.

PB: By the way, in shooting that drunk scene with Cotten, I understand he was so tired that he accidentally said the line "dramatic crimitism" that way, instead of "criticism," and you left it in.

OW: It happened that way in rehearsal and then it was performed. He was that tired because he had to go to New York to join the road tour of *The Philadelphia Story*, which he originated on the stage. And we all worked something like twenty-four hours, around the clock, with nobody going to bed, to get him finished.

PB: Would you agree, in general, that *Kane* is more self-conscious directorially than any of your other films?

OW: Yes. There are more conscious shots—for the sake of shots—in *Kane* than in anything I've done since. It has things like that shot where they're all posed around that trophy which is just a "let's see if we can make that shot" kind of shot. I'm not that pleased with it, looking back.

PB: No, it's studied.

OW: Yeah. I've tried to avoid that kind of thing since then.

PB: Well, *Ambersons* is much more relaxed.

OW: Much.

PB: Perhaps that's something one feels making one's first picture. A sort of inhibition—which you combatted by being daring to the point of self-consciousness at the time. Whereas *Othello* is very second-nature—as is everything you've done since.

OW: I think that's absolutely true. I stopped trying after *Kane*. There's a kind of unjustified visual strain at times in *Kane*, which just came from the exuberance of discovering the medium. And once you get used to it and learn how to swim, then you don't have to flex so many muscles. Now let's talk about something else.

PB: Well, we've barely scratched the surface of *Kane*.

OW: I'm sure—but I'm expiring.

PB: Well, OK. Let's talk about your name. Why'd you choose to be called by your middle name, Orson, instead of your first name, George?

OW: There wasn't any choice involved. I've been Orson all my life. I first learned my name was George when I was nine years old. It came as a terrible shock. Children started screaming, "Georgie, Porgie, puddin' and pie, kissed the girls and made them cry." This enraged me. I kicked out at my little playmates and got black eyes for it. How wrong I was. What a name to be born with and not use—George Orson Welles!
PB: All of it? You trust people with three names.
OW: With a name like George Orson Welles I wouldn't need to be trusted—I'd be Emperor of the World!
PB: Were you named after someone?
OW: George Ade, the great American humorist. Orson is a family name—descending (so the legend goes) from the Orsinis. Also because, by a bewildering and rather tiresome coincidence, my mother and father were on holiday in Rio—with George Ade and a man whose name was Orson Wells, without the "e," but *with* $30 million. I'd have those millions now if only I'd gone to visit my godfather. I hesitated, fearing old Mr. Wells would suspect my motives. I'd go *now*—on my knees. But as a twelve-year-old I had my pride. And then the news came that he'd gone to dwell with the morning stars.
PB: Was your father a great influence in your life—being an inventor?
OW: He didn't do much inventing in the years I knew him. I admired and loved him, but he was bitterly opposed to my interest in music and painting and everything like that. As far as he was concerned, if I was going to be an artist, it'd be better to be a cartoonist, like his friend George McManus, who drew "Jiggs and Maggie," otherwise known as "Bringing Up Father"—that's where the money was.
PB: But your mother was—
OW: The artist—the musician. Because of her I was a sort of *Wunderkind* of music: a child conductor, violinist, pianist. Then, when I was nine, she died. I've never done anything in music since.
PB: What was the influence of your guardian, Dr. Bernstein? And why did you give that name to the character in *Kane?*
OW: You're sneaking in *Kane* again.
PB: Sorry.
OW [*laughs*]: That was a family joke. He was nothing like the character in the movie. I used to call people "Bernstein" on the

radio all the time, too—just to make him laugh. . . . I sketched out the character in our preliminary sessions—Mank did all the best writing for Bernstein. I'd call that *the* most valuable thing he gave us. . . .

PB: Where did Jed Leland [Joseph Cotten] come from?

OW: Jed was really based on a close childhood friend of mine—George Stevens' uncle Ashton Stevens. He was practically my uncle, too.

PB: Did you tell Stevens the character was based on him?

OW: Oh God, he could see it—I didn't have to *tell* him. I sent him the script before we began, of course, and while he was visiting me on the Coast, I brought him on the set during shooting. Later he saw the movie and thought the old man would be thrilled by it. As it turned out, after *Kane* was released, Ashton was forbidden by his Hearst editors to even mention my name. . . . What I knew about Hearst came even more from him than from my father—though my father did know him well: there was a long story about putting a chamber pot on a flagpole, things like that, but I didn't get too much from *that* source. My father and Hearst were only close as young swingers. But Ashton had taught Hearst to play the banjo, which is how he first got to be a drama critic, and, you know, Ashton really was one of the great ones. The last of the dandies—he worked for Hearst for some fifty years or so, and adored him. A gentleman . . . very much like Jed.

PB: Jed Leland is really not all that endearing a character—I mean, you like him, but one's sympathies somehow are with Kane in the scene where he attacks Kane so strongly.

OW: Well, you know—when a man takes a stand on some question of principle at the expense of a personal friendship, the sympathy has to go to the victim of the righteousness, now, doesn't it?

PB: Getting back to your guardian, Dr. Bernstein—did he have any influence on your creative life?

OW: Well, he was an enormously important *element* in my life. But we seldom had the same tastes in anything. I'd say the biggest influence was Roger Hill, who became headmaster of the school to which I went for three years, and with whom I later wrote four textbooks on Shakespeare. He's still a great, a valued, friend.

Roger Hill's introduction to Everybody's Shakespeare [*1934; later,* The Mercury Shakespeare, *1939*], *which he edited with Orson, begins like this:*

ON STUDYING SHAKESPEARE'S PLAYS

Don't!

Read them. Enjoy them. Act them.

Shakespeare might not be surprised to know that his plays are still bringing money to producers and fame to actors throughout the world. He would be greatly surprised, however, to know that they are studied (by compulsion) in the classroom; that they are conned by scholars, dissected by pedants, and fed in synthetic and minute and quite distasteful doses to students, much in the same manner as are capsules of Cicero's Letters and pellets of Euclid's Geometry. . . . Put Shakespeare where he belongs—on the stage.

OW: Roger is now eighty-something, runs a chartering service in Florida, and he helped me with the boats on *The Deep* when I shot in the Bahamas. He's always been a great boat fellow—he was called "Skipper" at school.

PB: Todd School?

OW: Yes. He was the son of the owner. When I was there, he was the athletics coach. He only became the headmaster after I left. But he was a great influence in that school.

PB: How old were you?

OW: Well, I went there three years, and my last year I was fourteen.

PB: And he?

OW: Must have been twenty-eight, thirty—I really don't know. I can't imagine life without him, and I go ten years without seeing him but it doesn't seem like ten years, because I think of him all the time. He was a great direct influence in my life—the biggest by all odds. I wanted to be *like* him. Everything he thought, I wanted to think, and that wasn't true of Dr. Bernstein.

PB: Or your father?

OW: Or my father. My father was a very strange man. Fascinating. Great wit and great raconteur.

PB: Did you take up painting right after—

OW: I painted, always, from the minute I could walk.

PB: Is it true that you still can't add or subtract very well?

OW: What would make you think I'd learn at this advanced age? I can't do it at all.

PB: Really?

OW: No. I got through school because I paid a boy called Gug-

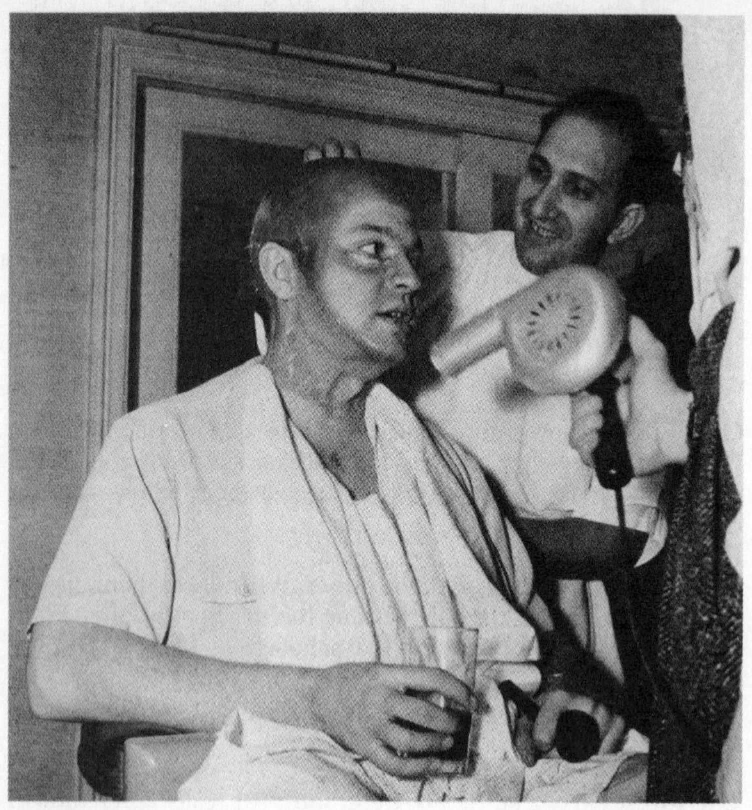

Welles' makeup for Kane.

genheim to take that sort of drudgery off my shoulders. For a fee, Guggenheim did most of the paperwork on Latin declensions and geometry. I graduated *magna cum laude*.

PB: I read in the Alva Johnston pieces in *The Saturday Evening Post* [January 20, 27, February 3, 1940] that you never wanted to be a child—that you wanted to escape childhood.

OW: That's true.

PB: Have you ever wanted to return?

OW: To childhood? I've been back there ever since I left.

PB: I read that you dislike *A Midsummer Night's Dream*.

OW: Because it was my reading primer. You'll have to try it—just read the first scene of *Midsummer Night's Dream* and imagine it's the first thing you've ever had to spell out.

PB: Well, since you were two years old, it's hard to imagine it anyway.
OW: Johnston wrote that I was. In fact, I believe I achieved literacy somewhat later on in life. He got that, I suppose, from Dr. Bernstein, who gilded the lily pretty thickly. I don't think I was very advanced in that way. I was a musician, all right, but as to book learning, I think I was rather backward.
PB: Were you really a bad student in school?
OW: All three years of it. I attacked the textbooks rather than mastered them. I led student revolutions—comic ones.
PB: You acted in and directed some school plays. Did you have a particular love of makeup even then?
OW: Yes, I used to when I was younger, and it was impossible for me to play any part that didn't look like a juvenile killer. Getting older, I discover I don't have to paint those lines under my eyes, and it's nice.
PB: But *Kane* is a masterpiece of makeup.
OW: There you go again—you had that whole chain of thought planned. God, you're crafty. . . . *Kane* had to be. Look at all those ages.
PB: Well, movies that have somebody age in them are usually quite bad.
OW: Yes, but you have no idea what work there was to that, because it was long ago; we didn't have sophisticated things for makeup which made it easy. In those days—you don't know what it was—I came to work many days on *Kane* at two-thirty in the morning, to be made up to start work at nine. It took that long, with the spraying and building. Maurie Seiderman was one of the two or three great makeup men of our time, and he's never really been allowed to do anything in the industry.
PB: Because he's too good?
OW: Yeah. How he worked! Two-thirty in the morning was normal all the time. With the contact lenses I wore, which in those days drove you mad with pain. Because I was a baby; you know, it's very hard to be seventy years old and make it believable. But the thing that's never been printed is the truth about me as a young man in that film. I was then twenty-five, twenty-six—I've forgotten how old I was—but I had my face lifted up with fish skin and wore corsets for the scenes as a young man.
PB: Why? Were you heavier than you looked?
OW: Of course. Not only heavier, but I always had that terrible

round moon face and it was all faked up with fish skins and tucked under the hair. Everything. Just as though I were some terrible old leading man at the end of his day [*laughs*]. So I was just as heavily made up as a young man as I was as an old man! I could hardly move for the corsets and the fish skin and everything else. I read once—Norman Mailer wrote something or other—that, when I was young, I was the most beautiful man anybody had ever seen. Yes! Made up for *Citizen Kane!* And only for five days!

PB: You mean you never looked like that?

OW: Never! I wish I had! On the other hand, Everett Sloane, who aged with me, never wore any makeup at all! We just shaved his head and put the white around it. And he couldn't have been more than twenty-one. It had a profound effect on him. Because he thought, "How can I represent a seventy-five-year-old man without makeup? It must be that my nose is too big." And he began bobbing it. He must have had twenty operations before he killed himself. He must have thought, "If I could ever bob my nose right, then I'll be a leading man."

PB: But that's incredible.

OW: Terrible story, yes.

PB: He was brilliant in *Kane.*

OW: Yes. Much better than in *The Lady from Shanghai.* He'd already begun to go to pieces. And he became a very bad actor in the last ten years of his life. But in *Kane* he was wonderful.

PB: Yes, that scene with the reporter [William Alland]—

OW: That was *all* Mank, by the way—it's my favorite scene.

PB: And the story about the girl: "One day, back in 1896, I was crossing over to Jersey on the ferry. . . . There was another ferry pulling in, and . . . a girl waiting to get off. A white dress she had on. . . . I only saw her for a second . . . but I'll bet a month hasn't gone by since, that I haven't thought of that girl."

OW: It goes longer than that.

PB: Yes, but who wrote it?

OW: Mankiewicz, and it's the best thing in the movie. "A month hasn't gone by that I haven't thought of that girl." That's Mankiewicz. I *wish* it was me.

PB: Great scene.

OW: If I were in hell and they gave me a day off and said, "What part of any movie you ever made do you want to see?," I'd see that scene of Mank's about Bernstein. All the rest could have been better, but that was just right.

PB: You wanted all the actors in *Kane* to be new faces, didn't you?
OW: That's true—but I was tricked [*laughs*]. My whole idea of having only new faces was ruined by the first day of shooting—which was, as I said, the first of several days when we pretended to be testing but were actually shooting the picture. The scene was in the nightclub with Susan when she's grown old. For the waiter in that nightclub, casting sent me a tubby little round-faced Italian [Gino Corrado] who is the waiter in every movie ever made! And I couldn't possibly send him away on the basis that he was too well-known a face because I was claiming to be testing. So there he is—spoiling the whole master plan in one of the first shots that I made!
PB: And you couldn't even rationalize it as an *hommage* to Hollywood, since I know that's not the sort of thing you do.
OW: I don't believe in *hommage*. Of course, nobody knew about it in those days, thank Christ—in our innocence—and I am terribly against all forms of *hommage*.
PB: I'm beginning to agree with you.
OW: You don't have to say that.
PB: No, I am. What was the big advantage of having actors inexperienced in movies?
OW: They didn't have terrible movie habits.
PB: Was Dorothy Comingore really a discovery of Chaplin's?
OW: Yes, but he didn't use her.
PB: And you liked her—
OW: After testing a lot of strippers. I tested about ten, none of whom were any good. I tested a lot of people for that part.
PB: You wanted that kind of cheapness?
OW: Yeah.
PB: Had she ever acted before?
OW: I don't think so. And she was such a success in it. Everybody said she was so wonderful that she turned down every offer she got for three years. And then there were no more offers, and that was the end of it. She was waiting for another part like that one.
PB: Was she an intelligent actress?
OW: Yes. Of course, her old-age scenes were tremendously tricked up. We blew dangerous drugs in her eyes and sprayed her throat so she couldn't talk, and everything else. But she was still great. "Well, what do you know—it's morning already." That's another favorite moment.

PB: What's so uncanny is that she reminds me so much of performances Judy Holliday was to give years later.
OW: Yes. Judy began with our theatre, you know. She was two years in the Mercury.
PB: I didn't know that. Perhaps she was influenced by Comingore—
OW: No, I don't think so.
PB: Well, there's a marked similarity.
OW: Yes, very much. She didn't have the humor or richness of Judy, but there's a great big similarity.
PB: Did she sing her own things?
OW: No.
PB: You had to get a singer who could make it sound bad.
OW: That's right. That was big work—very well done by the girl. Worked a long time on that.
PB: How did you find Fortunio Bonanova, who played her singing teacher?
OW: I saw him as the leading man with Katharine Cornell in *The Green Hat* when I was about eight years old. I never forgot him. He looked to me like a leading man in a dirty movie. Sent for him the minute I wrote that part. He was a great romantic leading man. When he was prompting her in the opera, he was so marvelous. God, he was funny.
PB: Had he ever done a picture before?
OW: Yes, I think so—he was living in Hollywood. But nothing much, you know. He was another one of the exceptions in the film.

PB: Why did you use that shrieking cockatoo?
OW: Wake 'em up.
PB: Literally?
OW: Yeah. Getting late in the evening, you know—time to brighten up anybody who might be nodding off [*laughs*].
PB: It has no other purpose?
OW: Theatrical shock effect, if you want to be grand about it—you can say it's placed at a certain *musical* moment when I felt the need for something short and exclamatory. So it has a sort of purpose, but no *meaning*. What's fascinating, though, is that, because of some accident in the trick department, you can see right through the bird's eye into the scenery behind.
PB: I always thought that was intentional.

OW: We don't know why it happened. Some accident . . . I'm very fond of parrots.
PB: There's one in *Mr. Arkadin*.
OW: Yeah. I have a wonderful one at home in Spain.
PB: How'd you do the scene just after the cockatoo, where Kane breaks up Susan's room?
OW: Just did it, with four cameras—broke up the whole set in one take. Tore my wrists and hands apart. I was bleeding like a pig when I was done with all that glass and everything.
PB: William Alland has been quoted as saying, "He came off exhilarated and said it was the first time he'd ever felt the emotion while acting a scene."
OW: Naw. I'm sure that's one of those memories after the event that are more creative than accurate. I came off with a bleeding wrist—that's what I came off with—and I don't enjoy bleeding, I'm not one of those. Five hours of makeup, and then get on and break it all up. Very rough. But the set was wonderfully done by Perry Ferguson. Marvelously dressed—made it very easy to play. My God, it was a wonderful set. I can see it now. He was just brilliant—I think Ferguson did a marvelous job.
PB: I agree. What did Van Nest Polglase do, who's also listed as art director?
OW: That shows your youth. In the days of the big studios, and the system of department heads, every picture carried a credit for art direction which went not to the man who really did the job, but to the head of the department. The man who actually did the work was always listed as assistant. Thus Cedric Gibbons was apparently the art director of every Metro picture, but he didn't even make a sketch. He and Van Polglase and the other art-department chiefs were much too busy for any actual creative work.
PB: Then you had no contact with Van Polglase at all?
OW: Just in budget meetings, costings—that was the regulation setup.
PB: Well, the set director, Darrell Silvera, told me that those ice sculptures of Leland and Bernstein in the party scene were a last-minute idea.
OW: Yes. We got them from the Brown Derby or someplace like that. It took a long time to shoot that sequence—five days. I threw all the girls out and waited till we got prettier ones—and they were marvelous girls, finally.
PB: Did you yourself design sketches on *Kane*?

OW: I do on everything, and I almost always design shows for the theatre. Let's go get another drink—I see this is going to be endless. . . .

> *An article could be devoted just to the "News on the March" digest that comes at the start of* Kane. *Apart from its perfection as an imitation news short, it is at the same time one of the most devilish parodies of vintage* Time-*style ever made: the inverted sentences, the taut fact-filled portentous reportage, the standard clichés.*

OW [*with a new drink*]: I showed it to Luce. He was one of the first people to see the movie—in New York. He and Clare Luce loved it and roared with laughter at the digest.
PB: They saw the parody?
OW: They saw it as a parody and enjoyed it very much as such—I have to hand it to them. He saw it as a joke—or *she* saw it as a joke and he had to because she did.
PB: There's a *March of Time* sequence indicated in *Smiler with a Knife.*
OW: Yes, that's where the idea for it in *Kane* came from. Of course, I'd been years on *The March of Time* radio program. Every day. It was a marvelous show to do. Great fun, because, half an hour after something happened, we'd be acting it out with music and sound effects and actors. It was a super show—terribly entertaining.
PB: Did you write some of them?
OW: Never. I only acted. I began as an occasional performer, because they had a regular stock company, and then I was finally let in—one of the inner circle. And then I had the greatest thrill of my life—I don't know why it thrilled me (it does still, to think of it now), I guess because I thought *March of Time* was such a great thing to be on. One day they did as a news item on *March of Time* the opening of my production of the black *Macbeth,* and I played myself on it. And that to me was the apotheosis of my career—that I was on *March of Time* acting *and* as a news item. I've never felt since that I've had it made as much as I did that one afternoon.
PB: And did you use the *Time* announcer, Westbrook Van Voorhies, for *Kane?*
OW: Oh, no. That was William Alland who imitated him. Great

imitation, but he's pretty easy to imitate. [*Doing it:*] "This week, as it must to all men—death came to Charles Foster Kane." We used to do that every day—five days a week! And, of course, there was a lot of "it must to all men" every week, and I used to play all these people. I played Zaharoff—it was one of my first parts on the show. As a matter of fact, I got the idea for the hidden-camera sequence in the *Kane* "news digest" from a scene I did on *March of Time* in which Zaharoff, this great munitions-maker, was being moved around in his rose garden, just talking about the roses, in the last days before he died. It was a radio show, but I remember the idea of an old tycoon being pushed around a rose garden.

PB: There's a wonderfully real sound cut during Thatcher's news conference in the "News" digest. A long shot of Thatcher sitting at the table with all these people around, but when you cut to a closeup of him as he starts to read his statement, the sound cuts a moment late, the way it often does in newsreels. I've always loved that touch.

OW: Yes, a slight mistake in the sound cutting. I'm glad you noticed it. You know how it was in those days—there was no tape, all the sound was on film. You can't imagine what mixing the sound was in those days—and what a cost in effort it was to get that little effect.

PB: Is it true that that news conference was reminiscent of a real J. P. Morgan news conference?

OW: No, but there *was* a famous J. P. Morgan news conference where a midget was put on his lap. I just know vaguely about it.

PB: Did you feel the newsreel was necessary so the juggling of time was possible?

OW: It was expository—to tell more about him than could be told in other ways.

PB: Were the shots for the "News" digest made depending on what makeup you were in?

OW: Yes, end of the day or during the day. There was a big back lot, and as we were moving from one place to another, we'd say, "Well, let's get on the back of the train and make me with Teddy Roosevelt," or whoever it was. It was all kind of half improvised—all the newsreel stuff. It was tremendous fun doing it. And did I tell you the reaction that sequence had in Italy when the film opened?

PB: No.

Shooting the Kane *newsreel.*

OW: They all stood up and hissed and booed because the quality of the film was so bad.
PB: They missed the point entirely.
OW: Yes! [*Laughs.*] You know, the total run in Rome in the entire life of *Citizen Kane* is three days—since it was made!
PB: That's about rock bottom, isn't it?
OW: Yeah. But I'm rock bottom in Italy. I've only started to come up in the last five or six years.
PB: Even among intellectuals?
OW: Oh, always low. Very low.
PB: Really?
OW: Because I came and lived there. And, you don't know this, but in many countries you're only respected if you're not living there. They think there must be something wrong with you if you come and stay there. So I had a great week when I arrived for *Black Magic* with every intellectual in the world—and after that I became nobody because I lived there. "Who is he? Must be some-

thing wrong with him or he wouldn't be in Italy." [*PB laughs.*] It's been true in an awful lot of countries—Ireland and Italy and Yugoslavia; I know a lot of smaller countries that never respect either their own countrymen until they leave, or a foreigner who lives there. In Yugoslavia, I'm beginning to lose a lot of face because I'm there too much. It's a very basic thing. I remember when we toured with Katharine Cornell—we were going to open up the theatre again in America—a thrilling ten-month tour, playing all over in theatres where no play had been for twenty, thirty, forty years. There we were, bringing really good actors and a repertoire of three plays, and the people would say, "What's wrong with Katharine Cornell, that she's here? She must be slipping." In other words, if she's any good, she'd stay in New York. It's just like the Yugoslavs or the Italians. They want to know why you aren't back in Hollywood!

PB: That's similar to American critics putting down Westerns and other typically American films.

OW: Yes, it's only the foreigners who appreciate the Western as a serious form. And comedy. There are very few people anywhere who take comedy seriously.

PB: That's true.

OW: You know, not one serious film festival in the world has ever given a first prize to a comedy.

PB: The Oscars rarely do, either.

OW: It's so idiotic, because it's quite easy to show that maybe the best movies and plays *are* comedies—or certainly as good as any tragedy. It's so idiotic to think that it's some kind of second-class tourist kind of entertainment. But these solemn boobs who talk about movies or anything else just cannot believe that a comedy is serious.

PB: Yes. [*Picking up notes:*] Why did you do the projection-room scene in such darkness?

OW: Because most of the actors play different parts later on. They're all doubling, except the head fellow. We didn't *dare* turn on the lights.

PB: It's dramatic.

OW: Of course, you've got a big excuse for that strong single light. It was the first scene I shot in the movie.

PB: Really?

OW: Yes, and I was supposed to be testing, so in case it was good

I wanted to save it, and I didn't want to hire a lot of actors if it wasn't good. So I used the whole Mercury cast, heavily disguised by darkness.

PB: And you shot it in a real projection room?

OW: Yes, because we didn't want to alert anybody to the fact that we were shooting. And there they all are—if you look carefully, you can see them. Everybody in the movie is in it.

PB: Not you, too?

OW: Yes, I'm there.

PB: Peter Noble's book indicates that the projection-room scene was influenced by a stage effect in a play you had acted in—Sidney Kingsley's *Ten Million Ghosts* [1936].

OW: That is one of the biggest pieces of *Schweinerei* I've ever heard in my life. In *Ten Million Ghosts*, there is a scene in which a home movie of war atrocities is run off in an apartment somewhere in Europe. I never saw the scene, because I was in my dressing room during it the six days the play ran, but the fact that a home movie is shown is the only possible connection with a projection room. Wow!

PB: Not having seen *Ten Million Ghosts*, I don't—

OW: Well, almost nobody did. I fell asleep on the stage on opening night, but that's another story. Next.

PB: Someone criticized the actor who did the editor, saying he was hammy, but I liked that—he was an editor, aware of the role he was playing.

OW: Yes, he's supposed to be a kind of a parody. That's the point.

PB: Is it true that Alan Ladd's in there somewhere?

OW: Not in that one. He's the leading reporter when all of them gather at Xanadu at the end. And you can't miss him—it was his first movie part, and there he is, wearing his hat the way he wore it for thirty pictures afterwards.

PB: How did you find him?

OW: He was brought in by his agent, who was later his wife. He read for me and I thought he was very good.

PB: He had a good voice.

OW: Yes. And very effective and intelligent. He's one of the only people I didn't know who's in the picture. There were very few—only three or four. You know, you are boring me to death—

PB: OK, I'll change the subject—

OW: No, *you* talk for a while—

PB: Well, OK. There's a good story I heard about John Ford.

OW: Tell it.
PB: The producer came down on the set, and Ford immediately stopped shooting. He sat down and started talking to the producer. And the producer noticed that everybody else sort of stopped working, and after a while he said, "Don't you think you ought to, you know, go back to work, Jack? I mean—" And Ford said, "Oh no! Gee, that would be rude. I mean, if *I* came into *your* office you'd stop making phone calls, wouldn't you, or whatever you do? You wouldn't keep making phone calls and talking to people while I was in your office. You'd sit and talk to me, wouldn't you? Well, I'm just doing the same thing—"
OW: That's great.
PB: I heard you once did a similar thing by telling the cast on *Kane* to play baseball when—
OW: Yes, we did, but that was intended as a practical joke and was friendly. It was when George Schaefer [head of the studio] came with all the bankers from New York, and they'd all heard, you know, about crazy Welles. We thought it would be nice if they came down and found us hard at work—playing baseball.
PB: Did it go over as a joke?
OW: Yes—it was quite benevolent. Don't think I didn't notice how you sneaked *Kane* in again.
PB [*laughs*]: OK—You had a fifteen-week schedule.
OW: Yes, and that included all the trick shots and everything else. There were so many trick shots—it was a big fake, full of hanging miniatures and glass shots and everything. There was very little construction.
PB: Did you purposely work for economy in making the picture?
OW: Of course. I wanted to go on working in Hollywood. I'd spent a year there before I made it, and I'd found out how important economy was. More important in those days than now, because grosses weren't as big.
PB: The trick shots are very good—
OW: I hope so. My God, I was months and months and months turning down versions of them, day after day, until they got good enough. Trick work *can* be good enough, but you must be brutal about it. Just refuse it, refuse it, refuse it till it gets better.
PB: Trick work in color gets to be almost impossible; it immediately looks phony.
OW: Yes, it *is* impossible. You mustn't do it in color—color looks like trick work anyway. It's only for black-and-white.

PB: I like the way real night looks in color, if it's very black.
OW: I like fog and fire and smoke in color, and winter snow. But it's pretty limited.
PB: All the dissolves were very carefully designed, it seemed to me.
OW: They're done electrically instead of optically.
PB: Could you describe that?
OW: We actually dimmed down lights on the stage—leaving lit the one key thing you wanted to see longer—and brought up the lights the same way for the incoming scene. In other words, if the last thing you want to see is Susan, that's the last thing you see, because all the other lights are fading out around her by dimmer, just as you would do it in the theatre. When you add the dissolve electrically, Susan lingers there, instead of the whole picture going out and another whole picture coming in. They were very carefully designed. All so that the dissolve would be more beautiful. And I still do it all the time.
PB: On the incoming shot, did you place the object you want to see in a different area on the screen?
OW: That's right, so it would complement the outgoing shot.
PB: I've never heard of anybody doing that before.
OW: No, nobody had. I thought that's the way they must do dissolves. After I had done several of them, Gregg broke it to me that it was not the way it's usually done. It just seemed to me from the theatre that that's what you would do. Innocence led me to it. . . . And, of course, we sent *them* back to the lab over and over again until they were right.
PB: You once said about the editing of *Kane*, "There was nothing to cut." What did you mean?
OW: When I made *Kane*, I didn't know enough about movies, and I was constantly encouraged by Toland, who said, under the influence of Ford, "Carry everything in one shot—don't do anything else." In other words, play scenes through without cutting, and don't shoot any alternate version. That was Toland in my ear. And secondly, I didn't *know* how to have all kinds of choices. All I could think of to do was what was going to be on the screen in the final version. Also, I had a wonderful cast.

I only learned about cutting when I got to Europe and had people who didn't speak English—or people who weren't even actors in the roles, wearing wigs and standing with their backs to the cameras—so that I had to fake things, and learn how to cut in order to cover troubles I was in. Now I'm in love with cutting. Transitions, yes—I knew about those instinctively for *Kane*, and they were written into the way we shot it, not discovered during cutting. But nothing was covered from other angles; there was no alternate to the master scene. Whenever I have a good enough cast, I never cover myself. So, of course, there wasn't anything to cut. It was just put together. There were hardly any closeups—I think there are four in the whole picture. And they were the only four closeups we made. And the only thing we deleted was a two-minute scene of me in a whorehouse, which was cut in its entirety very early in the cutting by general agreement, because we knew the censors wouldn't let it get by. It originally followed the dancing scene; I go off to a whorehouse—

PB: With the same women?

OW: No, with some other women. And it wasn't that good, so there was no reason to have it. That was the only *cut;* the picture was never previewed. There was never any alternate version of anything—it was simply put together as shot.

PB: Why did you decide not to have credits at the beginning of *Kane*? No one had ever done that before.

OW: The script dictated that. Look at all the other things that go on at the beginning, before the story starts: that strange dreamlike prologue, then "News on the March," and then the projection-room scene—it's a long time before anything starts. Now, supposing you'd added titles to all that. It would have been one thing too much to sit through. You wouldn't have known where you were in the picture.

PB: In that prologue you just mentioned, why does the light in his bedroom suddenly go off—and then come on again after a moment?

OW: To interest the audience. We'd been going on quite a while there with nothing happening. You see a light in the window—you keep coming nearer—and it better go off, or a shadow had better cross, or something had better happen. So I turned the light off—that's all.

PB: Then you cut inside.

OW: That's right. Maybe the nurse turned it off because it was getting in his eyes. Who knows? Who cares? The other answer is that it symbolized death. Got that? All right.

PB: We can use both answers—in different chapters.

OW [*laughs*]: Yes—use 'em both. In fact, that's really what was in my mind. He was supposed to die when the light went off, and then you go back a few minutes and see him alive again—if you really want a reason. The other, low-class reason was to keep the audience interested. And they're both valid.

PB: What did you mean by the mirrors at the end, when Kane walks by and you see his image reflected many times?

OW: I don't think a moviemaker should explain what he means. About anything. Leave it to the customers. Why spoil things for people who enjoy finding their own meanings?

PB: But you just explained the light going off—

OW: Next.

PB: The black smoke at the end has been said to symbolize the futility of his life. . . .

OW: I don't know—I hate symbolism.

PB: Fritz Lang said he dropped the use of symbols when he came to America because somebody at M-G-M said to him, "Americans don't like symbols."

OW: I'm one of those Americans. I never use it. If anybody finds it, it's for them to find. I never sit down and say how we're going to have a symbol for some character. They happen automatically, because life is full of symbols. So is art. You can't avoid them; but if you *use* them, you get into Stanley Kramer Town.

PB: I know you hate to think up titles—

OW: No! I love to think 'em up, but can't! *Citizen Kane* came from George Schaefer—the head of the studio, imagine that! It's a great title. We'd sat around for months trying to think of a name for it. Mankiewicz couldn't, I couldn't, none of the actors—we had a contest on. A secretary came up with one that was so bad I'll never forget it: *A Sea of Upturned Faces*.

PB: Can we talk about Leland's betrayal of Kane?

OW: He didn't betray Kane. Kane betrayed him.

PB: Really?

OW: Because he was not the man he pretended to be.

PB: Yes, but, in a sense, didn't Leland—

OW: I don't think so.

PB: I was going to say something else. Didn't Leland imagine that Kane was one thing and then was disappointed when he wasn't?

OW: Well, it comes to the same thing. If there was any betrayal, it was on Kane's part, because he signed a Declaration of Principles which he never kept.

PB: Then why is there a feeling that Leland is petty and mean to Kane in the scene when he gets drunk?
OW: Because *there* he is—only there, because he's defensive. It's not the big moment. The big moment is when he types the bad notice afterwards. That's when he's faithful to himself and to Kane and to everything.
PB: I wonder if that's as simple as your answer is now, because if you were put in a position like that—
OW: *I'm* not his character. I'm a totally different kind of person from Jed Leland. I'm not a friend of the hero. And he's a born friend of the hero, and the hero turned out not to be one. He's the loyal companion of the great man—and Kane wasn't great; that's the story. So of course he's mean and petty when he's discovered that his great man is empty inside.
PB: Well, maybe one feels that Leland could have afforded to write a good review.
OW: Not and been a man of principle. That Declaration of Principles Kane signed is the key to it. Leland couldn't—no critic can. He's an honest man. Kane is corrupt. I don't think he betrays Kane in any way.
PB: Well, one has an emotional response to Kane in the picture, and I certainly felt that Leland betrays him—I felt that emotionally.
OW: No, he doesn't. You're using the word "betrayal" wrong. He's cruel to him, but he doesn't betray him.
PB: Well, he betrays their friendship, then.
OW: He doesn't. It's Kane who betrayed the friendship. The friendship was based on basic assumptions that Kane hadn't lived up to. I strongly and violently disagree with that. There is no betrayal of Kane. The betrayal is *by* Kane.
PB: Then why do I somewhat dislike Leland?
OW: Because he likes principles more than the man, and he doesn't have the size as a person to love Kane for his faults.
PB: Well, then, there you are.
OW: But that's not betrayal. "Betrayal" is a dead wrong word. He simply doesn't have the humanity, the generosity of spirit, to have been able to endure Kane—
PB: OK, he had a certain meanness of spirit.
OW: That's right. At that moment. He doesn't later, when he talks about him.

PB: He's not very nice about Kane to the reporter.
OW: Not very terrible.
PB: There are certainly ambiguous moments even there.
OW: Not to me. It's very clear how he feels about him. There's no ambiguity in my mind about it. He has an affectionate memory of a man who turned out to be an empty box. That's it. And it's not as bad as you think. Or, if it is, the effect is not what I intended. As author of the film, I regard Leland with enormous affection. I don't see him as a mean person—he's much superior to Bernstein.
PB: Well . . .
OW: He's the only true aristocrat. . . .
PB: In the story?
OW: Yeah. He's talking my language. With all his meanness, you see, he's essentially an aristocrat. I have deep sympathy for him.
PB: Do you think that Thompson, the reporter, is changed by going through the Kane story? Is he altered?
OW: He's not a person. He's a piece of machinery—
PB: To lead you through.
OW: Yes.
PB: Was there any "mystery" before the Rosebud element? I mean, did you try anything else?
OW: Yes. And there was a scene in a mausoleum that I wrote—it was a quotation from a poem or something, I can't remember—and Mankiewicz made terrible fun of it. So I believed him and just said, "All right, it's no good." It *might* have been good—I don't remember it, because I was so ashamed from Mankiewicz's violent attack on it.
PB: Why did you begin and end with the "No Trespassing" sign?
OW: What do you think? Anybody's first guess has got to be right.
PB: A man's life is private.
OW: Is it? That should theoretically be the answer, but it turns out that maybe it is and maybe it isn't. . . .
PB: Is the name Kane a play on Cain?
OW: No, but Mankiewicz got furious when I used that name, because he said that's what people will think. We had a big fight about that.
PB: The original name was Craig.
OW: Yes. And I said I thought Kane was a better name—
PB: Just *because* it was a better name—
OW: Yes. And Mankiewicz made the other point: "They'll think

you're punning on Cain" and all that, because we had a big murder scene in the original script. And I said they won't, and he said they will, and so on. I won.

The first report:

HEARST OBJECTS TO WELLES FILM
Mention of RKO in His Press Barred as the Withdrawal of "Citizen Kane" Is Demanded
Studio Head Unmoved
Schaefer Says "No Serious Consideration" Is Given—Actor Denies Biography Intent

—*New York Times*, January 11, 1941

The Hearst press is under strict orders to ignore Welles, except for a series of articles pointing out that he is a menace to American motherhood, freedom of speech and assembly, and the pursuit of happiness.

—*The New Yorker*, May 10, 1941

OW: In the original script we had a scene based on a notorious thing Hearst had done which I still cannot repeat for publication. And I cut it out because I thought it hurt the film and wasn't in keeping with Kane's character. If I'd kept it in, I would have had no trouble from Hearst. He wouldn't have dared admit it was him.
PB: Did you shoot the scene?
OW: No, I didn't. I decided against it. If I'd kept it in, I would have bought silence for myself forever. They were really after me. Before *Kane* was released, I was lecturing—I think it was Pittsburgh, some town like that—and a detective came up to me as I was having supper with some friends after the lecture. He said, "Don't go back to your hotel. I'm from police headquarters. I won't give you my name." I said, "Why not?" He said, "I'm just giving you advice." I said, "What are you talking about?" He said, "They've got a fourteen-year-old girl in the closet and two cameramen waiting for you to come in." And of course I would have gone to jail. There would have been no way out of it.

I never went back to the hotel. I just waited till the train in the morning. I've often wondered what happened to the cameramen and the girl waiting all night for me to arrive. But that wasn't Hearst. That was a hatchet man from the local Hearst paper who thought he would advance himself by doing it.

PB: What was your personal reaction to the whole Hearst business?

OW: What do you mean, "personal reaction"?

PB: How did you feel?

OW: He was right! He was dead right. Why not fight? I expected that. I *didn't* expect that everyone would run as scared as they did. And, then, the mistake that Schaefer made was not to believe me when I made the best showmanship suggestion I've ever made, which was that *Citizen Kane* should be run in tents all over America, advertised as "This is the picture that can't run in your local movie house." If we'd done that, we would have made $5 million with it. But he couldn't—I can see why not. Still, I *know* that I would be a rich man today if they'd listened to me. Because it didn't play in any major movie houses. It never played in any chain. Ever. Anywhere. It was always in independent houses. And my idea was to make it sound worse and take it to big tents, and they would've come. It would have been great.

PB: Is it true you offered to buy *Kane* from RKO?

OW: Yes. When RKO wouldn't show it in tents, I was willing to. Because I could have made a fortune on it. If they'd only sold it to me—they would have got out from under, and I would have been independently wealthy for the rest of my life—everybody would have been happy. And they wouldn't do it. I could have raised the money easily to buy it. Everybody was willing to buy in on it.

PB: So you had reckoned on Hearst's anger, but you hadn't realized how effective it would be.

OW: Of course not. And I always thought that courageous showmanship could have turned it to good account. Also, I didn't conceal anything. RKO had read the script and they went ahead and put up the money for it. So they then should have been willing to go all the way, theoretically. Although I have no criticism of Schaefer, that's the basic situation. Nothing was slipped over on them.

PB: There was talk about reshooting some scenes, wasn't there?

OW: No, not that I ever heard of. Only to burn it.

PB: Was Schaefer really a partisan?

OW: Oh, he was great. Schaefer was a hero—an absolute hero. He was marvelous with me.
PB: But he got fired afterward.
OW: Not as a result of that. He was fired during *Ambersons*, but as a result of a whole program of pictures. He was basically a New York–based salesman and not a production head. Floyd Odlum bought control of RKO and took over. But Schaefer stood by the picture finally; if he hadn't, it might never have opened.
PB: Do you think it was because of Hearst that the picture didn't really do the business it should have?
OW: It *did* all the business it should have in the theatres it played in. It did capacity business. But it played in no chains, no major theatres.
PB: In other words, it just didn't get the exposure.
OW: That's right. But wherever it played it did tremendous business. Not in England, where it was a disaster. Not in Italy. But in America it did very well wherever it was shown, because of my reputation on radio.
PB: But it couldn't get the bookings because of Hearst.
OW: Nobody would book it—they were scared. Nobody would put it in.

That fear often took devious shapes. Theatres would pay for the film to avoid blacklist suits, but refused actually to play it. This item appeared in the New York Times, *September 7, 1941, over three months after* Kane*'s premiere:*

> The controversial *Citizen Kane* . . . has been sold to the Fox–West Coast chain, a segment of the National Theatre organization, but it will not be displayed in any of the circuit's 515 theatres on the Pacific Coast, the Mountain States and through the Midwest although they will pay for it. The reason for National's generosity is obscure but whatever the motive, the deal has aroused Orson Welles to new heights of fury. . . .
>
> This week Welles's associates said that if the deal is consummated, the actor-producer will sue RKO, the distributors, and attempt to force the picture's exhibition. In many cities National controls all theatres and in others the picture will be relegated to back-street houses where it will have no standing

> because it has not been shown in the first run theatres. According to RKO, in the three cities in which it has been shown at popular prices—San Francisco, Denver and Omaha—the film's revenue on opening day exceeded that of *Kitty Foyle* [one of RKO's biggest money-makers].

PB: Did you notice an influence on Hollywood films from *Kane*?
OW: You couldn't mistake it. Everybody started having big foreground objects and ceilings and all those kind of compositions. Very few people had ever even used a wide-angle lens except for crowd scenes.
PB: But the effect wasn't in terms of story construction?
OW: No, the things that I *valued* didn't seem to have much effect on anybody. But the most obvious kind of visual things, everybody did right away.
PB: A quote from Andrew Sarris: "*Citizen Kane* is still the work that influenced the cinema more profoundly than any American film since *The Birth of a Nation*."
OW: I don't think that's true. Because *The Birth of a Nation* had genuine innovations—the closeup, the moving shot, everything—the whole language of film is in it. And people could take that in a simple, direct way. I think *Citizen Kane* has influenced more movies in the last years than it did before. In the early days, all it did was put some ceilings on sets and some deep focus; it changed *setups*, which don't mean a thing. But the use of time and all that has only begun now. And it isn't direct, that influence.

I'm not a pro-innovation man. But I am supposed to be an innovator, and I have quietly given myself a few bows for all of these things that it turns out I didn't invent. I *did* invent, but my big inventions were in radio and the theatre. Much more than in movies. Nobody knows that. I invented the use of narration in radio.
PB: Yeah.
OW: Which made [Norman] Corwin possible and all that. He never wrote till I started. I'm the man who took the gelatins out of lights in the theatre.
PB: And made it just a white light?
OW: Yes. White light. That's the basis of all lighting. That I know I did. But in the movies I'd thought I'd done all these things and I find they've already been done. So it's a good argument in favor of my point that directors shouldn't look at too many pictures.

PB: But the important similarity between the two films is that *The Birth of a Nation* summed up all the techniques that had come before in silent films. It brought everything to a head, and *Kane* did that, too, for the sound film.
OW: Yes, it summed things up, to a point. But it's not the technical advances that I think are important about *Kane*, it's the use of time and the way people are handled—that kind of thing.
PB: From the technical point of view, the most important thing in *Kane* perhaps is the use of the sound track.
OW: Yeah, but nobody followed that. They can't. They don't know how. That's a particular trick, and it hasn't influenced anybody. They could learn to do it, but they don't. You can't just say, "Now let's do the overlapping thing." But it can be learned very easily. In movies, though, nobody asks anybody anything. In the great days of painters, they used to go and stay in the atelier and see how the man made that brush stroke. But now everybody sees a movie and says, "I can do it." Nobody really wants to learn—except in an academic way, on a theoretical basis.
PB: But in practice—
OW: In practice—just go and find out how Gregory La Cava got that joke across. You can go to him and he'll tell you. But nobody has the chutzpah to just do it.
PB: All right, how do you do it?
OW: It can be taught in about two hours. We need three very good actors and a little exercise in it. I can't explain it, we have to illustrate it.
PB: I made some stabs at it in *Targets*—
OW: And it worked.
PB: No, it was sloppy because you couldn't understand what was being said as well as—
OW: That's the thing—you have to drill them so that the right syllable comes at the right moment. It's exactly like conducting an orchestra. You have to say, " 'Can't' comes in now. Once again." Because the operative word is "can't" and you come in under there. It's very, very mechanical. It's cold as hell, ice cold—exactly like conducting.
PB: When you first went to Hollywood, you were quoted as saying, "If they let me do a second picture, I'm lucky."
OW: I was so right.
PB: You knew that even before you went out there.
OW: Yes.

PB: You've always been aware of what you were getting yourself into.

OW: Damn right.

PB: You had an awareness of your own character.

OW: And of Hollywood.

PB: Well, I mean *you* within your circumstances. Like you and Hearst, and you and the *War of the Worlds* broadcast. You always seemed to know what you were getting into. That's much more interesting than if you didn't know.

OW: Much more fun. The surprises have been in degree, that's all.

PB: What did you think when you got the Oscar for the Best Original Screenplay?

OW: You're a rat. I always deny that. I always pretend I never got an Oscar.

PB: Well, the picture was nominated in nine categories that year, for Director and—

OW: Never mind. You're spoiling my fun.

Orson is not without justification in denying the Oscar he shared with Mankiewicz—it was almost an insult. The Academy Awards are notoriously influenced by sentiment. Welles was the outsider, and not a humble one, either, on whom sanction could be generously bestowed. Envy, jealousy, fear, whatever—the Hollywood majority just didn't like him. In every category, the Award went to one of their own. (Even Best Screenplay was no doubt more a gesture to "old-time pro" Mankiewicz than an award to Welles.) Best Picture: Darryl Zanuck's production of How Green Was My Valley, *which also won Best Direction (John Ford's third Oscar), Best Art Direction, and Cinematography (Toland* was *a Hollywood man, but, tinged by Welles, his trend-setting photography was officially ignored). Best Actor went to an old favorite, Gary Cooper, for Howard Hawks'* Sergeant York. *I'd be the last to say these pictures were without merit, Ford and Hawks being two of my favorite directors; they were certainly at the forefront of the films of that year, but* Kane *was the film of a decade. The most telling Oscar was for Music: Bernard Herrmann was nominated twice that year—for* Kane *and for* All That Money Can Buy *(another RKO release), and the*

Academy gave him the Award—for All That Money Can Buy.

When the Oscars were announced (February 26, 1942), Welles was in Rio shooting It's All True. *On April 5, 1942, he sent his co-winner a belated note:*

Dear Mankie:

Here's what I wanted to wire you after the Academy Dinner:

"You can kiss my half."

I dare to send it through the mails only now I find it possible to enclose a ready-made retort. I don't presume to write your jokes for you, but you ought to like this:

"Dear Orson: You don't know your half from a whole in the ground."

Affectionately,
Orson

Even now, after thirty years, Citizen Kane *is like watching a consummate artist grappling for the first time with the intoxication of his found vocation. All his passions—theatre, magic, circus, radio, painting, literature—suddenly fused into one. This may explain why to so many people—even those who've seen Welles' other pictures (not so many have, actually)—*Kane *remains the favorite. It is not his best film—either stylistically or in the depth of its vision—but its aura is the most romantic: not just because he was twenty-five when he made it and strikingly handsome* in *it, not the content or thrust of the narrative that gives it romance, but the initial courtship of an artist with his art.*

No other director discovering the medium was as ready or as mature. The signs were right. So *were the circumstances, and they were never the same again: free choice of material, complete control before and during shooting, final word on the cutting, the full financial and technical resources of the best moviemaking facilities in the world; Orson never had all these elements combined on one movie again. (It's also the only film of his to receive, if not exactly decent distribution, at least national prominence and publicity.)* Kane, *therefore, is the only time Orson Welles was able to put on the screen* exactly *what he wanted from every standpoint.*

It was late in Guaymas. The sun was down, but there was still an orange glow on the bay. Orson was struck by the beauty of the scene, and we looked at it for some time without speaking. He seemed melancholy. Kane *was his first film, and the fact that, despite all the fine work in movies he has done since, people still remember him mainly for that one is not a small source of unhappiness. It is a similar situation in radio. So many of his programs were far better, more inventive and beautiful than* The War of the Worlds, *but that's the only one people want to talk about. And here we'd spent the whole day on* Kane, *the one film he least likes to discuss. Still, I chanced a final comment.*

PB: It seemed to me that your memory of your mother is reflected in the scenes with Kane's mother.
OW: Not at all. She was so different, you know.
PB: I don't mean the character, but the affection of Kane—
OW: Really no comparison. My mother was very beautiful, very generous, and very tough. She was rather austere with me.
PB: Well, the mother in *Kane* was not a sentimental mother—
OW: It isn't that. There's just not any connection.
PB: It's not so much the mother herself but the emotion of *remembering* a mother. As in the scene where you meet Dorothy Comingore and tell her you're on a trip in search of your youth, and she has that line, "You know what mothers are like." And you say, in a sad, reflective tone, full of memories, "Yes." It's one of my favorite moments in the picture.
OW: No, Peter, I have no "Rosebuds."
PB: But do you have a sentiment for that part of your past?
OW: No . . . I have no wish to be back there. . . . Just one part of it, maybe. One place. My father lived sometimes in China, and partly in a tiny country hotel he'd bought in a village called Grand Detour, Illinois. It had a population of 130. Formerly it was ten thousand, but then the railroad didn't go through. And there was this hotel which had been built to service the covered wagons on their way west through southern Illinois (which is real Mark Twain country, you know, and people like Booth Tarkington). My father spent a few months of his year there, entertaining a few friends. They never got a bill. And any legitimate hotel guests who tried to check in had a tough time even getting anyone to answer that bell you banged on the desk. Our servants were all retired or "resting"

from show business. A gentleman called Rattlesnake-Oil Emery was handyman. One of the waitresses had done bird calls in a tent show. My father was very fond of people like that.

Well, where I do see some kind of "Rosebud," perhaps, is in that world of Grand Detour. A childhood there was like a childhood back in the 1870s. No electric light, horse-drawn buggies—a completely anachronistic, old-fashioned, early-Tarkington, rural kind of life, with a country store that had above it a ballroom with an old dance floor with springs in it, so that folks would feel light on their feet. When I was little, nobody had danced up there for many years, but I used to sneak up at night and dance by moonlight with the dust rising from the floor. . . . Grand Detour was one of those lost worlds, one of those Edens that you get thrown out of. It really was kind of invented by my father. He's the one who kept out the cars and the electric lights. It was one of the "Merrie Englands." Imagine: he smoked his own sausages. You'd wake up in the morning to the sound of the folks in the bake house, and the smells. . . . I feel as though I've had a childhood in the last century from those short summers.

PB: It reminds me of *Ambersons*. You do have a fondness for things of the past, though—

OW: Oh yes. For that Eden people lose . . . It's a theme that interests me. A nostalgia for the garden—it's a recurring theme in all our civilization.

PB: Kane lost his Eden when the bank took him from his home, and you lost yours—

OW: —in Grand Detour? It was called Grand Detour because the Rock River circles there—it's almost an island. I never even saw the ruins of my father's hotel. It really was a marvelous little corner in time, a kind of forgotten place. . . .

PB: How old were you in those years?

OW: I don't know exactly. It was just before and during my time at Todd. It burned down the year before he died, with all his jade collection in it. And he came out of the fire in his nightshirt after everybody thought that all was lost—came out of the flames with a bird cage and, under his arm, a framed picture of Trixi Friganza. She'd been one of his old girlfriends. . . . Can I go now?

PB: OK.

OW: Good night.

3.

NEW YORK

THE MAGNIFICENT AMBERSONS ▪ TARKINGTON AND TWAIN ▪ *DON QUIXOTE* ▪ *THE DEEP* ▪ *CHIMES AT MIDNIGHT* ▪ *BLACK MAGIC* ▪ GRETA GARBO ▪ *CYRANO DE BERGERAC* ▪ ALEXANDER KORDA ▪ RUSSIAN WRITERS ▪ *AROUND THE WORLD IN 80 DAYS*

ORSON WELLES: *Ambersons* is the only picture of mine I've seen after it was finished and released.
PETER BOGDANOVICH: When?
OW: One evening, when they had a special showing in Paris, André Gide, who'd invited me to dinner, told me we were going to it, so I was trapped. It was most unpleasant. I would have been happier never to know and just *hear* what had been done to it. For five or six reels things weren't so bad. I thought, "Well, that isn't so bad. They didn't do too many things—only a few stupid little

The Magnificent Ambersons.

cuts." And then all hell broke loose. . . . It was a much better picture than *Kane*—if they'd just left it as it was.

> *Orson's suite at the Plaza Hotel. He's there preparing to tape a couple of TV shows for Dick Cavett as well as several for David Frost, whose program he has agreed to appear on and then to host for three days. He is also trying to raise money for a film called* The Other Side of the Wind. *The phone has been ringing all day, and since Orson always manages to run away when it does, I've been answering it for him. Then he always gestures broadly to me to hang up immediately. But it's late in the afternoon now, and things have quieted down.*

PB: How did you come to do the film of *Ambersons*?
OW: Well, we'd had success with it on radio; I played a recording of the show for George Schaefer and we agreed to it. Tarkington's an extraordinary writer—
PB: He's out of fashion now.

OW: Unjustly. He deserves to be taken much more seriously. If the movie of *Ambersons* has any quality, a great part of it is due to Tarkington. What doesn't come from the book is a careful imitation of his style. What was all my own was a third act which took the story into a darker, harder dimension. I can't pay enough tribute to Tarkington. The trouble is that so much of his stuff—particularly on kids—is hopelessly dated now. The kids have changed so much.

PB: You mean the *Penrod* stories.

OW: You just can't imagine kids like that anymore. But the stories themselves are marvelous—wildly funny.

PB: Why isn't Twain dated, then?

OW: Because Twain wasn't writing about children in a middle-class atmosphere. He put them into a kind of invented anarchistic world where middle-class values only exist in parody, and very much on the periphery of things—out in the wilderness, on the river and in caves, and not on Main Street under the shadow of the elms. Also, Twain is a giant, and Tarkington isn't quite that. Twain wrote more trash than Tarkington; it's only his masterpieces that last. You can't read the rest—I can't. But you can read all kinds of Tarkington with great joy. He had a great deal of grace.

PB: That's the thing you admire most, isn't it? That and gallantry. Isn't *Ambersons* as much a story of the end of chivalry—the end of gallantry—as *Chimes at Midnight*?

OW: Peter, what interests me is the *idea* of these dated old virtues. And why they still seem to speak to us when, by all logic, they're so hopelessly irrelevant. That's why I've been obsessed so long with *Don Quixote*.

PB: The idea of your *Quixote* film is to make him contemporary?

OW: He can't *ever* be contemporary—that's really the idea. He never was. But he's alive somehow, and he's riding through Spain even now. . . . The anachronism of Don Quixote's knightly armor in what was Cervantes' own modern time doesn't show up very sharply now. I've simply translated the anachronism. My film demonstrates that he and Sancho Panza are eternal.

PB: When do you think you'll be able to finish it?

OW: That's what I'm going to call it—*When Are You Going to Finish Don Quixote?* [*Laughs.*] After all, we began in 1955. Well, I hope pretty soon. There's *Man of La Mancha* coming. Maybe we shouldn't have spent the money on *The Deep*. But I felt it was high time to show that we could *make* some money.

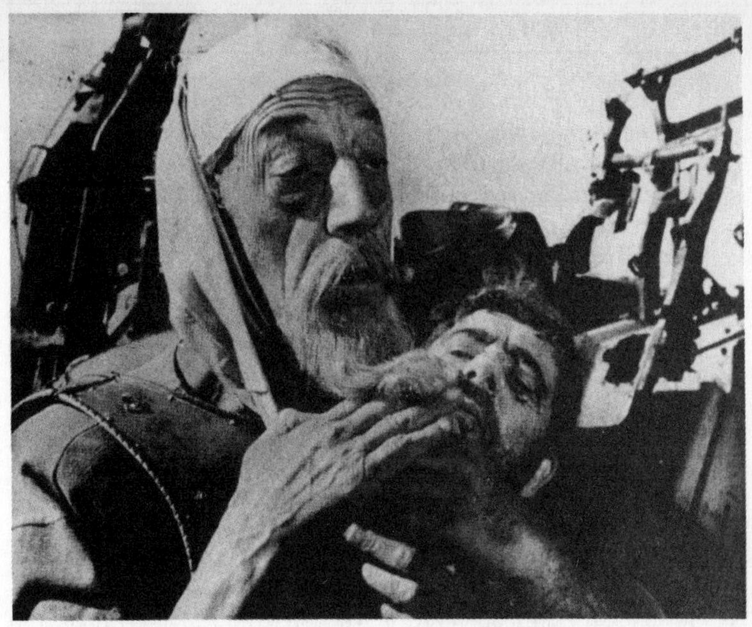

Francisco Reiguera and Akim Tamiroff in Don Quixote.

PB: *The Deep* is based on a novel?
OW: Yes, a good story called *Dead Calm*—about as deadly a title as one could possibly think of, wouldn't you say? It all takes place on the sea and in the boats. We're never on land from beginning to end. . . . We started very late, a year ago. The weather closed in on us, and, worse, our leading man, Michael Bryant, had a commitment in the London theatre. So we had to stop and wait a year for him to get free again.
PB: I thought Laurence Harvey was your lead.
OW: He's got the best part.
PB: I read in an interview with Harvey that you asked him to come down and do it for nothing.
OW: What Larry *said* was that he offered to do it for free and then I told him that I'd need a week to think it over. It's one of his funny stories. In fact, he asked for a big piece of the picture, and I needed a week to think *that* over. He got it, plus $15,000 living expenses—just for two weeks' work.

While Chimes at Midnight *is a lament for "Merrie England,"* The Magnificent Ambersons *reflects the loss of innocence and "the sense of moral values" that was destroyed by the coming of the automobile. Although the film is critical of the dying plutocracy, Orson also makes us feel compassion and affection for the frail figures in the story, and manages at the same time to evoke a pervasive nostalgia for what becomes another of those "lost Edens" that haunt his work.*

PB: François Truffaut once said that, if Flaubert reread *Quixote* every year, why can't we see *Ambersons* whenever possible? Did you ever hear that quote?
OW: No. Thank you for passing it along.
PB: Tim Holt's character, who represents the dying plutocracy, is quite unpleasant; and Eugene [Joseph Cotten], the representative of the mercantile machine age, is very attractive.
OW: Well, just because he's bringing with him the whole stinking hell of the automobile age doesn't mean he isn't a nice human being. He admits himself that what he's doing may be a bad thing. My father felt that way about it. He was a motorcar pioneer, but he abandoned it early on.
PB: For what reason?
OW: Got tired of it, I guess. Then he invented a bicycle lamp which, as it turned out, was on practically every automobile in the world! He was a friend of Tarkington's, and really there's a lot of my father in that character. An early automobile fellow with a deep suspicion of what the automobile would do—fascinated by it, and very much afraid of what it was going to do to the world. Cotten played the role quite marvelously, I think.
PB: For his big speech in the dinner scene, did you give him that piece of business—playing with the spoon as he talks?
OW: I wonder. I rather think it was probably his. Those kind of things usually come from actors.
PB: You know, it wasn't until about the fourth or fifth time I'd seen the picture that I saw any social points.
OW: One shouldn't ever be conscious of the author as lecturer. When social or moral points are too heavily stressed, I always get uncomfortable.
PB: Well, in *Ambersons*, the social observation is so integral to the story of the people that it never intrudes.
OW: Had to be careful about that. The only points I don't mind really stressing are ones that deal with character.
PB: Actually, Tim Holt's character is very ambiguously treated—

Welles as Falstaff in Chimes at Midnight.

which is not unusual with your so-called heavies—
OW: Except he's also the tragic hero, in a way.
PB: Because his love for his mother is genuine though it destroys her—but there's no judgment made on him. Not even by the mother—
OW: I'm not very fond of judgments. They're limiting and they don't work very well. When one character makes a judgment on another, I signal wildly to the audience that they're not to take it as an indication of the author's intention.
PB: You don't make a judgment on Prince Hal, either, in *Chimes*, though he does behave terribly to Falstaff.
OW: Well, Hal didn't just happen to grow up to be King Henry V. He has a beady Welsh eye on future dignity and glory, right from the start. He tells us that all the way through the story—he serves good notice. Here is a complicated young man with a curious,

rather spooky internal coldness. And there's also the charm, the comradely *joie de vivre*—all part of his vocation, the basic equipment of Machiavelli's perfect prince. In other words, that terrible creature, a great man of power.

PB: That's a further extension of a theme in all your pictures—an examination of power and what it does to people.

OW: There's the triangle: the prince, his king-father, and Falstaff, who's a kind of foster father. Essentially the film is the story of that triangle. Opposed to Falstaff, the king stands for responsibility. But what is so fascinating in Shakespeare is that the king himself is an adventurer—he who has usurped the throne speaks for legitimacy. And Hal must betray the one good man in the story to protect a doubtful heritage and realize his coolly chosen destiny as an English hero. And, of course, Falstaff is in himself a reproach and rebuke to all those royal and heroic pretensions.

PB: You called him "the one good man."

OW: I think he's one of the only great characters in all dramatic literature who is essentially *good*. He's good in the sense that the hippies are good. The comedy is all about the gross faults in the man, but those faults are so trivial: his famous cowardice is a joke—a joke Falstaff seems to be telling himself against himself; a strong case could be made for his courage. But his goodness is basic—like bread, like wine. He's just shining with love; he asks for so little, and in the end, of course, he gets nothing.

Even if the good old days never existed, the fact that we can *conceive* of such a world is, in fact, an affirmation of the human spirit. That the imagination of man is capable of creating the myth of a more open, more generous time is not a sign of our folly. Every country has its "Merrie England," a season of innocence, a dew-bright morning of the world. Shakespeare sings of that lost Maytime in many of his plays, and Falstaff—that pot-ridden old rogue—is its perfect embodiment. All the roguery and the tavern wit and the liar and bluff is simply a turn of his—it's a little song he sings for his supper. It isn't really what he's about.

PB: That's clear in the picture.

OW: And of course it sacrifices some of the biggest comedy effects. I know that. I had to deliberately give up some of the biggest jokes in order to play him that way.

PB: Well, there's that reverie for the past—

OW: Of course, it's wonderfully set up by those two old men, Shallow and Silence. It shows you what a drag the whole idea of thinking of the past is—how Falstaff hates hearing about it. "We have heard the chimes at midnight. . . ."

PB: You don't sentimentalize it—just as you didn't in *Ambersons*.

OW: You must *cherish* it but not sentimentalize it. At least that's what I try to do.

PB: One critic, Andrew Sarris, pointed out that there is more in common between you and Ford than one would think at first glance—because both of you have a great respect and love for the past.

OW: Well, we're hooked on different pasts, of course. I'm interested really in the myth of the past, *as* a myth. Jack Ford is one of the myth-*makers*.

From "Orson Welles' Almanac," New York Post, *February 6, 1945:*

Not long before he was killed, the Prince of Denmark visited England. Suppose he'd stayed there and avoided the ghosts and graveyards (he didn't like them, anyway), and lived to be old and fat. . . . Did he change his name? . . .

Shakespeare's great people, in their great moments, are transported with a high and passionate revulsion at the wickedness of the world. All except Hamlet. Exiled from tragedy and living sinfully in London, he laughs at the world, and it's the greatest laughter in our language. We catch him only once without a joke. "I am old," says John Falstaff of Elsinore. ". . . I am old."

The good life is about to be the death of him. He's ruined himself, but it's been fun. Hamlet or Falstaff—call him what you will—only regretted his sins because there weren't more of them.

Shakespeare, a sociable sort who liked to trade gags with the boys at the Mermaid, surely wished that Hamlet could have joined him for a drink after the show. I think Falstaff is Hamlet—an old and wicked Hamlet—having that drink. . . .

PB: What is the meaning of the exchange of looks between Prince Hal and the king and Falstaff over Percy's body?

OW: If that isn't clear, it speaks pretty badly for me. Because the film scene isn't really Shakespeare's. Falstaff, you remember, has come forward with the claim (who knows? perhaps as a sort of black joke) that he has killed Hotspur. When it's obvious that he's lying, the king looks at Hal as if to say, "These are the kind of friends you have. . . ." The prince could say, "No, I killed him," but he refused to do it. Why? Out of the sheer stubborn orneriness of the father-son relationship.

PB: Fascinating . . .

OW: Because of Gielgud—he's extraordinary, I think. It's a great role, and he fills it superbly.

PB: That character is quite ambiguous.

OW: He's obsessed with legitimacy and the whole mystique of the crown, precisely because he himself is not the true heir to it. The crown, as conceived of in Shakespeare, bears a very special kind of magic. And when the last of the Plantagenets was gone, that magic was gone out of England. Chivalry died with it. The very moment of the death of chivalry is the death of Hotspur—the last of the true knights.

PB: You give Hotspur a sort of ridiculous quality, too.

OW: That's Shakespeare—it isn't a distortion. We laugh at Hotspur sometimes, but we know that he could never betray a friendship.

PB: Hal, in a sense, could be called a symbol for modern—

OW: Oh, he's the modern man, all right. The Renaissance Man, the Tudor—the new kind of prince.

PB: You could extend it to the automobile in *Ambersons*. A different story, but—

OW: Tarkington didn't write Shakespeare, and neither did I. But I know what you mean. It's the same kind of moral takeover. Shakespeare was very conscious of what that signified. It began with the Renaissance.

PB: There's a moment in *Chimes at Midnight* that recalls Richard Bennett's scene by the fire in *Ambersons*.

OW: When *we're* sitting by the fire?

PB: Yes, old men contemplating their death. From the beginning —in all your pictures—I also sense a great concern with old age.

OW: It's not a very good preoccupation for a dramatist to indulge in, not in any medium, because it's the thing the public is least happy to hear about. But it's always fascinated me—just as much when I was twenty as it does now, when the fact starts looming ahead. . . .

I hate to think I repeat myself, but maybe you're right. There was that fire. . . . Hell, the only place we could sit in that room *was* the fireplace. That scene was originally to have been shot in the skeleton of an orchard with poor little black trees in the snow. The two old men beside Falstaff were going to be roasting some little birds over a brazier—a sort of terrible, greasy-fingered-old-men scene. We moved indoors for it because we couldn't get the snow. David Lean, making *Doctor Zhivago* next door to us, took off for Finland with a company of thousands chasing snowflakes. But I found an old house. . . . So much for the echoes of *Ambersons*.

PB: You don't like these things called to your attention, but aren't they a way of identifying a particular artist?

OW [*laughs*]: The fact that it's an amusing line of critical speculation doesn't change the fact that I don't enjoy having it applied to me!

PB: The influence of radio is very apparent in *Ambersons*.

OW: The narration, you mean? I'd like to do more of it in movies.

PB: Using a narrator who is not a participant?

OW: Yes, who just comes out and tells the story. I like that very much.

PB: Aren't you doing that with *Don Quixote?*

OW: Sort of, yes.

PB: It's supposedly uncinematic.

OW: I think words are terribly important in talking pictures.

PB: I was very interested in the use of the townspeople as commentators.

OW: A sort of chorus, yes.

> *In fact, Orson used this device in the radio production, which is particularly interesting to hear in light of the movie. Sensitive, somber, and compelling, the show's good qualities—the unusual construction, Orson's beautiful narration and sense of period—were greatly worked over and improved upon in the film. In almost every way, the program is like a fine simplified sketch for what was to become a great painting.*

PB: The script for *Ambersons* is one of the tightest ever written. For instance, the prologue establishes all the characters in three or four situations, sets up the period and the customs of the era, all within the first few minutes.

OW: I don't like to dwell on things. It's one of the reasons I'm so bored with Antonioni—that belief that, because a shot is good, it's going to get better if you keep looking at it. He gives you a full shot of somebody walking down a road. And you think, "Well, he's not going to carry that woman all the way up that road." But he *does*. And then she leaves and you go on looking at the road after she's gone.

PB: You wrote the script for *Ambersons* alone?

OW: Yes. Quite a lot of it on King Vidor's yacht off Catalina. And the rest of it in Mexico. With Molly Kent, the script girl from *Kane*, doing the secretarial work on it—best script girl that ever existed. Then we rehearsed it—longer than I've ever rehearsed anything in movies. It was a relatively small cast, and everybody worked very hard. I think we were five weeks—not on the set or anything, no movements, just rehearsing. And then we recorded every scene, for reference, so we could listen to the way we'd decided that it ought to sound like—even if we were going to change our minds, you know, later.

PB: Does it save time?

OW: It should have, but our cameraman [Stanley Cortez] was so slow that we took longer to shoot than any picture I've ever done.

PB: You couldn't get Toland back?

OW: Gregg had gone to Goldwyn on a long-term contract. We learned that at the last minute, so we had to make a last-minute change.

PB: The opening prologue has a slightly mocking tone mixed with nostalgia.

OW: I think we tend to look back on the immediate past—the past that isn't history but still a dim memory—as being faintly comic. It's an American attitude. I remember my own parents looking at old pictures of themselves and laughing.

PB: Why did you make fun of men's clothes and not women's?

OW: Because the men's clothes *were* funny and the women's weren't. The women's clothes were beautiful.

PB: Did you have to study that period, or was it second nature to you?

OW: It was a real one for my father and mother—and I was only that step away from it. It was much easier to do that period, because you could find the props and costumes for it in storage. It's very much harder to make an eighteenth-century movie, because the clothes and the furniture and the wigs aren't ever really right.

PB: So it wasn't a question of studying up on the times?

Gregory Ratoff during the shooting of Black Magic.

OW: You do it for the picture, then, but you've done it all your life if you're interested in those things, as I am. Costume pictures are more successful when there's a living tradition in the theatre for them. That's why the Japanese pictures are so good—it comes right out of the Kabuki, they *know* it. You really believe you're in the eighteenth century in Japan in a way you can't believe you're in eighteenth-century France when out come the Max Factor wigs and the Westmore mouth and the padded shoulders and all the rest of it.

PB: The women's hair is never worn properly in period films.

OW: It was in *La Kermesse héroïque* [*Carnival in Flanders*]. The costume designer enforced that—Georges Annekov. He did the costumes for that movie about Cagliostro.

PB: *Black Magic.*

OW: I guess that's what they called it.

PB: That was your first movie job in Europe.

OW: Yes, we were the first important film company in Europe after the war. That was a riotous experience—the funniest, most amusing time I've ever had in movies. Grischa [Gregory] Ratoff [the director] was a funny man. He hired all the Russians in Western Europe—you couldn't hear a word of Italian spoken on the set, much less English. The Russian costume designer had put on my hat a Masonic emblem—because, of course, Cagliostro *was* a Mason. And when they showed it in America, the Masons took great umbrage at this, so the studio had to hire a Japanese who painted out my Masonic emblem on every single frame . . . for two reels. That's some spicy matte shot!
PB: Was Ratoff good?
OW: A good comic, a great raconteur. He was at Fox for years—a kind of court jester of Zanuck's. Played gin rummy with the big producers and lost, so they cast him in every movie to get their winnings back. Poor Grischa was always in hock to them, and always dreaming up grand schemes.
PB: Why did you accept the role in the first place?
OW: To try to begin recouping my losses on that stage production of *Around the World*, on which I personally dropped about $350,000. Ratoff had been chasing me around the Fox lot for years saying: "Cagliostro! Think of it! Swordsman! Lover! Magician!" In fact, I'd been asked to play Cagliostro a few years earlier by Garbo. She was interested in that strange woman who was his mistress. Salka Viertel kept after me about it on her behalf and I kept stalling—I can't think why. This was just before *Two-Faced Woman* and her big decision to quit.
PB: What did you think of her?
OW: The greatest . . . I see from your silence that you don't agree.
PB: I just think if it hadn't been for *Ninotchka* and *Camille* you might not say that, because—
OW: If it hadn't been for *Don Quixote*, I don't think you could say that Cervantes was the greatest writer in Spanish literature.
PB: My point is, she wasn't great when she didn't have a really good director.
OW: There you are, plugging the directors again.
PB: Well . . . back to period pictures. Some directors spend months preparing a period story. Do you?
OW: Well, I spent months doing it when I was going to make *Cyrano de Bergerac*. It's a period I didn't know too well and never

even liked very much. I don't fancy that mixture of leather and lace and feathers—it sets my teeth on edge. Alexandre Trauner and I steeped ourselves in all that stuff in the most Germanically thorough sort of way—and all for a picture which I never made! I think every person feels more at home in some periods than others. You have to do your homework on others, because you don't feel you've been there.

PB: There are a couple of period pictures Ingmar Bergman has made that have a great feel for it.

OW: I liked *The Seventh Seal*—

PB: And *Wild Strawberries*.

OW: There's a truly great performance in that by old Victor Sjöström, one of the giants. Whenever I've failed to react to Bergman, it's because of a temperamental lack of sympathy with the preoccupations of his particular, Northern world.

PB: You were going to direct and play *Cyrano* for a movie?

OW: Yes. I lost about nine months on that project. That's why I left America. I never would have gone to Europe if it hadn't been for *Cyrano*. . . . I had a new idea for it. Cyrano, I think, is generous to Christian too soon in the story. He learns that Christian is also in love with Roxanne, and the very next instant he says, "Fine, I'll win her for you!" In my version, he was doing that in order to trip him up later and reveal himself as the true source of all those beautiful words. It's only when Christian dies in battle that he feels honorably *obliged* to keep the lie intact. It could have made a hell of a picture. Trauner designed marvelous things, all based on Callot drawings. I always thought I was wrong physically for Cyrano; I think he ought to be very short—a little bantam rooster poking his nose *up* at everybody. So I was going to make a lot of tricks so that I looked shorter, with doors made bigger and all that. Then I was going to steal something from Coquelin, the actor for whom the play was written. He did such a fabulous thing in it: *his nose got smaller every act!* Isn't that great? Each time just slightly smaller, so by the last act you stopped noticing it at all. I told that to a Hungarian actor who was rehearsing it in Budapest last year. He looked at me coldly and said, "I am playing it with *one* nose," and stalked away! By the way, my favorite people in the world are the Hungarian Jews—all those clever, charming, warm, and witty men, like [Ferenc] Molnár and Alex Korda.

PB: Wasn't Korda going to produce *Cyrano?*

OW: Yes. I lost several years of my life *not* making pictures for

Korda. I feel no bitterness about this; it was my own fault to let myself become so fascinated.

PB: Korda was actually quite a good director.

OW: Very good, but without *vocation.* He really wanted to be Prince Metternich, and he was better casting for it than Prince Metternich himself. No Baron Rothschild ever touched him for style, and there was nobody near him that didn't worship him. Extraordinary man: the only producer who really could have received a delegation from outer space with perfect aplomb and known how to seat everybody.

I prepared about six films for him, including *Henry IV* (in an American context), *Salome, War and Peace, Around the World in 80 Days,* and two originals. And, of course, there was *Cyrano.* . . . After finishing a new shooting script with Ben Hecht, I went to Paris with Trauner [the art director] and worked in the museums on the sets and costumes. The sets were starting to be built when Alex came to me and said, "My dear Orson, don't you really think that man with the nose is rather a bore? I have a chance of making $150,000—hard currency, my dear Orson—so I'm selling it to Columbia. You won't be angry, I know. . . ."

He was right, I wasn't. And that happened over and over. He needed dollars. Even while he was living it up on his yacht, he was still running for his life.

PB: What happened with *War and Peace*?

OW: That was my *first* nonpicture for Alex. We were going to shoot it in the Soviet Union. They were ready to give us just about everything—the whole Red Army for the retreat from Moscow. The same kind of sky's-the-limit backing they gave [Sergei] Bondarchuk later. As for Alex, he was going to deliver Vivien Leigh, Larry Olivier, Robert Donat, Ralph Richardson, old Uncle Tom Cobbley, and me.

PB: You were going to play Pierre.

OW: It's my part.

PB: You wrote a script?

OW: Yes, which is no mean job for somebody like myself who can't figure out the diminutives on Russian names.

PB: Why did it collapse?

OW: The Cold War killed us off. And M-G-M and Alex came to a parting of the ways.

PB: Where are all these scripts?

OW: I only keep 'em as long as I think there's some kind of chance for them. Most of 'em, of course, burned up in Spain.
PB: You were also going to do *Crime and Punishment* at one point. . . .
OW: Not for Alex, but, yes, I got a kind of offer, and nothing happened. I don't think I would have done it well. There are lots better Dostoevsky men than me. My Russian writers are Tolstoy and Turgenev, Gogol and Chekhov.
PB: What happened on the other Korda projects—*Salome*, for instance?
OW: There was a lot more Wilde than Welles in the shooting script, and it was Alex's idea. He promised the title role to Eileen Herlie. I wanted a kitten and he wanted a cat; we hated disagreeing, so we were both relieved, I think, when he got bored with it.
PB: Of course, you'd done *Around the World in 80 Days* on the stage—
OW: Yes, with Alex as a junior partner. When I first got the notion of making a musical of it, I took it to Cole Porter. It was Cole who persuaded me to have Mike Todd do the producing, because Mike was such an inspired hustler. So I wrote the script and Cole wrote the score and then we took it to Mike. He said, "Great," and we went into rehearsal—but after about five days we suddenly realized that Todd was broke. I had the choice of sending all the kids home or keeping the show going, and, like an idiot, I did *Around the World* with all my own dough. Or most of it. Alex was in for a bit, and, besides, he owned the Jules Verne rights.

After New York we were going to bring it to London, where Alex thought it would have been an enormous success at Drury Lane. But the English unions wouldn't allow us to use the American sets and costumes. It would have cost too much to make them over, so they were all taken out and burned. Then we thought of a movie. When I was in North Africa, I even shot a few days for the picture—second-unit stuff. Once again I wrote a script; and once again Alex sold it away from under me. And who did he sell it to? Mike Todd.
PB: Including the script?
OW: Just the rights, I guess. Todd's movie had only a few ghosts of things left over from me. For instance, when we were getting ready for the Broadway show, and Mike was supposed to be producing it, I explained to him that the sets—we had thirty-eight in

Around the World in 80 Days.

the show—were going to be based on [Georges] Méliès's films. "Who's that?" said Mike, and I told him about Méliès. Now, for no good reason, Mike's movie begins with a clip from Méliès's *Trip to the Moon*.

PB: What did you think of him?

OW: Toots Shor had the greatest line. Todd was supposed to be an old friend of Toots, and when he crashed in that plane they came to Toots—who's always good for a tear when one of the old chums goes away to that big barroom in the sky—and they told him, "Mike Todd's just been killed in a plane." Toots said, "Well, I don't know about Mike when he crashed, but when he got *into* the plane, he was a son-of-a-bitch."

PB: Then why on earth did you participate in that TV special about Todd?

OW: Needed the money. But his son, after I finished the job, told me and my secretary at the end of the day that there was no money to pay us. And since we had no contract, what were we going to do about it?
PB: Not really?
OW: Yes, but then the report came back from the lab that some of the material had been ruined, so he had to come back to me. One of those rare little moments of pleasure . . .
PB: And you said—
OW: "A little more money this time, and on the line before we start."
PB: Your stage production of *Around the World*—
OW: I wish you'd seen it, Peter.
PB: You liked it?
OW: Yes, really, with no shame at all.

> *Bertolt Brecht attended a matinee of the stage production during its Boston tryout (spring 1946), and according to Richard Wilson—an eyewitness—he came backstage afterward to tell Welles it was the greatest American theatre he had ever seen. Wilson himself, who worked on the show in several capacities, has described it as "a shoestring production—but on a grand scale."*

PB: Wasn't that the start of your tax problems, since they refused to allow all your expenditures on the production?
OW: Yes—I had the wrong advice on that one.
PB: Did you have movies in it?
OW: Yes, storm at sea, bank robbery, several things like that.
PB: Did Todd ask you to play a cameo in his movie?
OW: I'm the only one he didn't ask. But how could he?
PB: What did you think of the picture?
OW: Hard to make a bad movie of that subject. David Niven, a delightful actor, was all wrong for the lead. The whole point of Phileas Fogg is that he's not any sort of swinger but, rather, the supreme square of all time. But Niven, you know, wears his hat on the side of his head. Fogg has to have it straight over his ears. But I liked that balloon.
PB: Why do you think the movie was so successful?
OW: Salesmanship. Mike could sell anything. He would have made a fortune with a medicine show. . . .

PB: The staircase seems to dominate one's memory of *Ambersons*.
OW: Well, the heart of a pompous house was its pompous staircase. It's all that imitation-palace business. These people haven't got any royal processions to make, but they wouldn't admit it. I had great-aunts who lived in houses exactly like that one. There was one house that had a ballroom on the top floor, just like the Ambersons'.
PB: The top floor?
OW: The third floor, not the attic. And at some stage somebody changed it into an indoor golf course—some second husband, I guess. I remember those terrible little green felt hills built all over the old ballroom.
PB: Tim Holt was awfully good in the film.
OW: Extraordinary . . . One of the most interesting actors that's ever been in American movies, and he *decided* to be just a cowboy actor. Made two or three important pictures in his career, but was very careful not to follow them up—went straight back to bread-and-butter Westerns.
PB: He lives somewhere in Oklahoma now.
OW: Right. He was the most marvelous fellow to work with you can imagine. We ran every picture you can think of before we found him. And then we ran all kinds of six-day movies Tim had made before we were absolutely certain. It was a lucky decision.
PB: He had a small role in *Stagecoach*.
OW: And he did an awful lot of the stunts in that film, during which he claims Ford did everything possible to kill him. He loved Ford—but like somebody who's been through the wars. I used to pump him about Jack for hours.
PB: This part in *Ambersons* was the largest part he'd done. *And* Anne Baxter's—that was one of her first roles.
OW: Yes. She's Frank Lloyd Wright's granddaughter, you know.
PB: Oh?
OW: Yes. The old man used to visit us all the time we were shooting and made withering remarks about the sets. I kept saying, "But, Mr. Wright, we agree with you. That's the whole point." But he couldn't get over how awful it was that people ever lived in those kind of houses. Oh my God, what a marvelous old man. What an artist, and what an *actor*!
PB: How did you come to cast Dolores Costello?
OW: I'd thought of Mary Pickford. I talked to her a lot and she

almost did it—and I'm glad she didn't, I don't think she'd have been right. Finally, we thought of Miss Costello. Brought her back from total retirement. You might have thought she'd want to watch what we were up to. In rehearsals, I mean. But she was quite unfocused. Nothing naughty—just not wanting to be an actress.

PB: She was the daughter of the first silent male star Maurice Costello?

OW: Yes—who worked as an extra in *Kane*. And she was Jack Barrymore's ex-wife, you know.

PB: Did he make any comments to you about her?

OW: Yes, something about "your *bizarre* ideas of casting"—something like that.

PB: It's a heartbreaking moment when George's mother dies. You tell it by having Aunt Fanny embrace him and say, "She loved you, George," and then fade out immediately.

OW: It's hurt by the fact that they cut out some of the scenes that preceded it.

PB: Some of that's there.

OW: Some of it—but arbitrary. The full version made that sharp finish much more effective.

PB: I read a newspaper interview with Jo Cotten recently in which he said you'd been planning to shoot a new ending to *Ambersons*, since the old one was destroyed.

OW: Yes, I had an outside chance to finish it again just a couple of years ago, but I couldn't swing it. The fellow who was going to buy the film for me disappeared from view. The idea was to take the actors who are still alive now—Cotten, Baxter, Moorehead, Holt—and do quite a new end to the movie, twenty years after. Maybe that way we could have got a new release and a large audience to see it for the first time.

You see, the basic intention was to portray a golden world—almost one of memory—and then show what it turns into. Having set up this dream town of the "good old days," the whole point was to show the automobile wrecking it—not only the family but the town. All this is out. What's left is only the first six reels. Then there's a kind of arbitrary bringing down the curtain by a series of clumsy, quick devices. The bad, black world was supposed to be too much for people. My whole third act is lost because of all the hysterical tinkering that went on. And it *was* hysterical. Everybody they could find was cutting it. . . .

PB: When did you record the narration?
OW: The night before I left for South America to begin *It's All True*. I went to the projection room at about four in the morning, did the whole thing, and then got on the plane and off to Rio—and the end of civilization as we know it. . . .

Since Orson left for Rio barely a week after the end of shooting Ambersons, *he had to direct the cutting from there by telephone and telegram. It was not an ideal situation, but the Rio Carnival they had to film for* It's All True *began precisely at that time. There was no way to postpone a national holiday, and therefore no way to push back the start-date. Robert Wise was the cutter; he wrote me recently:*

For almost the last half of the actual shooting of *The Magnificent Ambersons*, Orson was directing that film during the day and acting most nights in *Journey into Fear*, a film he suddenly decided to activate in order to get rid of all of his commitments with RKO by the time he left for Rio.

We had done much of the preliminary editing work on *Ambersons* before Orson had to leave for a meeting in Washington pursuant to his trip to South America. I still had final decisions to be made on certain areas of the preliminary cut of the film. . . . There simply wasn't time to get all of this done before Orson had to be in Washington, so we proceeded in the following manner:

I went to Miami and set up shop in the Fleischer Cartoon Studio there, taking with me a number of reels of the film that needed some additional work. Orson came on to Miami after his Washington meeting and we spent 3 days and nights, practically around the clock, doing this additional work. I saw Orson off just after dawn the 4th morning when he left in a Mars flying boat for South America. I returned immediately to Hollywood with the film and set about completing the editing as per all of our decisions, and completing the sound and music work to get a print, originally intended for me to take to South America to show Orson. . . . [However], the government embargo on civilian flying just at that time stopped my personally going. So it was this cut of the film that I finished up back in Hollywood after Orson had gone on to Rio, that was sent on to him for viewing and from which we tried to work in this unfortunately long-distance situation in getting a final cut of the picture.

The cutting continued in full force, with no real problems, for over a month. George Schaefer was extremely anxious for the film to be released as RKO's Easter attraction, and since it was February by the time Welles left, there was considerable time-pressure to get the job done by the deadline. Plans were even made for the world premiere to be held in Rio—one of Orson's ideas for promoting good relations with South America—and he intended to record his narration personally in Portuguese, which he was learning.

As the work was nearing completion, on March 16, 1942, Orson suddenly received this cable from Wise:

Dear Orson: Reporting developments *Ambersons* Mr. Schaefer unexpectedly requested running *Ambersons* today for himself and Koerner [Charles W. Koerner, who was soon to become head of RKO, replacing Schaefer; he was also instrumental in causing the studio's disastrous break with Welles] and 4 other men unknown to me probably Eastern executives. Following showing Schaefer inquired regarding shortening length. He has ordered me to prepare picture for sneak preview Tuesday Nite with following cuts: both porch scenes and factory. Have advised Jack Moss [Welles' business manager and, in his absence, the film's acting producer].

The first preview was held the following day, March 17, at the Fox Theatre in Pomona, California. At this point the film ran a little over two hours, with three of Welles' scenes already cut. It followed The Fleet's In, *a Dorothy Lamour musical—not exactly an audience in the mood for a movie like* Ambersons, *though actually, of the 125 "comment cards" collected, 53 were positive. But the 72 negative ones and the audible bad reaction is what affected the executives attending.*

The cards asked, among other things, "Did you like this picture?" Here's a sampling of the answers:

Yes. This picture is magnificent. The direction, acting, photography, and special effects are the best the cinema has yet offered. It is unfortunate that the American public, as represented at this theatre, are unable to appreciate fine art. It might be, perhaps, critized [*sic*] for being a bit too long. . . .

No, the worst picture I ever saw.

. . . Too dramatic and strained but very artistic in spots . . .

I did not. People like to laff, not be bored to death.

Yes. Picture will not be received by the general audience because they as a whole are too darn ingorant [*sic*]. . . .

I did not like it. I could not understand it. Too many plots.

No. A horrible distorted dream . . .

Yes, I liked it but I feel that it was above the audience. I think it was very depressing and nerve-racking, but still when I think about it in retrospect, I can see its good points.

It stinks.

The picture was a masterpiece with perfect photography, settings and acting. It seemed too deep for the average stupid person. I was disgusted with the way some people received this picture which truly brings art to the picture industry. Each artist is deserving of a great deal of praise.

Rubbish.

Exceedingly good picture. Photography rivaled that of superb *Citizen Kane*. . . . Too bad audience was so unappreciative.

. . . Too many wierd [*sic*] camera shots. It should be shelved as it is a crime to take people's hard-earned money for such *artistic* trash as Mr. Welles would have us think. . . . Mr. Welles had better go back to radio, I hope.

. . . Too many shadows and the scenery was too dark.

No, it's as bad if not worse than *Citizen Kane*.

I think it was the best picture I have ever seen.

We do not need trouble pictures, especially now. . . . Make pictures to make us forget, not remember.

. . . Why do you like any good piece of art? A little hard to say in five lines, isn't it?

Previews are notoriously unreliable as a gauge of true audience response. Yet many producers still hold this ritual sacred—few have learned from Darryl Zanuck's example: The year before the Ambersons *sneak, Fox had previewed John Ford's* The Grapes of Wrath *to a reaction almost as bad as the one for Welles' picture. When confronted with the situation, Zanuck thought it over and came up with the answer. "Ship it—don't touch a foot of it." His confidence was more than rewarded, since* The Grapes of Wrath *became one of the most popular and critically acclaimed films in Fox's history.*

RKO, however, had no such intention. After further cuts in the film, a second preview was held on March 19 at the U.A. Theatre in Pasadena—following Captains of the Clouds, *a James Cagney flying story. The film had been cut by 17 minutes from Welles' original, and ran 115 minutes. At this running, only 18 of the 85 cards collected were unfavorable.*

Had the film remained in this form, it would still have been fairly close to Welles' version; despite the deletion of 17 minutes, the spirit of the work was not diminished. Above all, no new scenes had been shot and the crucial "last act" was still intact. But nothing evidently could erase the memory of the first preview, and panic set in.

Along with copies of the preview cards, Welles received a friendly but alarmed letter from Schaefer dated March 21, describing both previews. It reads in part:

Never in all my experience in the industry have I taken so much punishment or suffered as I did at the Pomona preview . . . especially in the realization that we have over $1,000,000 tied up. It was just like getting one sock in the jaw after another for over two hours.

In all our initial discussions, you stressed low costs, making pictures at $300,000 to 500,000, and on our first two pictures, we have an investment of $2,000,000. We will not make a dollar on *Citizen Kane* and present indications are that we will not break even. The final results on *Ambersons* is [*sic*] still to be told, but it looks "red."

All of which reminds me of only one thing—that we must have a "heart to heart" talk. Orson Welles has got to do something commercial. We have got to get away from "arty" pictures and get back to earth. Educating the people is expensive, and your next picture must be made for the box-office.

After that, things only got worse. Many exchanges of cables between Welles and Jack Moss continued between March 23 and 25—with Moss detailing the exact cuts that had been made for each of the two previews and outlining more drastic cuts suggested by Wise, Joseph Cotten, and himself, and Welles responding:

My advice absolutely useless without Bob [Wise] here . . . Sure I must be at least partially wrong but cannot see remotest sense in any single cuts of yours Bobs Joes,

along with a suggestion for redubbing one line that produced laughter—it gradually became clear that Wise would not be coming to Rio. A print did arrive, however, and Wise sent a detailed breakdown of how the film had been shown at both previews, together with suggestions for further cutting.

On March 27, Orson cabled eight pages of finely detailed and carefully explained, often minute changes he was willing to make—many of them drastic in themselves, knowing how he feels about it now. But his alterations, as he put it,

cut nothing which promotes story or reveals character where not otherwise revealed.

Many of his instructions were not incorporated. He even sent the text for a couple of new scenes to be made, as well as instructions for how they were to be shot—all in a desperate attempt to retain the shape and substance of the film:

New scene where [George] finds [Isabel] unconscious should be terrific if camera in close enough and moving with him as he drops to feet—takes her in his arms for fade out. Again emphasize tremendous importance this shot be beautifully done—music very strong.

This was never filmed.

He continued to try to improve the film, giving instructions typical of postproduction work:

Narration . . . throughout entire picture slightly too low consonants and sibilants too sharp. This must be filtered out also music sometimes fights me.

Welles concluded his cable:

FADE IN Eugene's car coming to stop in front of boarding house. Then play boarding house scene through as in present version. Only change necessary here is comic record. Norman [Foster, director of *Journey into Fear*] sounds too legitimate. Get Ray [Collins] to play straight man who should sound like bright tight voiced vaudevillian. . . .

. . . As to credits, these must be done in plaque style. One half plaque style or negative effect. Indeed, any effect but straight cuts as in present version. If no photographic tricks satisfactory, suggest pen and ink drawings in somewhat simplified Gibson style white lines on black field or some such vague pleasant stylish effect. . . . [This was never done; the credits remained in straight cuts.]

PB: Why did you yourself suggest so many cuts from Rio?

OW: I was trying to protect *something*. I was trapped down there. I couldn't leave, and all I kept getting were those terrible signals about this awful movie I'd made. My own chums were running, frightened—not just RKO.

PB: And you are affected by what your friends think and feel. Were you shaken in your confidence?

OW: Shaken. You bet. I remember even Jo Cotten writing me in South America. I had no idea, he said, now that they'd seen the whole picture *with an audience*, how terrifying and frightening that last part really was. So even those people who truly had my interests at heart felt that I'd gone too far. I didn't believe I had. And I still don't.

Excerpts from Cotten's letter, dated March 28, 1942, and written less than two weeks after the first preview:

Dear Orson,

In cases such as this Great Difference of Opinion in the editing and cutting of *Ambersons*, people usually say "nothing personal, of course" as an excuse to say whatever they think. . . . In my case, I have no business interest in *Ambersons*, Mercury or you; but a great personal feeling about all three, especially you, and whatever I say I know you will take in a personal way, and I want you to.

I have often been wrong in discussing scripts and plots with you, and I agree that I'm wanting in intellectual concept and understanding of art. I do, however, have a reliable instinct, and as often as I have been wrong about actual ideas, I have been right about audience reactions. I also know by now just about what your reaction to audiences is, and I am writing this to you because I know you would have been far from happy with the feeling in the theatre during the showings last week. The moment the temporary title was flashed on the screen *The Magnificent Ambersons*, a Mercury production by Orson Welles, there was a wonderful murmur of happy anticipation, which was warming and delightful to hear and feel. And the first sound of your voice was greeted with applause. Certainly I was fair in assuming at this point that the audience was with us. Then something happened. . . . It happened gradually and awfully and the feeling in that theatre became disinterested, almost hostile and as cold as that ice-house they had just seen and my heart as heavy as the heart of Major Amberson who was playing wonderful scenes that nobody cared about.

You have written doubtless the most faithful adaptation any book has ever had, and when I had finished reading it I had the same feeling I had when I read the book. When you read it, I had that same reaction only stronger. The picture on the screen seems to mean something else. It is filled with some deep though vague psychological significance that I think you never meant it to have. Dramatically, it is like a play full of wonderful, strong second acts all coming down on the same curtain line, all proving the same tragic point. Then suddenly someone appears on the apron and says the play is over without there having been enacted a concluding third act. The emotional impact in the script seems to have lost itself somewhere in the cold visual beauty before us and at the end there is definitely a feeling of dissatisfaction . . . chiefly, I believe, because we have seen something that should have been no less than great. And it can be great, I'm sure of that. It's all there, in my opinion, with some transpositions, revisions and some points made clearer . . . points relating to human relations, I mean.

. . . Our cables that fly back and forth I know present everything in a very unsatisfactory manner. They often must be misinterpreted at both ends. Jack [Moss], I know, is doing all he can. He is trying his best to get Bob Wise to you. His opinions about the cuts, right or wrong, I know are the results of sincere, thoughtful, harassed days, nights, Sundays, holidays. *Nobody in the Mercury* is trying in any way to take advantage of your absence. *Nobody anywhere* thinks you haven't made a wonderful, beautiful, inspiring picture. Everybody in the Mercury is on your side always. I miss you horribly and will be a happier soul when you return.

We all love you . . . and until then remain forever, as all of us do,

Obediently yours,
Jo

PB: Well, it seemed to me that a lot of your cuts were somewhat drastic, too.

OW: I was bargaining. "I'll give you that if you'll leave me this." They'd got so spooked because of a bad preview, and there'd been no preview of *Kane*. Think what would have happened to *Kane* if there had been one! In Pomona on Saturday night—you can imagine what would have happened.

PB: There were some letter-writing scenes that you wrote in South America, which Robert Wise shot. Why did you write them?

OW: To try and cover up some of those wild cuts they were making. I didn't know Robert Wise did the shooting. That was his beginning, wasn't it? That's when he got off the pad.

One of Orson's several attempts to give the picture an upbeat ending without compromising it came in a cable dated April 2, 1942:

To leave audience happy . . . remake cast credits as follows and in this order: First, oval framed old-fashioned picture very authentic-looking of Bennett in Civil War campaign hat. Second, live shot of Ray Collins . . . in elegant white ducks and hair whiter than normal seated on tropical veranda ocean and waving palm tree behind him—Negro servant serving him second long cool drink. Third, Aggie [Moorehead] blissfully and busily playing bridge with cronies in boarding house. Fourth, circular locket authentic old-fashioned picture of Costello in ringlets looking very young. Fifth, Jo Cotten at French window closing watch case obviously containing Costello's picture tying in previous shot: sound of car driving away Jo turns, looks out window and waves. Sixth, Tim Holt and Anne Baxter in open car—Tim shifting gears but looking over shoulder—as he does this, Anne looking same direction and waving, then turn to each other then forward both very happy and gay and attractive for fadeout. Then fade in mike shot for my closing lines as before.

This was never done. His desperate attempts to save the picture became increasingly futile. Both RKO and the Hollywood contingent of the Mercury had lost their nerve. Telephone connections were terrible, which only increased the disastrous breakdown in communication between all the parties involved. After receiving a cable from Schaefer on April 9 that alluded to retakes, Welles was unable to get further clarification until he received this cable on April 14 from Cotten and Moss:

Dear Orson Schaefer ordered three Amberson scenes retaken says he is phoning you for approval. Shooting scheduled start Friday. No further word from Schaefer and not hearing directly from you we are plenty worried. If you have not talked to Schaefer you should with us so we could discuss situation. . . .

Orson couldn't get through to anyone—the phone wasn't

working. At the same time, he was having terrible problems with the Rio film, It's All True, *which was being produced in cooperation with the government's Office of the Coordinator of Latin American Affairs. On April 15, he cabled Moss:*

Have call in for you meantime please wire full details legality studio retakes and studio cuts. My position is I cannot allow retakes what can Schaefer do about it? Is connection Coordinators Office [of Latin American Affairs] with this picture [*It's All True*] strong enough to keep me from being recalled or suspended? Will talk to [Schaefer] right after talk to you situation here. . . . really desperate . . .

The following day, from Jack Moss:

Dear Orson carefully thoroughly checked. . . . legality definitely gives studio final rights on basis film their property. . . . My opinion there will be no recall no suspension. Waiting your call to relate Amberson details. . . .

PB: Didn't you have a contract which said they couldn't recut *Ambersons*? As you did on *Kane*?
OW: Once you're finished with something, the owners can do anything they want. You can only protect yourself by contract *during* work. Unlike the Code Napoléon, which protects the rights of the artist [in France], English and American law protects property—but the author of a work has no enforceable rights once the person who paid for it has taken delivery.

Orson sent another twelve single-spaced pages of instructions for fixing Ambersons. *Most of these were ignored, because in Hollywood the panic had only increased. RKO began inviting "experts" in to look at the film and tell them how to save it. One of these was producer Bryan Foy, whose work to that date included such films as* Broadway Musketeers, Girls on Probation, *and* Calling Philo Vance. *After the running—all this is according to Jack Moss—Schaefer, Koerner, and other studio executives crowded anxiously around Foy. "Wha'd'ya think, Brynie?" they said. Foy kept them in suspense for several moments, chewing reflectively on his cigar. Finally, he gave a reasoned verdict: "Too fuckin' long."*

*The executives only crowded in closer. "But where, Brynie, where?" "Whole damn thing," Foy said. "Too fuckin' long. Ya gotta take out forty minutes." "All right, Brynie," they said, "*what *do we cut?" Foy barely hesitated. "Well," he said, "just throw all the footage up in the air and grab everything but forty minutes—it don't matter what the fuck you cut. Just lose forty minutes." (Ultimately, more than forty-five minutes of Welles' footage was scrapped.)*

But who would do the cutting? RKO approached several directors—among them William Wyler—but all refused to touch the picture out of respect for Welles. The fate of the movie fell squarely into the hands of the remaining Mercury staff—Moss, Cotten, and Wise—who found themselves caught in the midst of a miserable situation. Though they were bound by their loyalty to Welles, each of them was convinced that RKO was at least partially right: the picture needed work and could not be released as it stood. Moss did not want the job he was handed, but since it had to be done, he determined to make the changes as faithful as possible—to Tarkington. This might have been acceptable if the main scenes in question were from the earlier parts of the film, since in these sections Welles had himself been remarkably true to the original. But Moss "went back to the book" just in those places where Welles had departed from it.

So the revisions went on: more cuts were made, new scenes were written. "Since Ambersons *has become something of a classic," Wise has said, "I think it's now apparent we didn't 'mutilate' Orson's film." Moss feels the same way. In truth, it's a testament to Welles' genius that the movie remains as effective as it is* despite *the amount of tampering that went on. But a consideration of the cut sequences [see Appendix] will give an idea of how much the picture was diminished.*

The film was finally released in August 1942*; since several sections were taken up with scenes Welles had not written or directed, there was actually even less Welles footage in its eighty-eight minutes.*

PB: Your ballroom sequence must have been rehearsed for a long time.

OW: It was a big job technically. But not as hard as you might think, because the sets were built for it. We didn't go into a set and *then* say, "Let's do these elaborate shots." We knew that this wall was going here and that wall was there—it was all planned before we started.

PB: Probably the silliest cut I know of comes in the middle of a long sustained shot during the ball when two characters make some comment about olives, which were evidently new to America at the turn of the century.

OW: Yes. You didn't get to see the little joke about the olives, because some lamebrain said, "What's olives got to do with it?" One of those things. They cut twenty seconds' playing time and cut into two pieces our crane shot that would have played for a whole reel without a cut. Too bad. I like digressions, don't you? Look at Gogol. Read the first few pages of *Dead Souls* again and you'll see how one mad little digression can give reverberation and density to ordinary narrative.

PB: Perhaps the best things in your pictures are the digressions.

OW: Maybe that's why I've suffered so much from the cutters.

PB: Anyway, the olives cut killed your shot.

OW: Not stone dead, maybe, but it was kind of a shame to have worked that hard: four rooms with everything rolling back—an absolute triumph of technical engineering on everybody's part.

PB: It must have been beautiful to watch it happen.

OW: It was. It really was. [The deletions are actually far lengthier than Orson remembered; see Appendix.]

PB: In the novel, they sing "The Star-Spangled Banner" during the outing in the snow—which probably would get roars today. Why did you change it to "The Man Who Broke the Bank at Monte Carlo"?

OW: That's partly to do with my father, who really *did* break the bank at Monte Carlo—or so he always claimed. Anyway, his old chums used to like to sing that song to him, so it was partly for that reason that I used it.

PB: Where did you shoot that snow sequence?

OW: All inside. The "ice house"—a refrigerated soundstage in downtown Los Angeles. Our snow scene in *Kane* was all shot on Stage 4 at RKO with cornflakes, and it worried me because you didn't see people's breath.

PB: You obviously saw quite a few silent movies as a child, and I wondered whether the beautiful iris-out which concludes that sequence was in any way an *hommage* to the silent film.

OW: Well, as I told you, we didn't know about "*hommages*" in those days, thank God. But it does seem a shame that people don't use the iris-out anymore. It's a beautiful invention. There are a lot of silent things that ought to be revived.

PB: One could say that, since the iris-out came from the innocent days of the movies, you used it as an end to the innocent days of the people in the film.

OW: You could say that.

PB: Is it true that the kitchen scene between Holt and Moorehead was improvised?

OW: In a way it was—the rhythm of it all was set. The precise words weren't.

PB: Sounds hard to do.

OW: It takes rehearsal. The actors have to be used to working together, and it gets to be great fun if you do it right.

PB: Was the scene in which George and Lucy go through town in the horse and buggy originally intended to be done with rear projection?

OW: Never.

PB: Where on earth did you do it? It must be the longest dolly shot in the world.

OW: Just the old RKO back lot. We didn't build anything—just everything that was standing, redressed.

PB: It must have been half a reel, at least.

OW: Well, they just ride along.

PB: And the other side of the street is reflected in the windows.

OW: Yes, we *used* the reflections instead of trying to avoid them.

PB: I noticed in the second long street scene with Tim Holt and Anne Baxter that they pass a movie house, and one of the films playing is Jack Holt in *Explosion*.

OW: An in-joke, I'm afraid—for Tim. His father was coming to visit us for lunch that day.

PB: Actually, it's sort of an anachronism.

OW: Of course—Jack Holt wasn't around *that* early.

PB: Over in the corner is a poster for a Méliès film, which would have been right.

OW: But not for Indiana.

PB: In the scene where the Major sits in front of the fire, Richard Bennett really *looked* like he was dying.

OW: Yes. Dear man, I loved him so. I'd been such a breathless fan of his in the theatre. He had the greatest lyric power of any actor I ever saw on the English-speaking stage.

PB: Really?

OW: There's no *way* of describing the beauty of that man in the theatre.

PB: He was the father of the three Bennett girls [Barbara, Constance, and Joan]?

OW: Yes, and he was great and famous on the stage. By that time, he was incapable of remembering even a single word of dialogue, so I spoke every line and he repeated it after me, and then we cut my voice from the sound track. . . . I'd found him out in Catalina in a little boarding house, which was, I guess, the inspiration for the boarding house at the end of my original version of *Ambersons*. He was living there—totally forgotten by the world—this great, great actor. And think what it meant to him at the end of his life to be brought back and to suddenly play an important role! And to have people admire and respect him, as we did—as we all did. . . . Right afterwards, he died.

February 11, 1942

Dear Orson Boy

I wanted so much to tell you so many things before you slipped away. But: I feel sure you understand my gratitude—lifting as you did "an old scow" from the mud banks and permitting it to see the sunshine once more.

Now: For you: my boy your life is too precious to cast entirely to the swine who would sap your vitality and leave you hungry for conquest.

The future is at your feet, use it well but: spare the vitality it would sap.

Expletives count little. *I thank you* Orson.

Simply but sincerely
Richard—*to you* Dick—Bennett

PB: George's "last walk home" before he gets his "comeuppance" —when we see the broken-down city at the end—were there miniatures in that?

OW: That's downtown L.A. I went and shot it, in what's now standard practice. Then it was just me walking around holding the camera. Nobody took that material very seriously in the cutting room. In those days, for a director to hold a camera was unheard-of.

PB: What's left is very affecting.

Richard Bennett, Agnes Moorehead, Tim Holt, and Ray Collins in The Magnificent Ambersons.

OW: They left in a sort of "Coming Attractions"–type montage. . . . Then, too, you know, we had the end of all the other characters—not just Tim Holt. These other people weren't incidental to the story—they were all of equal importance, as in a Chekhov play. You followed Ray Collins right to the finish of him. And Cotten and Moorehead, and—more fully—Richard Bennett. Again, what you have now is a sort of synopsized version.

PB: Is it true that you rehearsed Agnes Moorehead so often in her scene by the boiler that she really *did* become hysterical?

OW: Well, she became more and more *real.* I didn't put her into a state of hysterics; I don't work that way with actors.

PB: She was quite remarkable.

OW: Yes, but, again, it's only half of what it was because people laughed when it was previewed. Some lumpen Saturday-night audience . . . So they ran scared and clipped the scene. The whole distance would have flayed you alive—Aggie was just that good. Why she didn't get an Academy Award for that performance, I'll never know. [Moorehead did, however, win the Best Actress award from the New York Film Critics that year.]

PB: Anybody who knows something about your work can tell you didn't direct the last shot in *Ambersons*—it's the only one in the film where the actors are in closeup and the background's out of focus. They walk out of frame and then the background comes into focus.

OW: Well, that's coming back in style. And in those days, they were doing it all the time. We broke away from it. Now it's modish again. . . . Anyway, that scene was shot without my knowledge or consent.

PB: But there are *some* scenes of yours in the last two reels.

OW: Little bits and pieces glued together in a sort of patch-'em-up woman's-magazine sort of style.

> *The mutilators used some of the identical dialogue Welles gave Eugene, but, placed in diametrically opposed circumstances and with opposite emphasis, its effect is the antithesis of what Welles had done.*

PB: Did you have Agnes Moorehead in mind when you were writing the script?

OW: There wasn't any question about it. How could there be? She'd been all those years with us—it was going to be her great part, and indeed it was, particularly in its full version. If only you'd seen how she wrapped up the whole story at the end. . . . Jo Cotten goes to see her after all those years in a cheap boarding house and there's just nothing left between them at all. Everything is over—her feelings and her world and his world; everything is buried under the parking lots and the cars. That's what it was all about —the deterioration of personality, the way people diminish with age, and particularly with impecunious old age. The end of the communication between people, as well as the end of an era. Sure, it was pretty rough going for an audience—particularly in those days. But without question it was much the best scene in the movie.

PB: Wasn't there a Two Black Crows record playing as counterpoint in the background?

OW: Yes, one of those famous comic turns they used to sell in the early days of gramophone records. And there were all these awful old people roosting in this sort of half old folk's home, half boarding house. They're playing cards in the background, and others are listening to that record, with the elevated clanking by. . . . I wish the film at least existed.

PB: I liked very much the narrating of the credits at the end, and particularly your sign-off—"My name is Orson Welles."

The boarding house.

OW: I got a lot of hell because of that. People think it's egotistic. The truth is, I was just speaking to a public who knew me from the radio in a way they were used to hearing on our shows. In those days we had an enormous public—in the millions—who heard us every week, so it didn't seem pompous to end a movie in our radio style.

Some months later, in a Beverly Hills hotel suite, Orson was flipping the TV dial as usual when he happened on an early scene from Ambersons. *Almost before it was visible, he quickly switched channels, but I noticed it and asked him to leave it on. He loudly refused, but everyone in the room started badgering him to let us see the film—one of the people had never seen it—and finally, exasperated, he turned back to the channel and stalked out of the room.*

Now we all felt terrible, and called to him to come back; he yelled in jokingly that he was going into the "soundproof room." We watched for a while, and pretty soon Orson appeared in the doorway, leaning against the door, looking at the TV unhappily. We all pretended not to notice and went on watching the picture. A few minutes went by. Orson casually made his way across the room and sat on the very edge of a sofa, and looked at the TV intently, but with a kind of desperation combined with a terrible anxiety.

The film went on, and Orson loudly announced the loss of certain truncated scenes. Several minutes later, he stood up and, turning his back to us, went to the window and began fiddling with the venetian blinds. The rest of us exchanged looks. We'd all noticed there were tears in his eyes.

Then one of us said to Orson, cheerfully, that we'd best turn it off because it seemed to be upsetting him. He said it wasn't but he didn't turn back to the room. I switched to another channel, and we started to talk of something else. Orson eventually joined the conversation, and no one mentioned Ambersons *for the rest of the night.*

About a year later—we were in Paris—I asked Orson about that evening. I said I supposed it had been painful for him to watch the movie in its butchered form. "No," he said, "it wasn't that—not at all. That *just makes me angry. Don't you see? It was because it's the past—it's over. . . ."*

4.

VAN NUYS

CHARLIE CHAPLIN ▪ *MONSIEUR VERDOUX*
GRETA GARBO ▪ W.C. FIELDS ▪ FRANK CAPRA
FEDERICO FELLINI ▪ JEAN-LUC GODARD
CENSORED ▪ KENJI MIZOGUCHI ▪ VITTORIO
DE SICA ▪ DIRECTING ▪ JAMES CAGNEY
EISENSTEIN AND *IVAN THE TERRIBLE*
CARL DREYER ▪ HARRY D'ARRAST ▪ CECIL
B. DE MILLE ▪ STERNBERG AND STROHEIM
IT'S ALL TRUE ▪ ROBERT FLAHERTY ▪ THE
RKO TAKEOVER ▪ *JOURNEY INTO FEAR*
SEEING FILMS

Peter Bogdanovich: It seems to me that the South American fiasco of *It's All True* is the direct cause of all your troubles ever since.
Orson Welles: That's right, that was "the great scandal." No doubt about it, everything stems from that. The basis of the whole enormous anti-Welles edifice dates exactly from South America. When I came back from there, I didn't get a job as a director for four years.

> *At night in the garden of PB's house in Van Nuys. Orson has been invited here in the hopes of trapping him into watching the second of his two ninety-minute appearances on* The Dick Cavett Show. *By way of bait, I've promised to run Raoul Walsh's* White Heat *starring James Cagney. This will come later. Now the Cavett show is on, and Orson has come out into the garden to get as far away from the sound of it as possible.*
>
> *What is one to make of this? The show is widely considered a high point of this television year. I watched it being taped in New York. Producers and public alike were ecstatic—a great success. So what's Orson doing out in the garden? Affectation? I've learned by now that he's incapable of that.*
>
> *It is a warm evening, and Orson lies flat on the grass watching the lights of the planes getting into their flight patterns over the nearby airport as some friends watch the show inside. Enter PB with an armload of files and notes and the tape recorder.*

OW: We work? . . . Some host.
PB: I'd *rather* watch the show.
OW: You've seen it . . . Where's that movie?
PB: When you've earned it.
OW: What's all that, for God's sake? You look like a one-man filing cabinet.
PB: Research.
OW: Throw it all away, Peter—it can only cripple the fine spirit of invention.
PB: King Vidor was one of your first friends, wasn't he, when you first came to Hollywood?
OW: Yes, he was very kind. I used to see a lot of King—and *his* good friend Chaplin.

PB: But I thought you didn't like Chaplin—
OW: Chaplin's a great artist—there can't be any argument about that. It's just that he seldom makes the corners of my mouth move up. I find him easy to admire and hard to laugh at.
PB: Even in *City Lights*?
OW: At the situations. At the drunk, yes. Not at Charlie.
PB: But you had a couple of projects you wanted to do with Chaplin, didn't you?
OW: Yes. I had an inspiration in the subway—one of those real "Eureka!" kind of things. I saw an advertisement for an antidandruff remedy which had a picture of a bright-faced little hairdresser type making that gesture of the stage Frenchman which indicates that something or other is simply too exquisite for human speech. "*Avez-vous Scurf*?" he was asking us.
PB: It made you think of Chaplin?
OW: Chaplin *as* Landru. I'd gotten to know him by then, through Aldous Huxley and King, so I went and told him about it. He said, "Wonderful." I went away, wrote a script, and showed it to him. He said, "Wonderful—I'm going to act it for you!" But then, at the last moment, he said, "No. I can't—I've never had anybody else direct me. Let me buy it." So I did, and he made it as *Monsieur Verdoux*. My title was *The Ladykiller*.
PB: This was to be a Mercury Production at RKO?
OW: Yes, his first non–"little man" role. I had one scene in which the Chaplin character meets up with a lady whose profession is to murder husbands. They go on a walking trip in the Alps, and each one tries to push the other one off the mountain. "Come see the lovely view," says one. "Come pick the edelweiss," says the other. And off-scene, in the distance, you can hear people yodeling. But Chaplin couldn't stand that scene, because the woman's part would have been equal to his own. So he changed it to what was, in fact, the funniest sequence in *Verdoux*, with Martha Raye, where he tries to but can't kill her. He changed it from a professional like himself to just somebody he couldn't kill. But there are still people yodeling in that sequence, because it's left over from the other scene.
PB: You wrote a complete screenplay?
OW: He says no, but I've still got a copy of it.
PB: Did he retain a lot of your work?
OW: An awful lot was his. He "brought it up to date." My period was the First World War, with zeppelin raids, to escape which the

ladykiller takes his victims to the safety of the suburbs. He moved it ahead—gave us shots of Hitler and goose-stepping Nazis: you know, social significance. The opening was from my version: the neat little bourgeois in the garden of his little villa briskly, neatly, delicately clipping his hedge while in the background thick, black crematory smoke pours up out of the chimney. At least Charlie didn't change *that*.

PB: Was any of the ending yours, when he talks to the priest before going to the guillotine?

OW: No, none of that. My ending was the rum. I had the greatest piece of business for him—I'm really proud of this. But I have to act it out. In my story, Landru never takes a drink—he's a teetotaler. Now, in France they give you a glass of white rum before you put your head on the guillotine, so at the end of the movie, as I wrote it, he is given the rum. Now, imagine not me but Chaplin as a man who's never taken a drink through his whole life, and has killed twenty women. And he thinks, "Why not?" Once, you know. Picks up the rum and for the first time takes a drink. [Orson acts out a man tasting something indescribably good, then putting down the glass with wistful regret.] Thinking, you know, "What I've missed! I killed all these women, had this wonderful life, but I *could* have been doing *that*." And goes off to the guillotine.

PB: Marvelous. But you only got token credit for the script.

OW: Yes. There was a paternity suit and he had said to me, "I must keep your name off until I settle my suit, so it won't be on at all when the picture opens in New York—just to protect me till I win my suit—and then we'll put it on." Well, he was attacked terribly in New York when it opened; it was the worst lynching by critics you've ever heard. And the next day—after they'd all said, you know, "Who gave him this *awful* idea?"—up on the screen went my billing: "Based on an idea suggested by Orson Welles." It's the only credit I ever got on the picture. And I think he sincerely believes it now. In an interview with a London critic, I said that I wrote the script, and Chaplin wrote a letter to the Sunday *Times* denouncing me, saying that a man who could make a picture like *The Trial*, whom everybody holds up to ridicule—just unbelievable. The *Times* editor wrote me about it, enclosing a copy. He said, "We can't print a letter like this."

PB: I'd like to see that letter.

OW: It burned up with a lot of other things in my house in Spain.

Just as well—It was really pretty ugly. . . . I had a *second* idea for him. For Charlie and Garbo.

PB: What a team!

OW: Just think of it. I went to see them both about it. A picture based on the love affair between D'Annunzio and Elèonora Duse. Garbo had already done comedy in *Ninotchka*, so now I thought she could go further, into farce. But both of them said, "Oh, this beautiful story—how could you possibly play it for laughs?" So it never came to anything. Garbo maybe could have been persuaded —with the help of Salka Viertel—if *she'd* thought it was funny. But I guess D'Annunzio was a bit close to the bone for Charlie. He'd become rather a man of destiny himself. . . . You know the story about his visiting Churchill? Churchill asked him what his next part was going to be, and Chaplin said Jesus Christ. There was a long pause and Churchill said, "Uh—have you—uh—cleared the rights?"

PB: Weren't you planning to do Dickens' *The Pickwick Papers* around that time?

OW: A little earlier, yes—with Bill [W.C.] Fields, John Barrymore, and some other people like that. It might have happened, if Uncle Claude [Welles' nickname for Fields] and Jack had stayed alive and if I hadn't been kicked out of the studio.

PB: Were you friendly with Fields?

OW: Friendly? One of his pen names was an in-joke just for me: Mahatma *Kane* Jeeves. The Jeeves part of it came from my telling him he ought to read P. G. Wodehouse, because he's so funny. That kind of bothered Uncle Claude—that somebody else was funny. Generosity was not his salient virtue.

PB: What about Frank Capra?

OW: Enormous skill—but always that sweet *Saturday Evening Post* thing about him . . .

PB: His pictures have an incredible pace.

OW: Don't they just? I saw *Mr. Smith Goes to Washington* again a little while ago on television. That cast! Imagine a comedy today with a troupe of actors like that! And as you say, the speed of it! How much faster comedies were when directors were laboring under the terrible burden of producers who kept telling them to "snap it up." The performance by Jimmy Stewart is beyond praise.

PB: Did you enjoy the screwball comedies of the thirties?

OW: I have admiration rather than affection for most of them. I liked the low comics better than the high comedies.

PB: But you liked Gregory La Cava.

OW: Very, very much. But not, you know, the same feeling I have for Bill Fields or for Laurel and Hardy. Great comic performances like those must be greater than any comedy director.

PB: Even Lubitsch?

OW: Well, Lubitsch . . .

PB: Don't tell me you don't like *Lubitsch!*

OW: I was just pausing in search of the right superlatives. I think more highly of Lubitsch all the time.

PB: What do you think about Hitchcock? [*A short silence.*] You once said he was the first director to make you want to direct movies.

OW: That was when he made those English pictures like *The Man Who Knew Too Much* and *The Lady Vanishes* and *The Thirty-nine Steps*—especially *The Thirty-nine Steps.*

PB: That's his best English film.

OW: The American movie I liked most was the one Thornton Wilder wrote. Jo [Cotten] was in it. . . .

PB: *Shadow of a Doubt*—it's his favorite, too.

OW: Thornton's natural warmth was a big help. There's a certain icy calculation in a lot of Hitch's work that puts me off. He says he doesn't like actors, and sometimes it looks as though he doesn't like *people.*

PB: How about Fellini?

OW: How about a little rest? Anyway, what's Fellini got to do with Hitchcock?

PB: Just interested in your reaction. I know you didn't like *La Strada.*

OW: And I haven't seen *Juliet of the Spirits.*

PB: And *La Dolce Vita?*

OW: Fellini is essentially a small-town boy who's never really come to Rome. He's still dreaming about it. And we should all be very grateful for those dreams. In a way, he's still standing outside looking in through the gates. The force of *La Dolce Vita* comes from its provincial innocence. It's so totally *invented.*

PB: Maybe "the small-town" aspect is why I like *I Vitelloni* most of all his films.

OW: After *The White Sheik,* it's the best of all.

PB: Would you have been happier with *8½* if Fellini had played it himself? I somehow couldn't see [Marcello] Mastroianni as a movie director.

OW: Ah, but he was just exactly Fellini's idea of what he wanted to look like. . . . The good things in that film are marvelous.
PB: I think we'd better have your thoughts on Godard.
OW: Well, since you're so very firm about it. He's the definitive *influence* if not really the first film artist of this last decade, and his gifts as a director are enormous. I just can't take him very seriously as a *thinker*—and that's where we seem to differ, because *he* does. His message is what he cares about these days, and, like most movie messages, it could be written on the head of a pin. But what's so admirable about him is his marvelous contempt for the machinery of movies and even movies themselves—a kind of anarchistic, nihilistic contempt for the medium—which, when he's at his best and most vigorous, is very exciting.
PB: What American director do you like the least?
OW: [Censored.]

Here follows a full reel of tape in which Orson attacks a number of filmmakers whose work he detests. This material was very colorful indeed, but the following letter from Orson, which I received soon after he was sent the typed transcript of this day's work, leaves me no choice in the matter:

Dear Peter,
How do you like having another director lick into you? It hurts, doesn't it? You tell yourself that you are angry, but the truth is that you are hurt. I know I am. A bad word from a colleague can darken a whole day. We need encouragement a lot more than we admit, even to ourselves. There's quite enough poison floating in the Hollywood air as it is, why add to the pollution?

Of course, I hate those movies we were talking about the other day, but I don't hate the men who made them. Or want to distress them even a little bit. You told me on the phone it was very funny when I said that [name deleted] ought to be put in jail. Well, let's commute the sentence. The book doesn't need it.

Always remember that your heart is God's little garden.

Yours ever,
Louisa Mae [*sic*] *Alcott*

One may note that there are certain exceptions—Michelangelo Antonioni, in particular—who are not protected by Or-

son's delicacy of feelings. He is also cheerfully prepared to attack the dead. "The goddamn pantheon," as he once told me, "is a perfectly legitimate shooting gallery."

PB: This is from an interview with you in France in 1958. [*Reading:*] "*J'admire beaucoup . . .*"
OW: Move those papers around nearer to the microphone. I want your readers to appreciate the full inquisitorial pressure. . . .
PB: The tape won't do our readers any good.
OW: That's a little technical problem you ought to work out, Peter.
PB [*reading again*]: "*J'admire beaucoup . . .*"
OW: Just the French accent alone . . .
PB [*continuing*]: "*. . . Mizoguchi.*"
OW: *What?*
PB: Mizoguchi.
OW: What language are you speaking now?
PB: You know perfectly well who Mizoguchi is; I'm quoting you.
OW: I doubt it. What's that name again?
PB: Mizoguchi. [*OW roars with laughter.*] Come on, Orson—he's a great director.
OW: I don't know *what* I told 'em. They put down what they wanted to hear. I know just how it went: "*Qu'est-ce que vous pensez de Meezagooochee?*" "*Ah!*" I'd reply. "*Ah!*" The big, approving "*Ah,*" you understand, because I'd be getting too tired by then to compose anything more complicated by way of a sentence in cinematic French. "*Mizzagoochee . . . Ah!*" [*More laughter.*]
PB: And the truth is, I suppose, you've never even seen one of his pictures!
OW: You don't realize what these interviews do to a man. You experts with the tape recorders—just give you enough time, and there's nobody you can't break. . . . I guess maybe I'd been belting into Antonioni at the time, and thought I'd better say something good about *somebody*. In fact, all I *did* say was "*Ah!*" . . . You have some comment to make? Please feel free to do so.
PB: Well, you're shameless, but I think basically your taste is pretty—
OW: *Low!* . . . The truth is, Peter, I really am one of those I-don't-know-anything-about-art-but-I-know-what-I-like people. If there's no pleasure for me in it, I feel no *obligation* to a work of art. I cherish certain paintings, books, and films *for the pleasure of*

their company. When I get no pleasure from an author, I feel no duty to consult him. My interests and enthusiasms are pretty wide; and I do keep trying to stretch them wider. But no *strain*. No. I am, indeed, quite shameless, as you say, about not straining to encompass what doesn't truly speak to me.

PB: Well, there's nothing shameless about that. . . .

OW: You say that without much conviction.

PB: You're just making out a case for the straightforward, philistine simplicity of your tastes. But here in the files—

OW: Oh God, Mr. Hoover . . . ! Please don't quote me anymore. I didn't mean a word of it.

PB: That's just what I'm afraid of. Here, for instance, when you said De Sica was your favorite director—

OW: I've got a lot of those.

PB: I'll say.

OW: Some anti-neorealist must have been bugging me at the time.

PB: And someplace else I've got you dismissing De Sica for—what was it?—"rather facile lyricism." You change your mind according to your mood, is that it?

OW: I change my answers according to who's asking me the questions. Anyway, what do these opinions really matter? Why should I upset a strong Fellini man by telling him I think *Satyricon* was frightened at birth by *Vogue* magazine?

PB: Just a few minutes ago you told me—

OW: That I love Fellini? Well, I do. My point is that, in an interview, if I like the guy, I like to keep him happy. But if he's very irritating . . .

PB: What's my category?

OW: Unendurable—but only for your tenacity. No, I agreed to this so we could get the record straight, so I'm playing it straight. . . . OK . . . First, De Sica—for my money, the pizza scene in *Gold of Naples* is the funniest sequence ever made in talkies. . . . No, you really want to break me, don't you? You want me to admit I've given out some pretty large opinions on films which I have never seen. I got hooked on the habit at those film festivals. All those endless interviews with dim aesthetes from Albania.

"What do you think," they ask you, "of our Albanian motion pictures?" You tell them, of course, that you're mad for them. But then you're stuck. "Ah," they say, "which one do you like best?" So what do you do? You can't just say, "The one with the blonde

in it." That reminds me of a Goldwyn story. . . . This was when Sam had a beautiful ballerina called Vera Zorina under contract. . . . Do you want to hear a Goldwyn story, Peter?
PB: OK.
OW: He was preparing *The Goldwyn Follies*, and there was going to be a ballet in it for Zorina, so he's brought out George Balanchine to do the choreography, a word Goldwyn couldn't even pronounce. This is at a story conference, a big table clotted with Hollywood gag men and associate producers. George is asked to explain just what he has in mind, and George, you must understand, speaks a version of our English language even more opaque than Sam's. He brings out matchsticks to demonstrate the movements and employs the whole specialized vocabulary of the dance. This takes a good hour, and when he's finished there follows one of those numb, executive silences. Not one of all those blank-faced writers and department heads can think of anything to say. Then Goldwyn speaks. "I like it," he says, "*and I understand it.*" That's the kind of thing I used to tell the Albanians.

What have you got *now*—another quote to qualify?
PB [*reading*]: "Writers should have the first and last word in moviemaking, the only better alternative being the writer-director, with stress on the first word."
OW: I'll stick with that. Just plain *directing* is the world's easiest job.
PB: You'd better qualify *that* one!
OW: Peter, there isn't another trade in the world where a man can go blithely on for thirty years with no one ever finding out that he's incompetent. Give him a good script, a good cast, and a good cutter—or just one of those elements—all he has to say is "Action" and "Cut," and the movie makes itself. . . . I mean it, Peter. Movie directing is a perfect refuge for the mediocre. But when a good director makes a bad film, the entire universe knows who's responsible.
PB: Hmm . . .
OW: The true author-director has to be so much better than any ordinary pro. When he isn't, it shows badly. The hacks are safe; the originals are out on a limb—which is just where they belong, of course.
PB: Are there more originals today, or less?
OW: Are movies almost finished, or have we scarcely started? Who knows? It's like that great remark of Chesterton's: "Nobody

knows," he said, "whether the world is old or young."

Later, the same night, in the living room; Orson in fine fettle now. The 16mm print of White Heat *has just been shown.*

OW: Cagney—since you've got that thing on again—has just got to be called the number-one screen-filler in movie history.
PB: Screen-filler?
OW: A displacer of air. The real test of that awful term "star quality"—the French call it "*présence.*" And here's a paradox for you—no, I won't call it a paradox, it's just simply the proof of what I've always claimed: that there simply isn't such a thing as "movie acting."
PB: As opposed, you mean, to acting in the theatre?
OW: There's just acting—good, bad, adequate, and great. All this talk about the special technique required for playing to camera is sheer bollocks. Stage actors are supposed to be too big. Well, Cagney was a stage actor and nobody was ever bigger than that. He came on in the movies as though he were playing to the gallery in an opera house.
PB: Bigger than life?
OW: Well, not any bigger than *truth.* He played right at the top of his bent, but he was always *true.* Sure, acting *can* be too *broad.* Broad is wide—spread out. Cagney was *focused.* Christ, like a laser beam!
PB [*reading*]: "When I began in films, apart from John Ford, I liked Eisenstein."
OW: That would be me, of course, sounding off again to the Albanians.
PB: 1958. How about now?
OW: Jesus, Peter, I liked lots of people: Hawks and Walsh, too, Lang and Lubitsch, Murnau, René Clair . . . and Jean Renoir! I've loved him most of all. . . .
PB: Apropos of Renoir, he told me that he's had difficulties with producers, but that his biggest difficulties have always been with the writers.
OW: That's because he's worked mostly in France. In the old Hollywood, when a writer accepted a movie job he felt that he'd already degraded himself to such a point that there wasn't much fight left in him. Nowadays, whatever *is* left is likely to be taken out of him by what are called "creative" producers. In Paris it was

always different. First-rate men are proud to write films, so, naturally, Renoir would have the kind of prickly difficulties one does get into with self-assured collaborators.

PB: OK. What about Eisenstein? Do you think of him as a poet?

OW: "Rhetoric" isn't a bad word, you know—look it up. Eisenstein was supremely the master of film rhetoric. . . . We had a very lengthy correspondence, you know.

PB: Really?

OW: Sustained for the most part by Mr. Eisenstein, I'm afraid, and triggered, I'm sorry to tell you, by a rather cool review I wrote of his *Ivan the Terrible.*

PB: You're sorry you wrote it?

OW: Who needs cool reviews? What does another cool review add to the sum of human knowledge? I should have kept my trap shut.

From "Orson Welles Today," May 23, 1945 (a daily column Orson wrote in the New York Post):

> . . . I took the wife around to the United Nations theatre the other evening and . . . treated her to two hours of Sergei Eisenstein's *Ivan the Terrible.*
>
> Well, sire, it's the darndest thing you ever saw. Like the little girl with the curl in the middle of her forehead, when it is good this new Russian film is very, very good, and when it is bad, etc. It isn't this week's movie "must," since it hasn't been publicly released here, and shouldn't be till a few English titles are tacked on to help you along. . . .
>
> . . . the arts and artists of our theatre have been so busy for so long now teaching their public to reject anything larger than life unless it be stated in the special language of glamor and charm that I'm afraid many good citizens who read the comic strips with the utmost solemnity will laugh out loud at Eisenstein's best moments. Our culture has conditioned us to take Dick Tracy with a straight face. But nothing prepares us for *Ivan the Terrible.*
>
> What's wrong with it, when it's wrong, is what goes sour in the work of any artist whose bent is for eloquence. Eisenstein's uninhibited preoccupation with pictorial effect sometimes leads him, as it has led others of us who work with the camera, into sterile exercises, empty demonstrations of the merely picturesque.

> The Tsar's beard, for instance, cutting like a mighty sickle through the hammer blows of the drama, isn't nearly as entertaining to the audience as it was to the director. And the great eye of the Ikon is permitted to stare so hypnotically out of the screen that it finally puts you to sleep. Anyway, my wife says I was asleep. I tell her I was just listening to the music. . . .

PB: What happened to that correspondence?
OW: Burned up in my house in Spain.
PB: You lost a lot, didn't you?
OW: Manuscripts, letters—a really marvelous long one from Roosevelt. A cup that Lincoln gave my grandfather when he was a little boy—
PB: How terrible.
OW: I try not to think so. I've got a thing about possessions. All my life I've tried to avoid letting them possess *me*.
PB: The house burned to the ground?
OW: Just the wing of it where everything I own was stored—all the things I hadn't been able to lose.
PB: Yeah, I've got a clipping on it.
OW: I'll just bet you do—you've got a clipping about everything.
PB: Well, thinking of posterity.
OW: No. That's a subject to avoid. It's another thing of mine.
PB: You don't think about posterity?
OW: Let's say that concern for it is just as vulgar as concern for worldly possessions. Or worldly success. Posterity is another form of worldly success. Jot that down, if you will, please, on a slab of marble.
PB: Well, shall we do some more directors?
OW: Damned mud-turtle . . .
PB: Carl Dreyer . . .
OW: You never let go, do you? . . . I think he's a rather tremendous talent. Not *The Passion of Joan of Arc*, I don't like that, but the so-called boring Dreyer movies are the ones I love. I even liked the very last one—what was it called? The one he made in his great old age.
PB: *Gertrud*, but I'll bet you never saw it.
OW: I do get stuck occasionally in these festivals. As I recall, the *salle* [auditorium] was rather disapproving. I don't know that I can say I *liked* it. You know, if he were a great success like the other

Scandinavians now, I probably wouldn't be so enthusiastic, but everybody snarled at it, and it seemed to me to be informed by some kind of authority and conviction, and that's enough for me. He ought to be defended.

PB: Yes. It was hooted out of every place it was shown. It was his last film, and he died . . . rather sad.

OW: What do you mean, "rather"? [*Slight pause.*] All right, who's next—Harry D'Arrast?

PB: He was good.

OW: Harry D'Arrast was actually a very considerable talent. And what a charmer he was, too. A sort of Michael Arlen figure—his gifts were fragile, and he spent the last half of his life, like Arlen, lounging about in elegant repose, wearing a faint, ironic smile. Am I holding your interest?

PB: Well, I've got you nailed to the wall on Mizoguchi. You tried to pretend you thought I was just making him up, and here I've found some solid quotes from you praising him to the skies.

OW: He can't be praised enough, really.

PB: You even go into detail—correct titles of a lot of his pictures and everything. But a little while ago—

OW: Consistency, as Oscar said, is the refuge of small minds.

PB: Oscar Wilde?

OW: No, Oscar Serlin—producer of *Gaslight* on the Broadway stage, Peter; don't look at me like that. He took over when Ruth Gordon quit on me. She and I were all set to go into rehearsals, but at the last moment Ruth decided that the play wasn't strong enough. That's one of several reasons why I'm not a multimillionaire.

Are we too far afield? I know, I know; our subject is the Cinema, and you're all poised to record some more of my lightning judgments on our distinguished colleagues. Well, where did we get to, the letter K? Kazan? Let's say he's even better in the theatre. Korda? The one, supreme seigneur. Kubrick—

PB: Did you like *2001*?

OW: Bet I'll love it.

PB: You'll never *see* it.

OW: I will, too—when and if a shorter version is released. I won't see anything that keeps me in a theatre seat for more than two hours.

PB: That would rule out your own version of *Ambersons*.

OW: Sure it would. I've got a bad back.

PB: Did you ever know De Mille?
OW: Sure. He was very nice to me. I liked him. A fascinating old showman, you know, in his way.
PB: I always thought he had a good narrative sense.
OW: Plus a wonderful sense of his own persona. As a director on the set he had the greatest act that's ever been seen, I suppose, except for the two ersatz "vons."
PB: Who?
OW: Stroheim and Sternberg.
PB: Ersatz?
OW: Well, both of them took out their own patents on nobility; you won't find either in the *Almanach de Gotha*. Does that sound snide? Really, I don't mean it to be.
PB: I'm sure you loved them both.
OW: Von *Sternberg?* The only one I know who loved Joe was Marlene. And when he wrote his book he called her, among other things, a stupid puppet.
PB: But as a director—
OW: He had a perfect, really an immense visual command over what is finally kitsch.
PB: I don't agree.
OW: Well, let's not let it spoil our friendship. My own "von" is the other one, whom I knew well and loved. He was just a nice Jewish boy, and I was always on to that—that's what I think is so great about him! [*Laughs.*] A genius of a Jewish boy, and a great charlatan as a figure, and a true artist—my God, he had talent! He was a great actor, too; he had everything. He's way out there, all by himself.
PB: There are certain parallels in your career and his which—
OW: What am I doing, Peter?
PB: Doing? You're making a funny face.
OW: I'm wincing. How can I do otherwise when you suggest that parallel? There's that von Stroheim legend . . . and there's mine. He was supposed to have been "irresponsible," "capricious," "self-destructive"—those words are only too familiar, aren't they? They were repeated in that book about me [Charles Higham's *The Films of Orson Welles*], and it cost me, as you will remember, the financing of a picture. Well, I want to make a suggestion. And before you turn me down, let me remind you of my reasons for agreeing to this project we're involved in now. From my point of view, the whole consideration was to get the record straight. That's why I

want you please to stop right here in your book and put in that letter. . . .

PB: Orson, I don't think it would be very chic to revive that controversy.

OW: Oh, I know. There were people who criticized you for it then. One of them was actually a critic—Charles Champlin of the *Los Angeles Times*. Well, he wrote the other day that my movies are all lacking in *content*, so, whatever he may be as a critic, I know he's not a friend.

PB: Well, he's a friend of *mine*. . . .

OW: He'll forgive you, Peter. . . . Just think, when we talk now about von Stroheim, we haven't any notion of *his* side of the story, much less the facts. So, please—let's be undignified. . . . Here you start a new chapter; I'll give you the heading: "Against My Better Judgment."

Two months before this conversation, I received the following letter from Orson in New York:

Dear Peter,

I think you've already met Dick Wilson. If you spend time with him, as I hope you will, you're going to find that he's invaluable. He was not only my right hand during those years but in South America deserves the title of executive producer. You'll find him very fair-minded, the very opposite of a yes-man. Trust him. I'll tell you in a minute why this matters.

I'm coming back to screenland. . . . Why? To look for some acting jobs, that's why. And what, you'll ask, has happened to my picture? Well, let's say (as I've had to say so often before all through the years) that there has been a temporary delay due to lack of funds.

I'm writing this to beseech your thoroughness in the matter of research. Certainly, I've nothing to reproach you for in this department, but regarding South America there are new and pressing reasons for the most exhaustive fact-finding on your part.

You will be talking to the witnesses in the case—bear down on them, get all the testimony you can.

I haven't bought the Higham book but managed to sneak a few pages of free reading in Brentano's the other day. That's as far as I'm going: no use eating up what's left of my liver. . . . He thinks I hate to finish my movies because I equate completion with death. I should think he'd realize that not finishing a job is not really to do it at all—which isn't suicide but murder. If he had his facts straight he'd see who's been guilty of that. I guess that's why he refused to take me up on my offer to check his material for purely factual inaccuracies: it would have robbed him of the source of some pretty ripe theorizing. On the other hand, it might have helped to get me off a hook which—after 25 years or so—is really starting to hurt. As for Dick, there's something stubborn—almost mulish—in his regard for the facts. And he *has* the facts—all of them—on paper. It's going to be a bore for you, but do please cast a long, cool, non-partisan eye on all that documentation. Get the truth about *It's All True*, and then put it down, just as you find it.

The South American episode is the one key disaster in my story, so of course, you'll want to get it straight. For my part, I *need* to get it straight—as a simple matter of survival. This is newly urgent for me, because, once again, the legend that grew up out of that affair has lost me the chance to make a picture.

As I've mentioned, that lovely money out in the middle west suddenly dried up. Mr. Higham seems to have spooked them. A quote from it in tagging the review in *Newsweek* sent them scampering. Once again I am the man who "irresponsibly" dropped everything to whoop it up in the carnival in Rio, and, having started a picture down there, capriciously refused to finish it. No use trying to explain that I didn't flit down to South American for the *fun* of it. . . .

I don't know of any more fun than making a movie, and the most fun of all comes in the cutting room when the shooting is over. How can it be thought that I'd deny myself so much of that joy with *Ambersons*? I felt then as I do now that it could have been a far better film than *Kane*. How can anyone seriously believe that I would jeopardize something I loved so much for the dubious project of shooting a documentary on the carnival in Rio? Jesus, I didn't like carnivals anyway—I associated them with fancy dress, which bores me silly, and the touristic banalities of the New Orleans Mardi Gras. You know why I went? I went because it was put to me in the very strongest terms by Jock [John Hay Whitney] and Nelson [Rockefeller] that this would represent a sorely needed contribution to inter-American affairs. This sounds today quite unbelievably silly, but in the first year of our entering the war the defense of this hemisphere seemed crucially important. I was told that the value of this project would lie not in the film itself but *in the fact of making it*. It was put to me that my contribution as a kind of Ambassador extraordinary would be truly meaningful. Normally, I had doubts about this, but Roosevelt himself helped to persuade me that I really had no choice.

Why else would I have agreed to make a film for no salary at all? Any appetite I may have felt for high-life could have been satisfied with a few flying weekends to New York. By preference I would have heard the chimes at midnight in Billingsley's Cub Room and in Dickie Wells' up in Harlem. But I was getting all the kicks I needed at the moviola. Dick's file will show you that I only agreed to the Brazilian junket on the firm guarantee that the moviolas and all the film would immediately follow me. What happened instead? The film never came. A takeover in RKO brought in new bosses committed, by the simple logic of their position, to enmity. I quickly lost the last vestiges of control over *Ambersons*, and friends at home collapsed in panic. Who can blame them? Even if I'd stayed I would have had to make compromises on the edition, but these would have been mine and not the fruit of confused and often semi-hysterical committees. If I had been there myself I would have found my own solutions and saved the picture in a form which would have carried the stamp of my own effort.

The point is that the tragedy of South America didn't end with the mangling of *Ambersons* by RKO. No, it cost me a hell of a lot more than the two years I spent making the picture. It cost me many, many other pictures which I never made; and many years in which I couldn't work at all.

For the new men who came to power in RKO it was all too easy to make this giant, this scriptless documentary in South America look like a crazy waste of money. And to justify their positions, it was very much in their interest to do so. A truly merciless campaign was launched, and by the time I came back to America my image as a capricious and unstable wastrel was permanently fixed in the industry's mind. You know all this, of course, but the documentation may surprise you. The extent of that campaign and its virulence is hard to exaggerate.

When I'd left, the worst that can be said for me was that I was some kind of artist. When I came back I was some kind of lunatic. No story was too wild—the silliest inventions were believed. The friendliest opinion was this: "Sure, he's talented, but you can't trust him. He throws money around like a madman; when he gets bored he walks away. He's *irresponsible*."

The legend was established, founded on the firm rock of popular conviction. Soon it was so large and life-like people couldn't see the reality which it obscured. Nobody cared about the facts; the fiction was so vastly more amusing.

I have carried that legend on my shoulders for more than a quarter of a century. Just lately, for the first time—and for no very obvious reason—it did seem to have expired finally of old age. Not quite old myself, I have been looking forward to as much use as the years will leave me to rather eagerly function as a movie-maker.

Then came that book. . . . The very well-intentioned review of it in *Newsweek* would seem to be what's cost me the financing for this new picture, *The Other Side of the Wind*. When the money people read that in the world's first news magazine they can scarcely be reproached for second thoughts in the matter of gambling on a Welles movie.

So now the legend walks again, Peter, and I've no choice but to go back to hustling those cameo jobs in other people's films. . . .

You have on-the-spot witnesses to consult and Dick has the documents. When you get to this chapter I'm hoping that you'll find the hard facts in this matter and will make it honestly possible to do a little job of disinfecting. . . .

This time, it's not just that I'd like to have the record straight—I'd like to go to work again. . . .

As a good, if relatively minor, example of how certain Welles legends get born, consider Raymond Sokolov's on-location report of the filming of Catch-22 *in* Newsweek, *March 3, 1969, which contained the following:*

A master of camera angles, cutting, focus and all the theater arts, Welles continually reblocked his own movements, suggested camera angles, and got editor Sam O'Steen's back up by persuading Nichols to shoot an unorthodox cut. To some of the actors it looked as though Welles wanted the sequence cut in half to save himself trouble learning lines—and as part of some egomaniac scheme for directing his own scenes.

In one of them, where Buck Henry and Martin Balsam were originally supposed to run behind his jeep at 30 miles an hour, Welles improvised a way to save them from heart attacks. He thought up a trick platform, invisible to the camera, on which Balsam and Henry frantically ran in place as it followed Welles in his speeding jeep. Like most of Welles' ideas, this helped, but also delayed, the shooting.

By this time, the cast had taken to mocking the Welles grand manner. Alan Arkin barely spoke a word to him. . . .

Nichols remained undaunted. He knew no actor can take a film away from a director, because the actor leaves, while the director stays and edits the film. Besides, Welles was turning in a great performance. And Nichols had the perspective to see that a great director's advice was worth having. . . .

PB: Did you really tell them how to do that jeep shot?

OW: You were there, Peter.

PB: I wasn't out there when it happened.

OW: Neither was Sokolov. He got it secondhand, so it's not surprising that he got it wrong. That article was well meant but harmful to me in Hollywood. It just fed the legend again. "There he is again, being difficult . . . giving 'unorthodox' cuts to the director." It was a *textbook* cut, Peter. Mike was just wondering if it would work, and I told him it would, that's all.

PB: You trail legends and false myths like Johnny Appleseed. Someone said to me, "Wasn't the first shot great in *Touch of Evil*? You know, it took him a whole week to shoot it!" Imagine anyone thinking that.

OW: It was scheduled for one night and that's what it took. . . . It'd be great if I were Howard Hughes, with all his money. Let them tell all the Howard Hughes stories they want to. But *I* have to hustle for the dough. . . .

Richard Wilson, who eventually became a good picture director, was moved to respond to the chapter from Higham's The Films of Orson Welles *on* It's All True—*which appeared in the Spring 1970 issue of* Sight and Sound—*in the same spirit of defense. He has kindly allowed me to reprint portions of his reply, since they throw considerable light on the* It's All True *affair, and carry not a little weight, since Dick was actually there. His report was called "It's Not* Quite *All True"* (Sight and Sound, *Autumn 1970):*

Books and articles about Welles, published mainly in England, France and Italy, abound in misinformation. One of the chief fonts of inaccuracy, I recognize, has been Orson himself. . . . After all, rationalizing defeat and exorcizing misery comes very naturally to filmmakers. . . .

Charles was given free access to the files from which I'm going to quote and chide him. . . . I am talking about the fifteen or so drawers of working memoranda, the frantic cables, the more expository letters, the successive drafts of scripts making up the files that happen to be in my safekeeping. [*Editor's note:* these files are now in the possession of the Lilly Library at Indiana University, which purchased them in 1979.]

. . . The numbers game I play . . . in what follows about planes, people, cameras and money may seem petty. On the contrary, numbers are the very heart of my objection to the portrait of Orson portrayed by Charles' article. It exudes an aura of profligacy on Orson's part, and stems directly from the accusations that hounded him *during* the making of the picture, and from which he never escaped. Accepted as fact and converted into publicity both covert and overt, these rumors about *It's All True* kept Orson from making any films at all until he made *The Stranger* in 1946. That publicity, still accepted as fact, in large measure inhibits his practical freedom to make films even now. The insidious damage of Charles' piece is that, by its tone and—time and time again—by its slightly distorted detail, it is perpetuating a myth about Orson which is not deserved.

What's really and ironically true about *It's All True*, and I don't think it has ever been stated, is that Welles was approached to make a non-commercial picture, then reproached for making a non-commercial picture. Right here I'd like to make it a matter of record: both RKO and Welles got into the project by trying to do their bit for the war effort. However: RKO, as a company responsible to stockholders, negotiated a private and tough agreement for the U.S. Government to pay it $300,000 to undertake its bit. This speaks eloquently enough for its evaluation of the project as a non-commercial venture. I personally think that Orson's waiving any payment whatever for his work, and his giving up a lucrative weekly radio program, is even more eloquent. For a well paid creative artist to work for over half a year for no remuneration is a most uncommon occurrence.

. . . I'd like to try clarifying the core issue which is raised in the sentence, "Unfortunately, Welles allowed himself to be pressured into agreeing to get to Rio for the Carnival . . ." Here is a statement which is worse than inaccurate, it's ridiculous. The "pressure" was self-imposed. What might have been argued against Orson was, first, whether he should have given in to the pressures to do this Inter-American venture at all. Second, whether the Carnival should, indeed, have been the main film subject.

About Carnival: that came from Brazil itself. They were a little drunk with the potency of the motion picture medium. It's not too hard to see how their DIP (Department of Press and Propaganda) would conceive luring one of the world's most creative filmmakers to make a fantastic tourist come-on (effective after hostilities ended, to be sure) centered around their fabulous Carnival. So they beckoned the gullible Yankees. I suggest the record is made even clearer when it is noted that the Brazilian official put in charge of working with us on the film was the head of the Departamento de Turismo. The weakness of the whole notion was that not Orson, not any RKO Production or story executive, not one of us knew anything about Carnival. The most we could really learn was that it was a sort of super Mardi-Gras which had to be seen to be believed. This latter turned out to be the literal truth.

Orson was very reluctant to give up the jazz segment of the original *It's All True*, a project of four true stories, as Charles describes. So it was not until he learned that the soul of the Carnival was the samba; that this music, like jazz, was a most

> powerful influence in the country's popular culture; that it, like jazz, was essentially a Negro contribution, that the Carnival subject began to seem usable to him. Even so, it was all hearsay and had to be experienced (and photographed and recorded) before it could possibly be developed into a film. . . .

PB: How did *It's All True* originate as a project?
OW: It was supposed to be three movies, and then it was changed to one movie of three parts. (But I went to South America thinking there were going to be three movies.) The first one was called *My Friend Bonito,* based on Robert Flaherty's story which he had written for us, and which I had planned to do before they even sent me to South America. It was set in Mexico and was the story of the bull who, because he was so brave, was pardoned and allowed to live. You saw the little boy who watched the bull grow up and was his friend and lived with him on the ranch; and then, when the bull was brought to the capital city, the matador went to church to pray for his life, and the boy went to the church to pray for the life of the bull. And the bull comes out and kills twenty horses, until finally the boy comes down in the ring—and all of this is nonsense except that it's true, and has happened about forty times in the last hundred years—and he says, "Hey, come here," and the bull follows him out like a little dog. Norman Foster shot for eight or nine weeks in Mexico—all the difficult bull stuff, not the actual story—while we were making *Ambersons* in Hollywood.

All that footage fell into darkness when I was fired by RKO. The little Mexican boy we found for the leading role is today a strong man of thirty. Anyway, fifteen years later, a movie arrived with the same story, produced by the King brothers, called *The Brave One* (1956), which got an Academy Award for Best Screenplay. Dalton Trumbo wrote it under a pseudonym; he couldn't take credit because he was a victim of the blacklist. So nobody came up to get the Oscar, and everybody said, "What a shame—poor Dalton Trumbo, victim of McCarthyism." But, in *fact,* the story was not his or mine but Robert Flaherty's. The King brothers were with RKO, and they just got the rights for it—and Trumbo took a great big invisible bow. Which Flaherty deserved.
PB: Did you get to know Flaherty well?
OW: Very well. We worked on two stories together at great length. The other was called *The Captain's Chair*—a wonderful

story about the Arctic and the Hudson Bay Company. I wish I could make it now. What a fellow he was! Oh boy, a marvelous man.

PB: How did you come to hire him?

OW: I loved his pictures, and he wasn't getting any work, and I thought, "Wouldn't it be nice?" At that time I felt I was powerful and could do that. I also had some people on small salaries experimenting in abstract movies and in animated cartoons. And there was Flaherty. Instead of being a favor for him, it turned out to be a favor for me. I wanted him to direct *The Captain's Chair* and he didn't want to, because it would have involved actors, you know, and he didn't like that. He wanted me to do it. I tried to persuade him but he said no, and then I thought of somebody else directing it. I wanted to start other people directing and all that—I thought I was beginning a great thing, you know.

PB: *It's All True* was to be made in collaboration with the Office of the Coordinator of Latin American Affairs?

OW: *For* them—only that—and for no other reason.

PB: They put up the money?

OW: No. RKO put up the money, because they were being blackmailed, forced, influenced, persuaded—and every other word you would want to use—by Nelson Rockefeller, who was also one of its bosses then, to make this contribution to the war effort. And I was never to get any salary. Going down there was my contribution.

PB: For six months.

OW: Eight months—for nothing. And RKO and everybody was doing it for nothing. Promoting inter-American affairs. I didn't want to do it, really; I just didn't know how to refuse. It was a nonpaying job for the government that I did because it was put to me as a sort of duty. And I hooked the *Bonito* story onto it, saying, you know, "Since you want Latin America, it just so happens I have in my pocket a Mexican story."

PR: What did you actually go down to shoot?

OW: Carnival.

> *From "Orson Welles' Almanac,"* New York Post, *February 13, 1945:*
>
> Now, there are some who disapprove of Carnival because they think it is only an excuse for getting drunk. . . . I was in Rio three years ago for the last great Carnival in that greatest

Carnival crowd in Rio.

of Carnival cities, and I saw with these two eyes a couple of million people dancing and singing (most of them didn't even go to bed for three days), and nobody anywhere in that enormous jamboree stopped celebrating long enough to take a drink.

. . . Carnival isn't a religious observance, but it is fundamentally the celebration of religious people. Wherever the money-changers have taken over, Carnival is no more. Wherever work is so hard that a holiday means rest instead of a good time, Carnival is only a word for a tent show. . . .

OW: I was literally thrown into it—ten days' notice, no script or anything—just true documentary, with no story even. I'd never heard of Carnival, any more than anybody else had. It was just something that went on down in Rio, and we went there and filmed whatever the cameras could show of it. The important thing about that was mainly what we recorded and what our little unit of researchers managed to assemble on the subject of samba,

Carnival sequence shot in Cinédia Studio.

which was then a dying art in the same way that jazz would have died in New Orleans if it hadn't gone up the river to Chicago, and would have died again if the French intellectuals and later the American intellectuals hadn't picked it up. Samba has not been picked up by intellectuals and is now dead. It has been revived very interestingly as bossa nova, but the pure old samba died. *That* was interesting—and samba clubs in the *favelas*—all that footage would have to have been organized to explain what it was socially. It would have made an interesting 50 percent of a total film and would have been a commercial enterprise in those days, because, as it turned out, in the ensuing six or seven years Latin American music swept the world, and this would have been the picture of it. But it's no longer new now, or fresh, and *Black Orpheus* has since plowed that ground.

PB: Did you like that film?

OW: I saw about two reels on French television—didn't like those.

PB: Actually, the samba project doesn't sound like the sort of thing you'd be interested in.

OW: No, it wasn't. I *was* interested in the idea of doing a documentary *since* they'd asked me. As it turned out, I became fascinated with samba. But I went groaning with horror at the thought of making a Carnival, because I hate those kind of events.

PB: And what was the third story to be?

OW: *The Trip of the Jangadeiros.* I think that was the most valuable story. The Jangadeiros were four sailors who felt they weren't getting a right price on their fish—they were the middlemen—so they went out on one of those rafts made of six logs and a sail, and they sailed from their hometown down the whole length of Brazil—made this heroic journey from the top corner of Brazil right down to Rio—to complain to the Brazilian President of their condition. By the time they arrived there, they were so famous—just by virtue of their voyage—that the President couldn't say, "I won't

Jangadeiros sequence.

see you," so he did see them, and they got what they wanted. When we re-enacted the voyage, halfway through, the head Jangadeiro fell off his raft and was never found. And the newspapers said that I'd done it—to get a thrilling shot. We weren't even shooting.

PB: Was he taking an unnecessary risk or something?

OW: That's right—he was a hero. They're a very noble people, very proud. He took a ridiculous chance. All his life in the water and, right near the beaches in Rio, Barra da Tijuca . . .

PB: There's another famous incident attached to the picture. Evidently you threw furniture out of an apartment window one day. Is that true?

OW: Yes. You know, when you rent an apartment or a house in any country, they sometimes charge for wear and tear of furniture. And I hadn't worn and torn anything—I'd hardly been *in* the apartment, it was in perfect condition—and there was this big sum of about two months' rent that I had to pay. At lunch one day, I was telling the Mexican Ambassador about it. He said, "That's just ridiculous." There was a small coffee table in front of him and he said, "If you really break something, let's see what they'll say to that"—and he threw the coffee table out of the window. So I took a chair and threw that, and we started throwing everything out. It just began like that—it was a great joke, we were howling with laughter. Since we'd paid for it, let's *do* some damage. That was the point of the joke.

PB: The story goes that a maid came in with some carrots, and you threw the carrots out the window—

OW: No. Nobody was there—Dick Wilson wasn't there. There are no eyewitnesses except the Ambassador from Mexico. Dick was deeply shocked. I thought it was so funny, and Dick was just white-faced and thin-lipped about it.

PB: Didn't it actually bring about some bad publicity in South America?

OW: A few papers—just anxious to knock the Americans. But everybody was out in the street cheering as we did it. The people loved it. You know, it didn't have any meaning. Gregg Toland was very shocked, too. He arrived the next year in uniform on a mission, and he made long speeches about how terrible it was that I didn't take my duties as a citizen seriously. All we'd done was throw furniture we'd *paid* for out in the little garden in front of the house.

Jangadeiros funeral sequence.

PB: Well, it's usually used against you: "some kind of drunken orgy."

OW: Yeah, I know, but nobody was drunk at all. It was a lunch party, you know—middle of the afternoon. Just terribly high-spirited.

PB: What caused the final collapse of the film?

OW: RKO was taken over by Floyd Odlum. Out went Rockefeller and in came Odlum and the Atlas Film Corporation. They really did think that the South American caper was crazy, and you can see why they would. They got rushes of the samba sequence, and, one of their executives defined it as: "A lot of jigaboos jumping up and down." Thousands of feet of it. And they said, "Where's the script?" "There is no script." Imagine what they thought. I entirely sympathized with them, but it wasn't my idea or my project—that's the whole point of it. And the fact that I might be making something that might be interesting, they had no way of knowing.

PB: And they didn't trust you?

OW: No. Also, they had people like Sid Rogell [an RKO executive] at their ear. But I can't really blame them. Their only mistake was that they thought it was my idea to be down there spending that money. It wasn't. I didn't even like it particularly. I liked samba, but I didn't want to go down and live in South America—it's my least favorite part of the world.

PB: You were particularly interested in the Jangadeiro story.
OW: That I liked, but that was a desperate act. When we were recalled from Brazil—owing to the change of government in RKO—I took what money was left and went up with Dick Wilson and a cameraman—a Hungarian [George Fanto] who is now the owner of Simpson's Department Store in London—and we made the Jangadeiros documentary. Three or four of us for about two months with the Jangadeiros, following their voyage. That was an extraordinary experience—funny and terrifying and strange—and I've never seen any of what we shot, not a foot. Nobody ever saw the rushes. I think it was never even developed—and it was by far the best of everything we made down there. Some people saw the samba stuff, because that was in color and that's what they were spending all the big money for.
PB: How much of the samba *was* there?
OW: Oh God, who knows? I had this enormous crew sent down—I didn't want them, but they gave me two camera crews. So I'd send a crew out there and said, "Shoot 'em marching up and down." I had to keep them busy; they were always saying, "We want to get home—we're trapped here." I had to put them to work to keep 'em happy. So there must have been an awful lot of junk shot, because I wasn't even there.
PB: How did RKO effect the break? You once said they did a very South American thing—they changed presidents at night.
OW: Well, they did—when Odlum got in. It was one of those takeovers. And Sid Rogell, who had been a sort of stooge, a clown of sorts, when I was there—a quiet enemy—suddenly arrived at our offices. I heard all this—I wasn't there—and he said, "You have to move out." We had all these offices—we'd built a Turkish bath, and we had our own kitchen with a chef to cook for us. You know, we were living it up pretty good. And Jack Moss, Jo Cotten, Norman Foster, and all these people who were running it said, "Well, you know, when? Next week?" And Rogell said, "You have six hours." And the next night he went into the Turkish bath to enjoy what he'd never been invited to sit in, and they had taken out the one little unit that made it work.
PB: Small compensation.
OW: I got back at him years later. I was at Fox, making *Compulsion* [1959], when he was technical head of the studio. And he came on the set with a group of bankers to watch me shooting. I saw him and I said—in front of everyone—"Mr. Rogell gets off

the set before I continue." He said, "Ha-ha, Orson, you're a great kidder." I said, "Out, Sid." And he had to go off. It was me or Rogell. And at that moment, you know, I had the part. . . . And I didn't really hate him. It just seemed to me, you had to get at him some way. So I shamed him in front of the bankers and made him crawl out. And it wasn't devastating—it was just a bad moment for him. But it was a pleasure to give it to him, because he'd been so mean—not really to me, but to everybody in our little organization. He was cruel and vindictive and bad.

PB: But, legally, could RKO just throw you out?

OW: Certainly. I'd been paid for those pictures. They had the right, owning those pictures, to cut them the way they wanted to and to screw them up however they wanted. And there was no renewal—so just get out of the offices, no more work. There were no more pictures pending. It was just assumed there would be. I had no long-term contract.

PB: And so they just allowed *It's All True* to become a total loss.

OW: And *Ambersons* and *Journey into Fear*. Because if they had not been total losses they would have looked pretty silly not to have kept me. If either picture had been a success, they would have been fools. And the slogan for RKO Pictures that year, which they printed on all their stationery, was "Showmanship Instead of Genius." Because there had been all that boring genius talk. So, in other words, they were selling their product on the basis that they no longer had me. And yet they had two pictures of mine to sell—it was that idiotic a situation. And so *Ambersons* and *Journey into Fear* were both deliberately released to be failures. That's not sour grapes—it really is true. *Ambersons* opened everywhere without proper advertising, without press showings—dead. Everything was done so that nothing would happen, and nothing did. Except in England, where it was such a total disaster, as was *Kane*. There's never in history been such empty theaters—that was really just a dislike of the English public for the picture. That's a special thing.

PB: But several of your pictures have received the kind of distribution that could only lead to disaster.

OW: Most of them. And I found out about *Ambersons* in the Amazon. I met a group of doctors who were a leprosy commission, paid for by some foundation, and flying to the upper reaches of the Amazon, in the tributaries where nobody ever gets to; in those days, even planes hadn't been there. And I had this marvelous three-week trip among headhunters, with blowguns shot at us and everything. I was pretending to be a leprosy doctor, because there was only one free seat on the plane—and in an incredible place, where the natives were from the Stone Age, out of a hut came a Jesuit father about your age who said, "Mr. Welles, it's marvelous seeing you. I saw *Magnificent Ambersons* last week in Washington and I loved it." And that was the first word I'd heard of it. I didn't even know it had been released.

PB: RKO's story was that you spent a great deal of money on *It's All True*.

OW: We spent only a little over half of the money that was supposed to have been spent.

PB: In other words, RKO mounted an assault against you in order to justify their firing of you.

OW: That's right.

PB: While you were out of the country and couldn't protect yourself.

OW: That's right.

As Herbert Drake, the Mercury's press representative, wrote to Welles on June 1, 1942:

> Nothing you can say and nothing I can say (as I have sadly discovered) can impress anybody with the importance of the expedition as opposed to the picture itself. I can always sell them the idea that your pictures will be magnificent but they have been hearing about neighborly expeditions for some years now and Disney took the cream off the idea.
>
> However, if somebody in Washington will come out with a thank you statement to you, you will return a conquering hero.

PB: Did you ever try to buy back the South American footage?

OW: Yes, all through the years I kept thinking I was gonna be able to finish *It's All True*, and I kept being promised that I could. Part of my deal with *Jane Eyre* was that they would buy it for me and that I would be allowed to cut and finish it, and then that fell through. Always a big effort to do it—because I knew there was a fortune in it during those years when that kind of Latin American music was what was sending everybody. And there was the original thing. It really would have been quite commercial in its time—not now. But it never worked. I tried everything. I was near it, near it,

Welles between takes on Journey into Fear.

near it. And I wasted many years of my life. If I'd just forgotten it —turned my back on it the way the studio did—I would have been way ahead. But I kept trying to be loyal to it, trying to finish it. And I began a pattern of trying to finish pictures which has plagued me ever since.

PB: Were you supposed to direct *Journey into Fear*?

OW: Never at any time. I produced it and Jo Cotten and I wrote the script, based on Eric Ambler's novel. The director was Norman Foster, who was a great friend of mine.

PB: Did you have anything to do with directing the sequence on the building ledge in the rain?

OW: Well, we all did—whoever was nearest the camera; there was no other way to get it made, because of the difficulties. It was a terrible situation: We'd all been up for twenty-four hours to get me finished so I could go to South America. And everybody was fairly well rocked, lurching around up on this thing—the way it's cut, it doesn't look as though it's very high, but we were at the top of the highest studio. And the double for Jack Moss [playing the lead heavy] fell and was killed the day after I left. So it was very dangerous, but we were feeling no pain and we were all helping, Jo, Norman, and myself; Norman, being on the crane, was out of touch sometimes. It was a collaborative effort.

PB: Well, there are parts of it that look like you had something to do with the direction.

OW: I wasn't even in the country for most of the picture. I was only there for three weeks. But I did the sets and I supervised the planning of the way it was going to be done. That picture was also ruined by the cutting. It was horrible what they did with it, because it was really quite a good script we did—it should have been a very decent picture. Good cast and everything. It was the opposite of an action picture, since it was based on the kind of thing that Ambler does so well, which is antiaction, antiheroics, and all that. And they just took out everything that made it interesting except the action—trying desperately to turn it into an action-B—and made quite a lot of nothing out of it. They even have a man looking through a porthole two reels after he's supposed to be dead. You could hardly even call it cutting—you know, run through a broken lawnmower.

PB: It was meant to be a straight entertainment-thriller?

OW: Yes, but with lots of brilliant character performances which all got chopped out and thrown away. I'm pretty awful in it. I happened to see a piece of it by accident on French television last year—

PB: It looked as though you were parodying it—

OW: And I didn't mean to. That's what people keep saying about my acting in other people's pictures. They think I'm this clever cynic who jokes about what I'm doing. Not at all. Now, *that* character was supposed to be a cynical sort, and that's the way I played it—but I think it missed.

PB: Did you design any of the setups on paper before you left?

OW: "Designed" is a pompous word. We planned it together, working with a model of the ship—that sort of thing. But if it's good, they deserve the credit, and if it's bad, I don't deserve the blame. That's about what it amounts to.

I used to think I invented for that picture what is now the cliché of all movies, which is a long sequence before the titles. We did the scene with Banat—played by Jack Moss, my business manager—loading the gun while a gramophone record plays in the background, and he goes out the door and then comes the titles. I genuinely believed it had never been done in pictures—and I have since found out that three years earlier it was done in *Of Mice and Men* (1939) by Lewis Milestone, a picture I never saw. There was a big controversy in the London *Sunday Times* about it. Now, if I had gone to movies all the time, I might even have hesitated to do it because Milly had done it. Today every picture does it, and all these years I thought, "Well, that's one of those things I did—they're all doing it now." Not at all—Milly, an old friend, did it. What a nice fellow he is, too. Good director.

PB: I'm not as fond of his pictures.

OW: Well, I never saw any of them! [*Laughs.*] Yes, I did. I saw *All Quiet on the Western Front* when I was a boy and thought it was good. But I didn't see *Of Mice and Men,* and I hated the book. I'm an anti-Steinbeck man. I liked *Travels with Charley* very much, though. It's the only Steinbeck thing I ever really liked except descriptions of animals scattered here and there.

PB: By the way, what do you think of Rossellini? He's made some very good documentaries lately—

OW: Oh, Peter, Peter . . . !

PB: You *don't* like him?

OW: I don't like this conversation. I don't like talking about movies. I'm bored with movie *talk.* I'll bet your readers are, too.

PB: Let's hope not.

OW: Right. Right. Of course, you're right. If our beloved cinema (and of course I mean that word "beloved," Peter—we do love it very passionately, indeed)—well, once it quits being the big contemporary obsession, then the whole beloved ball of wax is going to be left to the distributors. Thrown to the dogs, in other words—and *then* where are we? But what the hell have I got to contribute to this business of critical appraisals? I hardly see a film from one year to the next.

PB: That's not quite true, you know.

OW: There is no "film culture," Peter—just an awful lot of films. We must "keep up with things," of course, but with the whole, wide world—not just the movies. We must find out what we can about this place we're living in—this place in time—but we've got to be awfully careful, it seems to me, never to make ourselves too perfectly a part of it. Modishness is the sure sign of the second-rate. We're finally to be judged not by the degree of our involvement in the mainstream, but by our individual response to it.

I try to believe somehow that everything is for the first time. That's what I mean by innocence—like Adam in the first garden of the world making up names for all the beasts and flowers. Like my story about the opening of *Journey into Fear*—I really thought it was new.

PB: That's why you see so few films?

OW: Good ones, in particular. I stay away from most of them out of sheer self-protection, to cherish what's left of my own innocence. . . . You smile. I'm being serious. Innocence is really quite a serious concern. The better another man's film may be, the more I stand to lose by seeing it. No, when I look through the camera I need to look with my own innocent eye—to stand alone with every new scene, not in the company of other directors, however august. They keep crowding in, you know, unless you're very careful. . . . Please—let Mr. Mizoguchi keep his distance.

PB: You think that should be true for all of us?

OW: Of course not. Nothing's true for everybody. It's just that at my age virginity is rather fragile.

My own special case is that, to function happily, I like to feel a little like Columbus: in every new scene I want to discover America. And I don't want to hear about those goddamn Vikings. Each time I set foot on a movie set, I like to plant a flag. The more I know about the intrepid discoverers who've come before me, the more my little flag begins to look like the one on the golf course which you take out of a hole so you can sink a putt. I don't pretend at all that my own delicate feelings in this matter should be taken as dogma, but I will say this: let filmmakers beware of films. They really are bad, you know, for the eyes. Filmmakers spend too much of their lives in projection rooms. They should come out more often into the sunshine. Other men's films are a poor source of vitamins. . . . You follow me?

PB: I think I agree.

OW: Other men's films are full of good things which really ought to be invented all over again. Again and again. Invented—not repeated. The good things should be found—*found*—in that precious spirit of the first time out, and images *discovered*—not *referred* to.

PB: Well, it's a big problem for anybody starting now—

OW: Everything's been done, you mean? No, that's not the problem. The trouble is that everything's been *seen*. Directors see too many movies. Sure, everything's been done, but it's much healthier not to know about it. Hell, everything had all been done when *I* started. . . .

5.

BEVERLY HILLS

THE OTHER SIDE OF THE WIND ▪ *THE STRANGER* ▪ *JANE EYRE* ▪ *THE MERCURY WONDER SHOW* ▪ MAGIC ▪ *FOLLOW THE BOYS* ▪ *TOMORROW IS FOREVER* ▪ FDR ▪ *DUEL IN THE SUN* ▪ *THE LADY FROM SHANGHAI* ▪ MEMO TO HARRY COHN ▪ CAMERA ANGLES ▪ JACQUES TATI FOOLS, FELINES, MARTYRDOM

PETER BOGDANOVICH: When you saw that you couldn't work as a movie director, did you actively decide to become a movie star?
ORSON WELLES: Well, you know, I *was* a movie star by virtue of having been starred in *a* movie; so, until further notice, that's the way I was known. I didn't *actively* decide—I have never made an active decision in movies; it's always been what's going . . .

A bungalow in the Beverly Hills Hotel. Orson is here organizing the shooting for his new film, The Other Side of the

John Huston, Welles, and Bogdanovich during the shooting of The Other Side of the Wind.

Wind, *which is set in Hollywood and deals with an aging movie director and the last film he makes. (See Introduction.) Back in Guaymas, we had talked about old directors like John Ford, Fritz Lang, and Jean Renoir. Tonight, Orson tells me some more of what he's been thinking:*

OW: I was sleepless, and then I suddenly thought, "I've got a story—I've worked on it for years—about an old director. And I am crazy not to do it now, in preference to anything else." Because what you told me touched some kind of nerve with me. My character, Jake Hannaford, is one of the machos, hairy-chests.

I'm going to use several voices to tell the story. You hear conversations taped as interviews, and you see quite different scenes going on at the same time. People are writing a book about him—different books. Documentaries . . . still pictures, film, tapes. All these witnesses . . . The movie's going to be made up of all this

The Other Side of the Wind: *Orson Welles.*

raw material. You can imagine how daring the cutting can be, and how much fun.

PB: Have you written a screenplay?

OW: Four of them. But most of it's got to be ad-libbed. I've worked on it for so long—years. . . . If I were a nineteenth-century novelist, I'd have written a three-volume novel. I know everything that happened to that man. *And* his family—where he comes from—everything; more than I could ever try to put in a movie. His family—how they were competing with the Kennedys and the Kellys to get out of the lace-curtain-Irish department. I love this man and I hate him.

Later on, he reads me a scene from the movie.

JAKE (*His face is pale, his eyes glazed with liquor. He's not drunk, but he's been drinking heavily.*): The Medusa's eye. Know what I mean? Whatever I look upon finally dies under my gaze. The Medusa's eye. Yeah. Somebody once

The Other Side of the Wind: *John Huston*, *Gary Graver*, *Orson Welles*.

The Other Side of the Wind: rear, *Rick Waltzer*, *unidentified*; front, *Bill Weaver*, *Orson Welles*, *Oja Kodar*.

The Other Side of the Wind: *Peter Bogdanovich, John Huston, Orson Welles.*

told me about that. Maybe it's true. The eye behind the camera. Maybe it's an evil eye at that. There were some Berbers once up in the Atlas Mountains that wouldn't let me even *point* a camera at them. They think it dries up something in the soul. Who knows? Maybe it can. Aim too long at something. Stare too hard. Drain out the virtue. Suck out the living juices. The girls and boys, even the places, I've shot 'em all. Shot 'em dead. Whiskey, Mother?

In an interview in 1966, Orson had said—about himself:

When I shoot on location, I sense and see the place in such a violent way that now—when I look at those places again—they're like tombs, completely dead. There are spots in the world that to my eyes are cadavers; because I have already shot there—for me, they are completely finished. Jean Renoir said something that seems to be related to that: "We should remind people that a field of wheat painted by Van Gogh can arouse a stronger emotion than a field of wheat in nature." It is important to remember that art surpasses reality. And film becomes another reality. . . .

So now we are in Beverly Hills and Orson has been doing cameo parts in films and some television appearances in order to finance this new movie, the money men he'd been courting in New York having been scared away by the old Welles myth. In other words, he is following a pattern he set for himself years before—first on Othello*—after he'd become fed up with the system.*

PB: After *It's All True*, you didn't direct a film until *The Stranger*, about four years later—though I don't really consider it one of your most personal movies. How did it do?
OW: Very well—made a lot of money—so everything was fine. I had a chance to go on directing for the system, but I didn't want to do that. Somebody who isn't an actor *has* to do that in order to live. But I decided that I'd rather do what I didn't like very much as an actor than what I didn't like very much as a director. So I've kept my virtue slightly less sullied in the megaphone-holding department. Also, I try to maintain myself somehow as some sort of a movie name, because it's an important asset for me as a movie producer—I can always provide one character man for free. But if I could, I'd just direct. I was so happy on *Ambersons* not being in it; it's the only picture I was allowed *not* to act in. I'm less secure in front of a camera—always have been. I don't get as much pleasure out of acting as I ought to, considering that it's been my means of livelihood for thirty years—a lot less pleasure out of it than most actors. Too much pain, really—too much nerves and too much knuckle-chewing miseries.
PB: You don't even like to see yourself on the screen.
OW: Or hear my voice. I never listened to a recording of any radio show I ever did.
PB: How can you cut your pictures?
OW: Well, there are other things going to get my mind off the sheer ache of it.
PB: Maybe that's why you wear so much makeup.
OW: Sure—camouflage.
PB: How did you actually get the job directing *The Stranger*?
OW: It was offered me. There were going to be two producers, Sam Spiegel and Bill Goetz. And I'd had a happy time with Goetz

on *Jane Eyre* and *Tomorrow Is Forever*—that helped.
PB: So they "took a chance."
OW: Yes, but it wasn't such a big chance, because I was then being a director within the producer system—where a director is called in to work on a script that's been thought up by somebody else and all that; it's the only picture of that kind I ever made. Or ever will make.
PB: Besides acting in it, how much did you have to do with *Jane Eyre?*
OW: I produced it.
PB: Without credit?
OW: Yes. I don't think an actor should be a producer unless he directs, so I didn't use the credit. But it was in my contract, and I was in fact the actual producer.

> *David O. Selznick had originally prepared* Jane Eyre, *and when he sold it to 20th Century–Fox, he also loaned them his star, Joan Fontaine, still retaining some contractual power. In a July 15, 1943, letter to Fox, a Selznick lawyer, agreeing to give Welles credit on the film as producer if he wanted it, wrote, "We have only just learned that Mr. Welles did a great deal more producing on the picture than we had previously known. We have been informed by people from your studio that Mr. Welles worked on the sets, changes in the script, in casting, among other things, and that he had charge of the editing. . . ."*

PB: Why did you choose Robert Stevenson to direct?
OW: He had been chosen when I came on. And he was all right. I thought he did a good job. The picture is notable for being the first with Elizabeth Taylor in any sort of role.
PB: I didn't know that.
OW: Yes. She's Jane Eyre's little friend who cuts off her hair. I found her from interviewing a lot of girls.
PB: You had done *Jane Eyre* on the radio?
OW: Repeatedly—it was an old war-horse of ours.
PB: Parts of the film looked as though you had directed.
OW: Oh, I invented some of the shots—that's part of being that kind of producer. And I collaborated on it, but I didn't come around behind the camera and direct it. Certainly I did a lot more than a producer ought to, but Stevenson didn't mind that. And I

don't want to take credit away from him, all of which he deserves. It was an impossible situation for him, because the basic setup is wrong if an actor is also a producer—it shouldn't happen. In fact, we got along very well, and there was no trouble.

PB: Had you ever wanted to direct *Jane Eyre*?

OW: No. Not my kind of picture. I was delighted to act in it, and very happy to do it, but I would never have chosen it. I think, if I had a chance of directing sixty movies, *Jane Eyre* wouldn't be one of them.

PB: In a book of that period [*Orson Welles: A First Biography*, by Roy Alexander Fowler (London: Pendulum, 1946)], someone computed that *Jane Eyre* was your 5,028th performance in film, theatre, or radio.

OW: There might have been that many, with all the radio and all the theatre. Radio built it up especially. It'd be proportionately less now.

PB: John Houseman is credited on the script.

OW: He must have worked on it when Selznick owned it. They hired Aldous Huxley, and perhaps Houseman worked with him on the original draft of the script. And then the entire package was sold to 20th Century–Fox, where Bill Goetz was in charge of production. When I came on as its producer, Houseman was no longer even on the lot. My work began with the rewriting of the script with Huxley and the preparation of the sets and so on. He probably made a valuable contribution to the writing of the script, but we had no contact at any time.

PB: He says he mentioned you to Stevenson for the part of Rochester.

OW: Let's not talk about Houseman; I want to enjoy the afternoon, and he's one of the few subjects that depresses me so deeply that it really spoils my day to think of him. In *fact*, Stevenson had no choice in the matter of my casting—he was a hired director; it came entirely from Fox—he doesn't get either credit or blame. Fox at that time was offering me a part a minute. They offered me *Anna and the King of Siam* and I didn't want to act in it with Irene Dunne, for several reasons—none of them personal. I told them they ought to get Alfred Lunt, but they didn't want him, so I said "You ought to bring an actor over from England named Rex Harrison." And that was the beginning of Rex Harrison's American career.

PB: Why was Fox so anxious for you—?

OW: I don't know, it makes no sense—it's like the M-G-M story I told you. For a few weeks, somebody there wanted me.

PB: Around that time, you staged *The Mercury Wonder Show* [1943] in Los Angeles, for the war effort?

OW: Yes. And for fun. It's one of our great works, as any and all who were concerned with it will say. We're as proud of that as anything we ever did. Ask Aggie Moorehead or Jo Cotten. And Marlene Dietrich. And Rita Hayworth, until she was forced to quit. Marlene came in to take Rita's place when Harry Cohn wouldn't let her go on doing it.

PB: Why?

OW: "She's my star and I'm not going to have her entertaining for nothing out there on Cahuenga Boulevard." And Jean Gabin used to act as the propman backstage. And we had a lot of pretty girls. Very gay show. Later I did magic in a less elaborate form—various reduced versions of this—in all kinds of army camps, alone and with Marlene, but the original was done in a tent on Cahuenga Boulevard; it was a big spectacle.

PB: What was it like?

OW: It was just like a circus—I would have adored it if I'd been a member of the audience, I know that. Agnes Moorehead played the calliope outside. All the servicemen got in free, and they were 90 percent of the public. We had twenty-five or thirty seats which was called the Sucker Section and cost $30 each; they were for the Hollywood celebrities who wanted to come and see it—this small, highly paying public that got hell from us every night. We broke eggs over their heads and gave them blocks of ice to hold and demeaned and humiliated them in front of the servicemen. There was one seat that cost $70, and that was behind a pole so you couldn't see anything. Everybody'd want to get that good seat, and they always ended up straddling the pole—they had to look around from either side.

PB: Always somebody very rich—

OW: —and very important. Usually Sam Goldwyn or Jack Warner or somebody like that. And they had to pretend it was all good fun, because our boys in khaki were there, you know. We really gave it to them. If any of them came late, we'd stop the show dead and escort them to their seats, and I explained everything that had gone before and introduced them in a humiliating way to all the soldiers. I was watching Johnny Carson the other night, and he was interviewing somebody and talking about me and magic and

The Mercury Wonder Show

FOR • SERVICE • MEN

PROGRAM

ORSON THE MAGNIFICENT

Defies the laws of science in feats of legerdemain never before presented in America. The occult secrets of antiquity and the present day reproduced for your delight and fascination in: Born in Flames, A Rabbit From a Headpiece, Le Chapeau en l'air, The Devil's Orchard, Horticulture From Hell, The Strange Aquarium, Birds From the Blue, The Fourth Dimension, Audubon's Dream, The Hindu Mango Mystery (as advertised), Fruit Under a Spell, and THE HAUNTED AVIARY with Invisible Pigeons and Transparent Doves.

THE MIRACULOUS CHICKEN FARM

Twenty-five (25) Living Hens Manufactured as You Watch, Without the Aid of a Single Egg. DE- and RE-CAPITATION: A Strange Feat of the Barnyard as Never Before Presented in the Western Hemisphere; Ballet of the Roosters; Chanticleer Takes It on the Lam; The Hens' Delight.

Dr. Welles presents his

Original Experiments in Animal Magnetism

(All Nature Freezes at His Glance)

Psychic Readings

The MAGIC CRYSTAL

Due to the unbelievable strain on the practitioner of this incredible feat the management must reserve the right to change this portion of the program without notice.

Secrets of the Sphinx

THE ANCIENT LORE OF THE DARK CONTINENT ASSEMBLED FOR THE FIRST TIME UNDER CANVAS

CHAINED IN SPACE

WITCHES' FARMYARD

An Incredible Assortment of Sortilege Not To Be Duplicated in the Most Famous Repertoires in the History of Thaumaturgy, presenting: Bovine Obedience; At the Shooting Gallery (including "Markmanship's Reward); Evaporation in the Mystic Dairy; The Dalai's Milk Pail (direct from Tibetan Lamaseries); The Flight of the Hare; Fowl Elusive; La Rapiere du Diable; A Voice From the Dead; Faster Than Light; THE WORLD FAMOUS "BALSAMO'S SECRET," and the CASKET OF COUNT CAGLIOSTRO.

PEKIN NIGHTS

An Interlude from Old Cathay

The Manchu Marvel; The Cages of Han Lun; Enchanted Porcelain; Rain-making "Orientale"; Drought by Witchcraft (including Feats of Dexterity — a Dazzling Display); Hungkwei's Downfall; The Fan of Fu Ling.

THE CHEF'S SURPRISE

A Fantasy in Smoke; Shampoo Sorcery; The Indestructible Playing Card (Culled from the Secret Archives of Jared Higgenbottom); Humpty Dumpty Restored; Battledore.

ARTISTES: Miss Hayworth, Mr. Cotten, Mr. Welles, Miss Agnes Moorehead Miss Linda Brent, Miss Mary Rowland, Miss Merry Hamilton, Miss Lolita Leighter, Miss Eleanor Counts and Miss Martha Norman; The Messrs. Tommy Hanlon, Shorty Chirello, Jan

STAFF: Jackson Leighter (General Manager), John Tucker Battle, Dr. M. A. Bernstein, Peggy Vaughn, Shifra Haran, Clemmie Galloway, Paula Millard, and Norman Thomson (Stage Manager). Pete Dameron, Manfred Gruen. *SITE: Courtesy Metro-Goldwyn-Mayer

THE BAND—GENTLEMEN OF THE ORCHESTRA: Professor Bill Provost, Harry Wallace, Willie Martinez, Cal Earle, Henry Apperson. * * * * * * DECOR: Kay Lake.

The Mercury Wonder Show gratefully acknowledges the aid and cooperation of The Assistance League of Southern California.

THE ANCIENT LORE OF THE DARK CONTINENT
ASSEMBLED FOR THE FIRST TIME
UNDER CANVAS

→ CHAINED IN SPACE ←

WITCHES' FARMYARD

An Incredible Assortment of Sortilege Not To Be Duplicated in the Most Famous Repertoires in the History of Thaumaturgy, presenting: Bovine Obedience; At the Shooting Gallery (including "Markmanship's Reward); Evaporation in the Mystic Dairy; The Dalai's Milk Pail (direct from Tibetan Lamaseries); The Flight of the Hare; Fowl Elusive; La Rapiere du Diable; A Voice From the Dead; Faster Than Light; THE WORLD FAMOUS "BALSAMO'S SECRET," and the CASKET OF COUNT CAGLIOSTRO.

PEKIN NIGHTS

An Interlude from Old Cathay

The Manchu Marvel; The Cages of Han Lun; Enchanted Porcelain; Rain-making "Orientale"; Drought by Witchcraft (including Feats of Dexterity — a Dazzling Display); Hungkwei's Downfall; The Fan of Fu Ling.

THE CHEF'S SURPRISE

A Fantasy in Smoke; Shampoo Sorcery; The Indestructible Playing Card (Culled from the Secret Archives of Jared Higgenbottom); Humpty Dumpty Restored; Battledore.

$ Ten Thousand Dollars Challenged! $

(Performed Under Rigid Test Conditions)
IMPROVISATIONS
THE GOOSE, THE GUINEA PIG AND THE LADY

The Girl with the X-Ray Eyes

An Extraordinary Demonstration by Miss Rita Hayworth of Strange Powers Recognized, but *Unexplained by Science. Featuring* Thought Transmission and Projection, Extra-Sensory Perception, Lightning Calculation, and Second Sight.

The Great Joseph

The Wizard of the South Presents Split Second Escapology. The redoubtable J. Cotten Risks His Life at Every Performance.

The Death of the Silken Cords

FIRST TIME IN THE WEST

MILLION $ MYSTERY

Miss Hayworth and Mr. Cotten Make You Doubt Your Senses in a Bewildering Display.

INTERMISSION AND CONCERT

Scenes from a Hindoo Marketplace

THE FAKIRS OF INDIA OUTDONE
THE WORLD'S FASTEST CANARY
(Three Surprises and a Miracle)

Death Casket

The Flight of Time

Painless SURGERY

Doctor-Sorcerer and His Apprentices Defy Laws of Dissection

THE HUMAN SEWING MACHINE

Must Be Seen To Be Believed

Princess Nephrotite

The Queen of Egypt Brought Back From the Dead. Her Materialization, Levitation, Evanishment and Lightning Reappearances.

Grand Finale VOODOO!

A re-enactment of Mr. Cotten's Interesting Experiences Among the Witchdoctors in Dark Africa

LIGHTING: Otto K. Olesen. ★ ★ ★ ★ ★ WARDROBE: Iola C. Willis, Alma Weintraub. ★ ★ ★ ★ ★ ★ BANNERS: Caldwell Banner Co. ★ ★ ★ ★ ★ ★ THE BAND—GENTLEMEN OF THE ORCHESTRA: Professor Bill Provost, Harry Wallace, Willie Martinez, Cal Earle, Henry

★ ★ ★ ★ ★ ★ ★ ★ ★ PRESS: Al Parmenter & 'ack Kelly. ★ ★ ★ ★ ★ ★ ★ ★ The Mercury Wonder Show gratefully acknowledges the aid and cooperation

...n, Miss Lolita Leighter, Miss Eleanor Counts and Miss Martha Norman; The Messrs. Tommy Hanlon, Shorty Chirello, James Caffery, Norman Thomson, Fred Goetz, Gil Scherer, Melvin Eicher, Dick Owen, and "Death Valley" Mack. ★ ★ ★ ★ ★ ★ ★

...'s Millard, and Norman Thomson (Stage Manager). Pete Dameron, Manfred Gruen. ★SITE: Courtesy Metro-Goldwyn-Mayer Studios. ★ ★ ★ ★ ★ ★ COSTUMES: Western Costume Company, Jacks, Peggy Vaughn. ★ ★ ★ ★ ★ ★ CANVAS & BUNTING: Downie Brothers. ★ ★ ★

said, "You know the first time I was ever on the stage? I came up on *The Mercury Wonder Show* and held the girl's legs when he sawed her in half." I never knew that.

PB: You've done a lot of magic?

OW: Played Las Vegas twice. I am a professional magician since I've never found friends who were willing to "take a card, any card." All my friends hate magic, so I can't come under the heading of "amateur magician." I've only done it for money—except the *Wonder Show*, which was done for the army. I guess I'm the highest-paid magician in the world, come to think of it. Certainly the best . . .

PB: Of course. And you did some of the *Wonder Show* in a movie called *Follow the Boys*.

OW: Yes, there's a short little version of what we did in that. I cut Marlene in half. I saw it not long ago on television; she looks beautiful, but it's just a horrible picture.

PB: Had a lot of stars. Wasn't it sort of a war-effort movie?

OW: Pretending to be. It was a Charlie Feldman effort to make money—and he made a lot of money with it—showing how brave all the Hollywood actors were to entertain the boys. Disgusting morally. But I'd spent so much money on this *Wonder Show* that a chance to make fifty grand—you know, I couldn't say no, and not give Marlene a chance to make whatever she got, which must have been pretty good, too. She wasn't working—just in the army—so how could you say no? We needed it. But we were ashamed to be in the picture. She was, and so was I.

PB: Did you direct that sequence?

OW: Yes.

PB: Camera-wise?

OW: I think Eddie Sutherland directed it, but, you know, it was my act, our show.

PB: Magic usually doesn't work in movies, because audiences just assume it's all a camera trick.

OW: That's right. In fact, the end of this sequence *was* a camera trick, because if you do the real thing it's boring. So we saw her in half standing up, and her legs walk off alone. You *know* nobody can do that on stage, and we didn't even ask the audience to believe it. Just a way to get off. Everything before was real magic.

PB: Do you think magic has influenced your work in pictures?

OW: No. By the way, magic is directed almost entirely to men, you know. And it's a return for them to boyhood, childhood. It

Dietrich and Welles in Follow the Boys.

has nothing to do with women, who hate it—it irritates them. They don't like to be fooled. And men do.

PB: I never would have thought—

OW: All magicians know that. And the big thing is to conquer the women by interesting them in something other than the trick—because they don't like not to know how it's done. They'll say, "Well, it's just a trick." And a man likes *not* to know how it's done. That's the essential difference in the sexes.

The thing I like about magic is that it's connected with circus, and with a kind of corny velvet-and-gold-braid sort of world that's gone and that fascinates me and that I like. That's really it. It's not the skillful wonder-worker part of it but the ambience, the atmosphere of a magic show that delights me. I never saw anything in the theatre that entranced me so much as magic—and not the wonder of it: it's the kind of slightly seedy, slightly carnival side of it. I'm a terrible pushover for all forms of small-time show business anyway. Small theatres, small circuses, magic, and all that. It isn't the facility—that's not a conscious part of it to me.

Magic calls for real suspension of disbelief, except when you do mentalism, which is what I've done the last few years more than other things. *That* you can do with women, too, because you get them to believe you *are* reading their minds and all that. It's straight charlatanism, you know. Precognition and all that sort of stuff: they'll believe anything if you give them a spiel about that. But magic to me is a very special kind of thing. It's just what Robert-Houdin, who was the greatest magician of all time, defined a magician as being: "A great actor playing the part of a magician." I don't recognize magic as a style that can be applied to the theatre or movies. Maybe it's true of my work, but I just don't see it. To me, magic begins and ends with the figure of the magician who asks the audience, for a moment, to believe that the lady is floating in the air. In other words, be eight years old for a minute. And that has no connection with movies or the theatre, I think.

PB: Harry Houdini once told you never to perform a trick until you had practiced it a thousand times. Have you applied that to any of your work?

OW: He told me that, and immediately afterward Carl Brema, who was a manufacturer of magic, came into the dressing room with a vanishing lamp and said, "Look at this, Harry, I just made this." Harry said, "Great! I'll put it in the show tonight." So the effect of his advice only lasted about six minutes—until Carl Brema came in with his vanishing lamp.

PB: Why did you do *Tomorrow Is Forever*?

OW: For money. What a silly question.

PB: Did you direct any of it?

OW: No, nothing. I was deeply ashamed but in need of money.

PB: What did you think of the director, Irving Pichel?

OW: He's a perfectly competent man. I don't know what you can say about *Tomorrow Is Forever.* I don't think the audience knew, although they came in the millions. It was a very successful but ridiculous little charade.

PB: Did you rewrite your own lines?

OW: To the extent that I always rewrite what I'm going to say. But I didn't work very hard on it. I was not only writing a daily newspaper column but doing two daily political radio programs and writing articles in *Free World* magazine [see Chapter 9]—I was so busy between takes that I just got on to do it. I didn't make any contribution. And that's when I got into the vicious habit of getting up so early, which I've never broken since. Because I had to get that column out before I got to the studio.

PB: One of your lines is "Forget the past, because tomorrow is forever." Do you hold any personal opinion about that sentiment?

OW: I have no philosophical feelings about forgetting the past—I certainly couldn't put it into a pretty maxim. I'm concerned as little as possible with it. Of course, we all live with our past, but I try not to encourage it to misbehave.

PB: Well, do you have a theory about possessions, or just an inability to keep things from getting lost?

OW: Both. The things you own do have a way of owning you.

PB: How about things like letters and books?

OW: I'm not laying this down as the law for anybody else. It's just that I feel I have to protect myself against *things.* So I'm pretty careful to lose most of them.

PB: I read somewhere that you once wrote a book just for yourself and threw it away.

OW: Sure, a whole big long book about the art of government—it took me months.

PB: And threw it away?

OW: If it had been any good, I might have saved it.

I have trouble sometimes thinking things out clearly unless I

write my thoughts down in some consecutive order, so I write myself quite a good deal of disposable prose.
PB: And the hell with posterity?
OW: The hell with it. Isn't it just as vulgar as any other form of worldly success? No, I don't feel indebted to posterity, just to what God gave me; and I'm certainly way behind in my payments. . . .

> *FDR died during the making of* Tomorrow Is Forever, *and Welles wrote: "Desperately we need his courage and his skill and wisdom and his great heart. He moved ahead of us, showing a way into the future. If we lose that way or fall beside it, we have lost him indeed. Our tears would mock him who never wept except when he could do no more than weep. If we despair because he's gone—he who stood against despair—he had as well never lived, he who lived so greatly."*

PB: Didn't you write some of Roosevelt's speeches?
OW: Oh, we all did on those campaigns, you know.
PB: You went on the campaigns.
OW: Sure—I campaigned three times with him.
PB: Do you think it was that last campaign that killed him?
OW: No, he was fine on the campaign—it was afterwards. . . . I had breakfast with him on the morning he went to Yalta, and you could see that he was sick, in his face. But not on the campaign.
PB: People say the strain of the last campaign was—
OW: No, he just had the stroke—who knows why he had the stroke? I don't think it was the strain; he enjoyed the campaign—he had a wonderful time. He loved campaigns.

I wish I had the letters he wrote to me. He sent me three letters that I've lost—it's so shocking. One of them is three pages long, about world cooperation; he suddenly wrote me a long letter about world government. Luckily, it was printed in the paper. Very good letter. I must find it—I just never keep anything, though I do have one small thing he wrote on the back of half an envelope. I was booked to speak somewhere in the West, as principal speaker. And I suddenly got word that Mr. Roosevelt wanted me to bow out of that thing and go instead to somewhere in Pennsylvania where Henry Wallace was speaking as his vice-presidential candidate. It seemed very ridiculous that I should go there, but on the back of this envelope was written, "Please go and see that Harry keeps his shoes on." Wallace used to get up early in the morning and jog around the block in his bare feet, you see, which created a sort of nutty impression—those crazy professors and all that. And because Wallace and I were good friends, I was to go on and literally see that he kept his shoes on. That was it. So I went and saw that he did.

PB: Did Roosevelt ever say anything to you about your films?

OW: No—always radio. In his mind, I was a radio star. And theatre. We got along terribly well, you know, and laughed and screamed together. He was a very funny man. And they were always trying to keep me out. "He has to get to bed," they'd say. "Don't let Mr. Welles in with him, because then he'll never get to bed."

PB: Wasn't there a period when you were very interested in politics?

OW: Yes, I quit everything to try to go into politics. And found no proper outlet for my interests—none that seemed to me very constructive.

PB: In politics?

OW: Politics and world government. I was quite ready to stop. Another time I was quite ready to quit show business and go into adult education. I went and tried to get big foundation grants and so on, and I saw that I would be in the hands of an enormous bureaucracy, so I gave it up. But if I'd had any encouragement, you wouldn't be here with your microphone.

PB: I'm glad you weren't encouraged.

OW: No, I think it would have been much more interesting—using movies and the media not just as entertainment.

And one time I very nearly ran for the Senate in Wisconsin. My opponent would have been Joe McCarthy—so I've got him on my conscience—but that's another story.

PB: How did you happen to narrate the beginning of *Duel in the Sun*?

OW: Well, I did that for Selznick. I asked $35,000 for it, and he said that was an absurd price, so I said, "All right, $25,000." And he said, "Why do you do that? You'll just pay it away in income tax. Let me give you a really nice present." So I did the narration, and I waited for this custom-built Rolls-Royce to drive up, or whatever it was going to be. I knew David very well—we were uneasy but fairly intimate friends—and he used to say, "Wait'll Christmas. Wait'll you see—" What can it be? Undoubtedly he wasn't going to spend as much as $25,000, but maybe it was $18,000 worth of something—a painting—what was it going to be? And on Christmas morning I got a box with a pair of dueling pistols in it together with a card explaining their value, from an antiquarian point of view, which came to about $125. And that's my experience with *Duel in the Sun.*

PB: The present was sort of to remind you of the film's title—

OW: Yes—sentimental association! I never saw the picture. But from then on, every Christmas I sent him two of those glass pistols that used to have candy in them—I never let him forget—but he didn't think it was funny. I told all his friends; he suffered from that. But we were always having terrible set-tos; he tried to hit me on two or three occasions. Once he got drunk at a party of Walter Wanger's in Hollywood; we were all sitting around the port, the way the men used to in Beverly Hills—the ladies were elsewhere —and he was talking of making movies of old stage plays, and I said, "Why don't you do *The Yellow Ticket*, David?" And he said, "Who's yellow?" He hadn't heard of it and he was pissed, you see. So I said, "Oh, David, *you* are." So he stood up, took his glasses out, put them on, and then took a swing at me.

PB: Getting back to *The Stranger*, how much did you work on the script?

OW: I *worked* on all of it during general rewriting with Anthony Veiller and Spiegel—wrote all the stuff in the drugstore as well as the first two or three reels of the picture, which were almost entirely cut out because they didn't have anything to do with the story in the New England town. It was a decision by Sam Spiegel and Goetz to take that out.

PB: Did you shoot it?

OW: I shot it. It was much the best thing in the picture—or at least the stuff I liked the best, probably because I wrote it. But I do think it was the best to look at.

PB: Was it like the few scenes in the beginning—on the boat and so on—very atmospheric?

OW: Yes. A big chase in South America, with a whole series of very wild, dreamlike events that worried Spiegel and Goetz, so they took them out, but I think it was a mistake. The picture would have been much more interesting visually with them in; it was really the only chance to be interesting visually in the story. But considered irrelevant. That's always been the great thing that happens when a movie is turned over to the supereditor in the editorial department of the studio. The decision is made on this basis: does

Billy House and Welles in The Stranger.

it advance the story? And out go all the things that give a movie its real interest. They removed at least two reels of material which was certainly more original than the rest.

I also wanted the [Edward G.] Robinson civil-servant part to be played by Agnes Moorehead. I thought it would be much more interesting to have a spinster lady on the heels of this Nazi.

PB: That's bizarre!

OW: I couldn't persuade them to do that, either. And I think Robinson is one of the best movie actors of all time, but I thought it was too obvious casting. Anyway, I couldn't sell them on that. As I remember, Tony Veiller liked the idea, and I think Spiegel teetered back and forth but he had no real power, and the decision was with Bill Goetz. Spiegel was only allowed in because Goetz wanted the picture as a package and Spiegel was part of it—very much against Goetz's wishes. That's what got Spiegel's foot in the door as a producer. He promoted *The Stranger* through John Huston, who wrote most of the script—under the table, because he was in the army at the time and couldn't take credit. It was "No picture *or* Huston unless you take Sam."

PB: Was the Billy House character in *The Stranger*, the druggist who played checkers, based on your experience somewhere?

OW: No, I invented him. He was mostly written on the set. Had great trouble with Eddie Robinson—he went to the front office about it.

PB: Why?

OW: You know: "I'm a star and who's this fellow Billy House?"

PB: That was the best stuff in the picture, I thought.

OW: So maybe Eddie was right. It's the only stuff I really liked. I'd seen Billy in burlesque and always wanted to work with him. Well, the first three days he was so *miserable*. And I thought to myself, "Why can't I manage to put this marvelous performer at his ease?" I do rather flatter myself that I give actors a good time when they're working with me, and here was a man who was in a continual cold sweat—trembling. Then I discovered he had been eyeing the stand-in, who was, of course, another fat, bald man—and Billy, never having been in a movie, was under the impression that this stand-in was an actor waiting to take over if Billy wasn't good enough. He finally said to me: "Look, if you don't like me, get the other son-of-a-bitch and put him in—I can't stand it any longer!" He was a very funny man. He had some great old-fashioned slang that I've treasured through the years.

PB: For instance?

OW: "Fuzz castle" for a whorehouse. Too bad that "fuzz" has come to be a word for the cops; we can't use it now.

PB: "Billy House" couldn't have been his real name—

OW: No, it's obviously a burlesque name, like "Sliding Billy Watson."

PB: What is the true story about the famous closeup argument with Loretta Young on *The Stranger*?

OW: There was a fight scene in it, in which she was very good, and it played straight through from beginning to end in a medium full shot. We saw it in the rushes and it seemed to work and Sam Spiegel said, "OK, but we need a closeup of Loretta." It would have been fatal. I told that to Loretta, and she said, "Well, then, we're not going to make it." She was wonderful. But Spiegel came on strong as the producer for the first time. Finally we had to bring in Loretta's agent. Imagine getting a star's agent in to ensure that she *wouldn't* get a closeup! . . . There's another story like that. An album that I did with Bing Crosby of Oscar Wilde's *The Happy Prince* [1946]. It wasn't released for a year, because neither of us would take first billing. In the end, they had to toss a coin just to get the thing out.

PB: It's an interesting thing about your playing heavies—you're always so sympathetic. In *The Stranger*, I find myself rooting for you instead of Robinson, which throws the picture into a kind of ambiguous—

OW: Well, I think it was intentional even in the script. But I think *most* heavies *should* be played for sympathy. All the good ones in the theatre are.

PB: There's an extraordinary shot between you and Konstantin Shayne—a long, long walk outside the school that ends when you kill him.

OW: Yeah, I had to be a young man for that, Jesus, that was a physically tough shot—it nearly killed both of us.

PB: Doing it without a cut?

OW: Yes, everything was done in one. He's a very fine actor. Akim Tamiroff's brother-in-law.

PB: Is he still alive?

OW: Yes. He's a farmer. I saw him in a movie called *Mission to Moscow* [1943] and wrote him a letter to tell him how good he was, and that's how I got to know him. That's also how I got to know Akim—through him. Terrific actor.

PB: *The Stranger* was the first commercial film to use footage of Nazi concentration-camp atrocities.

OW: Was it? I'm against that sort of thing in principle—exploiting real misery, agony, or death for purposes of entertainment. But in that case, I do think that, every time you can get the public to look at any footage of a concentration camp, under any excuse at all, it's a step forward. People just don't want to know that those things ever happened.

I had a terrible experience. I was in a rather poor picture called *Is Paris Burning?* [1966] in which we had a scene where they were loading Jews into cattle cars in the station in Paris and sending them away. It was at exactly the same station where it actually happened, probably the same cars, and about 60 percent of the people were real veterans of this experience. They kept opening up their sleeves and showing me their tattoo numbers. And a lot of the Germans were real Germans—if not from that scene, at least they were from the German army—and it was so unpleasant I really could hardly get through the day. The whole Pirandelloish mystery of reality was morbidly mixed up in it. Intolerable.

PB: Where did the idea come for your death scene at the end—being impaled on the clock tower and all that? Was it yours?

OW: I'm afraid so. Pure Dick Tracy. I had to fight for it. Everybody felt, "Well, it's bad taste and Orson's going too far," but I wanted a straight comic-strip finish.

PB: I thought *The Lady from Shanghai* was a far more interesting thriller than *The Stranger.*
OW: So did I.
PB: But what was the Hollywood reaction generally to it?
OW: Friends avoided me. Whenever it was mentioned, people would clear their throats and change the subject very quickly out of consideration for my feelings. I only found out it was considered a good picture when I got to Europe. The first nice thing I ever heard about it from an American was from Truman Capote. One night in Sicily, he quoted whole pages of dialogue word for word.
PB: I guess that's called being ahead of your time.
OW: It's called being in trouble.
PB: How'd you come to make the movie?
OW: I was working on *Around the World in 80 Days* and we found ourselves in Boston on the day of the premiere, unable to get the costumes from the station because $50,000 was due and our producer, Mr. Todd, had gone broke. Without that money we couldn't open. I called Harry Cohn in Hollywood and I said, "I have a great story for you if you send me $50,000 by telegram in one hour. I'll sign a contract to make it." "What story?" Cohn said. I was calling from a pay phone, and next to it was a display of paperbacks and I gave him the title of one of them, *Lady from Shanghai.* I said, "Buy the novel and I'll make the film." An hour later, we got the money.
PB: There's a quote from Peter Noble's book: "*Lady from Shanghai* cost a fortune, lost a fortune, and finished Welles' career at any of the big Hollywood studios."
OW: The truth is that it cost about the same as any other Rita Hayworth picture in that period, and if it didn't do as well at the box office as some of the others, I don't think it did either of us any real harm. I went to Europe after that and stayed there, but I wasn't run out of town.

Harry Cohn told me, "I'm never going to make a picture like this again." He had a good point. His reasons were: "Not because of the script, you understand—it's the script I approved and I liked it and I don't care what anybody says. It's just because nobody should be the director *and* producer and also the leading actor in any picture. There's no way that he can be fired. Somebody has a deal like that—what's the use of me owning my own studio? I might as well be janitor."

PB: Going through the records, I found that the delays in shooting hadn't anything to do with you. Most of them were caused by Rita Hayworth's illnesses.

OW: I'd forgotten that. Yes, that's what got the home office into such a tizzy about Mexico.

PB: Also, according to Dick Wilson, there was a production manager from Columbia who insisted on doing things at the studio that could have been done cheaper on location.

OW: In those days, there was a deep distrust of all locations. They did let us go in the first place. But then—just three days too early—they yanked us all back to Gower Gulch. Three days more and we'd have wrapped up the whole thing in Mexico. Interrupting that meant that all sorts of bits and pieces had to be patched together in the studio in front of a process screen, with poor Rudy Maté endlessly fiddling about when we could have knocked it all off very briskly at the real location. And yet, you know, some of that tricking we had to do gave that part of the picture a dreamlike air which I rather liked. The scenes with Rita at night, and down by the sea . . .

PB: Somebody wrote that you began shooting with only a sixteen-page screenplay—

OW: Well, you've got the files on that.

PB: Yes, I've seen several versions of the script.

OW: There was a report on that script made for Cohn by Helen Deutsch. And in our first meeting he held this in his lap, with my script propped in front so I couldn't see the report—using it as a sort of pony from which he was cribbing.

PB: What kind of report?

OW: Most favorable, as I learned later from my spies. I had some of my own. Harry had hundreds.

PB: What did you mean by one of Rita's last lines in the picture, "Give my love to the sunrise"?

OW: I guess my character, O'Hara, was one of those poor sods who watches sunrises and quotes poetry.

PB: You don't watch sunrises?

OW: I almost never quote poetry.

PB: But you read poetry?

OW: Yes.

PB: Write it?

OW: I try.
PB: Why did you have Rita sing in the picture?
OW: How could she not?
PB: And you recorded it rather lovingly.
OW: How could I not? [According to Richard Wilson, the song sequence was actually added at the request of Cohn.]
PB: Would you agree the picture was a kind of sad farewell to Rita Hayworth?
OW: [*Unidentifiable grunt.*]
PB: It's been read that way.
OW: We'd been separated for a couple of years. She wanted to do the picture, and that brought us back together for a while. *Lady*

Welles cutting Rita Hayworth's hair.

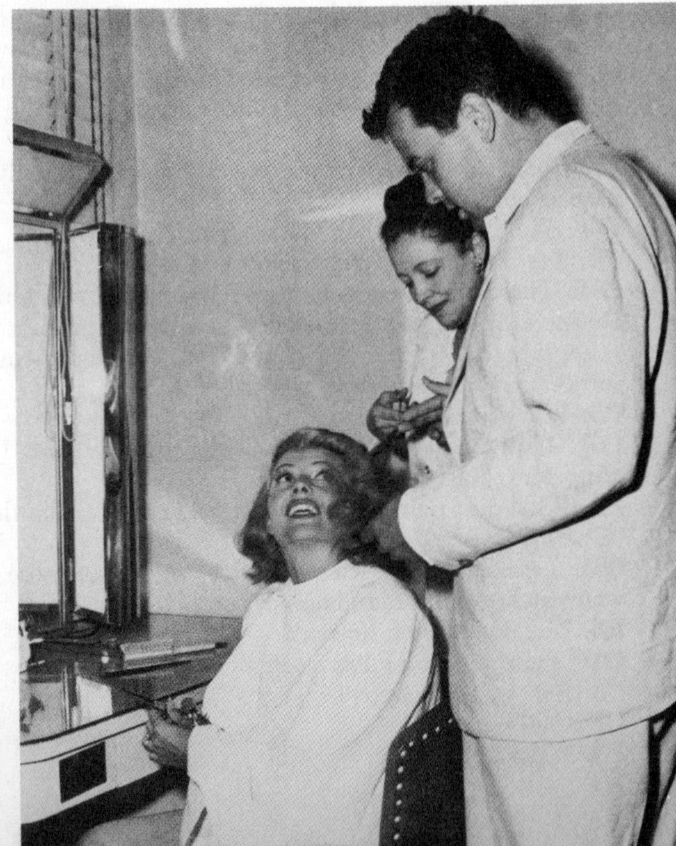

from Shanghai was written, as you know, for quite another actress [Barbara Laage]—not for an important star. And then, of course, when we were divorced soon after shooting, a theory got around that the whole project was some kind of sinister vengeance on poor Rita. Actually, it was Harry's idea *and* hers that she play that part, thus making it a big, expensive Hayworth A picture—which was the last thing I wanted to be involved with, working as I was, on that, for free.

PB: Free?

OW: Well, my money—such as there was of it—had all gone to that costume company in New York, *Around the World* ate it all up six months earlier, and all I wanted was to work off the obligation and get clear. . . . But as it turned out, I was lucky to have her. Rita's awfully good in it, don't you think? And at the time, people didn't even notice—she was too famous as a cover girl. Oh, the French loved her. But, then, the French do not automatically assume that if a girl is beautiful it follows that she's a lousy actress.

PB: Why did you cut her hair and try to change her image, so to speak?

OW: Well, don't forget, Petér, she was going to play a kind of person she'd never been on the screen. She couldn't come on as the well-established pinup; she needed a whole new look. So we made her platinum-blonde with very short hair. You can imagine how delighted Harry Cohn was when he found out about that!

PB: Did he ever say anything to you about it?

OW: Yes, indeed. But we never really quarreled. He had my office bugged, though, with about three microphones—and at the beginning of the day, when I came in for work, I used to make an announcement: "Good morning!" I'd say. "This is the Mercury office—we welcome you to another day of fascinating good listening." And we'd sign off with music: "Tune in again to us next morning. . . ."

PB: You rather liked him, didn't you?

OW: Yes. In a sort of awful way, he was quite admirable. He had guts and knew what he wanted. He wasn't a faker. He was totally ruthless and a self-confessed vulgarian and I suppose cruel, too, but I didn't really suffer at his hands. Though that's a picture that was ruined for me to a great extent by what happened to the sound track—

PB: Oh?

OW: We had to preview it—that's the only movie I personally ever previewed. Took it out to Santa Barbara. And for that one preview performance I made a temporary music track out of old stock stuff from the library. It was quite effective. I felt confident that, in constructing the real score, if they would just follow that, bringing it in and out just as I'd done, we couldn't go far wrong. I assumed I'd made a clear-cut blueprint for both music and effects. But in the event it was just hastily hashed together. Instead of allowing me to get a composer who would work with me, Cohn snuck in some fast fellow who put terrible music wherever he felt like it. I didn't mind the theme song, but the *incidental* music was clumsily handled throughout. For example, the mirror scene at the end should have been absolutely silent except for the crashing glass and ricocheting bullets. Like that, it was terrifying. All that was lost, of course, with that corny string choir snoring away under it: "Please don't kiss me—but if you kiss me—don't take your lips away." You know—while they were shooting it out among their own reflections.

PB: You like mirrors.

OW: I like reflections—as long as they aren't mine.

PB: What do you think of the picture yourself?

OW: In life I tend to forget the worst of the bad moments. But in your own movies the bad moments are unforgettable. . . . That first scene in the park, for instance. When I think of it, my flesh crawls. The whole sequence has no *flavor*. . . .

PB: It's true that it has a different look from the rest of the film.

OW: It's just like any Columbia program picture—you could clip it into any old B. Even Rita doesn't look like she does in the rest of the picture.

> *Orson's right, this sequence is perhaps the worst in any Welles-directed movie; he fought to have it cut out before release. Here are excerpts from a nine-page "Memo to Mr. Cohn from Mr. Welles," written after Orson had seen Cohn's edited version of the picture:*

> . . . The *preview* title music was written by a first rate composer, George Antheil. Although *not* written for our picture at all, this *temporary* title music had an atmosphere of darkness and menace combined with something lush and romantic which made it acceptable. . . .
>
> The only musical idea which seems to have occurred to

this present composer [Heinz Roemheld] is the rather weary one of using a popular song—the "theme"—in as many arrangements as possible. Throughout we have musical references to "Please Don't Kiss Me" for almost every bridge and also for a great deal of the background material. The tune is pleasing, it may do very well on the Hit Parade—but *Lady from Shanghai* is not a musical comedy. . . .

Mr. Roemheld is an ardent devotee of an old-fashioned type of scoring now referred to in our business as "Disney". In other words, if somebody falls down, he makes a "falling down" sound in the orchestra, etc., etc. . . .

If the lab had scratched initials and phone numbers all over the negative, I couldn't be unhappier about the results. . . .

Just before I left to go abroad, I asked Vi [Viola Lawrence, the editor] to make a cut which would involve dropping the near accident with the taxi-cab and also quite a bit of dialogue. I am convinced that this would have been an excellent cut . . . saving much needed footage in the slow opening sequence. . . . [*This was not done, accounting for the main weaknesses of the film's opening reel.*]

. . . There is nothing in the fact of Rita's diving to warrant a big orchestral crescendo. . . . What does matter is Rita's beauty . . . the evil overtones suggested by Grisby's character, and Michael's bewilderment. Any or all of these items might have inspired the music. Instead, the dive is treated as though it were a major climax or some antic moment in a *Silly Symphony*: a pratfall by Pluto the Pup, or a wild jump into space by Donald Duck.

There is no *sound atmosphere* on the boat. A little wind and water is sorely missed. There's no point in photographing a scene on a real boat if you make it sound as though it all happened in front of a process screen. . . .

At the start of the picnic sequence . . . in the temporary score, we used a very curious, sexy Latin-American strain. . . . This has been replaced with a corny "dramatic" sequel—bad stock stuff. . . . This sort of music destroys that quality of strangeness which is exactly what might have saved *Lady from Shanghai* from being just another whodunit. . . .

There is a big musical outburst after Grisby's line, "I want you to kill him." This is absurd. . . .

The Hawaiian guitar music which comes out of the radio

. . . was supposed to be corny enough to make a certain satirical point. As it stands now, it's on about the same level as the rest of the scoring. Nobody in the audience could possibly suspect that we're kidding.

The aquarium scene needs more *echo. "Please Don't Kiss Me" is in again!* . . .

A bad dubbing job and poor scoring has destroyed the character of Michael's run down the pier. From the gunshot through to the phone call, a careful pattern of voices had been built up with the expenditure of much time and effort. For some reason, this has all been junked in favor of a vague hullabaloo. As a result, the whole sequence seems dull. . . .

The audience should feel at this point, along with Michael, that maybe they are going crazy. The new dubbing job can only make them feel that maybe they're going to sleep. . . .

The gun battle with the breaking mirrors *must not be backed with music.* . . .

The closing music again makes reference to "Please Don't Kiss Me." . . .

This finale is obvious to the point of vulgarity, and does incalculable injury to the finish of the picture.

Every single one of Welles' points was ignored.

PB: But the cutting was mostly yours. . . .
OW: Pretty much. The most interesting sequence, in the fun house, has all but vanished. I was up every night from ten-thirty until five in the morning for a week painting that fun house. Cyril Connelly came one night and helped me—I had all kinds of strange people lending me a hand. This was *the* big tour-de-force scene. All you get now is one bad long shot which *I* was going to cut because it was banal compared to the way the sequence had been built. Too crazy for its time . . . "What's all that about?" yelled Harry Cohn, and yanked it out. People would have remembered it much more than the mirrors at the end—it was much more of a tour-de-force.
PB: Is the proverb in the picture—"One who follows his nature, follows his original nature in the end"—really Chinese? Or an Orson Welles proverb?
OW: Chinese.

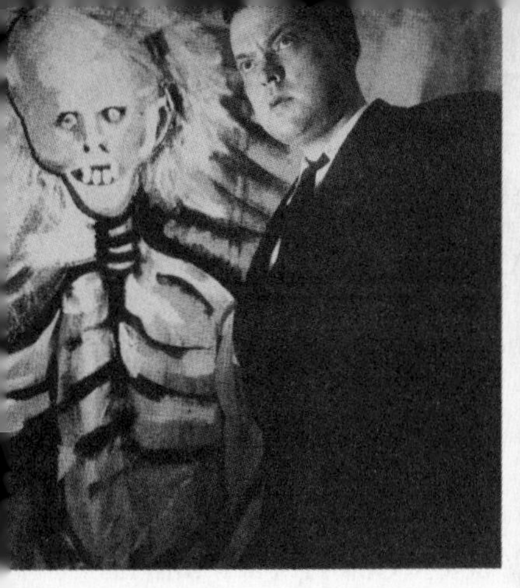

From the fun-house sequence.

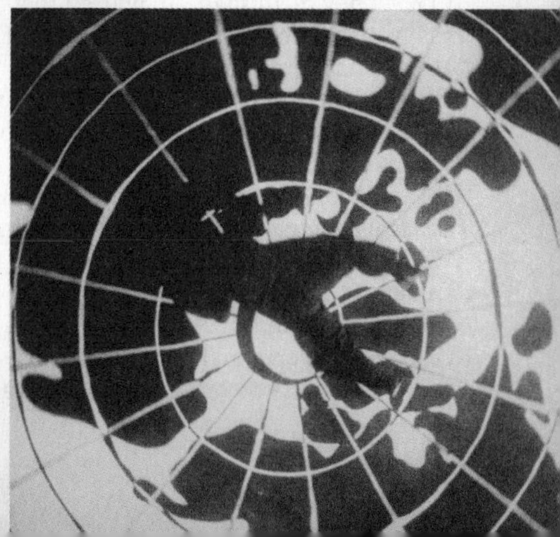

PB: Is it true that you moved a fishing village and rebuilt it in a more accessible spot?
OW: We didn't build a thing. We used Acapulco just as we found it.
PB: Was the love scene in the aquarium meant to relate back to the sharks story?
OW: Next question.
PB: Why *did* you shoot it there?
OW: In the aquarium? Why not?
PB: And the Chinese theatre?
OW: Well, that was a real sequence before Cohn got at it with his scissors. Same as the fun house. Now it's very bitty.
PB: Why did you cripple Bannister so completely—both legs?
OW: Because Everett Sloane was basically a radio actor; he'd never really learned to *move*. He was like a marionette. That was OK for Bernstein in *Kane*. But it didn't seem to me that a marionette would be a great criminal lawyer. So I made him an elaborate sort of cripple. And, of course, he loved it. All actors like to play cripples.
PB: Both the lawyer in *Lady from Shanghai* and the one you play in *The Trial* are rather shady, disreputable figures.
OW: I'd like to do twenty pictures taking the mickey out of the lawyers.
PB: Do you have little respect for the law?
OW: Well, we might say that one's respect is high enough for the law and low enough for the lawyers. And the doctors—most of them.
PB: Why?
OW: They're human. It figures that not many are going to be really up to their calling. . . . Kafka, of course, hates the *law* itself. What I hate are the abuses.
PB: In *Lady from Shanghai*, you have the judge playing himself at a chess game, then you cut to the empty courtroom—an interesting juxtaposition of images.
OW: I get a little nervous when I think about that. We're right on the jagged edge of symbolism there, I'm afraid.
PB: You staged a mockery of a trial in that picture, with an exceptionally stupid judge.
OW: Judges, in our American system, are political appointments. A judge in a criminal case (which calls for the least knowledge of the law) is likely to be an old political hack.

Welles with Betty Leong and other members of the Mandarin Theatre of San Francisco.

PB: And that terrible jury, sneezing and coughing all the time. What do you think of trial by jury?
OW: Oh, I could do lots of trials and make 'em all look idiotic, but that doesn't mean I think the *system* is wrong.
PB: Somehow I thought the Advocate, whom you played in *The Trial*, was sort of evil incarnate.
OW: I don't think I've ever projected a character who was evil incarnate. Not even Iago, because he's merely destructive and mischievous to the point of sin. I don't believe in such a thing as evil incarnate.
PB: The lawyer is pretty evil.
OW: He's pretty corrupt. I believe in the existence of evil, I believe in good and evil—I'm not one of those people who don't believe in evil—and I've got Jake in *The Other Side of the Wind* carrying on about that at great length, but in his terms. I really don't believe that evil or good is ever incarnate.
PB: Probably the slowest dolly shot I've ever seen takes place when Rita Hayworth and Everett Sloane are sitting in a corridor

before the trial. I had to look at the edges of the screen to see if it was really moving.
OW: That doesn't speak well for the film—when you start studying the edges of the screen.
PB: People sometimes look at your films and say, "God, what an insane, great shot." But when I've expressed something like that to you, your blank look shows me that clearly to you the shot was *normal*—or, rather, not *unusual*—simply the way you saw it.
OW: I like it when you answer your own questions.
PB: I'm right, aren't I?
OW: I don't often try to be crazy, no.
PB: But most people think just the opposite of your work.
OW: Sure, they think it's deliberate eccentricity—virtuoso hamming. That implies a certain strain. I just do what comes naturally. It's like that terribly old corny joke: The fellow goes to a doctor and says, "You know, doctor, I have these terrible headaches in the morning. Every morning after I get up and vomit and brush my teeth and have breakfast, I get this headache." The doctor says, "*What?*" "Sure," the fellow says. "After I get up and vomit and brush my teeth, I get this headache." "You mean," says the doctor, "you vomit every morning?" "Sure," says the fellow, "doesn't everybody?" Well, that's the point. That's my answer to those crazy shots: "Doesn't everybody?"
PB: Somebody said to Chaplin once, "You never have any interesting camera angles." And Chaplin said, "I don't need interesting camera angles—*I* am interesting."
OW: He was right.
PB: He also said that comedy was life in long shot and tragedy was life in closeup.
OW: What does that mean?
PB: The theory being that, when you show a man walking down the street in long shot and he slips on a banana peel, it's funny. But when you get in close, it stops being funny because the pain becomes apparent.
OW: Fair enough, but I think, if we want to be really accurate, comedy is a medium full shot. The true long shot is tragedy again.

You know, there are *performers*—Jacques Tati, for instance—who are only good in a full figure. Move in on Tati and he literally disappears.
PB: You like him?
OW: Yes. In a very nervous way—always waiting and hoping for

him to be just that little bit more *professional*—which is most unfair, of course, from a congenital amateur like myself. But it takes one to know one. . . . I think he has a sort of genius at moments, some kind of real greatness, but you just never know from one minute to the next what the action is going to be like.

PB: Speaking of long shots, the last shot of you in *Chimes at Midnight* is a good example—that small figure lumbering away.

OW: That was dangerous—the rejected figure scuffling away into the sunset. But there wasn't any other way.

Most of my closeups are made because I'm forced to. It's always better to avoid them when you can. . . . A long-playing full shot is what always separates the men from the boys. Anybody can make movies with a pair of scissors and a two-inch lens.

PB: Preminger once said that ideally, if he could, he would never cut. He would like a picture all in one take.

OW: That will come when tape is perfected and they stop putting film in the camera. I saw that kind of insane flash of ignorance when I first started. I said to Toland, "Isn't it basically ridiculous that the film is in the camera?" And he said, "Yes. Eventually it will just be a sort of electric eye. We won't be carting the film around or the motor—we'll just be carrying the lens."

PB: There's a line in *Lady from Shanghai*, "When I start out to make a fool of myself, there's little enough that can stop me. . . ." Do you feel that's been true in your life—have there been times when you feel you've made a fool of yourself?

OW: That's one of those searching, penetrating questions I thought we'd avoid.

PB: You don't want to talk about it?

OW: There've been so many occasions I don't know how to begin.

PB: Regrets?

OW: Millions. But, you know, I like the people who are *ready* and *willing* to make fools of themselves—being, as I am, a full member of the fraternity. Still, there are lots of nice felines who just can't.

PB: Felines?

OW: If spiritually you're part of the cat family, you can't bear to be laughed at. You have to pretend when you fall down that you really *wanted* to be down there just to see what's under the sofa. The rest of us don't at all mind being laughed at.

PB: Then you're canine?

OW: I'm a comic, anyway, even if I don't wag my tail very often.

PB: Isn't that willingness to be a damned fool a kind of courage?
OW: Just the nature of the beast. Like people with tape recorders and searching questions—you can't help it, it's your nature.
PB: In your pictures you do things that only *you* could get away with.
OW: And don't [*laughs*].
PB: Do you sometimes feel like a martyr, Orson?
OW: They have to really be shooting at you with arrows before you have the right to come on like a martyr. I mean real arrows.
PB: Like Saint Sebastian?
OW: Sure.
PB: And even at your low points, it never becomes a temptation?
OW: Martyrdom? I haven't the vocation for it.

6.

HOLLYWOOD

MACBETH IN TWENTY-THREE DAYS · SHAKESPEARE · JEAN RENOIR · MOVIE AUDIENCES · REVIEWS: EUROPE VS. AMERICA · *THE THIRD MAN* · DAVID O. SELZNICK · *OTHELLO* · *MR. ARKADIN*

Orson Welles' *Macbeth* has a kind of crude, irreverent power. Clad in animal skins like motorists at the turn of the century, horns and cardboard crowns on their heads, his actors haunt the corridors of some dreamlike subway, an abandoned coal mine, and ruined cellars oozing with water. Not a single shot is left to chance. The camera is always placed just where destiny itself would observe its victims. Sometimes we wonder in what period this nightmare is unfolding, and when, for the first time, we see Lady Macbeth, before the camera moves back to situate her, it is almost a woman in modern dress that we are seeing, reclining on a fur-covered divan beside the telephone.

—JEAN COCTEAU, August 1949
(translated by Gilbert Adair)

Hollywood died on me as soon as I got there. I wish to God I'd gone there sooner. It was the rise of the independents that was my ruin as a director. The old studio bosses—Jack Warner, Sam Goldwyn, Darryl Zanuck, Harry Cohn—were all friends, or friendly enemies I knew how to deal with. They offered me work. Louis B. Mayer even wanted me to be the production chief of his studio—the job Dore Schary took. I was in great shape with those boys. The minute the independents got in, I never directed another American picture except by accident. If I'd gone to Hollywood in the last five years, virgin and unknown, I could have written my own ticket. But I'm not a virgin; I drag my myth around with me, and I've had much more trouble with the independents than I ever had with the big studios. I was a maverick, but the studios understood what that meant, and if there was a fight, we both enjoyed it. With an annual output of 40 pictures per studio, there would probably be room for one Orson Welles picture. But an independent is a fellow whose work is centered around his own particular gifts. In that setup, there's no place for me.

—ORSON WELLES, circa 1970

Orson has rented a house in the Hollywood Hills and, after taping a couple of Dean Martin TV shows and acting in one or two brief movie roles, he has started shooting The Other Side of the Wind. *He does this with the smallest of crews imaginable, with no sets, no costumes, little equipment, but great good spirits and incredible ingenuity. At first I was marshaled into playing a thinly disguised parody of myself—or at least myself in my "serious-cinema-interviewer" role, doing a book on Jake, the film's central character. (Joseph McBride, now of* Variety, *took over this character's basic function when Orson later moved me to a leading role.) We shot at the L.A. airport, just under the spot where the planes come in for a landing—and, with careful instruction, improvised the dialogue. We've just finished shooting some hilarious party sequences in Orson's house, during which I found myself doing the sort of comic caricature I had no idea I was capable of even attempting in the privacy of the shower, much less in front of a dozen people. But acting for Orson is really easy—or, rather, he makes it seem easy. He is the kind of director who makes you better than you really are. Of course, he does that in life, too.*

Now the crew and the few other actors have gone, and we're alone, drinking Frescas amid the ruins of the living room. Orson has cut down on his cigars in order to put all his money into the new film, so he has just lit up the first of the day, and I am probably spoiling it by reminding him of an old quote of his, but I can't help it, so appropriate is it to the day we've just spent. He said once: "The great danger for an artist is to find himself comfortable. It's his duty to find the point of maximum discomfort, to search it out."

PETER BOGDANOVICH: OK, then, speaking of "maximum discomfort," how did you come to do *Macbeth* in only twenty-three days?

ORSON WELLES: Because we couldn't get the money to do it in twenty-four. Actually, "principal photography" took twenty-one days. It kept us pretty much on the tips of our toes. I slept two hours a night in a motel next door to the Republic lot.

Our best crowd scene was a shot where all the massed forces of Macduff's army are charging the castle. There was a very vivid sense of urgency to it, because what was happening, really, was that we'd just called noon break, and all those extras were rushing off to lunch.

PB: Do you think the film suffered from having been made so quickly?

Macbeth *(1948)*.

OW: Of course. Larry Olivier's big-budgeted *Henry* V and *Hamlet* didn't do us any good, either. I'd imagined, in my innocence, that allowances would be made for the modest size of our canvas. I should have known better. Too bad. If we'd been a bit more successful, we could have done a lot of other, more difficult subjects in the same way.
PB: I like small-budget pictures.
OW: Too bad there aren't more of you.
PB: I made my first picture on a tiny budget—
OW: That's how I'll make my last one.
PB: But I was interested to know whether you would've liked to have made—
OW: I'd love to make *Macbeth* again with lots of [Hugh] Hefner bread, as Polanski's done. Who wouldn't? Nowadays, people go to Shakespeare—at least they went to Zeffirelli's *The Taming of the Shrew* and *Romeo and Juliet*. Even in England, where the Bard, you know, has always been box-office poison—in the cinema, I mean.
PB: Even Olivier?
OW: Sure. *Henry* was his only really big one commercially, and the non-English receipts were what made all the difference. As for me, I wish I'd had just one chance at a Shakespeare movie where the money was just normal. . . . *Othello* was made, you know, in

installments, on the easy payment plan. (What do I mean, "easy"?) And *Chimes at Midnight* just managed to squeak through with all our biggest battle scenes boasting a maximum extra call of two hundred.

PB: If you had a "normal" budget offered you, what Shakespeare play would you film now?

OW: I would have said *King Lear*, but after Peter Brook's version . . . *The Tempest*, maybe, or an Edwardian *Twelfth Night*. The truth is, I'm more interested these days in . . . well, in these days.

PB: How did you convince Herbert Yates of Republic, which was noted for its Westerns, to let you do *Macbeth* in the first place?

OW: I didn't. That was my chum and partner Charlie Feldman. He had a deal with Yates for several pictures, and he simply told him one of them was going to be *Macbeth*. Yates didn't know who or what *Macbeth* was.

PB: And how did you sell it to Feldman?

OW: We used to live together in the same house. He wasn't really sold: he just groaned and gave in.

PB: Was the film really shot on old Roy Rogers and Gene Autry sets?

OW: It just looked that way. My own designs turned out, at the last minute, to be just a bit beyond our means, so what was left to photograph was cheesy cardboard. We did shoot in the old salt mine that the cowboys always used to get lost in—that became the great hall of the castle. Our costumes, lamentably, were all rented from Western Costume, except for Mr. and Mrs. Macbeth. Mine should have been sent back, because I looked like the Statue of Liberty in it. But there was no dough for another, and nothing in stock at Western would fit me, so I was stuck with it.

PB: Was there any remnant of your all-black stage production of *Macbeth* [1936] left in the movie?

OW: Yes. When Macbeth goes up to Duncan's bedchamber, for me—I don't know why—he simply has to move stage right to left. That's all [*laughs*].

PB: It has to be that way?

OW: I'd be in big trouble staging it even now if I had to turn it around!

PB: Was Jeanette Nolan your original choice for Lady Macbeth?

OW: She's a fine actress—from our radio days—but, actually, no. Among several others, I wanted Vivien Leigh, but Olivier wouldn't hear of it.

The Voodoo Macbeth *(1936).*

PB: Why?
OW: I didn't ask him.
PB: Why did you want her?
OW: I wanted a sexpot, Peter—and she could speak the lines.
PB: I read that you also considered Tallulah Bankhead.
OW: Except for one titled tragedian from Australia, we considered everybody.
PB: You staged the play up in Salt Lake City [1947] before shooting, didn't you?
OW: Yes.
PB: Pretty much as you did the picture—as a kind of rehearsal?
OW: Yes, very much.
PB: How long did you actually rehearse?
OW: A couple of weeks, including prerecording.
PB: You prerecorded the dialogue?
OW: Not just for reference, as we did in *Ambersons*. We actually acted to a playback. That meant the technicians could be roaring out instructions about where the crane went, and clattering and howling away off camera, while we were busy getting on with the filming. A foolish way to work, but on that schedule it was the only

way we could have got it made. We all got pretty good at following the records.

PB [*laughs*]: Like a musical?

OW: They spend money on musicals. But, yes, we had those clicks. Wherever the pauses were, there were clicks on the recording so you knew when to start moving your lips again.

PB: What was the famous problem with the Scottish brogues?

OW: A slight "burr," that was. People didn't like it, so in the end we took the whole show into the dubbing room.

PB: Why did you want the burr?

OW: If Shakespeare could tune in on us now with a time machine —or a time radio—he'd think that modern English actors were speaking in a foreign tongue. All our spoken English has become another language. So how do you speak Shakespeare? Oxbridge? West End? BBC? There are a lot of his gutsier moments which suffer very much from that particular refined, upper-class, southern-English way of speaking, which is mainly what we hear now. It's marvelous when a well-spoken Irish or Scotch actor does Shakespeare. Even the right sort of American voice, too—as long as those middle consonants are kept vigorous. Anyway, why

The Salt Lake City stage production.

shouldn't all the Scotsmen in *Macbeth* sound like Scotsmen? The Scottish lilt and color is so right for all that gooseflesh and grue. If I could make the picture in heaven, I'd make it with a Scottish burr all over again.

PB: But?

OW: Feldman had been so nice about everything that, when he asked for the Scottishness to be muffled, I muffled it. That meant postsynching, of course, and made splendid nonsense of my whole proud experiment in miming to playback.

PB: Evidently there was some objection because it was difficult to understand.

OW: In fact, it's easier to understand with Scotch accents, because that speech is clearer, purer, more incisive. It's just a great excuse for people who don't understand Shakespeare anyway to blame it on the burr.

PB: One could say that you made Shakespeare entertaining and exciting, as opposed to a cultural treasure—the way Shakespeare is taught.

OW: Yes, and performed—except by the old Mercury (if you'll excuse me) and the very newest generation of directors in the English theatre.

PB: Your Shakespeare book is still a tonic.

OW: It's terrible what's done to Shakespeare in the schools. You know, it's amazing that people do still go to him after what they've been through in the classroom.

Some excerpts from Orson's introduction to The Mercury Shakespeare*:*

Shakespeare said everything. . . . He speaks to everyone and we all claim him but it's wise to remember, if we would really appreciate him, that he doesn't properly belong to us but to another world; a florid and entirely remarkable world that smelled assertively of columbine and gun powder and printer's ink, and was vigorously dominated by Elizabeth. . . .

About sixty years earlier, Columbus had bumped into a couple of new continents and the Conquistadors were busy opening them up and exploiting them. Down in Italy . . . men had taken the hoods of the dusty, dusky old Middle Ages off their heads and had begun to look around. . . . Books were being written instead of copied; people had stopped taking Aristotle's word for it and were nosing about the world, taking it apart to see what made it run. All kinds of established convictions were being questioned and money in huge sums was being made. . . . This bustle and uncertainty and excitement had gotten across the channel and into the moist English air. . . .

To know something about Shakespeare we must know something about that England in which he was born; still more important we must know something of that peculiarly pure theatre he found in London and for which he wrote. It was neither new nor clumsy. It was not a rude thing but rather, like the classic theatres of high convention in China and Japan, a refinement. England's stage came out of the church when the actors got too entertaining. It lingered for a couple of hundred years in front of it in the marketplace and then moved into the inn yard. . . .

Poetry has since then been neither necessary nor possible because when you can make the dawn over Elsinore with a lantern and a pot of paint there's no call for having a character stop in the middle of the action and say a line like, "*But look, the morn, in russet mantle clad, walks o'er the dew of yon high eastern hill,*" even supposing you could write a line like it. You can't see and hear beauty, fully, at the same time . . . because poetry is its own scenery and because we've stuck to physical scenery and isolated our actor from his audience . . . we've stuck to prose. Before the Restoration, theatres were courtyards around platforms where you went to hear and be heard. Since then they've been birthday cakes in front of picture-frames where you go to see and to be seen. . . .

PB: Would you agree that Shakespeare was the biggest influence in your life?

OW: After you. Next.

PB [*laughs*]: Well, you once said that you think Shakespeare was a pessimist.

OW: Yes, but, like many of us, he was also at least a part-time idealist. The optimists are incapable of understanding what it means to adore the impossible. Shakespeare, remember, was very close to the origins of his own culture: the language he wrote had just been formed; the old England, the old Europe of the Middle

Ages, still lived in the memory of the people of Stratford. He was very close, you understand, to quite another epoch, and yet he stood in the doorway of our "modern" world. His lyricism, his comic zest, his humanity came from these ties with the past. The pessimism, of course, is closer to our modern condition.
PB: You also said he wasn't interested in the bourgeoisie.
OW: That was an age, you see, where there was lots of room at the top. In his plays, the common folk are mainly clowns.
PB: You'd say he was a snob.
OW: He was a country boy, the son of a butcher, who'd made it into court. He spent years getting himself a coat of arms. He wrote mostly about kings. We can't have a great Shakespearean theatre in America anymore, because it's impossible for today's American actors to comprehend what Shakespeare meant by "king." They think a king is just a gentleman who finds himself wearing a crown and sitting on a throne.

In this context, it may be interesting to quote Jean Renoir; I'd asked him what he thought of Orson and he said:

> I read an article by [Herbert] Marcuse, and his theory is that silent films were made for the working classes because they could appeal to all levels, which perhaps explains the great popularity of people like Chaplin and Keaton. But the man of the working class now has two cars and sends his children to the best schools; in fact, the working class has become the middle class. And almost all films today and for the last twenty years have been made for the middle class. Actually, most directors—even the greatest ones—are bourgeois directors. Orson Welles is one of a handful of aristocrats. And his films are aristocratic works. It is probably for that reason that they often are not financially successful. He is also a great actor who so submerges himself in a role that his own personality does not even exist any longer while he is in that character. I like his work so much that I even like him when he is not good, because at all times he remains an artist.

PB: You had a lot of very long takes in *Macbeth*.
OW: They were enormously long: never shorter than five minutes and often right up to a full reel in length. I think about five reels were like that—in other words, without cuts.
PB: Which Hitchcock did later in *Rope* [1948].

OW: Well, we'd already done it in *Ambersons*. Originally we had a whole reel that was a single take—
PB: At the dance?
OW: Yes, and that was cut into for a few stupid seconds by some cloth-headed expert in a darkened room. By the way, I saw Roddy McDowall the other night and he said, "Whenever I want to really enjoy myself I get a print of *Ambersons* and run it again." And I said, "You idiot! You're *in* a pretty good picture of mine called *Macbeth*. Why don't you run a print of that?" "Oh?" he said. I had to remind him that he was our Malcolm, and very convincing he was, too.
PB: In terms of schedule and budget, which is cheaper—long takes or a lot of short ones?
OW: That depends on what you've got to work with—your equipment and your cast. If you have a big efficient unit, a long take is certainly cheaper than a short one. If you have a small unit, it's the opposite.
PB: Do you think the length of shots or the angle of shots has a subconscious effect on an audience?
OW: I never think of an audience for the movie. That's the advantage of film over the theatre—when you do a play, you make it for an audience; when you do a movie, you make it for yourself.
PB: To please yourself?
OW: Well, it's impossible to conceive of what a movie audience *is*: a bunch of Sikhs; a band of Bedouins; a tribe of gypsies; four hundred widowed ladies from Ohio on a bus tour. . . . What *is* that audience? How can you set out to please it? You can't address yourself to it, because it's inconceivable. So you make it for yourself.
PB: Well, if that's true, then the whole idea of a preview is ridiculous.
OW: Sure.
PB: Because, in order to have a proper preview, you'd have to show it in every major city in the world.
OW: And how about the villages? All right, previews give the producers something to talk about. So they have some purpose. But really, you know, it's like writing a book. I don't think most people who write books *seriously* think much about the people who will buy them.
PB: Yet on *The Deep* you told me you purposely set out to make something you thought might be more appealing to—

OW: You're getting a bit close to the bone, Peter. My hope is that it won't turn out to be an art-house movie. I hope it's the kind of movie I enjoy seeing myself. Let's say I open a play Off Broadway or the West End of London or in the Greek Theatre in Syracuse in Sicily. I can imagine who's going to sit there by the time the lighting is set up. I can place myself in the tenth row center, where I sit during rehearsals, and imagine that I bought a ticket. I can't do that with a movie. It'll be in far too many kinds of theatres. Everybody's going to sit in that seat—and nobody.
PB: You once wrote, "Film is a very personal thing, much more than the theatre, because the film itself is a dead thing—"
OW: Yes, because you don't get anything back from the audience; it can't nourish itself on that audience. A movie doesn't come to life *because* it's in a theatre. Finally and forever, it's as dead as a book. And, potentially, as everlastingly alive.

> Our story is laid in Scotland—ancient Scotland, savage, half-lost in the mist that hangs between recorded history and the time of legends. . . . The cross itself is newly arrived here. Plotting against Christian law and order are the agents of Chaos, priests of hell and magic—sorcerers and witches. Their tools are ambitious men. This is the story of such a man, and of his wife. A brave soldier, he hears from witches a prophecy of future greatness and on this cue murders his way up to a tyrant's throne, only to go down hated and in blood at the end of all. . . .
>
> —Opening narration of Welles' *Macbeth*

OW [*commenting on the above*]: That reads like a trailer. I had to write it when two reels were pulled out of the movie just before release. People were getting a pretty brisk version of the tragedy; we had to set things up for them. The main point of that production is the struggle between the old and new religions. I saw the witches as representatives of a Druidical pagan religion suppressed by Christianity—itself a new arrival. That's why the long prayer of Saint Michael (not in Shakespeare at all)—that's why the screen is constantly choked with Celtic crosses. These people are holding off not just the forces of darkness but the old religion, which has been forced underground. The witches are the priestesses. Nobody ever paid any attention to that. The whole device of the picture is based on the struggle between two religious systems. I only wish I hadn't failed so badly with the witches themselves. They were lousy. Too bad. They were so good in Harlem when we imported them from Africa. . . . By the way, I think it's important that the witches don't really *prophesy*—they give Macbeth ideas which *make* things happen.

PB: They plant the seeds. . . .

OW: Sure. The witches cue the whole thing. They aren't foretelling the future, they're making it happen. That's why I end the movie with the three of them. I won't quote what they say. Bad luck.

PB: Is that a superstition?

Welles and witches in Salt Lake City stage production.

OW: Known to every Shakespearean actor in the world.
PB: Well, I know *Macbeth* is supposed to be a jinx to everyone who plays it.
OW: And there's a reason for that. I've played it in the theatre twice and produced it in the theatre a third time and made a film of it—so I *know*. When you do that play it has a really oppressive effect on everybody. Really, it's terrifying—stays with you all day. The atmosphere it generates is so horrendous and awful that it's easy to see how the old superstition lives on.
PB: And things go wrong?
OW: You *notice* things going wrong if you're in that state—you help *make* them go wrong. It's all those things operating. That play has a sort of terrible magic.
PB: The movie has that quality—very dark and oppressive—
OW: I think our second half worked better, after the first murder. The second half is a study of the decay of a tyrant. Nobody can play the first *and* second half. An actor who can do one can't do

Christopher Welles in Macbeth *(1948).*

the other. It requires an entirely different kind of person from the man who is the victim of his wife—the fearful tool of her ambition. I've never seen that problem successfully bridged. Certainly, I didn't. The victims of ambition are all, in one way or another, weaklings. When Macbeth is made king, we're only in the middle of the third act. There are still two and a half acts for Shakespeare to breathe in, finally, and to say: "I have finished with this damned ambition; now I can start to talk about a great man, who knows good wine and has lost the taste for it."

PB: You did the cutting on *Macbeth* in Italy while you were acting in *Black Magic*?

OW: Yes. Then they asked me to take out two reels and I did—but *I* cut out the two reels, they didn't. I thought they shouldn't have been cut out, but I'm the one who cut it. Not some idiot back at home.

PB: What kind of cut was it?

OW: All the way through—just whatever you could take out to cut two reels. That's a lot of time. They didn't care what.

PB: They just said, "Take out twenty minutes."

OW: Yeah. So I did. It was better twenty minutes longer.

PB: I would think so—

OW: The story was better told. It's a little too hustled now.

PB: You've said that Shakespeare never wrote pure tragedy—he wrote melodramas.

OW: His plays have tragic heroes. The framework, of course, is always rip-roaring blood-and-thunder—the Elizabethan theatre was *steeped* in melodrama.

PB: In *The Mercury Shakespeare*, you wrote that Shakespeare didn't invent his plots. Do you think plots are unimportant as far as your movies are concerned?

OW: Peter, I really can't make a comparison between a movie-maker and Shakespeare. No movie that will ever be made is worthy of being discussed in the same breath.

PB: But your attitude to the plays is often called irreverent.

OW: Because I make shooting scripts out of the texts, I guess.

PB: Your versions of both *Othello* [1952] and *Macbeth* don't have the "respectability" of "classics"—you think that's why the critics frowned upon them?

OW: Well, critics "frowned upon them" mainly in America.

PB: Well, in the English-speaking countries?

OW: Oh yes, in England, too.

The best that can be said of Welles' *Macbeth* is that it proves at least one Hollywood producer is willing to tackle Shakespearean tragedy. If Welles has failed utterly to live up to the standard set by Laurence Olivier's *Hamlet*, he has at least failed honestly.

—*Newsweek*, October 18, 1948

Orson Welles' *Macbeth* is made over and above all tradition, with evident changes in the order of certain scenes, with scenery and costumes which are purely imaginative and in reality far more truthful to the Shakespearean spirit than [those] in Olivier's *Hamlet*. . . . While Olivier only tried to adapt a theatre production for the cinema, Welles tried to use every possible dramatic means to express himself in a wholly new manner.

—JACQUES BOURGEOIS,
La Revue du Cinéma (Paris), October 1948

Shakespeare wrote *Macbeth* as a melodramatic tragedy. Mr. Welles has demoted it into a rather shabby Class B adventure story in costume.

—MARJORY ADAMS, *Boston Globe*, October 8, 1948

I love too much natural settings and natural light not to love also the fake light and the cardboard settings of *Macbeth*.

—ROBERT BRESSON, quoted in *Le Figaro* (Paris),
November 12, 1948

Responding to Dick Wilson's suggestion that he write an answer to the American critics, Orson cabled him from Florence on October 19, 1948:

Recording the music of The Third Man.

> Dearest Dick . . . Cannot imagine what you expect me to write for newspapers beyond simple apology for having been born. Please advise.—Orson

OW: The film was put into the Venice Film Festival. But after it was officially entered and the festival was under way, I was suddenly commanded by the American Ambassador to withdraw it because of supposed plots against the American film industry. I never understood the politics of this, but I had to stand up in front of an angry, jeering festival audience and pretend to explain how American films were being discriminated against at the festival, and thus why America was pulling out. High policy in that particular fiasco was somehow framed—believe it or not—by Elsa Maxwell. Result: a perfect storm of hisses and boos.

PB: Well, despite the bad notices on *Macbeth*, you still spent the next four years acting in other people's films to finance and shoot *Othello*. I guess the best of those films was *The Third Man*—you even did *that* one for *Othello*, didn't you?

OW: Yes, I could have had a third of *The Third Man* if I hadn't needed cash.
PB: Besides playing Harry Lime, what else did you do on it?
OW: I wrote my part—
PB: Every word of it?
OW: Carol Reed is the kind of director who'll use any ideas—anything that's going. I had notions for the dialogue, and Carol liked them. Except for my rather minor contribution, the story, of course, was by the matchless Graham Greene. And the basic idea—though he took no credit for it—was Alex Korda's.
PB: Who produced.
OW: Yes, it's the only film Alex and I ever really did together.
PB: Did you have anything to do with the actual setups and shots in the picture?
OW: Just a very few *ideas*, like the fingers coming through the grille.
PB: What about the first time we see you in the doorway?
OW: Pure Carol. He had a little second-unit specially set up for it, and at the end of every day we went there and tried it again, over and over, till he thought it was right.
PB: Was the last scene at the funeral your touch?
OW: No, it was not. It was a great shot invented by Carol—not by Greene or anybody else. Wonderful idea. I was there when they shot it. I wish I could pretend I'd contributed, but I was just standing there, watching them shoot it.
PB: The picture seemed influenced by you . . . perhaps because of the casting of [Joseph] Cotten.
OW: It was Carol's picture, Peter—and Korda's.
PB: Well, you have the smallest part but it dominates one's whole memory of the film.
OW: That's the part, you know. Every sentence in the whole script is about Harry Lime—nobody talks about anything else for ten reels. And then there's that shot in the doorway—what a star entrance that was! In theatre, you know, the old star actors never liked to come on until the end of the first act. *Mister Wu* is a classic example—I've played it once myself. All the other actors boil around the stage for about an hour shrieking, "What will happen when Mister Wu arrives?," "What is he like, this Mister Wu?," and so on. Finally a great gong is beaten, and slowly over a Chinese bridge comes Mister Wu himself in full mandarin robes. Peach Blossom (or whatever her name is) falls on her face and a lot of

coolies yell, "Mister *Wu!!!*" The curtain comes down, the audience goes wild, and everybody says, "Isn't that guy playing Mr. Wu a great actor!" *That's* a star part for you! What matters in that kind of role is not how many lines you have, but how few. What counts is how much the other characters talk about you. Such a star vehicle really is a *vehicle*. All you have to do is ride. Like Jean Gabin in this last epoch of his career; he now has written in his contract that he never shall be required to bend over. Literally!

Under the Ferris wheel in The Third Man, *Harry Lime has his most famous speech. Orson wrote it (which is acknowledged in Greene's published screenplay):*

LIME *(to Holly Martins, played by Joseph Cotten)*: . . . And don't be so gloomy. . . . After all, it's not that awful—you know what the fellow said: In Italy for 30 years under the Borgias they had warfare, terror, murder, bloodshed—they produced Michelangelo, Leonardo da Vinci and the Renaissance. In Switzerland they had brotherly love, 500 years of democracy and peace, and what did that produce? . . . The cuckoo clock.

PB: Your Ferris wheel speech about Switzerland and the cuckoo clock is so convincing that we seem to agree with you even though you're the heavy.
OW: When the picture came out, the Swiss very nicely pointed out to me that they've never made any cuckoo clocks—they all come from the Schwarzwald, in Bavaria!
PB: Is it true that you unknowingly threw Lady Eden off the set?
OW: Not unknowingly. Clarissa Churchill wasn't then married to Eden; she was doing publicity for Alex. He liked having all kinds of fashionable folk on his payroll. . . . Well, one day, Clarissa brought all these society friends of hers to visit the set, and they wouldn't keep quiet. Carol was far too nice and much too English to tell her to shut them up, so I did it *for* him. I didn't throw her out, but she went, and that was the end of our friendship. I'm sorry about that.
PB: Many people still associate you with that role—Harry Lime.
OW: In every way, the picture broke every known record, and the people went insane. Wherever you went, you heard nothing but that zither. To borrow Cotten and Alida Valli from Selznick,

Korda had to make a deal giving David American distribution. So in America the picture arrived as "David O. Selznick presents / A David O. Selznick Production / Produced by David O. Selznick," and so on. All David had done was to loan Alex a couple of actors. Alex dreamed up the whole project, in every sense of the word *produced* it, but David took the bows.

I was sitting with them about two years after the picture had opened—when all Europe was still reverberating with the strains of the "Third Man Theme," and Alex said, "You know, David, I hope I don't die before you do." "Oh!" said David. "Why?" And Alex said, "I hate the thought of you sneaking out to the graveyard at night and scratching my name off the tombstone."

> It's a little too early to predict the Oscar-winning player for the best supporting actor next year, but Henry King has picked him—Orson Welles as Borgia in *Prince of Foxes*. Henry said everybody told him he would have trouble with Welles; that he'd never be on time; and some days wouldn't even show. "I've never worked with anyone as cooperative," says King. "He came on location two days ahead of schedule, and after the first morning always beat me on the set at 8 A.M."
>
> —"HEDDA HOPPER's Hollywood,"
> *New York Daily News*, March 31, 1949

OW [*referring to the above*]: I used to hide and wait until he'd start to scream, "Where *is* he? I know the son-of-a-bitch is away in Venice shooting that goddamn Shakespeare!" And then I'd step out of the bushes fully dressed and say, "Do you want me, Henry?"
PB: Again, for *Othello*.
OW: Sure.
PB: How was Henry Hathaway on *The Black Rose?*
OW: Hathaway is a famous "cruel-to-actors" director. Real Jekyll-and-Hyde stuff—sweet, nice man in private life, and turns into this raving maniac on the set. People go off to rest homes afterward. Well, he tried pretty hard to break me, and it was fun watching him try. But we're still very friendly.
PB: And then there was some French film called *Le Portrait d'un assassin* [1949], which you worked on as a writer.

OW: Great cast: Erich von Stroheim, Pierre Brasseur, Arletty, and Maria Montez. Charlie Lederer and I were hired to doctor the script. We wrote a new one, but it wasn't used.
PB: Something about a wall-of-death rider in a circus.
OW: That's right. We locked ourselves in a room at the Lancaster Hotel for a few weeks and turned out something that wasn't bad at all. But nobody would read it. The producer failed to make our last payment, and then—taking the line that attack is better than defense—sued us. I don't know why he wanted us to begin with. The director wasn't even speaking to him.
PB: Had you worked with Lederer before?
OW: Not officially; unofficially we'd helped each other out on several things. Those writing bees were standard procedure in what might be called the Ben Hecht circle. Only way to meet all those deadlines.

Micheál Mac Liammóir and Welles in Othello *(1952).*

PB: Would you say *Othello* was the most arduous to make of all your pictures, since it took so long to finish?
OW: It was almost two years between starting it and finishing it because of lack of money, but "arduous" is maybe not the word—just maddening, because I had all the money and the contract early on. I went to Rome after the collapse of *Cyrano* to do *Black Magic*, which I made at Scalera Film Studios, then the biggest studio in Italy. And Mr. Scalera, the head of this great outfit, decided that he wanted to finance my making *Othello*, and we wrote a contract together. I gathered together my actors and [Alexandre] Trauner [art director] and my Italian crew, and away we went to Mogador to shoot it. We arrived in this condemned area—a little-known, out-of-the-way port on the Atlantic coast of Morocco—and everybody checked into hotels. Two days later, we got a telegram saying the costumes wouldn't come because they hadn't been completed. A day later, a telegram came saying they hadn't been started. And then a telegram came saying that Scalera had gone bankrupt. So I had a company of fifty people in North Africa and no money—though we had film and we had our cameras—but how can you shoot *Othello* without costumes?

That was how I got the idea to shoot two reels in a Turkish bath, because if people are in a Turkish bath they won't be wearing clothes. And we worked in a Turkish bath for about three weeks while a lot of little tailors in the village—with Carpaccio reproductions pinned on their walls—made the clothes; the costumes were all based on his paintings. My plan was to show much more of the corruption of the Christian Venetian world—this world of what Othello called "goats and monkeys." But everything I'd thought up for that had to go when I was obliged to film without costumes.
PB: How would you have done that?
OW: I don't know how to describe it: the same scenes, but it was just the way they would appear. You can't show people being very goatlike and monkeylike just sitting, sweating it out in a Turkish bath! Anyway, I shot until the money in the bank ran out—
PB: Your own money.
OW: Sure. And then everybody had to go home until I could earn some more or find some more. In fact, we stayed a little longer by virtue of a fellow who arrived and arranged for sales of the film for some strange countries like the Dutch East Indies and Turkey—places like that; we got together about $6,000 or $7,000 and stayed

Turkish bath sequence.

on a week or two more, thanks to him. And I gave him a role in the film. He wasn't an actor and he's very poor in it, but he was a big help in getting us the money. And then *that* ran out and everybody had to go home. [Micheál] Mac Liammóir, who was playing Iago, and his partner, Hilton Edwards [who played Desdemona's father], went back to Dublin to open their theatre season, and they couldn't be brought back just when I wanted, because of their theatre schedule. So, even when I got the money, I had to wait until my actors were free, which made a long wait—even longer than it took me to get the money. And when they were free, we went back again to Africa and then to Italy, where we shot all over the place and finished it. But that began the story of how long it takes me to make a movie. You know: "Look at him—even on his own pictures, it takes him over three years to finish it."

PB: That's how *that* myth got started—

OW: Yes, it's still very prevalent, and it all began with *Othello*. But the movie wasn't arduous—we had tremendous fun doing it, and everybody got along awfully well. Our headaches were all riotous and amusing; it wasn't anguish like *Mr. Arkadin* [1955] was. *Arkadin* was just anguish from beginning to end. No, it was a very happy experience for me in spite of these terrible troubles.

PB: Trauner told me he loved making the film, and remembers it as sort of an insane experience.

OW: He's a wonderful art director and an extraordinary fellow; I'm devoted to him. Marvelous at his job—of course, there wasn't much he could do with no money, but he still kept a very large staff. Imagine: the picture was being shot in a real location where there's no money except what I happened to have left in the bank, and Trauner had three assistants. So, when he remembers it as a crazy experience, there was nothing as crazy as Trauner, who insisted on keeping three assistants in Mogador drafting pictures of where we would put the matting that we bought—which is all they had to do, since there was nothing we could build.

PB: Well, then, what *did* he do?

OW: It was all going to be built originally in the south of France. All sets. And he designed everything. Then, when we decided on real places, he found Mogador—he found all the locations.

PB: The castle?

OW: Well, that's partly Safi and partly Agadir—all different places made to look like the same.

PB: Really?

OW: It's shot in four different towns in Morocco and about five places in Italy. And there is even a set that he *did* design, the palace in Cyprus, which he built in a studio in Rome. Poor Trauner was reduced to a mere wisp of what his original conception was.

PB: Is it true that Trauner sued you on *Othello?*

OW: No. The part of the work that Trauner did was financed by a French coproducer who failed to give him his last payment, as he did a lot of people. And Trauner, I think, sued with my cooperation. There was no quarrel between us.

PB: Is it true that you had Lea Padovani and Cécile Aubry as Desdemonas before Suzanne Cloutier?

OW: Never shot Cécile Aubry, but I did have Padovani—only for a day or two—and Betsy Blair for about a week.

PB: Why did you call Suzanne Cloutier the "Iron Butterfly"?

OW: Well, the phrase was invented by Jack Holt as a description of Mary Pickford, so it's not anything to do with me.

PB: You borrowed it.

OW: In the course of a lot of other things I called her—in a friendly way—
PB: Did you get along with her?
OW: Very well, sure. It was just jokes.
PB: You must have spent a lot of your time trying to raise money.
OW: Yes. One time I am in Venice trying to promote some money from a crazy Russian; we're at the Excelsior Hotel on the Lido. Churchill had been voted out of office and is there with Clemmie, and they're together just sitting at a table in the restaurant. And as I came in, for some reason, there was all this Italian gafuffle: "Hello—" "Here he comes—" And as I passed Churchill's table, I bowed to him. And Churchill—I don't know why, for reasons of irony, to send me up, I can't imagine why—half stood up, bowed, and sat down. I suppose it was some kind of joke. Well, the Russian afterward said, "You're close to Churchill," and the deal was closed right there. So the next day I'm swimming, and on the beach I find myself next to Mr. Churchill. And I said, "Mr. Churchill, you don't know what you did for me. By acknowledging my greeting that way, I've got the money for my picture—settled the whole thing."

All right. Finished swimming. That night, at dinner, we came in again. Churchill *stood up!* And for the rest of the time we were in Venice, every time I came in the restaurant, he *stood* when I passed! Thinking, you know, "Get some money for him." And no matter who I was with—somebody I *couldn't* get any money from—he stood. And people said, "What is this? Every time Churchill sees this actor, this great man—the greatest living fellow—is standing up!" And he thought, "Well, every time I stand up, he gets some more dough—so why not?" Oh God, what a wonderful man he was. And then, the same season, there was the great Bestigui Ball in Venice, where everybody's invited. And I happened to be invited, and of course Churchill was, too, but he was hoping to get back into office and everybody was attacking the ball as conspicuous luxury and all that, so he couldn't go. And here we are all going off in our speedboats to the ball, and there was Churchill down at the end of the dock watching us leave, ready—and miserable. . . . He would have come dressed as anything, you know, but he just couldn't go. Miserable!
PB: Not to be at the ball.
OW: Yes! He came to *Othello* and—

PB: You mean the play [1951]?
OW: Yes. Came backstage afterward and sat in the dressing room. There was a long pause, and I was waiting—I didn't know what he would say—he just sat there. And finally he said, "Most potent grave and reverent seignors—my most approved good masters . . ." Began reciting from the play—long speeches.
PB: To show that he knew them?
OW: Yes! Yes!
PB: I heard Richard Burton say that Churchill came to *Hamlet* and sat out front, reciting it right along with him.
OW: He was nice enough not to do that with me. What an adorable man he was. I ran some documentary footage for him once during the war which was all silent. And as we were watching it, we suddenly began to hear these strange sounds, and finally realized it was Churchill supplying the *sound effects* for the battle action on the screen!
PB: You cut *Othello* to ninety-one minutes.
OW: Yeah, it's my thing again about shows being too long.
PB: And you took out some of what is, I guess, dated comedy.
OW: It's very good comedy, but the movie I wanted to make didn't have room for it, that's all.
PB: And you feel quite free to change whatever you like for that reason.
OW: I don't see why there's any argument about it: A movie is a movie, and if we're going to take movies as a serious art form, then they're no less so than opera. And Verdi had no hesitation in doing what he did with his *Otello*, which is an enormous departure from the play; nobody criticizes him. Why is a movie supposed to be more respectful to a play than an opera?
PB: Or to a novel or anything else?
OW: Yes.
PB: You are basically doing your own variations on Shakespeare's theme.
OW: Yes. Of course, there's nothing can be done without Shakespeare—but you can't put a play on the screen. I don't believe in that—I don't think Shakespeare would have believed in it. He would have made a great movie writer.
PB: It's one of your best performances.
OW: I was much better in the theatre, which I did *after* the movie. Just the reverse. I should have done it first.
PB: You improved.

OW: I knew much more about it, had more time to think about it. Though I've always had a great feeling for *Othello*. The two plays I've most wanted to do in movies have always been *Othello* and *King Lear*.
PB: I have noticed that all the music you've put in your films—with the exception of *Touch of Evil*, where it wouldn't fit—has a classical quality to it.
OW: I attach an awful lot of importance to it.
PB: But it must go back to your early love of music.
OW: Yes, all of those things. I was very lucky in having Benny Herrmann for a while, and since then I've used some good composers, but I tend more and more to get music that isn't composed for the picture—so that I can control it, so that I'm not at the mercy of what the composer turns up with after he's already under contract.
PB: Well, the music in *Othello* is most memorable.
OW: Yes. That's an extraordinarily talented man, Lavignino—he did the music for *Chimes at Midnight*, too. Extraordinary music for the battle. But I took it out and recorded it three times over each other, did all those kinds of Beatles tricks with it. But still awfully good. *Othello* was superb. We used forty mandolins at one time. And that opening theme of the funeral, the main one, is just hair-raising. He makes too many movies now—does forty a year. He's an ex-professor of music at Vienna with a big classical background. And he wrote an entirely different score for *Othello* when I did it in the theatre.
PB: The first line in the movie—"I hate the Moor"—sets everything up. You do that sort of thing quite often—begin by telling what it's going to be about. You did it in *The Trial*.
OW: I like it in Elizabethan plays. In the primitive theatre, too, you find somebody coming out front and telling what it's all about. I just got through writing an opening exactly like that for *The Other Side of the Wind*. We tell what it is—and then, really, you could go home if you want to [*laughs*].
PB: Why did you decide to begin *Othello* with the funeral?
OW: Why not? [*Laughs.*] I don't know. Have another drink.
PB: Well, it couldn't be coincidental that *Kane*, *Othello*, and *Mr. Arkadin* all begin with the death of the leading character. . . .
OW: Just shows a certain weakness of invention on the part of the filmmaker.
PB: You can give me a better answer than that.

The traveling shot.

OW: Peter, I'm no good at this sort of stuff. I either go cryptic or philistine. All I can say is, I thought it was a good idea; whether you get me in the morning or the evening, I'm always going to say that [*laughs*].

PB: I loved the classic unity of that film. Beginning with Othello's head and then into the funeral—ending with his head and then the funeral. And it's not precious.

OW: Well, the shooting script, as such, was quite painstakingly developed.

PB: I think you're saying that as a reaction to some critics, who probably said it was thrown together. Where did you get the idea for the cage they put Iago in? Was that, in fact, the kind of punishment they might have used?

OW: You do see cages in museums sometimes, of one kind or another. Wasn't it Abd el-Krim, the great North African insurrectionist leader, who was driven in a cage tied to a donkey all over North Africa to show to the tribes? That's where I got the idea.

PB: Why did you shoot the long scene on the beach between Othello and Iago in one continuous traveling shot?

OW: Because the picture was made in pieces. Three different times I had to close it and go away and earn money and come back, which meant you'd see me looking off-camera left, and when you'd cut over my shoulder, it would be another continent—a year later. And so the picture had many more cuts than I would have liked; it wasn't written that way, but had them because I never had a full cast together. Now, for *that* shot we had the entire cast—Iago and Othello—and a great long place where we could do it all in one. So, for once in the picture, we could do a single sustained scene. Just as simple as that.

PB: Beautiful scene.

OW: It's a marvelous set. Trauner found it for me.

PB: In the scene before the mirror that follows—where Iago continues to poison his mind—did you mean his removing of Othello's armor as a symbol of what he's doing to him emotionally at the time?

OW: Well, it's not exactly a symbol. When the visual thing is so direct and so basic that you don't have to cerebrate, then it's OK. In other words, when it doesn't present the director in front of the curtain for his comments, then it's all right. It's so clear what's happening—you don't have to think about it—it's a kind of physical fact.

PB: It becomes a metaphor.

OW: Yes, a metaphor—you've found a good definition. I rather like metaphor.

PB: It's integral to the scene.

OW: There was a moment at the end of that scene that has remained a standing joke between Micheál and myself for years. He had to pick up Othello's cloak and go. And he picked it up and looked very meaningful and all that sort of stuff, and I finally said to him, "Micheál, pick up the cloak and go!" And that's become since then a sort of basic thing I use when an actor wants to enrich his performance—I say, "Pick up the cloak and go!"

I bring up the fable of the scorpion and the frog (see the Introduction) that the title character, played by Orson, tells at a party in Mr. Arkadin*:*

PB: What is the origin of the fable of the scorpion and the frog?

OW: Who knows? I heard it from an Arab.

PB: It relates to a lot of your films beside *Mr. Arkadin—Othello,* for example. Do you believe the world is divided between frogs and scorpions?

OW: No, there's lots of other animals.

PB: But you could probably divide an awful lot of the characters in your pictures into one camp or the other.

OW: I hope I don't. Judge not lest ye bore the audience.

PB: Why do you think Othello is destroyed so easily? Do you think he's a weak man?

OW: He's destroyed easily because of his simplicity, not his weakness. He really is the archetype of the simple man, and has never understood the complexity of the world or of human beings. He's a soldier; he's never known women. It's a favorite theme of Shakespeare's. A curious thing about Lear, too: Lear clearly knows nothing about women and has never lived with them at all. His wife is dead—she couldn't exist. Obviously, the play couldn't happen if there were a Mrs. Lear. He hasn't any idea of what makes women work—he's a man who lives with his knights. He's that all-male man whom Shakespeare—who was clearly very feminine in many ways—regarded as a natural-born loser in a tragic situation. Othello was another fellow like that. Total incomprehension of what a woman is. His whole treatment of her when he kills her is the treatment of a man who's out of touch with reality as far as the other sex is concerned. All he knows how to do is fight wars and deal with the anthropophagi and "men whose heads do grow beneath their shoulders."

PB: *That's* his tragedy, then.

OW: Yes.

PB: He could not imagine a person like Iago.

OW: No, and neither could a lot of Shakespeare's critics. As a result of which we have eight libraries full of idiot explanations of Iago—when everybody has known an Iago in his life if he's been anywhere.

PB: There are several moments in the movie which give the impression that Iago does what he does because it's in his character, rather than that he's plotting for some particular reason.

OW: Oh, he *has* no reason. The great criticism through all the years has been that he's an unmotivated villain, but I think there are a lot of people who perpetuate villainy without any motive other than the exercise of mischief and the enjoyment of the power to destroy. I've known a lot of Iagos in my life. I think it's a great mistake to try to motivate it beyond what is inherent in the action.

PB: You could say he was like the scorpion that followed his own character.

OW: Well, yup [*laughs*].

PB: Iago is certainly the most interesting part in the play.

OW: Shakespeare is like no other artist when his characters start to live their own lives and to lead the author against his wishes. In *Richard II*, Shakespeare is absolutely for Richard, but nevertheless he has to do justice to Bolingbroke. And, more than that, he has to make him seem real, human—so that suddenly this man Bolingbroke takes life and pulls off a large part of the play. You see Shakespeare trying to hold him back: nothing doing, Bolingbroke is launched! A very interesting theory has been put forward by some scholars; according to them, Shakespeare not only played small roles, but large ones. They think now that he played Iago and Mercutio—two second-level roles which steal the play from the stars.

All the great writers are actors. They have the actor's faculty of entering the skin of their characters, and transforming them—murderers or whatever—with what they give of themselves. This leads often to the fact that the protagonist of a story seems to speak for the author, even when he stands for things the author hates. . . .

PB: You said somewhere that there was an implication of impotence in your Iago.

OW: Yes. I don't think that is necessary to the truth of the play, but it was the key to Mac Liammóir's performance, that Iago was impotent. It isn't central, but it was an element that we used for the actor, as a means of performing the part. In the play, it's pretty clear that isn't so, and when I did the play in the theatre later, there was no suggestion of it. But I think it's a perfectly valid way of doing it, though I wasn't anxious for the audience to understand it, not trying to inform them of it—if the audience can find it, more power to them. To use the Stanislavsky argot, it was basically something for the actor "to use." I do a lot of that with actors. I'm always making fun of the Method, but I use a lot of things that are taken from it.

PB: Does Othello feel guilt at the end—after Iago's proven guilty?

OW: Depends on how you play it.

PB: In your picture.

OW: I've forgotten, because I remember my performance in the theatre much more clearly than in the movie, and I revised a lot of my ideas about playing it.

PB: Well, then, in the stage production.

OW: I don't think "guilt" is the right word. You know, *Othello* is so close to being a French farce. Analyze it! All he's got to do is say, "Show me the handkerchief," and you ring down the curtain. Being that close to nonsense, it can only come to life on a level very close to real tragedy—closer than Shakespeare usually gets. And Othello is so blasted at the end that guilt is really too small an emotion. Anyway, he's not a Christian—that's central to the character. And Shakespeare was very, very aware of who was a Christian and who wasn't, just as he was very aware of who was a Southern European and who was a Northern, who was the decadent and who was the palace man, and the outdoor man. These things run all the way through Shakespeare.

PB: There's an implication at the end that Othello understands, even almost forgives Iago for what he had done.

OW: He didn't forgive him.

PB: Well, understood.

OW: Yes, it was this terrible understanding of how awful he was which drains him of hate. Because when something is that awful you can't react to it that way. He becomes appalled by him. . . .

PB: The look between them is filled with ambiguity.

OW: That's a very interesting moment in the play.

PB: Do you think Othello is detestable in his jealousy?

OW: Jealousy is detestable, not Othello. He's so obsessed with jealousy, he becomes the very personification of that tragic vice. In that sense, he's morally diseased. All Shakespeare's great characters are sometimes detestable—compelled by their own nature.

PB: So are your characters.

OW: Well, you could say it, I think, about all drama, large or small, that attempts tragedy within the design of melodrama. As long as there is melodrama, the tragic hero is something of a villain.

PB: Why did you give Roderigo a white poodle?

OW: Because Carpaccio's full of them. And it's not a poodle, it's a tenerife—very special kind. We had a terrible time getting it. All the dandies in Carpaccio fondle exactly that dog—it's almost a trademark with them, like Whistler's butterfly; they're always clinging to those terrible little dogs.

PB: Where did you find that wonderful set with a thin layer of water all around?

OW: It's a beautiful Portuguese cistern in a town in Morocco called Mazagan.

PB: Is it the same place where Othello dies?

OW: No, it looks similar—I wanted it to. That's why I found a place in Viterbo, Italy, where *that* happens—so that it seems to be part of the same castle; that's why you believe it.

PB: In your style for the film, did you consciously proceed from bright light into shadows?

OW: Yes. I don't know that it was consciously. But I don't think anything visual that you see in a picture of mine is *un*conscious. Certainly deliberate—sure. It's not a kind of Germanic master plan that's made in the study before the picture is made, but it evolves and becomes a plan. Though I do make a master plan and then throw it away—

PB: I didn't know that.

OW: Yes. Not the shots, but I project the whole movie and then it never bears any relationship to that afterwards—none.

PB: None at all?

OW: Someday one of 'em will. There's always some reason why it

can't—there aren't any sets, so I have to shoot in a railway station or in a Turkish bath.
PB: You have to be very flexible?
OW: Yes, and I am. I like to be. Nothing depresses me more than rigidity in movies. It's terrible when they just sit down and wait for the cloud to go away or the noise to stop. I always go.
PB: Work through it.
OW: Find something else to shoot, eight reels later. There's always something to do; I never wait.
PB: Impatience?
OW: No. Because I think a movie dies. I don't mind waiting—I'm lazy physically, I'm very happy to sit. But I think the movie dies, the actors and the crew and everybody. It's a basic part of the way I work with a group of people—I always move. Not because I'm impatient, but because of what I think will happen to the picture if I don't.
PB: Keeping the energy up.
OW: Yes. I try to get it as close to a dress rehearsal as possible, and as far away from a first reading.
PB: How did you shoot that scene where Iago stabs Roderigo through the floorboards?
OW: Just put the floorboards up above the camera and monkeyed around.
PB: The lighting is very unusual.
OW: We had a very good cameraman—of the old school, but very fine. Never took a light reading, you know. . . . Toland told me that it was only a few years before *Kane* that no leading cameraman would be seen with a light meter. It was a sign of weakness. [Anchise] Brizzi was one of those. He went back to the days of the glass-roof studios—marvelous old man, and a great joy to work with, but very much the old school.
PB: Toland used a light meter, didn't he?
OW: Oh, yes. Claimed to be among the first to use them openly and without shame.
PB: Well, it's a little like your saying that the director shouldn't use a viewfinder.
OW: It's not the same thing—because one is precise and the other is not precise. You shouldn't use a finder because it is not precise —you *should* use the light meter because it *is* precise.
PB: Did *Othello* make its money back for you?
OW: Not for me. Of course not.
PB: But it was your own money, wasn't it?

OW: Yes, but the fellow who came in with the completion money made all the profit off it. Now he no longer owns it—it has reverted back to me, and I am now the owner of *Othello*. No—there's also a junior partner who was the heir of the mad Russian who put up part of the money. But it did well. And, you know, after Olivier's *Othello* [1965] there was a tremendous vogue for mine.
PB: Isn't it pretty much the way you shot it?
OW: Yes—exactly as I shot it. Nobody touched it.
PB: Which certainly was the opposite of *Mr. Arkadin*. How did you get the idea to make that next?
OW: I was doing a radio series based on Harry Lime for Harry Alan Towers, and I wrote about seven of those scripts in a couple of days. One of the plots I thought up in a rush suddenly was that plot—and I realized that the gimmick was super. It came from just throwing together a lot of bad radio scripts.
PB: Wasn't the original sequence of events in *Mr. Arkadin* told through an intricate series of flashbacks?
OW: Pretty intricate.
PB: The version that's in general release is told without any flashbacks at all. Some idiot must have decided it was confusing. Can you recall the correct continuity of *Arkadin*?
OW: I remember very well how it began, which was with a shot of an enormous empty beach and a naked girl being washed in by the sea. But I have a kind of block on the rest.
PB: Because you were so upset by the recutting.
OW: Yes, I just hate to even think of it. It was the best *popular* story I ever thought up for a movie, and really it should have been a roaring success. I'd love to make that story again.
PB: You could.
OW: I don't know whether I could; I don't know what my rights to it are. I'd like to find out, because it's a super movie story. It was blown, blown, blown by the cutting.
PB: What part of the story are you talking about—the man in search of his past?
OW: Well, no, he isn't in search of his past, as it turns out. That, I think, is the good gimmick. He's just trying to find out what somebody else could find out. He knows his past, and he wants to see what anybody could find—if there's anything to prevent him from getting the big army contract. And the only little thing is that he used to be a pimp. He doesn't want his daughter to know that. The other thing is that he's been rubbing everybody out all the time.

Paola Mori (Mrs. Orson Welles) as Raina Arkadin.

PB: Every time this fellow Van Stratten, whom he's sent out, finds out anything from anyone, Arkadin has that person killed.
OW: That's right.
PB: Why does Arkadin commit suicide?
OW: Because his daughter has found out a few of his untidy little secrets. Of course, in my version, you saw Arkadin as a sentimental, rather maudlin Russian drunk. Those scenes were cut out—there was another party scene, and another scene between Arkadin and Van Stratten, neither of which is in the picture now, and they're rather important to a story in which a man commits that kind of suicide at the end. Arkadin, you know, was based to some extent on Stalin.
PB: Really?
OW: He's a Georgian, if you'll remember—even his name tells you that.
PB: It's been said that he was patterned after Lowenstein, Kruger, and that munitions fellow Zaharoff.
OW: No, they were all *sly*. Arkadin occupies a position similar to theirs. But his character is something else: cold, calculating, cruel, but with that terrible Slavic capacity to run to sentiment and self-destruction at the same time. The beard came from a wig-maker and the character came partly from Stalin and partly from a lot of Russians I've known.

PB: When you wrote the novel of *Mr. Arkadin*—
OW: Peter, I didn't write one word of that novel. Nor have I ever read it.
PB: How could they publish it with your name on it?
OW: Somebody [Maurice Bessy] wrote it in French to be published in serial form in the newspapers. You know—to promote the picture. I don't know *how* it got under hardcovers, or who got paid for that.
PB: In a couple of books about you, they talk about the "beautiful" style of your writing in that novel.
OW: Maybe I did write it, at that.
PB: The characters in the movie are very lonely.
OW: Yes, that's true.
PB: They all look back to a strange, lost past. That's most movingly conveyed by that lovely scene with Katina Paxinou going through her scrapbook. I think it's the best scene in the picture.
OW: She's very fine in it. And Tamiroff as Zouk—in the full version it's the best he's ever done. It was almost the leading part. . . . And Redgrave. Wasn't it gutsy of him to put on that hair net?
PB: Behind Tamiroff, in that cluttered room, you put a photograph of Hitler upside down—why?
OW: Oh, this is after the war, remember, and we're up in the

Robert Arden and Welles in Mr. Arkadin.

Robert Arden and Katina Paxinou.

attic. There's been instant de-Nazification, so of course the attics all over Germany filled up with such sacred relics.

PB: Where did you get the idea for those Goya-like masks at the party?

OW: They are not Goya-*like!* Every one is an exact reproduction of a Goya etching.

PB: Why did you decide to do that?

OW: Why not? If you're going to have a party in Spain . . .

PB: Some critics have compared Arkadin with Harry Lime.

OW: Not comparable. First, Arkadin is a Slav, not Anglo-Saxon—

PB: —which changes it completely—

OW: Arkadin is a profiteer, an opportunist, a genial parasite who nourishes himself on corruption—and who doesn't look for ways to justify himself. He could be Greek, Russian, Georgian, Yugoslav. Arriving from some old, half-savage country, he sets himself up in modern Western European civilization, using his particular sort of energy and barbaric intelligence. His morality may be hateful, but not his spirit. I find it impossible to hate a passionate man. Harry Lime has no passion.

PB: And what about Van Stratten?

OW: The worst man in the story. He has no substance, no human substance. He's a shallow hustler.

Orson threw a little more light on Arkadin—as well as other characters he has played—in an interview in Cahiers du Cinéma, *no. 87 (September 1958):*

Many of the big characters I've played are various forms of Faust, and I am against every form of Faust, because I believe it's impossible for a man to be great without admitting that there's something greater than himself, whether it's the law, or God, or art. . . . I have played a whole line of egotists, and I detest egotism. . . . But an actor is not a devil's advocate: he is a lover. . . . In playing Faust, I want to be just and loyal to him, to give him the best of myself and the best arguments that I can find, because we live in a world that has been made by Faust—our world is Faustian.

. . . An actor never plays anything but himself . . . He simply takes out that which is not himself. And so, of course, in all these characters there *is* something of Orson Welles. I can't do anything about that. . . . And when I play someone I hate, I try to be chivalrous to the enemy. . . . I hate all dogmas which deny humanity the least of its privileges; if some belief requires denouncing something human, I detest it.

It's gotten pretty late and Orson has become irritable with me for only talking about movies. Packing up, I throw out a couple of general questions and reach for a memory of success:

Masks at party.

PB: What do you think of cynics?
OW: I despise them.
PB: Why?
OW: Don't need to explain that. If it isn't self-evident—
PB: Skeptics?
OW: Well, skeptics have nothing to do with cynics.
PB: No—it's another question.
OW: I don't care one way or another about skeptics. Cynics are intolerable, I think.
PB: Which do you value more highly—your instincts or your intellect? [OW *grunts*.] It's a key question.
OW: Isn't it better to leave these key questions to the kind of people who enjoy them?
PB: Then what must you think of psychoanalysis?
OW: About as valuable as—but considerably more expensive than—consulting your local astrologer.
PB: By the way, I forgot, your *Othello* won the first prize at Cannes.
OW: Yes, and the Russian *Othello* [1956] got it a few years later. There have been two *Othello* first prizes at Cannes.
PB: They must like the play.
OW: Yes—it's very big in the south of France! Did I tell you how I found out I'd got the prize?
PB: No.
OW: You see, you cannot release a picture without what is called a "certificate of origin," for which the picture has to have a nationality. And you also need that in order to get it into a festival. The Italians and the French, and the Americans—who might have been able to enter *Othello*—didn't want to; they had their own pictures. So, because it had been shot in Morocco, I entered it as a Moroccan picture. Well, you're never told if you've won until the end, you know, but I was sitting in my hotel room, and the director of the festival, Robert Favre Le Bret, called me on the phone and said, "What is the Moroccan national anthem?" And that was how I knew I'd won the first prize. Because they always play the national anthem of the winning country. And, of course, there *is* no Moroccan national anthem, or wasn't then, so they played something out of *Chu Chin Chow* or something, and everybody stood up. There was no Moroccan delegation or anything. I think I'm the sole winner in the Arab world of a great international prize.

PARIS

THE TRIAL ▪ SETS ▪ *CHIMES AT MIDNIGHT*
THE IMMORTAL STORY ▪ ISAK DINESEN
CUTTING ▪ TEACHING FILM ▪ THE ANGLE
OF THE MIRROR ▪ ACTING FOR THE MONEY
TREASURE ISLAND ▪ PIER PAOLO PASOLINI
YIDDISH THEATRE ▪ DREAMS

PETER BOGDANOVICH: You once said that your tastes don't shock the middle-class American, they only shock the American intellectual. Do you think that's true?
ORSON WELLES: Yes.
PB: Why?
OW: Because I'm a complete maverick in the intellectual establishment. And they only like me more now because there's even less communication between me and them. I've become kind of exotic, so they start to accept me. But basically I've always been

completely at odds with the true intellectual establishment. I despise it, and they suspect and despise me. I am an intellectual, but I don't belong to that particular establishment.
PB: Well, it's true that America likes its artists and its entertainers to be either artists *or* entertainers, and they can't accept the combination of the two.
OW: Or any combination. They want one clear character. And they don't want you to be two things. That irritates and bewilders them.

We're in a suite at the Georges V on the Champs-Élysées. I've come over to do some publicity work for a film of mine, The Last Picture Show, *which is about to open in Europe. Orson, since I saw him, has acted in several movies and TV shows to raise money for his own projects—in particular* The Other Side of the Wind *and* Don Quixote*—and he has become involved with another. He now calls it* Hoax *[later retitled* Question Mark, *or* ?, *and finally* F for Fake*], and it began as a documentary by François Reichenbach on art fakery through the ages. But one of the people interviewed—along with Orson —was Clifford Irving, the man who faked Howard Hughes' autobiography. When the big Hughes-Irving scandal broke, Orson became fascinated with the idea of turning the documentary into a unique kind of free-form essay on fakery, using the Irving-Hughes affair as a springboard. He persuaded Reichenbach to let him buy into the footage, and has now been shooting new material and cutting on it for several weeks; the end is in sight. Orson is very excited about the project and has shown me one or two brief sequences that were indeed fascinating. We've just had a lovely meal at the Lucas Carton restaurant, which I am now spoiling for him by bringing out a borrowed tape machine.*

PB: Didn't *The Trial* begin here in Paris?
OW: *The Trial* began as *Taras Bulba.* I did a one-day job for Abel Gance in *Austerlitz,* which was produced by a couple of Russians named Salkind—father and son. And they came to me a couple of years later and said they wanted me to act in *Taras Bulba.* Now, at that same time, an American company was about to shoot a *Taras Bulba* with Yul Brynner and Tony Curtis, and I said, "Well, we're going to have trouble fighting that big, expensive American pic-

Welles and Oja Kodar in F for Fake.

ture." They said, "We're willing to go ahead." So I said, "I'll only do it if you let me direct it and write it." They said all right. So I wrote a script for *Taras Bulba*—the real one—because it's a wonderful movie story, and when I'd finished, I went to see them and they said, "Well, we decided you're right. The Americans are nice." So I was stuck with the script of *Taras Bulba*—but now I had what's called "a relationship" with them. And the old man, who had made Garbo's first picture out of Sweden—an angelic, dear man—gave me a list of about a hundred books, saying, which one did I want to make? They had Kafka's *The Trial* on the list, and I said I wanted to do *The Castle* because I liked it better, but they persuaded me to do *The Trial.* I *had* to do a book—couldn't make them do an original. It was as negative as that.

PB: Do you remember some of the other titles on the list?

OW: No. Almost entirely Russian, very heavy.

PB: All public domain?

OW: Most of them were Dostoevsky and Turgenev and from the Russian theatre. They thought *The Trial* was public domain, and then had to pay for it—but that's another story. When they had these conversations with me—they later told me—they had to borrow the money in order to drive up to the Eagles, in the Austrian Alps, where I was. They not only didn't have the money for the picture, they didn't even have the money to come *talk* about

the picture. But that's what makes those kind of people great, and you have to love them, because they've made hundreds of pictures without any money. And here they were, willing to go ahead with me when nobody else was, and I was most grateful to them for that. And they went ahead and got the money together from various sources, some mysterious, and gave me absolute freedom from the beginning of the picture to final cut. There was only one thing: I had to use their composer, and I argued about that for months until I finally realized he was one of the principal backers.
PB: I *liked* the score—using jazz juxtaposed with the classical music.
OW: Had some good French jazz musicians do that. And all that was put in very late—because I was struggling with the backer—so I had to find, as I did, classical music to take the place of his score. Anyway, the Salkinds had a deal with Yugoslavia, and we were going to make half the picture there and half in France in order to enjoy French nationality on a coproduction basis. Despite that and the fact that we had a French crew, French cameraman, Madeleine Robinson, Jeanne Moreau, Suzanne Flon, and all that, Mr. Malraux, the washerwoman of Paris, Minister of Culture, wouldn't give us the French nationality. So they lost out on that.

I spent months designing the sets for all the interiors. We were only going to shoot the actual big office and the streets of Prague and Zagreb for the last walk with the murderers. And during the time we were in Zagreb, my sets were to be built in the studios. The art director who was to realize my designs had made all the blueprints, everything was ready to go, and, the night before we were to leave for Yugoslavia, Mr. Salkind the elder came to me and said there was no money to build any sets of any kind.

Now, that was the main body of the picture—totally designed for a special visual effect by myself, square inch by square inch. What to do? I was living here, at the Hôtel Meurisse—it was late at night—wandering around in the sitting room, trying to figure out how to shoot without sets, *this* story in particular. And the moon is a very important thing for me, and I looked out of the window and saw *two* full moons. And then realized that they were the two clock faces of the Gare d'Orsay glowing in the night, and it was really a sign. I went down at four in the morning and got in a taxi and went to the Gare d'Orsay and went in. And from four in the morning until dawn, I wandered around the deserted old railway station and found everything I needed for the picture.

Shortly before completing The Trial, *Orson elaborated on this discovery when he was interviewed by Huw Wheldon on the BBC-TV show* Monitor:

> I discovered the world of Kafka: the offices of the Advocate, the law court offices, the corridors—a kind of Jules Verne modernism, which seems to me quite in the taste of Kafka. . . . The thing that gave it a particular force is that it's not only a very large place to work in, and a very beautiful place to photograph, but that it's full of sorrow—the kind of sorrow that accumulates in a railway station where people wait. . . . I know this sounds terribly mystical, but really a railway station is a haunted place. And the story is all about people waiting, waiting, waiting for their papers to be filled. It is full of the hopelessness of the struggle against bureaucracy. Waiting for a paper to be filled is like waiting for a train, and it's also a place [of] refugees. People were sent to Nazi prisons from there. Algerians were gathered there. . . .

OW: We left that morning for Zagreb and I said, "It's all right, when we come back we'll shoot without sets—I've got everything." That's how it happened. And we shot there for seven weeks.
PB: All because of—
OW: Yes, the two moons. And some terrible bastard I told that to —I think he was from *Réalités*—did a long, quite good piece but said this is a lie because he'd seen photos of the Gare d'Orsay which were made long before the picture started and which Welles had studied. And the *fact* is that for the exterior of the Palace of Justice in the story—where K comes out and is picked up by his little niece and walks home—we *had* pictures of the façade of the Gare d'Orsay along with about thirty other big old-fashioned buildings in Paris. And I decided against it and, in fact, shot that scene in front of the Ministry of the Navy in Rome. Just a case of somebody saying, "Ah, it's a good story—but here's the truth." And the truth was that I *had* heard of the Gare d'Orsay and seen its pictures only in terms of a façade for the exterior of a big pompous building. But it was really one of those moments like the Turkish bath in *Othello*. In one case no costumes; in the other, no sets.
PB: You're very good at getting out of situations like that. I wonder why you couldn't pull off some larceny and get more money for films.

OW: It's larceny that I'm not very good at. I'm an escape artist!
PB: You didn't have any trouble getting permission to shoot in the Gare d'Orsay?
OW: No. Nothing's terribly easy here in France, but nothing's impossible. It's not owned by the government—it was owned by a little old lady then—and one or two ghost trains came into it. [*In the 1980s, the Gare d'Orsay became the Musée d'Orsay, the newest French art museum.*]
PB: Why do you say nothing's easy here?
OW: I mean, it's not easy to work in Paris, as it is in Rome, for instance, or Madrid, or Zagreb, which is heaven. You didn't even need special police permission for the streets. You just go out and ask people to move aside. Nobody says, "Who says you can shoot here?" The whole town is like a back lot. You say, "Get out of the way, please, we're shooting," and that's all there is to it. Can't find a policeman—don't need one. The only place where we bogged down completely was in a cathedral, because we had to have K go in the front door of the cathedral and the Archbishop wouldn't allow it. And to the good party-member officials of the studio, I said, "Get us in—he just has to walk in." And they said, "We couldn't interfere with the Archbishop."
PB: In a communist country—
OW: Yes. Finally, I waltzed him around a little and persuaded him that it was all right. Of course, the *interior* was the Gare d'Orsay again.
PB: Is that why the cathedral pillars are covered with rivets?
OW: Yes, of course. But I also built a couple of false ones and put rivets onto them—because I liked them, too. I used a lot of foreground miniatures of those.
PB: Somebody pointed out that you were constantly cutting from one country to another in *The Trial.*
OW: Well, I did it in *Othello*, between Italy and Africa—five different African towns and five different Italian ones. And in *The Trial*, constantly: over-shoulder shots that go from Yugoslavia to France all the time. I think nothing of it—I just leave, saying, "The over-shoulder will be three weeks from now somewhere else."
PB: It doesn't bother you?
OW: I prefer it, because I hate to be held down by what exists. I like to manufacture what I want. Particularly because I'm always in real places. If you get deprived of the sets you design, you at least want to be free with what you've got.

PB: Didn't you design sets for *Chimes at Midnight*?
OW: We only built one set—The Boar's Head, in a garage.
PB: Why a garage?
OW: A hell of a lot more economical than a film studio.
PB: You designed that set yourself, didn't you?
OW: What's worse, I painted it myself, and blowtorched it—the whole damn thing. I never seem to be able to get people to do that work properly. . . . Had to paint by hand everything in Michael Redgrave's antique shop.
PB: In *Arkadin*?
OW: Sure. Night after night—all night long, by myself, when the day's shooting was over. God, the work that went into that.
PB: What about the palace?
OW: The *Chimes* palace? Well, we had a week in a ruined church. After that, all I had was one little piece of wall against the side of the garage. All those interiors were done with one piece of plastered wall and lots of miniature columns in the foreground.
PB: Didn't you design the costumes, too?
OW: Yes, I spent a whole summer doing the most detailed costume sketches. They were all almost *too* carefully done—you know, "suitable for framing." But every last one—there were about a hundred—was stolen. Served me right for making them too pretty.
PB: How much did *Chimes* cost?
OW: A million-one.
PB: Cheap. How did you do it?
OW: Cutting corners—and then cutting the cuts.
PB: For instance?
OW: Well, things like finishing Sir John Gielgud in the major role of Henry IV in just ten days. Then, after he'd gone home, we did all the reverse shots over his back with a Spanish extra standing in for him in a crossover wig. There was one scene in which literally none of the seven principal actors being photographed were who they were supposed to be. Phony Gielguds, false Hotspurs—everybody a stand-in!
PB: Did you therefore have to cut around a lot more than you'd have liked?
OW: I won't say it wouldn't have been nicer to have had a full cast.
PB: Films cost so much that a filmmaker becomes by necessity a businessman, don't you think? Worried about costs and—
OW: And how to promote the bread in the first place. Without a

Beatrice Welles with her father during the shooting of Chimes at Midnight.

studio behind you, or a promoter for a partner, you've got to do all the hustling yourself.
PB: I understand that you had offers of backing for *Chimes* in color, but you only wanted to do it in black-and-white. Why, specifically?
OW: Well, it was primarily an actors' film, and color, you know, is a great friend in need to the cameraman but it's an enemy of the actor. Faces in color tend to look like meat—veal, beef, baloney—
PB: And makeup doesn't help.
OW: Makes it worse. Only hope is no makeup.
PB: You've done your color films so far without makeup.
OW: Oh, I wore one of those noses of mine in *Immortal Story*.
PB: I liked that performance a lot.
OW: It sure in hell wasn't *great*. I think every really great performance that's ever happened in movies—up to now, anyway—has been in black-and-white. But, then, you know my feeling about the importance of actors. They're the ones who finally count. Much more than people think.

PB: I'll give you that, but perhaps the great performances have been done in black-and-white because most of the great actors flourished in the black-and-white era.
OW: That's one *you* can have—good point.
PB: How did you get that very contrasty, sharp black-and-white in the forest scenes?
OW: Red filter. Every foot of film was shot through red filters—including the interiors. And we used only arcs. Not a single incandescent light in the whole picture.
PB: It gives almost the quality of a woodcut.
OW: "Almost" is the word. I wanted more *real* black, *real* white—
PB: Speaking of *The Immortal Story*, weren't you originally going to do several Isak Dinesen stories in one movie?
OW: Yes. One was called "A Country Tale"—a tremendous story, shattering. It's about aristocratic obligation, particularly the landowner's obligation to the land, and the peasant's feeling about the land. And it's the story of a changeling. Peter O'Toole was going to play in it.
PB: And that was to have been the companion piece to *The Immortal Story?*
OW: There were three companion pieces of hers besides. We actually shot for one day in Budapest, and then the English backer backed out on us and then we had to scurry out of town. *The Immortal Story* was supposed to have been called *The Guinea Piece*, and everybody agreed it was a better title, and then they released it as *The Immortal Story*. I don't know why.
PB: You love Dinesen's work?
OW: Who doesn't? I saw Hemingway after he got the Nobel Prize, which Ordoñez, the bullfighter, used to call "the Swedish Prize." I don't know why that always struck me as a funny name for it. Well, when Ernest got the Swedish Prize—not in his official speech, but to the press when he arrived—he said, "You shouldn't have given it to me—you should have given it to Isak Dinesen. . . ." There he was in Scandinavia, so it was very nice for her. I didn't know *how* nice until I mentioned it to him one day in Paris. He flew into a rage. It seems he hated her. The old Baron Blixen—her husband—was Hemingway's great pal out of Africa, and she'd left him for another man. Finch-Hatton, wasn't it? The white hunter.
PB: Did you ever meet her?
OW: No, I never even saw a picture of her until just lately. But I

Welles in The Immortal Story.

once flew to Denmark to visit her. People told me how to find her in that place she lived in on the road to Elsinore, but I just stayed in the hotel in Copenhagen for three days and left.

PB: Why?

OW: I'm not sure. But I went back and started to write her a letter—a love letter—a very long one. I worked on it for years. I was still working on it when she died.

PB: Someone commented that the idea of *Immortal Story* relates to the whole notion of a director making things actually happen. Is there anything to that? Do you think that's part of what interested you?

OW: No.

PB: Because a director basically does what Charlie Clay tries to do in the movie.

OW: "Charlie Clay"—the name's *Charles*. Certainly no one ever called him "Charlie" in his life; it was "Mr. Clay." No—he was trying to be God, not a director.
PB: Isn't a director trying to be God in a sense—?
OW: No, I think that's straining a point. He was really trying to make something happen—literally happen in *life*. I don't see any connection. That certainly didn't interest me—just the story line. And I had two other scripts of her stories; I wanted to do more. I only did that one because we would get the money from French TV if Jeanne Moreau was in it and there was no part for her in the other two Isak Dinesen scripts I'd written. It was just one of the three best movie stories, but it doesn't hold any particular obsessive interest for me as a story beyond its own quality.
PB: But you were interested in the idea of power. . . .
OW: No. He doesn't have the power—you show that it's meaningless.
PB: He fails—
OW: It doesn't even begin to work—it's a dream. That's the whole point of the story. He has no power: not that he does have it, but that he pretends that he does. It all turns to ashes.
PB: Why does he die?

Jeanne Moreau and Norman Eshley in The Immortal Story.

OW: He's getting ready to die when the story begins. And he dies when the thing can't work. He dies of disappointment. In his last gasp of frustrated lust—dusty lust department.

PB: When you're cutting a picture, do you sit with the cutter for—
OW: *I* cut it.
PB: Physically?
OW: Yes, and when I don't I mark the film so that my instructions are there on the precise frame. Nowadays I just can't do it any other way. It's the decisive thing that keeps me from working in England, where the union forbids you to lay a hand on your own film. And in America there are those terrible moviolas—like *What the Butler Saw* and a noise like a coffee grinder. Yes, I have to do it myself.
PB: Because of the question of diplomacy that enters into it?
OW: Diplomacy about cutting?
PB: Dealing with the cutter's ideas.
OW: Well, you can't be diplomatic about that. It's your own work, not his. If there's something another fellow can or should add to your picture after you've made it, then it doesn't seem to me that you're really in command of your own work.
PB: You got in the habit of doing it yourself in Europe, I suppose. Because of the difference in moviolas?
OW: Yes. In the Italian and German table models, film doesn't go through sprockets, so it's absolutely silent. I don't bother anymore with projection rooms. I go from shooting right onto the moviola.
PB: German or Italian . . .
OW: Yes, but never French. They have something which combines the worst qualities of every system. On a French moviola it's virtually impossible to stop accurately within fifteen frames—which may well account for much of that freshness of style in the Nouvelle Vague.
PB: Bad moviolas!
OW: I've put in incredible hours. The battle scene in *Chimes at Midnight*, for example: ten days to shoot, six weeks to cut, for six minutes of playing time. That's an extreme example, of course.
PB: Do you enjoy cutting?
OW: It's like writing—it's lonely. You need a huge capacity for common drudgery, total drudgery—ten hours a day, every day, month after month.

PB: It's instinct when you're cutting, isn't it? Deciding on the exact frame.
OW: A sense of rhythm—that's what it's all about. The true shape of a film is musical.
PB: And you can't teach it.
OW: Oh, you can teach it up to a certain point. If I'd ever try to teach filmmaking, I'd hold most of my classes around the moviola.
PB: What's your feeling about dissolves and fades at the end of scenes, now that everyone simply cuts to the next scene?
OW: I used direct cuts right from the start—in the middle of sentences, even—and also very long dissolves. I still don't think there's a rule, or ought to be. It's a shame when anything becomes merely fashionable.
PB: A lot of directors always have a cutter on the set at all times.
OW: Most directors on the big-time, big-budget pictures. And the cutter's always going to say, "Let's get some protection—let's *cover* it." Naturally—to cover *himself.* But if a man can tell a director what is a good cut, then he's either faking or he ought to be a director himself.
PB: Do you think, ideally speaking, that a director should only shoot what he knows he will need?
OW: Peter, I think it's possible for a director to make a fine movie without being interested in cutting, or the camera, and even without being really interested in the actors. First-rate movies get themselves made according to any system you can think of.
PB: Do you print more than one take?
OW: Usually just one.
PB: Then you must be a rather economical director, because—
OW: Well, there's no dogma about it. I'm willing to go to an awful lot of takes for an actor; any number he needs. But I print only one.
PB: And you don't plan out the cuts on paper?
OW: Never. That's too Germanic.
PB: Well, a lot of *American* directors . . .
OW: That Germanic mentality knows no national frontiers.
PB: You never plan.
OW: I make the damnedest, most elaborately detailed plans you ever saw, and then I throw them all away. The plans aren't made in order to be realized, they're made in order to prepare me for improvisation. That way, an awful lot of thinking is behind me, and I'm ready for what the actors have to surprise me with. The

camera has to serve the actors, not the actors the camera. I make up four or five whole movies in my head and never even try to shoot them when I get on the set. They are like exercises. . . . An actor reaches out a hand, the sun is there, a cloud moves, and the whole story is changed.

PB: Yes.

OW: You have to be awfully Germanic to say, "No, we don't change it, because it's in my shooting script, it's like this."

PB: Someone very sympathetic to your films wrote that you shoot like an egomaniac but you cut like a censor. What do you think of that?

OW: Shooting like an egomaniac must mean trying to call attention to your camera, and I hate that. I shoot, I hope, generously, *seeing* what's going on. An egomaniac by definition means somebody who thinks that what *he's* doing is great. I'm interested in what everybody's doing. I'm interested in what's *happening*. . . . That's why I'm not most pleased when people tell me how much they liked that opening crane shot in *Touch of Evil*. I don't want to be remembered for "great shots."

PB: Can I jump back to something you touched on a few minutes ago? Do you think that filmmaking *can* be taught in school?

OW: It seems to work in some countries—Poland and Czechoslovakia, for instance—so there must be something to be said for it. You can provide historical and technical information. But actually teaching somebody to be an artist isn't quite so easy. You can cram a lot of poems into kids, but reaching them through the poetic experience—that calls for such gifts on the part of the teacher that it certainly isn't something we can look for as a regular thing.

PB: You don't like theorizing.

OW: For those who enjoy theory, it's fine. Those serious minds who *need* theory—why not give it to them? But let's keep focused on what really matters—on the thing itself. Let's try to get into it, not walk around it with calipers and quiz glasses. You know what I mean: this filmmaker has returned constantly to the water closet; this seems to be a recurring leitmotif.

PB: Well, it *is* interesting to find recurrent themes.

OW: If you'd look at all my trunks full of unproduced film scripts, you'd find every kind of theme. All this scrambling after themes for textbook chapter headings—there's no use wasting time on that. . . .

I have a theory that the *success* of a movie always depends on one man—but he may very well be the cutter or the actor or the writer instead of the director.

PB: I agree with you—there are many examples of that—but not generally speaking; there are always many exceptions that prove the rule.

OW: That's right. I'm speaking of exceptions, I'll give you that. But I think we're in a blind alley—or at least a minor thoroughfare.

PB: I was just trying to argue about your impatience with the search for themes.

OW: Luckily, we know almost nothing about Shakespeare and very little about Cervantes. And that makes it so much easier to understand their works. The more we know about the men who wrote them, the bigger chance there is for all the Herr Professors in the academic establishment to befuddle and bemuse.

PB: In other words, everything's in the work itself, and all we need to know about the artist is what he has to say for himself?

OW: It's an egocentric, romantic, nineteenth-century conception that the artist is more interesting and more important than his art.

PB: Somebody once said, "There are no works, there are only artists."

OW: This emphasis on the artist himself—this glorification of the artist—is one of the bad turnings civilization has taken in the last two hundred years. In other words, the whole purpose of a book like this is what I quarrel with.

PB: Well, on my part I think it's a reaction to the common idea that an industry, a studio, an entire team always makes a movie.

OW: I think you're worrying a different bone. Why *not* talk about a team? Who cares if somebody discovers a grip or a propman who says I didn't make *Citizen Kane?* Maybe it's true—what of it? Maybe Houseman wrote it and the grip directed it. What does that matter? What matters is the film.

PB: But surely it's like trying to ascertain, when you find a lost work, who wrote it.

OW: You have a good point, but it's another subject. . . . To get back to this business of teaching filmmaking, I think that people should be taught just about everything *except* movies. Doctors have to learn an awful lot of things considered part, not only of the discipline, but of the culture which has been built up around the subject of the practice of medicine. And if that's true about something as pragmatic and untheoretical as doctoring, how much more true is it about the teaching of art? What the student movie director should be taught is as much of our whole culture as we are capable of synthesizing. Synthesizing, not specializing. To make a film for today's world, we should strive to comprehend as much as possible of the human accomplishment in these last twenty thousand years. We understand something at least of what it was to live under the pharaohs, of what made Elizabethan England great, how the Industrial Revolution happened, and why and what Puritanism and the Roman church has meant to Western civilization. I'm just reaching wildly around for things that should be taught—instead of seminars on Howard Hawks or Orson Welles or anybody else. Because anybody that's any good is going to get right on to Hawks or me or anybody else after he sees some of our movies. Who cares how Hawks felt about his mother, or what he said in a newspaper interview in 1927? There just isn't time for all that.

PB: You're not just talking about teaching the appreciation of films, but in fact teaching the making of movies.

OW: Well, I don't know how you teach the appreciation. A great teacher can certainly help you to experience, if his enthusiasm is contagious. My own point is that teachers should not be just purveyors of information or masters of chapter headings. I saw a television documentary three weeks ago in England, made by Bronowski, in which he talked for two hours about da Vinci. My interest in da Vinci had flagged and dimmed over a period of a quarter of a century to the point where there was very little left indeed. And after two hours' exposure to this man, I went rushing back for a fresh look at da Vinci. That's teaching!

PB: What would you say to someone who asked you what to teach a group of people who wanted to be movie directors?

OW: Hold a mirror up to nature—that's Shakespeare's message to the actor. How much more does that apply, and how much more is it true, to the creator of a film? If you don't know something about the nature to which you're holding up your mirror, how limited your work must be! The more film people pay homage to each other, and to films rather than to life, the more they are approximating the last scene of *The Lady from Shanghai*—a series of mirrors reflecting each other. A movie is a reflection of the entire culture of the man who makes it—his education, human knowledge, his breadth of understanding—all this is what informs a picture.

PB: A director creates his own world, then. . . .

OW: Sure, and the degree to which that can be done depends on what he has of himself by way of raw materials. The movie director must always remain a slightly ambiguous figure, after all, because so much of what he signs his name to came from elsewhere, so many of his best things are merely accidents over which he presides. Or the good fortune he receives. Or the grace.

PB: And the mechanics of making a film—

OW: —can be taught over the weekend to any intelligent person.

PB: Just as Toland taught you the mechanics of the camera.

OW: Yes. The rest of it is what you have to bring to the machinery.

PB: What you are . . .

OW: The *angle* at which you hold that mirror. What's finally interesting is not the romantic tilt or spastic quirk at which you hold it—but what the mirror has to show back to you.

PB: The subject, not the technique.

OW: Oh, I'm not attacking technique. . . .

PB: Isn't that what you meant by the angle of the mirror?

OW: Which is determined by moral, aesthetic, and ideological orientation. We know to what an extraordinary extent everything depends upon that angle. A mirror is just what it is.

PB: Your Mercury production of *Five Kings* [1939] was an early version of *Chimes*, wasn't it? Using the same Shakespeare plays, I mean.

OW: *Five Kings* was going to be in two evenings. We did only one, using *Richard II*, *Henry IV*, *Parts I* and *II*, and *Henry* V. The second night would have included *Henry VI*, *Parts I*, *II*, and *III*, and *Richard III*. The whole sweep of the English history plays. Peter Hall did much the same thing years later at Stratford, but without the condensations.

PB: And you played Falstaff.

OW: Twice in the theatre. In Dublin not long ago [1960]—a sort of tryout for the movie. Same title, even.

PB: Didn't you also take some scenes from *The Merry Wives of Windsor?*

OW: Not scenes. Just some dialogue of Falstaff's.

Welles in partial makeup for the role of Falstaff in Five Kings, *1939.*

PB: And you used Holinshed's writings for narration in *Five Kings*, as you did in *Chimes at Midnight?*
OW: Right.
PB: By the way, who was that actor who can't speak?
OW: Walter Chiari.
PB: I don't think the character is written that way in Shakespeare. . . .
OW: No, but he's called Silence, and that seemed a good cue to

make him practically incapable of speech by reason of a horrible stutter.

PB: You made him funny-looking by using a wide-angle lens, didn't you?

OW: Made him up, too: fake nose, cotton under his cheeks. Actually, he's a good-looking ex–football player—a superb low comedian and a great star of the Italian *rivista*.

PB: I was struck again in *Chimes at Midnight* by its remarkable economy of expression; it's a very moving film, but all the emotional scenes are held very firmly in check. You're often accused of being—

OW: Oh yes: "eloquent and all of that, but a complete lack of measure and balance . . ."

PB: You play your last scene with Hal with almost Spartan restraint.

OW: How else? That's such a tremendous moment in Shakespeare. It has to be treasured; it's too delicate for actors to get rough with. The whole movie, of course, is a preparation for that scene.

PB: There are many other scenes in the movie that anticipate that moment.

OW: Oh, sure . . .

PB: Though they are almost all played for comedy.

OW: Lots of people think we didn't play for comedy enough. But, you know, the closer I thought I was getting to Falstaff, the less funny he seemed to me. When I'd played him before, in the theatre, he seemed more witty than comical. And in bringing him to the screen, I found him only occasionally, and then only *deliberately*, a clown. That last, great scene was the very center of our film, and all the "comedy" had to be played in that perspective.

> *Orson, speaking about passport regulations, on the May 7, 1955, episode of the BBC-TV series* Orson Welles' Sketch Book:
>
> A free citizen is always more of a nuisance to the policeman than the criminal—he [the policeman] knows what to do with the criminal. . . .
>
> The regulations do pile up, forms keep coming in. We keep being asked to state our grandmother's father's name in block

letters and to say whether we propose to overthrow the government in triplicate, why, and all that sort of thing. But, you see, the bureaucrat—I'm including the bureaucrat with the police as part of one great, big, monstrous thing—the bureaucrat is really like a blackmailer. You can never pay him off; the more you give him, the more he'll demand. If you fill in one form, he'll give you ten.

PB: Did you like the novel *The Trial?*
OW: Yes, I like Kafka very much.
PB: You evidently rearrranged the order of the chapters.
OW: I don't remember—I'm sure I did. I don't suppose there's any novelist except Conrad who can be put directly on the screen.
PB: Eisenstein said he thought Dickens could be done that way, too—he did a long article proving that.
OW: Maybe.
PB: A lot of Dickens' scenes read like a shooting script. Eisenstein took a page and broke it into cuts.
OW: Yes, just as you can put them right on the stage, too. Oh, there are some more besides Dickens and Conrad, but very few. Though, you see, Dickens was an actor—and he was not a writer who acted, he was an actor who wrote. I believe it was his real vocation.
PB: And that's why he wrote all those great parts for actors. . . . Are you an actor who writes?
OW: Yes, of course, when I write and when I direct. I think there is part of the acting process which expresses itself in writing. Because everybody is an actor.
PB: You think so?
OW: Everybody in the world is an actor. Conversation is acting. Man as a social animal is an actor; everything we do is some sort of a performance. But the actor whose profession it is to act is then something else again. As I think I've told you, in my view he's a member of the third sex. I'm not making a joke—I think there are men, women, and actors. Actors are a different race in spite of the fact that everybody's an actor. I think, once they become an actor, they then become something different—which is not a difference in race but a difference in sex. They're generically distinct. Too bad that Mrs. Sartre [Simone de Beauvoir] has already used the title; it'd be a great one for a movie about actors, *The Third Sex*. But certainly all the great dramatists have been actors of

one sort or another. And all great directors and author-directors are actors.
PB: Even if they've stopped acting.
OW: That's right. Or never actually did it much—but they are essentially actors. A totally nonacting director is simply a producer with the word "director" written on the back of his chair.
PB: Do you think it's impossible for a movie to be good if the acting isn't?
OW: Yes—that's all that really counts after the story. I cannot buy a story that's badly acted or consider that a director's made a good picture if somebody says parenthetically it was badly acted. It seems to me that ends the conversation. The director hasn't made a picture if it's badly acted.
PB: I don't believe that's necessarily so.
OW: Well, we're totally at odds on that.
PB: If I were to make a picture that was badly acted, I would feel I'd failed, but I can appreciate some other pictures that are not very well acted.
OW: I don't understand what a picture is if there is bad acting. I don't understand how movies exist independently of the actor—I truly don't. I deny that such a thing exists. Otherwise, it's just an exercise in directorial virtuosity, and who cares about that except another movie director? As I've said, the director is the most overrated job in the world.
PB: Only *you* could say that. Though in most cases you're right.
OW: And in the exceptional cases, it's still overrated [*laughs*]. Next.
PB: *You've* been acting in more films lately than ever.
OW: Smaller parts and more movies. Wait till you see the one from Romania—it's right up there with *David and Goliath*!
PB: What's the name of that one?
OW: I don't know—*Erasmus and the Forty Krauts*! A great, huge, cut-rate German spectacle. I play Justinian, and have very little to add to what is going on.
PB: Who directed?
OW: Robert Siodmak.
PB: He used to be good.
OW: You can't blame him for this one. We were all of us bogged down there in Bucharest in the midst of an almost indecipherable plot. As it happens, the period is one in which I'm something of an expert—it being an old dream of mine to make a film about

Justinian and Theodora. But they had characters in this one—leading characters—I never heard of. All based, we were told, on heavy German research.
PB: Did you direct anything in *David and Goliath*?
OW: Guilty. It wasn't just a question of rewriting. The whole situation was so chaotic that I said I'd play the part if I could direct my own sequence in it—just to make sure that it began and ended, you know, *some* way. I hoped nobody'd ever blow the whistle on that one.
PB: Very noticeable because the—
OW: You mean you've seen it? My God! I didn't think a print ever got to America.
PB: I could tell that you'd directed one scene, because there's this moving shot around the pillar as you come by as Herod—
OW: Saul!
PB: Saul—or whoever it was.
OW: Shows how forgettable the whole thing was. . . .
PB: When some people go to see many of the films in which you're just an actor, the feeling persists that you did, in fact, have something to do with the direction.
OW: In that case, I inherited this terrible papier-mâché set, a lot of sleepy extras in bad costumes, and a few feeble torches, and away we went.
PB: Is there anything we can say about *Ferry to Hong Kong*? I haven't seen it yet.
OW: Well, it was the only time I ever had a difficult time with a fellow actor.
PB: Curt Jurgens?
OW: I was most inclined to like him very much and everything. But I didn't want to do the picture. I said I would only do it if we could change it and make it into a comedy. The plot is that a man, Jurgens, gets on the ferry from Hong Kong to Macao, and can't get off, because the governments at both ports won't let him. It really happened in life; a man got stuck on a ferry. I don't see *how* you can take that seriously.
PB: Yeah, it's pretty funny.
OW: I was the captain of the ferry, and I'm stuck with this fellow through the years, riding back and forth. Seems to me a very good comedy situation.
PB: But they tried to make it a drama?
OW: Yes, adventure drama, written in a rather straightforward

dramatic way. So there's a lot to be said for Jurgens' point of view —he wanted to do it as an adventure story with the big storm at sea and his befriending the children and all that, expecting me to just be the bad man who's unhappy about his being on the boat. And I was doing it as a farce and sending him up all the time, see?
PB: Yeah.
OW: And humor is not Curt's strongest point. He was very unhappy. But the picture, I believe, was an outstanding failure, and Lewis Gilbert, the director, said to me years later, "I learned something from that picture—and I'll never again make another failure." And I didn't have the courage to ask him what it was he'd learned, because I'd like to know.
PB: Why?
OW: Because since then he's never made a picture that hasn't grossed millions! But I had a marvelous time—it was wonderful being back in China again.
PB: All shot on location—
OW: In Hong Kong, yes. Everybody was nice, Sylvia Syms became a great friend—she's an adorable girl—but, like many pictures that are tremendous fun to make, it didn't work out well.
PB: I've seen photos of you in it. You had a funny sort of clown nose.
OW: It was a low-low-comedy character.
PB: And you played it that way?
OW: Yes, as a low-comedy character. And there was Curt Jurgens playing it dead straight, you see. So *that* only made it funnier—his playing it that way. And it only made Curt angrier that it went on like that. So, through the years, he's snarled at me as the "little genius." And then we found ourselves with a long scene to play up in the mountains of Yugoslavia in *The Battle of Neretva*.
PB: Yes, and what happened?
OW: Well, studiously polite on both sides, and we got through it all right. I only did *Neretva* so I could make *The Deep* in Yugoslavia. They gave me their services in exchange for mine. Jurgens has finally forgiven me. It took him a long time. I was never cross with him, he was just cross with me.
PB: Where was Lewis Gilbert? Just caught in the middle?
OW: He was on my side, and he expected that I was going to make a great hit in it and thought his picture was home because the crew used to fall about on the set, screaming with laughter at me. And the film opened and apparently the audience never

cracked a smile from beginning to end. It was one of those things that broke up everybody on the set and that's the last laughter ever heard.

PB: Well, perhaps nobody told people it was supposed to be a comedy. Audiences take things very seriously when they think it's supposed to be serious.

OW: No, perhaps I tried too hard. I don't know—seemed pretty funny. But there never was a good word said for it by anybody, friends or foes; it must be very poor. And we really thought we were making quite a funny, funny picture. It may just be that, by Jurgens' continuing to come on as an aging romantic fellow (and he was pretty long in the tooth to be trying to be the juvenile), and my playing it low comedy—that these two styles canceled each other out. Because the whole picture was between us; it wasn't just that we occasionally met. In fact, I haven't really played a full-length part since then. It washed me up for everything except cameos!

PB: Except in your own pictures.

OW: Yeah, where I'm running the store. But it really was a mess, because the company took sides against Jurgens. And I felt a funny kind of sympathy for him and still do, which has never been returned. And I understand why not. I am completely sympathetic with his indignation. Nothing to be done. I couldn't really come and play a serious heavy-man who's the captain of the ferryboat going back and forth—a four-hour trip—stuck with a passenger. It can't be anything except a farce situation.

PB: Do you remember a picture called *The Tartars*?

OW: With Victor Mature. That made a lot of money—it got back its cost in New York alone.

PB: That's another of yours I missed.

OW: Well, it's a very interesting picture for one reason: Victor Mature and I had an extended sword fight, on which I worked day after day. And in no shots—full, long, medium—at any moment is Victor Mature *ever* involved! Not even to hold the sword and look menacing.

PB: Really?

OW: Yeah. He said, "Oh, I don't want to do any of that stuff."

It was a perfectly legible drive-in kind of movie, directed by Richard Thorpe. Victor Mature had been told—incorrectly—by the costume department that I had built up my shoes by two inches to make myself look taller. So he went and got *his* sandals built three inches high and he could hardly walk. Very funny sandals, too—you look like a brassiered carioca girl in a carnival. And he could barely get across the stage in those things—just so he would be taller than I was, you see, neglecting to look at the script and see that in all our scenes I am sitting on the throne! His whole exercise in who was going to be the highest was a terrible waste of time. And when he came to have the sword fight, his double was *definitely* shorter than I was. . . .

PB: You went to Africa to do *The Southern Star*?

OW: Yes, to Senegal, to play a part written as a terrifying heavy. I did it as a comic gay Cockney.

PB: Funny?

OW: Not too bad, maybe. But nobody noticed it. The picture bombed.

PB: How was *Oedipus the King*? I haven't caught that yet, either.

OW: How do I know? I was only on it one day. Had that one speech—you know what those Greek tragedies are like. It was rather an odd idea, it seemed to me, to film *Oedipus* in a ruined Greek theatre, but costumed in the period in which the story is supposed to have originally happened. Bewildering.

PB: What about those two films you made with Sacha Guitry?

OW: Dear God in heaven, they were lousy; but Sacha was superb. A truly great type, you know—from another, happier, hammier world, and hugely endowed for success in it.

PB: One of the pictures was *Napoleon*. . . . You played Napoleon?

OW: Just his jailer. In another [*Royal Affairs in Versailles*, 1953] I was Benjamin Franklin—a part for which no actor in the world is less suited.

PB: Why?

OW: In that particular wig, it's impossible for me to look like anything except, you know, a dirty old man. And I've played Franklin twice!

PB: In *Lafayette* [1961].

OW: I don't know in which I was worse. Both times I looked exactly like Werner Krauss in *The Cabinet of Doctor Caligari*. But the Guitry pictures were fun to be in because of Sacha.

PB: I haven't seen any of his films.

OW: Well, you should. If you love him, as I do, you enjoy his showing off. We had long dinners during his last years when he tried to dream something up for us to do together. I couldn't imagine anything that would work. That wasn't because I didn't admire him—I just didn't think we were going to be the biggest team since Abbott and Costello.

PB: You mentioned another Napoleon movie before—*Austerlitz.*

OW: Yes. In that one I invented the steamboat.

PB: How was it?

OW: Well, it was nice to be with old Abel Gance. He invented an awful lot of things in movies that are coming back in style now. . . . They call me in for all the Napoleon movies, though. *Waterloo* is the latest—the big one by Bondarchuk.

PB: Do you remember an Italian epic called *L'Uomo, la Bestia e la Virtù?*

OW: Pirandello. I was "the beast," and "the man" was a comic called Toto, who claimed to be the direct descendant of someone like Charlemagne and was always addressed as "Your Highness" because he also claimed to be a prince. Maybe he was. It was very funny: "Ready for the next scene, Your Highness," they'd say, and he'd step into the shot and get a custard pie in his face. Viviane Romance was "the lady." She spent all of her time trying to hide me from the lens with great, long handkerchiefs. A real old-fashioned movie diva—the kind I'd never been near. I don't know how to describe the picture; it was so odd.

PB: Who was the director?

OW: A fellow called Steno. He worked with some writer—they were a team. But Viviane Romance's husband, who was an Egyptian, wrote her dialogue, which bore no relationship to Pirandello, Prince Toto, me, or anything else. And she spoke it in French. The prince and I spoke in Italian, and none of the dialogue made any sense at all. Complete non sequiturs.

PB: People do think you sometimes make fun of these awful films you're in.

OW: They're wrong; I've never done that. I really do try—no matter how ashamed I am.

PB: You finally did *Treasure Island* [1972].

OW: As an actor, yes—and they used my script. But I almost made it myself twice. I wrote a script, had a contract signed with 20th Century–Fox, and then the Disney people, who had an old and rather shop-soiled version of their own, plus a dreary TV series, frightened them into not letting me go through with it. Another time it was supposed to have been made by the backers of *Chimes at Midnight.*

PB: You were going to direct it?
OW: And play Long John Silver, sure. Finally I just got to play the part. We had a good script. It was loyal to Stevenson; my own contribution was to keep it clear about just where the people were on the island, which Stevenson didn't always bother about. You don't notice it when you're reading, just when you're making a film script. It happens all the time in adventure stories—the narrative carries you along, cloudy geography doesn't show up on the printed page.
PB: You like Stevenson?
OW: Oh yes, and *Treasure Island* would make a beautiful film. [Roman] Polanski told me he'd like to do it, too.
PB: You did it on the radio.
OW: Lots of juicy stuff for the actors—not interesting for you but for those who really love acting. . . .
PB: Come on, I like acting.
OW: You mustn't just *like* acting, Peter—you've got to *love* it. At least if you want to do *Treasure Island*.
PB: In *The VIPs*, I thought you seemed to be playing somebody you knew.
OW: My claim that I've never seen a picture I've been in breaks down there, because I saw *The VIPs* (couldn't help myself—they ran it in a plane). And I didn't recognize myself as anybody.
PB: I thought maybe it was a combination of people like Korda and Ratoff and Pascal.
OW: Well, in a way. Not Korda—he was much more stylish—but it had a little Gaby Pascal in it, certainly, because I used a Hungarian accent. Gaby, you know, was a wild, intense, dramatic kind of Hungarian—not *cheerful* like the character I played.
PB: What kind of director was Anthony Asquith?
OW: One of the nicest, most intelligent people who was ever in films. His nickname was Puffin. You couldn't judge him on *The VIPs*: the picture was made by the Burtons and written for them by Terry Rattigan—an old-fashioned Metro potboiler, sort of junior *Grand Hotel*. Rod Taylor and Maggie Smith were wonderful in it. And, of course, Margaret Rutherford. We were all very fond of Puffin; I'd known him for years, and was very happy to be with him—though he wasn't in real control of that picture. How could he have been? And, my God, he was polite. I saw him, all alone on the stage once, trip over an electric cable, turn around, and say "I beg your pardon" to it.

PB: How about *Rogopag*?
OW: Can't believe that. I was never in a picture with a name like that.
PB: In one episode directed by Pasolini. You played a movie director.
OW: Oh yes . . . Censored, in Italy at least, after one single screening in Venice.
PB: I didn't think it was very good.
OW: No? Why?
PB: It was sort of obscure and arty—
OW [*laughs*]: "Obscure and arty." Simply because it didn't happen on the banks of the Mississippi, it's obscure and arty. . . . You mustn't be asked about anything that isn't, you know, *Judge Shit on the Range* or something—
PB [*laughing*]: Well, among other things wrong with it, they dubbed you into Italian.
OW: I *played* it in Italian! The exhibitors must have thought the Italian public couldn't stand my accent. They have a terrible snobbism about accents in Italy. So much so that lots of their leading actors—the girls especially—have never been heard in Italy speaking their own language in their own voices; they're dubbed by radio actors.
PB: I didn't know that.
OW: Yes. If your accent is vaguely of the north, let's say, then everybody in the south hoots with laughter. So of course my own little touch of Kenosha would have been fatal. I read a poem in that one, and Pasolini told everybody that he'd never heard an Italian actor read Italian poetry with such simplicity and directness. He tried to get me to play a pig a couple of years ago when I was in Vienna.
PB [*laughing*]: Really a pig?
OW: A *German* pig. Something *really* obscene.
PB: You like Pasolini?
OW: Terribly bright and gifted. Crazy mixed-up kid, maybe—but on a very superior level. I mean Pasolini the poet, spoiled Christian, and Marxist ideologue. There's nothing mixed up about hin on a movie set. Real authority and a wonderfully free way with the machinery.
PB: Do you remember *Marco the Magnificent*?
OW: Belgrade in the deep winter of—what was it?
PB [*consulting notes*]: 'Sixty-four.

OW: A great year. The producer was the man who inspired *Catch-22*, Raoul Lévy.
PB: Oh?
OW: According to Raoul Lévy, yes, he was the original Yossarian. Fascinating type—you had to like him.
PB: Didn't he commit suicide?
OW: Well, he threatened to in front of Norm Geves' house and the gun went off. The Marco Polo film was a sort of suicide, too. He made that picture twice: The first time, with Alain Delon, he went broke and almost shut down the Yugoslavian film industry in the process. Then he got some more money together and made it all over again with Horst Buchholz. In both versions he had no script at all. Most of us just made it up as we went along. I did write a long scene for Omar Sharif, though. He was standing around looking gloomy because he'd been forced to be in that thing by Spiegel, to work out his contract from *Lawrence of Arabia*. So I borrowed a typewriter and did what little I could. Tony Quinn came to town with his own private writer. He played Kubla Khan, who, it turned out in Tony's authoritative version, was kindly, brave, benevolent, good, handsome, and irresistible to women. There was no grace or virtue which was not written into that character. And then he played it like Charlie Chan.
PB: Who directed your sequence in *Casino Royale*?
OW: Joe McGrath—until he was fired. He was taken off at four in the afternoon, and two minutes later, from another door, came Bob Parrish. Bob is an old friend and McGrath isn't, but I had no part in that ugly little moment.
PB: That was Charles Feldman producing?
OW: That was Feldman running scared. How that picture was a success, I can't imagine.
PB: Neither can I. . . . What about *A Man for All Seasons?*
OW: That came right after the *Casino Royale* caper, so you can imagine how grateful I was to be associated with something decent. I enjoyed acting with Scofield. It was a wonderful day—that's all it took.
PB: You've done the narration for several documentaries—
OW: Yes, and I never saw the movies. That's always been a condition of mine in narrating a film—that I don't have to see any footage. Otherwise, I won't accept the job.
PB: How do they time it?
OW: I say, "What's the timing?," and I'm a radio actor and I do it

in the time. But spare me the projection. . . . I had to see *Masters of the Congo Jungle* when the ex-King of Belgium did, because he showed it to me himself and there was no way I could say I wouldn't to His Royal Highness. That's the only one I ever saw.
PB: At one point it was announced that you were going to direct *The Bible* for Dino De Laurentiis, though it always seemed a little unlikely.
OW: Well, at first it was going to be Fellini and Bresson and myself—all three of us. Then, for a moment, Dino tried to persuade me to do the whole picture. Well, I couldn't imagine doing the Garden of Eden, just for a start. And, really, I didn't want to be responsible for the whole picture. So I got some kind of golden handshake for the script I'd done for the Abraham and Jacob sequences, and that was that. Bresson and Fellini weren't so lucky—they're still suing him, I think.
PB: Did you actually work with Bresson or Fellini preparing the picture?
OW: Well, we were *photographed* together. Repeatedly.

> Before the Law there stands a guard. A man comes from the country, begging admittance to the Law. But the guard cannot admit him. Can he hope to enter at a later time? "That is possible," says the guard. . . .

PB: The fable that opens *The Trial*—
OW: —is from Kafka, but it doesn't open the novel; it's told toward the end, by the priest in church. It's his sermon. [*Orson's translation of the story is a far more dramatic and graceful rendering than the published English version.*]
PB: Weren't you going to play the priest in the movie?
OW: I shot it, but when we couldn't find an actor for the Advocate's part, I cut those sequences in which I play the priest and started again. I really didn't want to be in *The Trial*. The only reason I did was because we couldn't find an actor for the part—everyone we asked refused. I wanted Jackie Gleason, but he wouldn't fly.
PB: I had no idea you wanted a comic for the part.
OW: No. I wanted Gleason being a legitimate actor—I think he's a marvelous actor. I don't much like him as a comic, but he's a superb serious actor, and I think he would have been marvelous

Anthony Perkins and Welles in The Trial.

in it. I didn't want to be in it, and the priest was nothing—a day's work—and the fable at the start would have made more sense if I'd been the priest.

PB: What about the illustrations you used for the fable-prologue?

OW: All those pictures were made by the shadows of pins. Thousands of pins. These two deliriously lunatic, highly civilized, elegant, and charming old Russians—a man and his wife [Alexandre Alexeieff and Claire Parker]—sit and on huge boards they place pins. And the shadow of the pin is what makes the chiaroscuro on the picture. They're two of the nicest and happiest people in the world. I think the pictures are very beautiful.

PB: Yes, they are. How did you come across them?

OW: I can't remember. I think I must have seen a sample of it on TV or somewhere. I think they've spent sixty years or something making a feature picture and have just got past the first three minutes, you know—something like that—which was shown on TV. So I went to see them and persuaded them to stop their major work for a mere matter of five months and stick in pins for me, which they did, and did it beautifully, I thought.

PB: Yes. That was, in fact, one of my favorite parts of the picture.

OW: We should have got them to make the whole movie with pins! Then we wouldn't have had any actors and it would have been your ideal sort of movie—just the kind of thing you and Hitchcock like! Movies without acting [*laughs*].

PB: No, no, it's because I like to hear you tell a story—that's what I meant.

OW: I like to hear anybody tell a story.

PB: Would you say that K dies in the picture because he rejects the Advocate?

OW: He rejects defeat. That's how he dies. Oh, you mean, why he dies. We don't know why they're executing him. It's a murder, but so's an execution, and it has the quality of both—of an assassination and of an execution—as indeed it does in Kafka; that's very true to the book. But not his defiance at the end. That's mine. In the end of the book he lies down there and they kill him. I don't think Kafka could have stood for that after the deaths of the six million Jews. That terrible fact occurred *after* the writing of *The Trial* and I think made Kafka's ending impossible. If you conceive of K as a Jew, as I did. I don't mean as a Jewish Jew, but as a non-Christian. It just made it morally impossible for me to see a man who might even possibly be taken by the audience for a Jew lying down and allowing himself to be killed that way.

PB: And you're really saying that, if Kafka had written the book after the war—

OW: I hope he wouldn't have done that. I think he wouldn't. Maybe the whole execution would have been different, and who knows? Anyway, that's what's behind it. And I don't think my solution was very good. But it was the only one I could find that would end the picture.

PB: Is Israel fighting that past now, too, nationally?

OW: Yes, sure they are. And it's admirable, but makes them rather boring company. All nationalists are terrible bores if you have to talk to them. I'm certainly *for* them in principle, though I wish they hadn't given up the Yiddish culture, because I'm so pro-Yiddish.

PB: You like that.

OW: Adore it. I would love to do Yiddish material. Not *Fiddler* *on the Roof*, but the real stuff. That's my dream—to play a great Yiddish part.

PB: Have there been any great plays?

OW: Not plays, except for Shylock. But there's the great Yiddish literature. The Yiddish theatre, of course, is divine nonsense, but the Yiddish literature is beautiful. The plays were all riotous—I used to go to them night after night. God, I'm a great expert on the Yiddish theatre.

PB: What are some of the plays?

OW: Oh, I've forgotten all of them now—*Moishe Itznik, the Village Idiot* was one. And great tragedies like the Yiddish *King Lear*. It's a retelling of the Lear story in terms of a Polish Jewish town in the last century. And he comes back to the wedding of Cordelia with a lot of beggars who are invited in for the food, and nobody recognizes him—except there's a follow-spot on him! Sitting with all the other beggars—with a nice big spotlight on him.

PB: Where did you see these plays?

OW: In the Yiddish theatre.

PB: In New York?

OW: Everywhere. The Yiddish theatres were everywhere—London, Paris, Rome, Buenos Aires. It was the only international theatre in history. Movies are the second. The first was Yiddish, because there were these great Yiddish-speaking communities all over the world. Maurice Schwartz and Jacob Adler and Max Gabel—people like that—played the world. And, every town they'd come to, there'd be another illegitimate son saying, "How do you do, Father. I haven't been seeing you in two or three years." Be a great movie about the old Yiddish theatre.

PB: Why did you decide to end the picture with the atom-bomb mushroom?

OW: It *isn't* an atom bomb. That's the way the cloud forms after any explosion.

PB: But you held on it a long time.

OW: I didn't have any more film to go to—I really didn't mean that big atom-bomb thing. It was a real mistake, a blooper on my part; it didn't register with me as an atom bomb. It just seemed to me to be all bombs—including the atom bomb—and all explosions and all destruction, and not the atom bomb. That's bad rhetoric, and I was very unhappy to find that that's the way it hit some people, and I would have gone back and changed it if I could have afforded to. Because, if it came off as just the atom bomb, it's a failure and was surely unintentional. I hate it, but that was finished about a day before the picture was released.

PB: Why were things so tight?

OW: Because the only theatre they could open it in was ready. I ran the picture the day before it was released—it was the only time I ever saw it from beginning to end. And it just gave me time to take out the scene with Katina Paxinou, and nothing else. And I think I was already rushing up the aisle by the time the atom bomb was on to try to get something else fixed. It was a blooper and a terribly stupid one. I can't explain that.

PB: What was the Paxinou scene about?

OW: K has his fortune told by the computer—that's what it amounts to. It was my invention. The computer tells him his fate.

PB: And it's correct.

OW: You don't know what it is, and neither does he. It's just a piece of punched tape. . . .

> K [*Anthony Perkins*]: . . . I suppose a computer is rather like a judge. . . . yes, why not? Why shouldn't an electronic brain replace a judge? That would be a great step nearer to perfection. Errors would no longer be possible and everything would become neat, clean and precise. Instead of trying to take advantage of us behind our backs, lawyers would be forced to be as exact as accountants or scientists. Imagine a tribunal working like a laboratory. . . .

PB: Some critic pointed out that the prominence of hands in *The Trial*—

OW: Well, those kind of people are happiest when writing about Buñuel, whom I hasten to say I like. He's a rich feeding ground for that sort of critic, because it's true about him. You can take off and say he likes feet and all that. Jesus, it's all true. He's that kind of intellectual, and that kind of Catholic. He is a deeply Christian man who hates God as only a Christian can, and, of course, he's very Spanish. I see him as the most supremely religious director in the history of the movies. A superb kind of person he must be. Everybody loves him. His son was my assistant director on *Don Quixote* for a while.

PB: The film isn't really told from K's point of view, is it?

OW: It's not K's point of view, but I made an effort throughout

the picture to move the audience into his viewpoint—the first person—many times. So that he is sufficiently ambiguous; he is sometimes in front of them and sometimes themselves.
PB: You mean by showing things from his point of view.
OW: No, not literally, but you are seeing it through his eyes many times in a visual sense of the word.
PB: One critic commented that, since K is asleep at the start of *The Trial*, it is possible that the whole film is a dream from which we don't see him wake up. [*OW snores.*] The picture starts with long takes and then, from about the courtroom sequence on, the cutting becomes more and more accelerated.
OW: Yes, that was planned—not an accident of economics.
PB: Was it an acceleration of pace?
OW: That's an oversimplification. Cutting does a lot of things besides pace. As you know, it creates a difference—not only in mood—it's almost a different dimension. You begin to tell the story in an entirely different way.
PB: Was that your invention in the first scene, with K throwing the inspector's words back at him?
OW: Yes. That scene is almost entirely new.
PB: I like when he accidentally says "pornograph" instead of "phonograph," and all that.
OW: Yes, that's mine.
PB: You told someone you dubbed eleven of the voices in the picture.
OW: Yes, I even do ten lines of Perkins' dialogue. I've defied him to find it and he hasn't been able to. . . . I'm about five voices in *Chimes at Midnight*.
PB: The running pattern of bars in *The Trial* reminded me of *Othello*.
OW: Yes, but I rather frizzle up at those things about how one picture reminds you of another. I think they do, but I'm not happy about hearing it. And if they do, I just have no comment to make except to squirm.
PB: You used reflected light in *The Trial*.
OW: Yes. Well, I did it first in *Kane*.
PB: When?
OW: The morning after the all-night working session at the newspaper, when Erskine Sanford goes home. I said to Gregg, "I want to see that light before the sun comes up." He said, "Well, we never have that in movies. We should." I said, "It's a diffused light,

so I suppose if you got enough reflectors, put enough diffusion in, you could get it." He said, "Yes, we can try that. Or we can try reflecting it." And I know we tried both, and I think we ended with the reflected light. Anyway, that was my first experience with it. Then I used it more and more and, of course, in *The Trial* there are long sequences with it. The whole first scene in the bedroom is lit by enormous arcs outside hitting onto white panels and bouncing back. *The Trial* is almost totally reflected light. Now, of course, it's become very fashionable, particularly for color photography. It's the only thing the good people do. There's no more direct light any more with the modern cameraman.

PB: When did you shoot the scene where the woman drags the trunk? The light is extraordinary.

OW: End of the day. The second the streetlights went on, we made a shot, and poor Suzanne Flon had to carry that trunk eight blocks.

PB: And it doesn't mean anything in terms of a symbol.

OW: No. Except what is immediately apparent. I don't want to be too cryptic, but there it is.

PB: You've said you don't like symbolism . . .

OW: Hate it.

PB: But I felt that *The Trial* . . .

OW: It's the kind of subject maybe that makes you feel you ought to look for symbols. It smells and looks like the sort of Middle European dream world that should be loaded with them.

PB: A symbol-hunter's dream—it's one of the reasons that I don't like it so much, I suppose.

OW: Well, it's full of do-it-yourself stuff. You can make your own symbols if you want to. But there isn't a single symbol in it.

PB: Well, is there a reason for the children to pursue Perkins after he leaves the painter's studio?

OW: The only answer to that is the old Yiddish story: Poor old Jewish gentleman is dying in a boarding house that is run by an Irish lady, and he's got his back turned to the wall. She goes and gets a priest, who opens up all his stuff and begins. Says, "Do you believe in the Father, the Son, and the Holy Ghost?" Fella says, "I'm a dying man and he asks me riddles."

PB: By the way, how did you do that sequence—K running through the slatted corridor?

OW: I built a long kind of slatted chicken coop in a field and lit it with arcs at night; the camera was on a wheelchair and we ran backwards pulling the wheelchair because there was no kind of dolly that would fit in there. And I had a Yugoslav runner to pull the chair. That was one of the only things left from my original design. That and the painter's tank with the ladder the girls chased him up are the only two things left. We built that great big thing.

PB: Well, now, in that scene, one has the feeling that those children coming to torment him through the lattice work are a symbol of something.

OW: Why?

PB: Well, then, what's the point of it?

OW: What's the point of a dream?

PB: Then that's really what the whole picture is—

OW: Yes, it's a dream—a particular nightmare—inspired by Kafka. It's surrealist, if you want. But the good surrealists aren't symbolists.

PB: Yes, you start off the picture by saying that the story has "the logic of a dream, a nightmare—"

OW: That was intended for people like you to jot down and remember.

PB: I'm liking the picture better.

OW: Keep on trying.

PB: But I think I always *understood* that about the film—

OW: *That's* probably why you don't like it. If only I'd mystified you a bit! [*Laughs.*]

PB: I told you I liked it better the second time I saw it.

OW: See it a third time!

PB: And I never actively *disliked* it, I just—

OW: Never mind all that.

PB: —didn't like it as much as your others.

OW: Well, you know why I defend it—I suppose because it's my own picture, unspoiled in the cutting or in anything else. That's why I hate to hear that it is not as good, because I can't blame anybody for it [*laughs*]. You see, even in *Chimes at Midnight* I was limited in money, much more than in *The Trial*, even though at one time I had to pay Madeleine Robinson's salary, because she wouldn't go on unless she was paid. We had those kind of moments. The producers were heroic and got it made, and there isn't anything I had to compromise—except no sets, and I was happy with the other solution, as it turned out, even though I was kind of in love with all the work I'd done. Still, I was happy enough to scuttle it, as I always am.

PB: Apropos of dreams, you said once, somewhat cryptically—though you may want to let it stand—"A film is a dream but a dream is never an illusion."

OW: Ah, you know what the British politicians say: "I require notice of that question." I think it sounds absolutely great but I haven't got any idea of what it means. It's like that awful moment on radio: I had a daily show at twelve o'clock when I was the Voice of Cornstarch, about which there need be no comment. And it was a fifteen-minute program [*Musical Reveries*] right across the board on CBS for the makers of Crisco or one of those things. And they had an orchestra, which played sweet music for the housewives—and then I would read a poem, and then there was more music. I got fifty bucks each time, and it was terribly nice money to have, because I just turned up five minutes ahead of time and read a poem and ran away with fifty dollars—it was a blessing. That went on for years. And I used to write a little lead-in for the poem. Particularly if it was obscure and I thought the housewives toiling over their stoves needed a little help, I'd make a little remark to "humanize it," as they say. And when this incident happened, I hadn't been asleep for four days. We were rehearsing two different plays—one in Harlem and one down at the Maxine Elliott—and doing sixteen radio shows a minute. And living it up in between times, too, I may as well confess. And I came into that studio and was handed, as the day's poem, one of Elizabeth Barrett Browning's *Sonnets from the Portuguese.* Out of which I could make neither head nor tail. And I remember, from having acted in a play called *The Barretts of Wimpole Street* with Miss Cornell, that there was a well-received joke made by Robert Browning—a real quote of his, used in the play, in which he was asked the meaning of a poem, and he read it, reread it and reread it, and finally said, "When this was written only God and Robert Browning knew what it meant. Now only God does." It is a good line.

PB: Very.

OW: So I thought I'd say that, because I knew the way I would read this poem would be jabberwocky. So I told the nice little story to the housewives, and when I got to the punchline, what I said was this: "When this was written only Bravin Drivet Griving—When Grompit Drivet—When this was written only Gropit Drivet—When Gris was Drivet Grinning—" There were twenty account people in the control room and they began waving and turning purple and everything, and I just put down the script and said, "Good morning, ladies," and walked out of the studio and was never seen again. I never had the nerve to come back. That was the end of my career with Cornstarch. Anyway, I think that remark applies very nicely to that splendid quote you found. Sounds to me like one of those remarks you make at a film festival.

PB: The people in the waiting room reminded me of the Nazi victims.

OW: Yeah, because they're Middle European—they're more like Nazi victims than like Russian victims or anything else.

PB: Did you intend any association of guilt with the torture by the Nazis in the concentration camps?

OW: It's *all* DP camps, not just Nazis. That isn't in the book at all. I suppose the film's greatest weakness is its attempt at universality. Perhaps on one level a picture always loses by being deliberately universal; that probably accounts for a lot of what you don't like about it.

PB: That we're not basically in any one country.

OW: Yes. Well, we're essentially in Middle Europe. . . . Of course, I never stopped thinking we were in Czechoslovakia.

PB: In your mind.

OW: Yes, it had to be. You can't make a picture *nowhere*—then it must be no good. It is Middle European, you see from the streets and everything. But, as in all of Kafka, it's supposed to be Czecho-

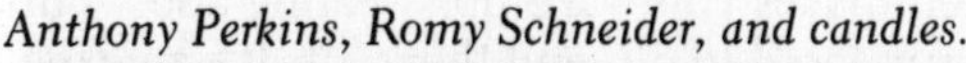

Anthony Perkins, Romy Schneider, and candles.

slovakia. The last shot was in Zagreb, which has old streets that look very much like Prague.
PB: What was the meaning of all the candles in the Advocate's room?
OW: There's *a lot* of candles in those rooms! [*Laughs.*] Just started lighting them and didn't know how to stop [*laughs*].
PB: Well, it was very effective visually.
OW: Well?
PB: Perhaps that was the problem with my reaction to the picture. I kept feeling that everything was supposed to mean more than it did.
OW: Nothing except what you saw. Do you know that, very strangely, the picture was best understood and best liked by the simplest people, who hadn't the kind of education that made them feel from the very word "Kafka," and from the nature of the film and so on, that it must be full of keys to things? They just saw it, you know. I underestimated the population of eggheads. I made it for the nonegghead public and forgot that, the minute we said the word "Kafka," we were stirring things in the bloodstream of normally nonintellectual folk.
PB: I guess it had that effect on me.
OW: It's a *dream.*
PB: And dreams aren't specific.
PB: Well, they can be specific, but some aren't, and this wasn't, because it's the very formlessness that is the horror of that story. It is supposed to project a feeling of formless anguish, and anguish is a kind of dream which makes you wake up sweating and whining. That's what that's supposed to do, and that's all. It's an experience.
PB: And the lack of specifics is similar to the lack of specifics in a dream.
OW: Well, there are all kinds of specifics—as there are millions of candles. But you've got to be simple enough or, excuse me, bright enough, to accept an awful lot of candles [*laughs*].
PB: There's a jealousy theme in the picture, too.
OW: It's *all* those things we have anguish about.
PB: Well, his guilt is never specified. . . .
OW: Maybe he's innocent. It's totally ambiguous. And he is the audience, too, in a way. What made it possible for me to make the picture is that I've had recurring nightmares of guilt all my life: I'm in prison and I don't know why—going to be tried and I don't

know why. It's very personal for me. A very personal expression, and it's not at all true that I'm off in some foreign world that has no application to myself; it's the most autobiographical movie that I've ever made, the *only* one that's really close to me. And just because it doesn't speak in a Middle Western accent doesn't mean a damn thing. It's much closer to my own feelings about everything than any other picture I've ever made.

PB [*after a pause*]: I've always felt that, unlike the rest of your films, *The Trial* is not really entertaining—just on that simple level.

OW: I've never really tried to make a film entertaining.

PB: No, but I think you *want* your films to be entertaining.

OW: Naturally; I'm out of business if they aren't. But it never crosses my mind whether a picture's entertaining or not. If I'm making a comedy, I'd want it to be funny. If I'm making a horror story, I want it to be horrifying. If I'm making a sad scene, I want it to be sad. But to say I want a thing to be entertaining . . . I don't know, the word unsettles me. Probably snobbishly. I didn't intend it to be entertaining—I intended it to be an experience of some kind for the audience.

PB: *That* I think it is.

OW: Well, that would be enough for me, and I'm pretty philistine, as you know. If a picture is an experience, I'd be very happy about it, but it has to be a real experience, not a demonstration of the director's skill. And if *The Trial* is that, then it's a failure, but if it comes off as an experience and not as exhibitionism on my part, then it's a success. By the way, I think it's very important to this book that you stick by your negative opinion of it—because your high opinion of me I cherish, but in order to make the book credible, you've got to make a stand against one of the films. And it's more entertaining that way. I think it's more important for a book like this to be entertaining than a movie!

PB: I was going to say that I think the chemistry between you and the material didn't produce that tension which was so interesting in *Touch of Evil*.

OW: Well, you write that in the book. I'm not interested in *hearing* it. I have a much poorer opinion of my life's work than you possibly could guess, and every negative thing that I hear from a friend or read from a person that I vaguely respect, reduces the little treasure that I have. So I don't want to hear it. You can print it in the book, but I'll skip it. I'm not being funny.

PB: I know you're not. Well, the scene in the office—now, I don't remember what scene that was. . . .

OW: Well, if you don't remember, go to the next question. An unforgettable picture! [*Laughs.*]

PB: Perhaps it's a deficiency in viewers who come to Kafka by Welles with a preconceived notion of a symbol-full movie.

OW: I don't think Kafka was interested in symbols, either. Although it's my own film and not illustrated Kafka, it's still true to what I take to be the spirit of Kafka; and that is a spirit of hauntings and anguish and all kinds of feelings that stir in the bloodstream of the race, and they're far above and beyond and too essential, too noble, to be reduced to shoddy UFA symbolism.

PB: Perhaps my reaction was actually simpler than that. I think it succeeds as an awful experience of a dream, and I didn't like that experience.

OW: Oh yes, a very unpleasant experience.

PB: I simply didn't *enjoy* the picture.

OW: Then great success! You weren't supposed to enjoy more than a few moments of it. There are some enjoyments. But you are supposed to have a very unpleasant time. That's the idea. In other words, you can argue that it shouldn't be made, but you have to give me what I was trying to do—which is to give you a rough time there in the theatre.

PB: I've had dreams in which I think I've murdered somebody.

OW: We all have. I've had that recurring dream since I was about twelve—that I murdered somebody and buried him under the floorboards. I wake up and say, "Where did I do it?"

PB: It isn't that I have grave reservations about the film's artistic success, but it simply isn't a picture I really like to see.

OW: You're using my own attitude toward moviegoing to get at me now—which is that I only go to the movies that I like to see. And here I go and make movies that I want people to see and not like. That's the paradox at the heart of all my work [*laughs*].

PB: But it's *not* true of all your pictures. This is the only one. All the others I could see joyously over and over.

OW: Yes, and of course you can't see *The Trial* joyously. It's perfectly fair.

PB: You can't say, "Let's all go down and see *The Trial* tonight and have fun."

OW: Unless it happens to strike you as it does me. I must say, there are areas of it that I expected might give more pleasure than

Akim Tamiroff in The Trial.

they apparently do. I thought everything to do with the lawyer and his office and the girl and Tamiroff and all that is enjoyable and funny.

PB: It's amusing.

OW: To me, it's funny. Makes me laugh all the time. We roared when we made it—you can't imagine the hysterical laughter with which that picture was made. Everything broke us up. Only way you could make it without going off your rocker. I still think of those scenes and they make me laugh.

PB: It's a very cold film, too.

OW: I believe it's full of passion—human stuff. I'm not coldly spooking you. But, of course, it's an icy atmosphere. Dank, horrible atmosphere. And the eroticism is dirty and morbid.

PB: Irmie and Mrs. Grumbach are the only normal ones in the picture.

OW: Yes, they are. True.

PB: Where did the business of the dirty pictures in the judge's textbook come from?

OW: From Kafka. And I got all the dirty eroticism of the rest of the movie out of that one thing.

PB: "K is guilty at the time he's born." Is that the feeling you had?

OW: Who said that?

PB: I don't remember—I read it in a book.
OW: Well, K is not metaphysically guilty at birth as conceived of by Kafka, since Kafka was a Jew. The idea of guilt at birth is Christian.
PB: Is that your view of K? That he feels guilty even when he's innocent?
OW: The point is not whether he's guilty or innocent. It's an *attitude* toward guilt and innocence—that's the point of the story. Because what is the guilt? The guilt of what? Kafka comes at it in one way, and I come from a slightly different angle. Still, I think that's essentially true of the book and the movie, that what counts is the attitude, not the fact.
PB: He's not guilty, but he feels guilty.
OW: Or he's guilty, and he feels guilty. It's totally without meaning whether he's guilty or not.
PB: The point is that he feels it.
OW: No, not that he feels it—that's oversimplifying it. It's a study of the various changing attitudes toward guilt, the way they can be used.
PB: Did you want K to be sympathetic or not?
OW: I don't think he's either. I don't think you're for him much, or against him much.
PB: Well, I think you're *with* him.
OW: Yes, but sympathetic is not the same thing as being with him. And he's pretty tough in the book, you know. He's a rising junior executive in a bank and he's a man on the make.
PB: When K comes into the court in the book nobody pays attention to him, and in the movie everybody pays attention to him. Why did you change that?
OW: Another sort of director would take off on that and it'd be very interesting to hear what he'd have to say. It isn't just that I'm being mulish; I really have nothing to say except—there it is. Unless I can give you a reason like "We didn't have any scenery" or something like that. They're indifferent to him in the book, as I remember; then, later on, they are interested in him. I think you ought to read the book. It's short. And see the movie once more.
PB: Well, I think *The Trial* succeeds completely in what you intended to do.
OW: You just don't know whether that's good enough for you. It may *not* be enough of a thing for a movie.
PB: No, I think it *is* like some terrible dream.

OW: But it isn't a reproduction of a dream—that's a very important point to make.
PB: It gives you the *feeling* of a dream.
OW: Yes, related to the experience of dreaming. And, you know, the magical part of dreaming is what I was looking for, trying to achieve. Because dreams do have something to do with magic, and I believe in magic as the main source of poetry. We create entire worlds in our dreams—full of people we've never seen, places we've never been to—that seem to echo and reverberate with worlds and memories that we've never experienced. And yet there they are, real, within the context of that sleeping experience—when we're in touch with whatever we're in touch with, which people have only begun to guess at. And so it would have been disastrous to have symbolism in the ordinary sense of the word in it, because a symbol is my statement to you and the audience, and I'm not there. I mustn't tell you anything. I must make you think that there are things happening in the next room that you don't know about; that's the thing of a dream. That they are richly happening. Totally ambiguous, you know. Signaling to us magically, but never in the sense of the egghead symbol, only in the symbolism of magic.

That symbolism is very valid, and I prefer not to talk about it. That's why candles—that's magic, you see. It doesn't mean something to do with guilt or innocence in a lawyer's office—it's an invocation of something. I know that I'm alibi-ing, because if somebody has reservations about a picture nothing you say will change it, but I believe that everybody who's had reservations about that film has them because they've asked from it something other than what I was intending to do.

8.

CAREFREE

***THE FOUNTAIN OF YOUTH* ▪ OTHER TV PILOTS ''TWILIGHT IN THE SMOG'' ▪ ARISTOCRACY *COMPULSION* ▪ *TOUCH OF EVIL* ▪ JOHN WAYNE *JULIUS CAESAR* ▪ HOWARD HUGHES ▪ WORKING WITH ACTORS ▪ DRUGS ▪ MARLENE DIETRICH WORKING IN AMERICA**

ORSON WELLES: I decided to throw a party for all the little Hollywood grandees from the old days who'd been friends and whom I hadn't seen in so long, having been in Europe for almost ten years, to show that I still remembered my friends—Sam Goldwyn and Jack Warner and all those kind of people. And I was late. I'd been shooting *Touch of Evil* and I thought, "I won't take time to remove this terrible, enormous makeup that took forever to put on"—padded stomach and back, sixty pounds of it, and horrible old-age stuff. When I came into my house, before I had a chance to explain that I had to get upstairs and take my makeup off, all these people came up and said, "Hi, Orson! Gee, you're looking great!"

We are outside a town called Carefree, for God's sake, a suburb of Phoenix, Arizona. Orson has rented a house built against a mountain where he has been shooting extensive sequences for The Other Side of the Wind, *using the same skeleton crew he'd gathered in Hollywood. The place is filled with equipment and props, some rather bizarre—like a dozen dummies all made to resemble one of the leading characters in the picture—and these are strewn around in various attitudes, which is not a little disconcerting when you think you're entering an empty room and find these bodies lying around. Everyone's gone for the day, and we're alone by the pool in the early evening, talking about Orson's last movie in Hollywood,* Touch of Evil, *which was released in 1958. It had also been his first there in a decade. And here we were nearly two decades later shooting a movie about a famous director's last movie.* [*And this,* The Other Side of the Wind, *would eventually turn out to be Orson's last too.*]

PETER BOGDANOVICH: What happened when you first got back to Hollywood?

OW: Nothing; that was the trouble. I had really a very unhappy time—the worst—getting no work. I went a year with almost nothing, just sitting at home waiting for the phone to ring. And then I got a couple of jobs: *The Long, Hot Summer* [1958], which I hated making—I've seldom been as unhappy in a picture; and imagine *Man in the Shadow*, a Jeff Chandler Western and a true deep-dyed B. He was a terribly nice, sad fellow whom I liked very much, but that was really hitting the bottom, you know, playing the head of the big ranch. And then came *Touch of Evil* and a tremendous high point—I thought I had it made and was going to stay and do a whole series of pictures with Universal.

PB: Didn't you do some television while you were waiting around?

OW: Yes, I did a pilot for Desilu—*The Fountain of Youth*—which they couldn't sell.

PB: But it was later sold as a special and won the Peabody Award

Joi Lansing in The Fountain of Youth.

in 1958. It's really the best television show I've ever seen—created for the medium, as you said. I especially like what you did with the ticking of the clock all the way through. And didn't you do another pilot around that time?

OW: Yes, and I did a half-hour thing about Dumas called *Camille, the Naked Lady and the Musketeers* [1956].

PB: For Desilu?

OW: I made it for myself. I spent my own money. I wanted to do a series of half-hour portraits of people. This was just me telling the story of the three Dumas, with pictures of them and drawings by me. In a purely narrative form, but quite visual in spite of that. Nobody would have any part of it. I thought I could sell it—syndication or something. Not a chance; nobody would look at it. I don't know what's ever happened to that; I wish I could find it.

At that dinner party I mentioned earlier, I showed them these two shorts—and Sam Goldwyn walked out of the first one and said, "I didn't come here to see a lot of shorts." I don't know what possessed him that night.

Then I spent a fortune—I wanted to do thirty-six weeks on the life of Churchill—which was later done with [Richard] Burton narrating. I must have spent $12,000 on research and things like that, and the tax people wouldn't let me deduct it. They said, "What did you do? You didn't sell it. You say you worked in your home—that's what every movie star says."

PB: What was the television documentary you prepared about Gina Lollobrigida [circa 1958]?

OW: It was about the Roman movie world. She was the leading subject, but a lot of other people were in it—De Sica and so on. The film was made as a pilot for ABC of a proposed series, a sort of magazine—a serious one, not variety. And they hated it and that was the end of that.

PB: Was it ever broadcast?

OW: No. They said it was technically incompetent and couldn't be shown. Had a lot of new ideas in it—done with Steinberg's drawings, many still photos, conversations, little stories—and they regarded that as technical incompetence. I spent a lot of time photographing movie posters. That bothered them, too.

It was made for *that screen* [TV], in the newspaper tradition. Me on a given subject, Lollobrigida, and not what she is in reality. An essay. Anyway, they hated it.

PB: What was Martin Ritt like directing *The Long, Hot Summer*?

OW: Well, he's the one who said to me, "I want you to relate to those windows," and I said, "Marty, you mean you want me to *look* at them?" But I enjoyed very much working with Joanne Woodward—we had nice scenes together—and with Angela Lansbury. I love her. But I wasn't very happy, although the picture was an enormous success. That's the one where the critic for the *New York Times* [Bosley Crowther] wrote, "Orson Welles, believe it or not, was quite good" [*laughs*].

PB: Did you know Faulkner yourself?

OW: Yes. That movie, of course, had nothing to do with the book [*The Hamlet*]—it was largely an imitation of Tennessee Williams, using the name Faulkner. But I knew Faulkner pretty well.

PB: What kind of man was he?

OW: I don't really know—I never saw him anything except wildly drunk through the years. He must have been sober to produce that great body of work.

PB: You like his writing?

OW: Not as much as other people do, but I admire him, yes. I prefer the others—his rivals of that generation—Fitzgerald, I'm very fond of Hemingway, and I'm a great fan of a very underrated American writer, John O'Hara.

PB: What do you think of Fitzgerald's Hollywood novel, *The Last Tycoon*?

OW: It always seemed to me to be a great failure of a book by a great writer.

PB: Well, it wasn't finished.

OW: But even what's there—I don't think he understood Hollywood for a minute. I don't think he knew what he was talking about.

PB: You wrote a good article for *Esquire* around that time about the death of Hollywood.

OW: I remember that the editor felt he had to write a little thing in his column that, after all, Hollywood had treated me well.

PB: An apologia.

OW: Yes. I've never complained about Hollywood, but I'm not really one of the *outstanding* beneficiaries of the system [*laughs*].

PB: That must be one of the great understatements of—

OW: Nor did I think my article was very bitter *about* it. It seemed to me that his comments were totally unnecessary.

Some excerpts from Orson's piece, "Twilight in the Smog," published in Esquire, *March 1959:*

> . . . It was Fred Allen who said, in his fair-minded way, that "California is a wonderful place if you're an orange." I guess what Fred was actually referring to was the general region of Los Angeles, or, as it's called, Greater Los Angeles (greater than what?). Like so many of us, this was the part of the state he knew best and liked the least.
>
> Anyway, as the citrus people are the first to admit, smog has taken the fun out of life even for the oranges. . . .
>
> According to the map, Hollywood is a district attached but not belonging to the City of Los Angeles. But this is not strictly accurate: Los Angeles—though huge, populous and rich—has never quite made it as a city. It remains a loose and sprawling confederation of suburbs and shopping centers. As for downtown Los Angeles, it's about as metropolitan as Des Moines or Schenectady. . . .
>
> There has never been a real metropolis that did not begin with a market place. Hollywood is a way station on a highway.

Drive as far as you like in any direction: wherever you find yourself, it looks exactly like the road to an airport. Any road to any airport . . .

Is Hollywood's famous sun really setting? There is certainly a hint of twilight in the smog and lately, over the old movie capital there has fallen a grey-flannel shadow. Television is moving inexorably westward. Emptying the movie theatres across the land, it fills the movie studios. Another industry is building quite another town; and already, rising out of the gaudy ruins of screenland, we behold a new, drab, curiously solemn brand of the old foolishness.

There must always be a strong element of the absurd in the operation of a dream factory, but now there's less to laugh at and even less to like. The feverish gaiety has gone, a certain brassy vitality drained away. TV, after all, is a branch of the advertising business, and Hollywood behaves increasingly like an annex of Madison Avenue.

Television—live, taped or on film—is still limited by the language barrier, while by nature and economics moving pictures are multi-lingual. Making them has always been an international affair. Directors, writers, producers and, above all, the stars come to Hollywood from all over the world and their pictures are addressed to a world public. The town's new industry threatens its traditional cosmopolitanism and substitutes a strong national flavor. This could not be otherwise since our television exists for the sole purpose of selling American products to American consumers. . . .

With the biggest of the big film studios limping along on economy programs administered by skeleton staffs, the gold-rush atmosphere which once was Hollywood's own dizzy branch of charm is just a memory.

In its golden age—in the first years of the movie boom—the mood and manner were indeed much like that of a gold rush. There was the frenzy and buccaneering hurly-burly of an earlier California: the vast fortunes found in a day and squandered in a night; the same cheerful violence and cut-throat anarchy. All of that Western turbulence has been silenced now. . . .

Architectural fantasy is in decline, the cheerful gaudiness is mostly gone, the more high-spirited of the old outrages have been razed or stand in ruins. In the "better" residential and business districts a kind of official "good taste" has taken charge. The result is a standardized impeccability, sterile and joyless, but it correctly expresses the community's ardent yearnings toward respectability. . . .

Right down to this last moment in a long, long history, show folk have been kept quite firmly segregated from respectability. Significantly, the theatre profession had no contact (or contamination) with the middle class. Indeed, it's just recently that we began to employ that very middle-class word, "profession." This was when the mention of art began to embarrass us, and this was the beginning of our fall from grace: when we suddenly aspired to the mediocre rank of ladies and gentlemen. Before that, and in common with all other artists, we had no rank at all, and stood in our own dignity outside of protocol. . . .

What had been invulnerable in our position was the fact that we really had no position whatsoever. For just as long as there was no proper place for us—neither above nor below the salt—an actor was at liberty to sit wherever he was welcome, and this was very often next to the king. (It may be noted that our most distinguished cousins in the British theatre are not today the easy intimates of royalty.) I hold that we had more to give to our art and to our audiences when we ourselves were royal bums, draped in our own brand of imperial purple. Our crown was tin, but it was a crown, and we wore it, with a difference, among such other diadems as happened to be gold. . . .

[At first, the movies were] an institution "legitimate" actors could look down on with all the priggish contempt formerly lavished by middle-class respectability on the playhouse itself. Hollywood became a word in the language, and in this unlikely outpost—unfettered, unbracketed and largely unconsidered—a motley crew of show folk, in spirit far closer to the circus, to burlesque and the *commedia dell'arte* than to the starchy stage world of that epoch, was gaily producing a new art form, and celebrating in the process a brief but exciting renaissance of the old royal nonsense and glory.

That glory had all but died out as the theatre reduced itself into a mere profession. Now—as the making of motion pictures began to be spoken of and to be organized as a mere industry—the glory started dimming in Hollywood.

What's valid on the stage or screen is never a mere professional effort and certainly not an industrial product. Whatever is valuable must, in the final analysis, be a work of art.

There should be no need to repeat that originality is one of the essential definitions of any work of art, and that every artist is an individual. Just as obviously, the industrial system, by its nature, cannot accommodate originality. A genuine individual is an outright nuisance in a factory.

There used to be something spoken of as "the Hollywood influence." What is more noticeable today is that the rest of America is influencing Hollywood.

As always, much fun is provided by the current sex symbols, but Jayne and Elvis are too patently creatures of the publicity experts—fuzzy carbon copies of the old freewheeling originals, the vamps and the sheiks who invented themselves and lived up so gorgeously to their own legends. The recent crop of "Method actors" and the official representatives of the beatnik constituency are rather too sullen in their personal style to add much color to the pallid scene. . . . They have their own conformism, these eagle scouts of The Actors Studio—there is no madness in their method.

Of the authentic mavericks the youngest, men like Mitchum and Sinatra, are in their forties. Rock 'n' roll throws up an occasional odd ball of a minor sort, but such types are "cool" in the dictionary sense of the word and do nothing to the tepid temperature of the new Hollywood one way or another. Their kind of egotism rages in a sort of monotone and with no exuberance. They hold the mirror up to their own generation. So do their pseudo-suburbanite elders in the film colony. These two groups, the T-shirts and the sports jackets, are more accurate reflections of today's America than were those dazzling pioneers who blazed screenland's frontiers.

One of our producers, by way of explaining the school of neo-realism in the Italian cinema, told me that over there, instead of actors, they use people. For good or evil it's certain that the town is overrun with characters who are quite reasonable facsimiles of today's people. It's a solemn thought, but maybe that's what's wrong with Hollywood.

PB: Have you ever secretly yearned for respectability?
OW: No! My goodness, no.

PB: To be accepted by the academicians—?
OW: Oh, indeed not, no. I think it's the duty of the artist to be as nimble as possible in avoiding that.
PB: Did you direct any of *Compulsion*?
OW: Dick Fleischer is a director who doesn't need and wouldn't welcome any help from me. Anyway, the part of [Clarence] Darrow was so difficult—that final speech to the court lasts two full reels—I was delighted to be doing it, and it took all my energy. I did it all in one take, without cuts.
PB: In that case, they made a big mistake cutting away from you so often. That's what's wrong with the scene.
OW: They didn't have the courage to stay with it. Not because I think I was so good, but if you're going to have a speech like that, you really don't need to have to resort to all those other things. They really should have had the guts to stay with the man and watch him. I saw what they did because I looped it—every word of it is postsynched.
PB: Well, and you had to learn it all. . . .
OW: I had a teleprompter.
PB: Oh, really?
OW: Certainly. Everybody was terribly embarrassed and kept the press off. I'm not at all embarrassed. Entirely too long to try to get straight [*laughs*]. I brought in a teleprompter. I knew the speech, but the fact that the teleprompter was there took that awful, nervous strain out of it. They moved it around outside of the shot, and I don't think I glanced at it—but, knowing it was there, I was at ease.
PB: I only suffered through your other Fleischer picture, *Crack in the Mirror*, because you were in it.
OW: I tried to pretend I wasn't as much as possible. Spent all my time cutting out my own lines. I couldn't literally hide, but I did reduce the verbiage to a point where I was as close to being invisible as possible—considering I was playing not one but two of the leading parts.
PB: Darryl Zanuck produced—
OW: Well, he was otherwise occupied when he made that picture. . . . I'm very fond of Darryl. He was by all odds the best and brightest of the big studio bosses. *Crack in the Mirror* was one of those things that happens to a man when he finds himself in the wrong country and stuck on the wrong girl.
PB: How did you get the chance to direct *Touch of Evil*?

OW: I had just acted in the Jeff Chandler Western for Universal [*Man in the Shadow*], and they sent me another script—a very bad one that took place in San Diego, with a crooked detective in it. And they said, "Do you want to play it?" I said, "Maybe," and I was still wondering whether I could afford *not* to make it when they called up Chuck Heston and said, "Here's a script—we'd like you to read it. We have Welles." And he misunderstood them and said, "Well, any picture that Welles directs, I'll make." So they got back on the phone quick and said to me, "Do you want to direct it?" And I said, "Yes, if I can rewrite it." Well, they said they'd let me do that if I wouldn't get paid as a director or a writer—just my original salary as an actor. So I had about three and a half weeks to go before it began, and I locked myself up with four secretaries and wrote an entirely new story and script.
PB: How do you work with four secretaries?
OW: Well, I rewrite an awful lot, you see. I write the dialogue without anyone around, but I redraft constantly and I like to look at fair copies. So they have to go bang, bang, bang and do it again and again each time I rewrite.
PB: But you do the actual writing physically—you don't dictate it?
OW: No, no. And it was hard work, because *everything* had to be done—a whole new story. There was just a good basic situation about a detective with a good record who plants evidence because he *knows* somebody is guilty—and the fellow turns out really to be guilty. That was from the original script.
PB: Did you bother to read the novel?
OW: No, I read the novel after the picture was made. There wasn't a copy around and I never would have had time to read one if there were. I think I didn't even *know* it was a book then. But about three or four years later, I happened to see it somewhere and I read it. The actual title is *Badge of Evil*, which was also what the picture was called originally. I don't know where they got *Touch of Evil* or what it means, but it sounds all right. You know me and titles—"thing" is about all I can come up with. I wish I could hire someone like Tennessee Williams or Irwin Shaw to write titles for me. Anyway, the book is better than the script they gave me—it isn't that bad a book.
PB: You don't approve of Vargas [Heston] using Menzies [Joseph Calleia] at the end to betray Quinlan [Welles]?
OW: No, and I think it's terrible what Menzies does. Betrayal is a

big thing with me, as you know from *Chimes at Midnight*—it's almost a prime sin.

PB: You must disapprove, then, of Cotten's betrayal of Harry Lime in *The Third Man*.

OW: Of course . . . What an actor—Joseph Calleia.

PB: How'd you find him?

OW: I fell in love with him as a ten-year-old boy. I saw him in a play in New York, a small miracle called *24 Hours to Kill* or something like that. A very well-staged melodrama which was an enormous hit for about a year—it was made as a movie later with somebody else. He had the leading role, and I never forgot him. And through the years I'd seen him in movies—little things. And I could never forget that performance of his. He's always played very stereotyped parts in pictures but is one of the best actors I've ever known. I have such respect for him. You play next to him and you just feel the thing that you do with a big actor—this dynamo going on.

PB: Did you write it with him in mind?

OW: No. My first choice for the part was Lloyd Bridges, who's a marvelous actor, but they turned him down at the studio because of some dumb reason. I wrote it for him, but I was more than happy with Calleia. And I was very lucky with that cast—nobody let it down at all.

PB: François Truffaut wrote that, at the end of *Touch of Evil*, "the stool pigeon and mediocrity triumph over intuition and justice." Is he right?

OW: It's a perfectly factual statement—doesn't cover the whole scene, but there's no error in that as a statement.

PB: But the implication would be that Quinlan is preferable to Vargas.

OW: I don't think that's what Truffaut is trying to say. I hope not. The point is that Quinlan has been betrayed. But Quinlan himself has betrayed his profession—and he is humanly betrayed as well. It's all about betrayal, isn't it?

PB: Well, Heston says, "Who's the boss—the policeman or the law? That's the question." Which is the theme of the picture on one level, isn't it?

OW: Yes. Damn right. That's very clearly stated. And I was widely attacked, all the way from the Soviet Union to France, for this incredible decadence and fascism and everything else as evidenced by *Touch of Evil*, which seems to me the most—

PB: —antifascist—
OW: And if anything *too clearly* antifascist. I can't understand how all that got started. The French are convinced it's the absolute proof that I'm a fascist. It's because an awful lot of the *Cahiers du Cinéma* people are fascists, and they *wanted* it to prove that I was fascist—not as an attack. The Russians got it wrong because they saw all these dirty things and said, "That's a sign of decadence." They didn't understand that I was *against* the decadence—they thought I reveled in it. One leading film director, [Sergei] Yutkevich, wrote a long piece against it.
PB: Well, the theme is restated several times. Somebody says, "It's a tough job to be a policeman," and Heston says, "It's supposed to be tough—a policeman's job is only easy in a police state."
OW: Yes. I decided that, since I was doing a melodrama, I'd do one about good and evil, and it's a quite simple statement of what I considered to be good and evil. Spelled right out for everybody.
PB: I wonder why people assume that, because you made a film like that, there's an element of autobiography—
OW: Yes, isn't that boring? Anybody who ever interviews you on any sort of serious level about movies is only digging for autobiography. They can't believe that you just think something up because that's what you want to think up.
PB: Heston, whose character is basically good in the picture, is, in fact, tainted by the corruption, isn't he? He resorts, finally, to *means* that are wrong.
OW: That's right. And I'm betrayed by my friend, you see.
PB: And there was something cut which had indicated Heston's disgust with the bugging device he uses. In fact, they took out several moralistic points—
OW: All they could. There's some still there in it, because you've been quoting from it. But they got a lot of moral stuff out. Jokes and morals went.
PB: Is that why you staged the entire last scene through all that machinery—making it even more difficult for Heston?
OW: He is an intruder—it's a scene where there's no place for him. I thought that he should have to seem to dig, like you dig for gold—and climb, like scaling a mountain. This work doesn't suit him and he hates it, as he told Menzies in that scene that was cut. And at this point, Vargas loses his integrity. He sneaks, he listens behind doors. I tried to work out some kind of apparatus that would seem to guide him—so he would be the victim of the appa-

Caesar.

ratus, rather than just a victim of his curiosity. He doesn't know how to make very good use of his recorder, he can only follow it and obey it, because the machine doesn't belong to him. He isn't born to be a spy.

PB: The whole thing must have been very rough to cut.

OW: That's why I was so long—they got mad at me—I was a month too long in the cutting.

PB: Do you have sympathy for Quinlan?

OW: Yes. Even though he doesn't bring the guilty to justice, he assassinates them in the name of the law. He wants to assume the right to judge, and I think no one has the right to judge except under the authority of law. Still, I have to like him because he loved Marlene Dietrich and saved his friend from a bullet. But what he stands for is detestable.

PB: Like Kane?

OW: Yes. Kane, in abusing the power of the popular press, stands against the law, against civilization. He tries to make himself a king in a world without law. All these people express, each in his own way, things I hold in loathing, but we have human sympathy for these characters. He has a human disposition, for want of a morality.

PB: When Heston says, "I'm no cop now. What did you do with my wife?" and then breaks up the bar, you don't condemn him for it.

OW: He's lost his control as a cop. He says it and does it, and what could be clearer than that?

PB: *Julius Caesar* is really about betrayal, too, isn't it?

OW: No. It is in *history*, not in the play. Because the character of Caesar is a ridiculous, pompous poseur in Shakespeare. He'd read it: the line, "Et tu Brute," in Plutarch, that's all. He just put it in because everybody knew it. They would have said, "Why didn't you have the line in?" But there's nothing to prepare for it. There's no relationship between Brutus and Caesar. Caesar is almost a cartoon dictator; he doesn't have to be played that way, but he can never be played sympathetically. He can either be full of pompous boast or an ice-cold genius, but there's no love between him and Brutus. There's nothing that makes it a story of betrayal at all.

In 1953, King Farouk of Egypt offered to finance a modern-dress film of Julius Caesar *entitled* Caesar!, *which Welles scripted and planned to shoot with Richard Burton, in newsreel style, playing the role of Brutus himself. Word of a Hollywood version being planned by John Houseman and Joseph Mankiewicz effectively ended the project.*

OW: You would have seen the Roman ruins everywhere, all plastered with great posters of the new Caesar. I'd done, I thought, a rather good script; I mean, it was a good use of the text—like a newsreel in blank verse, if such a thing is possible. And I thought they might find it useful, or at least be interested; so I sent a copy to Houseman, along with all my sketches for set-ups and scenery. It came back with enormous seals and a long letter from Houseman's lawyers: "This has not been opened—*will* not be opened. . . ." They were so afraid I was then going to claim that they had stolen things from me. I just meant it as a friendly gesture. . . .
PB: I take it you'd have played Brutus in the film, just as you did on the stage.
OW: It's my part.
PB: Why do you say that? It's not really a popular part. No one ever wants to play him—but you.
OW: Yeah. Except perhaps Paul Scofield. He *should* want to, because he would be the best Brutus of our century.
PB: Is he, to your mind, another aristocratic character?
OW: No. He *was* in history, but not in Shakespeare. He's a typical upper-middle-class liberal.
PB: Well, why do you like to play him?
OW: Because that's the kind of part I can play: thinking people. And so does Scofield. There are very few actors who can make you believe they think—not that they're thinking about what they're saying, but that they think outside of the scene. And Scofield is very good at that. He'd be a great Brutus, too, because of his enormous personal sweetness.
PB: I've seen some wonderful photos of your stage production—it looked very exciting.
OW: The photos are all bad compared to what it looked like. I was miserable with the photos. They never showed what it looked like, really.
PB: The lighting's so stark—
OW: Yeah, but you can't imagine what it was like. Mrs. Patrick Campbell said, "Why do you have everybody dressed up like

chauffeurs?" And it's true! It spoiled it for me. Ever since then, it looks like a whole convention of Rolls-Royce drivers! [*Laughs.*]

PB: What else was cut from *Touch of Evil*?

OW: There were about twenty minutes of comedy cut out of it—a big piece. They didn't monkey much with my cutting, they just lifted whole sequences. And, strangely enough, they couldn't take anything of my character out, because I was in the plot part, and the comedy was all nonplot. All Tamiroff and his team—really far-out black comedy—and it shocked and distressed them.

PB: Some of it was left—

OW: Which there was no way of them taking out—but I regret it. And they put in some things. They did a half day's work without me, you know—

PB: After the picture had been edited.

OW: Yes. Heston kept phoning me to say what he was doing and to ask if it was all right, because if I didn't approve he would walk off.

They had loved the rushes and—it's a very weird thing—when they saw the whole thing put together they just hated it. And there was a man who'd been in charge of part of their European sales for years, and he put the movie into the [Brussels] World's Fair at a special festival. The studio had about ten pictures they wanted instead of that and said no. He insisted. And the picture got the prize, and they fired him.

PB: Incredible.

OW: And they put it into a theatre in Paris for a couple of weeks and it ran a year and a half. It did tremendous business all over the world except—

PB: Except in America, where they snuck it out.

OW: Yes, on a double bill with no press showing. But, even so, it's made quite a lot of money, according to Chuck Heston, who owns a piece of it.

All their new scenes didn't amount to much—about four or five little bits and pieces were stuck in to glue it together in the absence of those comedy scenes that joined the plot. . . . On the other hand, the music, which I didn't have anything to do with, was, I thought, quite well done.

PB: But didn't you tell [Henry] Mancini what you wanted?

OW: Yes. But I wasn't there as I would normally be—like a mother hen, on every note.

PB: He says you talked with him extensively.

OW: Yes, I did. But I didn't stay through it all. I think he did a fine job.
PB: I noticed two short scenes between Heston and Janet Leigh in the hotel that didn't look like your lighting.
OW: And there's one with Heston and the District Attorney in the hotel. Some utility scene. Just because it wouldn't make any sense having taken out all those jokes that drove them mad.
PB: Didn't they cut a scene that would have explained your now cryptic line to Menzies—"That's the second bullet I stopped for you, partner"?
OW: Yes. Menzies tells Janet Leigh about it in a car scene: some years before, Quinlan courageously protected him in a gunfight—got shot saving his life—that's why he has a limp and walks with a cane. And then I mention "the second bullet" at the end, I'm torturing my friend, reminding him sadistically. Yes. The whole point of my limp and the whole point of Calleia's relationship to me was thus cut out—and it's a very important scene for him. They cut a lot of his part out; it's a shame. It was just stupid. You know the kind of editorial thing—"That doesn't advance the story" —and in the meantime you don't even know why some things happen. But they didn't absolutely murder it. I was very sorry about the things they did, but the story was still *roughly* intact when they were finished. That wasn't true of *Arkadin*, which was just made meaningless by the cutting. And that happened in Europe, not in America.
PB: What was Heston like?
OW: He's the nicest man to work with that ever lived in movies. I suppose the two nicest actors I've ever worked with in my life are Gielgud and Heston.
PB: Gielgud in *Chimes at Midnight*?
OW: Yes. They're two kinds of angels. We had seven *weeks* of night shooting—beginning at eight at night and ending at dawn—and I'll never forget Chuck Heston one night, at the end of those seven weeks. He was on the far side of the bridge, and I told him to quickly cross over in a shot. Dawn was about to rise. And he said, without irony or anger, very sweetly, "Do you mind telling me *why* I'm crossing the bridge?" And I said, "No, just cross the bridge, and when you get over here I'll tell you!"
PB: You were losing your light—
OW: Yes—*that's* why he was crossing the bridge, as I later explained to him.

PB: I thought he was very good in that picture.

OW: Wonderful in it. We rehearsed for two weeks before we shot, and he was an absolute soldier all the way through. I think he has the makings of a great heroic actor. And I don't know what movies may lead him into doing, but he has all the equipment—the voice, the physique, the intelligence, and everything—he's a big American heroic actor. If he isn't, then it's the movies' fault or the theatre's fault for not giving him enough to do.

PB: His performance in this film is one of his best, I think.

OW: He has a theory, he told me, that what went wrong with the film is that *my* part turned out to be too good. He forgot that it was the best part even when I was offered it as an actor in somebody else's script. And it was the *most* I could do to turn Heston's part into anything at *all*, because he was just the leading man, with absolutely no character. I had to make him a Mexican. I had to give him twenty problems. Everything to make him good. It wasn't that I built up *my* part. But now, as he remembers it, I built up my part and that's the only thing that went wrong with the picture.

PB: Well, your part was the lead.

OW: Yeah, but it always was—when I inherited the old story. You don't *know* what I did to make him interesting—to make it a character leading man. But he was angelic to work with. And could be a great big American actor.

PB: He did all the overlapping things very well.

OW: Oh, anything. All you have to do is point and Chuck can go in any direction. He's just spent a lot of years being a movie star. . . .

As one can read in Heston's journals, rehearsals began on February 9, 1957, and shooting started nine days later and continued through April 2. Editing and dubbing under Welles' supervision continued through the summer. After viewing a rough cut in early November, the studio requested another day of shooting to clarify certain aspects of the plot (at this point, Orson was acting in The Long, Hot Summer *at Fox), and by mid-November Heston was informed that Universal didn't want Welles to carry out this work, which was scheduled for November 18. He received a letter from Orson on November 17:*

Dearest Chuck:

I want you to read this before we talk—there are some points that should be made as unemotionally as possible, and I'm afraid I don't quite trust myself to keep the exposition of them as cool and clear as I'd like. . . .

Your telegram has arrived in which you speak of yourself as "legally bound" to the studio. But this is the advice —not of your own lawyer—but "the legal department of MCA." . . .

Even if I were not available, don't you think it would be sweetly reasonable on your part to insist on a certain standard of professional capacity and reputation in the choice of an alternate director? . . . UNLESS THE STUDIO IS STOPPED THEY ARE GOING TO WRECK OUR PICTURE—AND I MEAN WRECK IT, BECAUSE IT IS NOT THE KIND OF ONE-TWO-THREE, ABC VARIETY OF COMMERCIAL PRODUCT THAT CAN BE SLIGHTLY WRECKED. WITHOUT MY HELP THE RESULT WILL BE VERY MUCH LESS SATISFACTORY THAN THE MOST ORDINARY PROGRAM ITEM, THE RESULT WILL NOT SIMPLY BE SOMETHING LESS THAN YOU HOPED. THE RESULT WILL BE GENUINELY BAD. . . .

You must realize that if you have a financial interest in the picture, I have a professional one. If I were now directing another picture—or about to direct one—and if I hadn't been away so long, I might be tempted to write off my own investment as a bad loss. But as things are with me in this industry I simply cannot afford to sustain such a blow. . . . I'm heartsick at the thought of having to involve you. But you really cannot avoid some involvement—now or later.

If you are tempted to think of yourself as the helpless victim of sinister Hollywood forces over which you have no control, I must tell you that you're wrong. You aren't helpless at all, and it's well within your own power to save much of a rather large investment of time, money and—yes—love.

You can do this by getting a little tough now. . . .

Much love as always,
Orson

After receiving this letter Heston canceled the next day's shoot at his own expense (just over $8,000). But after further consultation with his lawyer and a final, unsuccessful appeal to studio chief Edward Muhl, he agreed to proceed with the retakes on November 19, with Harry Keller directing. Around this time, Orson sent him another letter:

Dearest Chuck:

The way I hear it, you and Janet are growing more cooperative by the minute. The fact that the dialogue you are speaking is not absolute hogwash—the fact that your director is not, after all, a certifiable incompetent and above everything, the fact that all this added work is involving a great quantity of close footage on both of you bums—I suppose makes this cheeriness inevitable.

This is to remind you that what is happening over there is still the ruination of our picture. The spoiling process may be a bit less obvious than we expected, but the essential fact remains, and I beg you not to permit the merry stimulation of work to interfere with that air of reticence you had sworn to maintain.

There's this character—(known and loved by all)—he might be called "Cooperative Chuck" . . . he is not merely well disciplined in his work, but positively eager —even wildly eager—to make things easy for his fellows on the set and for all the executives in their offices. . . . In a word, he's the Eagle Scout of the Screen Actors' Guild.

The purpose of this communiqué is to beg him to leave his uniform and flag in the dressing room. . . .

There's nothing I can do about meeting the excitations of the close-up lens, but I can implore you to curb your peace-making instincts and to maintain an aloof and non-committal silence. That goes for Janet, too, dammit.

In a word, keep your yap shut.

Much love,
Orson

PB: The opening four-minute crane shot is one of the great shots in movies.

OW: I've always regretted that they put titles over it, because it was meant to be done in the clear, with the titles at the end of the movie. It's a shame to see stuff written all over something that's important—the whole story was in that opening shot.

PB: How was that done technically? Were there many problems?

OW: No, because I had a great camera operator—one of the last great ones. Right after that picture, he became a lighting cameraman and we lost one more great operator—there aren't many of them. His name is John Russell. And we had a marvelous key grip, which is, as you know, a key thing in crane shots. That's why you can never make those kind of shots in Europe—you can get an operator who can do it, but never a grip like an American one.

PB: What do the grips do here that they can't do there?

OW: Well, he's the man who steadies that arm on its truck marks, and he's as important as the operator. And if he hasn't got a marvelous touch and absolutely sure grasp of what he's doing, you're lost. A chief grip in America sends his kids to college and has two cars and is a well-thought-of technician, and in Europe he's a poor miserable laborer, and you can't expect him to be good on that kind of dough. So those kind of shots can't even be attempted in European pictures. But there's, technically, a much more difficult crane shot in *Touch of Evil* which nobody ever recognizes as such; it runs almost a reel, and it's in the Mexican boy's apartment—it's in three rooms—where the dynamite is found in the bathroom and all that; it has inserts and long shots and medium shots and everything. We had breakaway walls—

PB: Without a cut?

OW: Without a cut.

PB: It must have been fun to do.

OW: Yeah, sure—and nobody realizes it. That's a success. It's much more of a shot than the famous opening. Of course, all the credit for those kind of shots goes really to the operator and the grip, because anybody can think it out—it's just who can do it? First day's shooting, that one was. And the unit manager kept saying under his breath on the phone: "He hasn't got anything yet. It's three-thirty, and there's nothing in the can. . . . Four forty-five . . . They're rehearsing—I don't know *what* they're doing. . . . Five-thirty—nothing yet . . ." Then—ten minutes of six—*fourteen* pages!

PB: Was it a real apartment?

OW: No, it was a set on the lot. But everything else was real. Only one room in the motel was a set; everything else was the real place.

They built sets, but we never went into them. I said I wouldn't, but they insisted on building them.

PB: That long take gives a great feeling of claustrophobia.

OW: Yes, they tend to. That's one of the things that you cannot do no matter how you cut—claustrophobia does require the long take. That's why I did a very long take in K's room—the opening scene of *The Trial;* it lasts about six and a half minutes.

PB: To give an oppressive feeling.

OW: Yes, and it does build up when you don't cut—you must lose in cutting.

PB: It's a subconscious effect on an audience, isn't it? I mean, do you think they're consciously aware that you haven't cut?

OW: It's only the bad things that they are aware of, isn't it? Whatever they're aware of is your failure as a director.

PB: You must be very much against all this currently fashionable technique that shows.

OW: Terribly. The directors I admire the most are the least technical ones—the ones freest of this very thing I'm strongly accused of being. In other words, the films I like best are the ones least like the sort of films I'm accused of making.

PB: John Ford and Jean Renoir.

OW: Yes, well, there you are. Even Pagnol, you know, who just turned the camera on—all those actors, and when they ran out of film they cut. Actually, that's why I always resist compliments about that opening shot in *Touch of Evil*—because it's one of those shots that *shows* the director making "a great shot," and I think great shots should conceal themselves a little bit. But that, by its nature, had to show it, because it told the plot. There was no way of not doing a kind of virtuoso shot that announced itself. But I prefer the ones that don't, that conceal themselves.

PB: You don't cut until Heston looks at the fire. And then do what looks like a zoom on the fire, though it's too short to be a zoom. Do you remember that shot?

OW: Yes. I think it's a zoom with frames pulled. Probably. When I use a zoom for that sort of thing, I almost always pull frames, because a zoom is never fast enough for me.

PB: How does that work?

OW: Take out every other frame in the shot—"skip-frame" is the right word. To me it should happen so fast that you hardly know you've moved in. It's almost like a cut—just short of being a cut. I always do a lot of skip-framing.

PB: Another thing you often do is break up one sentence with a lot of cuts. For instance, there's a brilliant exchange right at the beginning of *Touch of Evil*, when you first arrive. You're talking to Heston and you say, "You bet your sweet life you won't." And there's a very fast exchange of looks between the two of you, all during that one line.

OW: I like quick cutting very much. I didn't do much of it at the start. But the more I work the more I like it.

PB: How did you decide to shoot it in Venice, California?

OW: When it became clear that we couldn't shoot it in Tijuana—because of the Mexican censors; they'd never let us make it look scrubby. It would have been so marvelous if I could have shot in Tijuana. I've just come back through there now, and I thought, "Oh my God!" What a missed opportunity. What I would give to make a movie there! Perhaps one could steal in with a small crew. It's one of the greatest sets on earth, I think.

PB: Venice was a substitute.

OW: Yes—all dressed up. Pretty good equivalent: it looked a lot like Tijuana. Then, of course, we had the oil wells, which don't exist around Tijuana; that was a gift. And that wonderful canal—that dirty canal with typhoid in it, into which I threw myself bravely at five one morning, floated away with the ship. Oh Christ, that's love of art!

PB: I really loved the film—the sound and look of it—without following the plot completely about the first five times I saw it.

OW: I don't like that, but I don't think you can be blamed for it—because of the cutting that was done.

PB: No, I didn't mean that I *couldn't* follow the plot; it's just that it seemed to me the least important aspect that first few times I saw it.

OW: I know you don't bother with it, and *I* keep holding it against Howard Hawks because I couldn't follow the plot of *The Big Sleep* [1946]. I got furious.

PB: Well, he says he couldn't follow it, either. But it's true that sometimes the rhythm of your scenes is so exciting I don't really care what they're saying—it becomes like listening to music. And you could say the same thing for the film visually.

OW: I judge a scene by how it sounds—a difficult acting scene. I almost *prefer* to turn away from the actors. I think the sound is the key to what makes it right. If it sounds right, it's gotta look right.

PB: The tempo?
OW: Above all the tempo—the shape of it.
PB: Grandi [Akim Tamiroff] really wasn't the heavy. He was almost like a comic relief.
OW: Yes, he's a comic heavy. His sources—the world's full of comic heavies. There are more of them in life than in movies. I think most heavies are funny [*laughs*].
PB: But there's still a threat there.
OW: Yes, sure, he's a heavy and he's funny. The minute you have a gangster who has to perform a certain function in the melodrama, you're obliged to try and find something about him that doesn't make him identical to every other gangster and every other melodrama. It's as simple as that.
PB: That's funny, because in a certain way he behaves like the gangsters do in melodramas. And Janet Leigh makes fun of that in him.
OW: Which comes partly out of the fact that he has to perform certain gangsterish functions in the plot, and therefore in a way he's sent up. But it's not sending up the actor—it's sending up the man himself, that's the device.
PB: One agrees with her, in fact, that he probably has seen too many gangster films.
OW: Yes, that's the idea I got from knowing gangsters. I've known most of the famous ones—some of them better than I wanted to —and they did show strong influences as moviegoers. There certainly was a question of life imitating art; Grandi came from that observation.
PB: Which gangsters did you know?
OW: Oh, I knew Luciano and Costello, and even Capone, and lesser lights. It was easy to be in movies and not know them, but almost impossible to be in show business—Broadway—without knowing them, unless you never went out at night to a nightclub and never knew anybody in any form of show business. Unless you were the Lunts or Katharine Cornell, it was virtually impossible not to get to know them—they were so anxious for you to. Capone used to take four rows at the opening night of every play in Chicago and come backstage and see everybody. You couldn't get to a nightclub without Costello sending over a bottle of champagne, or sit in Lindy's without Luciano coming over. They were horrible people—I never thought they were glamorous or interesting or

anything—but there they were, part of the scene, and so one got to know them. Luciano and his gang used to descend on me in Rome and Naples during his exile, too.
PB: You didn't like their company?
OW: No. I think he was a particularly unsavory fellow—I disliked him more than the others. But there he was, and it was interesting to compare him to the old Warner Brothers gangster-movie prototypes. The similarity was extraordinary—he was just a little bit more polished and a little cheaper. That's class.
PB: Did you associate with him because you were scared of him?
OW: You didn't associate with him. You're sitting having coffee in the Excelsior Hotel in Naples and Lucky Luciano sits down at your table. That's associating with Luciano—until the coffee is finished; you say, "Yes, Charlie, glad to see you"—that's what you call him, Charlie—and a couple of the other boys sit down. "Wouldn't you like to make a picture about me, Orsten?" he used to say. "The real-life story of me?" He was always trying to promote —that's one of the reasons he kept chasing me around Italy. And I always used to say, "Oh, yes, yes," and wave wildly for the bill! [*Laughs.*]
PB: Supposedly he died in the arms of a film producer.
OW: I didn't know that. I knew he was poisoned, certainly by the Mafia. I'm anxious to see, by the way, what Howard Hughes will do with the Mafia in Las Vegas. He was seen walking around with two empty boxes of Kleenex on his feet instead of shoes one early morning in Las Vegas, according to gossip which may be as untrue as anything else. But he is a pretty wild fellow—rather an extraordinary one.
PB: You knew Hughes pretty well, didn't you?
OW: Pretty well considering we never had any reason to know each other. I ran into him more often than one is supposed to have. There were several times I talked to him in odd corners of the California scene, but I can't say I know him well, no.
PB: Did he ever ask you to make a picture?
OW: No. He was a director in those days. He was doing *The Outlaw* when I was cutting *Kane*, and Gregg Toland was coming back telling stories about him—he photographed *The Outlaw* and was sometimes phoned at 4:00 A.M. to come and shoot an insert of a rooster. Those things really happened.
PB: There are a lot of little signs in *Touch of Evil*, and I wondered if they were signs that were on location or if you put them there.

OW: No, there's nothing there that wasn't made.
PB: Like the sign on the door after Quinlan kills Grandi and leaves his cane behind—though we don't know it then: "Forget something? Make sure you didn't forget anything."
OW: Yes. I did all those and all the artwork—the pinups and everything—I painted myself, from blowups. You have to watch awfully carefully to see them, but I worked hard on those. Like Redgrave's antique shop in *Arkadin*—I was up every night from eleven o'clock till four or five in the morning working on that set myself, with one assistant.

It goes back to the beginning in Dublin in the theatre, when I used to not only design the sets, but paint the scenery myself.
PB: Why did you put a blind woman in the scene when Heston is telephoning his wife?
OW: There isn't anything to add to what's on the screen. There is the kind of director who *wants* to explain, but I haven't anything to say.
PB: Why did you make her blind?
OW: Why not? I know that sounds uncooperative, but I'm just absolutely flummoxed by those sort of questions, I don't have a reply. If I were standing before the Pearly Gates and had to tell why she was blind, I'd be stuck for an answer. I wasn't signaling something to the audience with it. I never am.

> *At this point I read to Orson a paragraph from his fifty-eight-page memo to Universal, written after he was allowed to see their rough cut:*
>
> In the scene in the blind woman's shop, I note with distress that the shot of Vargas at the telephone has been blown up in such a way as to eliminate the blind woman in the foreground. She was not there by accident. Her presence embarrasses Vargas and inhibits his phone conversation with Susan. This provides a curious note of minor tension which will be missed. Susan in the strange motel speaking with drowsy sexiness to her husband in the even more strange shop of the blind; his discomfort at the quiet, oddly attentive figure of the blind woman—these were elements in a rather carefully balanced little plan. It seems a shame to disrupt this simply because it struck someone that the woman sitting there in the foreground was rather peculiar. It was meant to be peculiar.

> If the dialogue between Susan and Mike was more significant, if vital plot points were being established, then, of course, the blind woman would be quite the wrong sort of distraction. As it is, she lends a special dimension to a scene which, on the face of it, advances our story not at all and must be perfectly routine.

PB: Why didn't you give *me* that answer?
OW: That's what you tell Eddie Muhl, not Pierre di Bogdanovich.
PB: How did the Dennis Weaver character evolve?
OW: Well, I had for years thought that Dennis Weaver in *Gunsmoke* was one of the greatest actors around. And I just got him out of *Gunsmoke* for three days and wrote a part for him—just because I wanted Dennis Weaver to be in a movie. That's the only reason the character was there. And what a joy it was to work with him—made my heart leap up. I felt in heaven working with him.
PB: How was Janet Leigh?
OW: Wonderful. And I gave her a very rough time, because she had to change her hairdo back and forth all the time, not knowing why. In the motel sequence we were shooting forty and fifty setups a day, and she never knew where she was in the plot. I just said, "The hair down. The hair up. Go to the window—don't ask me why"—you know—and she was going. Because we made it very quickly.
PB: You were shooting it out of sequence.
OW: I've never shot anything in sequence. I don't know how it is to shoot in sequence. Never done it in my life.
PB: You shoot for the way the lighting is—
OW: Have to. I've never been rich enough to shoot in sequence.
PB: How do you rehearse with actors?
OW: It depends on the actors. I think a director oughtn't to have a method he imposes on actors. I think the *actors* impose the method by their personalities, characteristics, and everything else. There are some actors who are unhappy and insecure unless you come on very strong, very firm, and give them an enormous amount of information. And others who are much better in a party, where you just kind of slip free information into their minds while nobody's looking—
PB: And you sense the different actors?
OW: Well, one tries to. I think that separates the boys from the men in directors. There *are* fine directors who are so much them-

Dennis Weaver and Charlton Heston in Touch of Evil.

selves that the actors have to toe the line and follow them. But I've always thought, as you know, that the job of the director is slightly overrated, overinflated, and I think the director must think of himself as the servant of the actors and the story—even when he wrote the story. Really, the big thing is what the actors are going to do—not that the actors are going to do what *you* want. It's to find out what they're going to do and bring it out of them. And I think you have to feel it sincerely—not just pretend that's what you think; you must mean it. I think you have to make an actor believe that he's better than he is. That's the biggest job.

PB: Give him confidence?

OW: More than confidence. Arrogance. He really has to think he's great, and that he's extending himself beyond what he thought he could do. There are so many ways of doing it, and it's dictated by the material itself and by the actor. It's so much a question of atmosphere and all those mysteries of personality and mood and everything else. So I don't have any method except that the basic atmosphere on the set with me—or on the stage—is always very gay and full of jokes, usually with someone playing the piano.

PB: You don't need silence?

OW: Well, we have silence when we need it. But the whole thing has to be "What fun it is to be here." Unless something in the story calls for creating a terrible, desperate atmosphere—something ominous—and then everybody has to get into that. But, basically, I think the actors should look forward to their work every day, not dread it.

PB: Well, in the theatre you said you like long hours.

OW: Yes, because there's such a short amount of rehearsal time given. The Russians take nine months to do a play, which is much too long, and Americans take three and a half weeks, which is much too short. The long hours is to get it done, that's all—I don't think it's any great advantage, everyone being dead tired. It's just no choice—if you go beyond that, they have to go on full salary, by Equity rules. Simple as that.

PB: So you don't do that in movies.

OW: No. I rehearse, but illegally. They'd come to my house before the picture started and we'd pretend we were talking over the script. But we really were rehearsing. We rehearsed *Touch of Evil* for about two weeks before we shot. Very hard.

PB: The staging as well.

OW: Some staging, and all the overlaps, and all those things you talk about, hour after hour, long before we came on the set. But you've got all that behind you.

PB: And they're so much more confident.

OW: That's right. You know, there are two great schools of lion training, the French and the German. In one, the French, the animals are kept strictly in their places. In the other, the German, they always seem to be fighting with their trainer. You'd rather expect the first school to be German, the second French, but it's just the opposite. Well, there are also two great schools of directors: one where the director dominates and terrifies: I belong to the other school.

PB: Mercedes McCambridge was very good in that really sick scene with Janet Leigh in the motel, where she comes in looking very butch and says, "I wanna watch."

OW: That's how I got the picture approved by Zugsmith. He was the producer. After he read that scene, it was "Go ahead and shoot!" [*Laughs.*]

PB: He never gave you any trouble at all?

OW: Nobody did until they saw the final cut.

PB: It was probably the first film to show a bunch of hopheads

and to drop marijuana loosely. What do you actually think of people who take drugs?
OW: Suicides. All real addicts are some form of suicide in my opinion.
PB: And marijuana?
OW: No, that's the beer of drugs. If there were no law against marijuana and no fuzz [police] connected with it, its popularity would diminish enormously. Because its effect is rather less potent than that of beer, and all it does is give you extremely bad breath. It's a socially very unpleasant thing unless everybody's on it. But there's nothing really against it. It was a terrible mistake to make it illegal, because it's quite an innocent thing in itself. All over the world, children of eight and ten smoke it with less harmful effects than from the few glasses of wine the French kids have. *Because* taking it is given an illicit feeling, and because it's now sort of connected with protests and is generally antiestablishment, anti-fuzz, and so on, the sort of neurotic who has the marijuana habit can be led into real drug-taking. But it's a terribly overrated drug; and it's very hard to get quantities of good enough quality to give anybody enough of a bang to be worth all the carrying on that they do about it.
PB: What do you think of the hallucinatory drugs in general?
OW: I'm against the principle of it, but not the adventure and experiment of it. I've never taken LSD, but years ago I took the hallucinatory mushrooms and all that kind of thing and, having done it, I've no desire ever to do it again.
PB: Did it help you in any way?
OW: Of course not.
PB: Does it help anybody?
OW: Maybe. I used to argue with Aldous Huxley, not for hours but for days, weeks—because we were great chums, and of course he was the guru of that sort of thing. And it's not something I want to fight about. I like involvement in society, but I think people have a right to cop out if they want to—though I think it *is* basically copping out.
PB: Well, it ties in with a whole way of making films that are basically onanistic. Much of the modern style is masturbatory.
OW: It's self-indulgent, as the great body of modern artwork is self-indulgent—to the point of at least narcissism, if not onanism. So to that extent it is true about movies, but movies should be

studied in the context of modern art in general, not alone—that is the point I keep making.

PB: Getting back to *Touch of Evil,* that's a very unusual shot when Heston hears his wife's been arrested and you cut to a big closeup of him and blur out.

OW: Yeah, it goes out of focus. I like doing that. I haven't used it as much as I'd like to—

PB: It goes out of focus so fast.

OW: We pulled frames again. That's the great secret—skip-framing. I do a lot of that, particularly for those kind of things—to hide zooms and cover out-of-focus shots.

PB: And to make the zoom faster?

OW: Yes, that's what I mean. To hide the mechanics, because the zoom is a deadly instrument when you feel it working. I think it's a great enemy to a lot of young directors who just can't get their hands off it—done a lot of harm. It's such an attractive toy, you can't blame them. But it's peculiarly dead optically in most of its uses. It can be staggeringly good but only very sparingly used, it seems to me.

PB: Where have you liked it?

OW: I've seen some good zooming around—particularly in European and English television. I see a lot more interesting things in television than I do in movies. And I think commercials are terribly interesting. The minute I arrive in America, or any country, I sit right down, turn off the sound, and stare at the commercials and look away during the shows, because I think some of the most interesting moviemaking is in the commercials. I don't mean they're all good, but every once in a while you see something that's staggering. And the more fast-cut commercials are made, the more sophisticated the public's eye becomes and the easier it is to do those things. The public is much readier to accept surprising things on the screen thanks to commercials. Quick transitions, too.

PB: I've never seen Dietrich as she was in *Touch of Evil*—she transcends everything and becomes almost a mythical figure.

OW: The whole character, you know, was written after the picture started. We were well along before I even thought it up. Then I phoned Marlene and said I had a couple of days' work for her and she'd have to have dark hair because, I told her, "I liked you as a brunette in *Golden Earrings.*" She didn't ask to read the script. She just said, "Well, I'll go over to Paramount—I think that wig is still there—and then I'll go to Metro for a dress. . . ." The front office didn't even know she was in the picture. You should have seen them in the projection room during the first rushes: "Hey! Isn't that Dietrich?" And I said, "Yes." They said, "We haven't got *her* in the budget." And I said, "No. Won't cost you anything as long as you don't give her billing." They decided they wanted to and paid her to be in it. But it was up to them.

PB: Well, it was actually a digression as far as the plot is concerned.

OW: Yeah, but it helped it enormously. Look what that does for the film—that scene when those two suddenly encounter each other. And when she sees him floating in the bay—it *makes* the picture, you know.

PB: That's what I think. Where did the pianola come from? It seems like a remembrance of *The Blue Angel* [1930].

OW: Honestly, I wasn't thinking of that. I've never seen *The Blue Angel*. I just think we found a pianola among the props. I think all that Dietrich part of it is as good as anything I've ever done in movies. When I think of that opening in New York without even a press showing . . . Really, Marlene was extraordinary in that. She really was the Super-Marlene. Everything she has ever been was in that little house for about four minutes there.

PB: All her past movies and everything—

OW: She was just an angel about it, you know.

PB: My favorite moment is the look between the two of you. You both just stand there looking at each other, and it's as though you knew each other for years.

OW: Forever—that's the whole thing.

PB: And it has all the reverberations of your past in the movies and her past in the movies—which is above and beyond anything you can put into a film, I think.

OW: Yes, an enormous mutual trust. We've been all these years —sawing each other in half eight times a day and being everywhere. She was never late by a minute. You can't *know* how close we are.

When I have seen him and talked with him, I feel like a plant that has been watered.

—Marlene Dietrich

PB: You have a flamboyant personality and critics sometimes think of you as a ham, but I've always thought that your acting was terribly simple. Just as your narration in *Ambersons* is so beautifully underplayed and low-key.
OW: As an actor, I'm always begging directors to let me do less, and they're always saying: "Can't we have a little more? And give it to us—a little bigger." And I keep saying, "No, please, no." I get flamboyant roles offered to me, and I take them because I have to live. I then try and deflamboy as much as possible.
PB: The truth is, you're often an underactor. *Touch of Evil* is a good example of it—that performance is just mumbled.
OW: Right in there with Lee Strasberg! [*Laughs.*]
PB: It's just another one of those clichés. Did you work harder on your performance in that than you usually do?
OW: It came very easily. I worked much harder for the five days on General Dreedle in *Catch-22* than I did on that fellow. I saw him clearly—I just played it. And I was greatly helped by Tamiroff—because a little word from another actor will help you. I came on with the hat and the makeup the way I'd worked it out; Tamiroff saw me and said, "You're the man."" The way Tamiroff said it, I knew it was right, and that was the end. I said, "I don't have to worry about that." And I just played it. I think, of all the performances I've ever given in movies, that was the one I was the least self-conscious about.
PB: I think it's one of your best.
OW: Probably for that reason. I wasn't worried about how to do it, thought it was going to be all right: "I'm doing it right—I'm on to it." And very rare for me to be not self-conscious, because I really do suffer as an actor too much, and worry, too. And that probably worked just because I didn't. I took very few takes. I knew exactly what to do—it just *worked*.
PB: The scene where you strangle Tamiroff is particularly gruesome.
OW: Terrible violence—it's a very unpleasant, horrible scene. And we felt awful when we were done with it.
PB: There was something vaguely sexual about it.
OW: Yes. It was perverse and morbid—the kind of thing I don't like to do too much. But it was one of those go-as-far-as-you-can-go—in that kind of dirty department. Tamiroff was great in it: when he looked at that gun, it was every cock in the world. It was awful, the way he looked at it—made the whole scene possible.

Welles, Leigh, and Tamiroff.

PB: You meant it to have a sexual connotation?
OW: Of course. It's a very ugly scene.
PB: How long did it take to shoot?
OW: A day.
PB: And how did you get the effect of his eyes bulging out after he's been strangled?
OW: Contact lenses. Painted.
PB: Terrifying.
OW: I've had people criticize that very strongly as in bad taste. Several people have told me, "You went too far with that." In fact, they're right to an extent—because it was almost subliminal in my cutting. And that's one of the things they changed: they added ten frames to that shot—
PB: Which made it just a little too long—
OW: Yes. My way, you didn't really know if you saw it—you were just left with that. And their way, you got a good long look at those eyes. And I didn't want you to. I wanted you not to be sure you saw it.

PB: Well, ten frames makes a big difference.
OW: Such a joy to work with all those great people—with [John] Russell on the crane, and with Tamiroff. *Touch of Evil* was, you know, unimaginably pleasurable to make, with everybody at the top of their bent. And you know that anything you think up, they'll just do.

That's why I was so heartbroken when it turned out I couldn't go on with it. I was so sure I was going to go on making a lot of pictures at Universal, when suddenly I was fired from the lot. A terribly traumatic experience. Because I was so sure. They went out of their way to compliment me every night for the rushes, and "When are you going to sign a four- or five-picture contract with us? Please come and see us." Every day they kept asking me to sign the contract. Then they saw the cut version and barred me from the lot.
PB: Wasn't it ever explained?
OW: Never. The picture was just too dark and black and strange for them.
PB: Awful story.
OW: Not just an awful story—a mystery. There's something missing there that I don't know about, that I'll never understand. It's the only trouble I've ever had that I can't begin to fathom. The picture rocked them in some funny way. They particularly loathed the black comedy—the kind people now like. Movies weren't nearly that black ten or twelve years ago. They just didn't know what I was up to. And I really thought I was home again, you know, and "I'm going to be at Universal three or four years making pictures"—the way they talked. Then suddenly I couldn't get on the lot.
PB: How were you apprised of that fact?
OW: They had a man at the gate to keep my car from coming in. They were deeply shocked—they felt insulted by the film in a funny way. And hurt and injured—I'd taken them for some kind of awful ride. It was sad for me it turned out that way, because I was ready to settle down in America.
PB: If you could have your way, you'd live in America?
OW: Well, I would certainly *work* in America, which means living here. I'd rather make pictures here than anywhere.

9.

WELLES' CAREER: A CHRONOLOGY

EDITOR'S PREFACE: The following account of Welles' career is compiled from many sources, in particular the original information and listings that were prepared by Bogdanovich for this book in the late 1960s and early '70s; these have been revised, expanded, and updated. Welles' work in commercials has been omitted. Due to space restrictions, credits are regrettably incomplete in most cases, but a balance has been sought between citing some of the most important names and including some information that is unavailable elsewhere. Like virtually all Welles' research, this compilation necessarily qualifies as work-in-progress rather than as an account that can pretend to be definitive or exhaustive.

Certain areas have been much harder to check than others. Welles' complete theatre credits in Dublin in 1931–1932 and the authorship of most radio scripts are especially difficult to pinpoint, because of the inadequacy of surviving records, although it is important to add, regarding the latter, that the scripts in Welles' radio series often tended to be written collaboratively. Drafts on the early shows were often done by outside writers, but Houseman or Welles usually took care of the final draft, with Welles almost always doing a polish; many of the later shows were worked on by several writers, and Ann Froelich was a significant collaborator with Howard Koch on some of the earlier ones.

All the material relating to *It's All True* was either supplied or checked by Catherine Benamou, whose dissertation on the subject promises to be extremely comprehensive. The compilation of much of the material from the mid-1960s on is indebted to Gary Graver and Oja Kodar, and the late Richard Wilson's detailed input on the earlier periods was indispensable.

The list of Welles' radio and TV appearances and his film narrations is, by virtue of the impossibility of tracking them all down, very far from complete.

The following abbreviations are used for names:

AA: Arthur Anderson
WA: William Alland
BB: Bea Benaderet
EB: Edgar Barrier
GB: Georgia Backus
JB: John Berry
JTB: John Tucker Battle
MB: Maurice Bessy
PB: Peter Bogdanovich
RB: Richard Baer (Barr)
GC: George Coulouris
HC: Hans Conried
JC: Joseph Cotten
RC: Ray Collins
BD: Brainerd Duffield
GD: George Duthie
KD: Kenneth Delmar
HE: Hilton Edwards
AF: Arlene Francis
AFT: Alice Frost
BF: Brenda Forbes
GF: Geraldine Fitzgerald
BG: Betty Garde
GG: Gary Graver
MG: Martin Gabel
WG: Will Geer
BH: Bernard Herrmann
JH: John Houseman
GK: Guy Kingsley
HK: Howard Koch
OK: Oja Kodar
FL: Francesco Lavignino
AM: Agnes Moorehead
HJM: Herman J. Mankiewicz
JM: Jeanne Moreau
MEM: Mercedes McCambridge
MM: Micheál Mac Liammóir
VN: Virginia Nicolson [Welles]
EP: Edgarton Paul
ER: Elliott (Ted) Reid
FR: Frank Readick
SR: Stephen Roberts
AS: Alfred Shirley
ERS: Erskine Sanford
ES: Everett Sloane
GS: Gus Schilling
GSP: Guy Spaull
HS: Hiram Sherman
PS: Paul Stewart
SS: Stefan Schnabel
WS: William Shakespeare
AT: Akim Tamiroff
HT: Howard Teichmann
EW: Eustace Wyatt
OW: Orson Welles
RW: Richard Wilson

Certain references are abbreviated in this chronology as follows:

MB: Maurice Bessy, *Orson Welles* (Paris: Seghers, 1963).

MB2: English translation by Ciba Vaughan of the above (New York: Crown, 1971).

FB: Frank Brady, *Citizen Welles* (New York: Charles Scribner's Sons, 1989).

PC: Peter Cowie, *A Ribbon of Dreams* (South Brunswick, N.J.: A.S. Barnes & Co., 1973).

RF: Richard France, *The Theater of Orson Welles* (Cranbury, N.J.: Associated University Presses, 1977).

RF2: ———, *Orson Welles on Shakespeare: The W.P.A. and Mercury Theatre Playscripts*, ed. Richard France (Westport, Conn.: Greenwood Press, 1990).

EAG: Eric A. Gordon, *Mark the Music: The Life and Work of Marc Blitzstein* (New York: St. Martin's Press, 1989).

CH: Charles Higham, *The Films of Orson Welles* (Berkeley, Calif.: University of California Press, 1970).

CH2: ———, *Orson Welles: The Rise and Fall of an American Genius* (New York: St. Martin's Press, 1975).

JH: John Houseman, *Run-Through* (New York: Simon and Schuster, 1972).

BL: Barbara Leaming, *Orson Welles* (New York: Viking, 1985).

RM: Richard Maney, *Fanfare: The Confessions of a Press Agent* (New York: Harper & Brothers, 1957).

JN: James Naremore, *The Magic World of Orson Welles*, 2nd ed. (Dallas: Southern Methodist University Press, 1989).

CV: Claudio M. Valentinetti, *Welles* (Firenze: La Nuova Stampa, 1981).

BW: Bret Wood, *Orson Welles: A Bio-Bibliography* (Westport, Conn.: Greenwood Press, 1990).

TOTI: *Theatre of the Imagination.* Criterion laser disc and audiotapes released by Voyager in 1988.

The following abbreviations are used in the credits:

D: Director
P: Producer(s)
Assoc p: Associate producer
Exec p: Executive Producer
Sc: Script or screenplay
Ann: Announcer
P mgr: Production manager
Asst d: Assistant director
Ph: Photography
Cam op: Camera operator(s)
Ed: Editor(s)
P des: Production designer
Art d: Art director
R t: Running time
Narr: Narrator

1915

May 6 George Orson Welles born, in Kenosha, Wisconsin, to Beatrice Ives Welles—pianist, champion rifle shot, and suffragette who once served a prison term for her radical views—and Richard Head Welles, a sometime inventor from a wealthy Virginia family. They already have one son, Richard, aged ten.

1918 Makes his stage debut as walk-on in *Samson and Delilah* at the Chicago Opera, followed by the part of "Trouble" in *Madame Butterfly* at the Ravina, Illinois, opera house.

1920 Costumed as a rabbit, he performs a ballyhoo for Marshall Fields department store. Because of his mother's influence, he is already showing marked signs of musical talent on the piano.

1924

May 10 Mother dies at the age of forty-three.

1925 At Camp Indianola, OW adapts, directs, and plays in a production of *Dr. Jekyll and Mr. Hyde*; at Washington Grade School in Madison, Wisconsin, he plays, among other roles, Scrooge in *A Christmas Carol*.

1926

Feb. 26 An article in the *Madison Journal* headlined "Cartoonist, Actor, Poet and Only Ten" describes some of OW's activities during this period, which include readings, performances, and editing and illustrating the *Indianola Trail*, a camp newspaper.

Fall Enters the Todd School for Boys in Woodstock, Illinois. Gives a magic performance there on Halloween; plays the Virgin Mary at the school's Christmas pageant. Later performances at Todd include Christ in *The Servant in the House*, Judas Iscariot in *Dust of the Road*, and Jim Bailey in *It Won't Be Long Now*, a musical revue that he writes with Roger Hill and Carl Hendrikson.

1928 Does the leading role of a young clubman engaged in amateur detective work in a Todd musical revue that he co-writes, *Finesse the Queen*, and becomes a scenic artist. Other productions at Todd that he directs, designs, adapts, and/or acts in over the next two years include *Wings over Europe*, Molière's *The Physician in Spite of Himself*, Marlowe's *Dr. Faustus*, *Everyman*, and *Dr. Jekyll and Mr. Hyde*; he also writes a radio play which he doesn't produce for a local broadcast around this time, based on Sherlock Holmes stories.

Spends summer at Grand Detour with his father.

1929 Stages, adapts, and plays the parts of Mark Antony and Cassius in WS's *Julius Caesar* at Todd.

Writes a theatrical column called "Inklings" for the *Highland Park News*.

In the summer, travels with two friends to England, Germany, France, and Italy.

1930 Stages, adapts, and plays the part of Ferovious in Shaw's *Androcles and the Lion* for the Woodstock Women's Club—another production performed with the Todd Troupers. Before graduation, he also stages, adapts, and plays Richard III in an amalgamation of WS's *Henry VI* and *Richard III* entitled *Winter of Our Discontent*.

Graduates from Todd, goes to Chicago Art Institute; in the summer, travels with his father to Japan and China.

Nov. 11 Ashton Stevens writes about OW in his column in the *Chicago Herald American*.

Dec. 28 Father dies at the age of fifty-eight.

1931

Jan. 1 Dr. Maurice Bernstein becomes OW's guardian.

Aug. Leaves the U.S. for Ireland to begin a sketching tour. Travels through the country and to the Aran Islands.

Sept. In Dublin, director Hilton Edwards engages him as a member of the new Dublin Gate Theatre company, which is just preparing its fifth season:

Oct. 13 *Jew Süss* (Dublin Gate Theatre Production) by Leon Feuchtwanger, adapted by Ashley Dukes. D: HE. Opens: Gate Theatre (through October 31). Cast: HE (Süss), OW (Duke Karl Alexander of Württemberg), Betty Chancellor (Naomi). (From OW's letter home, December 1931: "Karl

Alexander is a boorish product of his very physical age [eighty] . . . staggers magnificently through five acts to dukedom and destruction. . . . There are moments in the play when I feel I must make my voice ring and boom and make a gesture simple but studied and stagey but even in the moments of the most intense comedy or tragedy I must be Karl Alexander without a single tassel or tinsel. . . .") After this role, he is cast only in "character" roles at the Gate.

Nov. 3 *The Dead Ride Fast* (Dublin Gate Theatre Prod.) by David Sears. D: HE. Opens: Gate Theatre (through November 14). Cast: OW (Ralph Bentley), others. (OW, December 1931: "A rather bad thriller it was, trying desperately at the expense of the thrills to be highbrow. . . . My part [was as] the richest man in Montana . . . and I played him with a none too subtle flavor of burlesque, horn-rimmed spectacles, cigar, and an accent to fit the pre–Abraham Lincoln phrases in the script. . . . One of the critics remarked that while my performance was at once subtle, sincere, and amusing, my understanding of the American mentality was obviously slight!")

Nov. 20 *The Archduke* (Dublin Gate Theatre Prod.) by Percy Robinson. D: HE. Opens: Gate Theatre (through December 15). Cast: OW (Marshal François Bazaine/Mexican colonel), others.

Dec. 26 *Mogu of the Desert* (Dublin Gate Theatre Prod.) by Padraic Colum. D: HE. Sets: MM. Opens: Gate Theatre (through January 9, 1932). Cast: HE (Ali the Beggar), OW (Chosroes, King of Persia), Betty Chancellor, others.

1932

Jan. 12 *Death Takes a Holiday* (Dublin Gate Theatre Prod.) by Alberto Cassella and Walter Ferris. D: HE. Opens: Gate Theatre (through January 26). Cast: OW (Baron Lamberto), others.

Feb. 2 *Hamlet* (Dublin Gate Theatre Prod.) by WS. D: HE. Opens: Gate Theatre (through February 13). Cast: MM (Hamlet), HE (Claudius), OW (The Ghost/Fortinbras), others.

Twelfth Night *at the Todd School.*

March *The Circle* by W. Somerset Maugham. Opens: Abbey Theatre, Dublin. Cast: OW (Lord Porteus), others. OW's longest engagement at the Abbey.

While in Dublin, OW does a few productions of his own, including *The Chinese Bungalow* by Matheison Lang, Ibsen's *The Lady from the Sea*, Noel Coward's *Hay Fever*, OW's own adaptation of Lewis Carroll, *Alice in Wonderland U.S.A.*, Harry M. Vernon and Harold Owen's *Mr. Wu*, and *The Only Way*. He also designs the scenery for a production of Chekhov's *The Three Sisters*, and acts in several local productions, including the aforementioned *The Chinese Bungalow*, *Mr. Wu*, Ibsen's *Peer Gynt*, Strindberg's *The Father*, Sheridan's *The Rivals*, O'Neill's *The Emperor Jones*, Goldoni's *La locandiera*, Molnár's *The Play's the Thing*, Shaw's *Man and Superman*, Romains's *Dr. Knock*, Hodges and Percival's *Grumpy*, Capek's *The Marropouls Secret*, Milne's *The Dover Road*, Ben Jonson's *Volpone*, Patrick Hamilton's *Rope* (the role of David Kentley), and four WS productions (*Richard III*, *Macbeth*, *Timon of Athens*, and *King John*.)

During the same period, he contributes a column, "Chitchat and Criticism," to an Irish weekly tabloid under the pseudonym Knowles Noel Shane, mainly about theatre (and including much praise for his own performances).

1933

March OW proceeds to London in the hopes of doing more theatre there, but, unable to secure a work permit, he returns to the U.S.

May OW directs a Todd production of *Twelfth Night*, adapting Kenneth Macgowan's concept of using a giant "book" onstage with pages which he paints himself, opening to various scenes; he also designs the costumes. The production wins first prize in the annual Drama League contest held in the Chicago area for high-school and little-theatre groups. Roger Hill lends OW a silent-movie camera to film most of the dress rehearsal in color, which he shoots from a fixed position in the auditorium.

Spring–Summer Later that spring, he travels to Morocco and Spain, writes detective stories for pulp magazines, and does a little bullfighting on the side, returning to the U.S. circa August. He spends a short time in New York (where he is unable to get work), and otherwise remains mainly in Chicago with Dr. Bernstein and with Roger Hill in Woodstock, preparing with the latter a series of textbooks on WS and collaborating on a five-act play, *Marching Song*, based on the John Brown story, which is never produced or published. Around the same time, he writes a semi-autobiographical three-act play on his own, *Bright Lucifer*, about a demonic teenager (see JN and BL). Another early OW play, which may have been written during this period, and which appears not to have survived, is *Last Stand*, briefly described in a letter from OW to PB in the latter's article "The *Kane* Mutiny."

Sept. 18 Returns to New York. Through Thornton Wilder, who has heard of his Dublin successes, he is introduced to Alexander Woollcott, who brings him to the attention of director Guthrie McClintic and actress Katharine Cornell. They cast him for their thirty-six-week tour of:

Nov. 29 *The Barretts of Wimpole Street* by Rudolf Besier. D: Guthrie McClintic. Cast: Katharine Cornell (Elizabeth Barrett), OW (Octavius Moulton Barrett), BF, others, in repertory with:

Candida by George Bernard Shaw. D: Guthrie McClintic. Cast: Katharine Cornell (Candida), OW (Marchbanks), others. The tour begins in Buffalo, New York, and includes well over two hundred performances across the country.

1934 *Everybody's Shakespeare*, a series of textbooks by Roger Hill and OW, published by the Todd Press in Woodstock. Each volume contains the same introductory essays by Hill and Welles (one by each) followed by an "edited version for acting" of a WS play—*Twelfth Night, The Merchant of Venice*, or *Julius Caesar*—with OW illustrations.

Through actor-director Paul Stewart, OW meets radio director Knowles Entrikin, who gives him his first job on the radio:

School of the Air of the Americas (The American School of the Air) (CBS). D: Knowles Entrikin, Sc: Howard Rodman, others. Broadcast: every weekday afternoon. Cast: Dr. Lyman Bryson, RC, Parker Fennelly, Chester Stratton, Mitzi Gould, OW, JC, BG, others. Dramatizations of history, current events, and literature. This program is required listening in many U.S. classrooms.

Summer OW persuades HE and MM to come from Dublin and join him in a six-week "Summer Festival of Drama" staged at the Todd School in Woodstock:

Trilby by Gerald du Maurier. D: OW. Cast: MM (Little Billee), HE (Taffy), OW (Svengali).

Hamlet by WS. D: HE. Cast: MM (Hamlet), OW (Claudius), others.

The Drunkard by William H. Smith. D: OW.

Tsar Paul by D. S. Merejkowski. D: HE. Cast: HE (Tsar Paul), OW (Count Pahlen), VN (Elizabeth).

He also makes his first film:

Hearts of Age. D: OW, William Vance. P/Ph: Vance. Sc: OW Cast: OW (Death), VN (Old Woman), William Vance. 5 minutes (16mm, silent). Filmed at the old firehouse in Woodstock.

Fall A thirty-six-week tour of *Romeo and Juliet* by WS. D: Guthrie McClintic. Cast: Katharine Cornell (Juliet), Maurice Evans (Romeo), OW (Mercutio), Tyrone Power (Balthazar, later Tybalt), others.

Nov. 14 OW marries Virginia Nicolson, who had been his first leading lady in the movies (see Summer entry).

Dec. 21 A revised version of *Romeo and Juliet* opens at Martin Beck Theatre in New York. Cast: Katharine Cornell (Juliet), Basil Rathbone (Romeo), Brian Aherne (Mercutio), OW (Tybalt), John Emery (Benvolio), Edith Evans (nurse), George Macready (Paris), others. (See JH for a description of this production.)

1935 Continues radio work, mostly anonymous, on such shows as:

America's Hour (CBS). D: Knowles Entrikin. Cast: OW, JC, RC, FR, AM, BG, John Monks, others. A documentary series about American history, farming, industry, aviation, shipping, etc.

Cavalcade of America (NBC). D: PS, Homer Fickett, others. P: Roger Pryor. Sc: Norman Rosten, Arthur Miller, others. Cast: Jack Smart, AM, PS, Jeanette Nolan, John McIntire, OW, FR, JC, RC, ES, others. A distinguished series that begins this year and continues long into the 1940s (when OW is to make guest-star appearances), specializing in dramatizations of American history.

Columbia Workshop: Hamlet (CBS), adapted by OW from WS. D: Irving Reis. Music: BH. Cast: OW (Hamlet), others. Shown in two half-hour parts over successive Sundays. (OW: "We got one cue wrong in *Hamlet*—one cue off with Bernard Herrmann. He had broken his baton and thrown his script up in the air and walked out of the studio forty seconds before air time because of a quarrel with Irving Reis. And I dragged him back. We didn't have time to get the notes back in order on his stand, so he was one cue off all through it. So we had fanfares when it was supposed to be quiet, approaching menace when it was supposed to be a gay party, and all live; it was riotous. Nothing to do—he just went on. It got funnier and funnier, because Reis was an emotional-type director and Benny is an emotional-type conductor, and between the two of them . . .")

The March of Time (NBC-Blue). D/P: Arthur Pryor, Jr. D: Homer Fickett, others. Sc: Richard Dana, Carl Carmer, others. Sound effects: Mrs. Ora Nichols, others. Ann: Westbrook Van Voorhies. Cast: Bill Adams (FDR), AM (Eleanor Roosevelt), Maurice Tarplin (Churchill), Dwight

Weist (Hitler), Peter Donald (Chamberlain), Ted de Corsia (Mussolini), OW, RC, Arnold Moss, PS, WG, AF, MG, Jeanette Nolan, others. "*Time* . . . marches on!" Presented by Time Inc., this famous series, also produced as a newsreel for movie theatres, dramatizes weekly news events. OW, who appears on the show over the next four years, winds up making a parody of it in *Citizen Kane*. His first appearance is on March 22 (q.v.).

During this period, OW also reads poetry on Alexander Woollcott's radio show (NBC).

March 15 *Panic* (Phoenix Theatre Group Presentation) by Archibald MacLeish. D: James Light. P: JH, Nathan Zatkin. Choral movement: Martha Graham. Opens: Imperial Theatre, New York (3 performances only). Cast: OW (McGafferty), Zita Johann (Ione), Harold Johnsrud (Blind Man), Abner Biberman, Vincent Sherman, Bernard Zanville [later known as Dane Clark], others. A drama in blank verse about the Wall Street Crash in which OW plays a scheming manipulator; it is his first association with John Houseman.

March 22 OW performs a scene from *Panic* on *The March of Time*. On the same show, he also plays all five of the Dionne quintuplets in a report on these then-celebrated babies.

April Over the next month or so, OW plans, casts, and rehearses a stage production of John Ford's *'Tis a Pity She's a Whore*, to be produced by JH and featuring Miriam Batista, Alexander Scourby, and Hiram Sherman, but the financing falls through.

1936

Jan. 20 *Musical Reveries* (CBS). OW reads poems between musical selections.

April 14 *Macbeth* (A Federal Theatre Production of the WPA) by WS. D/adaptor/choreographer: OW. Managing P: JH, for the Negro Division of the Federal Theatre. Music: Virgil Thomson, performed by the Negro Orchestra. Opens: Lafayette Theatre, Harlem, New York (64 performances, until June 20); reopens at Broadway's Adelphi Theatre on July 6 for another two months; then goes on national tour of seven WPA theatres. Cast: Jack Carter (Macbeth), Edna Thomas (Lady Macbeth), Canada Lee (Banquo), Service

Bell (Duncan), others. In Indianapolis, OW performs the title role in blackface. "The idea of doing the tragedy with a colored cast was suggested by Mrs. Welles. Because Christophe, the famous black emperor of Haiti, had been a man after Macbeth's own heart, the action was transferred from Scotland to Haiti. The Birnam Wood that came to Dunsinane was a jungle of palms and bananas. The three weird women were translated into sixty black witch doctors." Alva Johnston and Fred Smith, "How to Raise a Child: The Disturbing Life—to Date—of Orson Welles," *Saturday Evening Post*, February 3, 1940. (See also RF2 (the original playscript), JH, RF, and BW.)

Autumn On the recommendation of PS, OW begins to appear regularly on *The March of Time* when it becomes a daily rather than a weekly show.

Sept. 26 *Horse Eats Hat* (A Federal Theatre Production, Project 891 of the WPA) by OW and Edwin Denby, freely adapted from the farce *Un Chapeau de paille d'Italie* by Eugène Labiche and Marc-Michel. D: OW. Managing P: JH. Music: Paul Bowles. Orchestration: Virgil Thomson. Opens: Maxine Elliott Theatre, New York (runs through December 5). Cast: JC (Freddy), OW [alternating with EP] (Mugglethorp), GD (Endwhistle), others. (OW to PB: "The farce *Horse Eats Hat* was the best of the Mercury shows—and, though successful, it divided the town. The press was mixed, yet it was always packed, and had an enormous following. Some people went to it every week as long as it ran." (See also JH, RF, and FB.)

Oct. 23 *Ten Million Ghosts* by Sidney Kingsley. D/P: Sidney Kingsley. Opens: St. James Theatre, New York. Cast: OW (peasant poet André Pequot), GC (Zacharey), Barbara O'Neill (Madeleine), MG, others. This antiwar drama about Zaharoff and the armaments racket is financed by Kingsley himself; it plays only 11 performances.

Autumn Late this year, Welles begins to appear on *The Wonder Show* (Mutual Broadcasting System). Cast: OW (Narrator and The Great McCoy), others. OW flies to Chicago to appear on this show for about six weeks; it features old-fashioned touring melodramas—e.g., *The Birth of the Sewing Machine Girl*, *Sweeney Todd*, and *The Relief of Lucknow*.

Welles in The Tragical History of Doctor Faustus.

1937

Jan. 8 *The Tragical History of Doctor Faustus* (A Federal Theatre Production, Project 891 of the WPA) by Christopher Marlowe. D: OW. Managing P: JH. Puppets: Bil Baird. Music: Paul Bowles. Lighting: A. H. Feder. Opens: Maxine Elliott Theatre, New York (runs through May 9). Cast: Charles

Peyton (Pope), J. Headly (Cardinal of Lorraine), OW (Faustus), Joseph Wooll [pseudonym for JC] (2nd scholar), Jack Carter (Mephisto), others. Presented on an apron stage with no scenery; the ticket prices are 55¢, 40¢, and 25¢. "A WPA Audience Survey Report" conducted during the play's run asks spectators whether they like this production and whether they want a permanent federal theatre. The replies to the first question are 940 affirmative (of which 282 are enthusiastic, 8 fair), 20 negative, and 143 "no answer"; the replies to the second are 1,064 pro, 18 con, and 21 "no answer." For detailed descriptions of the production, see OW's *The Cradle Will Rock: An Original Screenplay* (Santa Barbara, Cal.: Santa Teresa Press, 1993), JH, RF, and BW.

Radio activities in this period include guest appearances on the Federal Theatre Radio Division's series of classical plays; *Living Dramas of the Bible* (CBS); *Standard Brands Presents* (NBC); *Roses and Drums* (NBC), a weekly series about the Civil War; *Parted on Her Bridal Tour* (Mutual); the *Peter Absolute* series (NBC); *Streamlined Shakespeare*; continuing work on *Musical Reveries* and *The March of Time*; and regular appearances on:

March *The Shadow* (Mutual Broadcasting System). D: Dana Noyes, Harry Ingram, others. Sc: Peter Barry, Max Ehrlich, others; based on the magazine entries of Walter B. Gibson. Ann: André Baruch. Cast: OW (Lamont Cranston/The Shadow), AM (Margot Lane), Dwight Weist (Commissioner Weston), Keenan Wynn (Shrevie, cab driver), ES, Ted de Corsia, others. For the next two years, OW regularly plays Lamont Cranston (a role he did not create, although it is still identified with him), "wealthy young man-about-town" who had "several years ago in the Orient . . . learned a strange and mysterious secret . . . the hypnotic power to cloud men's minds so they cannot see him." (Only a selection of individual show titles are subsequently listed herein.)

April 11 *Columbia Workshop: The Fall of the City* (CBS). Verse play by Archibald MacLeish. P/D: Irving Reis. Music: BH. Cast: House Jameson (Studio director), OW (Announcer in isolation booth), Burgess Meredith (Pacifist orator), others. A polemic against totalitarianism written expressly for radio. (See FB.)

April 21 *The Second Hurricane* (Music School of the Henry Street Settlement) by Aaron Copland (music), Edwin Denby (libretto). D: OW. Conductor: Lehman Engel. Opens: Henry Street Settlement Playhouse, New York (runs for scheduled 3 performances). Cast: Vivienne Block (Queenie), Estelle Levy (Gwen), AA (Gyp), others. An operetta presented for the benefit of high school children. The onstage playing area is backed by a twenty-piece orchestra, and flanked by a Pupils' Chorus on the left and a Parents' Chorus on the right. (Note: although OW is usually credited with the direction, there is reason to believe that much of this work was carried out by HS while OW was preparing *The Cradle Will Rock*; see EAG.) Later this month, the production is broadcast on radio.

May Around this time, OW reads Ernest Hemingway's narration for Joris Ivens' documentary *This Spanish Earth* (which premieres on August 20); later his voice is discarded and replaced by Hemingway's own voice reading his own text. Both narrated versions still exist.

May 2 *Columbia Workshop: Macbeth* (CBS), adapted by OW from the WS play. D: Irving Reis. Music: BH. Cast: OW (Macbeth), others. Shown in two parts on successive Sundays.

June 16 *The Cradle Will Rock* (A Federal Theatre Production, Project 891 of the WPA). A play in music by Marc Blitzstein. Production by OW. Managing P: JH. Cast: Olive Stanton (Moll), George Fairchild (Gent/Gus), Guido Alexander (Dick), Howard da Silva (Larry), others. Blitzstein's radical pro-labor opera in ten scenes, set in Steeltown, U.S.A., during a strike, is originally scheduled to open on June 16 in its first public preview at the Maxine Elliott Theatre in a fully mounted production. On June 15, a dozen WPA guards padlock the theatre and take over the building, ostensibly because of Welles and Houseman's defiance in planning to put on the show in spite of government orders not to open any new shows before July 1 "because of impending cuts and reorganization." After much confusion, another theatre twenty-one blocks away, the Venice, is rented, and the audience is invited to walk that distance to see the show, without sets or costumes. Union regulations prevent the cast from appearing onstage, but Blitzstein appears there at an upright piano, reciting the stage directions and playing the score; the cast members deliver their lines and sing the songs from the audience, with the aid of a spotlight operated by A. H. Feder. The results are so successful that the show opens at the Venice in the same impromptu form on June 18, where it plays through July 1. During the same period, it is given an extra Sunday performance in an amusement park in Bethlehem, Pennsylvania, and a performance in Uncasville, New York, before touring the steel districts of Pennsylvania and Ohio. See EAG, JH, and OW's *The Cradle Will Rock: An Original Screenplay*.

June 24 Special midnight performance of *The Cradle Will Rock*.

June 27 At 8:30 P.M., New York radio station WEVD (named after socialist Eugene V. Debs) broadcasts *The Cradle Will Rock*.

July 23 *Les Misérables, Chapter 1: The Bishop*. D/adaptor: OW, from the novel by Victor Hugo. Cast: OW (Jean Valjean), MG (Javert), AFT (Fantine), VN (Cosette as adult), RC, AM, ES, BG, HS, FR, Richard Widmark, RW, WA, others. (OW to PB: "I first developed the idea of telling stories with first-person narration on a show I did for Mutual—which was my first job as a writer-director for radio—doing *Les Misérables* on a seven-week series.")

July 30 *Les Misérables, Chapter 2: Javert*.

Aug. 6 *Les Misérables, Chapter 3: The Trial*.

Aug. 13 *Les Misérables, Chapter 4: Cosette*.

Aug. 15 *Columbia Workshop: The Escape* (CBS), Part 1, adapted from John Galsworthy. Cast: OW, others.

Aug. 20 *Les Misérables, Chapter 5: The Grave*.

Aug. 22 *Columbia Worskshop: The Escape* (CBS), Part 2.

Aug. 27 *Les Misérables, Chapter 6: The Barricade*.

Aug. 29 "Plan for a New Theatre," by OW and JH, published in the Sunday *New York Times*.

Aug. 30 *Twelfth Night* (CBS), adapted from the WS play. Cast: OW (Orsino), Tallulah Bankhead (Viola), Cedric Hardwicke (Malvolio), Helen Menken (Olivia).

Sept. 3 *Les Misérables, Chapter 7: Finale.*

Sept. 26 *The Shadow: The Hypnotized Audience.*

Oct. Late this month, Marc Blitzstein's original, autobiographical, half-hour "song-play," *I've Got the Tune*, dedicated to OW, is broadcast on CBS. OW, announced to play the lead role of Mr. Musiker, the composer, is too busy rehearsing *Caesar*, so Blitzstein himself plays the role, with Shirley Booth, Lotte Lenya, and several Mercury players performing the other parts and BH conducting. (See EAG.)

Oct. 2 *The Shadow: The Black Abbot.*

Oct. 24 *The Shadow: The Temple Bells of Neban.* Along with many of the subsequent episodes listed here, this is released on record (Murray Hill M 51212) in 1979. For other episodes and/or editions, see Mark 56 608 (1973), Mark 56 657 (1974), Murray Hill 894599 (1976), Everest 5001 (1977), Everest 5029 (1978), Murray Hill S 55111 (1980), and Command Performance LP-3 (date unknown).

Nov. 11 *Caesar* (A Mercury Theatre Presentation), adapted by OW from WS's *Julius Caesar.* D: OW. P: JH. Music: Marc Blitzstein. Opens: The Mercury Theatre (formerly The Comedy Theatre), New York. Cast: Joseph Holland (Caesar), GC (Marcus Antonius), JC (Publius), OW (Marcus Brutus), MG (Cassius), HS (Casca), SS, ER, GD, AA, JB, others. Produced in modern dress, with contemporary political allusions (e.g., fascist salutes and "Nuremberg" lighting) and no scenery or intermission, this is the first production by the Welles-Houseman Mercury Theatre, and perhaps their greatest single success, prompting the headline "BARD BOFFOLA" in *Variety.* See RF2 for the original playscript.

(John Mason Brown, *New York Post*, November 13, 1937: "It is placed upon a bare stage, the brick walls of which are crimson and naked. That is all. And that is all that is needed. In its streamlined simplicity this set achieves the glorious, unimpeded freedom of an Elizabethan stage. It is a setting spacious enough for both the winds and victims of demagoguery to sweep across it like a hurricane. . . .

"In groupings that are of that fluid, stressful, virtuoso sort one usually has to journey to Russia to see, Mr. Welles proves himself a brilliant innovator in his deployment of his principals and the movements of his crowds. . . . He keeps drumming the meaning of his play into our minds by the scuffling of his mobs when they prowl in the shadows, or by the herdlike thunder of their feet when they run as one threatening body. It is a memorable device. Like the setting in which it is used, it is pure theatre: vibrant, unashamed and enormously effective.")

Nov. 18 OW as Haile Selassie on *The March of Time.*

Nov. 25 OW as amnesiac French soldier on *The March of Time.*

Dec. 5 *The Cradle Will Rock* reopens in a new "oratorio version" at the Mercury Theatre on Sunday nights—with the *Caesar* set, two rows of chairs, a reduced chorus of twelve, WG, Howard da Silva, HS, John Hoysradt, and Blitzstein himself at the piano, narrating and playing several of the smaller parts. The following year, Random House publishes the Blitzstein play with a short preface by OW (the latter dated January 10, 1938).

1938

Jan. 1 *The Shoemaker's Holiday* (A Mercury Theatre Presentation), adapted by OW from the play by Thomas Dekker. D: OW. P: JH. Opens: The Mercury Theatre (in repertory with *Caesar* until April 1 (64 performances). Cast: GC (King), Frederic Tozere (Sir Hugh Lacy), JC (Rowland Lacy), Vincent Price (Master Hammond), GD, HS, ER, SS, AA, WA, AFT, JB, RW, others. Unanimous raves again. Shown without an intermission, the play has a running time of 69 minutes. See JH and RF for detailed descriptions.

Jan. 4 *The Cradle Will Rock*, presented by the Mercury Theatre in association with Sam H. Grisman, reopens in New York at the Windsor Theatre. It runs for thirteen weeks (until April 2), with ticket prices ranging from 55¢ to $2.20.

Another Mercury Theatre production planned for this year, but eventually abandoned, is Oscar Wilde's *The Im-*

portance of Being Earnest with HS, Vincent Price, BF, and VN.

Jan. 6 In a feature devoted to the ten best movies of 1937 on *The March of Time*, OW impersonates Paul Muni (in both *The Life of Émile Zola* and *The Good Earth*), Fredric March in *A Star Is Born*, and Spencer Tracy in *Captains Courageous*.

Jan. 9 *The Shadow: The League of Terror.*

Jan. 16 *The Shadow: Sabotage.*

Jan. 20 *Caesar* begins a road tour in Providence, Rhode Island, with a new cast, including Tom Powers (Brutus) and Edmond O'Brien (Marc Antony). It goes on to play in Boston, Hartford, Washington, D.C., Cleveland, Chicago, and Toronto to excellent reviews but only moderate business.

Jan. 24 *Caesar* moves two blocks west from the Mercury to a much larger stage and auditorium at the National Theatre; two days later, *The Shoemaker's Holiday* moves to the National as well, where it stays through April 28. (JH: "So now during February and March, the Mercury had 124 actors performing in four shows in three theatres. Our three New York shows were playing within two blocks of each other on West 41st Street. We renamed it Mercury Street, and without permission from the city, put up temporary signs to that effect on the corners of 6th and 7th Avenues and Broadway. And we engaged a young specialist in industrial graphics to design an elegant poster, headed WELCOME TO MERCURY STREET, in which each of our productions was clearly symbolized by small, stylized figures: fascist-military; renaissance-comic; a cradle in a treetop in a rising wind.")

Feb. 6 *The Shadow: The Phantom Voice.* Later this evening, OW emcees and introduces each number at a benefit concert for *New Masses* at the 46th Street Theatre, where Blitzstein, Virgil Thomson, Alex North, Paul Bowles, Hanns Eisler, Harold Rome, Earl Robinson, and Lehman Engel present their works. Blitzstein's *I've Got the Tune* (see October 1937) receives its stage premiere, with Count Basie performing in one section; OW schedules it to run twice at the Mercury on Sunday nights later this month, on a double bill with Ben Bengal's *Plant in the Sun.* (See EAG.)

Around this time, excerpts of *The Second Hurricane* are presented on radio with commentary by OW, in a program sponsored by *New Masses*.

Feb. 28 *Columbia Workshop: Air Raid* (CBS) by Archibald MacLeish. D: William N. Robeson. Music: BH. Cast: OW, BG, RC.

March 7 In Chicago to supervise the opening of *Caesar* at the Erlanger Theatre, OW meets with thirteen hundred high school students and their teachers to discuss "The Modern Approach to Shakespeare."

March 10 OW as Fiorello La Guardia on *The March of Time*.

March 11 OW appears with Blitzstein and others at a symposium, "The Culture of the People's Front," at New York's Hotel Center.

March 17 OW as Sigmund Freud on *The March of Time*.

March 20 The last live episode of *The Shadow, The Silent Avenger*, is broadcast.

March 27 OW's first child is born to Virginia Welles—a girl, named Christopher.

April OW gives a series of talks at the Workers Bookshop Symposium for the Workers Bookshop Mural Fund, including "Culture and the People's Front" and "Theatre and the People's Front." The text of the latter appears in the *Daily Worker* on April 15.

This month, a slightly cut version of *The Cradle Will Rock*, with narration by Blitzstein, is released on records (Musicraft, album 18; later rereleased on American Legacy Records T1001)—the first full-length Broadway show ever to be recorded on disc.

April 29 *Heartbreak House* (A Mercury Theatre Presentation) by George Bernard Shaw. D: OW. P: JH. Opens: The Mercury Theatre (runs for 6 weeks, closes on June 11). Cast: GF (Ellie Dunn), BF (Nurse Guinness), OW (Captain Shotover), Vincent Price (Hector Hushabye), ERS, GC, EW, others. Shaw forbids OW to cut the play (although a few surreptitious cuts are made all the same); the production receives excellent reviews.

The same evening, OW appears as a featured speaker at the American Student Peace Ball held at the Mecca Temple ballroom.

May 9 In his makeup as the octogenarian Captain Shotover, OW appears on the cover of *Time* magazine, over the caption "From Shadow to Shakespeare, Shoemaker to Shaw."

May–June From mid-May to June 11, *Caesar* concludes its run at the National with members of the road company replacing OW and GC.

June In a lecture to a convention of English teachers in New York, OW argues that, in entertainment value, theatre has become "vastly inferior to the movies."

June 12 "The Summing Up" by OW and JH, a report on the Mercury Theatre's first year, is published in the Sunday *New York Times*.

July 11 *The Mercury Theatre on the Air* (CBS). D/P/Narr: OW. Assoc p/rehearsal director: PS. Sc ed: OW, JH. Sc: JH, OW, HK, others. Music: BH (with twenty-seven-piece orchestra). Sound engineer: John Dietz. OW sells CBS on a series of weekly dramatic radio programs as a summer replacement for Cecil B. De Mille's *Lux Radio Theatre*, each show adapted from a famous work of literature, with himself as narrator. He and the Mercury Theatre are signed, and the show—subtitled *First Person Singular*—is broadcast opposite Edgar Bergen and Charlie McCarthy. The staff remains basically the same throughout the show's run and therefore will not be repeated below; changes and additions are noted under the individual programs. Most of the scripts in this first series are written by JH in consultation with OW.

Dracula (*The Mercury Theatre on the Air*, CBS), adapted by OW and JH from the Bram Stoker novel. Cast: OW (Dr. Seward/Count Dracula), Elizabeth Farrell (Lucy Westenra), GC (Jonathan Harker), AM, MG, RC, others. Released on record: *The Great Radio Horror Shows* (Murray Hill 933977) in 1975, *Dracula* (Mark 56 720) in 1976.

Mid-July In preparation for a planned summer production of the farce *Too Much Johnson*, OW films what is supposed to be an introduction to the play:

Too Much Johnson (unfinished) (A Mercury Theatre Production). D/Sc: OW, based on the play by William Gillette. P: OW, JH. Assoc p/unit manager: RW. Cameramen: Harry Dunham, Paul Dunbar. Ed: OW, WA, RW. Asst d: JB. Cast: JC (Augustus Billings), EB (Dathis), EW (Faddish), VN, GD, Marc Blitzstein, GK, JH, JB, AF, others. Done in the style of a silent slapstick comedy, this short two-part movie is made in order to put across a lot of the play's difficult and wordy exposition in a prologue and to show a manhunt through a Cuban jungle at a later point in the action. (See CH.) But the summer theatre at which the production plays (see Aug. 16) has an inadequate throw for film projection, making it impossible to show the film. Ultimately, although the show is planned to open the new Mercury season in New York, OW and JH decide instead to begin with *Danton's Death*, to be followed by the farce. *Danton*, a large-scale production, encounters so many difficulties that, when it is finally produced, there is no money left to do *Too Much Johnson*. (The only copy of the film is destroyed in a fire at Welles' villa in Madrid in August 1970.)

July 18 *Treasure Island* (*Mercury Theatre on the Air*, CBS), adapted by OW and JH from the Robert Louis Stevenson novel. Cast: OW (Long John Silver), AA (Jim Hawkins), GC (Captain Smollett), RC, AM, EW, AS, WA, RW, others. Released on record (Radiola MR-1085) in 1978.

July 25 A *Tale of Two Cities* (*Mercury Theatre on the Air*, CBS), adapted by JH from the Charles Dickens novel. Cast: OW (Sidney Carton/Dr. Manette), Mary Taylor (Lucie Manette), EW, EB, MG, FR, BG, ERS, RC, KD, RW, WA, others. Opening scene released on record, *Bette Orson Ingrid* (Mark 56 848), in 1982; full program available on TOTI.

Aug. 1 *The 39 Steps* (*Mercury Theatre on the Air*, CBS), adapted by JH from the John Buchan novel. Cast: OW (Richard Hannay/Marmaduke Jopley), others.

Aug. 8 *My Little Boy/The Open Window/I'm a Fool* (*Mercury Theatre on the Air*, CBS), adapted by JH from three short stories, written respectively by Carl Ewald, Saki, and Sherwood Anderson. Cast: OW, EB, RC, others.

Aug. 15 *Abraham Lincoln* (*Mercury Theatre on the Air*, CBS), adapted by JH from the play by John Drinkwater and other sources. Cast: OW, RC, GC, Carl Swenson, AM.

Aug. 16 *Too Much Johnson* (A Mercury Theatre Presentation) by William Gillette. D: OW. P: JH. Opens: Stony Creek Summer Theatre, Stony Creek, Connecticut, for 2-week run. Cast: see film credits, mid-July entry.

Aug. 22 *Affairs of Anatol* (*Mercury Theatre on the Air*, CBS), adapted by JH from the Arthur Schnitzler play. Cast: OW, AFT, AF, Helen Lewis, RC.

Aug. 29 *The Count of Monte Cristo* (*Mercury Theatre on the Air*, CBS), adapted by JH from the Alexandre Dumas novel. Cast: OW (Edmond Dantes), RC (Abbé Faria), GC (Monsieur Morrel), EB, EW, PS, RW, VN, WA, JB, others. Released on record (Radiola MR-1145) in 1983.

Sept. 5 *The Man Who Was Thursday* (*Mercury Theatre on the Air*, CBS), adapted by OW from the G. K. Chesterton novel. Cast: OW (Gabriel Syme), EW (President Sunday), RC (Professor), GC, EB, PS, JC, ERS, VN. The series receives enough favorable response to be renewed after this, its ninth, broadcast.

Sept. 11 *Julius Caesar* (*Mercury Theatre on the Air*, CBS), adapted from the WS play, with narration by H. V. Kaltenborn adapted from Plutarch's *Lives*. Cast: abbreviated version of stage cast; see Nov. 11, 1937. Released on record (Ariel SHO 9, Fonodisc International).

Sept. 18 *Jane Eyre* (*Mercury Theatre on the Air*, CBS), adapted from the Charlotte Brontë novel. OW's first of several radio productions of the novel; he will also produce and act in the 1944 movie.

Sept. 25 *Sherlock Holmes* (*Mercury Theatre on the Air*, CBS), adapted from stories by Arthur Conan Doyle and the William Gillette play. Cast: OW (Holmes), RC (Watson), Mary Taylor (Alice Faulkner), BF, EB, RW, EW, AA, WA, others. Released in 1975 on record as *The Immortal Sherlock Holmes* (Radiola 1036).

Oct. 2 *The Shadow: The Black Abbot*. And the same night:

Oliver Twist (*Mercury Theatre on the Air*, CBS), adapted by OW from the Charles Dickens novel. Cast: OW (Oliver/Fagin), others.

Oct. 8 Russell Maloney's profile of OW, "This Ageless Soul," appears in *The New Yorker*.

Oct. 9 *Hell on Ice* (*Mercury Theatre on the Air*, CBS), adapted by HK from the book by Commander Lincoln Edward Ellsberg.

Oct. 16 *Seventeen* (*Mercury Theatre on the Air*, CBS), adapted by HK from the Booth Tarkington novel. Cast: OW (William Sylvanus Baxter), BG (Mrs. Baxter), RC (Mr. Parcher), Mary Wickes, JC, Ruth Ford, ER, others.

Oct. 23 *Around the World in 80 Days* (*Mercury Theatre on the Air*, CBS), adapted by HK from the Jules Verne novel. Cast: OW (Phileas Fogg), RC (Detective Fix), EB (Jean Passepartout), EW, FR, AF, SS, Al Swenson.

Oct. 30 *The War of the Worlds* (*Mercury Theatre on the Air*, CBS), adapted by HK from the H. G. Wells novella. Cast: OW (Professor Pierson), FR (Carl Phillips), RC (Last announcer), KD, Carl Frank, William Herz, SS, Howard Smith, PS, ES, RW. Probably the most famous of all radio broadcasts. Of the estimated nine million people who hear it, approximately 1,750,000 are frightened by it into some sort of action. Originally, thirty-six hours before the first rehearsal, HK favored dropping the show because he felt it was going to be boring; but when the only other available script proved to be "an extremely dreary version of *Lorna Doone* which I had started during the summer and abandoned" (JH), the company reluctantly returned to the Martian subject. The show has, of course, been released on record and audiotape in countless versions.

Nov. OW article "Experiment," *The American Magazine.* Also published this year: *The Director in the Theatre Today,* article in pamphlet form, available from the Theatre Education League; see JN for details.

Nov. 2 *Danton's Death* (A Mercury Theatre Presentation) by George Büchner (English text: Geoffrey Dunlop). Adaptation/d: OW. P: JH. Music: Marc Blitzstein. Opens: The Mercury Theatre (runs for 21 performances). Cast: Anna Stafford [VN] (Julie), MG (Danton), EB (Camille Desmoulins), OW (Saint-Just), ERS, GK, GD, AF, RW, EW, JC, JB, WA, EP, RB, SR, others. (JH: "It was rehearsed . . . in a set of which the dominant element was a huge, curved wall, formed entirely of human faces that filled the rear of the stage from the basement to the grid. . . . Jean Rosenthal went out and bought five thousand unpainted Halloween masks, each of which was colored by hand and glued onto a curved, stiffened canvas cyclorama by rotating crews. . . . When finished and lit, it was an effective and active device that suggested different things to different people: in one light it was 'the hydra-headed mob, impersonal but real, omnipresent as a reality,' in another 'it looked like a high canopy of staring faces which gave the strange ominous effect of a rigid dance of death.' ")

Nov. 6 *Heart of Darkness/Life with Father/The Gift of the Magi* (*Mercury Theatre on the Air,* CBS), adapted respectively from the Joseph Conrad novella (by OW and HK), the Clarence Day memoir, and the O. Henry story (latter two adapted by HK). Cast *(Heart of Darkness)*: OW (Narrator/Kurtz), RC (Marlow), AS, GC, EB, WA, VN, FR, ES; *(Life with Father)*: OW (Father), Mildred Natwick (Mother), AFT, AA, others.

Nov. 13 *A Passenger to Bali* (*Mercury Theatre on the Air,* CBS), adapted by HK from the Ellis St. Joseph novel. Cast: OW (Reverend Dr. Ralph Walkes), ES, SS, GSP.

Nov. 20 *The Pickwick Papers* (*Mercury Theatre on the Air,* CBS). Adapted by OW from the Charles Dickens novel. Cast: OW (Sergeant Buzzfuzz/Mr. Jingle), RC (Samuel Pickwick), AS (Augustus Snodgrass), FR, ER, EB, EW, BF, others.

Nov. 27 *Clarence* (*Mercury Theatre on the Air*, CBS), adapted by HK from the novel by Booth Tarkington. Cast: OW (Clarence), others.

Dec. 3 OW speaks at benefit, "Stars for Spain," for the Medical Bureau and North American Committee to Aid Spanish Democracy.

Dec. 4 *The Bridge of San Luis Rey* (*Mercury Theatre on the Air*, CBS), adapted by HK from the Thornton Wilder novel. As a result of the *War of the Worlds* program, OW and the Mercury are signed by their first sponsor, Campbell's Soup. And so, after this, its twenty-second broadcast, *The Mercury Theatre on the Air* changes its showtime and date, and as of December 9 becomes known as *The Campbell Playhouse.*

Dec. 9 *Rebecca* (*The Campbell Playhouse*, CBS), adapted by HK from the novel by Daphne du Maurier (interviewed in London by phone at the end of the show). Guest star: Margaret Sullavan (Mrs. de Winter). Cast: OW (Maxim de Winter), Mildred Natwick, RC, GC, FR, AS, EW, AM, others. Available on TOTI.

Dec. 16 *Call It a Day* (*The Campbell Playhouse*, CBS), adapted by HK from the book by Dodie Smith. Guest stars: Beatrice Lillie (Dorothy Hilton), Jane Wyatt (Catherine Hilton). Cast: OW (Roger Hilton), AM, BF, RC, FR, WA, RW, others.

Dec. 23 A *Christmas Carol (The Campbell Playhouse*, CBS), adapted by HK from the Charles Dickens story. Cast: OW (Ebenezer Scrooge) (Lionel Barrymore, scheduled to play Scrooge, is too ill to appear); HS, VN, BF, AFT, EB, AA, RC, FR, JC, AS, WA, RW, RB, others.

Dec. 30 A *Farewell to Arms* (*The Campbell Playhouse*, CBS), adapted by HK from the Ernest Hemingway novel. Guest star: Katharine Hepburn (Catherine). Cast: OW (Frederick Henry), AM, PS, ES, RC, FR, SS, RW, RB, JC, others.

1939 Harper & Brothers publishes a revised version of the 1934 *Everybody's Shakespeare*—"acting versions" of *Twelfth Night, The Merchant of Venice*, and *Julius Caesar* edited by OW and Roger Hill, with drawings by OW—called *The Mercury Shakespeare*. Separate editions of each play are printed along with the omnibus volume. The plan (never to be realized) is to issue a series that will embrace all the Shakespeare plays, releasing at the same time a matching series of phonograph records of each play, known as the Mercury Text Records on Columbia Masterworks:

Julius Caesar (Mercury Text Records [Columbia]). Recorded on March 1, 11, 21, and 25, 1938; released as five twelve-inch 78s on Columbia M-325. (Reissued on Entree EL 52 in 1953, Lexington LE 7570/7575 in 1967.) D/narr/adapter: OW. Cast: OW (Antonius/Cassius), GC (Brutus), EB, ES, VN, RB, JB, GK, ERS, WA, SR, Arthur Kennedy, others.

Twelfth Night (Mercury Text Records [Columbia]). Recorded on June 14, 16, and 17, 1938, released on ten twelve-inch 78s on Columbia C-7. D/narr/adapter: OW. Cast: LeRoi Operti (Feste), GC (Orsino), OW (Malvolio), WA, RW, EW, WG, GS, ERS, EP, others.

The Merchant of Venice (Columbia Records, C-6). Recorded on July 27, 28, 29, August 23, 25, and September 7, 14, 1938; released on twelve twelve-inch 78s as Columbia C-6. D/narr/adapter: OW. Cast: OW (Shylock/Prince of Morocco), Joseph Holland (Antonio), Norman Lloyd, EB, GK, BF, ERS, VN, GD, RW, WA, others.

Jan. OW article "To Architects," *Theatre Arts*.

Jan. 6 *Counsellor-at-Law* (*The Campbell Playhouse*, CBS), adapted by HK from the Elmer Rice play. Guest stars: Aline MacMahon (Regina), Gertrude Berg (Mrs. Simon). Cast: OW (Simon), RC, AF, JC, ES, FR, EB, SR, WA, others.

Jan. 13 *Mutiny on the Bounty* (*The Campbell Playhouse*, CBS), adapted by HK, JH, and VN from the Charles Nordhoff and James Norman Hall novel. Cast: OW (Captain Bligh), JC (Fletcher Christian), FR, EB, RC, RW, WA, EW, AM, others.

Jan. 20 *Chicken Wagon Family* (*The Campbell Playhouse*, CBS), adapted by HK from the Barry Benefield book. Guest star: Burgess Meredith. Cast: OW (Frank Fippany), RC (Hibbard), FR, JC, AM, ES, WA, RW, others.

Jan. 27 *I Lost My Girlish Laughter* (*The Campbell Playhouse*, CBS), adapted by HK from the Jane Allen book. Guest stars: George S. Kaufman (John Tussler), Ilka Chase (Madge Lawrence), Tamara Geva (Sarya). Cast: OW (Sidney Brandt), RC (Faye), Myron McCormick, FR, ES, AM, JC, WA, EB. A farcical and highly critical look at Hollywood; at the end of the show is a skit concerning the identity of the pseudonymous Jane Allen. This show is Kaufman's radio debut.

Feb. 3 *Arrowsmith* (*The Campbell Playhouse*, CBS), adapted by HK from the Sinclair Lewis novel. Guest star: Helen Hayes (Leora Arrowsmith). Cast: OW (Martin Arrowsmith), Al Swenson, RC, ES, FR, PS, others.

Feb. 10 *The Green Goddess* (*The Campbell Playhouse*, CBS), adapted by HK from the William Archer play. Guest star: Madeleine Carroll (Lucilla Crespin). Cast: OW (Rajah), RC, ES, AS, EW, EB, Robert Speaight, others. OW does this play in vaudeville later this year. (See July–August entry).

Feb. 17 *Burlesque* (*The Campbell Playhouse*, CBS), adapted by HK from the Arthur Hopkins and James Manker Watters play. Guest star: Sam Levene (Lefty). Cast: OW (Skid), AFT, AF, RC, ES, GS, others. Hopkins is interviewed.

Feb. 24 *State Fair* (*The Campbell Playhouse*, CBS), adapted by HK from the Philip Duffield Stong novel. Cast: OW (Pat), RC, ES, Effie Palmer, AFT, HT, others. Stong and comics Amos 'n' Andy (Freeman Gosden and Charles Correll) are interviewed.

Feb. 27 *Five Kings* (Part One) (A Theatre Guild/Mercury Theatre Presentation), adapted by OW from WS's *Richard II*, *Henry IV, Parts I and II*, and *Henry* V. D: OW. P: JH and The Theatre Guild. Music: Aaron Copland. Opens: Colonial Theatre, Boston. A 5-hour play with two intermissions, running from 8:00 P.M. to 1:00 A.M., later shortened by 40 minutes. Cast: Robert Speaight (Chorus), Morris Ankrum (Bolingbroke, later Henry IV), Burgess Meredith (Hal, later Henry V), OW (Brary/Falstaff), RB, GK, EW, John Emery, EB, GD, ERS, GS, JB, WA, EP, SR, RW, others. Preparing for a New York opening, OW's monumental production opens in three cities (see March 13, 20), but never gets to New York. (It is originally projected to play on two consecutive evenings, of which this is only the first.) This is OW's second version of what is later to evolve into the film *Chimes at Midnight* (1966). See RF2 for the original playscript.

March 2 *Royal Regiment* (*The Campbell Playhouse*, CBS), adapted from the Gilbert Frankau book. Guest star: Mary Astor (Camilla Wethered). Cast: OW (Tom Rockingham), RC, AS, ES, EW, HT, others. Frankau is interviewed.

March 10 *The Glass Key* (*The Campbell Playhouse*, CBS), adapted by HK from the Dashiell Hammett novel. Cast: OW (Paul Madvig), RC, ES, EB, PS, Elspeth Eric, others. Warden Laws of Sing-Sing is interviewed.

March 13 *Five Kings* opens at the National Theatre, Washington, D.C.

March 17 *Beau Geste* (*The Campbell Playhouse*, CBS), adapted by HT from the Percival Christopher Wren novel. Guest stars: Laurence Olivier (John Geste), Noah Beery (Sergeant Lejaune). Cast: OW (Beau Geste), RC, EW, HT, SS, others. Legionnaire Alphonse de Redenat is interviewed.

March 20 *Five Kings* opens at the Chestnut Opera House in Philadelphia, where it plays its final performances. This marks the close as well of the original Mercury Theatre, although OW will often revive the name.

March 24 *Twentieth Century* (*The Campbell Playhouse*, CBS), adapted by HT from the Charles MacArthur and Ben Hecht play. Guest stars: Elissa Landi (Lily Garland), Sam Levene (Owen O'Malley). Cast: OW (Oscar Jaffe), RC, GS, HT, ES, others. Broadway press agent Richard Maney is interviewed. OW will act in this play on TV, again playing Jaffe, in 1953.

March 31 *Show Boat* (*The Campbell Playhouse*, CBS), adapted from the Edna Ferber novel and play. Guest stars: Margaret Sullavan (Magnolia), Helen Morgan (Julie), Edna Ferber (Par-thy Ann Hawks). Cast: OW (Captain Andy Hawks), RC, William Johnstone, Carl Frank, ES, others. Ferber is interviewed.

April 7 *Les Misérables* (*The Campbell Playhouse*, CBS), adapted from the Victor Hugo novel. Narr: OW. Guest star: Walter Huston (Jean Valjean). Cast: OW (Javert), RC, ES, EB, AFT, WA, RW, others.

April 14 *The Patriot* (*The Campbell Playhouse*, CBS), adapted from the Pearl S. Buck novel. Guest star: Anna May Wong (Peony). Cast: OW (I-wan), RC, ER, ES, EB, HT, others. Buck is interviewed.

April 21 *Private Lives* (*The Campbell Playhouse*, CBS), adapted from the Noel Coward play. Guest star: Gertrude Lawrence (Amanda Prynne). Cast: OW (Elyot Chase), Naomi Campbell (Sibyl Chase), Robert Speaight (Victor Prynne), EB. Lawrence is interviewed.

April 28 *Black Daniel* (*The Campbell Playhouse*, CBS), adapted from the Honoré Morrow book. Guest star: Joan Bennett (Carolyn LeRoy). Cast: OW (Daniel Webster), RC, ES, WA, others. A retelling of *The Devil and Daniel Webster*.

May 5 *Wickford Point* (*The Campbell Playhouse*, CBS), adapted from the John P. Marquand novel. Cast: OW (Jim Calder), AM, RC, ES, PS, Carl Frank, others. Marquand is interviewed.

May 12 *Our Town* (*The Campbell Playhouse*, CBS), adapted from the Thornton Wilder play. Cast: OW (Stage Manager), AM, RC, John Craven, Patricia Newton, ES, ER, others.

May 19 *The Bad Man* (*The Campbell Playhouse*, CBS), adapted from the Porter Emerson Browne play. Guest star: Ida Lupino (Lucia Pell). Cast: OW (Pancho Lopez), FR, RC, AFT, ES, WA, others. Lupino is interviewed.

May 26 *American Cavalcade* (*The Campbell Playhouse*, CBS), an original historical dramatization, subtitled *Things We Have*, written by OW with the Mercury staff. Guest star: Cornelia Otis Skinner (Mary Scott/Frau Shurtz/Lady Townsend/Polish woman/Susan B. Anthony). Cast: OW

(James Scott/Professor Shurtz/O'Shaughnessy/The Limey/ John Brown), FR, KD, RC, AM, PS, Kingsley Coulton, others. Skinner is interviewed.

June 2 *Victoria Regina* (*The Campbell Playhouse*, CBS), adapted from the Laurence Houseman play. Guest star: Helen Hayes (Queen Victoria). Cast: OW (Prince Albert), RC, ES, EW, BF, AM, AS, VN. Hayes is interviewed. This is OW's last broadcast before going to Hollywood. Released on record—Mark 56 829—in 1979 as *Orson Welles and Helen Hayes at Their Best*.

June–July *The Green Goddess* (RKO Vaudeville Circuit) by William Archer. D/adapter: OW. Stage manager: JB. Opens: Chicago, then Pittsburgh, and various other spots on the RKO Vaudeville Circuit. Cast: OW (Rajah), Susan Fox (Lucilla), John Barrymore (occasional guest star), WA, JB, others. OW films a prologue for this abbreviated, twenty-minute version of the Archer melodrama; as with *Too Much Johnson*, it is meant to dispense with some tedious exposition, but is far briefer. Barrymore, in Chicago for another show, occasionally drops by and takes part in the matinees (there are four shows a day).

July 20 OW arrives in Hollywood in anticipation of a two-picture deal as producer-director-writer-actor with RKO Pictures; the first version of a summary agreement is signed two days later.

Aug. 21 OW signs a full-length sixty-three-page contract with RKO.

For the second season of *The Campbell Playhouse*, he initially has to commute to New York every Thursday night and return after the two Sunday broadcasts (the second for the West Coast). The show moves to Los Angeles circa mid-November, by which time most of the production staff and actors have already moved to the West Coast as well.

Sept. 10 *Peter Ibbetson* (*The Campbell Playhouse*, CBS), adapted from the George du Maurier novel and the John Nathaniel Raphael play. Guest star: Helen Hayes (Mary, Duchess of Towers). Cast: OW (Peter Ibbetson), John Emery, AM, RC, ES, EW, GC, EB, RW, others.

Sept. 17 *Ah, Wilderness!* (*The Campbell Playhouse*, CBS), adapted from the Eugene O'Neill play. Cast: OW (Richard Miller), RC, ER, AM, ES, AF, JC, FR, RW, PS, HT, Eda Heinmann. Critic George Jean Nathan, a friend of O'Neill's, is interviewed.

Sept. 24 *What Every Woman Knows* (*The Campbell Playhouse*, CBS), adapted from the James M. Barrie play. Guest star: Helen Hayes (Maggie Wylie). Cast: OW (John Shand), AS, ES, AM, Naomi Campbell, EW, RC.

Oct. 1 *The Count of Monte Cristo* (*The Campbell Playhouse*, CBS), adapted from the Alexandre Dumas novel. Cast: OW (Edmond Dantes), AM, GC, EB, FR, RC, RW, ES. Released on record (E.O.H. 99603).

Oct. 8 *Algiers* (*The Campbell Playhouse*, CBS), adapted by OW from the novel *Pépé le Moko* by Detective Ashelbé (Henri La Barthe) and the screenplay by John Howard Lawson and James Cain. Guest star: Paulette Goddard (Gaby). Cast: OW (Pépé le Moko), RC, EB, Benny Rubin, GS, ES, WA, RW, BB. Goddard is interviewed about her upcoming, still untitled Chaplin film *(The Great Dictator)*. One of the most ambitious and expensive Campbell shows in terms of aural effects and atmosphere.

Oct. 15 *The Escape* (*The Campbell Playhouse*, CBS), adapted from John Galsworthy. Guest star: Wendy Barrie (Lady in the hotel). Cast: OW (Matt Denant), EB, WA, RC, RW, ES, BB, others.

Oct. 22 *Liliom* (*The Campbell Playhouse*, CBS), adapted by JH from the Ferenc Molnár play. Guest star: Helen Hayes (Julie). Cast: OW (Liliom), AM, FR, JC, others.

Oct. 29 *The Magnificent Ambersons* (*The Campbell Playhouse*, CBS), adapted by OW from the Booth Tarkington novel. Narr: OW. Guest stars: Walter Huston (Eugene Morgan), Nan Sunderland (Isabel Amberson). Cast: OW (George Amberson Minafer), RC (Fred Amberson), Eric Burtis (Young George), WA (Neighbor), ES (Archie Smith), RW (Reverend Smith), BB (Mrs. Foster), Marion Barnes (Lucy Morgan), ER. Nan Sunderland is Mrs. Walter Huston; both she and her husband are interviewed. Available on the Voyager laser disc of the film *The Magnificent Ambersons*, which OW is to make two years later for RKO.

Nov. 5 *The Hurricane* (*The Campbell Playhouse*, CBS), adapted from the Charles Nordhoff and James Norman Hall novel. Guest star: Mary Astor (Germaine de Laage). Cast: OW (Eugene de Laage), RC, ES, EB, BB, GC, WA, RW, others.

Nov. 8 OW begins to make many guest appearances on comedy and variety shows. Among the first: *Town Hall Tonight* (*The Fred Allen Show*, NBC). D: Victor Knight. Sc: Fred Allen, others.

Nov. 12 *The Murder of Roger Ackroyd* (*The Campbell Playhouse*, CBS), adapted by HJM from the Agatha Christie novel. Guest star: Edna May Oliver (Caroline Sheppard). Cast: OW (Dr. Sheppard/Hercule Poirot), Alan Napier (Roger Ackroyd), BF, GC, RC, ES, others. OW plays both the murderer and the detective in this show, which is the first of several scripted by Herman J. Mankiewicz (with JH's editing and OW's suggestions) that is aired. Unfortunately, through an oversight, it omits a major clue in the mystery.

Nov. 19 *The Garden of Allah* (*The Campbell Playhouse*, CBS), adapted from the Robert Hichens novel. Guest star: Madeleine Carroll (Domini Enfilden). Cast: OW (Boris Androvsky), ES, GC, RC, Eddie Abdr.

Nov. 26 *Dodsworth* (*The Campbell Playhouse*, CBS), adapted by HJM from the Sinclair Lewis novel and the Sidney Howard play. Guest star: Fay Bainter (Fran Dodsworth). Cast: OW (Sam Dodsworth), Nan Sunderland (Edith Cortright), RC, EB, ES, BF, RW, WA, FR, others.

Nov. 30 *Heart of Darkness* (unrealized project). On this date, the Revised Estimating Script OW has adapted from the Joseph Conrad novella is completed and mimeographed. The film is to be his first RKO production, and over the next several months plans are made, sets designed, research done, casts discussed; a day of tests is shot with actors Robert Coote, Everett Sloane, Gus Schilling, and OW himself. The film is eventually shelved because of budgetary problems as well as RKO's probable reluctance concerning the projected experimental, first-person camera technique. OW's projected cast: OW (Marlow/Kurtz [just before cancellation, he decides to play only Marlow]), Vladimir Sokoloff (Doctor), EB (Strunz), Norman Lloyd (Adalbert Butz), ES (Ernest Stitzer), Dita Parlo (Elsa Gruner), Robert Coote (Eddie), GS (Frank Melchers), ERS (Schulman), GC (Carba de Arriaga), RC (Blauer), Jack Carter (Steersman), John Emery (de Tirpitz), FR (Meuss). (See Chapter 1.)

Dec. 3 *Lost Horizon* (*The Campbell Playhouse*, CBS), adapted from the James Hilton novel. Guest star: Sigrid Gurie (Lo Tsen). Cast: OW (Father Perrault/High Lama), ES, GC, Robert Coote, FR, RC, EB, others.

Dec. 10 *Vanessa* (*The Campbell Playhouse*, CBS), adapted from the Hugh Walpole novel. Guest star: Helen Hayes (Vanessa/Judith). Cast: OW (Benjie), John Hoysradt (Ellis), EW, AS, others.

Dec. 16 After a violent quarrel between OW and Houseman regarding finances, the latter leaves the Mercury and returns to New York; the next *Campbell Playhouse* show is the last one he scripts:

Dec. 17 *There's Always a Woman* (*The Campbell Playhouse*, CBS), adapted by JH from the Gladys Lehman work. Cast: OW (Bill Reardon), Marie Wilson (Sally Reardon), RC, ES, EB, GB, FR, RW, Mary Taylor.

Dec. 24 A *Christmas Carol* (*The Campbell Playhouse*, CBS), adapted from the Charles Dickens story. Narr: OW (as Dickens). Guest star: Lionel Barrymore (Scrooge). Cast: FR (Bob Cratchit), GB (Mrs. Cratchit), BB (Martha), RC, ES, GC, EB, ERS, RW, others. Released on record (Radiola MR-1114) in 1980.

At a Christmas party during this period, OW meets D. W. Griffith (see chapter 1). Around the same time, he narrates the RKO feature *The Swiss Family Robinson* (released early next year).

Dec. 31 *Come and Get It* (*The Campbell Playhouse* [CBS]), adapted from the Edna Ferber novel. Narr: ES. Guest star: Frances Dee (Lotta). Cast: OW (Barney), FR, RC, EB, GB, WA, others.

1940 During the year, OW and VN (aka Anna Stafford) are divorced; she is later to marry OW's good friend, writer Charles Lederer.

OW continues to propose and develop movie projects for RKO this year; among the titles registered with the Motion Picture Producers Association are *The Pickwick Papers* (a Dickens adaptation to star W. C. Fields and John Barrymore), *Cortez* (about the famous explorer), *The Borgias and Their Time*, *Around the World in 80 Days*, and *The Invasion from Mars* (at the urging of several RKO executives, who are hoping for a *War of the Worlds* spinoff). For Dolores Del Rio, he writes a screen adaptation of Federico Gamboa's novel *Santa* (published bilingually by the National University of Mexico in 1992, with commentary by David Ramón).

Jan. 7 *Vanity Fair* (*The Campbell Playhouse*, CBS), adapted by HJM from the William Makepeace Thackeray novel. Guest star: Helen Hayes (Becky Sharp). Cast: OW (Marquis of Steyne), John Hoysradt (Rawdon Crawley), AM, BG, EW, Joseph Holland, Edgar Kent, others.

Jan. 9 *The Smiler with a Knife* (unrealized project). On this date, OW's Revised Estimating Script is completed for this comedy-thriller based on the Nicholas Blake (C. Day Lewis) novel; according to OW, HJM also did some work on the screenplay. Casting problems (OW wanted Lucille Ball) and other difficulties abort this project. An exchange from the script:

> JOHN'S VOICE: The American people will never stand for a dictator.
>
> STRANGEWAYS: You mean they'll never give a politician that much power. How about a hero? We like heroes over here and this one won't talk like a dictator. He'll look like a movie star and everybody'll love him.

Mexican Melodrama (unrealized project). Another film project developed during this period (and subsequently reactivated in 1941 and 1942) is an untitled work very loosely based on the Calder-Marshall political novel, *The Way to Santiago*. Written by OW, who plans to produce, direct, and costar with Dolores Del Rio (although he announces in February 1942 that Norman Foster will direct), the film is to be shot by Gregg Toland, partially on location in Mexico—a thriller that, like both *Heart of Darkness* and *The Smiler with a Knife*, centers on a charismatic, fascistic figure (in this case, a propagandistic radio commentator). (See JN for more details.)

Jan. 14 *Theodora Goes Wild* (*The Campbell Playhouse*, CBS), adapted from the Mary McCarthy story and the Sidney Buchman screenplay. Guest star: Loretta Young (Theodora Lynn). Cast: OW (Michael Grant), RC, FR, GB, ES, WA, RW, others.

Jan. 20 The first in a three-part series of articles about OW, "How to Raise a Child: The Disturbing Life—to Date—of Orson Welles" by Alva Johnston and Fred Smith, appears in *The Saturday Evening Post;* further installments appear on January 27 and February 3. Although both CH2 and BW report that the series is highly inaccurate and that OW disliked it, OW tells PB in an interview (April 1969) that everything in it is true and that the authors had worked with him closely in preparing the piece.

Jan. 21 *The Citadel* (*The Campbell Playhouse*, CBS), adapted from the A. J. Cronin novel. Guest star: GF (Christine Manson). Cast: OW (Dr. Andrew Manson), Mary Taylor, EB, ES, GC, RC, GB, WA, RW, others. Released on record (Sandy Hook 15293).

Jan. 28 *It Happened One Night* (*The Campbell Playhouse*, CBS), adapted from the Samuel Hopkins Adams story "Night Bus" and the Robert Riskin screenplay. Guest stars: William Powell (Peter Grant), Miriam Hopkins (Ellie Andrews). Cast: OW (Mr. Andrews), ES, RC, RW, WA, others.

Feb. 4 *Broome Stages* (*The Campbell Playhouse*, CBS), adapted from the Clemence Dane book. Guest star: Helen Hayes (Donna Broome). Cast: OW (Edmond Broome/Harry Broome), AM, EW, ES, WA, RW, others.

Feb. 11 *Mr. Deeds Goes to Town* (*The Campbell Playhouse*, CBS), adapted from the Clarence Budington Kelland story "Opera Hat" and the Robert Riskin screenplay. Guest star: Gertrude Lawrence (Barbara Bennett). Cast: OW (Longfellow Deeds), ES, PS, FR, EB, AM, JC, HT, RW, others.

Feb. 18 *Dinner at Eight* (*The Campbell Playhouse*, CBS), adapted from the Edna Ferber and George S. Kaufman play. Guest stars: Lucille Ball (Kitty Packard), Hedda Hopper (Millicent Jordan), Marjorie Rambeau (Carlotta Vance). Cast: OW (Dan Packard/Larry Renault), Mary Taylor (Paula Jordan), EB, GC, RW, others.

Feb. 19 HJM joins the Mercury payroll to work on the script for a Welles film project, and starts work with JH and a secretary in Victorville, California, late this month or early March, continuing through early May. This original story and screenplay is first known as *Orson Welles #1*, then as *American*, and finally as *Citizen Kane*.

Feb. 25 *Only Angels Have Wings* (*The Campbell Playhouse*, CBS), adapted from the story and screenplay by Howard Hawks and Jules Furthman. Guest star: Joan Blondell (Bonnie Lee). Cast: OW (Jeff Carter), EB, Regis Toomey, GC, RW, WA, RB, others.

March 3 *Rabble at Arms* (*The Campbell Playhouse*, CBS), adapted from the Kenneth Roberts book. Guest star: Frances Dee (Ellen Phipps). Cast: OW (Benedict Arnold), GC, EB, Robert Warwick, GB, RB, RW, WA, others.

March 10 *Craig's Wife* (*The Campbell Playhouse*, CBS), adapted from the George Kelly play. Guest star: Ann Harding (Harriette Craig). Cast: OW (Walter Craig), Clara Blandick (Mrs. Harold), GC, BB, RB, RW, others.

March 17 OW appears as guest star on Jack Benny's *The Jell-O Program* (NBC).
The same evening, he does his own show: *Huckleberry Finn* (*The Campbell Playhouse*, CBS), adapted by HJM from the Mark Twain novel. Narr: OW. Guest star: Jackie Cooper (Huckleberry Finn). Cast: OW (Dauphin/Huckleberry Finn), Walter Catlett (Duke), Clarence Muse (Jim), ERS, GB, WA, RW, others. One of the more formally playful of OW's radio shows, this is partially constructed around the tug of war between Cooper and OW about who gets to play Huck. Released on record (Mark 56 634) in 1974; introduction to show available on *The Golden Days of Radio* (Mark 56 713), released in 1975.

March 24 *June Moon* (*The Campbell Playhouse*, CBS), adapted from the Ring Lardner and George S. Kaufman play. Guest star: Jack Benny (Frederick D. Stevens). Cast: OW (Candy Butcher on train), BB, GS, others.

March 31 *Jane Eyre* (*The Campbell Playhouse*, CBS), adapted from the Charlotte Brontë novel. Guest star: Madeleine Carroll (Jane Eyre). Cast: OW (Rochester), Cecilia Loftus (Mrs. Fairfax), Robert Coote (Mr. Brocklehurst), GC, EB, WA, others. This is the final broadcast of *The Campbell Playhouse.*

April 1 Delivers lecture, "The New Actor," at Pasadena Civic Auditorium. (The same lecture is given in Kansas City, Missouri, on April 11, followed by engagements in early May in Spokane, Portland, Tacoma, and Wenatchee, Wash.)

April 17 OW begins to record what will be the last of the Mercury Text Records, *Macbeth* (Columbia C-33), to be released later this year with an edition of the same play (published by Harper & Brothers) in *The Mercury Shakespeare* series. Adapted by OW from the WS play. Music: BH. Narr: WA. Cast: OW (Macbeth), Fay Bainter (Lady Macbeth), Robert Warwick (Banquo), RB, WA, ERS, EB, GC, RW, others.

May F. Scott Fitzgerald's short story "Pat Hobby and Orson Welles" appears in *Esquire.*

July 16 The third and final revised shooting script of *Citizen Kane* is completed.

July 22 OW begins shooting "tests" of *Citizen Kane* on the RKO lot; these continue through July 29, during which time the front office figures out that actual shooting has begun.

July 30 Official starting date of *Citizen Kane.* During principal photography, at Toland's urging, OW also shoots the *Kane* trailer—almost four minutes long, showing the leading cast members in street clothes and on RKO's soundstages, with various props from the film visible, narrated by OW offscreen, and containing all new material. (This trailer is available on the Voyager laser disc of *Citizen Kane.*)

Aug. 30 OW appears as a guest on an hour-long radio broadcast, *This Is Radio*, re-creating the history of radio.

Oct. 23 Shooting completed on *Kane*. OW spends remainder of the year cutting, supervising Vernon Walker's special effects, etc.

Oct. 25 Begins another lecture tour, speaking again on "The New Actor" in Lincoln, Nebraska, followed by Toledo, Fort Worth, Dallas, San Antonio, Houston, Detroit, and Des Moines. During his stay in Texas, he also appears on the *KTSA Texas News Show* and a special called:

Oct. 28 *H. G. Wells Meets Orson Welles* (KTSA). Broadcast from San Antonio on Charles Shaw's interview show, this 7½-minute discussion, the only meeting of these two men, includes such topics as the *War of the Worlds* broadcast, the effect of war on perception of the arts, and the forthcoming *Citizen Kane*. (Available on TOTI.)

1941 This year, a comedy series on Mutual called *The Great Gunns* about a modern stage family includes as one of its characters the actor-producer Lorson Snells (Marvin Miller), a parody of Orson Welles.

While waiting for *Citizen Kane* to be released, OW goes on a lecture tour, arranged by the Columbia Lecture Bureau.

A project considered during this period is the recently published *The Ox-Bow Incident*—according to RW, the only Western OW ever contemplates making.

The Life of Christ (unrealized project). OW, Gregg Toland, and Perry Ferguson scout locations in Mexico and Baja California and seek the approval of Bishop Sheen and other church leaders for this turn-of-the-century retelling of the story of Jesus Christ as "a kind of primitive Western," and OW writes a screenplay with dialogue taken exclusively from the Gospels of Mark, Matthew, and Luke. (A few years later, an unsuccessful effort is made to interest some publishers in a *Mercury Bible*.) (OW to PB: "Every word in the film was to be from the Bible—no original dialogue, but done as a sort of American primitive, set in the frontier country in the last century. Painters, until very recently, used to do all Biblical scenes in their own epoch. I was going to have the scribes and Pharisees as thin-lipped fundamentalist types. Now, the disciples could be flower children—dropouts. It's the greatest drama ever written, but it carries flowing robes and the terrible burden of all that bad lithographic religious art.") (In the mid-1950s, OW reactivates this film project and writes a second script, to be shot in Egypt, but this, too, is never brought to fruition.)

Jan. 16 *The Sealtest Program* (NBC). Host: Rudy Vallee. Guests: OW, John Barrymore, Lurene Tuttle. Sc: Abe Burrows, others. OW and Barrymore appear together on this show many times, often doing Shakespeare.

Feb. Article by OW, "Orson Welles Writing About Orson Welles," in *Stage*.

Feb. 14 Article by OW, "*Citizen Kane* Is Not About Louella Parsons' Boss," *Friday* (reprinted in *Focus on Citizen Kane*).

Feb. 22 *George Washington, American* (WNEW). Cast: OW (George Washington), others.

March 24 *Native Son* (A Mercury Production), adapted from the Richard Wright novel by Paul Green and Wright. D: OW. P: OW, JH, Bern Bernard (and, uncredited, Jack Moss). General stage manager: RW. Opens: St. James Theatre, New York. Cast: Canada Lee (Bigger Thomas), Evelyn Ellis (Hannah Thomas), Helen Martin, ERS, ES, Joseph Pevney, RC, PS, JB, SR, others. Presented without an intermission (ushers are instructed not even to hand out programs until *after* the show), this stark, gripping production of the grim Wright novel about a black man who kills a white woman receives excellent notices and runs for 114 performances. It is the last enterprise on which OW is to be associated with Houseman.

March 25 *Mexican Melodrama* (unrealized project). The third and final revision of OW's screenplay for RKO is completed. (See Jan. 9, 1940.)

March 30 *One Step Ahead (Silver Theatre)*, adapted from the John La Touche play. Cast: OW, Lurene Tuttle.

April 6 *His Honor—the Mayor* (*The Free Company*, CBS). Sc/d/narr: OW. Host: James Boyd. Cast: RC (Bill Knaggs), AM

Welles directing Native Son.

(Mary Knaggs), PS, ERS, RW, BG, AFT, ES. An original radio play about a mayor in a Mexican border town (RC) who defends the right of his enemies, a racist and antiunion group called the White Crusaders, to free speech and free assembly. (The unsponsored show is devoted to the Bill of Rights, and is performed without pay as a public service.) OW's play—published, like other *Free Company* shows, as a 10¢ pamphlet, and then reprinted the same year in a collection, *The Free Company Presents . . .* (New York: Dodd & Mead)—is attacked as subversive and communistic by leaders of the American Legion and the California Sons of the Revolution in the Hearst papers. The non-Hearst press defends OW, who issues a press statement of his own (reprinted in FB). In fact, OW's narration of the show, periodically interrupting the drama to remind the listener that it's an invented story, that it has no "message," and that he isn't even sure whether the mayor's approach to the problem is the correct one, makes this one of his least preachy broadcasts, and perhaps his most Brechtian.

April 17 OW makes guest-star appearance on *The Sealtest Program* (see Jan. 16) with Dorothy Lamour.

April 14 FBI director J. Edgar Hoover writes a "memorandum for the assistant to the attorney general Mr. Matthew F. McGuire" stating: "For your information the Dies Committee has collected data indicating that Orson Welles is associated with the following organizations, which are said to be Communist in character: Negro Cultural Committee, Foster Parents' Plan for War Children, Medical Bureau and North American Committee to Aid Spanish Democracy, Theatre Arts Committee, Motion Picture Artists Committee, The Coordinating Committee to Lift the Embargo, Workers Bookshop, American Youth Congress, New Masses, People's Forum, Workers Bookshop Mural Fund, League of American Writers [and] American Student Union. . . ." (See James Naremore, "The Trial: The FBI vs. Orson Welles," *Film Comment*, January–February 1991.)

May 1* *Citizen Kane* (Mercury Productions–RKO Radio Pictures). D/P: OW. Studio head: George J. Schaefer. Assoc p: Richard Barr (formerly Richard Baer). Original sc: HJM, OW (and, uncredited, JH). Ph: Gregg Toland. Music: BH. Art d: Perry Ferguson, Van Nest Polglase. Makeup: Maurice Seiderman, Mel Burns. Sd rec: Bailey Fesler, James G. Stewart. Ed: Robert Wise. R t: 119 minutes. Cast: OW (Charles Foster Kane), JC (Jedidiah Leland/Newsreel reporter), Dorothy Comingore (Susan Alexander), AM (Mary Kane), Ruth Warrick (Emily Norton Kane), RC (Jim Gettys), ERS (Mr. Herbert Carter/Newsreel reporter), ES (Mr. Bernstein), GC (Walter Parks Thatcher), WA (Jerry Thompson/"News on the March" narrator), PS (Raymond), Fortunio Bonanova (Matisti), GS (headwaiter), Philip Van Zandt (Rawlston), GB (Bertha Anderson, Thatcher Library curator), Harry Shannon (Jim Kane), Buddy Swan (Kane as 8-year-old), Guy Repp (reporter),

* *All dates for films denote either day of first public showing or of general release.*

others. (Bits include Gregg Toland [interviewer in newsreel]), HJM [newspaperman], Alan Ladd and RW [reporters], RB [Hillman]). Susan Alexander's singing voice is dubbed by Jean Forward. The shooting script (dated July 16, 1940) and the cutting continuity are published together with an extended essay by Pauline Kael, "Raising Kane," in *The Citizen Kane Book* (Boston: Atlantic/Little Brown, 1971).

May 8 Guest-star appearance on *The Sealtest Program* (see Jan. 16) with John Barrymore.

May 28 OW is interviewed on the radio in the lobby of the Gary Theatre at the San Francisco premiere of *Citizen Kane*—the third such opening he has attended.

Spring After the Mercury staff has been assigned to look for possible parts for OW to play, RW reads some articles about the infamous wife-murderer Landru and suggests this role.

June 20 Four related titles are registered by Mercury Productions with the Motion Picture Producers' Association: *The Ladykiller, The Life of Desire, Landru,* and *Bluebeard.* Around this time, OW writes a script and proposes that Charlie Chaplin play the lead, but eventually Chaplin decides to make his own film on the same subject, *Monsieur Verdoux.* (See April 11, 1947.)

Summer With Dolores Del Rio as his assistant, OW makes his debut as a professional magician at the California state fair in Sacramento, then tours at county fairs and in theaters.

July 6 *Between Americans* (*Gulf Screen Guild Theatre,* CBS). D: Harry Ackerman. Sc: Norman Corwin. Narr: OW. Host: Roger Pryor. A patriotic show performed with a live audience.

July 29 *It's All True* (unrealized project). On this date, OW registers the title for this omnibus movie which ultimately goes into production in Mexico (in the fall) and Rio (February). At this time, however, all but one of the stories that are to make up the picture are considerably different from what is done later: (1) *Jazz Story,* a history of American jazz as told through the life of Louis Armstrong, scripted by Elliot

Paul in collaboration with Duke Ellington (who will compose and arrange the score) as well as Armstrong, to feature Armstrong as himself and Hazel Scott as Lil' Hardin (Armstrong's first wife); (2) *Love Story*, story and screenplay by John Fante, about a young Italian couple, based on Fante's parents meeting in San Francisco. (See JN for details). (3) *My Friend Bonito*, adapted by Norman Foster and Fante from a story by Robert Flaherty. (4) *The Captain's Chair*, based on another Flaherty story about a boat captain in Hudson Bay, Canada.

Fall A more economical Mercury production of *Native Son*, with JB taking over as stage manager (and playing the role of Boris Max), opens in New York, then goes on a national tour for most of the remainder of the year.

Sept. OW goes to Mexico briefly to scout locations just before Norman Foster begins to direct *My Friend Bonito* as a Mercury-RKO production, filming of which continues through early December. Ph: Floyd Crosby, Alex Phillips. Cast: Jesús Vásquez (Chico, the boy), Domingo Soler (Miguel, his friend), and Jesús Solórzano (bullfighter), others.

Sept. 15 *Orson Welles Show* (CBS). "Almanac." D/P/host: OW. Sc: OW, Roger Quayle Denny, Carl Glick, others. Music: BH. Cast: OW, Blanche Yurka, Conrad Binyon, BF, HC, Dolores Del Rio, others. Program: (1) "Sredni Vashtar," adapted from the Saki story. (2) "Hidalgo," original radio play about Mexican history. (3) "An Irishman and a Jew," story by Geoffrey Household. (4) "Boogie Woogie" (Meade Lux Lewis, piano). The premiere of a new show, always done with the same basic crew (not repeated below), featuring adaptations, poetry, history, music, comedy, and commentary (called "Almanac") by OW. On many of the shows, the Disney character Jiminy Cricket (voice done by Cliff Edwards, who had done it for Disney) turns up between segments and banters with OW.

Sept. 22 *Orson Welles Show* (CBS). "Almanac" and Jiminy Cricket. (1) "The Right Side" with Elliot Lewis (Faust), RC (Devil). (2) "The Sexes," Dorothy Parker story, with Betty Field, Richard Carlson. (3) "Murder in the Bank," with Ruth Gordon. (4) "Golden Honeymoon," Ring Lardner story, with Ruth Gordon (Mother), OW (Father).

Sept. 29 *Orson Welles Show* (CBS). "Almanac" and Jiminy Cricket. (1) "The Interlopers," original radio play, with Elliot Lewis (narr), RC, OW. (2) "Song of Solomon" read by OW. (3) "I'm a Fool," Sherwood Anderson story, with OW, Nancy Gates. (Second segment available on TOTI.)

Oct. 6 *Orson Welles Show* (CBS). Cast: OW, Dorothy Comingore, JC, RC, PS, EB, ERS. (1) "The Black Pearl," original story by Norman Foster. (2) "There's a Full Moon Tonight." (3) "Annabel Lee," Poe's poem, read by OW.

Oct. 13 *Orson Welles Show* (CBS). "Almanac." (1) "If in Years to Come" by Earle Reed Silvers, with OW, Marsha Hunt, AM. (2) "Noah Webster's Library," skit with Lucille Ball, JC, Marsha Hunt. (3) Lucille Ball reads four poems by Dorothy Parker. (Two latter segments available on TOTI.)

Oct. 20 *Orson Welles Show* (CBS). "Almanac." (1) "Romance," story by Ellis Parker Butler, with JC (narr), Tim Holt, Anne Baxter, AM, RC. (2) "The Prisoner of Assiout," story by Grant Allen, with OW, ES, RC, ERS, EB, Marlo Dwyer. (3) Shakespeare sonnet read by OW.

Oct. 28 Shooting begins on *The Magnificent Ambersons*.

Nov. 3 *Orson Welles Show* (CBS). "Almanac." (1) "Wild Oranges," adapted by Roger Quayle Denny from the Joseph Hergesheimer novel, with Frances Dee, RC, PS, Gale Gordon, John Woodfolk.

Nov. 10 *Orson Welles Show* (CBS). (1) "That's Why I Left You," story by John Nesbitt, with RC (narr), Stuart Erwin, June Collyer, JC, AM. (2) "The Maysville Minstrel," story by Ring Lardner, with JC, RC, Stuart Erwin, June Collyer.

OW emcees a benefit in Hollywood for the American Committee to Save Refugees, the Exiled Writers' Committee, and United Spanish Aid.

Nov. 17 *The Hitch Hiker* (*Orson Welles Show*, CBS), original radio play by Lucille Fletcher (Mrs. Bernard Herrmann), with OW, others.

Nov. 24 A *Farewell to Arms* (*Orson Welles Show*, CBS), adapted from the Ernest Hemingway novel, with Ginger Rogers (Catherine), OW (Frederick Henry).

Dec. 1 *Orson Welles Show* (CBS). (1) "Something's Going to Happen to Henry," story by Wilma Shore and Louis Solomon, with Janet Gaynor, JC, RC, Glenn Anders. (2) "Wilbur Brown, Habitat: Brooklyn," story by Arthur Stander, with OW, RC, Glenn Anders. Second segment issued on TOTI.

Dec. 7 *Orson Welles Show* (CBS). (1) JC performs Ring Lardner text adapted by Vera Eikel, "Symptoms of Being 35." (2) OW reads from Walt Whitman's *Leaves of Grass*.

Dec. 15 *President's Bill of Rights* (*We Hold These Truths*, CBS, NBC, MBS). D/P/Sc: Norman Corwin. Music: BH. President Roosevelt concludes the program. Cast: Lionel Barrymore, James Stewart, OW, Edward G. Robinson, Walter Huston, Rudy Vallee, Edward Arnold, Walter Brennan, Marjorie Main.

Earlier the same night, OW does another show: *The Great Man Votes* (*Cavalcade of America*, NBC). Guest star: OW. Adapted by Peter Lyon from the screenplay by John Twist, based on the Gordon Malherne Hillman story.

Dec. 22 *Orson Welles Show* (CBS). (1) OW reads Saint Luke, chapter 2 (the Nativity). (2) "The Happy Prince," story by Oscar Wilde, with OW, RC, AM, JC, EB, ERS, GS, Tim Holt. (3) OW reads Christmas poem by G. K. Chesterton.

Dec. 29 *There Are Frenchmen and Frenchmen* (*Orson Welles Show*, CBS), adapted by JC from a Richard Connell story. Cast: Rita Hayworth, OW, Lurene Tuttle, JC. This is the first meeting between OW and Rita Hayworth, who is to become his second wife.

1942

Jan. 5 *The Garden of Allah* (*Orson Welles Show*, CBS), adapted from the Robert Hichens novel. Guests stars: Merle Oberon, Cedric Hardwicke.

Jan. 6 Shooting begins on the Mercury Production of *Journey into Fear*, Norman Foster (called back from shooting *My Friend Bonito* in Mexico) directing. OW plays Colonel Haki in the film some evenings after finishing the day's work on *Ambersons*.

Jan. 12 *The Apple Tree* (*Orson Welles Show*, CBS), adapted by Roger Quayle Denny from the John Galsworthy story, with OW (Frank), GF (Megan), RC (Phil). Issued on TOTI.

Jan. 19 *My Little Boy* (*Orson Welles Show*, CBS), adapted by Carl Ewald from his own story, with Dix Davis, OW, Ruth Warrick, RC, Barbara Jean Wong. The same story had been adapted on *Mercury Theater on the Air*, and, according to OW's introduction tonight, is the most popular story ever done on the Mercury. Issued on TOTI.

Jan. 22 Principal photography completed on *Ambersons*.

Jan. 26 Additional shooting on *Ambersons*. On the same day, OW appears as a guest star on the Red Cross program (CBS) with Alexander Woollcott and Ethel Barrymore, reading Kenneth Robinson's poem "American Laughter."

He also does his regular show: *The Happy Hypocrite* (*Orson Welles Show*, CBS), adapted from the Max Beerbohm story, with OW (narr), John Barrymore, Maureen O'Sullivan, AM, EW, ES.

Jan. 29 Additional shooting on *Ambersons*.

Jan. 31 OW's last day of shooting on *Ambersons*. (All subsequent retakes and new scenes are to be done in March, April, and May by others, when he is in South America.)

Feb. 1 OW completes his acting role in *Journey into Fear*.

The same night, after a repeat of Norman Corwin's *Between Americans* (done last December 7 for the *Gulf Screen Guild Theatre*) as the final *Orson Welles Show*, OW concludes the program as follows: "This is the last time for some while I'll be speaking to you from the United States. Tomorrow night the Mercury Theatre starts for South America. The reason, put more or less officially, is that I've been asked by the Office of the Coordinator of Inter-American Affairs to do a motion picture especially for Americans in all the Americas, a movie which, in its particular way, might strengthen the good relations now binding the continents of the Western Hemisphere. . . ."

Feb. 2 OW goes to Washington for briefing and continues to Miami, where he meets editor Robert Wise and, for nearly three days and nights, in the cutting-and-dubbing facilities of a cartoon studio, they work almost continually on the rough cut of *Ambersons*, including recording by OW of additional narration. It is planned that Wise will join OW with the film in Rio for final work once he has finished the rough cut—a plan that is never implemented.

Feb. 4 OW leaves Miami for Rio de Janeiro, to arrive four days later.

Feb. 8 Test shooting of pre-Carnival festivities in Rio begins, in Technicolor. (Lighting equipment does not arrive until March.)

Feb. 13 Technicolor and black-and-white footage of Carnival festivities continues through February 17, followed by footage on aftermath (black-and-white only, February 20–25). The main credits are: D: OW. Assoc p: RW. Sc: OW, Robert Meltzer. Research and writing staff: Clovis de Gusmão, Ernani Fornari, Aydano Couto Ferraz, Luiz Edmundo, Alex Viany, Rui Costa, Ayres de Andrade, Jr. B/W Cam op: Joseph Biroc. Cast: Grande Otelo, Linda Batista, others.

March 6 Lighting equipment arrives; OW leaves for Salvador, Bahia, en route to Fortaleza to scout locations (March 8–9).

March 10 Robert Wise shoots retakes on *Ambersons*.

March 12 Shooting completed in Hollywood on *Journey into Fear*.

April 14 *Pan American Day* (NBC-Blue). Speakers: OW, Oswaldo Aranha (Brazilian Foreign Minister).

April 17 Freddie Fleck shoots retakes on *Ambersons*. (He shoots further retakes on April 18, 20, and 22; the final scene in the release version is shot on April 20.)

April 18 *President Vargas' Birthday* (NBC-Blue). Speakers: OW, Linda Batista, others.

April 20 OW leaves for Buenos Aires to receive an award for *Citizen Kane*.

May 4 The recut *Ambersons* is previewed in Inglewood.

May 12 The recut *Ambersons* is previewed in Long Beach.

May 19 Jack Moss shoots the final *Ambersons* retakes; Jacaré, the leader of the Jangadeiros, drowns during the shooting of the re-enactment of their arrival in Rio in November 1941.

June 13 OW and his crew of five leave for Fortaleza to shoot the Jangadeiros sequence, *Four Men on a Raft*. D/sc: OW, based on research by Edmar Morel. Executive assistant RW. Ph: George Fanto. Camera assistant: Reginaldo Calmon. Cast: Manoel "Jacaré" Olímpio Meira, Manuel Preto, Jerônimo André de Souza, many others.

Summer A radio production of *Peter and the Wolf* narrated by OW is broadcast on the CBS series *Russian-American Festival.*

July 1 In Hollywood, the Mercury Productions staff are ousted from their offices at the RKO Radio Pictures Studio.

July 10 *The Magnificent Ambersons* (Mercury Productions, RKO Radio Pictures). At the end of the film, over a montage of moviemaking machinery, OW narrates the credits this way: "*The Magnificent Ambersons* was based on Booth Tarkington's novel. Stanley Cortez was the photographer. Bernard Herrmann wrote and conducted the music. Mark-Lee Kirk designed the sets—Al Fields dressed them. Robert Wise was the film editor. Freddie Fleck was the assistant director. Edward Stevenson designed the ladies' wardrobe. The special effects were by Vernon L. Walker. The sound recording was by Bailey Fesler, and James G. Stewart. Here's the cast: Eugene Morgan—Joseph Cotten, Isabel Amberson Minafer—Dolores Costello, Lucy Morgan—Anne Baxter, George Amberson Minafer—Tim Holt, Fanny Minafer—Agnes Moorehead, Jack Amberson—Ray Collins, Roger Bronson—Erskine Sanford, Major Amberson—Richard Bennett. . . . I wrote the script and directed it. My name is Orson Welles. . . . This is a Mercury Production." The following, therefore, are uncredited: D (new, non-Welles scenes): Robert Wise, Freddie Fleck, Jack Moss. Exec p: George Schaefer. P/narr: OW. Assoc p: Jack Moss. Sc (new scenes): Moss, JC. Ph (with OW): Harry J. Wild (almost half the picture), Russell Metty, Jack McKenzie; (new scenes and retakes): McKenzie, Nicholas Musuraca, Russ Cully. Additional music: Roy Webb. Original r t: 132 minutes.

Released r t: 88 minutes. The film opens without fanfare in Los Angeles at two theatres, on a double bill with *Mexican Spitfire Sees a Ghost*.

July 14 OW and crew leave Fortaleza for two days of shooting in Recife, then about a week in Salvador, Bahia.

July 22 OW returns to Rio; in another week he leaves for brief trips to Argentina, Bolivia, several other South American countries, and Mexico.

Aug. 22 OW returns to the U.S. He begins doing guest shots on various radio programs, including *The Kate Smith Show* and:

Sept. 2 *The Hitch Hiker* (*Suspense*, CBS), by Lucille Fletcher. P/D: William Spier.

OW is guest of honor at a benefit held in Croton-on-Hudson for the Russian War Relief.

Sept. 11 *Men, Machines and Victory* (NBC-Blue). Speaker: W. C. MacFarlane. Narr: OW.

Sept. 18 *Information Please* (NBC). Host: Clifton Fadiman. Guest panelist: OW. On the first of his many guest appearances on this show, in which panelists respond to questions submitted by listeners, OW answers every question correctly and even corrects the host on three occasions.

Sept. 25 *Crime Without Passion* (*The Philip Morris Playhouse*, CBS), adapted from the 1934 screenplay by Ben Hecht and Charles MacArthur. This is the first of many guest appearances by OW on this show.

Sept. 28 *Juarez: Thunder from the Hills* (*Cavalcade of America*, NBC). For Cavalcade staff, see 1935 entry. A verse play by Arthur Miller, adapted from *Juarez: Liberator of Mexico* by N. B. Baker. Narr/Juarez: OW. According to BW, this is the first time that OW is granted creative control on the show—a historical drama about the life of Mexican revolutionary Benito Juárez at the end of the nineteenth century which compares him to Lincoln, presented before a live audience. (See Arthur Miller's *Timebends*, New York: Harper & Row, 1987.)

Oct. 5 *Passage to More Than India* (*Cavalcade of America*, NBC). Guest star: OW.

Oct. 11 *Radio Reader's Digest* (CBS). OW reads the poem "High Flight."

Oct. 12 *Admiral of the Open Sea* (*Cavalcade of America*, NBC), adapted by OW, Robert Meltzer, and Norris Houghton from the book by Samuel Eliot Morison. D/narr: OW. Written to commemorate Columbus Day, this program about Christopher Columbus is translated into Spanish and Portuguese and rebroadcast to Latin America by the Coordinator of Inter-American Affairs. Under the title *Columbus Day*, the radio play is published in *Radio Drama in Action*, edited by Erik Barnouw (New York: Farrar & Rinehart), 1945.

Oct. 13 *Annual United Fund Appeal* (CBS). Radio play: *Hospitals in Wartime*. Narr: OW.

Oct. 16 OW speaks with Charlie Chaplin, Sam Jaffe, Lillian Hellman, Joris Ivens, I. F. Stone, Rockwell Kent, and others at Carnegie Hall in New York for the "Artists' Front to Win the War." The same evening, he makes another guest appearance on *The Philip Morris Playhouse*.

Oct. 18 *Texaco Star Theatre* (NBC; rebroadcast on Armed Forces Radio Service). Host: Fred Allen. D: Victor Knight, Howard Reilly. Sc: Fred Allen, others. Guest star: OW. Cast: Portland Hoffa, Parker Fennelly, KD, Alan Reed. Ann: Arthur Godfrey. OW and Allen tell jokes about OW's precocious childhood and do a comic version of *Les Misérables* on this long-running show, later known as *The Fred Allen Show*.

Oct. 20 OW gives an extemporaneous talk to film students at New York University; he is introduced by Robert Gessner as "the most original, creative force in motion pictures since D. W. Griffith."

Oct. 26 *In the Best Tradition* (*Cavalcade of America*, NBC). Sc: Peter Lyon. D/narr: OW. A celebration of the U.S. naval forces; OW "interviews" Commodore Perry and John Paul Jones and reads poetry by Carl Sandburg.

Autumn RKO allows OW to do some re-editing work on *Journey into Fear,* which includes shooting a brief final scene with JC and adding JC's voice-over narration. (Neither OW nor JC is paid for this work.)

Nov. OW begins broadcasting two shows a week for the Columbia network:

Nov. 9 *The Flying Fortress* (*Ceiling Unlimited,* CBS). D/host/narr: OW. Cast: OW, ES, RC, Patrick McGeehan, others. Music: BH. Sc: Ranald MacDougall, Norman Rosten. A wartime propaganda series presenting dramatizations of various aspects of air travel; Leonardo da Vinci is a featured character tonight. Arthur Miller, one of the principal writers, helps to develop the show's format.

Nov. 15 *Brazil* (*Hello Americans,* CBS). P/d/host: OW. Cast: OW, Carmen Miranda, Mercury Players. Sc: Robert Meltzer. Music: Lucien Moravec. A show dealing in part with the origins of the samba. (OW to PB: "They were good shows, I thought. All inter-American affairs. I did the A-B-Cs of the Caribbean. And they were very amusing. I didn't really do much of it—the writers were awfully good. And it was a good form. A-B-C: 'A' is for 'Antilles,' 'Antigua,' and so on. We went through like that, and did little things and big things, with music and stories each week. I'm queer for the Caribbean anyway—not as it exists, but as it was in my mind in the eighteenth and nineteenth centuries. The Caribbean is just great stuff. All of it. The whole idea of all these empires fighting over tiny little islands, and black independence and Spanish pride and the War of Jenkins's Ear and those great earthquakes.")

Nov. 16 *Air Transport Command* (*Ceiling Unlimited,* CBS).

Nov. 22 *Hello Americans* (CBS). Program: (1) *The Andes,* with Edmond O'Brien (Bolivar), AM, RC, ER, Barbara Jean Wong, HC, others. (2) Two musical compositions by Justin Erlie and Carlos Gomes. (3) Poetry by Norman Rosten.

Nov. 23 *The Navigator* (*Ceiling Unlimited,* CBS), by OW and Milton Geiger. Cast: OW, JC, RC, AM, ER.

Nov. 29 *The Islands* (*Hello Americans*, CBS), with the Haitian Chorus, RC, HC, ER. A program about the abolition of slavery in Haiti led by Toussaint-L'Ouverture and the reign of Henri Christophe.

Nov. 30 *Wind, Sand and Stars* (*Ceiling Unlimited*, CBS), adapted by OW from the book by Antoine de Saint-Exupéry. Cast: OW, Burgess Meredith.

OW serves as chairman on forum held in the Beverly Hills Hotel to raise money for the defense of Mexican American youths in the Sleepy Lagoon murder case (see June 1943).

Dec. 6 *The Alphabet: A to C* (*Hello Americans*, CBS). Guest singer: Miguelito Valdez. A program in part about the Venezuelan revolutionary Bolivar, with reference back to Christophe, the early nineteenth-century Haitian king.

Dec. 7 *The Ballad of Bataan* (*Ceiling Unlimited*, CBS). OW reads a Norman Rosten poem.

Dec. 10 RKO studio head Charles Koerner orders all of the footage that was cut from *Ambersons* destroyed.

Dec. 13 *The Alphabet: C to S* (*Hello Americans*, CBS).

Dec. 14 *War Workers* (*Ceiling Unlimited*, CBS). Sc: HC. OW "interviews" many people at an airplane factory, including a blind girl and a midget.

Dec. 20 *The Alphabet: Slavery (Abednego) to End of Alphabet* (*Hello Americans*, CBS), by OW, JTB. Cast: OW (Sir Barnaby Finch), ER (Abednego), Norman Field (Toussaint-L'Ouverture), Gerald Mohr (Henri Christophe).

Dec. 21 *Gremlins* (*Ceiling Unlimited*, CBS), by Lucille Fletcher Herrmann. Cast: OW, JC, AM, Lou Merrill. A Christmas show.

Dec. 27 *The Bad-Will Ambassador* (*Hello Americans*, CBS), by Richard Brooks. Cast: Norman Field, Pedro de Cordoba, JTB, HC, Martin Stone, OW.

Dec. 28 *Pan American Airlines* (*Ceiling Unlimited*, CBS), by Milton Geiger.

1943 *The Little Prince* (unrealized project). OW buys the rights to Antoine de Saint-Exupéry's novel and a first-draft script is written, with OW to star as the narrator and the aviator, and animation to be used for the interplanetary travel. He also begins discussions with Alexander Korda about an adaptation of Tolstoy's *War and Peace* to be shot in Russia, and later writes a script—a project abandoned circa 1946.

This year, OW plays the part of a crusading editor in one episode of *Nazi Eyes on Canada* for the Canadian Broadcasting Company.

Jan. 3– Jan. 4 Due to illness, OW is unable to appear on his two shows; in his place, Lud Gluskin provides Latin American dance music on *Hello Americans*, and Edward G. Robinson hosts *Anti-Submarine Patrol* on *Ceiling Unlimited* the following evening.

Jan. 10 *Mexico* (*Hello Americans*, CBS). The stories of Montezuma and Benito Juárez.

Jan. 11 *Finger in the Wind* (*Ceiling Unlimited*, CBS), by Myron Dutton.

Jan. 17 *Feed the World* (*Hello Americans*, CBS) by Milton Geiger. Narr: FR. Cast: Eddie Jerome (Gaucho), OW (Famine), Carl Swenson, Joseph Cheshire, Jack Moss, Louis Solomon.

Jan. 18 *Letter to Mother* (*Ceiling Unlimited*, CBS), by John Steinbeck. Cast: BG (Mother), OW.

Jan. 24 Lud Gluskin again substitutes for OW on *Hello Americans*.

Jan. 25 *Ceiling Unlimited*, CBS. (1) *Flyer Come Home with Your Wings* by John Steinbeck. (2) *Mrs. James and the Pot of Tea* by JTB.

Jan. 31 *Bolivar's Idea* (*Hello Americans*, CBS). The final show in the series.

Feb. 1 *The Future* (*Ceiling Unlimited*, CBS). The final show in the series, set three years in the future at La Guardia Airport.

Feb. 10 OW writes a guest column for Leonard Lyons, *N.Y. Post*.

Feb. 12 *Journey into Fear* (Mercury Productions, RKO Radio Pictures). D: Norman Foster (and, uncredited, OW). P (uncredited): OW. Assoc p (uncredited): Jack Moss. Sc: JC (and, uncredited, OW), based on the Eric Ambler novel. Ph: Karl Struss. Ed: Mark Robson. Original r t: 91 minutes. Release r t: 69 minutes. Cast: OW (Colonel Haki), JC (Howard Graham), Dolores Del Rio (Josette Martel), ES (Kopeikin), Ruth Warrick (Stephanie Graham), AM (Mrs. Mathews), Jack Durant (Gogo), EW (Dr. Haller), FR (Mathews), EB (Kuvietli), Jack Moss (Banat), SS (Purser), HC (Oo Lang Sang, the magician), Richard Bennett (ship's captain), Robert Meltzer, Shifra Haran, others.

March 6 OW gives a speech, "New Techniques in Mass Education," at the annual conference of the California Association for Adult Education, held at the Hotel Ambassador, Los Angeles.

March 14 For four consecutive weeks, while Jack Benny is ill, OW takes over as guest host of *The Jack Benny Program* (NBC). D: Robert Ballin. Sc: Bill Morrow, Ed Beloin. Cast: Mary Livingston, Dennis Day, Eddie Anderson (Rochester), others. A live half-hour comedy show.

April 11 When Benny returns, OW is his first guest.

May 23 *Something About Joe* (*The Free World Theatre*, NBC-Blue). Guest stars: OW, Lena Horne, Rex Ingram, Hazel Scott. OW reads a war ballad.

June OW contributes a foreword to a political pamphlet about a trial in which seventeen Mexican Americans are tried for murder, *The Sleepy Lagoon Murder Case* (Los Angeles: Mercury Press). During the same period, he serves as spokesman for the Citizens' Committee for the Defense of Mexican American Youth; see BL for further details.

July 25 Another guest column by OW for Leonard Lyons.

August 3 *The Mercury Wonder Show* (Mercury Productions). D: OW. P: OW, JC. R t: 150 minutes. Opens: Mercury Wonder Show Tent, 9000 Cahuenga Boulevard, Hollywood. Cast:

OW, Rita Hayworth (later replaced by Marlene Dietrich) (playing themselves), JC (Jo-Jo the Great), AM (Calliope Aggie), others. A magic-and-variety show staged free for the troops, involving twenty-three costume changes for OW, with regularly priced tickets for the public or "suckers" (see chapter 5); each performance is given for about eleven hundred servicemen and four hundred "suckers." The production plays for over a month, after which OW takes a reduced version of it to various army camps around the country. In October, he films a brief segment from his magic act for the feature *Follow the Boys* (see May 5, 1944).

Sept. 3 *Reading Out Loud.* OW reads and comments on John Donne's "The Sun Rising" and "No Man Is an Island" and a passage from George Jessel's biography on a new fifteen-minute program—a show that is not continued because of lack of audience response.

Sept. 7 OW marries Rita Hayworth. The same day, near the end of the run of *The Mercury Wonder Show,* he, Rita Hayworth, Marlene Dietrich, JC, OW's chauffeur "Shorty" Chirello, and various members of the audience are all interviewed on station KMPR during the show's intermission. OW notes that they've performed the show by now for about forty-eight thousand servicemen.

Sept. 11 OW gives a speech about racism at the Mass Rally to Win the Peace at the Chicago Stadium.

Sept. 23 *The Most Dangerous Game* (*Suspense,* CBS), adapted from the Richard Connell story. D: William N. Robeson. Guest stars: OW, Keenan Wynn. The first of many guest appearances on this popular series.

Sept. 27 Guest appearance on *The Pepsodent Show* (NBC) with Bob Hope.

Sept. 30 *The Lost World* (*Suspense,* CBS), adapted by Harry Julian Finke from Arthur Conan Doyle. Guest star: OW.

Oct. Editorial, "Moral Indebtedness," published in *Free World* magazine, edited by Louis Dolivet. This New York–based monthly is to print eleven more editorials by OW over the next two years.

Oct. 7 *The Philomel Cottage* (*Suspense*, CBS), adapted from Agatha Christie. Guest stars: OW, GF.

Oct. 12 Guest appearance on *Duffy's Tavern* (NBC-Blue), a weekly comedy series set in a New York diner where "the elite meet to eat." Cast: Ed Gardner, Shirley Booth, Charlie Cantor, others.

Oct. 14 *Lazarus Walks* (*Suspense*, CBS), adapted by Robert Richards. Guest star: OW.

Oct. 25 OW speaks at the Free World Dinner held at the Hotel Pennsylvania in New York.

Oct. 28 OW gives a speech to the Free World Congress.

Nov. 2 OW gives a speech at the Overseas Press Club, excerpts of which are reprinted in Elsa Maxwell's newspaper column on November 4.

Nov. 8 OW gives a speech to the Soviet American Congress at the Shrine Auditorium.

Nov. 11 OW gives a speech, "Moral Indebtedness," at a mass rally held at the Chicago Stadium for the United Nations Committee to Win the Peace—a revised version of the editorial published in the October issue of *Free World*.

Nov. 14 *New York Philharmonic Symphony* (CBS), conducted by Bruno Walter. Speaker: OW.

Guest appearance on *We, the People* (CBS), a popular series of human-interest stories.

Nov. 21 *New York Philharmonic Symphony* (CBS), conducted by Arthur Rodzinski. Speaker: OW.

Guest star on *Take It or Leave It*, a quiz show later known as *The $64,000 Question*.

Nov. 27 *Inner Sanctum* (CBS). D/P: Himan Brown. The first of many guest appearances on a mystery show introduced memorably by a squeaking door (see Sept. 23, 1944 and April 16, 1946).

Nov. 28 *New York Philharmonic Symphony* (CBS), conducted by Arthur Rodzinski. Speaker: OW.

Dec. Editorial in *Free World*, "The Unknown Soldier," reprinted in *Treasury for The Free Press*, edited by Ben Raeburn (New York: Arco Publishing, 1946; and Freeport, N.Y.: Books for Libraries Press, 1972).

Dec. 24 *Jane Eyre* (20th Century–Fox). D: Robert Stevenson. P: Kenneth Macgowan (and, uncredited, OW). Exec p: William Goetz. Sc: Aldous Huxley, Robert Stevenson, JH, from the Charlotte Brontë novel. Ph: George Barnes. Music: BH. R t: 96 minutes. Cast: OW (Edward Rochester), Joan Fontaine (Jane Eyre), Peggy Ann Garner (Jane as a young girl), Henry Daniell (Mr. Brocklehurst), Margaret O'Brien (Adele), AM, EW, Elizabeth Taylor, others.

1944

Jan. OW goes on a lecture tour arranged by the William Morris Agency. Title: "The Nature of the Enemy." Subject: Fascism.

Around this time, he discusses with Broadway producer Billy Rose a proposal to stage Donald Ogden Stewart's *Emily Brady* in San Francisco and New York, and works on editing *My Friend Bonito* with José Noriega (a project eventually abandoned in 1946).

OW is signed for a new season of live, weekly thirty-minute radio broadcasts with a loose variety format, featuring guest stars and drama, poetry readings, comedy sketches, music, and personal commentaries. Many of these shows (with the same basic staff, not repeated below) originate from army camps around the country where OW is entertaining the troops with his magic acts. Drawing, perhaps, some of its format from the Jack Benny radio show, on which OW appeared several times the previous spring, the show features a good many comic regulars, such as Jiminy Cricket (Cliff Edwards), Miss Grimace (AM, supposedly OW's secretary), Prudence Pratt (offering weekly household tips), and Dr. Snake Oil, with OW serving more as host and character in his own right than as performer; see BW for further details. (The summaries below are often incomplete.) The series is appropriately called:

Jan. 26 *Orson Welles Almanac* (CBS). D/host: OW. P: Harry Essman. Sc: Bud Pearson, Les White, Lou Quinn. Cast: AM, Arthur Q. Bryant, RC, Cliff Edwards, others. (1) Guest: Groucho Marx. (2) OW reads from Tom Paine.

Feb. 2 *Orson Welles Almanac* (CBS). (1) Guest: Lionel Barrymore. (2) Swing music. (3) "The Kiddie Show" (skit). (4) Tribute to Victor Herbert by Lud Gluskin. (5) Barrymore reads a text by George Washington.

Feb. 9 *Orson Welles Almanac* (CBS). (1) Guest: Ann Sothern. (2) "Abraham Lincoln's Prairie Years," adapted from the biography by Carl Sandburg.

Feb. 16 *Orson Welles Almanac* (CBS). (1) Guest: Robert Benchley (lecture on "the history of Eskimo love"). (2) "Colloquy to the States" by Archibald MacLeish.

Feb. 23 *Orson Welles Almanac* (CBS) (1) Guest: Hedda Hopper. (2) "The Sword in the Stone," adapted from the novel by T. H. White. Cast: AM, HC.

March Editorial in *Free World*, "The Bolivian Dilemma: The Good Neighbor Policy Reconsidered." ("The good neighbor policy has had too much to do with the front steps of the various presidential palaces and too little to do with the back door of Mr. and Mrs. America.")

March 1 *Orson Welles Almanac* (CBS). (1) Guest: Victor Moore. (2) "Sacre du Printemps," story by Ludwig Bemelmans.

March 8 *Orson Welles Almanac* (CBS). (1) Guest: Lucille Ball. (2) OW reads John Donne poem, "No Man Is an Island."

March 15 *Orson Welles Almanac* (CBS). (1) Guest: Charles Laughton. (2) Tent scene from WS's *Julius Caesar*, with Laughton (Cassius), OW (Brutus). (3) Dixieland jazz.

March 22 *Orson Welles Almanac* (CBS). (1) Guest: Betty Hutton. (2) "Ballad of Bataan," poem by Norman Rosten, read by OW.

March 29 *Orson Welles Almanac* (CBS). Program: *Cyrano de Bergerac*, adapted from the Edmond Rostand play. Cast: OW, Mary Boland.

April Editorial in *Free World*, "Democracy in Latin America."

Shooting begins this month on *Tomorrow Is Forever*, in which OW plays one of the three leading roles.

On weekends, he flies to San Francisco to attend the UN Security Council meetings.

April 2 OW is a guest on *The Chase and Sanborn Hour* (NBC) with Edgar Bergen and Charlie McCarthy. OW is to make several appearances (May 28, October 29, November 5) on this show, which had been his competitor when *Mercury Theatre on the Air* first began.

April 5 *Orson Welles Almanac* (CBS). (1) Guest: Dennis Day. (2) OW reads "O! what a rogue and peasant slave" speech from *Hamlet*.

April 12 *Orson Welles Almanac* (CBS). (1) Guest: Monty Woolley. (2) OW reads two psalms from the Bible.

April 13 *The Marvelous Borosco* (*Suspense*, CBS) by Ben Hecht. Sc: Harry Julian Finkle. Cast: William Spier, OW, others.

April 19 *Orson Welles Almanac* (CBS). (1) Guest: George Jessel. (2) OW reads from the Bible.

April 24 OW gives a speech for the Council for Civic Unity at the Philharmonic Auditorium in Los Angeles.

April 26 *Orson Welles Almanac* (CBS). (1) Guest: Carole Landis. (2) Scene from the last act of *Macbeth*, read by OW.

April 27 Guest appearance on *Suspense* (CBS).

Three of a Kind (*U.S. Treasury Show*, CBS). Cast: OW, Bert Lahr, Reginald Gardiner, Shirley Mitchell.

April 28 OW announces to the press that he, John Hammond, and F. O. Matthiessen have organized a Citizens' Committee to prevent the deportation of Harry Bridges.

May Editorial in *Free World*, "The Habits of Disunity."

May 3 *Orson Welles Almanac* (CBS). (1) Guest: Lucille Ball. (2) OW reads honor speech from *Henry V*.

May 4 *The Dark Tower* (*Suspense*, CBS), play by Alexander Woollcott and George S. Kaufman. Cast: HC, OW, others.

May 5 *Follow the Boys* (Universal Pictures). D: A. Edward Sutherland. P: Charles K. Feldman. Sc: Lou Breslow, Gertrude Purcell. R t: 122 minutes. Cast: George Raft, Vera Zorina, OW, Marlene Dietrich, Dinah Shore, W. C. Fields, others. As part of this wartime revue, OW saws Dietrich in half as he did in *The Mercury Wonder Show*. (His segment was filmed over five days the previous fall.)

May 10 *Orson Welles Almanac* (CBS). (1) Guests: Jimmy Durante, Aurora Miranda. (2) "Woodrow Wilson." Broadcast from the U.S. Army Air Force Redistribution Center, Santa Monica.

May 17 *Orson Welles Almanac* (CBS). (1) Guest: Ann Sothern. (2) Readings from *Romeo and Juliet*, with OW, HC.

May 18 *Donovan's Brain*, Part I (*Suspense*, CBS). P/D: William Spier. Adapted from the Curt Siodmak novel. Ann: Joe Kearns ("the man in black"). A tour-de-force radio performance in which OW as guest star plays Dr. Patrick Cory, an obsessed scientist who keeps alive a disembodied brain that gradually takes over his personality. OW dramatizes the transformation by alternating between the voices of both personalities, sometimes switching within the same sentence. (The complete show is available on audiocassette from National Recording Company.)

May 20 OW opens the fifth War Loan Drive with an hour-long radio show about American democracy from Thomas Paine to Thomas Wolfe. Guests include Charles Laughton, Lionel Barrymore, John Huston, Leopold Stokowski, Oscar Hammerstein II, and BH. (See CH2.)

May 24 *Orson Welles Almanac* (CBS). (1) Guests: The Wilde twins (Lyn and Lee), Lois Collier. (2) OW reads a public letter written by a missionary in 1890, printed in an Australian newspaper. Broadcast from the Air Service Command Training Center, Fresno.

May 25 *Donovan's Brain*, Part II (*Suspense*, CBS). See May 18.

May 31 *Orson Welles Almanac* (CBS). (1) Guest: Marjorie Reynolds. (2) A spoof of *Donovan's Brain*. (3) "High Flight," poem by John Gillespie Magee, read by OW.

June 3 *The Texarkana Program*. OW appears with Walter Huston, AM, JC, Danny Kaye, and Joe E. Brown to support the war effort, in a program broadcast live from Texas. (See CH2.)

June 5 *Jane Eyre* (*Lux Radio Theatre*, CBS), adapted from the Charlotte Brontë novel. D/P/host: Cecil B. De Mille. Guests: OW, Loretta Young. The first of several appearances by OW on this famous, long-running series (it started in 1936) which performs adaptations of current movies before a live audience in Hollywood.

June 7 *Orson Welles Almanac* (CBS). A special broadcast for D-Day dramatizing the lives of various Americans when they hear of the Normandy invasion, with OW, AM, others.

June 12 *The Summing Up: Fifth War Loan Drive* (CBS). Sc: OW. Guest speaker: Secretary of the Treasury Henry Morgenthau, Jr. Broadcast from Texarkana. Cast: OW, Keenan Wynn, Walter Huston, EB, AM, others.

June 14 *Orson Welles Almanac* (CBS). A follow-up to the above broadcast; Stephen Vincent Benét's "Prayer for the U.N." is featured.

Balance Sheet: Fifth War Loan Drive (CBS). P/D: PS. Sc: Peter Lyon. Guest speaker: Henry Morgenthau, Jr. Narr: Fredric March. Broadcast from Hollywood Bowl. Stars: OW, Lionel Barrymore, others.

June 19 *Fifth War Loan Drive* (CBS). Guest speaker: Henry Morgenthau, Jr. Broadcast from Soldiers Field, Chicago. Stars: OW, Lana Turner, Jack Benny, Ray Bolger, Paul Lukas. OW, uncredited, reads Walt Whitman's "You and Me" and presents a short play with Mercury actors about Americans during wartime.

June 21 *Orson Welles Almanac* (CBS). (1) Guest: Martha O'Driscoll. (2) Ethel Waters sings. (3) OW reads from WS's *Richard II*. Broadcast from Chicago's Wrigley Building.

June 28 *Orson Welles Almanac* (CBS). (1) Guest: Lynn Bari. (2) Jazz. (3) OW reads from the Bible. Broadcast from Camp Haan, Riverside, California, before an audience of servicemen.

July Editorial in *Free World*, "Race Hate Must Be Outlawed."

July 5 *Orson Welles Almanac* (CBS). A special program featuring "The Mercury Wonder Show No. 1," broadcast from the Los Angeles Port of Embarkation, Wilmington, before an audience of servicemen. Guests: Lana Turner, Keenan Wynn. OW sings "You Made Me Love You" to Turner.

July 12 *Orson Welles Almanac* (CBS). Guest: Susan Hayward. (1) Comedy. (2) OW reads speeches from *Richard II*. Broadcast from Camp Cooke, near Sacramento, before an audience of servicemen.

July 19 *Orson Welles Almanac* (CBS). Guest: Ruth Terry. (1) "With Your Wings," script by John Steinbeck. (2) Scenes from WS's *Hamlet*. Broadcast from Long Beach Coast Guard Camp, California, before an audience of servicemen. This is the twenty-sixth and last program in this series.

Aug. Editorial in *Free World*, "War Correspondents."

Aug. 13 Guest appearance on *The Gracie Fields Show* (NBC).

Sept. Editorial in *Free World*, "The American Leadership in '44."

Sept. 1 OW gives the first of many campaign speeches for Roosevelt, this time before a Democratic meeting held at the Shrine Auditorium. During this period, he stands in for FDR in a debate with Thomas Dewey at the Hotel Astor.

Sept. 11 *Break of Hearts* (*Lux Radio Theatre*, CBS), adapted from the screenplay by Sarah Y. Mason and Victor Heerman, based on the story by Lester Cohen. Guest stars: OW, Rita Hayworth. At the end of the show, Hayworth is asked how she copes with her husband; she replies, "He goes his way and I go with him."

Sept. 21 OW introduces Vice-President Henry Wallace at a rally for Roosevelt held at Madison Square Garden.

Sept. 23 *The Dream* (*Inner Sanctum*, CBS). D/p: Himan Brown. Sc: Milton Lewis. Guest star: OW (Judge Robert Branscome).

Oct. 2 *Let Yourself Go* (NBC). Special broadcast from Chicago. Guest star: OW.

Oct. 6 "Now Is the Time: A Soliloquy for Election Year." A campaign speech for Roosevelt, broadcast from Carnegie Hall in New York City.

Oct. 8 *Philco Radio Hall of Fame* (ABC). Guest host: OW. Guests: Milton Berle, Mary Martin, Burl Ives. A wartime variety show.

Oct. 9 Speeches for Roosevelt at a luncheon honoring Eleanor Roosevelt (Hotel Commodore, New York City) and at a rally held at the War Memorial Auditorium in Trenton, New Jersey.

Oct. 10 OW addresses a "Registration Week Luncheon."

Oct. 11 *Labor Party Broadcast* (CBS). Speakers: Franklin Roosevelt, OW.

The same day, OW delivers a campaign speech in Saint Petersburg, Florida.

Oct. 13 *Orson Welles for Roosevelt* (NBC)

Oct. 15 *The Dark Hours* (*The Kate Smith Show*, CBS). Host: Ted Collins. Star: Kate Smith. Guest star: OW. A radio play about Edgar Allan Poe is presented as a special program.

Oct. 16 Campaign speech for Roosevelt in Newark, New Jersey.

Oct. 17 Campaign speech in Wheeling, West Virginia.

Oct. 18 *Herald-Tribune Forum* (NBC-Blue). Speakers: Thomas E. Dewey, OW (the latter replacing FDR).

Oct. 27 *Welles for Roosevelt* (CBS).

Oct. 30 *Welles for Roosevelt* (Mutual).

Nov. 1 *Special Political Broadcast for the Democratic National Committee* (NBC-Blue). Speakers: OW, Quentin Reynolds, John Gunther.

Nov. 4 Campaigns with FDR at Fenway Park in Boston.

Nov. 6 OW buys the rights to the Richard Powell novel *Don't Catch Me* and begins to develop from it a "farce-melodrama" screenplay, in collaboration with Bud Pearson and Les White, the comedy writers on *Orson Welles Almanac*; the script is never sold. See BW for further details.

Democratic National Committee (four networks). Speech by OW.

Dec. Editorial in *Free World*, "Liberalism—Election's Victor."

Dec. 1 OW's third guest column for Leonard Lyons appears today, mainly about theatre.

Lecture on the GI Bill of Rights for the American Youth for Democracy, Roosevelt Hotel, Hollywood.

Dec. 4 Lecture, "The Survival of Fascism," for the Modern Forum, Wilshire Ebell Theatre, Los Angeles.

Dec. 10 OW is guest on *Chicago Round Table*, a local talk show on Chicago radio.

Dec. 17 OW's second daughter, Rebecca, is born to Rita Hayworth Welles.

Around this time, OW begins to appear on a new radio show with a live audience in Hollywood called *This Is My Best* ("America's Best Stars in the World's Best Stories"), inspired by the book edited by Whit Burnett, which he is soon to take over as producer-director-star. He appears in a dual role in Sinclair Lewis' *Willow Walk* and also acts in:

Dec. 19 *The Plot to Overthrow Christmas* (*This Is My Best*, CBS), radio play in verse by Norman Corwin. Cast: RC (Santa Claus), OW (Nero), John Brown (Devil).

Dec. 24 *The Happy Prince* (*Philco Hall of Fame*, NBC-Blue), adapted by OW from the Oscar Wilde story. Guest stars: Bing Crosby, OW.

Dec. 25 *The Happy Prince* (AFRS). A condensed version of the Dec. 24 show.

1945 Around this time, OW writes and records a series of eight programs that are never broadcast. On each show he appears speaking mainly on social and political issues, as he does on a series he launches this fall (see Sept. 16), *Orson Welles Commentaries;* in some ways, these initial programs can be regarded as trial runs for the later series. The titles of the programs are *Lobbying, G.I. Bill of Rights, New Year's, Post War, Epiphany, Shut-eye, Grable,* and *Inauguration.*

Among OW's many radio appearances for the AFRS (Armed Forces Radio Service) during the war are those for *Mail Call* and *G.I. Journal.* He also stars in one episode of Sherman Dryer's science-drama series, *Exploring the Unknown* (Mutual) called *The Battle Never Ends,* about man's fight against plagues, and appears on *Stage Door Canteen.*

OW contributes a brief foreword to *Hero's Oak,* a novel by William Castle and Robert Joseph (New York: Reader's Press), published this year.

Jan. Editorial in *Free World,* "G.I. Bill of Rights." A French translation of OW's December editorial appears in the French edition, *Le Monde libre.*

Jan. 19 A story on the back page of the *New York Post* announces that OW will begin a regular column in this spot on Monday. "Certainly, I love the stage and screen," he is quoted as saying in an interview at the Saint Regis Hotel. "But things are happening in the world today that are more important than the theatre."

Jan. 22 Speech, "The Nature of the Enemy," arguing for "active intervention in the affairs of Argentina," New York City Center. Soon afterward, he gives the same talk in Baltimore and Washington, D.C.

OW's first column appears, under the title "Orson Welles' Almanac." It continues on weekdays on a somewhat regular basis for much of the year—often divided into many sections, like his radio show of the same title, and dealing with everything from astrological and household tips to politics and films. This first column focuses mainly on presidential inaugurations but also notes, "Byron was born today, and so was D. W. Griffith, the greatest of all motion picture directors." See JN for more details on the column.

Jan. 28 Guest star on *The Kate Smith Show* (CBS).

March 7 *Special V-E Day Broadcast* (AFRS). Cast: Bob Hope, Bing Crosby, OW, Frances Langford, Dinah Shore, Judy Garland, Clark Gable, Loretta Young, Charles Boyer, others.

March 13 *Heart of Darkness* (*This Is My Best*, CBS), adapted by OW from the Joseph Conrad story. D/P: OW. Cast: OW (Marlow/Kurtz), others. OW takes over this show with his second radio version of the Conrad story—a good deal more effective than the first, and much closer to the conception of the film project. Available on TOTI. (John Dunning, *Tune in Yesterday* [Englewood Cliffs, N.J.: Prentice-Hall, 1976]: "He directed from a podium, puffing away on his eternal cigar and flashing directions with a specially designed cue box with colored lights [white = control room, red = sound effects, blue = orchestra, green = miscellaneous].")

March 20 *Miss Dilly Says No* (*This Is My Best*, CBS), adapted by Robert Tallman from the Theodore Pratt novel. Cast: OW (Producer), Ann Sothern (Miss Dilly), Rita Hayworth (Miss Dilly's friend), Francis X. Bushman (Mr. Flagstone). A satire set in a Hollywood studio where an inconspicuous secretary writes a best-seller and is much sought after.

March 26 *A Tale of Two Cities* (*Lux Radio Theatre*, CBS), adapted from the Charles Dickens novel. D: Earl Ebie. Cast: OW (Sydney Carton), Rosemary De Camp (Lucie Manette), Dennis Greene (Charles Darnay), Verna Felton.

March 27 *Snow White and the Seven Dwarfs* (*This Is My Best*, CBS), adapted by Robert Tallman from the Grimm story and the 1937 Walt Disney film. Songs also from the film. Narr: OW. Cast: Jane Powell (Snow White), Jeanette Nolan (Wicked queen), Bill Daves (Prince Charming), John McIntire (Magic mirror). OW mentions that this program was chosen for overseas broadcast and dedicates it to his daughter Christopher on her seventh birthday.

April 3 *The Diamond as Big as the Ritz* (*This Is My Best*, CBS), adapted by Robert Tallman from the F. Scott Fitzgerald story. Narr: OW. Cast: OW (Braddock Washington), David Ellis (John T. Unger), Sheila Ryan (Kismine Washington).

April 10 *The Master of Ballantrae* (*This Is My Best*, CBS), adapted by Robert Tallman from the Robert Louis Stevenson novel. Cast: OW, AM, RC, Alan Napier.

April 12 Special CBS broadcast in memory of President Roosevelt, who has just died. OW is among the speakers.

April 13 Another special CBS broadcast on the death of Roosevelt.

April 17 *I'll Not Go Back* (*This Is My Best*, CBS) by Milton Geiger (original radio drama). Guest star: Joan Loring. A program dedicated to Roosevelt and "the future of America."

April 23 OW's first column since Roosevelt's death, now retitled "Orson Welles Today."

April 24 *Anything Can Happen* (*This Is My Best*, CBS), adapted by Robert Tallman from the book by George and Helen Papashvily. Cast: EB, Konstantin Shayne, Peg La Centra. Although the next show is announced—a dramatization of *Don't Catch Me* (OW's film project—see Nov. 6, 1944) with Rita Hayworth—a rift develops between OW and the sponsors, and consequently this is the last broadcast in the series.

April 25 OW begins to edit a daily newsletter in San Francisco at the United Nations Conference on International Organization, published in English, French, and Spanish. Around the same time, he has a short-lived radio show featuring conference participants, *The Free World Forum*.

May Editorial in *Free World*, "In Memoriam: Mankind Grieves for Our Late President."

May 7 OW is among the speakers in a special V-E Day broadcast.

May 27 Talk about the United Nations Conference, California Labor School, San Francisco.

May 31 Talk about the United Nations Conference, for the National Citizens Political Action Committee, Los Angeles.

June 6 OW's last daily column in the *Post*—it is resumed on a weekly basis on September 4—as he prepares his first film-directing job in four years, *The Stranger*.

July Editorial in *Free World*, "World Citizenship and Economic Problems."

July 10 *New York: A Tapestry for Radio* (*Columbia Presents Corwin*, CBS). D/P/Sc: Norman Corwin. Narr: OW, MG. The first of many appearances on this series of original Corwin radio plays.

July 17 *French Press: The Liberation of Paris* (NBC). OW narrates a radio documentary about the French underground radio during the Occupation.

July 19 *Command Performance* (CBS/AFRS). Cast: OW, Peggy Lee, Larry Adler, the King Sisters, Danny Thomas, Alfred Drake.

Aug. 9 *Town Meeting of the Air* (*America's Town Meeting*, NBC-Blue). D: Wylie Adams. Ann: Ed Herlihy. Subject: "What Does the British Election Mean to Us?" Moderator: George V. Denny, Jr. Guest speakers: OW, Manchester Boddy, others. Published later as a pamphlet.

Aug. 14 *14 August* (*Columbia Presents Corwin*, CBS). Narr: OW. D/Sc: Norman Corwin. Subject: "The Japanese and the Bomb." A condensed version of Corwin's *God and Uranium* (see Aug. 21).

Command Performance (CBS/AFRS). Guests: OW, Ernst Lubitsch, Jack Benny, Ken Carpenter, Greer Garson.

Aug. 21 *God and Uranium* (*Columbia Presents Corwin*, CBS). Narr: OW. Guest star: Olivia de Havilland. Expanded version of Corwin's *14 August* (see Aug. 14).

Sept. Editorial in *Free World*, "Now or Never." This is the last of OW's *Free World* editorials.

Sept. 2 *Victory Extra* (*Command Performance*, all networks). A special V-J Day production. Cast: Bing Crosby, Frank Sinatra, Dinah Shore, OW, Bob Hope, President Truman, others. OW recites a prayer.

Sept. 4 "Orson Welles Today" resumes as a weekly column with "Says Bill: Blame Us All for Pearl Harbor" (on cartoonist Bill Mauldin).

Sept. 11 "Orson Welles Today": "Bey of Beverly Meets His Match" (pseudonymous account of a Hollywood producer).

Sept. 16 This month, OW begins a series of weekly commentaries, called *Orson Welles Commentaries*, most of them on social and political subjects, which runs for thirteen months on ABC. (OW misses an occasional week, but it has not been possible to confirm all the dates when he appears; only a few of these broadcasts are listed.)

Sept. 18 "Orson Welles Today": "What's in a Name? Poetry or Legend Perhaps."

Oct. 2 "Orson Welles Today": "Aunt Lou in the Labor Crisis."

Oct. 9 "Orson Welles Today": "An Open Letter to Mr. Secretary."

Oct. 21 *Request Performance* (CBS). D: William N. Robson. Cast: OW, Eddie Bracken, Virginia O'Brien.

Oct. 23 "Orson Welles Today": "The Actor's Role in Society."

Oct. 30 "Orson Welles Today": "On Listening to Mr. Truman."

Nov. 6 "Orson Welles Today": "I Get a Driver's License." The last of OW's columns.

Nov. 21 Shooting completed on *The Stranger*.
The same week, OW leaves for New York and continues *Orson Welles Commentaries* from there (WJZ).

Dec. 27 *In the American Tradition* (Decca Records). Readings by OW: (1) Thomas Jefferson's 1st Inaugural Address, March 4, 1801. (2) Abraham Lincoln's 2nd Inaugural Address, March 4, 1865. (3) Woodrow Wilson's Address to the Peace

Conference, Paris, January 25, 1919. (4) Franklin Roosevelt's 1st War Address Before Congress, January 6, 1942. Liner notes by Howard Fast.

Around this time, OW also records *The Song of Songs* for Decca; see CH2.

1946 During this year, Decca releases two more OW recordings:

No Man Is an Island. Readings by OW: (1) Pericles' "The World Is Their Sepulchre." (2) John Donne's "For Whom the Bell Tolls." (3) Thomas Paine's "Tyranny Is Not Easily Conquered." (4) Patrick Henry's "Liberty or Death." (5) Lazare Carnot's "The New World Teaches the Old." (6) Daniel Webster's "Liberty and Union, Now and Forever." (7) John Brown's "In Behalf of His Despised Poor." (8) Abraham Lincoln's Gettysburg Address. (9) Émile Zola's "Truth and Justice Cost Too Dear." Liner notes by Louis Untermeyer. (Reissued as long-playing album DL-9060).

The Happy Prince (Decca Records Album 420). D/adaptor/narr: OW, from the Oscar Wilde story. Music: BH. Conductor: Victor Young. With Bing Crosby as the prince.

OW also writes a brief foreword to Dave Dexter, Jr.'s *Jazz Cavalcade: The Inside Story of Jazz* (New York: Criterion), published this year ("The cultists are going to hate *Jazz Cavalcade.* I like it because a square can understand it, and because it isn't for the long-haired").

Jan. OW gives a talk to Eleanor Roosevelt's American Committee for Yugoslav War Relief in New York.

Jan. 16 *All American Jazz Concert* (NBC). Guest: OW. Stars: Duke Ellington, the Nat "King" Cole Trio, and Woody Herman.

Jan. 18 *Tomorrow Is Forever* (International Pictures/RKO Radio Pictures). D: Irving Pichel. P: David Lewis. Sc: Leonore Coffee, from the novel by Gwen Bristow. Cast: Claudette Colbert (Elizabeth MacDonald Hamilton), OW (John MacDonald Kessler), Natalie Wood, others.

Feb. 28 OW speaks at a Madison Square Garden Rally on employment practices.

March 1 *The Danny Kaye Show* (NBC). D: Goodman Ace. Sc: Goodman Ace, Sylvia Fine. Guest star: OW. Cast: Kaye, KD, others.

March 3 Guest appearance on *The Fred Allen Show* (NBC). (For credits, see Oct. 18, 1942.) OW and Allen re-create their *Les Misérables* parody-sketch.

March 4 OW gives a political talk in Tacoma, Washington.

March 15 Guest appearance on *The Kate Smith Show* (ABC).

March 20 *Ellery Queen* (CBS). D: Phil Cohen, others. Cast: Hugh Marlowe (Ellery Queen), others. Guest "Armchair Detective": OW. A mystery series with a different celebrity each week trying to guess whodunit.

March 31 *Radio Reader's Digest* (CBS). OW reads "Back for Christmas."

April 1–April 2 Marc Blitzstein's *Airborne Symphony*, a cantata for male voices, receives its premiere performances at New York's City Center, conducted by Leonard Bernstein, with OW speaking the role of the Monitor (narrator) and the eighty-five voices of Robert Shaw's Collegiate Chorale performing.

April 5 *The Phoenix*, a magic magazine, publishes OW's card trick "The Town Skryer."

April 16 Guest appearance on *Inner Sanctum* (NBC-Blue).

April 27 OW's gigantic musical production of *Around the World in 80 Days* opens its pre–New York tryout tour at the Boston Opera House, where it runs through May 4.

During this run, when Bertolt Brecht comes backstage after a matinee (see chapter 3), he asks Welles to direct his *Galileo*. But because of the debts incurred by *Around the World*, this never happens, despite the additional encouragement of Charles Laughton, who eventually stars in *Galileo* under Joseph Losey's direction. (OW to PB: "Brecht had an extraordinary brain. You could tell he'd been educated by the Jesuits—he had the kind of disciplined brain characterized by Jesuit education. Instinctively, he was more of an anarchist than a Marxist, but he believed himself a perfect Marxist. When I said to him one day—while we were talking about *Galileo*—that he had written a perfect anticommunist work, he almost became aggressive. I said, 'But this church you describe has to be Stalin and not the Pope. You have made something resolutely anti-Soviet!' ")

May 7 *Around the World* moves to the Shubert Theatre in New Haven, where it runs through May 11. During the engagement, OW takes over the role of Dick Fix, which he continues to play in Philadelphia and New York.

May 13 *Around the World* moves to Philadelphia, where it runs through May 20.

May 31–August 3 *Around the World in 80 Days* (A Mercury Production). Adapted by OW from the Jules Verne novel. D: OW. Assoc p: RW. Music/lyrics/incidental score: Cole Porter. [The orchestra comprises thirty-six musicians; the overall production requires fifty-five stagehands.] Film ed: Irving Lerner. Opens: Adelphi Theatre, New York. Cast: BD (Bank robber/Mr. Benjamin Cruett-Spew/Second Arab spy/Mr. Oka Saka, circus proprietor/Sol, San Francisco stationmaster), GSP (Police inspector/Mr. Ralph Runcible/Maurice Goodpile, conductor on the Great Indian Peninsula R.R.), OW (Dick Fix, a Copper's Knark), Nathan Baker (London bobby/Sinister Chinaman/Father clown/Dancing gentleman), Jack Pitchon (London bobby/Roustabout/Singing gentleman), Arthur Margetson (Mr. Phileas Fogg), Mary Healy (Mrs. Aouda, Indian princess), others. OW's personal favorite among all his stage productions, inspired by the films of Georges Méliès. It opens to mixed reviews—some unimpressed by the extravagance, others overwhelmed by it. Critic Robert Garland writes that the show has "everything but the kitchen sink," so the following evening, during his curtain speech, OW has a kitchen sink brought out. In the *New York Times*, Lewis Nichols writes, "The State Legislature should pass a bill prohibiting Mr. Welles from leaving the New York theatre." OW again uses films to bridge scenes and eliminate wordy exposition. Done in silent-movie style, complete with titles, this footage has since disappeared. Although the audience who comes loves the show, and even though OW invests much of his own money, he does not have enough—nor can he secure enough to keep the show running through the traditionally slow summer months; this, combined with the theatre's inadequate air conditioning, finally forces him to close the production after 75 performances. He personally loses $320,000, which, because of bad legal advice, the government refuses to allow him on his taxes. He is to spend many years paying this off.

In an effort to further employ the thirty-six musicians used in *Around the World*, OW plans a cantata version of *King Lear*, which he hopes to show on Tuesday, Thursday, and Saturday afternoons during the run, but this project is vetoed by six separate unions. (See RM.)

June OW signs with CBS for *Mercury Summer Theatre of the Air*, a series to be broadcast from New York that will reprise some of his old Mercury shows and present some new plays in a half-hour format.

June 7 *Around the World in 80 Days* (*Mercury Summer Theatre*, CBS). D/P/host: OW. Assoc p/rehearsal director: RW. Music: BH. (These credits remain constant and are not repeated below.) Cast: OW (Fix), Arthur Margetson (Phileas Fogg), Larry Laurence (Passepartout), Mary Healy (Princess Aouda), Julie Warren (Molly Muggins), GSP, SS, BD.

June 14 *The Count of Monte Cristo* (*Mercury Summer Theatre*, CBS), adapted from the Dumas novel. Cast: OW (Edmond Dantes), Julie Warren (Mercedes), SS, GSP, BD.

June 16 OW responds to a survey about fathers for Father's Day in the Sunday *New York Times Magazine*: "At the turn of the century my father began making automobiles but gave it up in favor of making bicycle lamps because he thought there was no future in the automobile business. He made a fortune in spite of himself, inasmuch as the automobile manufacturers bought the lamps for their cars."

Orson Welles Commentaries (ABC).

June 21 *The Hitchhiker* (*Mercury Summer Theatre*, CBS) by Lucille Fletcher. Cast: OW, AFT.

June 28 OW appears on *The Colgate Sports Newsreel* with Bill Stern.

Jane Eyre (*Mercury Summer Theatre*, CBS), adapted by Norman Corwin from the Brontë novel. Cast: OW (Rochester), AFT (Jane Eyre), GSP, SS, Mary Healy, Abby Lewis.

June 30 *Orson Welles Commentaries* (ABC), protesting both the end of the OPA (rent and price controls) and the A-bomb testing on Bikini scheduled for that night.

July 2 *The Stranger* (Haig Corporation/International Pictures/RKO Radio Pictures). D: OW. P: S. P. Eagle (Sam Spiegel). Exec p: William Goetz. Sc: Anthony Veiller (and, uncredited, OW, John Huston). Story: Victor Trivas, Decla Dunning. Ph: Russell Motty. P des: Perry Ferguson. Ed: Ernest Nims. Original r t: 115 minutes. Release r t: 95 min. Cast: OW (Charles Rankin/Franz Kindler), Edward G. Robinson (Inspector Wilson), Loretta Young (Mary Longstreet), Philip Merivale (Judge Longstreet), Richard Long (Noah Longstreet), Byron Keith (Dr. Lawrence), Billy House (Mr. Potter), Konstantin Shayne (Konrad Meinike), others. Working title: *Date with Destiny*.

July This month, Lear Radios, the sponsor of *Orson Welles Commentaries*, decides not to renew its option because of the program's failure to reach a large audience. ABC agrees to continue the show until a new sponsor is found (which never happens), and OW's weekly salary is cut from $1,700 to $50. (See BL).

July 5 A *Passenger to Bali* (*Mercury Summer Theatre*, CBS), adapted from the Ellis St. Joseph book.

July 12 *The Search for Henri Le Fevre* (*Mercury Summer Theatre*, CBS) by Lucille Fletcher. Cast: OW, MEM, Julie Warren, BD.

July 19 *Life with Adam* (*Mercury Summer Theatre*, CBS) by Hugh Kemp. Host: OW. D: Fletcher Markle. Cast: Fletcher Markle (Adam Barneycastle), Grace Mathews (Eve), John Drainie (Chester), BG (Jenkins), Hedley Rainie (Waiter/Producer/others), Patricia Loudry, MEM. As a departure on this show, OW presents a comic radio play originally produced for Stage 46 in Toronto by Andrew Allen the previous week, with the same director and many of the same cast—a satire on the popular persona of OW, represented here as "Adam Barneycastle." MEM and Markle, who meet on the show, are eventually married, and Markle later works for OW as a writer.

July 26 *The Moat Farm Murder* (*Mercury Summer Theatre*, CBS) by Norman Corwin. Cast: OW (Dougal), MEM (Cecile). An original radio play based on a real-life crime—an Englishman murdered his wife and eventually confessed.

July 28 *Orson Welles Commentaries* (ABC). OW reads an affidavit sent to him by the NAACP, signed by Isaac Woodward, Jr., a black veteran who served for fifteen months in the South Pacific and earned one battle star. On the previous February 12, he was beaten so brutally by police officers in South Carolina after an altercation with a bus driver that he was blinded in both eyes. In an impassioned response, OW promises to root out and expose the officer responsible. This powerful broadcast provokes a good many letters from listeners, both pro and con, as well as a threatened lawsuit and angry demonstrations from Aiken, South Carolina, whose mayor insists that it was not the town where the event occurred. (This later proves to be Batesburg.) Woodward becomes the major focus of the show over the next month (see Aug. 4, 11, 18, 25); the officer responsible is eventually uncovered in August, and sentenced to a year in prison in September. (See BL for further details.)

Aug. 2 *The Golden Honeymoon* (*Mercury Summer Theatre*, CBS), adapted from the Ring Lardner story. Cast: Julie Warren, BD, MEM, Mary Healy, Ted Osborne, SS, Santos Ortega. OW also presents excerpts from *Romeo and Juliet* on the show.

Aug. 4 *Orson Welles Commentaries* (ABC). On world peace negotiations, Congress, and the Woodward case.

Aug. 9 *Hell on Ice* (*Mercury Summer Theatre*, CBS), adapted from the Lincoln Ellsworth book. Cast: OW, John Brown, ER, Byron Kane, Norman Field, Earle Ross, Lurene Tuttle.

Aug. 11 *Orson Welles Commentaries* (ABC). OW reads from his July 1944 editorial, "Race Hate Must Be Outlawed," and comments further on the Woodward case.

Aug. 12 The Aiken, South Carolina, police ban the local screening of *The Stranger*.

Aug. 16 *Abednego the Slave* (*Mercury Summer Theatre* [CBS]) by OW and JTB (see Dec. 20, 1942). Cast: OW, Norman Field, Earle Ross, Joe Granby, Barbara Jean Wong, Carl Frank, Byron Kane, John Brown, William Johnstone, ER, WA.

Aug. 18 *Orson Welles Commentaries* (ABC). The police chief responsible for Woodward's blindness is uncovered; OW reads and replies to a letter from an irate Southern white supremacist, and reads his December 1943 editorial, "The Unknown Soldier."

Tonight, OW appears at a benefit for Woodward with heavyweight champion Joe Louis and contralto Carol Brice held at Lewisohn Stadium; twenty thousand people attend. (See CH2.)

Aug. 23 *I'm a Fool/The Tell-Tale Heart* (*Mercury Summer Theatre*, CBS), adapted from the stories by Sherwood Anderson and Edgar Allan Poe. Cast: OW, WA, Joe Granby, ER, Norman Field, Carl Frank, others.

Aug. 25 *Orson Welles Commentaries* (ABC). On Isaac Woodward, the Texas gubernatorial election, the Ku Klux Klan, Palestine.

Aug. 30 *Moby Dick* (*Mercury Summer Theatre*, CBS), adapted by BD from the Herman Melville novel. (Many Brainerd Duffield scripts, possibly including this one, were written with Emerson Crocker.) Cast: OW (Ahab), WA, Byron Kane, John Brown, Earl Ross, ER.

Sept. This month, OW replaces Henry Wallace as a speaker at a National Citizens' Political Action Committee in Providence, Rhode Island. (See CH2.)

Sept. 6 *The Apple Tree* (*Mercury Summer Theatre*, CBS), adapted from the John Galsworthy story. Cast: OW, Norman Field, Mary Lansing, Lurene Tuttle, Jerry Farber, others.

Sept. 13 *Scenes from King Lear* (*Mercury Summer Theatre*, CBS), adapted from the WS play. Narr: John Brown. Cast: OW (Lear), Lurene Tuttle, EB, AM, ER, WA, others. OW also reads Ernest Dawson's poem "Cynara." This is the last *Mercury Summer Theatre* show.

Sept. When *Around the World* closes, OW and his small company return to Hollywood to continue preparing a picture for Columbia Pictures—a film that is to become *The Lady from Shanghai*. While at Columbia, OW proposes and develops some other film projects:

Salome, a script by Fletcher Markle—very freely based on Oscar Wilde's play, with a contemporary framing device—for Alexander Korda, to be shot in color by Georges Perinal, with sets by Christian Bérard, and with OW as both Wilde and Herod (see BW; excerpts from another *Salome* script, written later by OW, are included in MB). He also hopes to film Wilde's *The Happy Prince* as a sort of appendage to *Salome*.

Two other Korda projects are Robert Louis Stevenson's *The Master of Ballantrae* (abandoned when they are unable to acquire the rights) and Edmond Rostand's *Cyrano de Bergerac* (from a script by Ben Hecht, later rewritten by Charles Lederer), with Alexandre Trauner designing the sets and Jean Simmons contacted to play Roxanne.

Another project, for Harry Cohn, is *Carmen* with Paulette Goddard: "Memo: To Harry Cohn from Orson Welles [upon submission of a screen treatment by BD]: Dear Harry: The treatment that follows sticks closely to the story line and duplicates the style of the original novel *Carmen* by Mérimée. The novel is in no way to be confused with the opera of the same name. Mérimée was the James Cain–Raymond Chandler of his time; and in his best vein can make Ernest Hemingway seem like a Vassar girl in a daisy chain. It is tough writing, rough and sexy, and unsentimental. . . . In my opinion the public is now ready for the true Carmen, the real Carmen, who has never been seen before . . . the original melodrama of blood, violence, and passion. It is a fast-moving story, hard-boiled and modern. And there are other strong commercial aspects. It is rich in color, music, dancing, pageantry, showmanship. It is a famous classic work, a title well-known the world around. It is a great star vehicle. . . . Orson." Cohn eventually signs Charles Vidor to direct a picture based on the novel, released as *The Loves of Carmen* in 1948, with Rita Hayworth and Glenn Ford, only five months after the release of *The Lady from Shanghai*.

Oct. 2 Shooting begins on *The Lady from Shanghai* in Hollywood (the opening Central Park sequence), and continues on location in Acapulco (from mid-October through early December) and San Francisco. Principal photography will take 98 days. Working titles include *Black Irish, Take This Woman,* and *The Girl from Shanghai.*

Oct. 6 *Orson Welles Commentaries* (ABC). The final broadcast. This is the last of OW's own radio shows.

Oct. 16 OW speaks on the FEPC at a mass rally held at the Second Baptist Church in Los Angeles.

1947 A theatre project that OW unsuccessfully attempts to produce in New York this year is an oratorio based on *Moby Dick*, with a script by BD and a score by BH. (See JN.)

Jan. 22 Shooting suspended on *The Lady from Shanghai* because Rita Hayworth falls ill.

Feb. 17 Filming resumes. OW concludes negotiations for the film rights to Isaac Asimov's science fiction story "Evidence," although the project never goes any further.

Feb. 27 Principal photography completed on *The Lady from Shanghai*; after two final days of additional shooting (March 10–11), OW spends the next several weeks editing the picture.

April 11 Charles Chaplin's *Monsieur Verdoux*, "based on an idea by Orson Welles," opens.

May 7 *Duel in the Sun*, with narration by OW, opens.

May 28 Preparing his low-budget film of *Macbeth*, OW stages the play in Salt Lake City with almost the same cast:

Macbeth (Mercury Production/Utah Centennial Commission and University Theatre in cooperation with the American National Theatre and Academy). P and adaptation (from the WS play): OW. Executive director: RW. Stage manager: WS. Production coordinator: Emerson Crocker. Opens: Utah Centennial Festival, University Theatre. Cast: OW (Macbeth), Jeanette Nolan (Lady Macbeth), Dan O'Herlihy (Macduff), ERS (Duncan), Roddy McDowall (Malcolm), EB (Banquo), BD, WA, others. The production plays through May 31, after which rehearsals continue in California.

May 29 OW appears on *Command Performance's* hour-long show commemorating the fifth anniversary of AFRS.

June 23 Shooting begins on *Macbeth* in Hollywood.

July 17 Filming is concluded on *Macbeth* (23 actual shooting days). Shortly thereafter, OW leaves for Europe, where he works on the cutting and prepares to shoot *Cyrano de Bergerac* and *Around the World in 80 Days*, another film project for Korda, for which he shoots a few days of location footage in Morocco that are never cut or used.

During this same period, in Italy, he plays Cagliostro in Gregory Ratoff's film *Black Magic* (and directs a few scenes) and begins preparing and trying to finance his own movie production of *Othello*. He has the idea of recording film sound on tape—an idea adopted by the film industry later—and asks RW to send him a portable tape machine for this purpose in Europe; RW secures the recorder from former Columbia Pictures sound man Lodge Cunningham. OW also writes another script for Korda, based on Pirandello's *Henry IV*. (OW: "I spent months on that. If I ever wanted a script of mine to be published, that would be the one. It was completely redone on the Pirandello theme—it wasn't a movie version of the play. It happens in Europe, but it's about an American. Tennessee Williams ruined it for me by using frontal lobotomy in *Suddenly Last Summer* afterwards. The idea was, the father of the man who believes he is—or is pretending to believe he is—Henry IV is living on an island off the coast of Italy, and is determined to call his son's bluff and shame him.")

Nov. 11 OW and Rita Hayworth are divorced.

1948 OW writes Introduction to Bruce Elliott's *Magic as a Hobby: New Tricks for Amateur Performers* (New York: Harper), which also contains an original trick by OW, "Fruit Cup."

May 30 *The Lady from Shanghai* (Columbia Pictures). D: OW. Sc: OW (and, uncredited, William Castle, Fletcher Markle, Charles Lederer, others), based on Sherwood King's novel *If I Die Before I Wake*. Assoc p: RW, William Castle. Exec p: Harry Cohn. Ph: Charles Lawton, Jr. (and, uncredited, Rudolph Maté, Joseph Walker.) Original r t (in rough cut):

155 minutes. Release r t: 86 minutes. Cast: Rita Hayworth (Elsa Bannister), OW (Michael O'Hara), ES (Arthur Bannister), Glenn Anders (George Grisby), Ted de Corsia (Sidney Broome), ERS (Judge), GS (Goldie), Carl Frank, RW, others.

Sept. *Macbeth* is entered and then withdrawn from competition at the Venice Film Festival. Around this time, OW begins filming *Othello* in Venice with Lea Padovani as Desdemona; this footage is later reshot with Suzanne Cloutier.

Oct. 1 *Macbeth* (Mercury Productions/Literary Classics Productions/Republic Pictures). D/P: OW. Sc: OW, based on the WS play. Assoc p: RW. Exec p: Charles K. Feldman. Ph: John L. Russell. Music: Jacques Ibert. Ed: Louis Lindsay. Dialogue director: WA. Original r t: 107 minutes (later recut by OW to 86 minutes.) Cast: OW (Macbeth), Jeanette Nolan (Lady Macbeth), Dan O'Herlihy (Macduff), Peggy Webber (Lady Macduff/Witch), Lurene Tuttle (Witch/Gentlewoman), BD (Witch/First assassin), EB (Banquo), John Dierkes (Ross), George Chirello (Seyton), ERS (Duncan), Roddy McDowall (Malcolm), Charles Lederer (Witch), WA, GS, others. Filmed at Republic Studios; editing done in Europe during the filming of *Black Magic*.

1949 *Invasion from Mars*, a collection of "interplanetary stories" including the radio script of *The War of the Worlds*, is published by Dell in New York. OW, credited as editor, signs the introduction ("Can a Martian Help It If He's Colored Green?"), although there is reason to believe that his work on this book was ghosted.

OW spends the next three years making *Othello* and acting in other films in order to raise money for the production. The first to be released:

April *The Third Man* (London Film Production/Selznick Releasing Organization). D/P: Carol Reed. Exec p: Alexander Korda. Presented by David O. Selznick. Sc: Graham Greene (and, uncredited, Reed, OW). Story: Graham Greene, Alexander Korda. Ph: Robert Krasker. Zither music: Anton Karas. R t: 104 minutes. World premiere: Cannes Film Festival (winner, Grand Prix). Released in U.S. February 1950. Cast: JC (Rollo "Holly" Martins), Alida

Valli (Anna Schmidt), OW (Harry Lime), Trevor Howard (Major Calloway), others.

April 17 OW article "Out of a Trance" (on hypnotism), *New York Times*.

During this same period, OW collaborates with Charles Lederer on the script for a French film, *Portrait d'un assassin* (1949); the film is made, with Erich von Stroheim, Arletty, and Maria Montez, directed by Bernard Roland, but their script is not used. Also, as a favor to Lederer when he is indisposed, OW writes part of one short chase sequence for Howard Hawks' *I Was A Male War Bride*, with Cary Grant and Ann Sheridan.

June 19 Shooting begins on *Othello* in Mogador, Morocco, after over two weeks of rehearsals; filming is also done in Safi.

July 24 Shooting suspended for lack of funds.

Aug. 19 *Black Magic* (Edward Small Productions/United Artists). D: Gregory Ratoff (and, uncredited, OW). P: Ratoff. Sc: Charles Bennett, Richard Schayer, based on Alexandre Dumas's novel *Memoirs of a Physician*. Cast: OW (Cagliostro/Josef Balsamo), Nancy Guild (Marie Antoinette/Lorenza), AT (Gitano), others.

Aug. 24 Shooting resumes on *Othello* in Venice, Italy.

Sept. 6 After a day's break for travel, filming continues at Scalera Film Studios in Rome.

Sept. 17 Shooting suspended for lack of funds.

Oct. 18 Filming resumes in Tuscania, Italy.

Oct. 23 Filming continues in Viterbo, Italy.

Nov. 1 Filming continues in Rome.

Nov. 18 Shooting suspended for lack of funds.

During the production of *Othello*, OW proposes a modern-dress film adaptation of *Julius Caesar* for HE to direct, with himself and MM featured. Another project developed during this period is an adaptation of Homer's *Odyssey*, scripted by Ernest Borneman, with OW in the title part, and financed by an Egyptian refugee. Production to be in the manner of Robert Graves' historical novels, of which OW was a great admirer.

PB: How were you going to do it?
OW: Realistically. The soldier coming home from the wars and taking all those years to do it. No gods or goddesses; all very concrete.

Dec. *Prince of Foxes* (20th Century–Fox). D: Henry King. P: Sol C. Siegel. Sc: Milton Krims, from the Samuel Shallabarger novel. Cast: Tyrone Power (Orsini), OW (Cesare Borgia), Wanda Hendrix (Camilla), ES (Belli), Katina Paxinou (Mona Zoppo), others. Filmed in Italy.

1950 In Taormina, Sicily, OW writes a preface to Kenneth Tynan's first book, *He That Plays the King*, in the form of a letter addressed to Tynan; the book is published later this year in London by Longmans, Green. OW also writes a preface to Frédéric O'Brady's autobiographical *Extérieurs en Venise*, published this year in Paris by Gallimard. Tribune Records in the U.S. issues *This Is the U.N.*, a record featuring commentary by OW.

Jan.–Feb. OW appears as a character in *Superman* comics in an episode entitled "Black Magic on Mars!"

Jan. 31 Shooting resumes on *Othello* in Mogador, and continues through early March in Safi and Mazagan; minor additional shooting continues intermittently over the next few months. Cutting the film will occupy the better part of the next year, between performances in other movies and a couple of stage productions (taken on to finance the film's completion).

June 15 *The Blessed and the Damned* (La Compagnie "Les Pleiades"). An evening of two plays by OW. D/sets/costumes: OW. P: Georges Baume, Pierre Beteille.

(1) *The Unthinking Lobster*, "a Hollywood fable." Cast: Suzanne Cloutier (Miss Pratt), Jamie Schmitt (Roland Zitz), OW (Jake Behoovian), George Lloyd (Leander Plaice), Frédéric O'Brady (Archduke), HE (Archbishop), others.

(2) *Time Runs . . .* , "a version of the old legend with the collaboration of many authors, among them Milton, Dante and Marlowe." Music: Duke Ellington. Lighting: HE. Cast: OW (Dr. John Faustus), HE (Mephistopheles), Eartha Kitt (Helen/Chorus), Lee Zimmer (First man), Jennifer Howard (Woman), others. Opens: Théâtre Edouard-VII, Paris.

(From OW's program notes: ". . . The two plays were written to be performed together. They deal, respectively, with a lost soul and with an inspired one, and are intended to develop, in contrasting styles, contrasting ideas regarding the state of Grace and the state of damnation. . . .")

(OW to PB: "*The Unthinking Lobster* takes place in Hollywood while the town is in the grip of a cycle of religious movies. On one set an Italian neorealist is making the story of a saint like Bernadette who worked miracles and cured the sick. He has just fired the star and replaced her with a secretary from the typists' pool because she seems to have a more spiritual quality. As it turns out, he's only too right. The scene they're shooting has a lot of cripples in it, and the Italian has insisted that, in the interest of believability, on the first day they must be real. So a lot of malformed, miserable people are brought in by the casting department. She blesses them and—behold!—they throw away their crutches—they are cured! She *is* a saint. So Hollywood becomes the new Lourdes. People go on their knees through the gates of M-G-M. Little pieces of film are sold as holy amulets. . . . Except for the trade in sacred relics, business is terrible. The industry is only saved by the arrival of an archangel who goes into conference with the studio heads and makes a deal with them: heaven is prepared to suspend any further miracles in Hollywood if, in exchange, Hollywood will stop making religious pictures.")

Presented in English, with both plays synopsized bilingually in the program, the production receives excellent notices ("a stage masterpiece," says *Le Monde*). For *The Unthinking Lobster*, which he later will hope to make into a movie, OW shoots an introductory film, *Le Miracle de Sainte Anne*, in the park of Buttes Chaumont, with Marcel Archard, Georges Baume, Frédéric O'Brady, and Maurice Bessy, among others. (OW to PB: "It's got a lot of distinguished Paris celebrities. . . . It's not supposed to be a very good film—it's just rushes. The play begins in a projection room where they're running rushes.")

Despite the good notices, the show is not a financial success, probably in part because of the language barrier. OW decides to tour Germany with a somewhat different version of the show, with him and MM freely selecting the scenes to perform in each city:

Aug. 7 *An Evening with Orson Welles* (La Compagnie "Les Pleiades"). D/lighting: HE.

(1) "*Time Runs* . . ." Cast: OW (Faustus), MM (Mephistopheles), Eartha Kitt (Helen), others.

(2) *The Importance of Being Earnest*, a condensation of the first act of Oscar Wilde's play. Cast: OW (Algernon), MM (John), Lee Zimmer (Lane, the butler).

(3) A song recital (in many languages) by Eartha Kitt.

(4) *Henry VI*, the last scene from WS's play. Cast: OW (Gloucester), MM (Henry).

(5) A magic act by OW.

Opens: Altjakobstheater am Zoo, Frankfurt. (Other scenes performed elsewhere in the tour include the tent scene from *Julius Caesar* and a scene from *Othello*.)

Aug. 15 Performances in Hamburg.

Aug. 21 Performances in Munich.

Aug. 30 At Geiselgasteig Studios, outside Munich, OW films the *Importance* and *Henry* vignettes, with George Fanto as cinematographer, but is dissatisfied with the results and scraps the footage.

Sept. *The Black Rose* (20th Century–Fox). D: Henry Hathaway. P: Louis D. Lighton. Sc: Talbot Jennings, from the Thomas B. Costain novel. Cast: Tyrone Power (Walter of Gurnie), OW (General Bayan), Cécile Aubry (Miriam), others. Filmed in North Africa.

MB's *Les Truquages au cinéma* (Paris: Éditions Prisma), with a preface by OW, is published.

Sept. 1 Performances of *An Evening with Orson Welles* in Düsseldorf (Staatsoper Theater).

Sept. 4 One performance for an audience of English soldiers at Bad Oynhausen.

Sept. 9 Final performance of German tour at Titania Palast, Berlin, after which the show plays for ten days in Brussels, and OW then resumes work on *Othello*.

1951 *Abraham Lincoln*, a record featuring speeches and poems, with contributions by OW, Carl Sandburg, Walter Huston, and AM, is issued in the U.S. on Decca.

March Article, "Thoughts on Germany," *The Fortnightly* (London); see JN.

In London, OW begins acting in (and, in some cases, writing for) a new half-hour radio show, *The Adventures of Harry Lime* (Lang/Worth Syndication). D: Tig Roe. P: Harry Alan Towers. Sc: OW, Ernest Borneman, others. Music: Anton Karas. Recorded in IBC Studios, Portland Place, London; broadcast on BBC. Cast: OW (Harry Lime), Agnes Bernelle, Dana Wynter, Sebastian Cabot, Robert Arden, others. OW plays in each of the thirty-nine programs in the series, which is inspired by his character in *The Third Man;* it is later syndicated for U.S. radio as *The Third Man: The Lives of Harry Lime.*

The episodes: *Too Many Crooks* (Sc: OW), *A Ticket to Tangier* (Sc: OW), *Two Is Company* (Sc: OW), *Operation Music Box* (Sc: OW), *The Golden Fleece* (Sc: OW), *Dead Candidate* (Sc: OW), *Buzzo Gospel* (Sc: OW; a show that is later developed into a film treatment by OW, *V.I.P.*, which is then published as a novel in French, *Une Grosse Légume* [see July 1953]. *Greek Meets Greek* (Sc: OW; a show that is later developed into the script for *Mr. Arkadin;* Frédéric O'Brady plays "Arkadian"; recorded in Paris), *It's in the Bag* (Sc: OW), *Blue Bride, The Bohemian Star, Casino Royale, Clay Pigeon, The Elusive Vermeer, Every Frame Has a Silver Lining* (Sc: Robert Cenedella), *Fool's Gold, Harry Lime Joins the Circus, Horseplay* (Sc: Peter Lyon), *The Hyacinth Patrol* (Sc: Virginia Cooke), *In Pursuit of a Ghost, It's a Knockout, The Little One, Love Affair* (Sc: Sigmund Miller), *Man of Mystery, Mexican Hat Trick, New York: 1942, An Old Moorish Custom* (Sc: Irvan Ashkinazy), *The Painted Smile, The Pearls of Bohemia, Rogue's Holiday* (Sc: Peter Lyon), *The Secret of Making Gold, See Naples and Live* (Sc: Sigmund Miller), *Suzie's Clue, The Third Woman, Three Farthings for Your Thoughts, Violets Sweet Violets, Vive la Chance, Voodoo, Work of Art* (Sc: Bud Lesser).

(Many of the uncredited programs are scripted by Ernest Borneman.)

The same year, OW narrates another half-hour radio show, a series of dramatizations of famous cases from the files of Scotland Yard, *The Black Museum* (Lang/Worth Syndication). P: Harry Alan Towers. D: Tig Roe. Presented by arrangement with M-G-M Radio Attractions. Sc: Kriswick Jenkinson. Episodes: *The Bathtub, The Bedsheet, The Blue .22, The Brass Button, The Brickbat, The Canvas Bag, The Car Tyre, The Chain, Four Small Bottles, The Gladstone Bag, The Hammer, The Key, Kilroy Was Here, The Mallet, Mandolin Strings, Open End Wrench, The Pink Powder Puff, The Raincoat, The Receipt, The Sash Cord, The Scarf, The Sheath Knife, The Sleeveless Unstitched Baby Jacket, The Straight Razor, The Tan Shoe, The Telegram, The .32 Calibre Bullet, The Walking Stick.* These shows are broadcast in the U.S. on Mutual (MBS) in 1952.

OW is seen (by very few) in two shorts released this year:

Désordre (Disorder). D/Sc: Jacques Baratier. R t: 18 minutes. An exploration of Paris's Left Bank, with glimpses of OW, Jean Cocteau, Simone de Beauvoir, Juliette Greco. OW is seen walking along the Champs-Élysées. (OW: "I didn't know it was being shot for a short. People film me all the time—you don't know what they're doing it for. Usually it's television. . . .")

Return to Glennascaul (Dublin Gate Theatre Productions). D/Sc: HE. P: T. R. Royle. Narr: OW. Cast: Michael Laurence, Shelah Richards, Helena Hughes, OW (as himself). Filmed in Ireland in January 1951. OW introduces this 23-minute ghost story as "your obedient servant."

Oct. 1 *Othello*. D/P/adapter: OW. Presented by Laurence Olivier and S. A. Gorlinsky. Music: FL. Cast: OW (Othello), Gudrun Ure (later known as Ann Gaudrun) (Desdemona), Basil Lord (Roderigo), Peter Finch (Iago), John Van Eyssen (Cassio), Edmund Purdom, others. Opens: Theatre Royal, Newcastle, England; runs through October 7.

Oct. 18 The same production opens at the Saint James Theatre in London, where it runs for six weeks (through December 15). Kenneth Tynan writes in the *Observer*: "Welles the producer gave us a new vista (based on five permanent golden pillars) for every scene; he used a russet traverse-curtain to wipe away each setting in the same manner that the film would use a dissolve; he sprinkled the action with some striking background music and realistic recording—in fact, he sacrificed much to give us a credible reading for a play which bristles with illogicalities. The presentation was visually flawless. . . . The St. James' stage seemed as big as a field."

During the run, OW performs a "midnight matinee" at the London Coliseum, doing a magic act before Princess Elizabeth and the Duke of Edinburgh, and announcing, "I have just come from the St. James Theatre, where I have been murdering Desdemona—or Shakespeare, according to which newspaper you read." (See CH2.)

1952 MM's *Put Money in Thy Purse*, a diary of the shooting of *Othello* with a preface by OW, is published this year in London by Methuen. *The Lives of Harry Lime*, by OW and others, stories based on radio scripts, is published in London by News of the World in a Pocket Book Edition (stories by OW: "It's in the Bag," "The Golden Fleece," and "A Ticket to Tangier").

This year, OW appears on the last show in a BBC radio series, *Sherlock Holmes*—an adaptation of Conan Doyle's "The Final Problem." P: Harry Alan Towers. D: Tig Roe. Cast: John Gielgud (Holmes), Ralph Richardson (Watson), OW (Moriarty).

May 10 *Othello* (Mercury Productions/Marceau Films/United Artists). D/P: OW. Sc: OW, from the WS play. Assoc p: Giorgio Pappi, Julien Derode, with Walter Bedone, Patrice Dali, Rocco Facchini. Ph: George Fanto, Anchise Brizzi, G. R. Aldo, with Obadan Troiani, Alberto Fusi. Music: FL, Alberto Barberis, conducted by Willy Ferraro. Ed: Jean Sacha, John Shepridge, Renzo Lucidi, William Morton. Art d: Alexandre Trauner. R t: 91 minutes. Narr: OW. Cast: OW (Othello), MM (Iago), Suzanne Cloutier (Desdemona), Robert Coote (Roderigo), HE (Brabantio), Fay Compton (Emilia), Nicholas Bruce (Ludovico), Doris Dowling (Bianca), Jean Davis (Montano), Michael Laurence (Cassio), JC (Senator), Joan Fontaine (Page), Abdullah Ben Mohamet (Page to Desdemona). Filmed at the Scalera Studios (Rome) and on locations in Morocco (Mogador, Safi, Mazagan) and Italy (Venice, Tuscany, Rome,

Viterbo, Perugia and Torcello). World premiere: Cannes Film Festival (winner, Golden Palm).

June 5 Two plays by OW are published in French (translated by Serge Greffet) in a single volume in Paris by La Table Ronde, *Miracle à Hollywood* (*The Unthinking Lobster*—see June 15, 1950) and *À bon entendeur* (*Fair Warning*, a two-act play). (OW to PB: "It's been played in Israel and Ireland—a few countries like that; I've never seen it done or put it on myself. It begins like a rather banal play and then the actors begin to forget their lines, and finally they can't think of a word of the play—not a word—they obviously don't even know what play they're in. There's no way of ad-libbing, because they don't know where they are. Then they try to persuade the audience in the theatre that they don't know who *they* are, either. There's been an attack on the theatre by an invisible gas which has rendered people totally amnesiac—on the stage and in the audience. And the representative of the country which has taken over the world comes to preside over the stage proceedings. We discover at the end that he is a croupier and the country is Monaco, because that's where scientists have to live. They want to keep people from blowing each other up, so they've given everyone a fair warning by making them forget for a while who they are. And if they don't behave themselves, then they're going to drop the big bomb and nobody will remember for a lifetime. 'You know who you are now,' they say, 'you can go home, you know which subway to take and which streetcar—but you haven't known that for an hour and a half. Unless you behave yourselves, we're going to drop the big one. You can go home now.' And that's the end of the play. It has a Pirandello beginning and a sort of Chicago Company Show ending.")

Sept. 2 OW speaks on *Portrait of Robert Flaherty*, a BBC radio program.

Dec. Article, "La Jeunesse décidera," *La Démocratie Combattante* (Paris; reprinted in MB and, abridged, in MB2.)

1953 This year, King Farouk of Egypt offers to finance a modern-dress film of *Julius Caesar* entitled *Caesar!* which OW scripts and plans to shoot with Richard Burton, in newsreel style, playing the role of Brutus himself. Word of a Hollywood version being planned by JH and Joseph Mankiewicz effectively ends the project.

This year, OW also acts in and narrates Walt Whitman's *Song of Myself* (released on Westminster WBBC-8004 in 1968) and acts in *Queen of Spades* (on the show *Theatre Royale*), both on BBC radio.

March 23 In Rome, OW completes a draft of *Masquerade*, a screenplay adapted from his radio script *Greek Meets Greek* (for *The Adventures of Harry Lime*); this project will later be known as *Mr. Arkadin*.

April–May Article by OW, "Il n'y a pas d'art apprivoisé," in *La Démocratie Combattante* (Paris; reprinted in MB.)

June 6 In New York, Dick Himber presents a live card trick that he performs with OW in a film segment—an act he takes on the road later this year. This long lost film was rediscovered in 1991 by Himber's widow and revived in David Copperfield's 1992 CBS-TV special.

July *V.I.P.*, a satirical film treatment written by OW for Korda, based on his radio script *Buzzo Gospel* for *The Adventures of Harry Lime*, translated into French (with OW's help) and adapted by MB, is published as a novel by Gallimard in Paris, with a preface by MB, under the title *Une Grosse Légume*. The story, set on an imaginary island in the Mediterranean on the brink of revolution, concerns the misadventures of an American soft-drink salesman who is mistaken for an undercover agent.

OW: It's about the Coca-Cola and Pepsi-Cola empire—a farce about capitalist imperialism, the communist menace, and all that. Set, I'm sorry to say, in one of those mythical kingdoms, someplace about the size of Luxembourg but in the Mediterranean—the last place on earth without either a Pepsi or a Coca-Cola concession. It's about competing imperialism and the Cold War. They've been living off American aid ever since the war in order to keep off the communist menace. The truth is, they have no communists—but that's their own well-kept secret.

PB: Did Korda buy the book?

OW: He didn't go that far. He gave me all the cigars I wanted and he died soon afterward [1956], so I didn't get to *not* make that one, either.

Other unrealized projects of this period (the first of which may have been written somewhat earlier):

Operation Cinderella.

OW: The best comedy script I ever wrote. . . . It's about the occupation of a small town in Italy. It's always been occupied—by the Romans and the Goths, the Saracens, the Barbary pirates, and then by the Germans and the English. Peace finally, and then suddenly a long line of trucks comes up the road. Who is it *now?* Hollywood! It's the story of the occupation of this town by a movie company. The population divides between the collaborators—those who play along with the movie company—and the underground who tries to get rid of them. Great part for Anna Magnani as the Passionaria of the underground.

PB: So what happens?

OW: Terror and resistance—the whole occupation bag. A man's sitting in his home eating his dinner and people come in with lights and make him stop. Nobody has any rights. You can't cross the street because they're shooting pictures; you can't get home, you can't go anywhere. So the underground gets organized, and the townspeople, who've been working as extras, go on strike and refuse to work, in this great knights-of-old sort of battle that has to be fought in the film. Subs are brought in from the next village. The two towns have hated each other for seven hundred years—and now there's a real battle between the home team in civvies and the strike-breakers in armor. They make a catapult out of the movie crane —you can imagine. . . . Meanwhile, the Hollywood crew has broken the statue of the town's patron saint. So, every time they're ready for a shot, just on the cry of 'action,' one tiny little cloud goes right in front of the sun.

The Cinderella is a local girl they've picked up. At the end she's leaving with them on the bus—going to Hollywood to be a big star. Her fiancé, who's been

> hoping to marry her all this time, is waiting for her when the bus stops at the crossroads. The doors open. Is she going to get out and join him, or go on? . . . She goes on. To Hollywood.

The leading character, modeled on Gregory Ratoff, would be played by OW.

Paris by Night. Written for Alexander Korda. A series of loosely connected sketches, all set in Paris and all original stories by OW except for an adaptation of Isak Dinesen's "The Old Chevalier."

Two by Two. A modern retelling of the story of Noah, also written by OW for Korda. (OW to PB: "I wrote a book, a movie script, and a musical play—a sort of comic fantasy on the Flood. They're all on the short side. . . . If the world, as we're told in the Bible, was indeed totally covered with water, then obviously we can't imagine what anything on earth was like before everything was destroyed. So why not assume that the world was just like what it is now? That's the premise: Noah—in a world just like ours—is living in a DP camp. He's a nice old drunk whom God happens to take a shine to.")

As a movie actor, OW appears in three European features this year:

L'Uomo, la Bestia e la Virtù (Man, Beast and Virtue) (Rosa/Paramount). D: Steno (Stefano Vanzina). P: Carlo Ponti. Sc: Steno, Italiano Brancati, from the play by Luigi Pirandello. Cast: OW (Captain Perrella), Viviane Romance (Mrs. Perrella), Toto (Professor Paolino) others.

Trent's Last Case (British Lion/Republic). D/P: Herbert Wilcox. Sc: Pamela Bower, from the E. C. Bentley novel. Cast: Michael Wilding (Philip Trent), Margaret Lockwood (Margaret Manderson), OW (Sigsbee Manderson), others.

Si Versailles m'était conté (Royal Affairs in Versailles). D/P/Sc: Sacha Guitry. Cast: Sacha Guitry (Louis XIV), Claudette Colbert (Madama de Montespan), OW (Benjamin Franklin), Jean-Pierre Aumont, Edith Piaf, Gérard Philippe, Micheline Presle, Jean Marais, Daniel Gélin, others.

Aug. Lecture by OW at the Edinburgh Festival, "The Third Audience."

Sept. 7 *The Lady in the Ice* (Ballet de Paris). A ballet based on an idea by OW. Libretto/costumes/sets: OW. Choreography:

Roland Petit. Music: Jean-Michael Damase. World premiere: Stoll Theatre, London. (Produced by Petit later in the year in Paris as *Une Femme dans la glace.*) Cast: Colette Marchand, George Reich, Joe Milan, Ballet de Paris de Roland Petit. (OW to PB: "It was very successful in London and only moderately so in Paris, where it was very badly lit —as everything always is in Paris. The plot is: A girl's been found, like dinosaurs have been found, in a block of ice. And she's on display in a sort of carnival. A young man falls in love with her, and his love melts the ice. And when she kisses him he turns to ice. A little parable for our times . . .")

Oct. 18 OW returns briefly to the U.S. in the fall to make his first television appearance: *King Lear* (*Omnibus*, CBS-TV). Adapted from the WS play. D/Sc: Peter Brook. P: Fred Rickey. Music/conductor: Virgil Thomson. Series host: Alistair Cooke. Cast: OW (Lear), Alan Badel (Fool), MM (Edgar), Beatrice Straight (Goneril), others. Available on videotape from Film Forum and Hollywood Video Library, r t: 75 minutes.)

During this period, OW is writing a lengthy book about international government and finance that he subsequently destroys.

1954 Article, "The Third Audience," based on Edinburgh lecture (see Aug. 1953), *Sight and Sound* (London), January–March. Reprinted in PC.

Early in the year, OW begins filming *Mr. Arkadin*; shooting progresses over eight months in Madrid, other Spanish locations, Munich, Paris, and Rome; after concluding in Spain, OW returns to Paris for dubbing and then to Rome for cutting.

Aug. 25 Article by OW, "Je combats comme un géant dans un monde de nains pour le cinéma universel," *Arts* (Paris). Reprinted in English translation as "For a Universal Cinema," *Film Culture* 1 (January 1955).

Dec. 25 OW fails to meet a Christmas deadline for completion of the editing of *Mr. Arkadin*, and producer Louis Dolivet subsequently removes the film from his control; final editing is then carried out by Renzo Lucidi, although OW continues to send instructions.

OW acts in three more European features this year:

Three Cases of Murder (Wessex Films/London Films/British Lion). Exec p: Alexander Korda. D: George More O'Ferrall ("Lord Mountdrago"), Wendy Toye ("In the Picture"), David Eady ("You Killed Elizabeth"). Sc: Ian Dalrymple, Donald Wilson, Sidney Carroll, Brett Halliday. "Lord Mountdrago" episode based on the W. Somerset Maugham story. Ph: Georges Perinal. Cast ("Mountdrago" episode only): OW (Lord Mountdrago), Alan Badel (Owen), Helen Cherry (Lady Mountdrago), others. R t: 99 minutes. Filmed at Shepperton Studios (London). U.S. release: March 15, 1955. OW unofficially codirected the performances in his own scenes in this three-part movie.

Trouble in the Glen (British Lion/Republic). D: Herbert Wilcox. Sc: Frank S. Nugent, from a story by Maurice Walsh. Cast: Margaret Lockwood (Marissa), OW (Sanin Cejador y Mengues), Forrest Tucker, Victor McLaglen, others.

Napoléon (Filmsonor/CLM/Francinex). D/Sc: Sacha Guitry. Cast: Sacha Guitry (Talleyrand), Michèle Morgan (Josephine), Daniel Gélin (Young Bonaparte), Raymond Pellegrin (Emperor Bonaparte), OW (Hudson Lowe), Erich von Stroheim (Beethoven), Maria Schell, Jean Gabin, others.

OW also flies to London for three days in the fall to play the part of Father Mapple in John Huston's *Moby Dick* (see June 30, 1956).

1955

Feb. In Paris, while OW is planning a stage version of *Moby Dick*, writer Wolf Mankowitz offers to help him get it staged in London. Mankowitz also helps OW out financially by selling the novelization rights of *Mr. Arkadin* to a French newspaper that will run the novel serially. This novel, ghosted by MB, is published later in the year by Gallimard, with OW listed as sole author. An anonymous English translation, also listing OW as sole author, is published by W. H. Allen (London) and Crowell (New York) in 1956, and subsequently appears in paperback editions—e.g., Pyramid (New York, 1958) and Kenington Publishing (New York, 1987).

March *Mr. Arkadin* (Mercury Productions/Filmorsa [Paris]/Cervantes Films/Sevilla Film Studios [Madrid]). D/story/Sc/art d/costumes: OW. Exec p: Louis Dolivet. Ph: Jean Bourgoin. Music: Paul Misraki. Ed: Renzo Lucidi. World premiere: Madrid. R t: 95 minutes. Narr: OW. Cast: OW (Gregory Arkadin), Paola Mori (Raina Arkadin), Robert Arden (Guy Van Stratten), Patricia Medina (Mily), AT (Jakob Zouk), Michael Redgrave (Burgomil Trebitsch), Mischa Auer (Flea trainer), Katina Paxinou (Sophie), Jack Watling, Gregoire Aslan, Peter Van Eyck, Suzanne Flon, Frédéric O'Brady, Tamara Shane, Gert Frobe, others. (OW dubbed some of the actors himself, including Auer and O'Brady, and supplied the voice of the Munich airport announcer.) A Spanish-language version of the film was shot simultaneously, with a different editor (Antonio Martinez) and some different actors, including Irene Lopez Heredia (Sophie) and Amparo Rivelles. (This is presumably the version that premieres in Madrid.)

April 24 Wolf Mankowitz arranges for OW to appear in a weekly TV series in London:

Orson Welles' Sketch Book (BBC-TV). P: Huw Wheldon, for the BBC-TV Drama Department. Commentator: OW. The first in a series of six 15-minute "talking-head" programs, all consisting of OW's commentaries on a broad range of subjects, often illustrated by his own drawings and sketches. A great success in England, this first show deals with his early days in the theatre.

April 31 *Orson Welles' Sketch Book* (BBC-TV). Topic: critics.

May 7 *Orson Welles' Sketch Book* (BBC-TV). Topic: the police. OW briefly relates the story of Isaac Woodward (see July 28, 1946), talks about passports and bureaucratic red tape, and at one point anticipates both the theme of and a particular speech from *Touch of Evil:* "I'm willing to admit that the policeman has a difficult job, a very hard job. But it's the essence of our society that a policeman's job *should* be hard. He's there to protect the free citizen, not to chase criminals—that's an incidental part of his job."

May 8 At Caxton Hall, municipal headquarters of Westminster, two days after his fortieth birthday, OW marries his third wife, Paola Mori, the actress who played the female lead in *Mr. Arkadin.*

May 14 *Orson Welles' Sketch Book* (BBC-TV). Topics: prompting, Houdini, John Barrymore.

May 21 *Orson Welles' Sketch Book* (BBC-TV). Topic: *The War of the Worlds*.

May 28 *Orson Welles' Sketch Book* (BBC-TV). Topics: bullfighting and the story of "Bonito the Bull" (see July 29 and Sept. 1941).

June 16–July 9 *Moby Dick—Rehearsed* by Orson Welles, adapted from the Herman Melville novel. D: OW. P: Wolf Mankowitz, Oscar Lowenstein, in association with MG, Henry Margolis. Assoc p: Herbert Chappel. Opens: Duke of York's Theatre, London. Cast: OW (Actor-manager/Father Mapple/Ahab), Gordon Jackson (Young actor/Ishmael), Joan Plowright (Young actress/Pip), Patrick McGoohan (Serious actor/Starbuck), others. (This play will be published by Samuel French in 1965.)

During this period, OW shoots about 75 minutes of this production at the Hackney Empire and Scala theatres in London with the same cast, Henry Margolis as producer, and Hilton Craig as cinematographer, with plans to sell it to the TV series *Omnibus* in the U.S., but stops filming when he is dissatisfied with the results.

Summer Hoping to form a new repertory theatre company, OW also plans stage adaptations of Hemingway's *The Sun Also Rises* (with Marlene Dietrich) and a novella by Wolf Mankowitz.

After the run of *Moby Dick—Rehearsed*, OW spends some time on the island of Torcello in the Gulf of Venice, where he prepares another TV series that is produced later this year for British commercial television, a series of filmed "travel essays": *Around the World with Orson Welles* (Associated Rédiffusion/ITA-TV). D/Sc/host: OW. P: Louis Dolivet. R t: 26 minutes each. (1) *The Basque Countries*. (2) *La Pelote basque*. (3) *The Third Man in Vienna*. (4) *St.-Germain-des-Près*. (5) *The Queen's Pensioners*. (6) *Bullfighting in Spain* (with Kenneth Tynan). (7) *The Dominici Affair* (unfinished). (OW: "They're all sort of home movies —a vacation documented. . . .")

While in Spain, OW shoots some tests of Mischa Auer for his long-planned production of *Don Quixote*, which he later discards when he decides on another actor for the role.

Aug. 11 *Mr. Arkadin* opens in London under a different title, *Confidential Report.*

Sept. 15 OW's film *Othello* finally opens in New York in a somewhat different version. (See Editor's Notes to Chapter 6.)

Oct. OW returns to the U.S. to mount his stage production of *King Lear.* Once again he hopes to establish a repertory theatre, with particular plans to stage Ben Jonson's *Volpone,* ideally with Jackie Gleason. (Other productions discussed include a restaging of *Moby Dick—Rehearsed* and a modern-dress *Twelfth Night.*) But five British actors selected for both productions are denied entry visas, and OW, in addition to having to abandon *Volpone,* has to assemble an American cast for *Lear.*

Nov. 13 Beatrice Judith Welles, OW's third daughter, is born in New York.

Nov. 22 Mayor Robert Wagner greets OW at City Hall and announces OW's upcoming City Center engagement.

Nov. 25 *Person to Person* (CBS-TV). Host: Edward R. Murrow. Guest: OW. OW is interviewed in a suite at the Sulgrave Hotel, where he introduces his wife and shows a picture of his twelve-day-old daughter, asleep in the next room. (See RM.)

1956 Introduction by OW, *S-F: The Year's Greatest Science-Fiction and Fantasy,* edited by Judith Merrill (New York: Dell).

Out of Darkness (*Continental Classroom,* CBS-TV News). D/Sc: Albert Wasserman. P: Irving Gitlin. Narr: OW.

Jan. 8 Article by OW, "Tackling *King Lear,*" *New York Times.*

Jan. 12– Jan. 29 *King Lear* (New York City Center Theatre Company), adapted by OW from the WS play. D: OW. P: Jean Dalrymple (for City Center), MG, Henry Margolis. Assoc d: Emerson Crocker. Music/harpsichord: Marc Blitzstein. Cast: OW (Lear), Alvin Epstein (Lear's Fool), GF (Goneril), Sylvia Short (Regan), Viveca Lindfors (Cordelia), others. Performed in 140 minutes, without an intermission. The week before *King Lear* opens, OW breaks his ankle during a preview. After limping slightly through his part on opening night, he injures a cartilage in his other leg while climbing the stairs to his dressing room. On the second night, after poor notices, he appears on a bare stage seated at a table, and asks the audience of 2800 not to ask for its money back from the nonprofit City Center, but to remain to hear him discuss the play, recite some of the major speeches, and answer questions. Roughly three quarters of the audience comply, and OW resumes the production the following night, playing his part for the remainder of the engagement in a wheelchair. There are 21 performances in all.

Feb. Around this time, OW makes two guest star appearances on "The Ed Sullivan Show" (CBS-TV).

March OW moves with his family to the Riviera Hotel in Las Vegas, where he performs a 25-minute act featuring magic and recitations from *Julius Caesar*, *King Lear*, and *The Merchant of Venice*. His four-week engagement is held over for an additional two weeks.

April OW returns to Hollywood for the first time in years, and settles there for a while.

April 7 *Twentieth Century* (*Ford Star Jubilee*, CBS-TV). Adapted by Robert Bruckner from the play by Ben Hecht and Charles MacArthur. D: Paul Nickell. P: Arthur Schwartz. Cast: OW (Oscar Jaffe), Betty Grable (Lily Garland), Keenan Wynn (O'Malley), RC (Webb), Harry Shannon, others.

May 8–May 11 For Desilu Productions, who recently filmed him in an *I Love Lucy* episode (see Oct. 15), OW shoots a pilot for a projected series of half-hour shows which he will direct, produce, write, and host. No sponsor or network buys the series, and the pilot isn't shown on TV until Sept. 16, 1958 (q.v. for credits).

Around this time, OW works very briefly with Charles Lederer on the script of *Tip on a Dead Jockey*, which he hopes to direct for M-G-M; it is eventually directed by Richard Thorpe and released in 1957.

June 2 *Mr. Arkadin* opens in France.

June 30 *Moby Dick* (Moulin Productions/Warner Brothers). D/P: John Huston. Sc: Ray Bradbury, Huston, from the Herman Melville novel. Cast: Gregory Peck (Captain Ahab), Richard Basehart (Ishmael), Leo Genn (Starbuck), OW (Father Mapple), others.

August Story by OW, "Diplomatic Crisis; or Fifi and the Chilean Truffle," *Ellery Queen's Mystery Magazine*.

Oct. 15 *Lucy Meets Orson Welles* (*I Love Lucy*, CBS-TV). D: James V. Kern. Sc: Madelyn Martin, Bob Carroll, Bob Schiller, Bob Weiskopf. Cast: Lucille Ball (Lucy), Desi Arnaz (Ricky), OW (himself), Vivian Vance (Ethel Mertz), William Frawley (Fred Mertz).

Around this time, with the $5,000 earned from this guest-star appearance, OW produces another half-hour TV pilot, on a much smaller scale, which he is also unable to sell: *Camille, the Naked Lady and the Musketeers (Orson Welles and People)* (Orson Welles Enterprises). D/P/Sc/designer/music arranger/narr: OW. Based on the life of Alexandre Dumas. R t: 27 minutes. (See chapter 8.)

During the same period, again with his own money, OW researches a planned TV series about Winston Churchill (one of the figures, along with P. T. Barnum, he had hoped to deal with on *Orson Welles and People*) which never comes to fruition.

Late this year, OW acts in a Hollywood picture, *Pay the Devil*, later retitled *Man in the Shadow* (see Jan. 11, 1958), and appears on "The Herb Shriner Show" (CBS-TV).

Dec. 25 Rebecca Welles' Christmas gift from her father is a handmade illustrated book he creates, *The Bravades*, about a French medieval pageant. (This book is auctioned at New York's Swann Galleries on March 22, 1990.)

Dec. 26 Invited to star in a Universal thriller in which OW is cast as the villain, Charlton Heston suggests that OW direct as well. A deal is closed two weeks later; OW rewrites the script in five days. (The film is eventually called *Touch of Evil*; see Feb. 1958.)

1957 Article by OW, "The Scenario Crisis," published in *International Film Annual*, no. 1 (London: John Calder).

This year, OW narrates a TV production of Archibald

MacLeish's *The Fall of the City*, and acts in abridged versions of *The Merchant of Venice*, *Macbeth*, and *Othello* for CBS.

Jan. 22 A final draft of OW's screenplay *Badge of Evil* is completed; it is trimmed and approved for shooting over the next few days.

Feb. 9 Rehearsals begin.

Feb. 18 *Badge of Evil* (later retitled *Touch of Evil*) begins shooting. First scene: the interrogation in Sanchez's apartment. (From Charlton Heston's journal: "We rehearsed all day. . . . We never turned on a camera all morning or all afternoon, the studio brass gathering in the shadows in anxious little knots. By the time we began filming at 5:45, I knew they'd written off the whole day. At 7:40, Orson said, 'OK, print. That's a wrap on this set. We're two days ahead of schedule.' Twelve pages in one take, including inserts, two-shots, over-shoulders; the whole scene in one, moving through three rooms, with seven speaking parts.")

March 14 OW films the opening shot of the film.

April 2 Last day of principal photography on *Touch of Evil*; OW spends the next two months editing the picture, mainly with Virgil Vogel.

June 6 OW flies to New York to appear on Steve Allen's TV show; when he returns, a new editor, Aaron Stell, has been assigned to the picture, and OW is asked to let him work alone.

June 29 Around this date, OW leaves for Mexico to work on *Don Quixote*. In his absence, Universal production head Ed Muhl looks at Stell's cut of *Touch of Evil* and objects to the rapid crosscutting between scenes in the first five reels. Postproduction head Ernest Nims, who had worked with OW on *The Stranger*, is assigned to recut these reels.

Aug. 28 OW returns from Mexico and views Nims' cut; he does more work on *Quixote* in Mexico in September and October.

Nov. 19 A day of retakes on *Touch of Evil*; OW is barred from participation.

Dec. OW flies to Chicago to attend the wedding of his daughter Christopher to Norman R. De Haan.

1958 *Man in the Shadow* (Universal-International). P: Albert Zugsmith. D: Jack Arnold. Sc: Gene L. Coon. Cast: Jeff Chandler (Ben Sadler), OW (Virgil Renchler), Colleen Miller (Skippy Renchler), others.

Early this year, OW returns with his family to Italy, eventually settling in Fregene, outside Rome. He proceeds to Paris to act in *The Roots of Heaven* (see Dec. entry).

Feb. *Touch of Evil* (Universal-International). D: OW (and uncredited, Harry Keller). P: Albert Zugsmith. Sc: OW, based on script by Paul Monash adapted from Whit Masterson's novel *Badge of Evil*. Ph: Russell Metty. Cam op: John Russell, Phil Lathrop. Music: Henry Mancini. Ed: Virgil Vogel, Aaron Stell, Edward Curtiss, Ernest Nims. R t: 93 minutes (a 108-minute version is discovered in the mid-1970s and subsequently released). Cast: Charlton Heston (Ramon Miguel "Mike" Vargas), Janet Leigh (Susan Vargas), OW (Hank Quinlan), Joseph Calleia (Pete Menzies), AT ("Uncle Joe" Grandi), Valentin De Vargas ("Pancho"), Joanna Moore (Marcia Linnekar), RC (D.A. Adair), Dennis Weaver (Motel clerk), Mort Mills (Schwartz), Marlene Dietrich (Tanya), MM (Gang leader), Joi Lansing (Zita), Harry Shannon, Billy House, Zsa Zsa Gabor, GS, JC, others. OW's last film for a Hollywood studio.

During this period, OW shoots another TV pilot: *Portrait of Gina* (ABC). D/Sc/host: OW. P: Leonard H. Goldenson. Cast: Vittorio De Sica, Rossano Brazzi, Gina Lollobrigida, Anna Gruber, Paola Mori. R t: 27 minutes. Shot in Rome and the Lazio countryside, including Subiaco. According to Goldenson's *Beating the Odds* (written with Marvin J. Wolf [New York: Charles Scribner's Sons, 1991]), OW was given $200,000 to produce a pilot for a series to be called *Orson Welles at Large*, and presented ABC with only one reel of film in 16mm. (See chapter 8.)

The Method (ABC-TV, London). A documentary on The Actors Studio in which OW appears.

April *The Long, Hot Summer* (Jerry Wald Productions/20th Century–Fox). D: Martin Ritt. P: Jerry Wald. Sc: Irving Ravetch, Harriet Frank, Jr., based on William Faulkner's novel *The Hamlet*. Cast: Paul Newman (Ben Quick), Joanne Woodward (Clara Varner), Anthony Franciosa (Jody Varner), OW (Will Varner), Angela Lansbury (Minnie), others. Shot partially on location in Louisiana.

April 6 *What's My Line?* (CBS). OW is guest panelist.

May 20 *The Vikings* (Bryna Productions/United Artists). D: Richard Fleischer. Narr: OW.

May 24 Letter from OW published in *New Statesman* (London), in response to a review of *Touch of Evil*.

June 8 *Touch of Evil* is shown at the Brussels World Fair, where it wins the grand prize, and OW holds a press conference. (See *Cahiers du Cinéma*, no. 87 [September 1958].)

June 24 Article by OW, "Un Ruban de rêves," in *L'Express* (Paris). Reprinted in English as "Ribbon of Dreams" in *International Film Annual*, no. 2 (London, 1958), and in French in MB. Some skeptical reflections on the new trend in widescreen formats:

"... Man is made in God's image. To enlarge that image is not to glorify but to deform it. It's a sort of joke, and one doesn't joke with God. That is not only religion but good aesthetics.

"A film is a ribbon of dreams.

"It can happen to us to dream in color and sometimes in black and white, but never in CinemaScope. We never wake from a nightmare shrieking because it has been in VistaVision. ..."

July *South Seas Adventure* (Stanley Warner). Narr: OW. A film in Cinerama.

July 12 OW contributes to a debate between Kenneth Tynan, Eugene Ionesco, Philip Toynbee, and others on art and politics in *The Observer* (London), later reprinted in Ionesco's *Notes and Counter Notes* (New York: Grove Press, 1964).

Sept. 16 *The Fountain of Youth* (Welles Enterprises/Desilu). D/Sc/designer/music arranger: OW. Based on John Collier's story

"Youth from Vienna." Exec p: Desi Arnaz. Ph: Sidney Hickox. Art d: Claudio Guzman. Ed: Bud Molin. Makeup: Maurice Seiderman. Telecast: *The Colgate Palmolive Theatre* (NBC-TV). Cast: OW (Host/narr), Dan Tobin (Humphrey Baxter), Joi Lansing (Carolyn Coates), Rick Jason (Alan Brody), Billy House (Albert Morgan), Nancy Kulp (Mrs. Morgan), Marjorie Bennett (Journalist). R t: 25 minutes. Shot as a pilot in 1956, and winner of a special Peabody Award this year. Available on videotape (with Peter Brook's 1953 *King Lear*) from Hollywood Video Library.

Dec. *The Roots of Heaven* (20th Century–Fox/Darryl F. Zanuck Productions). D: John Huston. Sc: Romain Gary, Patrick Leigh Fermor, based on the novel by Gary. Cast: Errol Flynn (Forsythe), Juliette Greco (Minna), Trevor Howard (Morel), OW (Cy Sedgewick), Grégoire Aslan, others.

1959 Films narrated by OW this year include *High Journey (Vu du ciel)* and *Masters of the Congo Jungle (Les Seigneurs de la forêt)*. Early this year, he travels to Asia to shoot *Ferry to Hong Kong*.

March Article, "Twilight in the Smog," in *Esquire*.

Article, "Lavorare è difficile," in *Cinema nuovo*, no. 138 (Milan). (Cited in CV.)

April *Compulsion* (20th Century–Fox/Darryl F. Zanuck Productions). D: Richard Fleischer. P: Richard D. Zanuck. Sc: Richard Murphy, from the novel by Meyer Levin, inspired by the Leopold-Loeb murder case. Cast: OW (Jonathan Wilk), Diane Varsi (Ruth Evans), Dean Stockwell (Judd Steiner), Bradford Dillman (Artie Straus), others.

May With *Compulsion* costars Stockwell and Dillman, OW shares the prize for best actor at the Cannes Film Festival.

Aug. OW shoots additional scenes for *Don Quixote* in Rome and Manziana.

David è Golia (David and Goliath). D: Richard Pottier, Fernando Baldi (and, uncredited, OW). Cast: OW (Saul), Ivo Payer (David), HE (Prophet Samuel), others. OW directs his own scenes. Filmed in Rome and on locations in Jerusalem and Yugoslavia. Released in the U.S. in 1961.

Ferry to Hong Kong (Rank Organization). D: Lewis Gilbert. P: George Maynard. Sc: Vernon Harris, Lewis Gilbert, from the novel by Simon Kent. Cast: Curt Jurgens (Mark Conrad), OW (Captain Hart), Sylvia Syms (Liz Ferrers), others. Released in the U.S. in April 1961.

OW is featured on two records released this year: *A Lincoln Treasury* (Decca DL 9065) and *Compulsion* (20th Century–Fox FEP 101 1-45).

1960 OW narrates *An Arabian Night* for ATV (in England) this year, and acts in three more films:

Crack in the Mirror (20th Century–Fox/Darryl F. Zanuck Productions). D: Richard Fleischer. Sc: Mark Canfield (pseudonym for Zanuck), from the novel by Marcel Haedrich. Cast: OW (Hagolin/Lamorcière), Juliette Greco (Éponine/Florence), Bradford Dillman (Larnier/Claude), others. Released in the U.S. in May.

Austerlitz (Lyre/Galatea/Dubrava Films). D: Abel Gance. P: Alexander and Michael Salkind. Sc: Gance, Nelly Kaplan. Ph (in Dyaliscope and color): Henri Alekan, Robert Julliard. Cast: Pierre Mondy (Napoleon), Martine Carol (Josephine), Claudia Cardinale (Pauline), Jean Mercure (Talleyrand), OW (Fulton), Leslie Caron, Vittorio De Sica, Rossano Brazzi, others. Belatedly released in the U.S. only on video. During the shooting of this film, producer Alexander Salkind proposes making a film with OW which eventually becomes *The Trial*.

I Tartari (The Tartars) (Lux Films/M-G-M). D: Richard Thorpe. Cast: OW (Burundai), Victor Mature (Oleg), Folco Lulli (Togrul), others. Released in the U.S. in June 1962.

During this period, OW does more shooting and editing on *Don Quixote*, and accepts a commission from RAI-TV in Italy to shoot a documentary in Spain that will permit him to continue this work (see Dec. 1964).

Don Quixote (unfinished). D: OW. P: OW, Oscar Dancigers. Sc: OW, from the Miguel Cervantes novel. Narr: OW. P mgr: Alessandro Tasca di Cuto. Ph: Jack Draper. Cam op: Giorgio Tonti, Ricardo Navarete. Asst d: Juan Luis Buñuel. Asst d/script girl: Paola Mori, Mauro Bonanni, Maurizio Lucidi. Ed: Renzo Lucidi, Mauro Bonanni. Cast: Francisco Reiguera (Don Quixote), AT (Sancho Panza), OW (himself), Patty McCormack (Dulcie), others. Filmed since 1957 in Mexico (Mexico, Puebla, Tepozlan,

Texcoco, Rio Frio), Spain (Pamplona, Seville), Italy (Rome, Manziana, Civitavecchia), and elsewhere.*

Feb. 13 *Chimes at Midnight* (Dublin Gate Theatre). Adapted by OW from WS's *Henry IV, Parts I and II, Henry V, Richard III*, and *The Merry Wives of Windsor*. D: HE. Production assistant: Michael Lindsay-Hogg. Cast: OW (Falstaff), Keith Baxter (Hal), Reginald Jarman (King Henry IV), Thelma Ruby (Mistress Quickly), HE (Narr), others. Opens: Grand Opera House, Belfast. Runs for 5 performances.

Feb. 20 The production moves to the Gaiety Theatre in Dublin. During its run (which ends in late March), OW also presents *An Evening with Orson Welles* at the Gaiety, consisting of a solo reading of *Moby Dick—Rehearsed* and a question-and-answer session with the audience. HE and OW originally hope to bring *Chimes at Midnight* to London, but after the lack of a success in Ireland makes this unfeasible, OW accepts an offer from Laurence Olivier to direct another play:

April 28 *Rhinoceros* (English Stage Company) by Eugene Ionesco, translated by Derek Prouse. D/designer/costumes: OW. P: Oscar Lewenstein, Wolf Mankowitz. Cast: Monica Evans (Bessie), Laurence Olivier (Berenger), Duncan MacRae (John), Henry Woolf (Grocer), Joan Plowright [later replaced by Maggie Smith] (Daisy), Alan Webb (Duddard), others. Opens: Royal Court Theatre, London. OW shifts the action of the play to England, and incorporates film footage of rhinoceroses. The production has a five-week run at the Royal Court, then moves to the Strand. (OW to PB: "We made a lot of money out of that production, and the critics liked it. I didn't like the play. I agreed to it because I thought the gimmick was good enough so that you could invent an evening in the theatre about it. And it worked—it always seems to work everywhere no matter

* A version of the film edited by Jesus Franco premieres in Spain at Expo 92 in 1992. Much of the surviving footage, including about 40 minutes edited and dubbed by OW, is now permanently housed at the Filmoteca Española in Madrid. As this book goes to press, additional edited and unedited footage is held by Mauro Bonanni in Rome.

how it's done. But throughout rehearsals, every day, it seemed to me that I liked Ionesco less as a playwright.")

1961 *Taras Bulba* (unrealized project). OW writes a screenplay based on the famous Gogol story for producers Alexander and Michael Salkind. (See chapter 7.)

OW spends much of this year writing the script and designing sets for *The Trial*, as well as shooting *Nella Terra di Don Chisciotte* (see Dec. 1964) and then editing it in his house near Rome.

June 11–August 12 The first retrospective devoted to OW's films is held at the Museum of Modern Art in New York, organized by PB, with a monograph by him entitled *The Cinema of Orson Welles* (Doubleday).

Oct. 13 *King of Kings* (M-G-M). D: Nicholas Ray. P: Samuel Bronston. Sc: Philip Yordan. Narr: OW (uncredited). Cast: Jeffrey Hunter, Siobhan McKenna, Robert Ryan, others.

Nov. 29 *Orson Welles on the Art of Bullfighting* (*Tempo*, ABC-TV). D/Sc/narr: OW. Series d: Reginald Collin. Produced in London for *Tempo*, a weekly show.

This year, OW also acts in *Lafayette* (Copernic/Cosmos Productions). D: Jean Dréville. P: Maurice Jacquin. Sc: Jean-Bernard Luc, Suzanne Arduini, others. Cast: Jack Hawkins (General Cornwallis), OW (Benjamin Franklin), Vittorio De Sica (Bancroft), Edmund Purdom, others. Filmed in France; released in the U.S. April 10, 1963.

1962 Around this time, OW contributes a preface to Conchita Cintrón's *Memories of a Bullfighter*.

OW narrates *Rivers of the Ocean (Der Grosser Atlantik)*, released this year.

Late this year, OW appears on the BBC-TV program *Monitor*, interviewed by Huw Wheldon, where he discusses his forthcoming film *The Trial*.

March 26 Shooting begins on *The Trial* at the Studio de Boulogne, Paris; location work follows in Zagreb, Rome, and Paris (at the Gare d'Orsay). During the shooting in Zagreb, OW meets a young sculptor, actress, TV anchor, and writer, Olga Palinkas, who later becomes his companion and (as Oja Kodar) collaborator on many of his film projects for the remainder of his life.

June 5 Shooting on *The Trial* completed; cutting proceeds until just before the Paris premiere in December.

Oct. 12 *Mr. Arkadin* opens in New York at the New Yorker Theatre, in a flashback version corresponding more closely to OW's original intentions and editing, found by PB in Hollywood in 1961.

Nov. 28 OW's adaptation, *Moby Dick—Rehearsed*, opens on Broadway at the Ethel Barrymore Theatre, staged by Douglas Campbell and starring Rod Steiger. OW has nothing to do with this production, which has only a brief run.

Dec. 21 *The Trial* (Paris-Europa Productions [Paris]/Hisa Films [Munich]/FI-C-IT [Rome]/Globus-Dubrava [Zagreb]). D: OW. Sc: OW, from the Franz Kafka novel. Exec p: Alexander and Michael Salkind. Ph: Edmond Richard. Pinscreen prologue: Alexandre Alexeieff, Claire Parker. Music: Jean Ledrut, the *Adagio for Organ and Strings* of Tomaso Albioni (and, uncredited, jazz by Martial Solal, Daniel Humair). Ed: Yvonne Martin, Fritz H. Mueller. World premiere: the Vendôme, Paris. R t: 120 minutes. Narr: OW. Cast: Anthony Perkins (Joseph K), JM (Miss Burstner), OW (Hastler, the Advocate), Elsa Martinelli (Hilda), Romy Schneider (Leni), Suzanne Flon (Miss Pittl), Madeleine Robinson (Mrs. Grumbach), AT (Block), Arnoldo Foà (Inspector), Fernand Ledoux (Chief clerk), William Chappell (Titorelli), Paola Mori (Librarian), others. The script is published in Spanish (as *Il processo*) in *Temas de Cine* (Madrid, 1962), in French (as *Le Procès*) in *L'Avant-Scène du Cinéma*, February 1963, and in English (London: Lorrimar, 1970, distributed in the U.S. by Frederick Ungar.)

1963 *Wide World of Entertainment* (ABC-TV). D/P/Sc: Barry Shear. Cast: OW, Michael Redgrave, Shirley Bassey, Douglas Fairbanks, Jr., others. A color variety show filmed in Paris.

Some of the film projects considered by OW during this period, according to FB and others, include adaptations of *Crime and Punishment* for the Salkinds, Guy Endore's *King of Paris* (a novel about Alexandre Dumas), Joseph Heller's *Catch-22*, a modern-dress *Julius Caesar* for Italian TV, *King Lear*, and *Treasure Island*. Meanwhile, he continues to work on *Don Quixote*.

Feb. 20 *The Trial* opens in New York.

Sept. *The VIPs* (M-G-M). D: Anthony Asquith. P: Anatole de Grunwald. Sc: Terence Rattigan. Cast: Elizabeth Taylor (Frances Andros), Richard Burton (Paul Andros), Louis Jourdan (Marc Champselle), OW (Max Buda), Elsa Martinelli, Margaret Rutherford, Maggie Smith, Rod Taylor, Robert Coote, others. Filmed in London.

Sept. 25 *Rogopag (Laviamoci il Cervello)* (Arco Film/Ceneriz/Lyre Film). P: Alfredo Bini. D/Sc: Roberto Rossellini, Jean-Luc Godard, Pier Paolo Pasolini, Ugo Gregoretti. Cast (of Pasolini episode, *La Ricotta*): OW (Film director), Laura Betti (Star), Mario Cipriani (Stracci), others. R t: 125 minutes.

1964 *Lord Jim* (unrealized project). OW writes a screen adaptation of the Conrad novel but is prevented from making the film when Columbia Pictures and Richard Brooks announce their production, released the following year.

Marco the Magnificent (La Fabuleuse Aventure de Marco Polo) (ITTAC/SNC/Prodi Cinematografica/Avala Films). D: Denys de la Patellière, Noel Howard. P: Raoul Lévy. Sc: Jacques Rémy, J.-P. Rappeneau, Denys de la Patellière, Lévy (and, uncredited, OW). Cast: Horst Buchholz (Marco Polo), Grégoire Aslan (Achmed), Robert Hossein (Nayam), OW (Akerman), Elsa Martinelli, AT, Omar Sharif, Anthony Quinn. Released in the U.S. September 1966.

OW narrates *The Finest Hours*, released in the U.S. in November. (The sound track, with Patrick Wymark, is released on Mercury SRP 2-604.)

Sept. OW begins filming *Chimes at Midnight* in Spain, and continues until shortly before Christmas.

Dec. *Nella Terra di Don Chisciotte (In the Land of Don Quixote)* (RAI-TV). P/ed/additional ph: OW. Exec p: Alessandro Tasca di Cuto. Assistant editor: Roberto Perpignani. Presented by Enrico Ghezzi and Marco Melani. An extended TV series produced in Spain for Italian television, aired between late 1964 and early 1965. The episodes: *Itinerario andaluso* (27 minutes), *Spagna santa* (22 minutes), *La feria di San Fermin* (27 minutes), *L'encierro di Pamplona* (26 minutes), *Le cantine di Jerez* (25 minutes), *Siviglia* (25 minutes), *Feria de Abril a Siviglia* (unaired episode, 25 minutes), *Tempo di flamenco* (26 minutes), and *Roma è Oriente in Spagna* (26 minutes). As with *Around the World with Orson Welles* (see Summer 1955), the programs are essentially black-and-white home movies, shot with a cameraman from Spanish TV (an Italian cameraman for the Prado) and an Italian sound person; they show OW on sightseeing trips through Spain with Paola Mori and Beatrice Welles. The version edited by OW contains no narration, but RAI adds a narration of its own, written by playwright and stage director Gian Paolo Callegari with the assistance of Antonio Navarro Linares and spoken by Arnoldo Foà. See Maurizio Ponzi's "Welles à la TV," *Cahiers du Cinéma*, no. 165 (April 1965). (Most of this series is screened at the National Video Festival in Los Angeles, 1986; the same year, it is aired again on RAI's third channel, this time without the commentary.)

1965

Feb. Shooting on *Chimes at Midnight* resumes, after delays caused by budgetary problems and OW's illness. Around the same time, OW does preliminary work in Spain on a film of *Treasure Island* that he scripts and in which he plays Long John Silver, directed by Jesus Franco; years later, this film is completed by John Hough (see Sept. 12, 1973).

April Shooting on *Chimes at Midnight* is completed; cutting continues in Paris for the remainder of the year and into 1966.

OW also rewrites a comedy script, *Beware of the Greeks*, originally written in the 1950s.

His play *Moby Dick—Rehearsed* is published by Samuel French (New York and London).

Sept. 10 OW narrates *Americans on Everest* in the first of the *National Geographic Specials* (CBS-TV).

Nov. 7 *The Profile of Orson Welles* (*Tempo*, ABC-TV). D: James Goddard. Telecast in England.

Dec. 22 OW narrates a BBC-TV documentary, *Miss Goodall and the Wild Chimpanzees*.

1966 Article by OW, "Il mio caro Falstaff," in *Cinema nuovo*, no. 182 (Milan). (Cited in CV.)

OW appears as one of the hosts in *Bloopers from "Star Trek" and "Laugh-In"* (NBC).

Spring OW acts in *Is Paris Burning?* (see Nov. entry).

May 8 *Chimes at Midnight* (Internacional Films Escolano [Madrid]/Alpine [Basel]). D/costumes: OW. Sc: OW, adapted from portions of WS's *Henry IV, Parts I and II*, *Henry V*, *Richard III*, and *The Merry Wives of Windsor*, and Raphael Holinshed's *The Chronicles of England*. Exec p: Alessandro Tasca di Cuto, Harry Saltzman. P: Emiliano Piedra, Angel Escolano. 2nd unit d: Jesus Franco. Asst d: Tony Fuentes, Juan Cobos. Ph: Edmond Richard. Ed: Fritz Mueller. Music: FL. Narr: Ralph Richardson. R t: 119 minutes. Cast: OW (Sir John Falstaff), Keith Baxter (Prince Hal), John Gielgud (King Henry IV), JM (Doll Tearsheet), Margaret Rutherford (Mistress Quickly), Norman Rodway (Henry Percy, called Hotspur), Marina Vlady (Kate Percy), Alan Webb (Justice Swallow), Walter Chiari (Silence), Fernando Rey (Worcester), Beatrice Welles (Page), others. World premiere: Cannes Film Festival. Filmed in Avila, Barcelona, Cardona Château, Calatanazor Village, Colmenas Viejo, Guipuzcoa, Madrid (including the Casa de Campo park), Pedraza, Puerta de San Vincente, and Soria Cathedral, Spain.

June Albert and David Maysles film an 8-minute documentary of OW in a Madrid bullring (later shown on French TV) describing to a group of Americans a feature he intends to make. Thc prefigured feature, which later develops into *The Other Side of the Wind*, concerns a "macho" American film director and a group of bullfighting aficionados.

Sept. Filming of *The Immortal Story* starts in Paris and Madrid.

The Bible . . . In the Beginning (Dino De Laurentiis/20th Century–Fox). D: John Huston. Sc: Christopher Fry (and, uncredited, OW [Abraham and Jacob sequences]). Ph: Giuseppe Rotunno. R t: 174 minutes. Cast: George C. Scott (Abraham), Ava Gardner (Sarah), John Huston (Noah), Michael Parks, Richard Harris, Peter O'Toole, Franco Nero, others. A version of the script is published this year by Pocket Books (New York); OW refuses a writing credit after his ending of the Abraham sequence is altered.

Nov. Shooting is concluded on *The Immortal Story*.

Is Paris Burning? (Paris brûle-t-il?) (Marianne Transcontinental Films/Paramount–Seven Arts). D: René Clément.

P: Paul Graetz. Sc: Gore Vidal, Francis Ford Coppola, Marcel Moussy, from the book by Larry Collins and Dominique Lapierre. R t: 173 minutes. Cast: Jean-Paul Belmondo (Morandat), Charles Boyer (Monod), Leslie Caron (Françoise Labe), OW (Nordling), Kirk Douglas (Patton), Glenn Ford, Simone Signoret, Alain Delon, others.

Dec. A *Man for All Seasons* (Highland/Columbia). D/P: Fred Zinnemann. Sc: Robert Bolt, based on his play. Cast: Paul Scofield (Thomas More), Wendy Hiller (Alice More), Robert Shaw (King Henry VIII), Leo McKern (Thomas Cromwell), OW (Cardinal Wolsey), others. Filmed in England. (The sound track is issued in 1967 on RCA Victor VDM-116.)

1967 OW spends part of this year shooting *The Deep* in boats around Hvar and Primòsten, Yugoslavia; the financing is entirely his and OK's.

He reanimates his project to film a modern-dress, documentary-style *Julius Caesar* in Rome, this time with Christopher Plummer as Marc Antony, himself as Caesar, and Paul Scofield as Brutus.

OW appears as one of the hosts in *Revenge of TV Bloopers*, an hour-long TV special.

March OW is interviewed by Kenneth Tynan in *Playboy*.

March 19 *Chimes at Midnight* opens in New York with a different title *(Falstaff)*, to mixed reviews.

April 14 *Casino Royale* (Famous Artists/Columbia). D: Robert Parrish, Joe McGrath, John Huston, Ken Hughes, Val Guest. P: Charles K. Feldman, Jerry Bresler. Sc: Wolf Mankowitz, John Law, Michael Sayers, from the Ian Fleming novel. Music: Burt Bacharach. Cast: Peter Sellers (Evelyn Tremble/James Bond), Ursula Andress (Vesper Lynd/007), OW (Le Chiffre), David Niven, Joanna Pettet, Woody Allen, Deborah Kerr, John Huston, others.

April 3 *The Levin Interviews* (Associated Rédiffusion). OW is interviewed by Bernard Levin on British TV.

April 24 *The Sailor from Gibraltar* (Woodfall Films.) D: Tony Richardson. P: Oscar Lewenstein, Neil Hartley. Sc: Christopher

Isherwood, Don Magner, Richardson, from the Marguerite Duras novel. Cast: JM (Anna), Vanessa Redgrave (Sheila), OW (Louis of Mozambique), Ian Bannen. John Hurt, Hugh Griffith, others. Filmed in England.

May OW is one of the narrators in *A King's Story*. (The soundtrack is issued on DRG SL 5185 in 1980.)

Sept. 14 *The Dean Martin Show* (NBC-TV). D/P: Greg Garrison. Guest stars: OW, James Stewart, Juliet Prowse. OW segments: song, "Personality," with Martin, Stewart; radio sketch with Martin; song, "Brush Up Your Shakespeare," with Martin; Shylock speech from *The Merchant of Venice*. The first of many appearances on this taped variety show.

Dec. 1 OW narrates *Ten Days That Shook the World* (NBC-TV).

1968 OW spends most of this year filming in Europe for a CBS-TV special, first called *Around the World with Orson Welles*, then *Orson's Bag*. He also continues to pick up remaining shots necessary for *The Deep*, and in Paris writes a short script with OK based on Poe's "The Cask of Amontillado" and "The Masque of the Red Death," originally intended for the anthology film *Spirits of the Dead*.

Jan. 25 *The Dean Martin Show* (NBC-TV). Guests: OW, Joey Heatherton. OW segments: magic act, speech from *Julius Caesar*.

April *I'll Never Forget What's 'is Name* (Scimitar). D/P: Michael Winner. Sc: Peter Draper. Cast: OW (Jonathan Lute), Oliver Reed (Andrew Quint), Carol White (Georgina), Harry Andrews, Michael Hordern, Marianne Faithfull, others.

May 24 *The Immortal Story* (ORTF/Albina Films). D: OW. Sc: OW, based on the novella by Isak Dinesen. P: Micheline Rozan. Ph (in Eastman color): Willy Kurant. Ed: Yolande Maurette, Marcelle Pluet, Françoise Garnault, Claude Farny. Music: Erik Satie piano pieces, played by Aldo Ciccolini and Jean-Joel Barbier. Narr: OW. Cast: OW (Mr. Charles Clay), JM (Virginie Ducrot), Roger Coggio (Elishama Levinsky), Norman Eshley (Paul, the sailor), Fernando Rey (merchant). OW is dubbed by Philippe Noiret in the French dubbed version. World premiere: on French TV and simultaneously in theatrical release in France as *Une Histoire immortelle*. R t: 58 minutes. A postproduction script of the film is published in *L'Avant-Scène du Cinéma*, July 1–15, 1982. Originally planned as part of an anthology of Dinesen stories; the second, "The Heroine," is abandoned after a day's shooting in Budapest with OK when the producer proves to be insolvent.

June *Oedipus the King* (Crossroad). D: Philip Saville. P: Michael Luke. Sc: Philip Saville, Michael Luke, based on Paul Roche's translation of the Sophocles play. Cast: Christopher Plummer (Oedipus), OW (Tiresias), Lilli Palmer (Jocasta), others. Released in the U.S. in December.

Orson Welles (ORTF). D/P: François Reichenbach, Frédéric Rossif. Sc: MB. Narr: JM. A documentary for French TV that wins the Golden Bear for Shorts at the Berlin Film Festival, its initial showing.

Sept. 8 OW narrates *Around the World of Mike Todd* (ABC-TV), an hour-long documentary. D: Saul Swimmer.

Sept. 26 *The Dean Martin Show* (NBC-TV). Guests: OW, Edgar Bergen, Patricia Crowley, Jack Gilford. OW segments: recalling the Martian broadcast; song, "Everybody Ought to Have a Maid," with Martin, Crowley, Gilford; Falstaff speech.

Oct. 5 *The Jackie Gleason Show* (CBS-TV). Guests: OW, Milton Berle, Gene Kelly. OW segments: magic act; song, "Old Rocking Chair," with Kelly, Berle, Gleason.

Nov.–Dec. Begins work with PB on this book, continuing off and on through 1975.

Dec. 19 *Der Kampf um Rom (The Last Roman)* (CCC [West Berlin]/Studioul Cinematographic [Bucharest]). D: Robert Siodmak. Sc: Ladislas Fodor, based on the book by Felix Dahn. Cast: Laurence Harvey (Cothegus), OW (Justinian), Sylvia Koscina (Theodora), Honor Blackman, Harriet Andersson, others. Filmed in Romania.

1969 Intermittent shooting and long periods of cutting on *Orson's Bag* and *The Deep* occupy much of this year, between acting jobs. Scripts written in this period include *Soldier, Soldier,* a period farce set around the period of *Tom Jones;* a comedy about female pirates for Pearl Bailey, Jane Fonda, and OK; *No Flowers for a Duchess,* about a murderous surgeon on a remote island; *Con Man;* and *Because of the Cats,* written with OK in Rome and based on a story by Nicholas Freeling. OW narrates a documentary by Adrian J. Wensley-Walker *(Barbed Water);* coscripts and plays the part of Winston Churchill in a Yugoslavian film directed by Stipe Delic called *Sutjeska;* and acts in:

Viva la Revolución (Tepepa) (Filmamerica/SIAP/PEFSA). D: Guilio Petroni. P: Alfredo Cuomo, Richard A. Herland, Nicolo Pomilia. Sc: Franco Solinas, Ivan della Mea. Cast: OW (General Cascorro), Tomas Milian (Tepepa), others. Filmed in Spain.

The Begatting of the President (Mediarts Records 41-2). P: Ben Brady, Alan Livingston. Sc: Myron Roberts, Lincoln Haynes, Sasha Gilien. Narr: OW. A satirical record album about Richard Nixon which may have led to OW's subsequent tax audit; the text is published by Ballantine Books (New York).

Jan. 9 *The Dean Martin Show* (NBC-TV). Guests: OW, Ben Blue, Nancy Ames. OW segments: song, "Só Danço Samba"; sketch, American tourists in Paris, with Martin.

March *House of Cards* (Westward). D: John Guillermin. P: Dick Berg. Sc: Irving Ravetch, Harriet Frank, Jr., James P. Bonner, from the Stanley Ellin novel. Cast: George Peppard (Reno), Inger Stevens (Anne), OW (Leschenhaut), others.

May 31 *The Southern Star (L'Étoile du sud)* (Euro-France/Capitole/Columbia). D: Sidney Hayers. P: Roger Duchet. Sc: David Purcall, Jack Seddon, Paul André, based on the Jules Verne novel. Cast: George Segal (Dan Rockland), Ursula Andress (Erica Kramer), OW (Plankett), others. Filmed in Senegal. CH2 reports that, according to director Hayers, OW directed the film's opening scenes.

July 21 OW narrates *How Science Fiction Viewed the Moon,* a CBS news feature done as part of its coverage of the Apollo 11 moon flight. The same day, OW is interviewed live in London by Mike Wallace about the event and his 1938 Martian broadcast.

Oct. 20 *The Joey Bishop Show* (ABC-TV). OW is interviewed and does card tricks.

Nov. *12 + 1 (Una su tredici)* (COFCI/CEF). D: Nicholas Gessner. Sc: Mino Guirrini, Marino Onorati (and, uncredited, OW, who wrote his own scene). Cast: Vittorio Gassman, Sharon Tate, Terry-Thomas, OW (Markan), others. Adapted from the same source as Mel Brooks' *The Twelve Chairs;* OW appears briefly to perform magic.

Nov. 28 *The Battle of Neretva (Bitka na Neretvi)* (Jadran/Bosna/Eichberg/Commonwealth United). D: Veljko Bulajic. Sc: Stevo and Veljko Bulajic, others. Music: BH. Cast: Yul Brynner (Vlado), Hardy Kruger (German captain), Franco Nero (Italian captain), OW (Chetnik senator), Curt Jurgens (German general), others.

Dec. 18 *The Dean Martin Show* (NBC-TV). Guests: OW, Gina Lollobrigida, George Gobel, Charles Nelson Reilly. OW segments: sketch with Martin; song, "Here's to You," with Martin; reading from *Richard II*.

1970 This year, OW narrates a BBC-TV adaptation of Jack London's story "To Build a Fire," directed by David Cobham; appears on the *ABC Comedy Hour* and in *A Horse Called Nijinsky* (an English documentary); signs a contract with *McCall's* to write his memoirs (see Dec. 1982); develops a film project, *Midnight Plus One*, for Jack Nicholson and Robert Mitchum; and does further work in Italy on *Orson's Bag* (CBS-TV; not telecast). D/P/Sc: OW. P mgr: Alessandro Tasca di Cuto. Music: FL. Ph: Giorgio Tonti, Ivica Rajkovic, Tomislav Pinter. Ed: Fritz Muller, Mauro Bonanni. Cast: OW (English clubmen/Shylock/others), Mickey Rooney, Senta Berger, Arte Johnson, Charles Gray (Tailor/Antonio), Jonathon Lind (Other tailor), Irina Maleva (Jessica), PB, others. R t: 79 minutes. Filmed in color on locations in London; Vienna; Trogir, Zagreb [Yugoslavia]; Venice, Rome, Ansolo [Italy]; and Los Angeles. Segments: "Swinging London," "Tailor's Shop," "Spying in Vienna," and a 40-minute condensation of WS's *The Merchant of Venice*. (Ultimately, CBS halts work on this special for tax reasons.)

The Deep (unfinished). D/P: OW. Sc: OW, from the novel *Dead Calm* by Charles Williams. Ph (in color): Willy

Kurant, Ivica Rajković. Cast: Laurence Harvey (Hughie Warriner), JM (Ruth Warriner), OW (Russ Brewer), OK (Rae Ingram), Michael Bryant (John Ingram). Filmed off the Dalmatian coast, 1967–69. Working title: *Dead Reckoning.*

Waterloo (Mosfilm/Dino De Laurentiis). D: Sergei Bondarchuk. Sc: H. A. L. Craig, Sergei Bondarchuk, Vittorio Bonicelli. R t: 132 minutes. Cast: Rod Steiger (Napoleon), Christopher Plummer (Duke of Wellington), OW (Louis XVIII), Dan O'Herlihy (Marshal Ney), others. Filmed in Italy and Russia.

Jan. 22 *The Dean Martin Show* (NBC-TV). Guests: OW, Virna Lisi, Lou Rawls, Rocky Graziano. OW segments: song, "Give Me the Simple Life," with Martin, others; Ahab speech from *Moby Dick.*

Feb. *The Kremlin Letter* (20th Century–Fox). D: John Huston. P: Carter De Haven, Sam Wisenthal. Sc: Huston, Gladys Hill, from the Noel Behn novel. Cast: Bibi Andersson (Erika), Richard Boone (Ward), OW (Aleksei Bresnavitch), others.

Feb. 7 *Start the Revolution Without Me* (Tandem). D/P: Bud Yorkin. Exec p: Norman Lear. Sc: Fred Freeman, Lawrence J. Cohen. Cast: Gene Wilder (Claude/Philippe), Donald Sutherland (Charles/Pierre), Hugh Griffith (King Louis XVI), OW (Storyteller), Jack MacGowran, Billie Whitelaw, others.

May 14 *The Dick Cavett Show* (ABC-TV). Guests: OW, Jack Lemmon.

June *Catch-22* (Filmways/Paramount). D: Mike Nichols. P: John Calley, Martin Ransohoff. Sc: Buck Henry, from the Joseph Heller novel. Cast: Alan Arkin (Captain Yossarian), Art Garfunkel (Captain Nately), OW (General Dreedle), Bob Newhart, Anthony Perkins, Paula Prentiss, Martin Balsam, Richard Benjamin, others.

June 4 *The David Frost Show* (Group W). Guest: OW. A ninety-minute interview.

June 8 *The David Frost Show* (Group W). Guest host: OW. Guests: Norman Mailer, Duke Ellington, Elly Stone.

June 9 *The David Frost Show* (Group W). Guest host: OW. Guests: Louis Armstrong, New Yorkers participating in a "teach-in" about city problems.

June 10 *The David Frost Show* (Group W). Guest host: OW. Guests: Darryl F. Zanuck, Tiny Tim.

Shortly after acting in *A Safe Place* (see Summer 1971), OW meets cinematographer Gary Graver, who is to shoot and work in other capacities on most of his subsequent film projects.

July 27 *The Dick Cavett Show* (ABC-TV). Guest: OW.

Aug. A fire breaks out in OW's villa in Madrid during his absence, destroying many personal possessions, including scripts, correspondence, and films.

Aug. 17 With GG, OW begins tests on *The Other Side of the Wind* in Los Angeles; shooting starts around August 30.

Aug. 28 *Upon This Rock* (Marstan/American Continental). D/Sc: Harry Rasky. P: Stanley Abrams. Ph: Aldo Tonti. R t: 90 minutes. Cast: OW (Michelangelo), Ralph Richardson (Guide), Dirk Bogarde, Edith Evans. A documentary on Saint Peter's Basilica, originally conceived as a TV special.

Aug. 31 With GG, OW starts to shoot six half-hour videos for Sears, Roebuck, including recitations of *The Happy Prince*, stories by G. K. Chesterton and P. G. Wodehouse, and speeches by Socrates and Clarence Darrow.

Sept. Shooting (and cutting) *The Other Side of the Wind* continues in Los Angeles, including the M-G-M back lot in Century City, through Christmas.

Sept. 14 *The Dick Cavett Show* (ABC-TV). Guest: OW.

Sept. 17 *The Dean Martin Show* (NBC-TV). Guests: OW, Petula Clark, Joey Bishop. OW segments: sketch with Martin about a pregnant pup; song, "Battle Hymn of the Republic"; song, "Everybody Has a Song," with Bishop, Clark.

Oct. 16 *The Enemy Before Us* (*The Name of the Game*, NBC-TV). D/P: Barry Shear. Sc: Joseph Cavelli. R t: 75 minutes. Cast: Tony Franciosa (Jeff Dillon), Susan Saint James (Peggy

Maxwell), OW (Thomas Wolfe narration), Katina Paxinou (Filomena Coria), others.

Oct. 26 *Rowan & Martin's Laugh-In* (NBC-TV). P: George Schlatter, Ed Friendly. Guest: OW.

Nov. OW narrates *Is It Always Right to Be Right?*, nominated for an Academy Award for Best Cartoon.

Nov. 3 Article by OW, "But Where Are We Going?," in *Look*.

1971 Filming *The Other Side of the Wind* with GG continues over four months early this year in Carefree, Arizona, and later in Beverly Hills.

La Décade prodigieuse (Ten Days Wonder) (Films La Boétie). D: Claude Chabrol. P: André Génovès. Sc: Paul Gégauff, Paul Gardner, Eugene Archer, based on the Ellery Queen novel. Cast: Marlène Jobert (Helene), Anthony Perkins (Charles), OW (Theo), Michel Piccoli (Paul), others. During the shooting of this film in France early this year, OW begins filming a one-hour 16mm film with GG in Strasbourg, a solo piece in which he recounts the story of *Moby Dick*. About half an hour is filmed.

Among the films narrated by OW this year are *Secrets of the African Baobab*, *Kelly Country*, *Sentinels of Silence* (winner of Academy Award for best live-action short), *Happiness in Twenty Years (Prague 48–68)*, *National Geographic* (NBC-TV, shown Oct. 9), *Silent Snow, Secret Snow* (*Night Gallery*, NBC-TV, Oct. 20), and *Freedom River* (Dec. 20).

Jan. 14 *The Dean Martin Show* (NBC-TV). Guests: OW, Charles Nelson Reilly, Don Rice. OW segments: three comic sketches with Martin; OW tells the story of Noah.

Jan. 26 *ABC Comedy Hour* (ITV/ABC-TV). D: Dwight Hemion. Guest host: OW (with Ron Moody).

March 11 *The Dean Martin Show* (NBC-TV). Guests: OW, Petula Clark, Norm Crosby, Leonard Barr, Eubie Blake. OW appears in three sketches.

May *Malpertius* (SOFIDOC [Brussels]/Artemis [Berlin]/Société Expansion du Spectacle [Paris]). D: Harry Kumel. Sc: Jean

Ferry, based on the Jean Ray novel. Cast: Susan Hampshire, Mathieu Carrière, Jean-Pierre Cassel, OW (Uncle Cassavius), others. A Belgian film with surrealist trimmings.

May 3 *Rowan & Martin's Laugh-In* (NBC-TV). Guests: OW, others.

July 5 OW is guest host on *The Tonight Show* (NBC-TV).

July 6 *The Silent Years* (PBS). P: Ricki Franklin. Host: OW. A 12-week Tuesday film series that premieres with *The Gold Rush*; OW's introductions were shot in London by GG. The remaining films, in order, are *Son of the Sheik*, *Intolerance*, *The Mark of Zorro*, *The General*, *Beloved Rogue*, *The Extra Girl*, *The Thief of Bagdad*, *Orphans of the Storm*, *Sally of the Sawdust*, *Blood and Sand*, and *The Hunchback of Notre Dame*.

Sept. 15 *Directed by John Ford* (California Arts Commission/AFI). D/Sc/interviewer: PB. P: George Stevens, Jr., James R. Silke. Assoc p: David Shepard. Narr: OW. R t: 90 minutes.

October A *Safe Place* (BBS/Columbia). D/Sc: Henry Jaglom. Exec p: Bert Schneider. Cast: Tuesday Weld (Noah), OW (Magician), Jack Nicholson, Gwen Welles, others.

Nov. 17 Letter by OW about the *Kane* script in the *London Times*.

Around this time, OW writes *Surinam* with OK for the Directors Company, a script adapted from Joseph Conrad's *Victory*, with parts for Ryan O'Neal, PB, OK, and OW.

Other film projects in this period include a feature about the Dumas family (developed with OK, with PB as young Dumas and OW as the father).

He finds a new title for his *Quixote* film—*When Are You Going to Finish Don Quixote?*—and begins to alter his conception of the film, planning to integrate it into an essay film about contemporary Spain.

1972 This year, OW begins work on an essay film that will eventually be called *F for Fake*.

Films narrated by OW: *The Crucifixion* (TV), *To Kill a Stranger* (D: Peter Collinson), *Salvador Dali par Jean-Christophe Averty*, *The Last of the Wild Mustangs* (ABC-TV, April 22).

Toy Factory. Cast: OW, Pamela Frankin, Michael Ontkean.

Necromancy (The Witching) (Zenith International). D/P/Sc: Bert I. Gordon. Cast: OW (Mr. Cato), Pamela Franklin (Lorie), Harvey Jason (Jay), others.

April 22 *Marty Feldman Comedy Machine* (ABC-TV). Guest: OW.

June 14 *Get to Know Your Rabbit (Warner Brothers)*. D: Brian De Palma. Sc: Jordan Crittenden. Cast: Tom Smothers (Donald Beeman), John Astin (Mr. Turnbull), OW (Mr. Delasandro), others.

Sept. 15 *Future Shock* (ABC-TV). D/P: Alex Grasshoff. Sc: Ken Rosen. Host/narr: OW. R t: 60 minutes.

Nov. 29 *The Man Who Came to Dinner* (*Hallmark Hall of Fame*, NBC-TV). Adapted from the play by George S. Kaufman and Moss Hart. D: Buzz Kulik. Cast: OW (Sheridan Whiteside), Lee Remick, Don Knotts, Mary Wickes, others.

Late this year, in Europe, OW and OK adapt a recently written story by OK, "Crazy Weather," into a script, and development work is begun on an adaptation of Paul Theroux's *Saint Jack* (years later to be done by PB).

1973

F for Fake (SACI [Teheran]/Les Films de l'Astrophore [Paris]/Janus Film und Fernsehen [Frankfurt]). Presented by François Reichenbach. D: OW. P: Dominique Antoine. Assoc p: Richard Drewett. Sc: OW, OK. Ph: Christian Odasso (France and Ibiza), GG (U.S. and Toussaint). Music: Michel Legrand. Sound: GG, others. Costumes/props: OK. Ed: Marie-Sophie Dubus, Dominique Engerer. With: OW, OK, Elmyr de Hory, Clifford Irving, Edith Irving, François Reichenbach, JC, Richard Drewett, Laurence Harvey, Jean-Pierre Aumont, Nina Van Pallandt, RW, PS, Howard Hughes, the voices of PB and WA, others. Incorporating some material as well as outtakes from a BBC documentary by François Reichenbach about Elmyr de Hory, this multifaceted essay film has several alternate titles: *Hoax*, *?*, *Fake*, and, in French, *Vérités et mensonges*. Although completed by late summer or early fall, it does not open for another year (see Sept. 1974). According to Dominique Villain, who interviewed the film's chief editor, the editing of this film took a year, working seven days a week (interrupted only by the time it took for Legrand to write the score), and required the use of three separate editing rooms. See Villain, *Le Montage au cinéma* (Paris: Éditions Cahiers du Cinéma, 1991). (OW quoted by Mary Blume, *International Herald Tribune*, December 9, 1983: "In *F for Fake* I said I was a charlatan and didn't mean it . . . because I didn't want to sound superior to Elmyr, so I emphasized that I was a magician and called it a charlatan, which isn't the same thing. And so I was faking even then. Everything was a lie. There wasn't anything that wasn't.")

Suspense (including *The Hitchhiker* and *The Master of Ballantrae*) is issued on Pelican LP 107.

Jan. *Power and Corruption* (The Learning Corporation of America). OW hosts and narrates a 34-minute educational film about WS's *Macbeth.*

June GG joins OW in France for shooting in Orvilliers and Paris on *The Other Side of the Wind*, which continues through mid-September.

Sept. 12 *Orson Welles' Great Mysteries* (syndicated). Host: OW. A British-made TV series of twenty-six 30-minute episodes premieres, introduced by OW in brief clips shot by GG in July; the series runs through 1974.

Later this month, GG does second-unit work in Spain on *Don Quixote*.

Treasure Island (National General Pictures). D: John Hough. P: Harry Alan Towers. Sc: Wolf Mankowitz, O. W. Jeeves [OW], based on the Robert Louis Stevenson novel. Cast: Kim Burfield (Jim Hawkins), Walter Slezak, OW (Long John Silver), Lionel Stander, others. (See Feb. 1965).

1974

Jan. Shooting on *The Other Side of the Wind* resumes in Carefree for three months; John Huston, the belatedly cast lead, comes for the last six weeks, and PB, replacing Rich Little as Brooks Otterlake, is also often present.

July 21 OW and GG begin shooting *Filming "Othello"* with HE and MM in a Paris hotel; work on *The Other Side of the Wind* continues soon afterward in Orvilliers (involving rear-projection for a car scene in the rain).

This year, a 90-minute documentary, *Une Légende, une vie: Citizen Welles*, produced by Monique Lefebvre and Claude-Jean Philippe, is presented on France's second channel.

Sept. *F for Fake* premieres at film festivals in San Sebastian and New York.

Nov.–Dec. OW edits *The Other Side of the Wind* in Paris and Rome.

1975 This year, OW narrates and hosts *Challenge of Greatness* (aka *The Challenge*, D: Herbert Kline), *Bugs Bunny Superstar, Magnificent Monsters of the Deep* (*Survival* [Anglia/NBC]), and *And the World Was Watching* (WMAQ-TV, October 3). He narrates the film *The Other Side of the Mountain* (D: Larry Peerce); and his voice is heard in *Ten Little Indians* (D: Peter Collinson). Preface by OW to Marion Davies' *The Times We Had* (New York: Bobbs-Merrill).

Jan. 9 *Rikki-Tikki-Tavi* (Chuck Jones Enterprises/ABC-TV). D/P/Sc: Chuck Jones. OW narrates and plays the voice of the title hero in this cartoon adapted from Rudyard Kipling's *The Jungle Book*.

Feb. 9 The American Film Institute presents its third Life Achievement Award to OW in Hollywood; OW presents two extracts from *The Other Side of the Wind*. The 90-minute ceremony is broadcast on CBS, and OW's speech is reprinted in the May 1975 issue of *Films in Review*.

Shortly afterward, filming on *The Other Side of the Wind* resumes (the party sequences) at PB's house in Los Angeles, continuing through mid-May.

April 8 *Tomorrow* (NBC-TV). Host: Tom Snyder. Guest: OW. The show is rebroadcast on May 1.

May OW moves to Beverly Hills; shooting on *The Other Side of the Wind* continues into June. After spending July and August in Europe, he resumes editing in the fall.

1976

Jan. Shooting and much of the editing completed on: *The Other Side of the Wind* (SACI [Teheran]/Les Films de l'Astrophore [Paris]). D: OW. P: Dominique Antoine. Sc: OW, OK. P mgr: Frank Marshall, Larry Jackson. Production associate: Neil Canton. Ph: GG. Cast: John Huston (Jake Hannaford, PB (Brooks Otterlake), Lilli Palmer (Zarah Valeska), Susan Strasberg (Juliette Rich), OK (Actress), Bob Random (John Dale), Howard Grossman (Charles Higgam), Joseph McBride (Mr. Pister), Tonio Sellwart (Baron), Cathy Lucas (Marvis Hensher), Norman Forster (Billy), Dan Tobin (Teacher), Edmond O'Brien (Pat), Cameron Mitchell (Matt), MEM (Maggie), Gene Clark (Projectionist), Curtis Harrington, Henry Jaglom, Paul Mazursky, PS, RW, Benny Rubin, John Carroll, Dennis Hopper, Claude Chabrol, Stéphane Audran, GG, others. Filmed in Los Angeles; Flagstaff and Carefree (Arizona); Paris and Orvilliers (France), 1970–1976.

Jan. 26 OW appears on *The Tonight Show* (NBC-TV). His subsequent appearances this year are on March 3 and 25, April 9, May 7, July 16, September 23, October 27, December 2 and 30.

June OW flies to Atlanta to begin filming *The Magic Show* with performers Abb Dickson and OK (doubling as asst d) and GG as cinematographer.

Nov. 21 *NBC—The First Fifty Years* (NBC-TV). D: Greg Garrison. Host: OW. R t: 150 minutes.

Dec. 7–Dec. 25 Preparing for the U.S. release of *F for Fake*, OW films and edits a lengthy trailer of mainly new material, 9 minutes long, featuring OW, OK, and GG. The U.S. distributor refuses to process it, and the workprint survives today only on video.

Dec. *Voyage of the Damned* (Associated General). D: Stuart Rosenberg. P: Robert Fryer. Sc: Steve Shagan, David Butler, based on a book by Gordon Thomas and Max Morgan-Witts. Cast: Faye Dunaway, Max von Sydow, Oskar Werner, Malcolm McDowell, James Mason, OW (Raoul Estedes), others. Original r t: 158 minutes.

1977 *Great American Documents*, featuring OW, Henry Fonda, Helen Hayes, and James Earl Jones, is released on CBS records and wins a Grammy for Best Spoken Word.

OW narrates *The World of Franklin and Jefferson, Tut: The Boy King*, Larry Jordan's animated *The Rime of the*

Ancient Mariner, The Late, Great Planet Earth (which he also hosts; recorded July 1977) and *The Greatest Battle.*

Scripts by OW during this period include *The Other Man* (an adaptation with OK of Graham Greene's novel *The Honorary Consul*), *Dead Giveaway* (an adaptation with GG and OK of Jim Thompson's novel *A Hell of a Woman*), and *The Assassin* (an adaptation with OK of a nonfiction script and book about Sirhan Sirhan by Donald Freed).

Jan. 7 At the opening of *F for Fake* in Boston, OW also screens *Othello*, and GG films a discussion with the audience afterward for later use in *Filming "Othello."*

Jan. 28 *The ABC Comedy Hour.* Guests: OW, Frank Gorshin, Rich Little.

Feb. 3 OW appears on *The Tonight Show* (NBC-TV).

April 1 *The Merv Griffin Show* (Metromedia). Most of the 90-minute show is devoted to a conversation with OW.

April 13 OW appears on *The Tonight Show* (NBC-TV).

July–Aug. Shooting for *The Magic Show*, mainly on weekends.

Aug. 27 OW shoots the moviola sequences for *Filming "Othello"* today and September 8 in his house near Beverly Glen.

Dec. 11 *It Happened One Christmas* (ABC-TV/Daisy Productions/Universal Television). D: Donald Wyre. Sc: Lionel Chetwynd, based on the Philip Van Doren Stern story "The Greatest Gift." Ph: Conrad Hall. Cast: Marlo Thomas (Mary Bailey Hatch), Wayne Rogers (George Hatch), OW (Henry F. Potter), Cloris Leachman (Clara), others. R t: 150 min. A made-for-TV remake of *It's a Wonderful Life* with a gender switch.

1978 This year, OW writes a screenplay, *Da Capo*, based on two stories by Isak Dinesen, later revised as *The Dreamers.*

The *Citizen Kane* sound track is released on Mark 56 810.

Jan. 12 Shooting resumes on *The Magic Show*, continuing sporadically through March and in June.

March 18 *Mysterious Castles of Clay* (NBC-TV). Narr: OW.

May 19 OW and GG both appear on *The Merv Griffin Show*.

June 9–June 12 In Sedona, Arizona, OW films conversations with Roger and Hortense Hill for *Orson Welles Solo*, a sort of scrapbook self-portrait he has been developing for years. (Ph: GG.) Other planned segments, scripted but never shot, include an abridged *Julius Caesar* (without Brutus, OW playing all the parts) and the telling of Isak Dinesen's story "The Old Chevalier," which OW later plans to shoot with video technician Frank Beacham in a Betacam format.

Aug. Shooting at the Ivar Theatre, a Hollywood burlesque house, for *The Magic Show*.

Sept. 7 With GG, OW begins shooting a 90-minute pilot for a TV talk show, with Burt Reynolds. Other guests include Angie Dickinson, the Muppets (taped October 1), Lynn Redgrave, and Patrick Terrail. Completed around February 1979, this pilot, like his earlier TV pilots, is never sold.

Nov. OW appears at a tribute held by the American Film Institute at the Directors Guild in Hollywood, "Working with Welles." Participants include Roger Hill, Dan O'Herlihy, Kenneth Tynan, Norman Lloyd, and John Berry.

Dec. 11–Dec. 12 *A Woman Called Moses* (NBC-TV/Henry Jaffe Enterprises). D: Paul Wendkos. Sc: Lonne Elder III, based on a novel by Marcy Heidish. Narr: OW. Cast: Cicely Tyson, Will Geer, Robert Hooks, others.

1979 This year, OW puts the final touches on *Filming "Othello."* D/sc/host: OW. P: Klaus and Jurgen Hellwig. Ph (in color and 16mm): GG. Music: FL, Alberto Barbaris. Ed: Marty Roth. With: OW, HE, MM. R t: 84 minutes. Made for West German television.

Other projects this year:

Never Trust an Honest Thief. D: George McCowan. Cast: OW (Sheriff Paisley), Michael Murphy (Jason), others. Never released. (See FB.)

The Muppet Movie. D: James Frawley. Guest star: OW (Lew Lord).

The Eleven Powers. Narr: OW.

The Double McGuffin. D: Joe Camp. Cast: Ernest Borgnine, George Kennedy, Elke Sommer, others. OW appears at the beginning to explain the film's title.

Bloods and Guns. Cast: OW, others.

Feb. 18 Article by OW, "Jean Renoir: 'The Greatest of All Directors' " (an obituary), *Los Angeles Times*.

Aug. 31 OW is guest on *The Merv Griffin Show*.

1980 *The Orson Welles Story* (*Arena*, BBC-TV). Leslie Megahey, Alan Yentob. Narr: Leslie Megahey. With: OW, PB, Charlton Heston, John Huston, JM, Anthony Perkins, Robert Wise, others. R t: 210 minutes. The longest and (in many respects) best of all the OW interviews done for TV, taped in Las Vegas and focusing mainly on OW's films. A version of this program, cut by about an hour and retitled *With Orson Welles: Stories from a Life in Film*, premieres in the U.S. ten years later (February 5, 1990) on the cable channel TNT.

Tajna Nikole Tesle (The Secret of Nikola Tesla). D: Krsto Papic. Sc: Papic, Ivo Bresan, Ivan Kusan, with John Hughes, John English (and, uncredited, OW). Cast: Peta Bozovic (Tesla), OW (J. P. Morgan), Strother Martin (George Westinghouse), OK, others.

The Shah of Iran. Narr: OW.

Aug. 26 OW begins shooting *The Dreamers* (see 1978 entry), mainly at his home in Hollywood, in color, with OK as Pellegrina and himself as Marcus Kleek; GG is cinematographer. More is filmed in September and October.

1981 This year, OW narrates a public-service short for United Way, *Real Heroes*, as well as *Greatest Adventure* (PBS-TV, March 8), *Genocide*, *The Greenstone*, and Mel Brooks' *History of the World, Part I*.

Butterfly. D: Matt Cimber. Cast: Stacy Keach, Pia Zadora, OW (Judge Rauch), Ed McMahon, others.

circa March At the urging of director Henry Jaglom, OW writes an original screenplay with OK, *The Big Brass Ring*. Over the next year and a half, Jaglom finds a producer, Arnon Milchan, who agrees to furnish an $8-million budget if a bankable male star can be found to play the lead. But all six of the actors approached effectively turn the part down. (See June 22, 1982).

April 26 More filming on *The Dreamers*, followed by cutting and dubbing in May.

July 14 OW appears with Pia Zadora on *The Merv Griffin Show*.

Nov. 14 With a University of Southern California audience, OW discusses *The Trial*; GG films the event for a prospective essay film, *Filming "The Trial."*

Dec. 18 Shooting resumed for ten days on *The Dreamers* and *The Magic Show*.

April 16 *J. Digger Doyle* (*Magnum, P.I.*, CBS-TV). OW plays the voice of Robin Masters in this hour-long crime series (see also Feb. 25, 1982; Feb. 10 and April 7, 1983).

1982 *The Muppets Take Manhattan*. D: Frank Oz. Guest star: OW.

Donovan's Brain (see May 18 and 25, 1944) is released on Radiola records and wins a Grammy for Best Spoken Word.

OW narrates Steven Paul's *Slapstick (of Another Kind)*.

Introduction by OW, Nancy Streebeck's *The Films of Burt Reynolds* (Secaucus, N.J.: Citadel Press).

Jan. *Magic with the Stars* (NBC-TV). Cohost: OW.

Feb. 23 OW is awarded the French Légion d'Honneur in Paris.

Feb. 24 At the Cinémathèque Française, OW speaks with and to a large gathering of French film students. A one-hour film is made of this event, *Orson Welles à la Cinémathèque*, by Pierre-André Boutang.

Feb. 25 *Double Jeopardy* (*Magnum, P.I.*, CBS-TV).

March 8 OW appears as one of the hosts on *Night of 100 Stars* (ABC-TV), a benefit for the Actors' Fund retirement home taped at Radio City Music Hall.

April 12 *Baryshnikov in Hollywood* (CBS). Narr: OW.

June 12 OW speaks at a massive antinuclear rally in New York's Central Park. (This speech is included in the 1984 documentary feature *In Our Hands*.)

June 22 OW completes a final draft of *The Big Brass Ring* (see March 1981), which is published in 1987 by Santa Teresa Press in Santa Barbara.

Aug. More shooting on *The Dreamers* this month and September 1.

Dec. OW writes and edits a section of a special Christmas issue of the French *Vogue*, which he dedicates to Georges Méliès, including excerpts in English from his autobiography-in-progress, several texts in French (including ones on Eduardo de Filippo, OK, and Isak Dinesen), and many drawings.

1983 *Shogun* (ABC-TV). D: Jerry London. For the rerun of this popular miniseries (originally shown September 15–20, 1980), additional narration by OW is used to help explicate the Japanese dialogue. He also narrates the Canadian (CBC) TV series *Tales from the Klondike* and appears briefly in Julien Temple's British documentary, *It's All True*.

Efforts continue to set up a film of *King Lear*.

Feb. 10 *Birdman of Budapest* (*Magnum, P.I.*, CBS-TV).

April 7 *The Big Blow* (*Magnum, P.I.*, CBS-TV). OW's final performance as the voice of Robin Masters.

The Merv Griffin Show. Guests: OW, JH. The only real reunion of OW and Houseman since the 1940s.

June 3 *Pleine Lune* (INA-TV). D: Philippe Grandrieux, in collaboration with Jérôme Prieur. An extended interview with OW about the media done for French television. (OW: "[Television] demands less from the public than any other medium. And the strongest mediums are those which ask the most from the public. When we had only black-and-white in the cinema, we demanded something from them. When we had no sound we demanded something. The closer we got to an approximation of life, the less was asked of the public, and therefore the less impact it had upon the public. That's why the theatre has a stronger impact than the cinema—because the audience must pretend that they aren't an audience. It is already part of the performance. In French you say you '*assister*,' [which] we do not say in English. It is a wonderful verb for being at a performance: you assist the performance by being there. You don't assist television; it's just on. . . . Sadat is killed, and Lux soap is used, and people sit eating food while a soldier bleeds to death in Lebanon, and it's unreal.")

1984 Around this time, OW appears in the TV specials *Natalie —A Tribute to a Very Special Lady* and *Dom De Luise and Friends* (Parts I and II) and narrates *King Penguins—Stranded Beyond the Falklands* and Jacques-Yves Cousteau's *Snowstorm in the Jungle*, two TV documentaries.

OW is featured on the pop single "I Know What It Is to Be Young," with the Ray Charles Singers and the Nick Perito Orchestra (GBNP Crescendo GNPS 1206). During this period, OW also narrates the tale "Dark Avenger" for the heavy-metal band Man-o-War on their album *Battle Hymns*.

Where Is Parsifal? D: Henri Helman. Cast: Tony Curtis, OW (Klingsor), others. Filmed in London.

Seven Days to Eternity. D: Yan Regin. Narr: OW.

OW also narrates the trailer for *Revenge of the Nerds*.

June OW is shown an original screenplay by Ring Lardner, Jr., *Rocking the Cradle*, about the 1937 stage production of *The Cradle Will Rock*, a script that Michael Fitzgerald plans to produce. Fitzgerald invites OW to direct it, and OW completely rewrites the script. A production schedule is worked out, sets are built, some casting is done (including Rupert Everett as OW and, tentatively, Amy Irving as Virginia Welles), and OW continues to revise the script through early November, but three weeks before the shooting is scheduled to start (exteriors in Hoboken, New Jersey, Staten Island, New York, and downtown Los Angeles; theater interiors and some studio work in Rome), the financing falls through. (The script is published in Santa Barbara by Santa Teresa Press in 1993 as *The Cradle Will Rock*.)

Sept. 30 *Scene of the Crime* (NBC-TV). Host: OW. The pilot of a new series that OW continues to host next year. (See April 14, 1985.)

1985 Michael Fitzgerald continues to try to raise money to produce *The Cradle Will Rock* this year; the $6-million budget is reduced to $3 million, but there are still no backers.

Around this time, OW records the narration for a remixed and remastered version of a 1976 pop album, *Tales of Mystery and Imagination: Edgar Allan Poe*, by The Alan Parsons Project. (The new version is released in 1987 on Polygram Records 0704.)

March 9 OW is awarded the Special Fellowship of the Academy of Magical Arts.

March 13 With GG, OW shoots a black-and-white video test for *King Lear*.

April 14 *Scene of the Crime* (NBC-TV). Host: OW. This series continues through May 26.

May OW's efforts to make *King Lear* in France finally collapse because of an artificially inflated budget, impossible production conditions, and broken promises.

OW adapts and records a series of literary works on audiocassettes for the Japanese market. The half-hour solo readings include *The Happy Prince*, *Huckleberry Finn*, Conrad's *The Secret Sharer*, Waugh's *A Handful of Dust*, Beerbohm's "A. V. Laider," Bemelmans' "Grapes for Mr. Cape," Capote's "Miriam," Cheever's "The National Pastime," John Collier's "The Chaser," Dinesen's "The Old Chevalier" and "The Heroine," Fitzgerald's "The Diamond As Big As the Ritz," Harte's "The Outcasts of Poker Flats," Hawthorne's "Wakefield," Hemingway's "Ten Indians" and "In Another Country," Kipling's "Rikki-Tikki-Tavi," O'Hara's "Malibu from the Sky," Poe's "The Tell-Tale Heart," Saki's "Sredni Vashtar," Saroyan's "The Summer of the Beautiful White Horses," Irwin Shaw's "The Girls in Their Summer Dresses," Stevenson's "Letter to the Reverend Dr. Hyde," OW's own "My Father Wore Black Spats" (from *Vogue*), and H. G. Wells' "The Red Room"; he also records a few short poems, including works by Byron, Graves, and Kipling.

Summer OW starts work on a new script, *Mercedes*, based on "Blind Window," an original story by OK.

Someone to Love. D/sc/ed: Henry Jaglom. Cast: Jaglom

(Danny Sapir), Andrea Marcovicci (Helen Eugene), Michael Emil (Mickey Sapir), Sally Kellerman (Edith Helm), OW (himself), OK (Yelena), others. R t: 105 minutes. Released in 1987 (a film "dedicated with love to Orson Welles").

Aug. *Almonds and Raisins.* D: Russ Kavel. Narr: OW. A documentary about Yiddish cinema, shown later this year on PBS.

Sept. The discovery of 314 cans of film relating to *It's All True*, including about 80 percent of *Four Men on a Raft*, is reported by Bill Krohn in *Cahiers du Cinéma.*

Sept. 21 Further work on *The Dreamers.*

Oct. 5 OW introduces a special hour-long "film-noir" show on *Moonlighting* (ABC-TV), "Dream Sequences Always Ring Twice," with Cybill Shepherd and Bruce Willis.

The Transformers. D: Nelson Shin. An animated feature in which OW does the voice of an evil planet.

Oct. 7 With GG at UCLA, OW lines up shots for *Orson Welles Solo* (the *Julius Caesar* sequence) and *The Magic Show* (see Oct. 10).

Oct. 9 Burt Reynolds proposes that OW direct an episode for the TV series *Amazing Stories* that Reynolds will star in.

The Merv Griffin Show (syndicated). Guests: OW, Barbara Leaming, Meredith Salenger. Appearing with his biographer Leaming, OW performs magic and discusses his career.

Oct. 10 OW dies of a heart attack early in the morning at his house in Hollywood while typing stage directions for the material he plans to shoot with GG at UCLA later today.

His ashes are buried on a remote Spanish farm, three hours by bus from Seville, where he had lived for a summer when he was eighteen.

APPENDIX:
The Original *Ambersons*

EDITOR'S PREFACE: This summary of the cuts and other alterations made in Welles' original version of *The Magnificent Ambersons* represents both a condensation and, in certain particulars (such as descriptions of screen action), a paraphrase of the original work done by Peter Bogdanovich. I have carried out this editorial work partially in order to avoid the less readable jargon and abbreviations of RKO's cutting continuity, and partially in order not to duplicate the textual work being carried out by Robert L. Carringer, who has been preparing a "reconstruction" and "scholarly edition" of *Ambersons* in book form to be published by the University of California Press. Carringer has already put together a superb "deluxe" edition of *Ambersons* on laser disc for Voyager, containing many valuable materials that I have drawn from in the editing of chapter 3, including a fine-grain print of the release version of the film taken from the original negative and many supplementary documents.

I should add, however, that, apart from this textual work, Carringer's work-in-progress is based in part on critical assumptions that are diametrically opposed to those of the present volume. Certain conclusions about these assumptions can be made on the basis of three texts: (1) the final chapter of Carringer's *The Making of "Citizen Kane,"* entitled "Collaboration and *The Magnificent Ambersons,*" (2) an article about his work-in-progress—"*The* (Not-so) *Magnificent Ambersons*" by Caroline Taylor, published in the July-August 1988 issue of *Humanities*—whose title seems an accurate indication of his approach, and (3) a lecture given by Carringer that I attended at New York University's Welles conference in May 1988, based on an early draft of his introduction (also alluded to in Taylor's article, under the title "Oedipus in Indianapolis.")

In (1), Carringer argues that "the heart of the problem" that led to the "undoing" of *Ambersons* was "in the production circumstances themselves. There was no screenwriter [Carringer basically discounts Welles' own work as an adaptor], and the art director and cinematographer were Welles' second choices. The production had major problems in all three areas. Collectively, these problems were enough to make the difference. If Welles had had the best talent available in these key roles . . . *The Magnificent Ambersons* might have rivalled *Citizen Kane.*" (As a corollary to this conclusion, one should note that the thesis of Carringer's book is that *Citizen Kane* was essentially a collaborative work—a thesis that Welles himself hotly contested, as Carringer acknowledges.)

In (2), Carringer again argues that *Ambersons* was fatally flawed at the outset, but this time he adds that Welles' psychological makeup was largely responsible: "He could not resolve the familial conflicts in *Ambersons* because they related to conflicts in his own childhood that he had never resolved. . . . He didn't appear in this picture and he didn't write a reconciliation because he couldn't." This notion is amplified in (3), in which Carringer argued that *Hamlet* was the "secret" source of Welles' *Ambersons*, imparting much significance to the fact that Welles never directed *Hamlet* onstage or as a film. He also follows the line of biographer Charles Higham in assigning the ultimate responsibility for *Ambersons*' undoing to Welles himself.

Regarding the final scene in Welles' original version, it is obviously impossible to evaluate a scene that no longer exists. But the outline given here (simplified somewhat in the interests of clarity), coupled with Welles' remarks in chapter 3, suggests that the most daring aspect of this scene—and probably the aspect that troubled spectators and studio personnel the most—is that nothing of dramatic consequence happens in it, apart from the exposition of George and Lucy's offscreen reconciliation and Eugene's forgiveness of George. As a kind of *tabula rasa* and sounding brass for everything in the film preceding it, it appears to function as a kind of chilling, tragic diminuendo that has few if any counterparts in the American cinema; indeed, the only rough parallels that come to mind are the last scene in Carl Dreyer's *Gertrud*—a film Welles expresses some sympathy for in chapter 4—and the last shot in Kenji Mizoguchi's *The Life of Oharu*. Finally, it might be argued that Carringer's linkage of *Ambersons* to *Hamlet*, another tragedy, makes sense only if George is viewed squarely as the film's tragic hero; but the last scene suggests that Eugene, Fanny, and Isabel—and the processes of time and history—may be equally important.

The following summary of Orson's original version is based on a "cutting continuity" which was copied directly from the screen and dated March 12, 1942, five days before that crippling first preview.

> *The first reel opens with Welles setting the period and fashion of the times through nostalgic pictures and evocative narration. One part of this sequence—Eugene's falling into the bass viol during the nighttime serenade and thus estranging himself from Isabel—was moved back several minutes to come closer to the scene where he is visibly turned away by her butler. It was more a part of the general flow of life in its original place—Welles focusing in on the story in a more leisurely way. The pace was also slightly accelerated by two cuts. The first ran for about one minute, came immediately after the amusing succession of shots of Eugene trying on different kinds of clothes, and contained the following offscreen narration while we see Eugene leaving his house with a box of candy and walking down the busy street toward the Amberson mansion, tipping his hat to others as he passes them (slash marks* [/] *indicate shot changes):*

The people were thrifty in that Midland town because they were the sons or grandsons of the "early settlers," who had opened the wilderness with wagons and axes and guns, but with no money at all. The pioneers / were thrifty or they would have perished; they had to store away food for the winter, or goods to trade for food, and they often feared they hadn't stored enough. . . . They left traces of that fear in their sons and grandsons. In the minds of most of these, indeed, their thrift was next to their religion. To save, even for the sake of saving, was their earliest lesson and discipline. No matter how prosperous they were, they could not spend money either upon "art" / or upon mere luxury and entertainment, without a sense of sin. . . .

Various townspeople comment on the Ambersons and their mansion. Their final exchange was cut:

HUMPHRIES: Well, sir, I presume the President of the United States'd be tickled to swap the White House for the new Amberson Mansion if the Major'd give him the chance. . . .

/ AUGUST: But by the Almighty Dollar, you can bet your sweet life the Major wouldn't.

BAXTER: Well, well . . .

After Isabel marries Wilbur Minafer and they have a single child, George Amberson Minafer, the latter is introduced as a young boy arrogantly riding through town in a horse cart, almost knocking down a laborer (who yells, "By Golly! I guess you think you own this town!") *George stops to answer him in a continuation of the scene that was cut:*

GEORGE *(offscreen):* I will when I grow up." / *(Onscreen as laborer approaches)* I guess my grandpa owns it now, you bet!

LABORER: Aw, pull down your vest!

GEORGE: Don't haf' to! Doctor says it ain't healthy! *(Driving off.)* But I tell you what I'll do. . . . *(Laborer runs after cart.)* I'll pull down my vest if you'll wipe off your chin!

When George, now a grown boy, comes home from school, we see him again in his cart, followed by an entire scene that was cut, running slightly less than three minutes, and adapted faithfully from Tarkington. Comprising sixteen shots and running into the second reel, the scene is set at the "Friends of the Ace" clubroom, where George enters a meeting in progress (the first four shots) and proceeds to take it over:

GEORGE: What's Fred Kinney doing in the president's chair? *(Fred raps on desk.)* Didn't you all agree I was to be president just the same, even if I was away at school?

/ FRED: All Friends of the Ace will take their seats! I'm president of the F.O.T.A. Now, George Minafer . . . / this meeting will now come to order. . . .

GEORGE: No it won't. You put down that gavel. *(Fred pounds on desk; George grabs gavel away from him.)* It belongs to my grandfather. Give it to me.

FRED: I was legally elected here.

GEORGE: All right. / You're president. *(He turns to other boys.)* Now we'll hold another election.

/ FRED *(leaping up)*: We will not! *(He sits down again.)* We'll have our regular meeting, and then we'll play euchre, a nickel a corner just what we're here for. . . . This meeting will now come to order. *(He pounds on desk with gavel; George leans over and grabs gavel again.)* [*Reel change.*]

/ GEORGE: That belongs to my grandfather. . . . Who's the founder of the F.O.T.A., if you please? *(He looks around at the other boys belligerently.)* / Who got the janitor to let us have most of this furniture? You think you could keep this clubroom a minute if I told my grandfather I didn't need it for a literary club any more? And another thing . . . / I want to say something on how you men been acting, too! If that's what you want, you can have it. I was going to bring some port wine down here and we'd have a little celebration some night, like we do in our crowd at school. / But, you men got a new president now! *(He goes to the door.)* I guess all I better do is . . . resign!

CHARLIE: All those in favor of holding a new election say, "Aye."

ALL: Aye! *(Boys raise their hands.)*

FRED *(leaping up in foreground)*: That's unfair!

GEORGE: *(in background)*: All those in favor of me being president instead of Fred Kinney say, "Aye."

ALL: Aye!

GEORGE: The "Ayes" have it. *(Grinning, he returns to the desk while Fred hurries to the door.)*

FRED: I resign! *(He slams the door behind him; the other boys laugh.)*

/ GEORGE *(taking off his hat)*: Old redhead Fred'll be around next week. He'll be around boot-lickin' to get us to take him back in again. / *(He takes a cigar from his pocket, sniffs it.)* Well, fellows . . . I suppose you'd like to hear from your president. I don't imagine there's any more business before the meeting. / *(He pounds on desk.)* Meeting adjourned . . . *(Laughter; boys rise and mill around.)* I had a pretty good time at the old school, back East. . . . *(Boys gather around a card table as he continues.)* Had a little trouble with the faculty and had to come home. But the family stood by me as well as I could ask. Anybody that's game for a little quarter-limit poker or any limit they say, why I'd like to have 'em sit at the president's card-table. . . . *(They sit down at table.)*

A lap dissolve takes us to the Amberson mansion decked out for a ball in George's honor. Over five minutes was cut from this sequence as a whole; the first deletion—just after George is introduced to Eugene's daughter Lucy—involves a rambunctious Uncle John and Aunt Fanny:

JOHN *(entering the frame as he describes the staircase):* Solid black walnut every inch of it . . . balustrades and all. *(He slaps railing.) Sixty thousand dollars* . . . worth o' carved woodwork in the house! Like water! Spent money like water! Always did! Still do! Like water! *(Fanny enters behind him and he turns.)* Gosh knows where it all comes from! *(To Fanny)* Hello . . . / Fanny!

FANNY: Hello, Uncle John . . .

(Lucy and George enter at left.) GEORGE: Aunt Fanny.

FANNY *(surprised):* Well . . .

JOHN: Hello.

FANNY: Is this Lucy Morgan?

GEORGE: Miss Morgan . . . Miss Minafer . . .

FANNY: You must favor your mother, my dear. I never knew her.

JOHN *(grabbing Fanny):* Come on . . . / *They enter hall.)* There's dancing going on. Hoopla! *(Lucy and George follow them.)* Let's push through an' see those young womenfolks crack their heels! Hoopse-daisy! Ha-ha-ha. *(He and Fanny start dancing, as do George and Lucy. The music stops and people applaud.)*

GEORGE: Give me the next one and the one after that, and every third one the rest of the evening.

LUCY: Are you asking?

/ JOHN *(to Fanny):* Well . . . I don' want any more o' that! *(Wilbur Minafer enters behind John.)* Jus' slidin' 'round!

FANNY: Wilbur . . . *(John passes them as Fanny and Wilbur whisper; Wilbur passes behind George and Lucy while following John.)*

JOHN *(to George and Lucy):* Call that dancin' . . . *(Wilbur grabs him to quiet him down.)*

WILBUR: John . . . John . . .

JOHN: Rather see a jig any day in the world! *(To Lucy)* Hello, young lady . . . *(He nudges her, winks, and they both laugh.)*

LUCY: Hello . . .

WILBUR *(to George, while pulling John away)*: I'll send Uncle John home. . . .

GEORGE: All right, Father . . .

JOHN *(laughing as Wilbur guides him away, George and Lucy following)*: Ain't very modest some of 'em. I don't mind that, though. Not me . . . *(Wilbur exits with John.)*

The last shot continues in the film as George gets jealous because so many of the young men know Lucy; he says they all used to belong to a club he'd been president of, but doesn't know why his mother invited them (a reference to the deleted F.O.T.A. scene).

The following scene, which was cut from the film, appeared much later in Tarkington's novel—after Wilbur's death and at the time of George's graduation. In fact, Welles took several scenes from other parts of the novel and set them at the dance. As George and Lucy went down the stairs to dance, the shot continued with the camera moving down to Isabel and Eugene as Jack went up the stairs, approaching them:

ISABEL: It's charming, isn't it?

EUGENE: Hm?

ISABEL: Those children. It's touching. But of course they don't . . . It's touching.

JACK *(to Isabel and Eugene)*: Do you know what I think whenever I see these smooth . . . triumphal young faces? / *(New angle shows Fanny beside steps as the other three start walking down.)* I always think, "Oh, how you're going to catch it!"

ISABEL: Jack.

JACK: Oh, yes. Life's got a special walloping for every mother's son of 'em.

ISABEL: Maybe some of the mothers can take the walloping for them. *(They cross to the right, joined by Fanny, the camera panning with them.)*

JACK *(laughing)*: Not any more than she can take on her own face the lines that are bound to come on her son's. . . . *(They stop walking as people pass.)* I suppose you know that all these young faces have got to get lines on 'em?

ISABEL: Maybe they won't. Maybe times will change and nobody will have to wear lines.

EUGENE: Times have changed like that for only one person I know. *(He laughs at Isabel; they move forward, following the camera as they talk.)*

JACK: What puts the lines on faces? Age or trouble? Ha, we can't say that wisdom does it. . . . We must be polite to Isabel. *(They all laugh.)*

EUGENE: Age puts some, and trouble puts some, and work puts some . . . *(They stop moving.)* . . . but the deepest wrinkles are carved by lack of faith. The serenest brow is the one that believes the most.

ISABEL: In what?

EUGENE: In everything . . . Oh, yes, you do.

ISABEL: Why, I believe . . . I believe I do.

(Jack laughs as they follow the camera through an arch.) JACK: Isabel. There're times when you look exactly fourteen years old.

The rest of this shot remains in the film—as Major Amberson, Wilbur, Isabel, Jack, and Eugene reminisce about Eugene's fall into the bass viol, and George and Lucy tease each other and have a drink of punch. Three inconsequential lines ("No, they're not. . . ." "No . . ." "No . . .") *between two women guests at the party (meant to lead to a discussion of olives in the next shot) were cut from the very end of this shot, which ended reel 2.*

The opening of reel 3—all done in one continuous shot—was deleted. (In Tarkington's novel, the scene played between Eugene and the father of Fred Kinney; the olive exchange is from the opening of the book.)

(As Lucy and George come into the foreground, George bumps into a man and ignores him; the man turns. Jack and Eugene are visible beside a table in the background.)

MAN: Look at that! Look at that boy! Sorry, your highness. *(He exits at right while Jack and Eugene approach, then stop, while the camera moves back.)*

JACK: I can't see why Isabel doesn't see the truth about that boy!

EUGENE: Hm?

JACK: Georgie . . .

EUGENE: What's the matter with him?

JACK: Huh, too much Amberson, I guess, for one thing. Yes, and for another, his mother just fell down and worshiped him from the day he was born. Oh, I don't have to tell you what Isabel Amberson is, Gene. Oh, she's got a touch of the Amberson high stuff about her, but you can't get anybody who ever knew her to deny that she's just about the finest woman in the world.

EUGENE: No, you can't get anybody to deny that. *(They approach the camera, following it through a doorway.)*

JACK: Well, she thinks he's a little tin god on wheels. Why, she actually sits and worships him! You can hear it in her voice when she speaks to him. See it in her eyes when she looks at him. My gosh! What *does*

she see when she looks at him? *(They stop by a woman at left before a mirror.)*

EUGENE: Huh, she sees something that we don't see.

JACK: What's that?

EUGENE: An angel.

JACK: Angel!

(A little man enters hurriedly.) LITTLE MAN *(to woman):* There they are.

EUGENE: I'll take one of these. *(He and Jack exit right; two figures hurry forward as the camera moves back.)*

MRS. JOHNSON: The olives.

WOMAN: Roger . . .

JACK *(offscreen):* Angel.

WOMAN: . . . come over here and look at the olives. *(The two stop beside a group around a butler holding a tray of olives, picking up olives and looking at them.)*

LITTLE MAN: You're supposed to eat them. . . .

MRS. JOHNSON: Green things they are, something like a hard plum.

ROGER: A friend of mine told me they tasted a good deal like a bad hickory nut.

MRS. JOHNSON: I hear you gotta eat nine. . . .

LITTLE MAN: And then you get to like them.

ANOTHER MAN: Well, I wouldn't eat nine bad hickory nuts to get to like *them*. . . .

ROGER: Kind of a woman's dish, anyway, I suspect.

MRS. JOHNSON: Well, I reckon most everybody'll be makin' a stagger to worm through nine of 'em, now Amberson's brought 'em to town. *(People laugh and return olives to tray. Mrs. Johnson reaches around behind the butler to grab a few.)*

JACK *(offscreen):* All mothers are like that. . . .

EUGENE *(offscreen):* Um-hm . . . *(Eugene and Jack enter frame, butler exists, Mrs. Johnson bumps into Eugene.)*

MRS. JOHNSON: Excuse me. . . .

EUGENE *(setting glass down on a passing tray):* Here you are. . . . *(The camera pans with him and Jack as they cross to left.)* Here, take this. *(They approach the foreground as the camera moves back through the room. To Jack:)* That's what she sees.

JACK: Angel? My nephew? Look at him. Do you see an angel?

EUGENE: No. All I see is a remarkably good-looking young fool-boy with the pride of Satan and a set of nice drawing-room manners.

JACK: What do you mean? *(They stop moving.)*

EUGENE: Mothers are right. Mothers see the angel in us because the angel is there.

JACK: Ah-ha—you mean Georgie's mother is always right.

EUGENE: I'm afraid she always has been. *(He crosses to left and Jack follows; the camera follows them to a burning fireplace, a mirror overhead reflecting the crowd dancing.)*

JACK: Yes, well, wait till you get to know young Georgie a little better.

EUGENE: Jack, if you were a painter, you'd paint mothers with angels' eyes, holding little devils in their laps. *(Jack laughs, Eugene moves into foreground.)* Me, I'll stick to the Old Masters and the cherubs. *(The music stops; the people in the mirror are seen applauding.)*

JACK: Well, somebody's eyes must have been pretty angelic if they've been persuading you that George Minafer is a cherub.

EUGENE: They are. They're more angelic than ever. . . . *(Music resumes.)*

Without a cut, Eugene goes to dance with Isabel, and George tells Lucy that he intends to become a yachtsman. A slow dissolve finds Isabel and Eugene still dancing much later, alone on the floor now, as the ball quietly comes to a close. . . . Riding home in Eugene's horseless carriage, Lucy and Eugene talk about George and Isabel. After Eugene admits he is still very fond of Isabel, these last four lines were cut:

LUCY: She's lovely. . . . lovely! . . . Papa, I wonder sometimes . . .

EUGENE: What?

LUCY: I wonder just how she happened to marry Mr. Minafer.

EUGENE *(laughing):* Ha-ha . . . oh, Wilbur's all right.

A lap dissolve returns us to the Ambersons. As reel 4 begins, George confronts Wilbur about "this man Morgan," insinuating that Eugene wants Jack and Major Amberson to invest in his autos. When Fanny and Wilbur tell him he's wrong, he persists: why did he bring his car with him, then? (His next line, delivered in a closeup —"People that own elephants don't take their elephants with 'em when they go visiting"—was cut.) George then gets into a family squabble with Fanny. This dissolved to a cut scene (about a minute long) of Eugene and Lucy arriving home:

(We see doors opening inside a stable and Lucy running inside; horses are heard neighing, and Eugene drives in.)

EUGENE: Look out, Lucy . . . look out, dear—

LUCY: Right. *(She follows him until he stops the car and climbs out.)* You know, I wish George wasn't so conceited and bad-tempered. . . . He's really quite nice.

EUGENE: What's that, dear?

LUCY: George! Maybe I shouldn't call him exactly bad-tempered.

EUGENE: Of course not. Only when he's cross about something. *(He crosses to the right, the camera panning with him, speaking to the stamping and neighing horses.)* Whoa . . . whoa . . . whoa . . . *(He walks around the car. Lucy laughs. He fixes a light.)* You know, dear, you need only three things to explain all that's good and bad about George. . . .

LUCY: What?

EUGENE *(to horses)*: Whoa . . . whoa . . . whoa . . . *(He and Lucy come into the right foreground; he kneels, fixing the light, while two horses stamp and rear in stalls behind them.)* Well, he's Isabel's only child. . . . He's an Amberson. He's a boy.

LUCY: Well, Mr. Bones, of these three things, which are the good ones and which are the bad ones?

EUGENE: All of them. *(Fadeout.)*

The celebrated sleigh-ride and car-ride sequence fades in: Lucy and George in the one-horse open sleigh; Isabel, Eugene, Jack, and Fanny in the Morgan car. After the sleigh overturns, they all pile into the car, which has trouble starting. George has to push, and the exhaust fumes make him choke; when they're finally on their way, everyone joins in singing "The Man Who Broke the Bank at Monte Carlo." After two verses of the song, the group gets into the following cut conversation, about two minutes long:

ISABEL *(in front, with Eugene):* When we get this far out you can see there's quite a little smoke hanging over town. *(The singing stops.)*

JACK: Yes, that's because the town's growing.

EUGENE: Yes, and as it grows bigger it seems to get ashamed of itself, so it makes that big cloud and hides in it.

ISABEL: Oh, Eugene . . . / *(Cut to a closer shot.)*

EUGENE: You know, Isabel, I think it used to be nicer.

ISABEL: That's because we were young.

EUGENE: Maybe. It always used to be sunshiny, and the air wasn't like the air anywhere else. As I remember it, there always seemed to be gold dust in the air.

/ *(Cut to shot of Lucy sitting on Jack's lap; George leans in behind them, looking disgusted.)* JACK: How about it, young folks? You notice any gold dust?

(Lucy laughs.) GEORGE *(derisively):* Gold dust?

LUCY: I wonder if we really do enjoy it as much as we'll look back and think we did—

JACK: Of course not.

LUCY: I feel as if I must be missing something about it, somehow, because I don't ever seem to be thinking about what's happening at the present moment. I'm always looking forward to something . . . thinking about things that will happen when I'm older.

(Jack starts whistling.) GEORGE *(to Lucy):* You're a funny girl . . . but your voice sounds pretty nice when you talk along together like that. *(He looks off to the left and yells.)* Hey, look at those fences all smeared. /

(Fanny, at right, whistles; George, at left, frowns.)

LUCY *(offscreen):* That must be from soot.

FANNY: Yes . . . there're so many houses around here now.

GEORGE: Grandfather owns a good many of them, I guess . . . for renting.

FANNY: He sold most of the lots, Georgie.

GEORGE: He ought to keep things up better. It's getting all too much built up. Riffraff! / *(Cut to Lucy laughing.)* He lets . . . / *(Cut back to George.)* . . . these people take too many liberties. They do anything they want to. . . . / *(Cut to Lucy whistling.)* / *(Cut back to George, speaking to Lucy.)* You know, you've got that way of seeming quietly . . . / *(Cut to Jack and Lucy, both whistling, George behind them, angry.)* . . . superior to everybody else. I don't believe in that kind of thing.

LUCY: You don't?

GEORGE: No. Not with me. I think the world's like this.

LUCY *(gesturing and singing loudly):* La . . . la . . . la . . .

GEORGE: *(glaring as Jack joins Lucy in song):* There's a few . . . there's a few people that, from their birth and position and so on, puts them on top, and they ought to treat each other entirely as equals. I wouldn't speak like this to everybody. / *(Cut to new angle on George without Lucy and Jack, who continue to sing.)* Oh, I had a notion before I came for you today that we were going to quarrel.

/ LUCY: No we won't. Takes two! *(The singing that precedes this deleted dialogue continues in the released version as the car rides off, and the reel ends with a famous and memorable iris-out.)*

Reel 5 begins with Wilbur's funeral; people file past his coffin. Part of the shot of the mourners was deleted (laughs at preview), along with a cut to Wilbur's tombstone in the Ambersons' family plot, which dissolved in from a closeup on Fanny, and was followed by a fadeout. It was replaced with an alternate version Welles had shot (and authorized) of a townsman saying, "Wilbur Minafer. Quiet man. Town'll hardly know he's gone."

The next two shots were deleted—an insert showing George's college diploma followed by an exterior shot of the Amberson mansion in the rain—and the film dissolves directly to the celebrated kitchen scene between George and Fanny.

This scene ends in the released version with George looking out the window at the rain. Originally, it went on like this:

JACK: You know, I think perhaps we ought to . . .

GEORGE: Holy cats! *(He runs to put on his coat.)*

JACK: What's wrong, Georgie? . . . Why, Georgie . . . / *(Cut to outside house, George running out followed by Jack, putting on his own coat.)* Georgie . . . *(Jack opens an umbrella.)*

/ *(Cut to excavations under the raging storm, partly erected buildings in the background, George running and turning.)* GEORGE: What is this? / *(Jack running forward.)* Looks like excavations. . . . / *(George and Jack both visible.)* Looks like the foundations for a lot of houses! Just what does grandfather mean by this? *(He rushes toward the building sites, Jack following.)*

JACK: My private opinion is he wants to increase his income by building these houses to rent. For gosh sakes, come in . . . / *(New angle of George.)* . . . out of the rain. . . . *(George running; Jack goes to him.)*

GEORGE: Can't he increase his income any other way but this?

JACK: It would appear he couldn't. I wanted him to put up . . . / *(Jack tries to hold umbrella over both of them.)* . . . an apartment building instead of these houses.

GEORGE *(shouting)*: An apartment building! Here?

JACK *(shouting)*: Yes, that was my idea.

GEORGE *(shouting)*: An apartment house! / *(George looks to right, shocked, water streaming down his face.)* Oh, my gosh!

JACK *(off)*: Don't worry! *(Jack under umbrella looking to left.)* Your grandfather wouldn't listen to me, but he'll wish he had, some day.

/ GEORGE: But why didn't he sell something or other, rather than do a thing like this?

/ JACK: I believe he *had* sold something or other, from time to time.

/ GEORGE: Well, in heaven's name, what did he do this for?

/ JACK: In heaven's name, to get money. That's my deduction.

/ GEORGE: I suppose you're joking . . . or trying to.

/ JACK *(shaking his head)*: That's the best way to look at it. *(Fadeout.)*

Isabel, Fanny, George, and Lucy visit Eugene's motorcar works—an event only mentioned in the novel. The very end of the sequence (and reel) was deleted:

(Lucy and George emerge from the entrance and he helps her up onto the buggy.) LUCY *(speaking of Eugene and Isabel)*: Gracious! Aren't they sentimental. *(She sits down; the camera pans to George sitting down beside her.)*

GEORGE: People that age are always sentimental. They get sentimental over anything at all. *(He drives the buggy out of frame. A car comes out of the factory—Eugene driving, Isabel and Fanny in the back seat —and the camera pans to the left as they continue down the street. / The car approaches the camera while pedestrians on both sides of the street watch; music is heard. After the car turns a corner and leaves the frame, the dust clears and the buggy with George and Lucy approaches.*

George and Lucy quarrel as the buggy moves down the street. (In the film as released, a conversation between Eugene and Isabel under a tree, which comes several sequences later in Welles' version, precedes this buggy scene.)

As George and Lucy drive off, we see Major Amberson and Jack in a horse and carriage; the Major says he feels that the town is "rolling right over" his heart "and burying it under." The last part of their dialogue was cut:

MAJOR: . . . When I think of those devilish workmen yelling around my house and digging up my lawn . . .

JACK: Never mind, Father. Don't think of it. When things are a nuisance, it's a good idea not to keep remembering 'em.

MAJOR: I try not to. I try to keep remembering that I won't be remembering anything now very long. . . . Not so very long, my boy. . . . Not so very long now, huh . . . not so very long!

There is a lap dissolve to a long night sequence that was cut from the picture, approximately 6½ minutes long; under pressure, Orson had authorized cutting only the "vision" at the end:

(A long shot of the empty yard to the left of the Amberson mansion, which is also visible, with lights from the passing street traffic in the background, lap dissolves / to a medium shot of the front porch. Music is heard.) FANNY *(her rocker creaking):* I don't believe we'll see as many of those automobiles next summer.

ISABEL: Why?

FANNY: I've begun to agree with George about their being a fad more than anything else—like roller skates. Besides, people just won't stand for them after a while. I shouldn't be surprised to see a law passed forbidding the sale of automobiles the way there is with concealed weapons.

ISABEL: You're not in earnest, Fanny.

FANNY: I am, though!

ISABEL: Then you didn't mean it when you told Eugene you'd enjoyed the drive this afternoon.

FANNY: I didn't say it so very enthusiastically, did I?

ISABEL: Perhaps not, but he certainly thought he'd pleased you.

FANNY: I don't think I gave him any right to think he'd pleased me.

ISABEL: Why not, Fanny? Why shouldn't you?

FANNY: I hardly think I'd want anyone to get the notion he's pleased me just now. It hardly seems time yet—to me. *(Isabel starts to whistle; Fanny stops rocking.)*

FANNY: Is that you, George?

GEORGE: Is that me what?

FANNY: Whistling "On Yonder Rock Reclining"?

ISABEL *(amused)*: Oh, it's I.
FANNY: Oh.
ISABEL: Does it disturb you?
FANNY: No, not at all. Just had an idea that George was depressed about something—wondered if he could be making such a cheerful sound.
ISABEL: Troubled about anything, Georgie?
GEORGE: No.
(Isabel laughs.) FANNY *(to Isabel)*: Are you laughing about something?
ISABEL: Pardon?
FANNY: I asked: were you laughing at something?
ISABEL: Yes, I was. It's that funny, fat old Mrs. Johnson across the street. *(She rises and steps behind George.)* She has a habit of looking out her bedroom window with a pair of opera glasses.
FANNY: Really!
ISABEL: Really. She looks up and down the street, but mostly over here. Sometimes she forgets to turn out the light in her room, and there she is, spying for all the world to see. Can you see her, Georgie?
GEORGE: Hm? Oh—pardon me, I didn't hear what you were saying.
ISABEL: It's nothing. Just a funny old lady . . . She's gone now. I'm going, too. *(George rises, Isabel moves away from camera towards the door.)* At least, I'm going indoors to read. It's cooler in the house, though it's not really warm anywhere, since nightfall. Summer's dying. How

quickly it goes, once it begins to die. *(We hear her go through the door; George sits down again.)*

FANNY: It seems queer how your mother can use such words—

GEORGE: What words?

FANNY: Words like "die" and "dying." I don't see how she can bear to use them so soon after your poor father—

GEORGE: Seems to me you're using them yourself.

FANNY: I? Never!

GEORGE: Yes, you did.

FANNY: When?

GEORGE: Just this minute.

FANNY: Oh—you mean when I repeated what she just said?

GEORGE: Mmm-hmm.

FANNY: That's hardly the same thing, George.

GEORGE: I don't think you'll convince anybody that Mother's unfeeling.

FANNY: I'm not trying to convince anybody. I mean merely, in my opinion . . . Well, perhaps it's just as wise for me to keep my opinions to myself. *(She slowly rises while speaking and exits.)* There is one thing I hope. I hope at least she won't leave off her full mourning the very anniversary of Wilbur's death.

/ *(A closer shot of George, leaning against the railing and staring off, lost in thought, as music is heard. / A medium long shot of him sitting up on the step at the left as a transparent vision of Lucy—kneeling and*

holding out her hands pleadingly to him—appears on the right as the music continues.) LUCY: George, you *must* forgive me! Papa was utterly wrong! I have told him so, and the truth is that I have come rather to dislike him as you do, and as you always have, in your heart of hearts.

GEORGE: Lucy, are you *sure* you understand me? You say you understand me, but are you *sure?*

LUCY: Oh, so sure! I shall never listen to Father's opinions again. I do not even care if I never see him again!

GEORGE *(gently):* Then I pardon you. *(Her vision disappears and he leans back. / A closer shot of him leaning back against a post; laughter and faint singing is heard, and a vision of Lucy with a group of boys on her own front porch appears over and behind him, at right. / A medium long shot of George sitting and then jumping up as this vision also disappears.)* Pardon nothing! Riffraff! Riffraff! *(He continues to yell as he heads for the door.)* Riffraff! *(He slams the door behind him.)*

Reel 7 begins with a brief scene of Eugene and Isabel beneath a tree; he asks if she doesn't think they should tell George about their plans to marry. She says they should wait.

Next comes an extended family-dinner scene at which George insults Eugene. The only line deleted here is George's sarcastic response (in closeup) to Jack suggesting that Eugene might think him "offensive": "I don't think I could survive that."

Then there is another lengthy scene between George and Fanny as they go up the stairs, during which he forces Fanny to admit she's heard Mrs. Johnson "across the way" talking about the affair and George storms off to confront and berate the neighbor, who throws him out of her house. While Uncle Jack is taking a bath (Welles' setting), he and George argue about the situation. Two brief exchanges were deleted from this scene. The first (which Orson agreed to cut from Rio) immediately follows Jack's riposte, "Why shouldn't they?":

(George looking down grimly.) JACK *(shouting offscreen):* I don't see anything— / *(Jack in tub.)* —precisely monstrous about two people getting married when they're both free and care about each other. What's the matter with their marrying?

/ *(George.)* GEORGE *(angry):* Then it would be monstrous! Monstrous if even this horrible thing hadn't happened. Now, in the face of all this — *(He starts to leave in a fury and Jack calls him back [in the released version he simply leaves, thus losing the end of the scene]. George reapproaches the camera; / cut to Jack in the tub.)*

JACK: You mustn't speak to your mother about this, George! . . . I don't think she's very well.

/ GEORGE *(impatiently)*: Mother? I never saw a healthier person in my life.

/ JACK *(sharply)*: She doesn't let anybody know. . . . She goes to the doctor regularly.

/ GEORGE: Women are always going to doctors regularly.

/ JACK *(warningly)*: I'd leave her alone, George. / *(George goes out the door, slamming it behind him as the camera pans down to follow him; fadeout.)*

Reel 8 fades in with a day sequence that was deleted, about one minute long:

(Reflected in a mirror, George unwraps a box and approaches a mantelpiece as music is heard; his hands appear in the right foreground as he places a picture of his father there, looks around, picks up the picture again, and turns around. / He approaches the camera, the camera tilting upward to follow him to the left foreground. He stops to look at the picture, then places it on a table facing the camera; the camera pans with him to the left as he sits down, back to the camera. The sound of a car is heard.)

Eugene comes to take Isabel for a ride—they had made a date—but George rudely turns him away and slams the door in his face. The next scene, about 2½ minutes long, was cut:

(George enters the room with Wilbur's picture from the front hall, approaching the camera, which then follows him to the window, where he looks out through the curtains; he turns and approaches the foreground, then sits down, his back to the camera; music is heard. / A reverse angle of him as Isabel enters, looks around, sees him.) ISABEL: Why, Georgie! Dear, I waited lunch almost an hour for you, but you didn't come! *(A bell is heard ringing.)* Did you lunch out somewhere?

GEORGE: Yes. *(A maid passes through the room.)*

ISABEL: Did you have plenty to eat?

GEORGE: Yes.

ISABEL: Are you sure? *(She calls to the maid in the hallway.)* I think it's Mr. Morgan, Mary, tell him I'll be there at once.

MARY *(offscreen)*: Yes, ma'am.

ISABEL *(to George, approaching the table where he sits)*: Wouldn't you like to have Aggie fix something now for you in the dining room? Or they could bring it to you here, if you think it would be cozier. *(She sits by the table.)*

GEORGE: No. *(He rises as she talks.)*
ISABEL: I'm going out driving, dear. . . .
(Mary appears in doorway.) MARY: 'Twas a pedlar, ma'am.
ISABEL: Another one? I thought you said it was a pedlar when the bell rang a while ago.
MARY: Mister George said so, ma'am; he went to the door.
ISABEL: There seems to be a great many of them. *(The maid exits.)* What did yours want to sell, Georgie?
GEORGE: He didn't say.
ISABEL: You must have cut him off rather short. *(She picks up the framed picture without yet identifying it.)* Gracious, you *have* been investing! Is it Lucy? *(She looks at the picture; George turns to her.)* Oh! That was nice of you, Georgie. I ought to have had it framed myself, when I gave it to you. *(She replaces the picture on the table; George goes to her, looks at her, and hurries out into the hallway. / A lap dissolve to George passing in the vestibule, looking offscreen and then down, then a lap dissolve to / Isabel sitting beside the table.)*

Jack comes from Eugene's and tells Isabel what had happened, offscreen, while Fanny prevents George from coming in on them. Reel 9: Isabel receives a letter from Eugene asking her to go against George's wishes and marry him. The following scene, set in George's bedroom, was almost entirely reshot by Robert Wise in order to soften George's manner and make him a little more sympathetic. (A slight difference in the filming of Dolores Costello is particularly apparent, since her facial blemishes show for the first and only time in the picture, and the cutting is also somewhat different.) Both versions begin with Isabel asking George if he has read Eugene's letter and George replying that he finds it "offensive" and "insulting." Here is Orson's original version of what follows:

ISABEL *(in a medium closeup):* You can see how fair he means to be.

/ GEORGE: Do you suppose it ever occurs to him that I'm doing my simple duty? / *(Cut back to Isabel, seated on the side of the bed.)* That I'm doing what my father would do if he were here? *(George, seated on the other side of the bed, rising and going over to the fireplace, the camera panning with him as he speaks.)* He said he and you don't care what people say, but I know better! *(He throws the letter into the fire; / a closeup of George turning toward the foreground.)* He may not care—but you do. / *(Isabel, tears in her eyes.)* You're my mother and you're an— / *(George.)*—Amberson—and you're too proud to care for a man who could write such a letter. *(He moves toward the camera; / cut to a medium shot as he passes Isabel toward the door, the camera panning with him. He opens the door and turns to her.)* Well, what are you going to do about it, Mother? / *(A closer shot of him.)* What kind of answer are you going to make to such a letter as that?

/ *(A medium closeup of Isabel, tears in her eyes.)* ISABEL *(brokenly):* Why —I don't quite know, dear.

/ GEORGE *(bitterly, frowning in the doorway):* It seems to me that if he ever set foot in this house again, I . . . I can't speak of it. *(He turns and exits. / Cut back to Isabel; fade dissolve.)*

The night scene that followed, about two minutes long, was cut:

(A letter is slipped under a door in closeup; a shadow moves and music is heard. / Lap dissolve to George picking up the letter and going over to his bed to open it, the camera panning with him. He lies down and reads the letter while Isabel's voice is heard offscreen.) ISABEL: George, my own dearest boy . . . I think it is a little better for me to write to you like this, because I'm foolish and might cry again, and I took a vow once, long ago, that you should never see me cry. I've written Eugene just about what I think you would like me to. *(George turns over on his stomach, his back to camera, and continues to read as the camera slowly approaches him.)* He'll understand about not seeing him. He'll understand that, though I didn't say it in so many words. He'll understand. *(George turns the page.)* My darling, my beloved. I think I shouldn't mind anything very much as long as I have you "all to myself"—as people say—to make up for the long years away from me at college. We'll talk of what's best to do, shan't we? And for all this pain you'll forgive your loving and devoted . . .

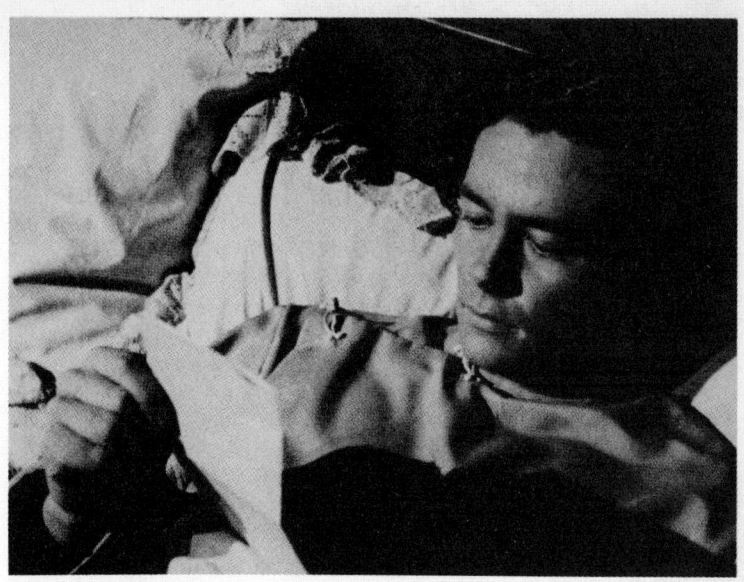

/ *(Closeup of George's face, the letter before it, as he whispers the last word.)* GEORGE: ". . . Mother." *(Fade dissolve as he frowns; music is heard.)* /

Walking down the street, George says goodbye to Lucy—he and Isabel are going off to Europe together; he tries to be tragic about their separation, but Lucy only makes light of his attitude, acting as though she doesn't care at all.

Reel 10: When George leaves, Lucy goes into a drugstore, asks for spirits of ammonia, and faints. We don't actually see her fall, and Welles shot two versions of this: one in which the clerk simply looks down at her, very surprised; the other in which he says, "For Gosh sakes, Miss!" The latter was used, after the previews, but the following brief night scene with the same clerk (Gus Schilling, a Welles regular), which clarified the fainting, was cut:

(The clerk, in a pool hall, turns toward the foreground, bragging.) CLERK: . . . An' if I hadn't been a bright, quick, ready-for-anything young fella— *(Camera moves back as he turns with cue, pushing markers above.)* —she'd a flummoxed plum'! *(He turns away and back while talking.)* One of the prettiest girls that ever walked in our place and

took one good look at me. I guess it must be true what some-a you town wags say about my face . . . huh? *(Fadeout.)*

Also cut was the night scene that followed, which ran for three minutes:

(Fade-in to the Amberson porch, where Fanny and Major Amberson are seated, autos passing in the street far behind them; music is heard.)

MAJOR: Funny thing—these new houses were built only a year ago. They look old already. . . . cost enough money, though. . . . I guess I should have built those apartments after all.

FANNY: Housekeeping in a house is harder than in an apartment.

MAJOR: Yes. Where the smoke and dirt are as thick as they are in the Amberson addition, I guess the women can't stand it. Well, I've got one painful satisfaction—I got my taxes lowered.

FANNY: How did you manage such an economy?

MAJOR: I said it was a *painful* satisfaction. The property has gone down in value, and they assessed it lower than they did fifteen years ago.

FANNY: But farther out—

MAJOR: Oh yes, "farther out"! Prices are magnificent "farther out" and farther in, too! We just happen to be in the wrong spot, that's all.

FANNY *(thoughtfully)*: There seems to be so many ways of making money nowadays. Jack had some scheme he was working on before he went abroad.

MAJOR *(laughing)*: Yes . . . that invention. "Millions in it!" Some new electric headlight. He's putting half he's put by into it. Had a letter from him the other day asking me to go into it, too.

FANNY: He seemed certain it would pay twenty-five percent the first year, and enormously more after that! And I'm only getting four on my principal.

MAJOR: Isabel wants to come home. Her letters are full of it. Jack writes me she talks of nothing else. . . . She's wanted to come for a long while. She ought to come while she can stand the journey.

FANNY: People are making such enormous fortunes out of everything to do with motor cars, it does seem as if . . . I wrote Jack I'd think it over seriously.

MAJOR: Well, Fanny, maybe we'll be partners. How about it? And millionaires, too! *(He laughs; fadeout.)*

In the day scene that followed, the dialogue was changed after previews through redubbing over the backs of Jack and Lucy, using the same first shot. The last three speeches and the entire second shot were cut. Jack has just returned from Paris:

(Fade-in to Jack helping Lucy out of a touring car. Both walk toward the Morgan mansion as he speaks.) JACK: I wonder, Lucy, if history's going on forever repeating itself. I wonder if this town's going on building up things and rolling over them, as poor father once said it was rolling over his poor old heart. It looks like it. *(They go up the steps.)* Well, here's the Amberson mansion again, only it's Georgian instead of nondescript Romanesque; but it's just the same Amberson mansion my father built long before you were born. / *(Cut to front door as they enter the frame and turn; music is heard.)* You're pretty refreshingly out of the smoke up here.

(A butler opens the door behind them.) LUCY: Yes, until the smoke comes and we have to move out farther.

JACK: No . . . no. You'll stay here. It'll be somebody else who'll move out farther. *(He chuckles slightly and takes her arm; they enter the hallway.)*

Jack tells Eugene and Lucy about seeing Isabel and George in Europe, commenting especially on Isabel's poor health. In the next sequence, George brings her home and the family meets them at the station. She is so weak that George has to carry her into the carriage. The following night scene was cut:

(In the Amberson hallway, George sits dejectedly, Jack stands beside him, and the Major stands nearby. A nurse enters through a doorway.) MAJOR: Nurse, when are they going to let me see my daughter? I think she wants— *(The nurse exits, and the Major goes up to George and Jack.)* —I think she wants to see me. *(He stops, somewhat bewildered; a*

doctor appears in the doorway.) A . . . a . . . a . . . I'm sure she wants to see me. . . . I've got something to say to her, too. *(Jack goes to him as he mumbles.)* If she don't want—

JACK: Father!

MAJOR: —to let me in to see . . . *(He turns to Jack; Jack looks at the doctor, and the Major turns to notice him as well. Jack glances at George as the Major approaches the room with the doctor.)*

(Fanny, climbing the steps at right, calls to George in a whisper.) FANNY: George . . . George . . . George . . .

ISABEL *(offscreen)*: Father . . . Father . . .

FANNY: George! *(The Major and doctor exit; Fanny approaches the foreground, still whispering.)* Eugene is here. . . . George!

GEORGE: Hm?

FANNY: He's downstairs.

GEORGE: What?

FANNY: Eugene is here. *(George rises and goes over to her as she continues, cautiously.)* He's downstairs. . . . He wants to know if he can't see her. I didn't know what to say—I said I'd see. I didn't know—the doctor said—

GEORGE *(grimly)*: The doctor said we must keep her peaceful. Do you think that man's coming was very soothing? Why, it would be like taking a stranger into her room. Doesn't he know how sick she is? *(He passes to the right behind her.)* You tell him the doctor said she had to be quiet and peaceful. That's what he *did* say, isn't it? *(She turns slowly and descends the steps while he watches her.)*

The continuation of this scene, which begins reel 11, was reshot by assistant director Freddie Fleck in order to take most of the blame off George and Fanny for not allowing Eugene to see Isabel. Here's how it originally played:

(Eugene, sitting in the hallway at right, rises as he sees Fanny approaching from the background at left. The camera moves closer to her as he passes out of the frame and she stops.) FANNY: The doctor said she must be kept quiet.

EUGENE *(offscreen)*: If I could only look into the room and see her . . . *(re-entering frame)* . . . just for a second.

FANNY *(tensely)*: The doctor said she mustn't see anyone—

EUGENE: All right, Fanny. *(He turns and exits, and she watches him leave down the hall to the front door, the camera panning as he goes out.*

George watches Eugene leave, then has a final scene with Isabel, who asks if Eugene had come to see her. He tells her the truth and she says sadly, "I'd like to have seen him—just once. . . ." It is the last thing she says in the film. The following shot was cut:

(Jack and Fanny are seated in George's room, and the Major is stretched out on his bed. They all rise when George enters; Fanny rushes out, and George addresses Jack.) GEORGE: The doctor in New York said she might get better! Don't you know he did? Don't you know he said she might?

(The Major lies back down; Jack stops by him, then goes over to the doorway and stands there.) /

Lap dissolve to the scene in which we learn of Isabel's death, when Fanny embraces George saying, "She loved you! She loved you!" Her last line, "Oh, how she did love you," was deleted.

As Major Amberson stares into the fire, Welles' voice describes his thoughts. The bits of narration in brackets and all of Jack and Fanny's offscreen dialogue were both deleted from this exquisite scene:

NARRATOR *(offscreen):* And now Major Amberson was engaged in the profoundest thinking of his life. [He was occupied with the first really important matter that had taken his attention since he came home after the Gettysburg campaign, and went into business;] and he realized that everything which had worried him or delighted him during this lifetime between then and today—all his buying and building and trading and banking—that it was all trifling and wasted beside what concerned him now. For the Major knew now that he had to plan how to enter an unknown country where he was not even sure of being an Amberson [—not sure of anything, except that Isabel would help him if she could.]

JACK *(offscreen):* That's true, Fanny. . . . You know, it's a funny thing about the deed to the house. Father—

FANNY *(offscreen):* But it *must* go right, we saw with our own eyes how perfectly it worked in the shop.

JACK *(offscreen):* I'm only glad you didn't go into the confounded thing, to the extent I did.

FANNY *(offscreen):* But the light was so bright no one could face it, and so there can't be any reason for it not to work. . . . It simply must.

JACK *(offscreen):* It certainly was a perfect thing—in the shop! Well, our headlight just won't work, Fanny.

Jack asks the Major if the house was in Isabel's name but he can't remember. Jack says, "The whole estate is about as mixed up as an estate can get." His following line, "I haven't helped out any by this infernal headlight scheme," was cut. Still staring into the fire, the Major ponders whether the earth came out of the sun, and in the released version, his voice fades out as he is talking. Originally the scene continued as follows:

MAJOR: . . . We go back to the earth we came out of, so the earth goes back to the sun it came out of . . . and in a little while we'll all be back in the sun together. And time means nothing, just nothing at all. I wish—

(He glances to the right as George speaks.) GEORGE *(offscreen):* Did you want anything, Grandfather?

MAJOR: Huh.

GEORGE *(offscreen):* Would you like a glass of water.

MAJOR *(speaking slowly):* No . . . no. I . . . I don't want anything at all. I wish somebody could tell me . . .

/ *(A day shot of the cemetery, where we see the tombstones for the Major and Isabel; music is heard. Fadeout.)*

Welles had authorized cutting the cemetery shot in exchange for retaining all of the Major's speech; both went.

Reel 12 begins with the railroad scene in which Jack says goodbye to George. The first half of it was cut:

(A crowded railroad station; day. Jack and George are seated on a bench; bells are heard, and George is taking out his wallet.)

JACK: Just a hundred, Georgie, I know you can't spare it, but I really must have something to tide me over in Washington till things are settled. *(The camera moves closer to them as George glances around nervously.)* Nobody's looking. *(George hands him the money.)* We'll survive, Georgie—*you* will especially. For my part, I'll just be content with just surviving. An ex-Congressman can always be pretty sure of getting a consulship somewhere. Oh, I'll live pleasantly enough with a pitcher of ice under a palm tree, and native folk to wait on me—that part of it will be like home.

GEORGE: I wish you'd take more. *(Jack declines, and George replaces his wallet.)*

JACK: There's one thing I'll say for you, young George; you haven't got a stingy bone in your body. That's the Amberson stock in you. *(They rise and the camera follows them; station noises and a train whistle is heard.)* Well, I may not see you again, Georgie. From this time on it's quite probable we'll only know each other by letter until you're notified as my next of kin that there's an old valise to be forwarded to you, and maybe some dusty curios from the Consulate mantelpiece. . . . Well . . .

The rest of the goodbye scene plays as written. When Jack leaves promising to "send back the money as fast as they pay me," this of course takes on a completely different connotation in the released

version, where we don't know that George has just lent *him the money.*

This is followed in the released version by three scenes Welles had placed later in the film (Eugene and Lucy in their garden; Fanny and George by the boiler; George with Bronson, a prospective employer). In Welles' original, after the railway scene came George's "last walk home" through "what seemed to be the strange streets of a strange city."

These shots were cut from the "last walk home":

(Clothes hanging on lines behind an apartment house as the camera moves to the left.) NARRATOR *(offscreen):* In this alley he'd fought with two boys at the same time, and whipped them. / *(Lap dissolve to the camera moving left past a shabby house and yard; music is heard.)* On that sagging porch a laughing woman had fed him and other boys with doughnuts and gingerbread. / *(Lap dissolve to the camera moving left to a fence across the street from a building.)* Yonder the relics of the iron picket fence he'd made his white pony jump, on a dare. / *(Lap dissolve to the camera moving left past a house.)* And in the shabby stone-faced house behind he'd gone to children's parties—and when he was a little older he'd danced there often and fallen in love with Mary Sharon and kissed her, apparently by force, under the stairs in the hall. . . . / *(Lap dissolve.)*

The sequence continues correctly for four shots in the released version; then this was cut:

NARRATOR *(offscreen):* Tonight would be the last night that he and Fanny were to spend in the house which the Major had forgotten to deed to Isabel.

After the lines "Tomorrow they were to move out. Tomorrow everything would be gone," the scene faded out, and the following night scene, partially cut, faded in:

(The camera moves back from George in the foreground, with his back to the camera, kneeling beside Isabel's dismantled bed.) NARRATOR *(offscreen):* The very space in which tonight was still Isabel's room would be cut into new shapes by new walls and floors and ceilings. And if space itself can be haunted as memory is haunted, then it may be that some impressionable, overworked woman in a "kitchenette," after turning out the light, will seem to see a young man kneeling in the darkness, with arms outstretched through the wall . . . / *(Lap dissolve to a more distant and static shot of George kneeling by the bed.)* . . . clutching at the covers of a shadowy bed. It may seem to her that she hears the faint cry, over and over. . . .

The above shot of George kneeling was retained, as well as his whispered "Mother, forgive me! God forgive me!" And, mercifully, the conclusion of Welles' most affecting speech also remains.

Reel 13 began with the aforementioned George-Fanny boiler scene, the beginning of which was partially reshot by Jack Moss—the dialogue transposed as well—because of some laughs in the preview. With this in mind, Moorehead's hysteria was keyed down considerably at the start of the sequence, which had originally played in one continuous shot, but is now in several pieces.

Here is how the beginning of the scene originally played:

(Fanny sinks down on the floor beside the boiler, staring up at George, who is standing in the right foreground, partly off-camera, his back to us.) FANNY *(hysterically):* You want to leave me in the lurch!

GEORGE: Get up, Aunt Fanny.

FANNY: I can't. I . . . I'm too weak. You're going to leave me in the lurch!

GEORGE: Aunt Fanny! I'm only going to make eight dollars a week at the law office. You'd have to be paying more of the expenses than I would.

FANNY: I'd be paying—I'd be paying—

GEORGE: Certainly you would. You'd be using more of your money than mine—

FANNY: My money! *(She laughs hysterically.)* I have twenty-eight dollars. That's all.

GEORGE: You mean until the interest is due again.

FANNY: I mean that's all. I mean that's all there is. There won't be any interest because there isn't any principal. I know, I told Jack I didn't put everything in the headlight company, but I did—every cent except my last interest payment and—and it's gone.

GEORGE: Why did you wait till now to tell me?

FANNY: I *couldn't* tell till I had to. It wouldn't do any good—nothing does any good, I guess, in this old world! I—I knew your mother'd want me to watch over you and try to have something like a home for you—and I tried—I tried to make things as nice for you as I could. . . . I walked my heels down trying to find a place for us to live—I walked and walked over this town—I didn't ride one block on a streetcar—I wouldn't use five cents no matter how tired I— *(She laughs wildly, hysterically.)* Oh—and now—you don't want—you want—you want to leave me in the lurch!

In the released film, some of these lines were cut or transposed. Fanny's shots in this section were all directed by Welles; a shot of George saying, "Oh, for gosh sakes, will you get up!" was inserted. The rest of the scene—as Fanny's hysteria builds up and George drags her into the next room and finally calms her down—was retained as shot.

After George goes to see Roger Bronson (Erskine Sanford) about a job, Eugene and Lucy have an oblique conversation in their garden. Orson's version of this scene had no score, but an "inspirational," upbeat theme by Roy Webb was added.

(These three scenes were moved ahead of the "comeuppance" scene, when George kneels at Isabel's bed, because Moss and others in Hollywood felt it was the climax of the film and should be as near the end as possible. Under pressure, Welles had agreed to this change but not to all the cuts.)

In Welles' original, the garden scene is followed by George's accident: he gets run over by a young man who says that George "run into me much as I run into him," and won't "get one single cent out of me. . . . I'm perfectly willin' to say I'm sorry for him. . . ." The rest of the scene was cut:

YOUNG MAN *(as the cop shoves him offscreen to the left):* We're both willin' to say. . . . Understand? *(Two cops shove people back as the camera follows them.)*

POLICEMAN: I guess he ain't got much case to give that fellow . . . *(His voice is covered by the sounds of the crowd and a passing truck.)* . . . and that's all he did . . . *(More obscuring noise.)* . . . broke both his legs for him and gosh knows what all. . . .

2ND POLICEMAN: I wasn't here then. What was it?

POLICEMAN: "Riffraff . . ." / (Fadeout.)

Reel 14: Except for the final credits, this whole reel—almost entirely invented by Orson and a considerable departure from the book—was cut; running a few seconds under eight minutes, it is by all counts the most disastrous omission in the film. Replacing it are two poorly acted, written, photographed, and directed (by Fleck) scenes that Welles had nothing whatever to do with, accompanied by "inspirational" music.

Here is the original final sequence (Eugene has just heard of George's accident):

(Inside his factory, Eugene sits in the shadows; he rises, goes to the window and looks out; music is heard. / A closer shot of him looking out grimly; lap dissolve to him leaving and approaching his car, parked inside the gate; / lap dissolve to him addressing the driver in the front seat through the left window.) EUGENE: I won't go home now, Harry. Drive to the City Hospital.

HARRY: Yes, sir . . . Miss Lucy's there. . . . She said she'd expected you'd come there before you go home.

EUGENE: She did?

HARRY: Yes, sir. *(Eugene gets into the car, and the driver starts the engine. / The car leaves the factory; / lap dissolve to the front of the hospital, where the car stops; Eugene gets out, goes up the steps, and enters. /*

Wipe down lap dissolve to Eugene re-emerging and getting back into the car, which drives off.

/ Lap dissolve to tall buildings with a few lit windows; the car stops in front of the building on the right, and Eugene gets out. Traffic noises are heard. / Eugene goes through gates toward the house. / A dark shot of the front door; the doorbell rings and the music we've been hearing stops. The door opens, revealing a man in the hall who is eating; a comedy record is heard indistinctly; the camera approaches the man as he turns away, then pans to the left, showing the landlady rising from a table in the background and approaching. As she crosses to the right, the camera swings to the left, showing Eugene and the landlady in the foreground and women in the background reflected in a mirror.

LANDLADY: What may I do for you, sir?

EUGENE: I'd like to see Miss Fanny Minafer, please.

LANDLADY: Just a moment. *(In the mirror, we see her retreat to the back of the room; Eugene follows more slowly.)* Miss Minafer—there's a gentleman to see you. *(We see Fanny rising from a table in the background while other women watch her curiously; she comes over to Eugene.)*

EUGENE: Hello, Fanny.

FANNY: Hello, Eugene.

(They approach the foreground as he speaks.) EUGENE: I missed you at the hospital. I'm sorry.

(Their reflections cross the screen to the right as she speaks.) FANNY: There's nothing to worry about. *(The camera pans to the right as they enter an adjoining room; the women visible in the mirror continue to watch them with curiosity.)* The doctor told me he's going to get him all well. . . .

EUGENE: Yes . . .

FANNY: I saw Lucy there.

EUGENE: Yes . . .

/ *(A man is eating at a table in the background; the talking comedy record is heard indistinctly.)* FANNY: Lucy looks very well.

EUGENE: Yes . . .

(Fanny sits down at left.) FANNY *(to man eating):* Will you excuse us, Mr. Fleck? You feeling any better? *(Her chair squeaks as she rocks; the man exits.)*

EUGENE *(still standing):* Yes, she got there before I did. How are you, Fanny?

FANNY: Oh, I'm fine. . . . / *(The victrola and its spinning record in the foreground; a man reading on a lounge visible along with Eugene and Fanny in the background.)* Fine . . . *(The man throws his book down and crosses to the right, the camera panning with him as he glances at*

Eugene and Fanny and exits into the hall, closing the doors behind him. / A closer shot of Eugene turning to look at Fanny, her rocking chair squeaking and the comedy record audible.

EUGENE: You look fine. *(He sits down.)* About your nephew—

FANNY: George?

EUGENE: I thought at first I wouldn't go to the hospital.

FANNY: No?

/ *(Cut to closer shot of Eugene.)* EUGENE: I thought it would be hard not to be bitter, but of course I went.

/ *(Cut to Fanny, unemotional, rocking. / Cut to new angle of Fanny from the victrola in foreground, which is making a scratching sound. / Cut to Eugene, who gets up, the camera panning with him as he goes toward the victrola. / Cut to Fanny glancing in his direction.)* FANNY: Think they'll get married . . . after all?

/ *(Cut to victrola in foreground as Eugene's hand lifts the needle off the record and stops the machine.)* EUGENE: Think so, Fanny. / *(Cut to Eugene, his face now visible, turning to Fanny.)* Lucy says so. *(He walks back to Fanny.)*

/ *(Cut to Fanny in rocker as Eugene's shadow passes over her. He enters*

frame at left and sits in the right foreground.) EUGENE: Funny how much like her he looks.

FANNY *(coldly)*: Who?

EUGENE: George.

FANNY: Oh . . .

EUGENE: Like Isabel.

FANNY: Oh . . . *(She smiles slightly.)* Well, it's nice to see you, looking well. . . .

EUGENE: Thanks, Fanny . . . *(He glances at her, hesitates. As he continues, she listens stony-faced.)* I just wanted to come here . . . and . . . you were always so close to Isabel . . . she was so fond of you. . . . You know what he said to me when I went into that room?

/ *(Closeup of Fanny.)* FANNY *(sharply)*: George?

EUGENE *(offscreen)*: He said— / *(Closeup of Eugene, speaking slowly and sadly.)* "You must have known my mother wanted you to come here today so that I could ask you to forgive me." / *(Closeup of Fanny glancing down as her chair squeaks.)* / *(Closeup of Eugene, smiling slightly.)* We shook hands. . . .

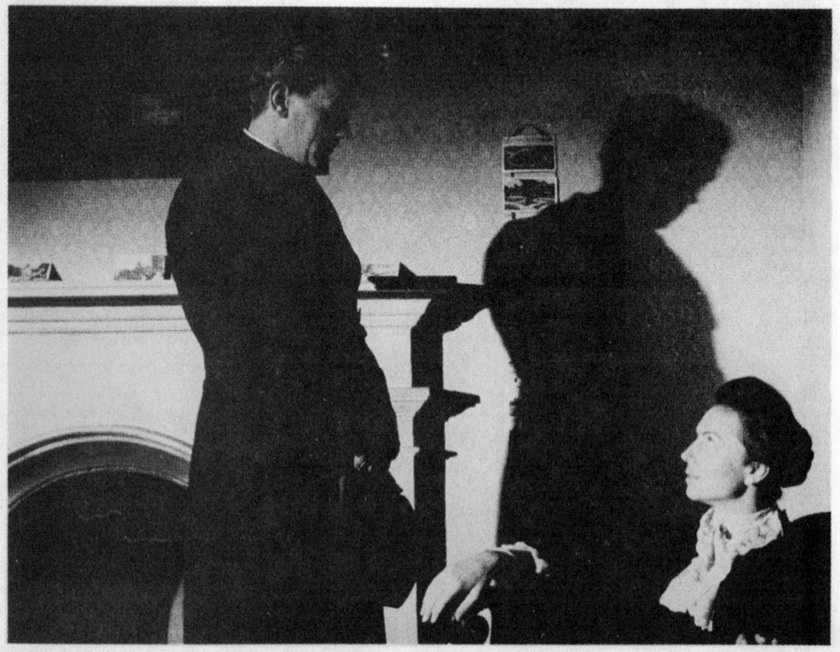

/ *(Closeup of Fanny; her chair squeaks.)* FANNY: Hm . . .

(Medium close shot of Eugene in right foreground, Fanny rocking behind him.) EUGENE *(wistfully):* I wish you could have seen Lucy. *(He looks down, rises, and exits at screen left. / Eugene's shadow passes over Fanny's face in closeup. She looks up to the left, her chair squeaking, as Eugene's voice continues offscreen.)* Fanny . . . you're the only person I'd tell this to . . . but it seemed to me as if someone else was in that room down there at the hospital. *(She stops rocking and stares off tensely; Eugene's shadow again crosses her face. / A low angle of Eugene passing from right to left foreground, the camera panning with him; he stops and looks down to the left.)* And that through me she had brought her boy under shelter again . . . that I'd been true at last to my true love.

/ *(Closeup of Fanny, staring off to the left; her rocking and squeaking resumes.)* FANNY *(looking down):* Yes . . .

/ *(A low angle of Eugene, standing at right in shadow, turning to the right. / Fanny stares down in closeup as his shadow crosses her face. / Eugene in shadow at left, Fanny seen partially at right, still rocking.)*

EUGENE: Well, I'll say goodnight, Fanny. *(She rises slowly and exits to the left; he turns and exits after her.)*

/ *(Cut to a shot of the hallway mirror reflecting women around a table in the background. A door at the right of the mirror opens and Eugene and Fanny enter, the camera panning with them as they approach the right foreground. As they stop, a door is heard closing and a man passes behind them to the left; Fanny looks down—another door is heard closing—and glances at Eugene, smiling grimly as a man enters the hallway in the background, watching them.)* FANNY: Well . . . goodnight, Eugene. *(The man exits.)*

EUGENE *(smiling slightly)*: Goodnight, Fanny. *(He approaches the left foreground; the camera pans as Fanny and then Eugene exit; the mirror reflects Fanny watching him leave and the women at the table in the background watching her curiously. Fanny turns and goes over toward them.)*

/ *(Cut to the car parked outside the boarding house; tall, lit buildings at the end of the street are in the background, and music is heard. The car starts up and drives away from the camera, turns a corner and exits; fadeout.)*

/ *(Music is heard over black leader.)* NARRATOR *(offscreen)*: Ladies and gentlemen, that's the end of the story. / *(The credits follow.)*

EDITOR'S NOTES

1. ROME

Orson Welles' work in theatre and radio represents by far the most prolific part of his career, and a comprehensive, chronological account of that work can be found in Chapter 9. For further information about the legendary *War of the Worlds* broadcast in 1938, see Hadley Cantril's *Invasion from Mars* (New York: Harper & Row, 1966) and Howard Koch's *The Panic Broadcast* (Boston: Little, Brown and Co., 1970; reprint, New York: Avon Books, 1971), both of which reprint Koch's script. Regarding

The Shadow, Frank Brady reports in *Citizen Welles* (New York: Charles Scribner's Sons, 1989) that, because Welles had some difficulty making Lamont Cranston's opening laugh on the show sound sufficiently chilling, Frank Readick's old introduction was used when Welles joined the series, "and no one knew the difference." An excellent evocation of this period can be found in Welles' autobiographical, unproduced screenplay, *The Cradle Will Rock*, written in 1984 (Santa Barbara, Cal.: Santa Teresa Press, 1993).

Among the many actors cited by Welles in this section: Rod La Rocque (1896–1969) was a popular matinee idol of the silent period who appeared in movies through the early 1940s; Werner Krauss (1884–1959), an actor on the German and Austrian stage as well as in many German silents, played the title role in *The Cabinet of Dr. Caligari* (1919); the only surviving film record of Vasili I. Kachalov (1875–1948), an actor in the Moscow Art Theater, apart from fragmentary records of his stage performances, is in Yakov Protazamov's *The White Eagle* (1928), where he costars with his mentor, Vsevolod Meyerhold. A tribute to actor-playwright Eduardo de Filippo (1900–1984) by Welles appeared in French in the Christmas 1982 issue of the French *Vogue*.

Regarding D. W. Griffith, the latter told reporter Ezra Goodman in 1947, "I loved *Citizen Kane* and particularly loved the ideas he [Welles] took from me. The various cycles, the goddam German pictures, I loved them all" (Ezra Goodman, *The Fifty Year Decline and Fall of Hollywood*; New York: Macfadden Books, 1962). It should be added that film scholars now generally believe that Griffith was not so much the inventor of the closeup and camera movement as the first filmmaker who used these and other techniques with the kind of dramatic force that impressed them on a very wide public.

The Merchant of Venice (1969)—probably the least known of Welles' completed films, and the last of his realized Shakespeare adaptations, which he was working on while the interviews in this section were taped —is a forty-minute condensation of the play in color which eliminates the role of Portia. It was originally made for a CBS-TV special that never aired called *Orson's Bag* (see 1970 entry in Chapter 9). Shortly after the film was completed—edited, scored, and mixed—the sound track of two of the three reels was stolen in Rome; it has still not been recovered. Welles willed the film (along with *The Deep* and other unreleased works) to his companion and collaborator, Oja Kodar, who has shown the reel with sound at various Welles tributes, and still hopes to recover the missing elements.

The Deep (1967–69), a film that Welles financed himself and which he left unfinished, was a thriller adapted from Charles Williams' novel *Dead Calm*. (In 1989, an Australian film of that title from the same source, directed by Philip Noyce, was released, with the story's original set of characters reduced from five to three.) Shot in color by Willy Kurant in Yugoslavia, it starred Welles, Jeanne Moreau, Laurence Harvey, Oja Kodar, and Michael Bryant. Conceived as a commercial venture, it was never completed for a number of reasons—including difficulties with the cast and budgetary problems—and the few people who have seen it in its unfinished form describe it as one of Welles' minor efforts, although interesting for Welles' own performance.

About three years after this portion of the interview was taped, I was unexpectedly invited to lunch by Welles in Paris, where I was living at the time, on July 3, 1972—the only time I ever met him. I had been researching his first Hollywood project, *Heart of Darkness*, for an article I was writing ("The Voice and the Eye," *Film Comment*, November-December 1972, published with the screenplay's introductory sequence), and when I discovered that Welles was editing a film in Paris (which was later called *F for Fake*), I wrote to him at his editing studio, asking him a few questions about the conception and casting of the project. I was more than a little surprised when a Welles assistant phoned me two days later, asking if I would care to join Mr. Welles for lunch.

My first question to Welles was why he had invited me. "Because I don't have time to answer your letter," he replied cordially. Although our conversation covered many of the same points about *Heart of Darkness* that are discussed here, a few additional details are worth noting. He had seen Carol Reed's Conrad adaptation *Outcast of the Islands* as well as Richard Brooks' *Lord Jim*, and regarded both with disdain; he had written scripts of his own adapting both *Lord Jim* and *Victory*, but showed less interest in the filmic possibilities of *Nostromo*. At one point, he had seriously considered shooting *Heart of Darkness* on location, and he emphasized the contemporary political implications of the project for him, making particular reference to Otto Skorzeny (1908–1975)—an Austrian who became an SS officer and was one of the models for Kurtz—and some of the then recent activities in the Belgian Congo. (It was only after our meeting that I looked up who Skorzeny was; considering that he became prominent in the news only after he rescued Mussolini from imprisonment in 1943, it is possible that Welles might have confused him with another Nazi of the 1930s.) When I asked Welles at what point he had abandoned the *Heart of Darkness* project, he replied that he had never abandoned it—he still wanted to do it—a point that he reiterated when the question of the casting of Kurtz came up. (He stressed that he might have taken the part himself only because he hadn't come up with anyone else, and added, "I'm still looking.") Seven years after our conversation, Francis Ford Coppola's *Apocalypse Now*, scripted by John Milius, Coppola, and Michael Herr—which transferred and updated Conrad's novella to Vietnam, and may well have been partially inspired by Welles' project—was released to wide acclaim.

According to Brady's *Citizen Welles*, William Vance, not Roger Hill, supplied the camera for *Hearts of Age*; and Welles' original two-picture contract with RKO, which was signed on July 22, 1939, was more restrictive than other accounts suggest, including the one given here. It should be noted, however, that because of this contract, Turner Entertainment was prevented from colorizing *Citizen Kane* in the 1980s.

No Welles scholarship to date has uncovered any of the stories for the pulps that Welles wrote as a teenager in Seville, all of which were apparently published under pseudonyms; but as a measure of how warmly he remembered this portion of his youth, at his own request his ashes are buried in that part of Spain today. For accounts of Welles' year in Ireland, see Micheál Mac Liammóir's *All for Hecuba* (London: Methuen, 1950), Brady's *Citizen Welles*, and Chapter 9.

2. GUAYMAS

Given the virtually mythological status of *Citizen Kane* in Welles' career, it isn't surprising that it has generated by far the most debate of all his films. Two publications in particular should be cited: "Raising Kane," by Pauline Kael, which appeared originally in two successive issues of *The New Yorker* (February 20 and 27, 1971), and then as a lengthy preface to the script, published later the same year (*The "Citizen Kane" Book*, Boston: Atlantic/Little, Brown & Co.), and Robert L. Carringer's *The Making of "Citizen Kane"* (Berkeley, Cal.: University of California Press, 1985). Kael's essay was replied to at length by Bogdanovich and Welles in a point-by-point refutation published by Bogdanovich, "The *Kane* Mutiny," in *Esquire* (October 1972), which included certain portions of the interview in Chapter 2. Other rebuttals included Ted Gilling's interviews with George Coulouris and Bernard Herrmann in *Sight and Sound* (Spring 1972), polemics by Joseph McBride (*Film Heritage*, Fall 1971) and myself (*Film Comment*, Spring 1972 and Summer 1972), and remarks in the Welles biographies of Barbara Leaming (*Orson Welles*, New York: Viking, 1985) and Frank Brady.

The major focus of Kael's essay is its defense and celebration of screenwriter Herman J. Mankiewicz as the principal, neglected creative force behind *Kane*. According to Kael, the script was written almost entirely by Mankiewicz, and Welles had actively plotted to deprive him of any screen credit.

> . . . Welles probably made suggestions in his early conversations with Mankiewicz, and since he received copies of the work weekly while it was in progress at Victorville, he may have given advice by phone or letter. Later, he almost cer-

tainly made suggestions for cuts that helped Mankiewicz hammer the script into tighter form, and he is known to have made a few changes on the set. But Mrs. Alexander, who took the dictation from Mankiewicz, from the first paragraph to the last, and then, when the first draft was completed and they all went back to Los Angeles, did the secretarial work at Mankiewicz's house on the rewriting and the cuts, and who then handled the script at the studio until after the film was shot, says that Welles didn't write (or dictate) one line of the shooting script of *Citizen Kane*.

. . . Mankiewicz began to realize that he'd made a very bad financial deal, and that the credit might be more important than he'd anticipated. After talks with Mrs. Alexander and the Mercury people who visited on weekends, he decided he was going to get screen credit, no matter what his bargain with Welles had been. Meanwhile, Houseman . . . discovered once again, and as so many others had, that it wasn't easy to get your name on anything Orson Welles was involved with. Houseman was apparently fed up with arguments, and he says he waived his claim when he saw how determined Welles was; he left for New York and got started on preparations for *Native Son*. But Mankiewicz was an experienced Hollywood hand and veteran of credit brawls who kept all his drafts and materials, and a man who relished trouble. He had ample proof of his authorship, and he took his evidence to the Screen Writers Guild and raised so much hell that Welles was forced to split the credit and take second place in the listing.

Later in the same essay, Kael recounts another story:

Nunnally Johnson says that while *Citizen Kane* was being shot, Mankiewicz told him that he had received an offer of a ten-thousand-dollar bonus from Welles (through Welles' "chums") to hold to the original understanding and keep his name off the picture. . . . Mankiewicz said he was tempted by Welles' offer. As usual, he needed money, and, besides, he was fearful of what would happen when the picture came out —he might be blackballed forever. William Randolph Hearst, like Stalin, was known to be fairly Byzantine in his punishments. At the same time, Mankiewicz knew that *Citizen Kane* was his best work, and he was proud of it. He told Johnson that he went to Ben Hecht with his dilemma, and that Hecht, as prompt with advice as with scripts, said, "Take the ten grand and double-cross the son of a bitch."

I asked Nunnally Johnson if he thought Mankiewicz's story was true, and Mankiewicz had actually got the offer and had taken Hecht's advice. Johnson replied, "I like to believe he did." It's not unlikely.

Bogdanovich's "The *Kane* Mutiny" replies to all three of these charges, beginning with the first:

> Over the years, Miss Kael has been writing against those of her fellow critics, like [Andrew] Sarris (and he is now in the majority), who believe that when a film aspires to the level of art, the man in charge of its making, the director, must be held responsible for the result or blamed accordingly. Miss Kael would have it otherwise. By taking a great director (Welles) and seeking to prove that a great film of his *(Kane)* was actually the creation of an "old-time" screenwriter (Herman J. Mankiewicz), a member and product of the old Hollywood system, she clearly hopes to demolish this idea forever.
>
> Welles was a shrewd choice. He's somebody people love to attack, anyway. Whether he deserves all that kicking around is another matter of opinion. It may easily be argued that he brings it on himself, and just as easily that it's not only in Hollywood that the price of real stature in a man is the eager venom with which others try to cut him down. For over three years now I've been working on a book about Welles, not so much straining for new aesthetic evaluations, but quite simply, trying to pin down what can be documented as the truth about his career to date as a filmmaker. Not an easy job, but, nearing the end of it, I think I can state with some authority that Ken Russell [in *Books and Bookmen*] does not exaggerate when he calls Miss Kael's article "Hedda Hopperish and Louella Parsonish." Strong words, but, unfortunately, Miss Kael does indeed manage to reach the level of the old gossipmongers when she claims that Mankiewicz, the credited co-author of the *Kane* script, "was blackmailed into sharing credit with Welles." Equally strong words, and the bitter fact is that in the published version of his own film Welles stands accused of being, in effect, a liar and a thief. Well, either he is or he isn't.
>
> Miss Kael passes on a particularly scabrous anecdote from screenwriter Nunnally Johnson, who, she says, told her Mankiewicz had once told him that Welles had offered a $10,000 bribe to Mankiewicz to leave his name off the screen. To speculate that Johnson, an able scenarist, may feel (as many others do) justifiably bitter about the degree of credit directors are often given at the writers' expense, would probably be playing Miss Kael's guessing game. But Johnson's reply to her when she asked him if he actually believed this piece of gossip speaks for itself. Said Johnson: "*I like to believe he did*" (italics mine). Charles Lederer, another screenwriter, one of the best and wittiest, and an intimate friend of Mankiewicz's, told me *he* didn't believe this story for a minute. But Miss Kael, like

Johnson, *would* "like to believe it," and leaves this ugly little rumor unresearched but on the record.

Bogdanovich quotes Lederer again a bit further in his article:

"Manky was always complaining and sighing about Orson's changes. And I heard from Benny [Hecht] too, that Manky was terribly upset. But, you see, Manky was a great *paragrapher*—he wasn't really a picture writer. I read *his* script of the film—the long one called *American*—before Orson really got to changing it and making his version of it—and I thought it was pretty dull."

Miss Kael turns this incident into a key event: the direct cause of the fracas which very nearly led to the film being suppressed. Hearst's mistress was the actress Marion Davies (a good portion of Miss Kael's attacks on the film are aimed at those places where it departs from the real Hearst-Davies story) and Mankiewicz asked Lederer, who was Miss Davies' nephew, to read the script and tell him if he thought the principals, particularly his aunt, would be angry with him about it.

Miss Kael writes that after reading it, Lederer was extremely concerned, as a result of which the Hearst lawyers were finally called in. "That," Lederer told me, "is 100 percent, whole cloth lying." He did not, as Miss Kael claims (she never bothered to check with him), give the script to Miss Davies: "I gave it *back* to him. He asked me if I thought Marion would be offended and I said I didn't think so. The script I read didn't have any flavor of Marion and Hearst—Robert McCormick was the man it was about." McCormick, the Chicago press lord, divorced his first wife, Edith Rockefeller, and married Gauma Walska, whom he tried to push into prominence as an opera star. Kane divorces his first wife (the daughter of an American president) and tries to make Susan Alexander an opera star. Miss Kael barely mentions this obvious parallel, and the weight of her piece plays it down. It should be clear that the story of the Chicago press lord and his fairly untalented mistress contributed even more to Kane's personal story than did Hearst's backing of the delightful screen comedienne Marion Davies often was.

Lederer went on: "Also, I knew Marion would never read it. As I said, it [Mankiewicz's script] was pretty dull—which is not to say I thought the picture was dull. Orson vivified the material, changed it a lot, and I believe transcended it with his direction. There *were* things in it that were based on Hearst and Marion—the jigsaw puzzles, Marion's drinking—though

> this was played up more in the movie than in the script I read, probably because it was a convenient peg for the girl's characterization. . . ."

Still later, Bogdanovich addresses the matter of the script's authorship more directly by quoting Richard Barr (formerly Richard Baer), the associate producer of *Citizen Kane* who was then (in 1972) president of the League of New York Theatres, and the producer of all the Edward Albee plays, among many others:

> "The revisions made by Welles were not limited to mere general suggestions, but included the actual rewriting of words, dialogue, changing of sequences, ideas and characterizations, and also the elimination and addition of certain scenes."
>
> This . . . is from an affadavit Barr swore out in May 1941 concerning the writing of *Kane* (the necessity for this document had arisen from trouble—or the threat of it—from the Hearst powers): "Mankiewicz was engaged by Mercury or RKO for the purpose of *assisting* [italics mine] in writing a script. . . ." Miss Kael failed to interview Welles' secretary. Her name is Katherine Trosper and she was with him from the rough-draft beginnings, through the final "mix" of the finished print of the film. Is there a better witness? Not for Miss Kael's purpose. She prefers to take on face value a statement by Mankiewicz's secretary that "Orson Welles never wrote (or dictated) one word of *Citizen Kane*." This secretary was employed by Mankiewicz when he was working quite separately, in another part of California, where he was sent by Welles to put together his own draft of a shooting script, based on their meetings together. She could have had no knowledge of Welles' script; she was never present during the working meetings between the two, when the conception and basic shape of the story was developed, nor could she have known what happened to the Mankiewicz drafts *after* they were passed on to Welles, changed and rewritten by him, and incorporated in his own screenplay. When I repeated to Miss Trosper recently Miss Kael's assertion that Mankiewicz was the sole author of *Kane*, her answer was not a little derisive: "Then I'd like to know," she said, "what was all that stuff I was always typing for Mr. Welles!"
>
> "It is not possible," says Mr. Barr in his affadavit, "to fix the actual number of complete redrafts [by Welles] as changes were being continuously made on portions that had previously been written." In my own conversations with Mr. Barr, he told me he remembered seeing Orson "fume about the pages that arrived from Mankiewicz. He thought a lot of it was

> dreadful." Barr says he, himself, was "in the room and saw" the writing of various important scenes in the script. Miss Trosper agrees. "Orson was always writing and rewriting. I saw scenes written during production. Even while he was being made up, he'd be dictating dialogue."
>
> Miss Trosper and Mr. Barr are active, in good health, accessible, and both are living, as Miss Kael does, in New York City. Neither received so much as an inquiry about their participation in the making of *Citizen Kane*. But then, neither did Welles. In fact, there is nothing to show that Kael interviewed anyone of real importance associated with the actual making of the film.
>
> In 1940, the year before *Kane*, screenplay credit was given to a director or producer on only five pictures out of 590 released in the U.S. In two cases out of these five the producers (Gene Towne and Graham Baker) were script writers who had become producers and always wrote their own screenplays. Yet, Miss Kael maintains that it was not only easy, but common practice for directors and producers to grab screenwriting credits which they didn't deserve, because at this period the real authors had no power to stop them. "That's one of the main reasons why the Screen Writers' Guild was started," says Lederer. "But by the time of *Kane* it was quite effective in preventing that sort of thing. It had to be *proved* by them, as it does now, that the director or producer contributed more than 50 percent of the script." The *Kane* case never came before the Guild's Board. "If *Kane* had gone to arbitration," Lederer concludes, "Orson would certainly have won, and Manky must have known that."
>
> Far from trying to bribe his co-author to consent to having his name taken off the screen, Welles, entirely on his own initiative, and not bound by any such contractual requirement, gave Mankiewicz top billing.

Indeed, the first of Kael's charges, which even Robert Carringer calls "a flagrant misrepresentation," has no factual basis beyond a willful confusion about how the script was written, apparently fostered by various statements from John Houseman—Welles' producer and partner in the Mercury stage and radio productions, who had gone through a violent break with Welles in Hollywood during the work on *Heart of Darkness*, and was later hired back to assist Mankiewicz on the *Kane* script.

Houseman repeated the notion that Mankiewicz was the script's sole author many times, in many contexts, up until his death, without ever explaining many anomalies about this—such as his own cable to Mankiewicz from New York, quoted by Frank Brady in *Citizen Welles*, which reads in part [passages in square brackets are my own]: "Leaving tonight for Carolina to confer with Paul Green and Richard Wright [on *Native*

Son]. . . . Received your cut version and several new scenes of Orson's. . . . After much careful reading I like all Orson's scenes with exception of Kane Emily sequence [apparently the breakfast montage, which is found in none of Mankiewicz's drafts]." It should be added that even though Houseman is often a relatively reliable source on certain matters regarding Welles' work, his memoirs are highly misleading and inaccurate concerning aspects of the *Heart of Darkness* project (which he claims never developed beyond a first-draft script, despite many scripts and other documents to disprove this) as well as *Kane*.

As Welles explained the screenwriting process of *Kane* in a letter to the London *Times* (November 17, 1971), in an account which no scholar has contested,

> The initial ideas for this film and its basic structure were the result of direct collaboration between us; after this we separated and there were two screenplays: one written by Mr. Mankiewicz, in Victorville, and the other, in Beverly Hills, by myself. . . . The final version of the screenplay . . . was drawn from both sources.

Although the printed shooting script of *Kane* credits both Mankiewicz and Welles, in that order, just as the film's final credits do (with the consequence that Welles, as legally established co-author, received royalties on *The "Citizen Kane" Book*, along with Kael and with Mankiewicz's heirs), Kael's first charge, which has remained unmodified in all subsequent editions of the book, continues to be believed by a good many readers. Her second charge—that Welles tried to deprive Mankiewicz of any screen credit—has never been substantiated either, although Carringer curiously concludes that "it seems to be true." Carringer's evidence is Mankiewicz's contract with the Mercury Theatre (he had no contract with RKO), which "contained the standard waiver of rights of authorship," and letters from Arnold Weissberger (Welles' lawyer) to Welles and RKO's legal department. All this *does* point toward a possible denial of screen credit to Mankiewicz—following the precedent of the Mercury radio adaptations, which assigned no scriptwriter credits and fostered the false impression of Welles as sole adaptor—but nothing in the evidence cited by Carringer indicates that Welles was an instigator of this plan, or even necessarily a supporter of it.

Kane can be seen in two diametrically opposed fashions. One can see it as the first feature of a maverick independent filmmaker, and the only one in which he was accorded both full use of a Hollywood studio *and* final cut. Alternatively, one can view *Kane* as the ultimate vindication of the Hollywood mainstream, showing that major creative talents (including Welles, Mankiewicz, and cinematographer Gregg Toland) could be brought together and used to their fullest advantage.

According to Kael, *Kane* is a culmination of 1930s newspaper comedies, a picture whose greatness stems from the collaboration of disparate talents rather than a single guiding intelligence (also Carringer's thesis), and a "*shallow* masterpiece" (her emphasis). The net result was to make Welles' best-known work also seem like one of his safest. (Years earlier, however, Kael had described *Kane* in a short review as "the most controversial one-man show in film history," making it clear that the "one-man" in question was Welles, not Mankiewicz; and she was one of the most eloquent and passionate defenders of Welles' *Falstaff*: see her book *Kiss Kiss Bang Bang* [Boston: Atlantic/Little, Brown & Co., 1968] for both reviews.)

Regarding Welles' troubled relationship with Houseman, which is alluded to only elliptically here, one should consult Barbara Leaming's Welles biography and Bogdanovich's "The *Kane* Mutiny" to get Welles' side of the story. [For Houseman's side, see the first volume of his memoirs, *Run-Through* (New York: Simon and Schuster, 1972).] During my meeting with Welles in 1972, described in the notes for Chapter 1, the question of Houseman and his memoirs came up when I alluded to some of Houseman's skeptical remarks about the *Heart of Darkness* project. After Welles insisted that Houseman was in no position to have known much about the project because he wasn't even around for any of the story conferences, he went on to say (I quote from memory), "He's the worst kind of enemy someone can possibly have, because he gives the impression to others"—meaning me in this case—"of being sympathetic." "That's really a pity," I replied, "because his discussion of the Mercury radio shows is probably the most detailed account of them that's appeared anywhere in print." There was a long, smoldering silence at this point—the only moment during our lunch when Welles betrayed any anger—after which he said quietly, with a touch of both sorrow and sarcasm, "So be it."

It's worth adding, however, that *Citizen Kane* was not the last Welles project that Houseman was involved with. Between the completion of *Kane* and its release, the two collaborated once again, on their last stage production together in New York, an adaptation of Richard Wright's powerful, best-selling novel about American racism, *Native Son*, starring Canada Lee as Bigger Thomas, which Wright himself helped to adapt, and which enjoyed a successful run. Like the Welles productions of *Julius Caesar* and *Shoemaker's Holiday*, the show ran without an intermission; its main action was set in a courtroom (where the audience was encouraged at certain points to regard itself as a jury), with eight flashbacks, and, like the novel, centered around Bigger Thomas' murder of a young white woman. (One of the flashback settings was the tenement flat of the Thomas family, where one of the Rosebud sleds used in *Citizen Kane* figured as a prop.)

When Welles recalls "playing himself" on *The March of Time* radio show, it is possible that he is misremembering the actual occasion and alluding to his performance of a scene from Archibald MacLeish's *Panic*, a week after he performed that play on the stage in March 1935, rather than his production of his black *Macbeth* two years later. (See Chapter 9, March 15 and March 22, 1935, entries.)

A few basic dates might be helpful in understanding Welles' discussion of his childhood. He was born May 6, 1915. His mother, Beatrice Ives Welles, died May 10, 1924; his father, Richard Head Welles, died December 28, 1930. His parents separated when he was six, and his relationship with Dr. Maurice Bernstein—who was close to his mother, and who became his official guardian after his father's death—virtually went back to his infancy. He attended the Todd School from 1926 through 1930. For the most detailed discussion of this period, see Barbara Leaming's *Orson Welles*.

Regarding Preston Sturges, his first play was *The Guinea Pig*, which ran for 64 performances; *Strictly Dishonorable*, which opened about eight months later in 1929, wound up running for 557 performances.

Thornton Wilder, whom Welles first met in 1933, was instrumental in getting Welles his touring job with Katharine Cornell by giving him an introduction to Alexander Woollcott; the tour lasted from 1933 to 1934.

Akira Kurosawa's *Rashomon* (1951), the first of his films to get worldwide attention, is set near Kyoto in the eighth century, and describes a rape and murder from the viewpoints of the four people present, each of whom contradicts the other three concerning the basic facts of what happened.

The term "pan focus" was used in *Life* magazine's May 26, 1941, article about Welles, shortly after *Kane*'s release. For the same illustrated story, Toland shot three still photographs to demonstrate the differences between "pan focus," "the old way," and "a conventional closeup."

Dorothy Comingore entered films as Linda Winters in Columbia comedy shorts of the mid-thirties after some stage experience in stock. She appeared in Three Stooges comedies and some low-budget Westerns and did some bits in a few other films in the late thirties (e.g., *Scandal Sheet* and *Mr. Smith Goes to Washington* in 1939) before landing the lead female part in *Citizen Kane*.

For further comments from Welles on the nonfunctionality of producers and agents, see his feisty and controversial article for the February 1941 *Stage*, "Orson Welles Writing About Orson Welles," reprinted in *Hollywood Directors, 1941–1976*, edited by Richard Koszarski (New York: Oxford University Press, 1977).

Regarding Welles' fondness for birds and his parrot in Spain, the latter can be seen with him in *Treasure Island* (1972)—a film that he scripted as well as acted in—along with his pet monkey, Mimi.

Targets (1968), Bogdanovich's first feature, scripted by him, with uncredited assistance from Samuel Fuller, and based on a story by Bogdanovich and Polly Platt, alternates two stories, both set in Los Angeles, which come together in the final sequence: a horror actor (Boris Karloff) decides to retire, claiming his films can't compete with the horrors of contemporary life, and a Vietnam veteran (Tim O'Kelly) goes mad, kills his family, climbs a tower, and shoots people passing on the freeway.

For more information about the cut brothel sequence in *Kane*, see Mankiewicz and Welles' shooting script in *The "Citizen Kane" Book* and (for illustrations) Carringer's *The Making of "Citizen Kane."*

3. NEW YORK

For a detailed account of part of the shooting of *Don Quixote*, see "*Don Quixote:* Orson Welles' Secret," by Audrey Stainton (who worked as Welles' secretary in 1958–1959), in the Autumn 1988 *Sight and Sound.* (See also the 1960 entry in Chapter 9.) Further information about *The Deep* can be found in the notes to Chapter 1. On *Chimes at Midnight*, Bridget Gellert Lyons' 1988 volume on the film in the Rutgers University Press Films in Print series is indispensable.

Perhaps the most important plot difference between Welles' radio adaptation of *The Magnificent Ambersons* and his subsequent film adaptation is the complete absence on radio of Aunt Fanny as a character. (This October 29, 1938, broadcast is available in Voyager's "deluxe" edition of *Ambersons* on laser disk.) Apart from Ray Collins, the casting of the radio show was completely different (see Chapter 9, October 29, 1939), and viewers of the film who think that Welles should have played George Minafer rather than cast Tim Holt in the part might revise their opinion after hearing Welles as George on the radio show.

For more details about Welles' various projects with Alexander Korda, see Chapter 9.

According to Joseph Cotten (*Vanity Will Get You Somewhere* [New York: Avon, 1987]), Frank Lloyd Wright expressed skepticism about the suitability of adapting a novel such as *The Magnificent Ambersons* into a film, until Welles arranged for him to see an hour of the rough cut, which caused him to reverse his position.

It's worth noting that some of the changes made in the order of certain sequences at RKO in Welles' absence conform to the order of sequences in his original script. As in many other Welles films, he revised many aspects while shooting and editing, and the final boarding-house sequence, for instance, cannot be found in the original script (which ended with Eugene writing a "letter" to Isabel in his diary, an entry he recites offscreen).

Perhaps the most important sequence scripted and shot by Welles for *Ambersons* and deleted by his own decision, before he left for Rio, was a virtuoso, lengthy subjective-camera sequence, shot in a single take, that moved through the dismantled Amberson mansion before fading out; this shot was to come immediately before the climactic shot of George kneeling at Isabel's bed. It would have been accompanied by narration about the fate of "the very space in which tonight was still Isabel's room" (see Appendix), and it is described in Welles' script as follows:

> On the Narrator's words, "move out" the door opens and CAMERA MOVES thru it into the house.
>
> MOVING SHOT as CAMERA WANDERS SLOWLY about the dismantled house—past the bare reception room; the dining room which contains only a kitchen table and two kitchen chairs; up the stairs, close to the smooth walnut railing of the balustrade. Here CAMERA STOPS for a moment, then PANS down to the heavy doors which mask the dark, empty library. HOLD on this for a short pause, then CAMERA PANS back and CONTINUES, even more slowly, up the stairs to the second floor hall where it MOVES up to the closed door of Isabel's room. The door swings open and we see Isabel's room is still as it always has been; nothing has been changed.

In my 1972 meeting with Welles in Paris, Welles admitted that this sequence—which represented his most sustained use of the subjective camera technique he had planned for *Heart of Darkness*—wound up making him feel somewhat disenchanted with the technique after he shot it. It's worth adding, however, that striking, less sustained uses of the subjective camera were employed in the sequence devoted to the mourning of Wilbur Minafer's death, as well as at the beginning of the boarding-house sequence that concluded Welles' original version (see Appendix), when Eugene arrives at the front door.

Finally, it is also worth noting that the use of a comedy record as ironic counterpoint in this sequence inspired Bogdanovich to make a similar use of a 1950s comedy record, "It's in the Book," in the final sequence of *The Last Picture Show* (1971), his second feature, a fact confirmed to me by Bogdanovich himself.

4. VAN NUYS

Welles' unfavorable review of Eisenstein's *Ivan the Terrible, Part I* in his newspaper column, nearly all of which is reproduced in the text, was followed in his next column (May 25, 1945) by an extended comparison of the film with the contemporary Hollywood release *Wilson*, a piece which concluded as follows:

> The star in a Russian studio is the director. When his camera performs as a principal actor we are offered great cinema. But when that camera dominates the action at the expense of the rest of the performers, it's as tiresome as any star hogging closeups, or taking pleasure in the sound of his own voice.
>
> Because of the inferiority of Russian film stock, lenses, and other equipment, the camera must assert itself by what it selects, and by the manner of selection. The Hollywood camera has a merchant's eye and spends its time lovingly evaluating texture, the screen being filled as a window is dressed in a swank department store.
>
> We have much to learn from each other.

Welles' characterization of Erich von Stroheim as a "nice Jewish boy" alludes to Denis Marion's discovery, several years after Stroheim's death in 1957, that the "von" in his name, his alleged military background and links with the Austrian aristocracy, and his family background were all basically fabrications (see Marion's "Stroheim, the Legend and the Fact," *Sight and Sound*, Winter 1961–1962; see also Richard Koszarski, *The Man You Loved to Hate*; New York: Oxford University Press, 1983). Welles' prescience about this matter can be noted in a French interview he gave in 1958 (published in *L'Express*, June 5) in which he described Stroheim's art as "Jewish baroque."

A few of the negative comments made by Welles about other directors that were originally removed from the manuscript have been reinstated here if the directors in question are no longer alive. (Very few of these directors, in fact, are still living.) I have retained Welles' letter to Bogdanovich about this matter, however, because of its own intrinsic interest, and have followed the wishes stated there. (For additional remarks by Welles about contemporary directors, see especially *Interviews with Film Directors*, edited by Andrew Sarris New York: Avon Books, 1969.)

On the matter of *It's All True*, more recent developments—both the recovery of certain unedited rushes that were previously thought lost, and significant advances in film scholarship—have confirmed the major thrust of Welles' remarks while sowing some doubts about a few of the individual details. For the record, Welles' statement that *It's All True* was originally supposed to be three separate films (rather than one three-part film) is unsupported by any of the detailed documentation in the Mercury files, and there is some evidence that he may have seen some portions of the Jangadeiros footage while trying to find backers for the project after his return to the United States (although most of this footage, one should stress, was processed only after his death.)

Because of widespread misunderstandings about *It's All True* which persist to the present day, I have elected to break a rule applied elsewhere in the editing of this book and have retained part of an article that has previously appeared in print, Richard Wilson's "It's Not *Quite* All True." Only a small part of the beginning of this piece, however, is quoted, and interested readers are strongly urged to look up the entire essay, one of the most useful and meticulous pieces of Welles scholarship that we have.

The discovery in the mid-1980s of about two thirds of the unedited material shot by Welles in Fortaleza at the very end of his Brazilian sojourn, most of which had never been seen (even by Welles) or even processed prior to its relatively recent discovery, represents one stage in a contemporary reevaluation. (Samples of this footage are visible in Richard Wilson's 1986 short *Four Men on a Raft*, and plans are afoot to expand this into a documentary feature.) Then came the revelatory research carried out in Brazil, Mexico, and the United States by Robert Stam and Catherine Benamou—research that is still in progress, but which has already yielded some fascinating discoveries. Drawing on an array of Hollywood and Brazilian documents, including the massive research conducted and commissioned by Welles at the time, Stam, for instance, persuasively argues that most of the complaints about Welles' profligacy in Brazil can be attributed to his radical pro-black stance, including his enjoyment of the company and collaboration of blacks, as well as his insistence on featuring non-whites as the central characters in both of the film's Brazilian episodes. Based on this reading, which Stam explores in detail, one is encouraged to reread most biographical accounts of Welles' "Brazilian episode" as unconsciously but unmistakably racist. (See, in particular, Stam's "Orson Welles, Brazil, and the Power of Blackness," and articles by Catherine Benamou and Susan Ryan, in *Persistence of Vision* [special Welles issue], no. 7, 1989; Benamou is currently preparing a book on the subject.)

In her Welles biography, Barbara Leaming points out two important references to *It's All True* in *The Lady from Shanghai*—the use of Grisby (Glenn Anders) as a parody of Rockefeller, and the mention of Fortaleza in Michael O'Hara's story about sharks devouring each other.

In his collection *Celebrity Circus* (New York: Delacorte Press, 1970), Charles Higham denies that Welles ever made an offer to check his facts in *The Films of Orson Welles* (Berkeley, Cal.: University of California Press, 1970), but adds, "Had he done so, I would certainly not have ruined the book by presenting his own doctored version of the facts." It should be stressed, however, that Higham's subsequent book, *Orson Welles: The Rise and Fall of an American Genius* (New York: St. Martin's Press, 1985), which silently corrects many of the errors in *The Films of Orson Welles*, is even more vituperative than the previous book, and contains numerous factual inaccuracies of its own.

In an article written for the Arts & Leisure section of the Sunday *New York Times* ("Is It True What They Say About Orson?," August 30, 1970), Bogdanovich responded both to Higham's first book on Welles and to Raymond Sokolov's sympathetic review of it in *Newsweek*; rebuttals from both Higham and Sokolov appeared in the September 17, 1970, issue of the Sunday *Times*.

5. BEVERLY HILLS

The first of Bogdanovich's Hollywood columns for *Esquire*, alluded to at the beginning of this section, is reprinted in the revised and expanded edition of Bogdanovich's collection *Pieces of Time* (New York: Arbor House, 1985) under the title "Over the Hill." At the time this piece was written, in January 1972, Josef von Sternberg had died three years previously at seventy-five, after sixteen years of inactivity; Fritz Lang was eighty-two and hadn't worked since 1961; King Vidor, four years younger, had not been employed for thirteen years; John Ford, then seventy-seven, had made his last film in 1966; Raoul Walsh had made his last film at seventy-seven in 1964.

According to Ephraim Katz's *The Film Encyclopedia*, *Jane Eyre* was not Elizabeth Taylor's first film role but her third, preceded by *There's One Born Every Minute* and *Lassie Come Home*.

On the subject of magic, it is worth pointing out that one film project Welles was still working on when he died was *The Magic Show*, a film featuring some of his best acts of prestidigitation, all done without camera tricks, which was shot intermittently between 1976 and 1985. (See Chapter 9, June 1976 entry and following, for further details.) A biography of Welles concentrating on his involvement in magic is presently being written by magic specialist Bart Whaley.

For more information about Welles' interest in politics and world government in the mid-1940s, see Barbara Leaming's biography and James Naremore's *The Magic World of Orson Welles*, 2nd ed. (Dallas: Southern Methodist University Press, 1989). The revised edition of Naremore's book also contains further information about Welles' original version of *The Stranger*, which was almost half an hour longer than the release version and also contained an expressionist dream sequence.

For the record, the lengthy take in the film discussed here that ends with the murder lasts four minutes and ten seconds.

Although I've retained Welles' standard explanation of the inception of *The Lady from Shanghai*—an amusing story that he told on many occasions—it is necessary to report that it is not accurate. A look at the autobiography of one of the film's two associate producers, William Castle (*Step Right Up! I'm Gonna Scare the Pants Off America* [New York G. P. Putnam's Sons, 1976]), provides some important clues. Castle's memories often aren't reliable—at one point he has Welles marrying Rita Hayworth circa 1945 rather than two years earlier—but it seems plausible that the truth exists somewhere between his and Welles' versions. The following account of the film's inception, at any rate, was approved for its accuracy by the late Richard Wilson, the film's other associate producer, shortly before his death.

Welles first became acquainted with Castle in 1938, when *Too Much Johnson* opened for two weeks for what proved to be its only run, at the Stony Creek Theatre in Stony Creek, Connecticut, a theatre owned by Castle. Six years later—not long after Castle directed a popular mystery, *The Whistler*, which spawned several sequels, many of which he directed himself—Castle purchased the film rights to an Inner Sanctum thriller by Sherwood King entitled *If I Die Before I Wake* for probable use as a film in that series, paying only $200, with $400 more due if and when the picture went into production.

The following year, in his newspaper column, Welles strongly recommended Castle's B film *When Strangers Marry* to his readers. ("It isn't as slick as *Double Indemnity* or as glossy as *Laura*, but it's better acted and better directed by William Castle than either.") Gratified by this plug, Castle, who was in New York for the film's opening, phoned Welles in Hollywood, and, as Castle reports it, Welles responded with a proposal: " 'Let's do a picture together, Bill. You direct and I'll produce—or I'll direct and you produce.' " Castle was then a contract director at Columbia, "but Welles assured me he could handle [studio head] Harry Cohn and told me he would send along some books and scripts that he thought would make great movies. If I had anything, I was to send it to him."

Castle subsequently wrote a ten-page treatment of the Sherwood King novel; when he learned that Cohn was away on holiday for several weeks, he showed it to a Columbia story editor, who rejected it and told Castle that Cohn would hate it because the leading lady was a murderess. On an impulse, Castle sent the book and treatment to Welles, who wrote back enthusiastically a month later (Castle reproduces his short letter in full), proposing that he play the lead and Rita Hayworth costar. (" 'The script should be written immediately. Can you start working on it nights?' ")

At some point afterward—Castle isn't clear on this point, or on whether or how he responded to Welles' letter—Castle was called into Cohn's office, given a treatment based on the King novel (apparently by

Welles), and told that Welles, who would be doing the picture for Columbia, had requested Castle as associate producer. "Furious, I reached Orson in New York. He excitedly told me how he had sold *If I Die Before I Wake* to Harry Cohn for $150,000. It was a package deal—Orson would produce, direct, write and costar. I had paid $200 and Columbia had turned it down.

" 'We'll be working together, Bill. Isn't that what we planned? Get to New York as quickly as possible so we can begin preparations.' " Despite his disappointment at not being able to direct, Castle concluded that "working with Orson in any capacity would be a great learning experience," and agreed to sign on as associate producer; the first of his many duties that he recounts was renting Errol Flynn's yacht, the *Zaca*, for use in the picture.

Complicating the above account somewhat are two other sources of information: (1) In the Mercury files, there is a copy of a contract, dated September 20, 1945 (and stating that the "agreement commences" the previous August 13), through which Welles acquired the rights to the Sherwood King novel and reassigned them to Columbia Pictures; Castle is not mentioned in the document, so presumably this happened after Castle's option expired. (2) The late Fletcher Markle, with whom I spoke several times before his death in 1991, recalled working on the film's treatment with both Castle and Welles in New York during the run of *Around the World in 80 Days* at the Adelphi Theatre. Later, he and Castle both did additional work on the script in Acapulco during the location shooting; Markle recalled working on both the extended night scene on the yacht and the aquarium sequence, and noted that a couple of other writers whom he never met collaborated with Welles on the script. (According to Welles himself in a portion of the interview that is not included here, Charles Lederer helped him with the narration at a later stage, during postproduction.)

For a fascinating speculative discussion of what *The Lady from Shanghai* was like in its prerelease form, when it was almost an hour longer, see the final chapter in the revised edition of Naremore's *Magic World of Orson Welles*, which draws upon some of the scripts and other materials housed at the Lilly Library at Indiana University.

6. HOLLYWOOD

The discussion of *Macbeth* took place several years before the rediscovery in 1980 of the original fine-grain positive film materials of the 107-minute version, which led to a restoration of this version by the UCLA Film Archives and the Folger Shakespeare Library in Washington, D.C. Twenty-one minutes longer than the release version, which is also still in circulation, this original *Macbeth* contains the original prerecorded sound track (complete with Scottish accents), a lengthy musical overture, and one of the full-reel, ten-minute takes alluded to by Welles in the interview (consisting of all the events that take place immediately before, during, and after the murder of Duncan)—a ten-minute take which, as Bogdanovich indicates, preceded Hitchcock's *Rope* (a film made up almost exclusively of very lengthy takes) by about a year (and which was preceded in turn by the ten-minute take shot for *Ambersons*). This restored version has subsequently become available both on film and on videotape (although the version on tape, distributed by NTA Home Entertainment, omits the extended musical overture); the release version, which contains the narrated prologue, is still available on film but not on tape.

For other accounts of the shooting of *The Other Side of the Wind* from other actor-participants, see John Huston's *An Open Book* (New York: Alfred A. Knopf, 1980); the second chapter of Joseph McBride's *Orson Welles* (New York: Viking Press, 1972) and McBride's article "The Other Side of Orson Welles," *American Film*, July-August 1976; and Mercedes McCambridge's *The Quality of Mercy* (New York: Times Books, 1981). See Barbara Leaming's *Orson Welles* for a detailed account of the legal problems that have prevented its completion or release.

Zeffirelli's popular film versions of *The Taming of the Shrew* and *Romeo and Juliet* were released in 1967 and 1968, respectively.

Welles' suggestion that there is virtually nothing of his 1936 "black *Macbeth*" (set in Haiti and staged in Harlem) in his movie of the same play is not quite accurate. In his 1978 film *Filming "Othello,"* during a question-and-answer session with an audience in a Boston theatre, a young man points out certain resemblances in the stage designs used in both versions, and Welles agrees: "The basic set had the same plan. . . . It wasn't the same set, but it had the same basic plan, because it worked before and we were in a great rush."

Regarding the "several other" actresses considered for the part of Lady Macbeth, one should include Geraldine Fitzgerald (though not Agnes Moorehead, who is cited in some accounts, and who played the part on radio); the "one titled tragedian from Australia" who Welles indicates was *not* considered was Dame Judith Anderson (who played the part opposite Maurice Evans in a 1959 made-for-TV production, as well as previously —in 1937 and 1941—on the stage).

The witches that Welles expresses some dissatisfaction with were played by three actors who doubled in other parts (Peggy Webber, Lurene Tuttle, Brainerd Duffield) and by Welles' screenwriter friend Charles Lederer. Their final words, which end the film—which are not the final words in the play—come from act I, scene iii: "Peace! the charm's wound up."

The tentative interest voiced here by Welles about making a film of *King Lear* subsequently grew into a full-fledged project in the 1980s, which Welles wanted to shoot in black-and-white and chiefly in closeups, with himself as Lear, Oja Kodar as Cordelia, and magician Abb Dickson (or, at an earlier stage, Mickey Rooney) as the Fool. Welles taped a six-minute proposal for prospective producers in the living room of his home in Hollywood, explaining directly to the camera how he wanted to adapt the play, which is quoted in full below (the punctuation and paragraphing are my own). It's worth bearing in mind that the apparent flippancy of Welles' throwaway remark in the interview about filming another Shakespeare play ("The truth is, I'm more interested these days in . . . well, in these days") actually points to a renewed interest in the present, probably stimulated by his current work on *The Other Side of the Wind*, which his *Lear* film, to judge from his proposal, would undoubtedly have reflected.

> *King Lear* is Shakespeare's masterpiece and, stripped of its classical or stage trappings, it's as strong now and as simple and as timeless as any story ever told. And what is simple for the story of *King Lear*—what is truly important—is not that the tragic hero is an old king, but that he's an old man. Just such an amiable, egocentric family tyrant as holds sway in the domestic scene even nowadays. Of course, we've been so famously liberated from the spice of the forbidden that nothing can be counted as truly obscene. But there is one exception: death.
>
> "Death" is our only dirty word. And *King Lear* is about death and the approach of death, and about power and the loss of power; and about love. In our consumer society, we are encouraged to forget that we will ever die, and old age can be postponed by the right face cream. And when it finally does come, we're encouraged to look forward to a long and lovely sunset.
>
> "Old age," said Charles de Gaulle, "old age is a shipwreck"—and he knew whereof he spoke. The elderly are even more self-regarding than the young. To their dependents the elderly call out for love, for more love than they can possibly receive, and for more than they are likely—or capable—of giving back. When old age tempts or forces a man to give away the very source of his ascendancy over the young, his power, it's they, the young, who are the tyrants, and he, who was all-powerful, becomes a pensioner.
>
> Of all the aches of the elderly, the loss of power is the most terrible to bear. The strong old man, the leader of the tribe—the city, the church, the state, the political party, or corporation—demands love as a tyrant demands tribute; and, bereft

of power, he must, like Lear, plead for it like a beggar. When, by self-abdication or forced retirement, such a one is suddenly deprived of his own life-sustaining tyranny, he can only flounder to the grave, struggling vainly to exact from those who have been the subjects of his whim some portion of that suffocating pity he now feels for himself. Impotent, from side to side he swings like the clapper in a bell, ringing soundlessly. He is then a castaway, banished to the desert island of his loneliness, cast out indeed from his own personal identity. "Who is it?" cries the old King Lear. "Who is it that can tell me who I am?" He has given up not only his crown, he has given up himself.

Well, you must forgive me if I've been telling you what our film will be about. To tell you what it'll be like won't be so easy. I can't really describe something which just at the moment is only in my mind. Even with a movie already on the screen, words don't get us very far. What I *can* tell you, though, is what this movie will *not* be. In any sense of the word, it will not be what is called a "costume movie." That doesn't mean that the characters are going to wear blue jeans; it does mean that a story so sharply modern in its relevancy, so universal in its simple, rock-bottom humanity, will not be burdened with the timeworn baggage of theatrical tradition. It will be just as free from the various forms of cinematic rhetoric—my own as well as the others—which have already accumulated in the history of these translations of Shakespeare into film. What we'll be giving you, then, is something new: Shakespeare addressed directly and uniquely to the sensibility of our own particular day.

The camera language will be intimate, extremely intimate, rather than grandiose. The tone will be at once epic in its stark simplicity and almost ferociously down-to-earth. In a word, not only a new kind of Shakespeare, but a new kind of film. I intend to keep the promise, and there's some basis for some optimism in the fact that I've invested so much time and energy and love in its preparation. Most importantly, the material from which this project will be realized is quite simply the greatest drama ever written.

Please forgive my outrageous lack of modesty, and thank you for giving me so much of your kind attention.

Finally, on the subject of Welles and Jean Renoir—probably the filmmaker whom Welles revered the most during his later years—it would be fitting to quote from Welles' Renoir obituary, published in the *Los Angeles Times* on February 18, 1979, particularly because it has some bearing on Welles' own relation to Hollywood during his final years:

For the high and mighty of the film industry, a Renoir on the wall is the equivalent of a Rolls Royce in the garage. Nothing like the same status was accorded the *other* Renoir, who lived in Hollywood and who died here last week.

If we exempt Islamic and Japanese newcomers, it's safe to say that the owners of Pierre Auguste Renoir's paintings in Bel-Air and Beverly Hills are all connected with the movies. And it's just as safe to say that not one of them has ever been connected, however distantly, with any movie comparable to the masterpieces of the painter's son, Jean Renoir.

He made his first film in 1924, his last in 1969. Here are his best known movies: *Tire au Flanc, Boudu Saved from Drowning, Toni, The Crime of M. Lange, A Day in the Country, La Grande Illusion, La Marseillaise, The Human Beast, The Rules of the Game, The Southerner, The River, French Cancan, Picnic on the Grass, The Elusive Corporal, The Little Theater of Jean Renoir.*

Some of these were commercial and even, in their time, critical failures. Some enjoyed success. None were blockbusters. Many are immortal.

. . . A number of his early silents were financed out of his own pocket, and when that money was gone, he sold some of his father's paintings to get more, and to make more movies. The price of a Renoir has gone up since then. Who knows? Some of those same paintings may be hanging today in the beautiful homes of the money-men in Bel-Air. For the price of one or two of those pictures, they could have bought themselves a moving picture—an original Jean Renoir of their very own.

It would be unjust, however, to reproach Hollywood for their ill-treatment without acknowledging that Renoir's troubles were just as painful during his years with the French film industry. . . .

A long-winded and murky dispute has ranged through the years over the question of which films are "true" Renoir and which are, if not "false," at least what many French aesthetes speak of as "deceptions." From his earliest beginnings, and many times throughout his long career, he has been charged with abandoning social realism, or with turning away from "nature" to a candid theatricality which outrages those who would tie his work to the impressionism of his father, or would rate the films according to their ideological content. . . .

As for Jean Renoir, he said, "The care of everyone who tries to create something in films is the conflict between exterior realism and interior non-realism." As for working "close to nature," he reminded us that, "Nature is millions of things. And there are millions of ways of understanding its preoccupations. . . ."

> There are no easy labels for such a man. The money-men catalogued him at least as inaccurately as the critics. "Producers," he told critic Penelope Gilliatt, "want me to make the pictures I made 20 years ago. No, I am someone else. I have gone away from where they think I am. . . ."
>
> He also said that every artist must be 20 years ahead of his time. And this was much harder for the artist of the cinema, "because the cinema insists upon being 20 years behind the public. . . ."

According to Carol Reed in an interview (Charles Thomas Samuels' *Encountering Directors* [New York: G. P. Putnam's Sons, 1972]), the hand coming through the grille in *The Third Man* was Reed's own, filmed on location in Vienna prior to Welles' arrival, and the preceding shot with Welles was filmed in a studio.

For many years unavailable in the United States, *Othello* was restored from the original negative of its U.S. release version by Michael Dawson and Arnie Saks for Beatrice Welles-Smith (who owns the rights) in early 1992—a complex task that included rerecording the music and sound effects in stereo and resynchronizing much of the dialogue—and is currently distributed by Castle Hill Productions. This second version, also edited by Welles, differs from the original in many respects: the original has credits spoken by Welles after the opening sequence but no narration, and there are many other differences in terms of individual shots and editing. The Castle Hill version, apart from the brightness or darkness of certain shots, conforms precisely to the second version in visual terms. In terms of sound, because of the refashioned music and effects (entailing some losses—such as the Latin chants of monks at the end of the first sequence—as well as some gains), it is different from both previous versions.

Perhaps the most detailed *and* entertaining account of the shooting of any Welles film, and a key document in understanding Welles' filmmaking methods from *Othello* on, is Micheál Mac Liammóir's wonderful *Put Money in Thy Purse* (London: Eyre Methuen, 1952; revised edition, 1976), a diary that extends from Dublin on January 27, 1949, to Mogador on March 7, 1950, in a book prefaced by Welles. (There are also a good many details in Welles' 1978 film *Filming "Othello."*)

I have been unable to determine whether the two missing scenes from *Mr. Arkadin* mentioned by Welles still exist. (They aren't in any of the various circulating versions or the producer's workprint materials now housed at the Cinémathèque de Luxembourg.) At least four different versions of the film *do* exist, however. The one closest to Welles' intentions is distributed in the United States by Corinth Films; the one that may be furthest from his intentions is, alas, the one most widely available on video (from several labels) and most often shown on TV, although the "Corinth" version can also be found on video (and is also in public domain). The other two *Arkadins* are the original European release version, entitled *Confidential Report*, now available in the United States on Voyager laser disc, and the Spanish-language version, which may exist only in Spain and which I have only been able to sample. For more details, see Chapter 6, my article "The Seven *Arkadins*" in the January-February 1992 *Film Comment*, and articles by Tim Lucas in *Video Watchdog*, nos. 10 and 12 (1992).

7. PARIS

The article in *Réalités* mentioned is by Jean Clay and appeared in no. 201, 1962.

The cut sequence featuring Katina Paxinou as a scientist is included in the version of the script published in English (London: Lorrimar, 1970, distributed in the United States by Frederick Ungar), pp. 119–22, although this is a translation of the French version published by *L'Avant-Scène du Cinéma* rather than the original English text.

As an unfinished novel, Kafka's *The Trial* was left by its author as a manuscript containing several ambiguities—including the precise order of at least seven of the ten chapters that were finished—so that Welles' so-called rearrangement of the order of certain chapters could be read as merely one of many possible interpretations of the original text. (For an interesting and detailed defense of the film as an essentially faithful literary adaptation, see Noël Carroll, "Welles and Kafka, *Film Reader*, no. 3, 1978.)

According to the executive producer of *Chimes at Midnight*, Alessandro Tasca di Cuto, the final cost of that film was $800,000, not $1.1 million—contrary to most accounts, which set the figure higher.

Several years after these interviews took place, in 1978, Welles wrote a script based on two Isak Dinesen stories, "The Dreamers" (from *Seven Gothic Tales*) and "Echoes" (from *Last Tales*), which became the most cherished of all his later unrealized film projects—initially called *Da Capo* and later entitled *The Dreamers*. In the first of eight drafts of the script that Welles wrote while trying to raise money for the project, he began with a spoken introduction by himself in which he recounted both his abortive plans to visit Dinesen in Denmark and his unsent letter to her, adding a partial explanation of why he held back from meeting or communicating with her:

> I'd been in love with Isak Dinesen since I'd opened her first book. . . . What could a casual visitor presume to offer except his stammered thanks? The visitor would be a bore, and the

> lover was too humble and too proud for that. I had only to keep silent and our affair would last—on the most intimate terms—for as long as I had eyes to read print.

It should be added that Welles' first attempt to adapt Dinesen for films was around 1953, when Alexander Korda bought the rights to her story "The Old Chevalier" (included in *Seven Gothic Tales*) for a sketch film to be made by Welles called *Paris by Night*. In the project that Welles was preparing when he died, *Orson Welles Solo* (see Chapter 9, June 9–June 12, 1978, entry), he planned to tell the same story. The three other Dinesen stories he wanted to make to go with "The Immortal Story" (included in her collection *Anecdotes of Destiny*) were "A Country Tale" (included in *Last Tales*), "The Heroine" (included in *Winter's Tales*), on which he did a day's shooting in Budapest with Oja Kodar, and "The Deluge at Norderney," (another one of the *Seven Gothic Tales*), in which he planned to play the part of Cardinal von Sehestedt.

Concerning Welles' work on moviolas, Dominique Antoine, the French coproducer of *The Other Side of the Wind*, recalls that he edited the rough cut of that film in the mid-1970s using eleven moviolas at once, arranged in a semicircle.

When Bogdanovich refers to a quote from "someone very sympathetic to [Welles'] films," the statement in question, which he slightly misremembers, comes from the June 17 entry of François Truffaut's "The Journal of *Fahrenheit 451*" (*Cahiers du Cinéma*, no. 180, July 1966; *Cahiers du Cinéma in English*, no. 7, January 1967): "Orson Welles' work is the prose which becomes music on the cutting bench. His films are shot by an exhibitionist and edited by a censor."

Sergei Eisenstein's essay on the relation of Dickens to film is "Dickens, Griffith, and the Film Today," included in his collection *Film Form* (New York: Meridian Books, 1967).

The Robert Siodmak spectacular alluded to is the two-part *Der Kampf um Rom* (1968), released in the United States in a highly edited, single-feature version, *The Last Roman*.

The Italian who dubbed Welles' part in Pasolini's episode of *Rogopag* was the highly respected writer Giorgio Bassani; and the film in which Pasolini tried to cast Welles as a German pig was *Porcile* (*Pigpen*).

"UFA symbolism" refers to the style of filmmaking associated with the large German studio UFA during the late 1910s and '20s.

8. CAREFREE

An invaluable document which was originally part of this book, and which has been excluded only because it has subsequently become available elsewhere, is a selection of entries from Charlton Heston's journals during the making of *Touch of Evil*. Interested readers should consult Heston's *The Actor's Life: Journals 1956–1976*, edited by Hollis Alpert (New York: E. P. Dutton, 1976; reprint, New York: Pocket Books, 1979); as a sympathetic and perceptive observer and participant, Heston provides an invaluable day-to-day account. Other useful materials can be found in Terry Comito's 1985 volume on the film in the Rutgers University Press "Films in Print" series, which includes a continuity version of the script based on the 108-minute version of the film discovered by UCLA film archivist Bob Epstein in 1975—the only version that is currently in circulation.

Although this version does not correspond precisely to Welles' original cut, and even contains additional material shot by Harry Keller after Welles was removed from the project, it is nevertheless closer to his conception than the 93-minute version originally released by Universal, the version that is discussed in the interview.

Welles' charge that "an awful lot of the *Cahiers du Cinéma* people are fascists" seems somewhat hyperbolic—even for the period during which *Touch of Evil* came out, when the right-wing tendencies of that magazine were at their most pronounced—but it is worth quoting André Bazin, normally one of the most liberal of the *Cahiers* critics, writing about the film in 1958: "Quinlan is physically monstrous, but is he morally monstrous as well? The answer is yes and no. Yes, because he is guilty of committing a crime to defend himself; no, because from a higher moral standpoint, he is, at least in certain respects, above the honest, just, intelligent Vargas, who will always lack that sense of life which I shall call Shakespearean. These exceptional beings should not be judged by ordinary laws. They are both weaker and stronger than others. Weaker . . . [but] also so much stronger because directly in touch with the true nature of things, or perhaps one should say, with God." (*Orson Welles: A Critical View*, translated by Jonathan Rosenbaum [Los Angeles: Acrobat Books, 1991].)

According to Yuri Tsivian, a contemporary Russian film scholar, Sergei Yutkevich's attack on *Touch of Evil* should not be taken as necessarily representative of Russian responses to the film, and should be read today in the context of the Cold War ideology of the period.

Perhaps the most striking differences between Welles' shooting script for *Touch of Evil* (dated February 1957) and the subsequent film in both its versions are the characters of Tanya (Marlene Dietrich) and the motel clerk (Dennis Weaver); the former does not figure in the script at all, and the part of the latter is expanded and developed from that of an "old man" who figures in only one scene (when Vargas arrives at the motel after Susan's departure). The most startling detail in the script that isn't in the film relates to the bottle of acid that is thrown at Vargas outside the strip joint. In the film, the acid hits a poster; in the script, it hits a cat in a "VERY CLOSE SHOT": "A flash of liquid whips over the cat—which had been half-asleep near a pile of garbage, and the bottle bounces near the animal's face. Instantly the cat is transformed into a writhing, screaming fury. In a perfect transport of burning agony the creature seems to be attempting to twist itself out of its own skin."

For a detailed three-way comparison between Whit Masterson's novel *Badge of Evil*, the script adapted from it by Paul Monash, and the film adapted by Welles from Monash's script, see the article by John Stubbs reprinted in the Terry Comito collection.

For more detailed accounts of the disagreements that arose between Welles and Universal over the cutting of *Touch of Evil*, see Barbara Leaming's *Orson Welles* and Heston's *The Actor's Life*.

The last TV pilot Welles made was a ninety-minute talk show that I haven't seen, made in late 1978 and early 1979; like all the others, it was never sold; to the best of my knowledge, it has never been shown except privately. For further details, see Chapter 9 entry for Sept. 7, 1978.

The genesis of *The Fountain of Youth* was Welles' friendship with Lucille Ball and Desi Arnaz; see Chapter 9 entry for Sept. 16, 1958, for further details. Contrary to nearly every published account of the making of this extraordinary TV pilot, the shooting was neither lengthy nor unusually costly; according to the Desilu files, which were recently checked by Welles scholar Bill Krohn, the shoot took only five days and the final, all-inclusive cost was $54,896—almost $5,000 more than the $49,832 Welles was originally budgeted for, but still only slightly more than half the cost of the first episode of *I Love Lucy* (about $95,000).

In a phone interview with Krohn for *Cahiers du Cinéma*, conducted in February 1982 and still unpublished in English, Welles said of *The Fountain of Youth*: "I was going to be the permanent star—not as a host like Ronnie Reagan coming on at the beginning and end of *Death Valley Days*, or like Hitchcock, but woven all the way through the show, and it's a style I'd like to go back to. I was very fond of it, that way of doing it. It was based entirely on back projection, there was no scenery. We just took the props from the prop department and put them behind the screen, and a few little things in front. It was entirely ad lib. . . . And of course, it's the only comedy I've ever made on film. I used to do an awful lot of comedy in the theatre, and radio. But in film I've always been pretty solemn. Comedy scenes in tragic movies . . . I was awfully glad to be liberated."

Regarding the TV pilot "about Dumas"—*Camille, the Naked Lady and the Musketeers*, which appears not to have survived—Fletcher Markle, a good friend of Welles during this period and one of the few people who have seen it, described it to me in his letter of February 10, 1987, as a pilot for a biographical series which would theoretically deal with such disparate figures as P. T. Barnum and Winston Churchill. It was made on a minuscule budget, using the $5,000 Welles had been paid for appearing as himself and performing part of a magic act on an *I Love Lucy* episode, and was shot in a single day, in "a cheap, non-union 16mm studio—a converted garage, as I recall, somewhere off Hollywood Boulevard," with Welles as narrator, armed with "masses of period photos and drawings of Dumas and the Paris of his day" that were "blown up for use on the insert stand." Judging from the comments of Markle—who incidentally had suggested the title *Orson Welles and People* for the series, just as he had previously come up with the title *The Fountain of Youth*—it was not a major work, but is nonetheless significant as one of Welles' many forays into the essay film, which would eventually lead to *F for Fake* and *Filming "Othello."* (On this subject in general, see my article "Orson Welles' Essay Films and Documentary Fictions: A Two-Part Speculation," *Cinematograph*, 4 [1991], pp. 169–79.)

Another such foray is *Portrait of Gina*, the three-reel pilot Welles shot in Italy, apparently in 1958. In the Bill Krohn interview cited above, Welles noted, "It was made for CBS. And sent to them, where there were cries of horror and disgust from Aubrey there [James Aubrey, Jr., later head of production at M-G-M], whose nickname, you may remember, was 'The Smiling Cobra.' I don't think it was very good. In that case, 'The Smiling Cobra' was right. I worked very hard on it and the result was a show that looked like it had been worked on very hard. . . . I suppose it was better than most."

In the late 1950s, Welles left behind what is apparently the only surviving copy of this film in his hotel room at the Ritz in Paris. As the cans were unmarked, they wound up in the hotel's lost-and-found department, and were eventually transferred to another storage area. Almost three decades later, in 1986, when the film was uncovered, an excerpt was shown on French TV (the only portion I've been able to see), then screened in its entirety at the Venice Film Festival in September. Gina Lollobrigida, who was in the festival audience, and apparently less than happy with the film (which shows Welles visiting her in her villa in Subiaco, where she discusses her tax problems), subsequently placed a legal injunction on the film, prohibiting any further public showings. Based on the segment I've seen, it is not an ambitious work, but clearly an eccentric and personal one that anticipates many of the strategies—including some very rapid cutting—later used in *F for Fake*.

Fortunately, the remarkable *Fountain of Youth* has survived as well, although, unfortunately, it is also prohibited for legal reasons from public showing—a situation that one hopes is only temporary. In the meantime, it is available at the end of a video edition of Peter Brook's 1953 *Omnibus* production of *King Lear* released by Hollywood Video Library.

INDEX

Page numbers in italic refer to picture captions.

PHOTOGRAPH CREDITS

All photographs courtesy of the Estate of Orson Welles except: page xxxviii, Pavelle-Jacobs; page 11, Gene Lester; page 19, Acme Photos; page 25, Candid Illustrators; page 56, copyright 1941, RKO Radio Pictures, Inc.; page 58, copyright 1940, RKO Radio Pictures, Inc./Alex Kahle; page 68, RKO Radio Pictures, Inc./Alex Kahle; page 95, copyright 1941, RKO Radio Pictures/Alex Kahle; pages 99, 206, courtesy James R. Silke; page 110 bottom, Richard Tucker—Graphic House; pages 129, 158, 458, 469, 473, 485, 486, copyright 1942, RKO Radio Pictures, Inc.; pages 170, 245, © Gary Grever; pages 171, 172, 173, © 1974 Kevin C. Brechner, Time River Productions; pages 187, 225, The Museum of Modern Art/Film Stills Archive; pages 192, 219, Larry Edmunds/Cinema Bookshop; pages 197 top left, 199, Columbia Pictures—photo by Cronewith/courtesy James R. Silke; page 208, WPA Federal Theatre Photos; pages 209, 215, Boyart Commercial Photography; page 260, Richard Tucker; page 315, © Universal Pictures; page 363, Eileen Darby—Graphic House.